Middle School 3-1

학교시험 완벽대비

1학기 전과정

# 적중 100 plus

## 영어 기출문제집

중3

지학 | 민찬규

*Best Collection*

# 구성과 특징

교과서의 주요 학습 내용을 중심으로 학습 영역별 특성에 맞춰 단계별로 다양한 학습 기회를 제공하여
단원별 학습능력 평가는 물론 중간 및 기말고사 시험 등에 완벽하게 대비할 수 있도록 내용을 구성

## Words & Expressions

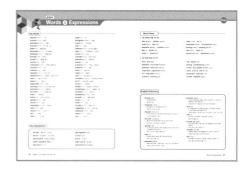

**Step1**    Key Words 단원별 핵심 단어 설명 및 풀이
              Key Expression 단원별 핵심 숙어 및 관용어 설명
              Word Power 반대 또는 비슷한 뜻 단어 배우기
              English Dictionary 영어로 배우는 영어 단어

**Step2**    실력평가 단원별 수시평가 대비 주관식, 객관식 문제풀이

**Step3**    서술형 대비 학업성취도 및 수행능력평가 대비 서술형 문제풀이

## Conversation

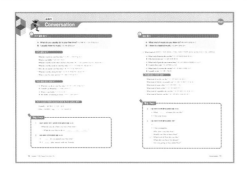

**Step1**    핵심 의사소통 소통에 필요한 주요 표현 방법 요약
              핵심 Check 기본적인 표현 방법 및 활용능력 확인

**Step2**    대화문 익히기 교과서 대화문 심층 분석 및 확인

**Step3**    교과서 확인학습 빈칸 채우기를 통한 문장 완성 능력 확인

**Step4**    기본평가 시험대비 기초 학습 능력 평가

**Step5**    실력평가 단원별 수시평가 대비 주관식, 객관식 문제풀이

**Step6**    서술형 대비 학업성취도 및 수행능력평가 대비 서술형 문제풀이

## Grammar

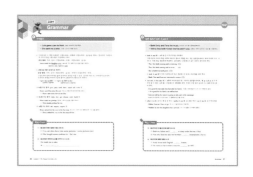

**Step1**    주요 문법 단원별 주요 문법 사항과 예문을 알기 쉽게 설명
              핵심 Check 기본 문법사항에 대한 이해 여부 확인

**Step2**    기본평가 시험대비 기초 학습 능력 평가

**Step3**    실력평가 단원별 수시평가 대비 주관식, 객관식 문제풀이

**Step4**    서술형 대비 학업성취도 및 수행능력평가 대비 서술형 문제풀이

## Reading

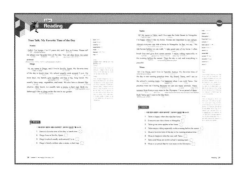

**Step1**    구문 분석 단원별로 제시된 문장에 대한 구문별 분석과 내용 설명
              확인문제 문장에 대한 기본적인 이해와 인지능력 확인

**Step2**    확인학습A 빈칸 채우기를 통한 문장 완성 능력 확인

**Step3**    확인학습B 제시된 우리말을 영어로 완성하여 작문 능력 키우기

**Step4**    실력평가 단원별 수시평가 대비 주관식, 객관식 문제풀이

**Step5**    서술형 대비 학업성취도 및 수행능력평가 대비 서술형 문제풀이
              교과서 구석구석 교과서에 나오는 기타 문장까지 완벽 학습

# Composition

## |영역별 핵심문제|

단어 및 어휘, 대화문, 문법, 독해 등 각 영역별 기출문제의 출제 유형을 분석하여 실전에 대비하고 연습할 수 있도록 문제를 배열

## |단원별 예상문제|

기출문제를 분석한 후 새로운 시험 출제 경향을 더하여 새롭게 출제될 수 있는 문제를 포함하여 시험에 완벽하게 대비할 수 있도록 준비

## |서술형 실전 및 창의사고력 문제|

학교 시험에서 점차 늘어나는 서술형 시험에 집중 대비하고 고득점을 취득하는데 만전을 기하기 위한 학습 코너

## |단원별 모의고사|

영역별, 단계별 학습을 모두 마친 후 실전 연습을 위한 모의고사

### 교과서 파헤치기

- **단어Test1~3** 영어 단어 우리말 쓰기, 우리말을 영어 단어로 쓰기, 영영풀이에 해당하는 단어와 우리말 쓰기
- **대화문Test1~2** 대화문 빈칸 완성 및 전체 대화문 쓰기
- **본문Test1~5** 빈칸 완성, 우리말 쓰기, 문장 배열연습, 영어 작문하기 복습 등 단계별 반복 학습을 통해 교과서 지문에 대한 완벽한 습득
- **구석구석지문Test1~2** 지문 빈칸 완성 및 전문 영어로 쓰기

# Lesson 1

# We Can Make a Difference

 **의사소통 기능**

- 걱정 · 염려 묻기
  What's the matter?
- 기원하기
  I hope these stickers will be helpful.

 **언어 형식**

- 관계대명사 what
  This is **what** we wanted.
- 지각동사의 목적격보어 – 현재분사
  I **saw** our cow **lying** on the ground.

# Words & Expressions

## Key Words

- **accept**[æksépt] 동 받아들이다
- **bazaar**[bəzáːr] 명 바자회
- **bump**[bʌmp] 명 도로의 튀어나온 부분
- **comfortable**[kʌ́mfərtəbl] 형 편안한
- **community**[kəmjúːnəti] 명 지역 사회, 공동체
- **complain**[kəmpléin] 동 불평하다, 항의하다
- **dangerous**[déindʒərəs] 형 위험한
- **decide**[disáid] 동 결정하다
- **device**[diváis] 명 도구, 장치
- **discover**[diskʌ́vər] 동 발견하다
- **disease**[dizíːz] 명 질병
- **elderly**[éldərli] 형 연세가 드신
- **electronically**[ilektránikəli] 부 전자적으로
- **exactly**[igzǽktli] 부 정확하게
- **excellent**[éksələnt] 형 훌륭한
- **experience**[ikspíəriəns] 명 경험
- **fence**[fens] 명 울타리
- **finally**[fáinəli] 부 마침내
- **float**[flout] 동 뜨다
- **freely**[fríːli] 부 자유롭게
- **hallway**[hɔ́lwei] 명 복도
- **headband**[hédbænd] 명 머리띠
- **ignore**[ignɔ́ːr] 동 무시하다
- **inform**[infɔ́ːrm] 동 알려주다
- **instead**[instéd] 부 대신에
- **invent**[invént] 동 발명하다

- **leave**[liːv] 동 남기다
- **lie**[lai] 동 눕다, 놓여 있다
- **lovely**[lʌ́vli] 형 사랑스러운
- **motorcycle**[móutərsàikl] 명 오토바이
- **national park** 국립공원
- **need**[niːd] 명 욕구, 요구
- **path**[pæθ] 명 작은 길
- **press**[pres] 명 언론
- **project**[prádʒekt] 명 과제
- **protect**[prətékt] 동 보호하다
- **raise**[reiz] 동 기르다
- **realize**[ríːəlàiz] 동 깨닫다
- **sadly**[sǽdli] 부 슬프게도
- **scarecrow**[skɛ́ərkrou] 명 허수아비
- **scholarship**[skálərʃip] 명 장학금
- **situation**[sìtʃuéiʃən] 명 상황
- **sort**[sɔːrt] 동 분류하다
- **southern**[sʌ́ðərn] 형 남쪽의
- **surprisingly**[sərpráiziŋli] 부 놀랍게도
- **trash bin** 쓰레기통
- **try**[trai] 동 맛보다
- **upset**[ʌ́pset] 형 기분이 상한
- **useful**[júːsfəl] 형 유용한
- **visitor**[vízitər] 명 방문객
- **work**[wəːrk] 동 작동하다, 효과가 있다

## Key Expressions

- **as a result** 결과적으로
- **be based on** ~에 바탕을 두다
- **be proud of** ~을 자랑스러워하다
- **be afraid of** ~을 두려워하다
- **collect donation** 기부금을 모으다
- **come up with** ~을 생각해 내다
- **even though** 비록 ~이지만
- **get paid** 돈을 받다
- **look down** 우울해 보이다
- **make a donation** 기부하다
- **make a difference** 차별을 두다, 변화를 가져오다
- **pay it forward** 선행나누기

- **pick up** ~을 줍다
- **prevent A from -ing** A가 ~하지 못하게 막다
- **sign up for** ~에 신청하다
- **such as** ~와 같은
- **set up** 설치하다, 세우다
- **scare away** 겁주어 쫓아보내다
- **take the place of** ~을 대신하다
- **thanks to** ~ 덕택에
- **turn away** 돌려보내다
- **try to** ~하려고 애쓰다
- **Why don't you** ~? ~하는 것이 어때?

## Word Power

※ 서로 비슷한 뜻을 가진 어휘

- □ **accept** 받아들이다 – **admit** 받아들이다
- □ **dangerous** 위험한 – **hazardous** 위험한
- □ **sort** 분류하다 – **classify** 분류하다
- □ **exactly** 정확하게 – **precisely** 정확하게
- □ **ignore** 무시하다 – **neglect** 무시하다

- □ **complain** 불평하다 – **grumble** 불평하다
- □ **device** 도구, 장치 – **apparatus** 장치
- □ **disease** 질병 – **illness** 질병
- □ **finally** 마침내 – **eventually** 결국
- □ **path** 작은 길 – **trail** 오솔길

※ 동사 – 명사

- □ **accept** 받아들이다 – **acceptance** 수용
- □ **decide** 결정하다 – **decision** 결정
- □ **ignore** 무시하다 – **ignorance** 무지
- □ **invent** 발명하다 – **invention** 발명
- □ **realize** 깨닫다 – **realization** 깨달음

- □ **complain** 불평하다 – **complaint** 불평
- □ **discover** 발견하다 – **discovery** 발견
- □ **inform** 알려주다 – **information** 정보
- □ **protect** 보호하다 – **protection** 보호

※ 명사 – 형용사

- □ **comfort** 편안함 – **comfortable** 편안한
- □ **decision** 결정 – **decisive** 결정적인
- □ **excellence** 훌륭함 – **excellent** 훌륭한
- □ **invention** 발명 – **inventive** 창의적인
- □ **information** 정보 – **informative** 정보를 제공하는

- □ **danger** 위험 – **dangerous** 위험한
- □ **exactness** 정확함 – **exact** 정확한
- □ **ignorance** 무지 – **ignorant** 무지한
- □ **protection** 보호 – **protective** 방어적인

## English Dictionary

- □ **comfortable** 편안한
  → making you feel physically relaxed
  신체적으로 느긋하다고 느끼는

- □ **bump** 혹, 요철, 고르지 못한 노면
  → a small raised area on a surface
  표면에 올라온 작은 부분

- □ **complain** 불평하다, 항의하다
  → to say or write that you are unhappy, sick, uncomfortable, etc.
  불행하거나 아프거나 불편하다고 말하거나 글로 쓰다

- □ **device** 도구, 장치
  → a machine or tool that does a special job
  특정한 작업을 위한 기계나 도구

- □ **fence** 울타리
  → a structure like a wall built outdoors usually of wood or metal that separates two areas
  두 지역을 분리하는 나무, 금속으로 외부에 지어지는 벽 같은 구조물

- □ **ignore** 무시하다
  → to refuse to show that you hear or see something or someone
  어떤 것 또는 어떤 사람을 보거나 들었다는 사실을 보여주기를 거절하다

- □ **scarecrow** 허수아비
  → a figure made to look like a person, that is dressed in old clothes and put in a field to frighten birds away
  새를 겁주어 쫓아 보내기 위하여 사람처럼 옷을 입혀서 들판에 세워 놓은 형상

- □ **scholarship** 장학금
  → an amount of money that is given by a school, an organization, etc.
  학교나 기관 등에서 주어지는 돈

[01~02] 다음 대화의 빈칸에 들어갈 말을 고르시오.

**01**

> B: I fell off my bike at Hangang Park this afternoon.
> G: Are you okay? How did it happen?
> B: I'm okay. I just rode over a big _____ on the bike path.

① mountain　② boat　③ truck
④ bump　⑤ sign

**02** 중요

> G: You look down. What's the matter?
> B: I signed _____ for the soccer team, but I couldn't join.

① down　② up　③ by
④ with　⑤ about

[03~04] 다음 빈칸에 들어갈 말로 적절한 것을 고르시오.

**03**

> It's such a _____ bed.

① pleased　② nervous
③ fence　④ responsible
⑤ comfortable

**04**

> There is a _____ in the middle of the field.

① situation　② value
③ price　④ dangerous
⑤ scarecrow

**05** 중요 다음 중 밑줄 친 부분의 뜻풀이가 바르지 <u>않은</u> 것은?

① They kill the animals that farmers are <u>raising</u>. (기르는)
② At first, I thought I couldn't do anything because I was <u>only</u> eleven. (겨우)
③ I thought lions were afraid of fire. But it didn't <u>work</u>. (일하다)
④ Then I realized I shouldn't <u>ignore</u> the problem. (무시하다)
⑤ At thirteen, I <u>finally</u> made what I called "lion lights." (마침내)

**06** 중요 다음 중 〈보기〉에 있는 단어를 사용하여 자연스러운 문장을 만들 수 <u>없는</u> 것은?

┌─ 보기 ─┐
useful　upset　trash bin　visitors

① Would you put the leftovers in the _____?
② You should _____ to save water.
③ I was _____ when he ignored me.
④ He gave me some _____ advice.
⑤ The doors of the museum opened and the _____ began to come in.

**07** 다음 밑줄 친 부분과 의미가 가장 가까운 것을 주어진 철자로 시작하여 쓰시오.

> I'm going to <u>complain</u> to your manager.

➡ g_____

**01** 다음 주어진 단어를 이용해 빈칸을 완성하시오.

> This _____ made him accept his situation.

➡ _____ (realize)

**02** 다음 짝지어진 단어의 관계가 같도록 빈칸에 알맞은 말을 쓰시오. (주어진 철자로 시작할 것)

> dangerous : safe = f_____ : sink

**[03~04]** 다음 빈칸에 공통으로 들어갈 단어를 쓰시오.

**03**

> • The police will _____ them from entering the building.
> • Regular exercise helps _____ weight gain.

**04**

> • He signed _____ for the basketball team, but he couldn't join.
> • She came _____ with a new idea for the class field trip.

**05** 다음 밑줄 친 부분과 의미가 가장 가까운 단어를 주어진 철자로 시작하여 쓰시오.

> They couldn't find the cause of the <u>disease.</u>

➡ i_____

**06** 다음 빈칸에 알맞은 단어를 〈보기〉에서 골라 쓰시오.

> ┤ 보기 ├
> set   result   donation   protect

(1) I made a small _____ to the Red Cross last month.
(2) She died as a _____ of the disease.
(3) Her mother _____ up a scarecrow in the field yesterday.
(4) The woman tried to _____ her children from the heavy rain.

**07** 다음 우리말에 맞게 빈칸에 알맞은 말을 쓰시오.

(1) 돈은 유일한 해답은 아니지만 차이를 만들어 낸다.
➡ Money is not the only answer, but it makes a _____.

(2) 이것은 그들이 적을 겁주어 쫓아버릴 수 있게 해 줘요.
➡ This can help them scare _____ their enemies.

(3) 그는 새로운 분야에서 딸의 성공을 자랑스러워한다.
➡ He's _____ of his daughter's success in a new field.

(4) 내가 매니저에게 항의를 했는데 그는 그것에 대해 아주 친절하게 해 주었다.
➡ I _____ to the manager and he was very nice about it.

# Conversation

## 1 걱정·염려 묻기

**What's the matter?** 무슨 일 있니?

■ 상대방에 대한 걱정 또는 염려를 묻는 표현으로 "What's the matter?"(무슨 일이야?)가 있다. 이와 비슷한 표현으로 "What's wrong?"(뭐가 잘못됐니?), 혹은 "What's the problem?"(무슨 문제가 있니?)도 있다. 반면에 "What's the occasion?"(무슨 일 있니?, 오늘 무슨 날이니?)는 평소와 달라 보여서 좋은 일이 있는지를 물을 때 주로 사용한다.

■ 염려스럽거나 걱정스럽다고 판단이 되는 상대방의 걱정, 슬픔이나 불만족, 실망의 원인에 대해 물을 때 사용되는 일반적인 표현으로 "What's the matter (with ~)?"가 쓰이며 "무슨 일[문제] 있니?"라는 뜻으로 다음 표현과 바꿔 쓸 수 있다. What's wrong? = What's the problem? = Is there anything wrong? = What happened? = Why the long face?

■ 걱정이나 두려움을 나타내는 표현은, "I'm anxious about ~" (~에 대해 걱정이다), "I'm worried about ~", "I'm concerned about ~"(~에 대해 걱정이다) 등이고, 상대의 걱정, 염려, 슬픔, 불만족, 실망에 대해 다음과 같은 위로하는 표현을 쓸 수 있다. Don't worry. / I'm sorry to hear that. / That's too bad. / Cheer up! 등

### 걱정·염려 묻기

- What's the matter? 무슨 일 있니?
- Is there anything wrong? 잘못된 일이라도 있니?
- What happened? 무슨 일이 있니?
- What's wrong? 뭐가 잘못됐니?
- What's the problem? 무슨 문제가 있니?
- Why the long face? 왜 우울해 보이니?

### 핵심 Check

1. 다음 빈칸에 들어가기에 적절하지 <u>않은</u> 것은?

> A: You look worried. _____
> B I forgot to bring my textbook.
> A: Oh, no. I'm sorry to hear that.

① What's the matter?
② What's wrong?
③ Is there anything wrong?
④ How is the problem?
⑤ What happened?

## ② 기원하기

**I hope these stickers will be helpful.** 나는 이 스티커들이 도움이 되면 좋겠다.

- 상대에게 좋은 일이 생기도록 기원하는 표현은 "I hope ~."를 사용한다. I hope 뒤에 접속사 that은 보통 생략하고, 기원하고자 하는 내용의 "주어+동사 ~"를 넣어 "I hope you succeed."(네가 성공하기를 기원해.)처럼 말한다. hope 이외에도 wish, pray 등을 사용하여 "I wish ~." 또는 "I pray ~."라고 하기도 한다.

- 상대의 구체적인 행동을 언급하지 않고 단순히 상대에게 행운이 깃들기를 기원하는 의미로 "행운을 빌어."와 같은 표현은 "Good luck to you."(행운을 빌어.), "I'll keep my fingers crossed (for you)."(행운을 빌어.), "Break a leg."(행운을 빌어.), "I hope everything goes well with you."(다 잘되기를 희망해.) 등을 사용하기도 한다.

### 기원하기

- I hope ~. 나는 ~하기를 희망한다.
- I pray ~. 나는 ~하기를 기도한다.
- I hope everything goes well with you. 다 잘되기를 희망해.
- I'll keep my fingers crossed (for you). 행운을 빌어.
- Break a leg. 행운을 빌어.

- I wish ~. 나는 ~하기를 기원한다.
- Good luck to you. 행운을 빌어.

### 핵심 Check

2. 다음 우리말에 해당하는 영어 문장을 쓰시오.

> A: What are you going to do for the festival, Sophia?
> B: I'm going to help people try flower tea.
> 　나는 그들이 즐거운 시간을 보내기를 희망해. (hope, great 포함) (7 words)
> A: You are very kind.

➡ _____

3. 다음 대화를 자연스러운 순서로 배열하시오.

> A: You look upset. What's the matter?
> (A) You're right. I hope they will stop running in the hallway.
> (B) Look! Some students are running in the hallway.
> (C) I hope so, too.

➡ _____

### Listen & Speak 1 A

B: What's the matter, Yura?

G: ❶I'm worried about this dog. I see it on the street ❷every time I go to school. I don't think it has a home.

B: Awww, what a cute dog! I'm sorry to hear that it doesn't have a home.

G: I know. What should I do with it?

B: ❸Why don't you take it to an animal care center and ask for help?

G: That's a great idea. Thanks.

B: 유라야, 무슨 문제가 있니?
G: 이 개가 걱정이 돼. 학교에 갈 때마다 길에서 봐. 집이 없는 것 같아.
B: 어이구, 정말 귀여운 개구나! 집이 없다는 말을 들으니 유감이다.
G: 알아. 어떻게 해야 할까?
B: 동물 보호센터에 데리고 가서 도움을 요청하면 어떨까?
G: 좋은 생각이야. 고마워.

❶ "be worried about"은 "~에 관하여 걱정이 되다"의 의미로 사람을 주어로 과거분사 worried를 쓴다.
❷ "every time"은 "~할 때마다"의 뜻으로 이 문장에서 접속사로 쓰여서 whenever와 같은 의미를 가진다.
❸ "Why don't you ~?"는 "~하는 것이 어떠니?"에 해당하는 의미로 권유, 제안을 나타내는 표현이다.

**Check(√) True or False**

(1) Yura always sees the dog when she goes to school.　　T ☐ F ☐

(2) Yura will bring a dog from an animal care center.　　T ☐ F ☐

### Real Life Communication

Henry: You ❶look upset. What's the matter, Mina?

Mina: Look at these comments, Henry. A lot of people say there aren't enough fun places ❷to see in our town.

Henry: That's too bad. I'm sorry that they didn't have a chance to visit the nice places here. We should do something about that.

Mina: Why don't we make a video that shows the famous places in our town and ❸put it on the internet?

Henry: That's an excellent idea. Let's do that.

Mina: Sounds good. I hope they enjoy their time here.

Henry: 너 속상해 보여. 미나야, 무슨 일이니?
Mina: Henry야, 이 댓글들을 봐. 많은 사람들이 우리 마을에 볼 만한 재미있는 장소가 충분하지 않다고 말해.
Henry: 그것 참 안됐다. 그들이 여기서 멋있는 장소를 방문할 기회를 가지지 못했다는 것이 유감이야. 우리가 무엇인가를 해야 해.
Mina: 우리 마을의 유명한 장소를 보여주는 비디오를 만들어 인터넷에 게시하는 것은 어떨까?
Henry: 그거 좋은 생각이야. 그렇게 하자.
Mina: 좋아. 그들이 여기서 즐거운 시간을 보냈으면 좋겠어.

❶ look upset: 속상해 보이다
❷ "to see in our town"은 앞에 있는 명사 places를 수식하는 형용사적 용법의 부정사로 "enough fun places to see in our town"은 우리 마을에서 볼 충분한 재미있는 장소"라는 뜻이다.
❸ 동사 put은 "Why don't we"에 이어지는 동사 make와 병렬 관계로 "Why don't we make ~ and put ~?"의 구조이다.

**Check(√) True or False**

(3) Mina and Henry read some comments from the visitors to their town.　　T ☐ F ☐

(4) Mina and Henry will put some pictures of famous places in their town on the internet.　　T ☐ F ☐

Listen & Speak 1 B

G: What's the matter, Mason? Are you hurt?

B: I ❶fell off my bike at Hangang Park this afternoon.

G: Are you okay? How did it happen?

B: I'm okay. ❷I just rode over a big bump on the bike path.

G: Weren't there any signs?

B: No, there weren't.

G: ❸How about writing about the problem on the community website?

B: That's a great idea.

❶ fall off: ~에서 떨어지다
❷ "ride over ~"는 "자전거를 타고 ~을 넘어가다"의 뜻이다.
❸ "How about ~ing?"는 "~하는 것이 어떠니?"의 의미로 제안을 나타낸다.

 Listen & Speak 1 C

A: You look worried. What's the matter?

B: ❶I forgot to bring my textbook.

A: Oh, no. ❷I'm sorry to hear that.

❶ "forget to"는 "(앞으로) ~해야 할 것을 잊어버리다"의 의미이다.
❷ "to hear that"은 감정(sorry)의 원인을 나타내는 부사적 용법이다.

 Listen & Speak 2 A

G: I love our stickers!

B: Me, too! ❶I hope these stickers will be helpful.

G: ❷I'm sure they will help people sort their waste for recycling.

B: Let's come back tomorrow to see if they work.

G: Sounds good.

❶ "I hope" 다음에 명사절을 유도하는 접속사 that이 생략되어 있다.
❷ "I'm sure" 다음에 접속사 that이 생략되어, "I am sure 주어+동사"의 구조이다.

 Listen & Speak 2 B

G: Hi, my name is Malala Yousafzai. I'm from Pakistan. ❶In my country, there were some people who believed that girls do not need to go to school. So they started to close down some girls' schools. I felt so bad. I wrote to the press about it and gave many talks. Thanks to the support from many people, an education law was finally passed in my country. Now I have a bigger dream. I hope ❷every child in the world can get an education.

❶ who는 some people을 선행사로 하는 주격 관계대명사이고, that은 접속사이다.
❷ every는 단수명사와 함께 쓰이고 주어 자리에 올 때는 단수 취급하여 단수동사가 온다.

 Listen & Speak 2 C

A: ❶What are you going to do for the festival, Sophia?

B: ❷I'm going to help people try flower tea. I hope they have a great time.

A: You are very kind.

❶ "What are you going to do ~?"는 앞으로의 계획을 묻는 말이다.
❷ 동사 help의 목적격보어 try는 동사원형으로 쓰였다. to부정사가 되어 "help people to try"의 형태로 쓸 수도 있다.

 Let's Check 1

G: ❶You look down. What's the matter?

B: ❷I signed up for the soccer team, but I couldn't join.

G: Why not?

B: There were already too many students on the team, so the coach won't accept any new students this year.

G: That's too bad. I hope you find another fun club.

B: Thanks.

❶ look down: 우울해 보이다
❷ "sign up for"는 "~에 신청하다"는 의미이다.

● 다음 우리말과 일치하도록 빈칸에 알맞은 말을 쓰시오.

### Listen & Speak 1 A

**B:** What's the _____, Yura?

**G:** I'm _____ _____ this dog. I _____ it _____ the _____ _____ _____ I go to school. I don't _____ it _____ a home.

**B:** Awww, _____ a cute dog! I'm _____ to _____ that it doesn't _____ a home.

**G:** I know. _____ should I do _____ it?

**B:** _____ don't you _____ it to an _____ care center and _____ for help?

**G:** _____ a great idea. Thanks.

### Listen & Speak 1 B

**G:** What's the _____, Mason? Are you _____?

**B:** I _____ off my bike at Hangang Park this afternoon.

**G:** Are you okay? _____ did it _____?

**B:** I'm okay. I just _____ over a big _____ on the bike path.

**G:** Weren't there any _____?

**B:** No, there weren't.

**G:** How about writing _____ the _____ on the community _____?

**B:** That's a great _____.

### Listen & Speak 1 C

**A:** You _____ worried. What's the _____?

**B:** I _____ to bring my textbook.

**A:** Oh, no. I'm _____ to hear that.

### Listen & Speak 2 A

**G:** I love our _____!

**B:** Me, too! I _____ these stickers will be _____.

**G:** I'm _____ they will help people _____ their waste for _____.

B: 유라야, 무슨 문제가 있니?
G: 이 개가 걱정이 돼. 학교에 갈 때마다 길에서 봐. 집이 없는 것 같아.
B: 어이구, 정말 귀여운 개구나! 집이 없다는 말을 들으니 유감이다.
G: 알아. 어떻게 해야 할까?
B: 동물 보호센터에 데리고 가서 도움을 요청하면 어떨까?
G: 좋은 생각이야. 고마워.

G: Mason, 무슨 일 있니? 너 다쳤니?
B: 오늘 오후 한강 공원에서 자전거에서 떨어졌어.
G: 괜찮니? 어떻게 하다 그런 일이 벌어졌니?
B: 괜찮아. 나는 단지 자전거 도로에 있는 큰 요철을 타고 넘었을 뿐이야.
G: 표지판이 없었어?
B: 아니, 없었어.
G: 동네 웹 사이트에 그 문제에 관하여 글을 쓰는 것이 어떠니?
B: 그거 좋은 생각이다.

A: 너 걱정스러워 보인다. 무슨 일 있니?
B: 나는 교과서를 안 가져왔어.
A: 오, 저런. 그 말을 들으니 안됐다.

G: 나는 우리 스티커가 아주 좋아!
B: 나도 그래! 나는 이 스티커들이 도움이 되기를 희망해.
G: 그것이 사람들에게 재활용 쓰레기를 분류하도록 도움을 줄 거라고 확신해.

B: Let's _____ back _____ to _____ _____ they work.

G: Sounds good.

해석

B: 그것들이 효과가 있는지 내일 다시 와 보자.

G: 좋아.

## Listen & Speak 2 B

G: Hi, my name is Malala Yousafzai. I'm _____ Pakistan. In my country, there _____ some people _____ _____ that girls do not _____ to go to school. So they started to _____ _____ some girls' schools. I _____ so bad. I wrote to the _____ about it and _____ many talks. _____ _____ _____ the support from many people, an _____ law was finally _____ in my country. Now I have a _____ dream. I _____ every _____ in the world can _____ an education.

소녀: 안녕하세요. 제 이름은 Malala Yousafzai입니다. 저는 파키스탄에서 왔습니다. 우리나라에서는 여자들은 학교에 갈 필요가 없다고 믿는 사람들이 있었습니다. 그래서 그들은 몇몇 여학교를 폐쇄하기 시작했습니다. 저는 매우 기분이 좋지 않았습니다. 그래서 그것에 관하여 언론에 글을 썼고, 많은 대화를 했습니다. 많은 사람들의 지지 덕택에 우리나라에서 교육법이 마침내 통과되었습니다. 이제 저는 더 큰 꿈이 있습니다. 나는 세계의 모든 아이들이 교육을 받을 수 있기를 희망합니다.

## Real Life Communication

Henry: You _____ upset. What's the _____, Mina?

Mina: Look at these _____, Henry. A lot of people say there aren't _____ _____ places to _____ in our town.

Henry: That's too bad. I'm _____ that they didn't _____ a _____ to _____ the nice places here. We should do _____ about that.

Mina: Why _____ we make a video that _____ the famous places in our _____ and _____ it on the internet?

Henry: That's an _____ idea. Let's do that.

Mina: Sounds good. I _____ they _____ their time here.

Henry: 너 속상해 보여. 미나야, 무슨 일 있니?

Mina: Henry야, 이 댓글들을 봐. 많은 사람들이 우리 마을에 재미있는 장소가 충분하지 않다고 말해.

Henry: 그것 참 안됐다. 그들이 여기서 멋있는 장소를 방문할 기회를 가지지 못했다는 것이 유감이야. 우리가 무엇인가를 해야 해.

Mina: 우리 마을의 유명한 장소를 보여주는 비디오를 만들어 인터넷에 게시하는 것은 어떨까?

Henry: 그거 좋은 생각이야. 그렇게 하자.

Mina: 좋아. 그들이 여기서 즐거운 시간을 보냈으면 좋겠어.

## Let's Check 1

G: You look _____. What's the _____?

B: I _____ _____ for the soccer team, but I couldn't _____.

G: Why not?

B: There were _____ too many students _____ the team, so the coach won't _____ any new students this year.

G: That's too bad. I _____ you find another _____ club.

B: Thanks.

G: 너 우울해 보인다. 무슨 일 있니?

B: 나는 축구팀에 지원했어. 그런데 가입할 수가 없어.

G: 왜 안 돼?

B: 이미 팀에 선수가 너무 많아, 그래서 코치가 올해는 새로운 학생을 받지 않을 거야.

G: 그거 참 안됐다. 나는 네가 다른 재미있는 동아리를 찾기를 바라.

B: 고마워.

[01~02] 다음 대화의 빈칸에 들어갈 말로 알맞은 것은?

**01**

B: What's the matter, Yura?

G: I'm worried about this dog. I see it on the street every time I go to school. I don't think it has a home.

B: Awww, what a cute dog! I'm _____ to hear that it doesn't have a home.

① pleased      ② sorry      ③ excited

④ happy      ⑤ tired

**02**

G: What's the matter, Mason? Are you hurt?

B: I fell off my bike at Hangang Park this afternoon.

G: Are you okay? How did it happen?

B: I'm okay. I just rode over a big bump on the bike path.

G: Weren't there any signs?

B: No, there weren't.

G: _____ on the community website?

B: That's a great idea.

① Did you find any information
② Why did you introduce the park
③ How did you post so many pictures
④ What did you post about the park
⑤ How about writing about the problem

**03** 다음 대화에 이어지는 순서가 바르게 배열된 것을 고르시오.

G: I love our stickers!

B: Me, too! I hope these stickers will be helpful.

(A) Let's come back tomorrow to see if they work.

(B) Sounds good.

(C) I'm sure they will help people sort their waste for recycling.

① (A) – (C) – (B)      ② (B) – (A) – (C)

③ (B) – (C) – (A)      ④ (C) – (A) – (B)

⑤ (C) – (B) – (A)

**01** 다음 빈칸에 들어가기에 가장 적절한 것은?

> A: What are you going to do for the festival, Sophia?
>
> B: I'm going to help people try flower tea.
> _____
>
> A: You are very kind.

① I think there should be many people.

② Do you suppose we will be busy?

③ How much tea should I prepare?

④ I think it is very helpful.

⑤ I hope they have a great time.

**02** 중요 다음 중 짝지어진 대화가 <u>어색한</u> 것은?

① A: You look down. What's the matter with you, Yura?

B: I signed up for the soccer team and the coach allowed me to join.

② A: You look worried. What's wrong with you?

B: I would like to go to the festival, but my dad didn't allow.

③ A: You look upset. Is there anything wrong with you?

B: I bought these shoes online, but they are too small.

④ A: What's the matter?

B: I studied hard, but failed at the test.

⑤ A: You look worried. What's wrong with you?

B: I lost my new phone that I had bought a week before.

**[03~04]** 다음 대화를 읽고 물음에 답하시오.

> G: You look down. What's the matter?
>
> B: I signed up for the soccer team, but I couldn't join.
>
> G: _____
>
> B: There were already too many students on the team, so the coach won't accept any new students this year.
>
> G: That's too bad. I hope you find another fun club.
>
> B: Thanks.

**03** 다음 빈칸 (A)에 들어가기에 가장 알맞은 말을 고르시오.

① How much did you pay?

② Why not?

③ What made you do it?

④ Why did you sign up?

⑤ When did you meet the coach?

**04** 중요 위 대화의 내용과 일치하지 <u>않는</u> 것은?

① The girl thinks that the boy looks worried now.

② The boy signed up for the soccer team.

③ There were too many students on the soccer team.

④ The girl suggests finding another fun club.

⑤ The coach will accept the boy as a new member for the soccer team.

[05~08] 다음 대화를 읽고 물음에 답하시오.

Henry: You look upset. (A)_____, Mina?

Mina: Look at these comments, Henry. A lot of people say there aren't enough fun places to see in our town.

Henry: That's too bad. I'm sorry that they didn't have a chance to visit the nice places here. We should do something about that.

Mina: (B)Why don't we make a video that shows the famous places in our town and put it on the internet?

Henry: (C)That's an excellent idea. Let's do that.

Mina: Sounds good. I hope they enjoy their time here.

**05** 빈칸 (A)에 들어가기에 적절하지 <u>않은</u> 것은?

① What's wrong
② What's the matter
③ Is there anything wrong
④ What happened
⑤ What's the cause

**06** 밑줄 친 (B)를 대신하여 쓰기에 적절한 것은?

① Where to see
② How to make
③ Let's to making
④ Should you make
⑤ How about making

**07** 밑줄 친 (C)That이 가리키는 것을 우리말로 쓰시오.

➡ _____

_____

**08** 위 대화를 읽고 대답할 수 <u>없는</u> 것은?

① Why does Mina look upset?
② Did Mina read the comments from the visitors?
③ Does Henry think the visitors didn't see the nice places of the town?
④ How many famous places are there in their town?
⑤ What will they put on the internet?

[09~10] 다음 대화를 읽고 물음에 답하시오.

G: You look down. What's the matter?

B: I signed up for the soccer team, but I couldn't (A)_____.

G: Why not?

B: There were already too many students on the team, so the coach won't accept any new students this year.

G: That's too bad. (B)_____

B: Thanks.

**09** 빈칸 (A)에 들어가기에 적절한 것은?

① find   ② join   ③ sign
④ think   ⑤ know

**10** 빈칸 (B)에 들어가기에 적절한 것은?

① I wish the students win the game.
② I think the coach will teach better.
③ I hope you find another fun club.
④ I think you should look up.
⑤ I hope more students play soccer.

**01** 다음 밑줄 친 단어의 적절한 형태를 쓰시오.

> A: You look worried. What's the matter?
> B: I forgot bring my textbook.
> A: Oh, no. I'm sorry to hear that.

➡ _____

[02~04] 다음 대화를 읽고 물음에 답하시오.

> Henry: You look upset. (A)_____'s the matter, Mina?
> Mina: Look at these comments, Henry. A lot of people say there aren't enough fun places to see in our town.
> Henry: That's too bad. I'm sorry that they didn't have (가)여기 있는 멋진 장소들을 방문할 기회. We should do something about that.
> Mina: (B)_____ don't we make a video that (나)(shows, put, the famous, in our town, on the internet, and, places, it)?
> Henry: That's an excellent idea. Let's do that.
> Mina: Sounds good. I hope they enjoy their time here.

**02** 빈칸 (A), (B)에 알맞은 의문사를 쓰시오.

➡ (A) _____ (B) _____

**03** 밑줄 친 (가)의 우리말에 해당하는 영어 표현을 쓰시오.

➡ _____

**04** 밑줄 친 (나)에 주어진 단어들을 문맥에 맞는 적절한 문장으로 배열하시오. (형태 변화 없음)

➡ _____
_____

[05~07] 다음 글을 읽고 물음에 답하시오.

> G: Hi, my name is Malala Yousafzai. I'm from Pakistan. (A)_____ my country, there were some people who believed that girls do not need to go to school. So they started to close down some girls' schools. I felt so bad. I wrote to the press about it and gave many talks. (가)많은 사람들의 후원 덕택에(thanks, support, from), an education law was finally passed (B)_____ my country. Now I have a bigger dream. I hope every child (C)_____ the world can get an education.

**05** (A), (B), (C)에 공통으로 들어가기에 적절한 한 단어를 쓰시오. (대·소문자 무시)

➡ _____

**06** 밑줄 친 (가)의 우리말에 어울리도록 주어진 단어를 포함한 영어 표현을 완성하시오.

➡ _____

**07** 위 대화의 내용에 어울리도록 아래 대화의 빈칸에 적절한 말을 쓰시오.

> A: What is your dream, Malala?
> B: I hope every _____ in the world can get an _____.

# Grammar

**1** 관계대명사 what

> • This is **what** we wanted. 이것은 우리가 원했던 것이다.
>
> • There's something in **what** he says. 그의 말에는 일리가 있다.

■ 관계대명사 what은 다른 관계대명사와 다르게 선행사를 포함한 관계대명사로 '~하는 것'으로 해석하며, the thing(s) which[that]를 나타낸다.
  • She doesn't always do **what** she promises. 그녀는 약속을 하고도 안 지키는 때가 있어요.
  (= She doesn't always do the thing(s) which[that] she promises.)

■ 관계대명사 what이 이끄는 절은 명사절로 문장에서 주어, 보어, 목적어의 역할을 한다.
  (1) 주어 역할
    • **What** I want is something really small. 제가 원하는 건 아주 작은 것입니다.
  (2) 보어 역할
    • Love is **what** helps mend a broken heart. 사랑이란 상처 입은 마음의 치유를 돕는 것이다.
  (3) 목적어 역할
    • I can't understand **what** he said. 나는 그가 말한 것을 이해하지 못하겠어요. (동사의 목적어)
    • I'm not interested in **what** other people think. 남이 뭐라고 생각하든지 관심없다. (전치사의 목적어)

■ 관계대명사 what의 관용적인 표현
  • He is **what is called** a young prince. 그는 소위 귀공자다.
  • He is content with **what he has** although he is very poor.
    그는 비록 매우 가난하지만 자기가 가진 것에 만족하고 있다.
  • **What's worse**, I have a bad cold. 설상가상으로, 나는 감기까지 걸렸다.

---

## 핵심 Check

**1.** 다음 괄호 안에서 알맞은 말을 고르시오.
  (1) (What / That) he wrote became very popular.
  (2) One lady was wearing (what / which) looked like two green chairs.
  (3) This is (what / that) she said.
  (4) He was hurt by (what / that) was said by her.

## 2 지각동사

- I **saw** our cow **lying** on the ground. 나는 우리 소가 바닥에 누워 있는 것을 보았어.
- I can still **feel** them **kicking**. 나는 여전히 그들이 발차기를 하는 걸 느낄 수 있어.

■ 지각동사는 감각기관을 통하여 인지하는 것을 나타내는 동사로, '보다, 듣다, 느끼다' 등의 의미를 갖는 see, look at, watch, observe, hear, listen to, feel 등의 동사를 말한다. '동사＋목적어＋원형부정사/현재분사'의 형태로 '목적어가 …하는 것을[~하는 중인 것을] ~하다'라는 의미를 갖는다. 목적격보어 자리에 원형부정사와 현재분사를 모두 사용할 수 있으나 의미상 그 동작이 진행 중인 것을 나타낼 때에는 주로 현재분사를 사용한다.

- I did not **observe** him **leave** the room. 나는 그가 방을 나가는 것을 보지 못하였다.
- Charles **listened to** her **singing**. Charles는 그녀의 노래에 귀를 기울였다.

■ '지각동사＋목적어＋원형부정사[현재분사]'로 쓰이는 경우, 목적어와 목적격보어는 능동 관계가 된다. '지각동사＋목적어＋과거분사'로 쓰이는 경우 목적어와 목적격보어의 관계는 수동이다.

- I **felt** something **creeping** on the back. 나는 등에 무언가가 기어가는 것을 느꼈다.
- David **heard** his name **called**. David은 그의 이름이 불리는 소리를 들었다.

■ 사역동사와 혼동하지 않도록 한다. 사역동사도 목적어와 목적격보어를 취하지만, 사역동사의 목적격보어로는 목적어와 능동의 관계일 경우 동사원형이 나오며, 수동의 관계일 경우 과거분사가 나온다.

- I'll **make** him **go** there whether he wants to or not. 나는 그가 원하든 원치 않든 그를 거기에 가게 하겠다.
- I **had** a new suit **made** last month. 나는 지난달 새 양복을 맞췄다.

### 핵심 Check

**2.** 다음 괄호 안에서 알맞은 말을 고르시오.

(1) Did you watch him (to play / playing) tennis?

(2) Have you ever heard her (sing / sang)?

(3) I'll see the work (doing / done) in time.

(4) I had my hat (washing / washed).

**01** 다음 두 문장이 같은 의미가 되도록 할 때, 빈칸에 알맞은 것은?

> I want to talk about the things that are happening now.
> = I want to talk about _____ are happening now.

① how         ② which         ③ who
④ that         ⑤ what

**02** 다음 괄호 안에서 알맞은 말을 고르시오.

(1) I saw something (burning / to burn) in the kitchen.
(2) She heard someone (answer / answered) the phone.
(3) This is (what / that) I could do for you.
(4) I didn't believe (what / that) he was telling everybody.

**03** 다음 두 문장을 한 문장으로 바꾸어 쓸 때 알맞게 표현한 것을 고르시오.

> • I saw her.
> • She was dancing on the stage.

① I saw her dance on the stage.
② I saw her danced on the stage.
③ I saw her dancing on the stage.
④ I saw her to dance on the stage.
⑤ I saw her had danced on the stage.

**04** 다음 우리말에 맞게 주어진 어휘를 바르게 배열하시오.

(1) 그가 제안한 것은 그가 실제로 생각한 것과 달랐다.
　 (he, he, what, what, different, thought, proposed, was, really, from)
　 ➡ _____

(2) 내가 네게 한 말을 잊지 마라.
　 (I, you, told, forget, do, what, not)
　 ➡ _____

(3) 나는 그녀가 들판을 가로질러 걸어가는 것을 지켜보았다.
　 (I, her, the field, walking, watched, across)
　 ➡ _____

**01** 다음 중 어법상 올바른 것은?

① Last night, I heard the dog barked fiercely.
② I saw our cow to lie on the ground.
③ She watched her sister done the dishes.
④ She listened to him call her name.
⑤ She made him does his homework right away.

**02** 다음 중 어법상 올바르지 않은 것은?

① I thought that I needed to make the lights.
② What is the thing that he bought at the shop?
③ Do you believe that she told you?
④ What I want is to take some rest as I worked all day long.
⑤ It made me remember what she said the other day.

**03** 다음 빈칸에 알맞은 말이 바르게 짝지어진 것은?

• Did you hear someone _____ on the door?
• This book is _____ Olivia bought last weekend.

① knock – that
② knocked – that
③ koncking – that
④ knocked – what
⑤ knocking – what

**04** 다음 괄호 안에서 알맞은 말을 고르시오.

(1) Eva watched her brother (making / to make) spaghetti.
(2) I heard him (close / to close) the door.
(3) Mom makes us (eat / eating) vegetables.
(4) Is this (that / what) you were looking for yesterday?
(5) Washing windows is the last thing (that / what) I want to do.

**05** 다음 대화의 빈칸에 들어갈 말로 알맞은 것은?

M: What do you want to do after school?
W: _____ I want to do after school is to go to the concert with my friends.

① What   ② That   ③ This
④ Which   ⑤ It

**06** 다음 문장의 빈칸에 들어갈 알맞은 것은?

I have set up lights at seven homes in my community and haven't heard anyone _____ about lions.

① complains   ② complain
③ complained   ④ to complain
⑤ to complaining

**07** 밑줄 친 부분의 쓰임이 올바른 것은?

① The fire helped the lions to better <u>watch the cows to move.</u>

② Didn't you <u>hear her said</u> she would be busy?

③ We can <u>see many people taking</u> a walk around the park.

④ Amy <u>watched the bottle filling</u> with water.

⑤ She <u>felt someone touched</u> her hand.

**08** 다음 주어진 문장의 밑줄 친 what과 같은 용법으로 쓰인 것을 모두 고르시오.

> <u>What</u> I want for my birthday is a guitar.

① <u>What</u> do you plan to do this weekend?

② She was very proud of <u>what</u> she was doing.

③ He gave me <u>what</u> I wanted.

④ He often hesitates <u>what</u> to do.

⑤ <u>What</u> made you think he was honest?

**서답형**

**09** 주어진 어휘를 이용하여 다음 우리말을 영작하시오.

> 나는 그 사람이 너에 대해 말하는 것을 들었어.
> (6 단어) (hear, talk about)

➡ _____

**서답형**

**10** 다음 문장에서 어법상 틀린 부분을 찾아 바르게 고쳐 쓰시오.

> They hoped to discover that is called the mechanism of the reaction.

_____ ➡ _____

**11** 다음 우리말에 맞게 빈칸에 알맞은 것을 고르시오.

> 난 그가 부르는 소리를 못 들은 체했다.
> ➡ I pretended I didn't hear him _____ me.

① called      ② calls

③ calling      ④ to call

⑤ has called

**12** 다음 빈칸에 들어갈 말이 나머지 넷과 다른 하나는?

① I finally made _____ I called "lion lights."

② College is a way to learn more about _____ I'm interested in.

③ At the moment we have no information _____ it is possible.

④ She doesn't think _____ you're doing is important.

⑤ She managed to ignore _____ people were saying.

**13** 다음 두 문장을 한 문장으로 바르게 연결한 것은?

> • This is not the food.
> • I ate it at the restaurant yesterday.

① This is not the food ate at the restaurant yesterday.

② This is not which I ate at the restaurant yesterday.

③ This is not that I ate at the restaurant yesterday.

④ This is not the food what I ate at the restaurant yesterday.

⑤ This is not what I ate at the restaurant yesterday.

**14** 다음 우리말과 일치하도록 빈칸에 알맞은 것은?

> 많은 사람들은 David이 하는 것이 시간 낭비라고 생각한다.
> → Many people think ＿＿＿＿＿＿ is a waste of time.

① that David do
② that David did
③ that David does
④ what David done
⑤ what David does

**서답형**
**15** 다음 문장에서 어법상 어색한 것을 바르게 고쳐 다시 쓰시오.

(1) I heard Steve played the guitar in his room.
　➡ ＿＿＿＿＿＿＿＿＿＿＿＿＿

(2) You can watch many people to walk their dogs in the park.
　➡ ＿＿＿＿＿＿＿＿＿＿＿＿＿
　　＿＿＿＿＿＿＿＿＿＿＿＿＿

(3) Did you see the window breaking?
　➡ ＿＿＿＿＿＿＿＿＿＿＿＿＿

(4) I tried to make myself understand.
　➡ ＿＿＿＿＿＿＿＿＿＿＿＿＿

(5) Did you read the book what I told you the other day?
　➡ ＿＿＿＿＿＿＿＿＿＿＿＿＿
　　＿＿＿＿＿＿＿＿＿＿＿＿＿

(6) Learning how to play the game is that I want to do now.
　➡ ＿＿＿＿＿＿＿＿＿＿＿＿＿
　　＿＿＿＿＿＿＿＿＿＿＿＿＿

 **16** 다음 중 어법상 어색한 것을 고르시오. (2개)

① Did you see the little girl to ride a bike?
② I watched rats running out of the house.
③ George listened to her sing on the stage.
④ I want you to wear the ring what I bought for you.
⑤ That is not what I was expecting you to say.

 **17** 다음 중 밑줄 친 부분의 쓰임이 나머지 넷과 다른 것을 고르시오.

① I felt my shoulders shaking.
② He saw the elephants walking over here.
③ Melanie is the girl talking on the phone with her friend.
④ Amy watched Jack making something in the kitchen.
⑤ Emily heard a man yelling at a girl.

**18** 다음 중 주어진 문장과 의미가 같은 것을 고르시오.

> The thing that I want to experience in Seoul is to visit Gyungbokgoong.

① I want to experience in Seoul is to visit Gyungbokgoong.
② The thing what I want to experience in Seoul is to visit Gyungbokgoong.
③ Which I want to experience in Seoul is to visit Gyungbokgoong.
④ That I want to experience in Seoul is to visit Gyungbokgoong.
⑤ What I want to experience in Seoul is to visit Gyungbokgoong.

**01** 다음 두 문장을 〈보기〉와 같이 하나의 문장으로 쓰시오.

┌─ 보기 ─┐
- I saw Sophie.
- She was singing a song at the park.
→ I saw Sophie singing a song at the park.

(1) • I woke up and saw our cow.
　　• It was lying on the ground.
➡ _____

(2) • I was in the library.
　　• Marianne was studying in the library.
➡ _____

(3) • He heard the girl.
　　• She walked out of the house.
➡ _____

**02** 다음 우리말에 맞게 주어진 단어를 바르게 배열하시오.

(1) 내가 하는 말이 이해가 안 될 때는 언제나 나에게 물어보세요. (you, I, ask, say, understand, don't, me, what, please, if)
➡ _____
_____

(2) 그녀는 그때 무엇을 했는지 기억할 수 있다. (she, she, time, can, did, remember, what, that, at)
➡ _____

(3) Rebecca는 누군가 그녀의 손을 만지는 것을 느꼈다. (Rebecca, her hand, someone, touch, felt)
➡ _____

**03** 그림을 보고, 주어진 어휘를 이용하여 빈칸을 알맞게 채우시오.

(1) _____ is a bird. (watch, she) (4 단어)

(2) He didn't give her _____ to have. (she, want) (3 단어)

**04** 다음 〈보기〉에 주어진 단어를 문맥에 맞게 알맞은 형태로 고쳐 쓰시오.

┌─ 보기 ─┐
runs　answers　shakes　calls

(1) I have never felt the ground _____.

(2) Miranda heard her name _____ in the crowd.

(3) Did you hear Christine _____ the phone?

(4) No one noticed him _____ back into the restaurant.

**05** 주어진 두 문장을 what을 이용하여 하나의 문장으로 쓰시오.

(1) • Let's review the thing.
　　• You learned it.
　　➡ _____

(2) • I think the thing keeps me young.
　　• It is the work.
　　➡ _____

(3) • You did it.
　　• It made me look like a fool.
　　➡ _____

(4) • Don't spend too much time doing something.
　　• It is trash.
　　➡ _____

**06** 다음 문장에서 어법상 어색한 것을 바르게 고치시오.

(1) I have seen the students to carry many things there.
　_____ ➡ _____

(2) Susan hears the train arrives at the station.
　_____ ➡ _____

(3) June watched Aaron walked down the street.
　_____ ➡ _____

(4) I felt myself lift up.
　_____ ➡ _____

(5) Let him tells you that it means.
　_____ ➡ _____

(6) The shop doesn't have the shirt what I want.
　_____ ➡ _____

(7) I can't imagine that she did yesterday.
　_____ ➡ _____

**07** 다음 두 문장의 의미가 같도록 빈칸을 알맞게 채우시오.

(1) There are some boys playing basketball in the park.
　= There are some boys _____ playing basketball in the park.

(2) I know the men doing things others did not ordinarily do.
　= I know the men _____ doing things others did not ordinarily do.

**08** 다음 우리말을 괄호 안에 주어진 어휘를 이용하여 영작하시오.

(1) 나는 그들이 그 집에서 떠들고 있는 것을 들었다. (hear, make a noise, in, 9 단어)
　➡ _____

(2) 나는 한 소녀가 꽃들의 향기를 맡고 있는 것을 보았다. (watch, smell, flowers, 6 단어)
　➡ _____

(3) 마지막으로 머리를 깎은 것이 언제입니까? (your hair, have, cut, last, 8 단어)
　➡ _____

(4) 오늘 할 수 있는 일을 내일까지 미루지 마라. (you, can, put off, do, until, 10 단어)
　➡ _____

(5) 그녀는 그가 그녀에게 한 것을 보고 감명받았다. (did, impressed, to her, with, 9 단어)
　➡ _____

# Reading
교과서

**The Idea That Brought Peace to My Town**

My name is Richard Turere. I live in Kenya in the <u>southern</u> part of Nairobi National Park. The <u>southern</u> part of the <u>park</u> does not have a fence, so wild animals like lions move out of the park freely.

<u>They</u> kill the animals <u>that</u> farmers are raising. As a result, farmers try to kill the lions <u>because</u> they want to protect their animals.

One morning, I woke up and <u>saw our cow lying</u> on the ground. It was dead, and I felt so bad. At first, I <u>thought</u> I couldn't do anything because I was only eleven. Then I <u>realized</u> I shouldn't ignore the problem. I really wanted to help the people in my town <u>in the same situation.</u>

My first idea was <u>to use</u> fire. I <u>thought</u> lions were afraid of it. Sadly, it didn't <u>work</u>. Instead, the fire <u>helped</u> the lions to better <u>watch the cows move</u>. Then I had another idea. It was to use a scarecrow. But the lions were very clever. The first day, they were turned away. <u>On the second</u> day, they jumped in and killed more animals.

peace: 평화
southern: 남쪽의, 남쪽에 위치한
national park: 국립공원
fence: 울타리
wild animal: 야생동물
raise: ~을 기르다
try to V: V하려고 애쓰다
protect: 보호하다
lie: 눕다, 누워 있다
realize: 깨닫다
ignore: ~을 무시하다
be afraid of: ~을 두려워하다
work: 효과가 있다
scarecrow: 허수아비

 확인문제

● 다음 문장이 본문의 내용과 일치하면 T, 일치하지 않으면 F를 쓰시오.

1  Richard lives in Nairobi National Park. ☐

2  Though there is a fence, wild animals move out of the park freely. ☐

3  Farmers kill the lions because they are afraid of them. ☐

4  Richard's first idea was to use fire. ☐

5  The lions were clever enough not to be fooled by a scarecrow. ☐

One night, I was walking around the cows with a light, and the lions didn't come. I discovered that lions were afraid of a moving light. So I came up with an idea. I decided to invent lights that move electronically. Because I like machines, I could find what I needed to make the lights. I found an old car battery, a small device from a motorcycle, a switch, and a broken electronic light.

At thirteen, I finally made what I called "lion lights." My father said, "I'm so proud of you, Richard!" Since then, I have set up lights at seven homes in my community and haven't heard anyone complain about lions. They thanked me, saying "This is exactly what we wanted, lovely boy!" Surprisingly, my idea is now used all over Kenya to scare away other animals, such as elephants. From this experience, I realized that I could make a difference in people's lives even though I am just a young boy. I was also able to prevent lions from being killed.

Thanks to my work, I got a scholarship to a great school in Kenya. I am really excited about this. In my new school, I am now teaching my friends how to make and use the lights. I tell my friends, "Our ideas can make a difference in people's lives!"

---

discover: ~을 발견하다
come up with: ~을 생각해 내다, 떠올리다
invent: 발명하다
electronically: 전자적으로
machine: 기계
device: 장치
set up: ~을 설치하다
community: 지역 사회
complain: 불평하다
scare away: ~을 쫓아버리다
prevent A from B: A가 B하지 못하게 막다, 예방하다
scholarship: 장학금

---

 **확인문제**

● 다음 문장이 본문의 내용과 일치하면 T, 일치하지 <u>않으면</u> F를 쓰시오.

1  When Richard was walking around the cows with a light, the lions came as usual. ☐

2  Richard discovered what the lions were afraid of. ☐

3  Richard's father felt proud of him. ☐

4  The lion light couldn't scare away elephants. ☐

5  It was impossible for Richard to make a difference in people's lives. ☐

6  Richard is excited about getting a scholarship to a great school in Kenya. ☐

● 우리말을 참고하여 빈칸에 알맞은 말을 쓰시오.

**The Idea That Brought Peace to My Town**

**1** My name _____ Richard Turere. I _____ _____ Kenya in the _____ _____ of Nairobi National Park.

**2** The _____ _____ of the park _____ not _____ _____ _____, so wild animals _____ lions move _____ _____ the park _____.

**3** They kill the animals _____ farmers _____ _____.

**4** _____ _____ _____, farmers try _____ _____ the lions _____ they want to _____ their animals.

**5** One morning, I _____ _____ and saw our cow _____ on the ground.

**6** It was _____, and I _____ so bad.

**7** At first, I thought I couldn't _____ _____ _____ I was only eleven.

**8** Then I _____ I shouldn't _____ the problem.

**9** I really _____ _____ _____ the people in my town in _____ _____ situation.

**10** My first idea was _____ _____ _____.

**11** I thought lions _____ _____ _____ _____. Sadly, it didn't _____.

**12** _____, the fire helped the lions _____ _____ _____ the cows move.

**13** Then I had _____ _____. It was to use _____ _____.

**14** But the lions _____ very _____.

**15** _____ _____ _____, they were turned away.

**16** On the second day, they _____ _____ and _____ more animals.

**17** One night, I was _____ _____ the cows _____ _____ _____, and the lions didn't come.

1 내 이름은 Richard Turere야. 나는 케냐의 나이로비 국립공원의 남쪽 지역에 살고 있어.

2 공원의 남쪽 지역은 울타리가 없어서 사자와 같은 야생 동물들이 공원 밖으로 자유롭게 나가.

3 그들은 농부들이 키우고 있는 동물들을 죽여.

4 그 결과, 농부들은 그들의 동물들을 보호하기를 원하기 때문에 사자들을 죽이려고 해.

5 어느 날 아침, 나는 일어나서 우리 소가 바닥에 누워 있는 것을 보았어.

6 소는 죽어 있었고, 나는 아주 기분이 좋지 않았어.

7 처음에는, 내가 겨우 열한 살이었기 때문에 아무것도 할 수 없을 거라고 생각했어.

8 그러고 나서 나는 이 문제를 무시하지 않아야 한다는 걸 깨달았어.

9 나는 같은 상황에 있는 우리 마을 사람들을 정말로 돕고 싶었어.

10 나의 첫 번째 아이디어는 불을 사용하는 것이었어.

11 나는 사자들이 불을 무서워 할 거라고 생각했어. 슬프게도 그것은 효과가 없었어.

12 대신에 불은 사자들이 소들이 움직이는 것을 더욱 잘 볼 수 있도록 도왔어.

13 그러고 나서 나는 다른 아이디어를 생각해 냈어. 그것은 허수아비를 사용하는 거였어.

14 하지만 사자들은 매우 영리했어.

15 첫날에는 사자들이 돌아갔어.

16 둘째 날에는 사자들이 뛰어 들어와서 더 많은 동물들을 죽였어.

17 어느 날 밤, 나는 전등을 들고 소들의 주위를 걷고 있었는데 사자들은 오지 않았어.

**18** I _____ _____ l i o n s _____ _____ _____ a _____ light.

**19** So I _____ _____ _____ an idea. I decided _____ _____ lights that _____ electronically.

**20** _____ I like machines, I could find _____ _____ _____ to make the lights.

**21** I found an old car battery, _____ _____ _____ from a motorcycle, a switch, and a _____ _____ _____.

**22** _____ thirteen, I finally made _____ _____ _____ "lion lights."

**23** My father said, "I'm _____ _____ _____ you, Richard!"

**24** Since then, I _____ _____ _____ lights _____ seven homes in my community and _____ _____ anyone _____ _____ lions.

**25** They thanked me, _____ "This is exactly _____ _____ _____, lovely boy!"

**26** _____, my idea is now _____ all over Kenya _____ _____ _____ other animals, _____ _____ elephants.

**27** _____ this experience, I realized _____ I could _____ _____ _____ in people's lives _____ _____ I am just a young boy.

**28** I was also _____ _____ _____ lions _____ being killed.

**29** _____ _____ my work, I got _____ _____ to a great school in Kenya.

**30** I am really _____ _____ this.

**31** In my new school, I am now _____ my friends _____ _____ _____ and _____ the lights.

**32** I tell my friends, "Our ideas can _____ _____ _____ in people's _____!"

• 우리말을 참고하여 본문을 영작하시오.

### The Idea That Brought Peace to My Town

**1** 내 이름은 Richard Turere야. 나는 케냐의 나이로비 국립공원의 남쪽 지역에 살고 있어.
➡ _____

**2** 공원의 남쪽 지역은 울타리가 없어서 사자와 같은 야생 동물들이 공원 밖으로 자유롭게 나가.
➡ _____

**3** 그들은 농부들이 키우고 있는 동물들을 죽여.
➡ _____

**4** 그 결과, 농부들은 그들의 동물들을 보호하기를 원하기 때문에 사자들을 죽이려고 해..
➡ _____

**5** 어느 날 아침, 나는 일어나서 우리 소가 바닥에 누워 있는 것을 보았어.
➡ _____

**6** 소는 죽어 있었고, 나는 아주 기분이 좋지 않았어.
➡ _____

**7** 처음에는, 내가 겨우 열한 살이었기 때문에 아무것도 할 수 없을 거라고 생각했어.
➡ _____

**8** 그러고 나서 나는 이 문제를 무시하지 않아야 한다는 걸 깨달았어.
➡ _____

**9** 나는 같은 상황에 있는 우리 마을 사람들을 정말로 돕고 싶었어.
➡ _____

**10** 나의 첫 번째 아이디어는 불을 사용하는 것이었어.
➡ _____

**11** 나는 사자들이 불을 무서워 할 거라고 생각했어. 슬프게도 그것은 효과가 없었어.
➡ _____

**12** 대신에 불은 사자들이 소들이 움직이는 것을 더욱 잘 볼 수 있도록 도왔어.
➡ _____

**13** 그러고 나서 나는 다른 아이디어를 생각해 냈어. 그것은 허수아비를 사용하는 거였어.
➡ _____

**14** 하지만 사자들은 매우 영리했어.
➡ _____

**15** 첫날에는 사자들이 돌아갔어.
➡ _____

**16** 둘째 날에는 사자들이 뛰어 들어와서 더 많은 동물들을 죽였어.
➡ _____

**17** 어느 날 밤, 나는 전등을 들고 소들의 주위를 걷고 있었는데 사자들은 오지 않았어.
➡ _____

**18** 나는 사자들이 움직이는 불빛을 두려워한다는 것을 발견했어.

➡ _____

**19** 그래서 나는 생각해 냈지. 나는 전자적으로 움직이는 전등들을 발명하기로 결심했어.

➡ _____

**20** 나는 기계들을 좋아했기 때문에 전등들을 만들기 위해 내가 필요한 것들을 찾을 수 있었어.

➡ _____

**21** 나는 오래된 자동차 배터리, 오토바이에서 찾은 작은 장치, 스위치, 그리고 부서진 전등을 찾았어.

➡ _____
_____

**22** 열세 살에 나는 내가 '사자 전등'이라고 불렀던 것을 마침내 만들었어.

➡ _____

**23** 나의 아버지께서는 말씀하셨어, "정말 자랑스럽구나, Richard!"

➡ _____

**24** 그때 이후로, 나는 우리 동네 일곱 가구의 집에 전등을 설치했고, 어느 누구도 사자들에 대해 불평하는 것을 듣지 못했어.

➡ _____
_____

**25** "이것이 바로 우리가 원했던 거야, 사랑스러운 소년아!"라고 말하면서 그들은 나에게 감사를 표했어.

➡ _____

**26** 놀랍게도 나의 아이디어는 이제 코끼리와 같은 다른 동물들을 쫓기 위해서 케냐 전역에 걸쳐 사용되고 있어.

➡ _____

**27** 이 경험을 통해 나는 내가 어린 소년이지만 사람들의 삶에 변화를 일으킬 수 있다는 것을 깨달았어.

➡ _____
_____

**28** 나는 사자들이 죽임을 당하는 것 또한 막을 수 있었어.

➡ _____

**29** 나의 작업 덕분에, 나는 케냐 최고의 학교에 장학금을 받고 입학하게 되었어.

➡ _____

**30** 나는 정말 기분이 좋아.

➡ _____

**31** 나의 새 학교에서 나는 지금 나의 친구들에게 어떻게 전등들을 만들고 사용하는지 가르쳐 주고 있어.

➡ _____

**32** 나는 친구들에게 "우리의 아이디어가 사람들의 삶에 변화를 일으킬 수 있어!"라고 이야기해.

➡ _____

**[01~03]** 다음 글을 읽고 물음에 답하시오.

One morning, I woke up and saw our cow lying on the ground. It was dead, and I felt so bad. At first, I thought I couldn't do anything because I was only eleven. Then I realized I shouldn't ignore the problem. I really wanted to help the people in my town in the same situation.

**서답형**

**01** 다음과 같이 풀이되는 말을 위 글에서 찾아 쓰시오.

pay no attention to something

➡ _____

**서답형**

**02** Write the reason why the writer felt sad. Answer with six words and use the word 'because', and 'find.'

➡ _____

**03** Why did the writer think that he could do nothing?

① He was too scared to do anything.
② He felt bored by the situation.
③ He was too young to handle the situation.
④ He felt uncomfortable to see his cow dead.
⑤ He was too afraid to see lions.

**[04~05]** 다음 글을 읽고 물음에 답하시오.

My name is Richard Turere. I live in Kenya in the southern part of Nairobi National Park. The southern part of the park does not have a fence, so wild animals like lions move out of the park freely. ⓐThey kill the animals that farmers are raising. As a result, ⓑfarmers try to kill the lions because ⓒthey want to protect ⓓtheir animals.

**04** ⓐ~ⓓ 중 같은 것을 지칭하는 것끼리 바르게 묶은 것은?

① ⓐⓑ, ⓒⓓ          ② ⓐⓓ, ⓑⓒ
③ ⓐ, ⓑⓒⓓ          ④ ⓑ, ⓐⓒⓓ
⑤ ⓒ, ⓐⓑⓓ

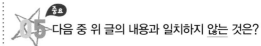

**05** 다음 중 위 글의 내용과 일치하지 않는 것은?

① Richard lives in Kenya.
② The southern part of Nairobi National Park doesn't have a fence.
③ Lions kill animals that farmers are raising.
④ Farmers raise wild animals like lions.
⑤ Wild animals can move out of the park freely.

**[06~08]** 다음 글을 읽고 물음에 답하시오.

My first idea was to use fire. I thought lions were afraid of (A)it. (①) Sadly, it didn't work. (②) Instead, the fire helped the lions to better watch the cows move. (③) It was to use a scarecrow. (④) But the lions were very clever. The first day, they were turned away. (⑤) On the second day, they jumped in and killed more animals.

**06** ①~⑤ 중 주어진 문장이 들어가기에 가장 적절한 곳은?

Then I had another idea.

①          ②          ③          ④          ⑤

**서답형**

**07** 밑줄 친 (A)가 가리키는 것을 위 글에서 찾아 쓰시오.

➡ _____

**중요**

**08** 다음 중 위 글을 읽고 답할 수 있는 것은?

① How many lions used to attack cows?
② When did lions usually move?
③ How did the writer make a scarecrow?
④ How many lions were turned away on the first day?
⑤ What happened on the second day?

[09~11] 다음 글을 읽고 물음에 답하시오.

At thirteen, I finally made what I called "(A) lion lights." My father said, "I'm so proud of you, Richard!" Since then, I have set up lights at seven homes in my community and haven't heard anyone complain about lions. They thanked me, saying "This is exactly what we wanted, lovely boy!" Surprisingly, my idea is now used all over Kenya to scare away other animals, such as elephants. From this experience, I realized that I could make a difference in people's lives ⓐ_____ I am just a young boy. I was also able to prevent lions from being killed.

**09** 빈칸 ⓐ에 들어갈 말로 가장 적절한 것은?

① unless          ② as soon as
③ even though     ④ because
⑤ no matter what

**중요**

**10** 다음 중 밑줄 친 (A)의 쓰임으로 가장 적절한 것은?

① to feed lions       ② to surprise lions
③ to catch lions      ④ to protect lions
⑤ to scare lions away

**서답형**

**11** 위 글의 내용에 맞게 빈칸에 알맞은 말을 쓰시오.

> The lion light scares away not only _____ but also _____.

[12~14] 다음 글을 읽고 물음에 답하시오.

One night, I was walking around the cows with a light, and the lions didn't come. I discovered that lions were afraid of (A)_____. So I came up with an idea. I decided to invent lights that move electronically. Because I like machines, I could find what I needed to make the lights. I found an old car battery, a small device from a motorcycle, a switch, and a broken electronic light.

**12** 글의 흐름상 빈칸 (A)에 들어갈 말로 가장 적절한 것은?

① a moving human being
② a moving machine
③ a blinking light
④ a moving light
⑤ a light using electricity

**서답형**

**13** According to the passage, what does the writer like? Answer in English with a full sentence.

➡ _____

**중요**

**14** Choose the one that was not used in making the lights that move electronically.

① a battery found in an old car
② a switch
③ broken electronic light
④ a small device from a motorcycle
⑤ a broken battery

[15~18] 다음 글을 읽고 물음에 답하시오.

My name is Richard Turere. I live in Kenya in the southern part of Nairobi National Park. The southern part of the park does not have a fence, so wild animals like lions move out of the park freely. They kill the animals that farmers are raising. (A)_____, farmers try to kill the lions because they want to protect their animals.

One morning, I woke up and saw our cow lying on the ground. It was dead, and I felt so bad. At first, I thought I couldn't do anything because I was only eleven. Then I realized I shouldn't ignore the problem. I really wanted to help the people in my town in the same situation.

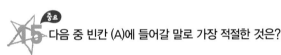

**15** 다음 중 빈칸 (A)에 들어갈 말로 가장 적절한 것은?

① For example        ② That is

③ As a result        ④ However

⑤ In other words

**16** 다음 중 위 글을 읽고 답할 수 있는 것은?

① How old is Richard now?

② How many animals do the farmers raise?

③ What kind of animals do the farmers raise?

④ What killed the animals that were raised by farmers?

⑤ How many cows did Richard raise?

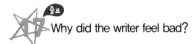

Why did the writer feel bad?

① Because farmers killed his cow.

② Because he woke up late in the morning.

③ Because lions attacked farmers.

④ Because his cow disappeared.

⑤ Because he saw his cow lying dead.

**18** Write the reason why wild animals move out of the park freely. Answer in English and use the phrase 'It's because.'

➡ _____

_____

[19~22] 다음 글을 읽고 물음에 답하시오.

My first idea was to use fire. I thought lions were afraid of it. Sadly, it didn't (A)work. Instead, the fire helped the lions to better watch the cows move. Then I had another idea. It was to use a scarecrow. But the lions were very clever. The first day, they were turned away. On the second day, they jumped in and killed more animals.

One night, I was walking around the cows with a light, and the lions didn't come.

(B) I decided to invent lights that move electronically. Because I like machines, I could find what I needed to make the lights.

(C) I discovered that lions were afraid of a moving light. So I came up with an idea.

(D) I found an old car battery, a small device from a motorcycle, a switch, and a broken electronic light.

**19** 밑줄 친 (A)와 쓰임이 같은 것은?

① I can't work if I'm hungry.

② She works for an engineering company.

③ The phone isn't working.

④ My plan worked and gave me a chance.

⑤ I'm still looking for a work.

**20** 자연스러운 글이 되도록 (B)~(D)를 바르게 나열한 것은?

① (B)–(D)–(C)        ② (B)–(C)–(D)

③ (C)–(B)–(D)        ④ (C)–(D)–(B)

⑤ (D)–(C)–(B)

**서답형**

**21** What did the writer use to turn lions away? Answer in English with a full sentence.

➡ _____

_____

**서답형**

**22** What was the writer doing with a light? Answer in English.

➡ _____

**[23~28]** 다음 글을 읽고 물음에 답하시오.

At thirteen, I finally made what I called "lion lights." My father said, "I'm so proud of you, Richard!" Since then, I have set up lights at seven homes in my community and haven't heard anyone complain about lions. They thanked me, saying "ⓐThis is exactly what we wanted, lovely boy!" Surprisingly, ⓑ my idea is now used all over Kenya to scare away other animals, such as elephants. From this experience, I realized that I could make a difference in people's lives even though I am just a young boy. I was also able to prevent lions from being killed.

Thanks to ⓒmy work, I got a scholarship to a great school in Kenya. I am really excited about ⓓthis. In my new school, I am now teaching my friends how to make and use ⓔ the lights. I tell my friends, "Our ideas can make a difference in people's lives!"

**중요**

**23** According to the passage, why was "lion lights" made?

① to make people's lives comfortable
② to find lions in the field
③ to turn away his neighbors
④ to scare away wild animals
⑤ to feel proud of himself

**24** 다음 중 위 글을 읽고 알 수 있는 것은?

① Elephants help people in Kenya.
② The writer's father made the lion light.
③ People didn't like lion light.
④ Lions used to be killed by people.
⑤ A young boy can't make any difference in people's lives.

**25** ⓐ~ⓔ 중 의미하는 바가 <u>다른</u> 하나는?

① ⓐ  ② ⓑ  ③ ⓒ  ④ ⓓ  ⑤ ⓔ

**중요**

**26** 다음 중 위 글을 읽고 답할 수 <u>없는</u> 것은?

① How many homes has the writer set up lights at?
② What did people say to the writer about the lion light?
③ How many years has the writer tried to make "lion light?"
④ What is now used all over Kenya to scare away other animals?
⑤ What did the writer get thanks to the lion light?

**서답형**

**27** 위 글의 내용에 맞게 빈칸에 알맞은 말을 쓰시오.

The lion light scares away not only _____ but also _____ _____ , _____ _____ _____ .

**서답형**

**28** What is the writer doing now in his new school? Answer in English with a full sentence.

➡ _____

_____

**[01~04]** 다음 글을 읽고 물음에 답하시오.

My name is Richard Turere. I live in Kenya in the southern part of Nairobi National Park. The southern part of the park does not have a fence, (A)_____ wild animals like lions move out of the park freely. They kill the animals that farmers are raising. As a result, farmers try to kill the lions (B)_____ they want to protect their animals.

One morning, I woke up and saw our cow lying on the ground. It was dead, and I felt so bad. At first, I thought I couldn't do anything (C)_____ I was only eleven. Then I realized I shouldn't ignore the problem. I really wanted to help the people in my town in the same situation.

**01** 주어진 단어를 빈칸 (A)~(C)에 써 넣으시오.

| (because / so) |
| --- |

➡ (A)_____ (B)_____ (C)_____

**02** 위 글의 내용에 맞게 빈칸에 알맞은 말을 쓰시오.

| Richard wanted to help people in his town whose animals were also _____ by lions. |
| --- |

**03** According to the passage, from what do farmers want to protect their animals? Answer in English with a full sentence.

➡ _____

**04** 다음 중 글의 내용과 일치하지 <u>않는</u> 것을 한군데 찾아 바르게 고쳐 쓰시오.

| Richard found his cow dead one afternoon and he felt terrible. But he did nothing at first because he was only eleven. However, he came to think that he shouldn't ignore the problem. |
| --- |

➡ _____

**[05~07]** 다음 글을 읽고 물음에 답하시오.

My first idea was to use fire. I thought lions were afraid of it. Sadly, it didn't work. Instead, the fire helped the lions to better watch the cows move. Then I had another idea. (A)It was to use a scarecrow. But the lions were very clever. The first day, they were turned away. On the second day, they jumped in and killed more animals.

**05** 밑줄 친 (A)It이 가리키는 것을 위 글에서 찾아 쓰시오.

➡ _____

**06** What did the writer think when he decided to use fire? Answer in English with seven words.

➡ _____

**07** What happened on the first day of setting up a scarecrow? Answer in English with four words.

➡ _____

[08~10] 다음 글을 읽고 물음에 답하시오.

One night, I was walking around the cows with a light, and the lions didn't come. I discovered that lions were afraid of a moving light. So I came up with an idea. I decided to invent lights that move electronically. Because I like machines, I could find what I needed to make the lights. I found an old car battery, a small device from a motorcycle, a switch, and a broken electronic light.

**08** What did the writer decide to invent? Answer in English with a full sentence.

➡ _____

_____

**09** According to the passage, what did the writer discover about lions?

➡ _____

_____

**10** What was needed to make the lights that the writer wanted to invent?

➡ _____

_____

[11~15] 다음 글을 읽고 물음에 답하시오.

At thirteen, I finally made what I called "lion lights." My father said, "I'm so proud of you, Richard!" Since then, I have set up lights at seven homes in my community and haven't heard anyone complain about lions. They thanked me, saying "(A)This is exactly what we wanted, lovely boy!" Surprisingly, my idea is now used all over Kenya to scare away other animals, such as elephants. From this experience, I realized that I could make a difference in people's lives even though I am just a young boy. I was also able to prevent lions from being killed.

Thanks to my work, I got a scholarship to a great school in Kenya. I am really excited about this. In my new school, I am now teaching my friends how to make and use the lights. I tell my friends, "Our ideas can make a difference in people's lives!" *I = Richard

**11** What did Richard call what he made at thirteen? Answer in English with nine words.

➡ _____

**12** 밑줄 친 (A)가 가리키는 것을 위 글에서 찾아 쓰시오.

➡ _____

**13** What did Richard realize from the experience? Answer in English with a full sentence.

➡ _____

_____

**14** Thanks to his work, what did Richard get? Answer in English.

➡ _____

**15** 위 글의 내용과 일치하도록 빈칸에 알맞은 말을 쓰시오.

In addition to making a difference in people's lives, Richard was also able to stop _____.

# 구석구석

## Communication Task Step 2

**A:** What's the matter, Minsu?
무슨 일 있니? = What's wrong with you?

**B:** There aren't many parks in our community.
There aren't many ~ = ~가 많지 않다.

I hope we can have some more.
I hope 뒤에는 접속사 that이 생략되어 있다.

**A:** Me, too. That would be nice.

구문해설 • Me, too. = 나도 마찬가지야.

해석
A: 민수야, 무슨 일 있니?

B: 우리 동네에 공원이 많지 않아. 나는 좀 더 많은 공원이 있으면 좋겠어.

A: 나도 그래. 그러면 좋겠다.

## Before You Read

It is Jessica's first day on a farm. She is painting the fence. Her mother is
비인칭 주어 It          현재진행형(~하는 중이다)

setting up the scarecrow. Her father is going to the market on a motorcycle.
~로 가는 중이다          교통수단을 나타내는 전치사(~을 타고)

They are a good team!
Jessica. her mother. her father

구문해설 • farm: 농장 • fence: 울타리 • set up: ~을 설치하다 • scarecrow: 허수아비

Jessica의 농장에서의 첫날이다. 그녀는 울타리를 칠하고 있다. 그녀의 엄마는 허수아비를 설치하고 있다. 그녀의 아빠는 오토바이를 타고 시장에 가고 있다. 그들은 좋은 팀이다!

## Let's Write

I have seen students carrying many things at school. So, I have brought my
현재완료(계속적 용법)   지각동사 see의 목적격보어          결과를 이끄는 접속사

favorite item, a bag, for you. If you want to carry many things, this bag is
        동격

exactly what you need. It is very light and comfortable. I hope it can be useful
선행사를 포함하는 관계대명사(= the thing that[which])                = the bag
for you. Thank you.

구문해설 • light: 가벼운 • comfortable: 편한

저는 학생들이 학교에서 많은 것들을 가지고 다니는 것을 봤습니다. 그래서 저는 제가 가장 좋아하는 물건인 가방을 여러분을 위해 가지고 왔습니다. 만약 여러분이 많은 것들을 가지고 다니고 싶다면, 이 가방은 정확히 여러분이 필요로 하는 것입니다. 이것은 매우 가볍고 편합니다. 저는 이것이 여러분에게 쓸모가 있기를 바랍니다. 감사합니다.

# 영역별 핵심문제

**01** 다음 빈칸에 공통으로 알맞은 것을 고르시오.

> • I hope they will _____ running in the hallway.
> • We had to _____ to buy some snacks.
> • The rain will _____ them from going out.

① stay      ② stop
③ discover      ④ invent
⑤ float

**02** 다음 밑줄 친 단어와 의미가 같은 것을 고르시오.

> I have to sort the data.

① classify      ② press
③ push      ④ complain
⑤ decide

**03** 다음 영영풀이에 해당하는 단어를 고르시오.

> a figure made to look like a person, that is dressed in old clothes and put in a field to frighten birds away

① scarecrow      ② fence
③ scholarship      ④ disease
⑤ harmony

**04** 다음 대화의 빈칸에 들어갈 말로 적절한 것을 고르시오.

> G: I love our stickers!
> B: Me, too! I hope these stickers will be _____.

① expensive      ② comfortable
③ dangerous      ④ ignorant
⑤ helpful

**05** 빈칸 (A)와 (B)에 들어가기에 적절한 것으로 짝지어진 것은?

> A: What are you going to do for the festival, Sophia?
> B: I'm going to help people (A)_____ flower tea. I hope they (B)_____ a great time.
> A: You are very kind.

    (A)     (B)
① plant      take
② plant      make
③ try      take
④ try      have
⑤ try      do

**06** 다음 (A)에 주어진 단어를 문맥에 맞는 적절한 형태로 바꾸어 쓰시오.

> A: You look upset. What's the matter?
> B: Look! Some students are running in the hallway.
> A: You're right. I hope they will stop (A) (run) in the hallway.
> B: I hope so, too.

➡ _____

**[07~10]** 다음 대화를 읽고 물음에 답하시오.

> Henry: You look (A)_____. What's the matter, Mina?
>
> Mina: Look at these comments, Henry. A lot of people say there aren't enough fun places to see in our town.
>
> Henry: ⓐThat's too bad. I'm sorry ⓑthat they didn't have a chance to visit the nice places here. We should do something about that.
>
> Mina: (B)Why don't we make a video ⓒthat shows the famous places in our town and put it on the internet?
>
> Henry: That's an excellent idea. Let's do ⓓthat.
>
> Mina: Sounds good. I hope ⓔthat they enjoy their time here.

**07** (A)에 들어가기에 적절하지 않은 것은?

① worried      ② down

③ upset      ④ disappointed

⑤ pleased

**08** 밑줄 친 ⓐ~ⓔ 중에서 쓰임이 같은 것끼리 짝지어진 것은?

① ⓐ, ⓑ      ② ⓑ, ⓒ

③ ⓐ, ⓒ      ④ ⓐ, ⓓ

⑤ ⓒ, ⓔ

**09** 밑줄 친 (B) 대신 쓰기에 어색한 것은? (2개)

① Can you make

② How about making

③ What about making

④ Shall we make

⑤ Will you make

**10** 위 대화의 내용과 일치하지 않는 것은?

① Mina is reading comments about her town on the internet.

② Many people who visited their town weren't satisfied.

③ Henry thinks there aren't any nice places in his town.

④ Mina suggests making a video showing the famous places in the town.

⑤ Henry and Mina will post the video on the internet.

**[11~13]** 다음 대화를 읽고 물음에 답하시오.

> G: You look (A)down. What's the matter?
>
> B: I signed up (B)_____ the soccer team, but I couldn't join.
>
> G: Why not?
>
> B: There were already too many students on the team, so the coach won't accept any new students this year.
>
> G: (C)That's too bad. I hope you find another fun club.
>
> B: Thanks.

**11** 다음 중 밑줄 친 (A)와 같은 의미로 쓰인 것은?

① The sun was going down.

② The bathroom is down the stairs.

③ The system was down all the morning.

④ I felt a bit down today.

⑤ The boys ran down the hill.

**12** 빈칸 (B)에 들어갈 전치사를 쓰시오.

➡ _____

**13** 다음 중 밑줄 친 (C) 대신 쓸 수 있는 것은?

① We are pleased to hear that.
② I am sorry to hear that.
③ He was sorry to be late.
④ I am sad to miss you.
⑤ He is glad to find the club.

Grammar

**14** 다음 밑줄 친 부분 중 어법상 틀린 것은?

① I saw some bottles <u>floating</u> in the water.
② She watched her husband <u>go</u> out.
③ Jim looked at her <u>to play</u> on the floor.
④ In big cities, you can't usually hear cars <u>come</u>.
⑤ She felt someone <u>following</u> behind her.

**15** 다음 그림을 참고하여 괄호 안에 주어진 어휘를 이용하여 빈칸에 알맞게 쓰시오.

➡ Sarah saw John _____ too much for breakfast. (eat)

**16** 다음 중 어색한 문장을 <u>모두</u> 고르시오.

① Would you tell me what you think of the job?
② I would like to do what I want when I want.
③ I watched him entered the room.
④ I never thought what we could love each other more.
⑤ I heard someone singing in an empty room.
⑥ I had a letter sent to him.

Reading

[17~19] 다음 글을 읽고 물음에 답하시오.

My name is Richard Turere. I live in Kenya in the southern part of Nairobi National Park. The southern part of the park does not have a fence, so wild animals like lions (A)_____. They kill the animals that farmers are raising. As a result, farmers try to kill the lions because they want (B)<u>to protect</u> their animals.

**17** 다음 중 글의 흐름상 빈칸 (A)에 들어갈 말로 가장 적절한 것은?

① eat their meat in the park
② don't move at all
③ walk in the park slowly
④ make loud noises
⑤ move out of the park freely

**18** 다음 중 밑줄 친 (B)와 쓰임이 같은 것은?

① He went out <u>to see</u> his sister off.
② Molly decided <u>to jog</u> every morning.
③ Ken needed something <u>to drink</u>.
④ It is possible for me <u>to get</u> there on time.
⑤ They felt sad <u>to hear</u> the news.

**19** 다음 중 위 글의 내용과 일치하는 것은?

① Richard Turere lives far from Nairobi National Park.
② Richard Turere likes lions.
③ Richard Turere moves out of the National Park freely.
④ Nairobi National Park lies in Kenya.
⑤ Farmers try hard to protect lions.

[20~22] 다음 글을 읽고 물음에 답하시오.

At thirteen, I finally made what I called "lion light." My father said, "I'm so ①proud of you, Richard!" Since then, I have set up lights at seven homes in my community and haven't heard anyone ②compliment about lions. They ③thanked me, saying "This is exactly what we wanted, lovely boy!" Surprisingly, my idea is now used all over Kenya to scare away other animals, such as elephants. From this experience, I realized that I could make a difference in people's lives even though I am just a young boy. I was also able to prevent lions from being killed.

④Thanks to my work, I got a scholarship to a great school in Kenya. I am really excited about this. In my new school, I am now teaching my friends ⑤how to make and use the lights. I tell my friends, "Our ideas can make a difference in people's lives!"                    *I = Richard

**20** ①~⑤ 중 글의 흐름상 어색한 것은?

①          ②          ③          ④          ⑤

**21** 위 글의 내용에 맞게 빈칸에 알맞은 말을 쓰시오.

Richard is really excited about _____
_____ _____ _____
_____ _____ _____ .

**22** According to the passage, when did the writer make what he called "lion lights?" Answer in English with five words.

➡ _____

[23~28] 다음 글을 읽고 물음에 답하시오.

**Pay It Forward**
*Paying it forward* means doing something nice for someone _____(A)_____ someone else did something nice for you. It could be as ⓐ[simple / complex] as carrying a large bag for an elderly neighbor or holding a door open for someone. It is about (B)_____.

**The Ice Bucket Challenge**
The Ice Bucket Challenge is a project to ⓑ[ignore / inform] people about Lou Gehrig's disease and collect donations. People throw a bucket of ice water on their head and make a donation. Then they choose three people (C)to do the same thing.

**Time Bank**
A time bank is a way of trading ⓒ[work / play]. It is based on the idea _____(D)_____ time takes the place of money. With time banking, a person does not pay or get paid for services. Instead, a person can use a skill or talent to help other members of their community.

**23** 위 글의 빈칸 (A)에 알맞은 것은? (2개)

① as               ② if
③ though          ④ while
⑤ because

**24** 주어진 단어를 바르게 나열하여 빈칸 (B)에 들어갈 말을 완성하시오. 필요하다면 어형을 바꾸시오.

(spread / others / be / to / of / the joy / kind)

➡ _____

**25** 밑줄 친 (C)가 의미하는 것을 위 글에서 찾아 쓰시오.

➡ _____

_____

**26** 위 글의 빈칸 (D)에 알맞은 것은?

① if         ② that
③ how        ④ what
⑤ which

**27** ⓐ~ⓒ에서 글의 흐름상 자연스러운 것끼리 바르게 짝지은 것은?

① simple – ignore – work
② complex – ignore – work
③ simple – inform – work
④ complex – inform – play
⑤ simple – inform – play

**28** 다음 중 위 글을 읽고 답할 수 있는 것은?

① Who made the Ice Bucket Challenge first?
② How many people have taken part in the Ice Bucket Challenge?
③ How many people do people choose after making a donation?
④ What kind of talent do we need to participate in the time bank?
⑤ Who invented the idea about a time bank?

**[29~30]** 다음 글을 읽고 물음에 답하시오.

(A)Pay It Forward

*Paying it forward* means doing something nice for someone because someone else did something nice for you. It could be as simple as carrying a large bag for an elderly neighbor or holding a door open for someone. It is about spreading the joy of being kind to others.

**29** What does 'paying it forward' mean? Answer in English.

➡ _____

_____

_____

**30** 다음 중 밑줄 친 (A)에 해당하지 <u>않는</u> 것은?

① Amie: I held a door open for an elderly man.
② Becky: I gave up my seat for an elderly woman.
③ Clara: I pushed a door for a boy sitting in a wheelchair.
④ David: I said 'Hi' to my classmates.
⑤ Emilia: I pushed an elevator button for a very little girl.

출제율 95%

**01** 짝지어진 단어의 관계가 같도록 빈칸에 알맞은 말을 쓰시오.

> accept : acceptance = c_____ : complaint

출제율 90%

**02** 다음 빈칸에 들어갈 말로 적절한 것은?

> The leaves _____ on the water.

① discovered    ② floated

③ decided    ④ accepted

⑤ ignored

출제율 90%

**03** 주어진 우리말에 맞게 빈칸을 채우시오. (철자가 주어진 경우 그 철자로 시작할 것)

(1) 그 회의는 지역 문화 회관에서 열릴 것이다.

➡ The meeting will be held in the c_____ culture centre.

(2) 주소가 조금이라도 변경될 경우에는 저희에게 알려 주십시오.

➡ Please i_____ us of any changes of address.

출제율 95%

**04** 주어진 말에 이어질 대화의 순서가 바르게 배열된 것은?

> A: You look upset. What's the matter?
>
> (A) You're right. I hope they will wait their turn.
>
> (B) Look! Some students are cutting in line.
>
> (C) I hope so, too.

① (A) – (C) – (B)    ② (B) – (A) – (C)

③ (B) – (C) – (A)    ④ (C) – (A) – (B)

⑤ (C) – (B) – (A)

**[05~07]** 다음 대화를 읽고 물음에 답하시오.

> G: What's the matter, Mason? Are you hurt?
>
> B: I fell (A)_____ my bike at Hangang Park this afternoon.
>
> G: Are you okay? ⓐ_____?
>
> B: I'm okay. I just rode over a big bump (B)_____ the bike path.
>
> G: Weren't there any signs?
>
> B: No, there weren't.
>
> G: How about writing about the problem (B)_____ the community website?
>
> B: That's a great idea.

출제율 95%

**05** 빈칸 (A), (B), (C)에 들어가기에 알맞은 것으로 짝지어진 것은?

| | (A) | (B) | (C) |
|---|---|---|---|
| ① | off | in | by |
| ② | with | of | under |
| ③ | off | on | on |
| ④ | in | about | at |
| ⑤ | over | of | in |

출제율 90%

**06** 내용상 빈칸 ⓐ에 들어가기에 가장 적절한 것은?

① How did it happen?

② Why did you ride a bike?

③ When did you hurt?

④ What did you ride?

⑤ Who rode the bike?

**07** 위 대화를 읽고 대답할 수 <u>없는</u> 것은?

① Where did he ride a bike?

② When did he hurt?

③ What was on the bike path?

④ What will he post on the website?

⑤ Where were the signs?

[08~10] 다음 대화를 읽고 물음에 답하시오.

Henry: (가)_____ What's the matter, Mina?

Mina: Look at these comments, Henry. ( A )

Henry: That's too bad. ( B ) I'm sorry that they didn't have a chance to visit the nice places here. ( C ) We should do something about that.

Mina: Why don't we make a video that ⓐ(show) the famous places in our town and put it on the internet? ( D )

Henry: That's an excellent idea. ( E ) Let's do that.

Mina: Sounds good. I hope they ⓑ(enjoy) their time here.

**08** 빈칸 (가)에 들어가기에 가장 적절한 것은?

① You are happy.

② You have a new friend.

③ You said hi.

④ You are wearing a new jacket.

⑤ You look upset.

**09** (A)~(E) 중 주어진 문장이 들어갈 곳은?

A lot of people say there aren't enough fun places to see in our town.

① (A)　② (B)　③ (C)　④ (D)　⑤ (E)

**10** 밑줄 친 ⓐ, ⓑ에 주어진 단어의 형태로 적절한 것은?

|  | ⓐ | ⓑ |
|---|---|---|
| ① | show | enjoys |
| ② | shows | enjoy |
| ③ | to show | enjoying |
| ④ | showing | enjoyed |
| ⑤ | shown | to enjoy |

**11** 어법상 빈칸에 알맞지 <u>않은</u> 것을 고르시오.

She _____ him open the window.

① watched　② made　③ saw

④ asked　⑤ heard

**12** 다음 빈칸에 들어갈 말이 나머지와 <u>다른</u> 하나는? (대·소문자 무시)

① _____ I want for my birthday is a pair of shoes.

② There was something heavy _____ I didn't know.

③ That is _____ I like best about my job.

④ She showed me _____ she had bought at the shop.

⑤ Please try to remember _____ you have been doing.

**13** 다음 문장의 빈칸에 알맞은 말은?

We observed them _____ in the water.

① swam　② swum

③ to swim　④ to swimming

⑤ swimming

**14** 다음 중 어법상 적절한 문장은?

① This isn't that I expected!

② The movie what I saw last night was fantastic.

③ I couln't understand what you meant.

④ That my friend cooked for me yesterday was really yummy.

⑤ You should learn the things what you have to do.

**15** 다음 두 문장의 의미가 같도록 빈칸에 알맞은 말을 쓰시오.

(1) She felt the building shaking. (1 단어)

= She felt the building _____.

(2) Dad bought me something that looked like a fish. (5 단어)

= Dad bought me _____.

(3) We can satisfy ourselves by eating the food we choose. (3 단어)

= We can satisfy ourselves by eating _____.

**[16~19]** 다음 글을 읽고 물음에 답하시오.

My first idea was to use fire. (①) I thought lions were afraid of it. Sadly, it didn't work. Instead, the fire helped the lions to better watch the cows move. (②) Then I had another idea. It was to use a scarecrow. (③) The first day, they were turned away. On the second day, they jumped in and killed more animals. (④) One night, I was walking around the cows with a light, and the lions didn't come. (⑤) I discovered that lions were afraid of a moving light. So I came

up with an idea. I decided to invent lights that move electronically. Because I like machines, I could find what I needed to make the lights. I found an old car battery, a small device from a motorcycle, a switch, and a broken electronic light.

*I = Richard

**16** ①~⑤ 중 주어진 문장이 들어가기에 가장 적절한 곳은?

But the lions were very clever.

①     ②     ③     ④     ⑤

**17** Write the reason why Richard could find what he needed to make the lights. Use the phrase 'It's because.'

➡ _____

**18** 위 글의 내용에 맞게 빈칸에 알맞은 말을 쓰시오.

Because of the fire Richard used, the lions could _____ _____ _____ _____ _____.

## 19 Choose the one that is NOT true.

① Richard kept thinking about the ways to turn away lions.

② It turned out that lions weren't afraid of fire.

③ A scarecrow didn't work from the first day.

④ Richard is fond of machines.

⑤ Richard could find what he needed to make the lights without difficulty.

**[20~21]** 다음 글을 읽고 물음에 답하시오.

### My Item for the Class Bazaar

I have seen students carrying many things at school. So, I have brought my favorite item, a bag, for you. If you want to carry many things, this bag is exactly (A)_____ you need. It is very light and comfortable. I hope it can be useful for you. Thank you.

## 20 빈칸 (A)에 들어갈 말로 가장 적절한 것은?

① which          ② that

③ whom          ④ what

⑤ why

## 21 Write the reason why the writer brought the bag. Answer in English.

➡ _____

_____

**[22~23]** 다음 글을 읽고 물음에 답하시오.

My name is Richard Turere. I live in Kenya in the southern part of Nairobi National Park. The southern part of the park does not have a fence, so wild animals like lions move out of the park freely. They kill the animals that farmers are raising. As a result, farmers try to kill the lions because they want to protect their animals.

One morning, I woke up and saw our cow lying on the ground. It was dead, and I felt so bad. At first, I thought I couldn't do anything because I was only eleven. Then I realized I shouldn't ignore the problem. I really wanted to help the people in my town in the same situation.

## 22 다음 중 위 글의 내용과 일치하는 것은?

① It is hard for Richard to see animals like lions.

② Richard found his cow dead when he was ten years old.

③ Richard wanted to help people in the same situation as his.

④ Farmers used to raise the lions.

⑤ There was no fence in the park because people try to protect the lions.

## 23 According to the passage, why do farmers try to kill the lions? Answer in English and use the phrase 'It's because.'

➡ _____

_____

[01~03] 다음 대화를 읽고 물음에 답하시오.

> G: What's ①the occasion, Mason? Are you hurt?
> B: I ②fell off my bike at Hangang Park this afternoon.
> G: Are you okay? How did it happen?
> B: I'm okay. I just ③rode over a big bump on the bike path.
> G: Weren't there any signs?
> B: No, there weren't.
> G: How about ④writing about the problem on the community website?
> B: That's ⑤a great idea.

**01** 위 대화의 내용을 아래와 같이 요약할 때 빈칸에 들어가기에 적절한 단어를 본문에서 찾아 쓰시오.

> I fell off my (A)_____ at Hangang Park this afternoon. I didn't know there was a (B)_____ on the path. There weren't any (C)_____. I think it is dangerous.

**02** 주어진 영영풀이에 해당하는 단어를 위 대화에서 찾아 쓰시오.

> a track that is specially made for people to walk or ride on

➡ _____

**03** 위 대화의 ①~⑤ 중에서 내용상 어색한 부분을 찾아 번호와 함께 쓰고, 올바르게 고치시오.

➡ _____

**04** 관계대명사 what을 사용하여 주어진 두 문장을 한 문장으로 바꾸시오.

(1) • I want to do something for the community.
  • It is to pick up trash.

➡ _____
_____

(2) • I liked it.
  • Yuna gave it to me last month.

➡ _____

(3) • Did you enjoy the movie?
  • We saw it at the theater last night.

➡ _____
_____

**05** 주어진 두 문장을 한 문장으로 바꾸시오.

> • I saw the airplane.
> • The airplane was flying low from south to north.

➡ _____

**06** 다음 우리말을 주어진 어휘를 이용하여 영작하시오.

(1) 당신은 당신이 찾을 수 있는 것에 놀랄 것입니다. (will, find, surprised by, 9 단어)

➡ _____

(2) 설상가상으로 비까지 내리기 시작했다. (worse, started, 5 단어)

➡ _____

(3) Samuel은 그의 이름을 부르는 소리를 들었다. (hear, call, 5 단어)

➡ _____

(4) 나는 Ann이 그녀의 개를 산책시키고 있는 것을 보았다. (see, walk, 6 단어)

➡ _____

[07~09] 다음 글을 읽고 물음에 답하시오.

My first idea was to use fire. I thought lions were afraid of it. Sadly, it didn't work. Instead, the fire helped the lions to better watch the cows move. Then I had another idea. It was to use a scarecrow. (A)But the lions were very clever. The first day, they were turned away. On the second day, they jumped in and killed more animals.

One night, I was walking around the cows with a light, and the lions didn't come. I discovered that lions were afraid of a moving light. So I came up with an idea. I decided to invent lights that move electronically. Because I like machines, I could find ⓐ_____ I needed to make the lights. I found an old car battery, a small device from a motorcycle, a switch, and a broken electronic light.          *I = Richard

**07** 빈칸 ⓐ에 들어갈 알맞은 말을 쓰시오.

➡ _____

**08** 위 글의 내용에 맞게 사건이 일어난 순서대로 나열하시오.

> ⓐ Lions didn't come when Richard walked around the cows with a light.
> ⓑ Richard determined to invent lights that move electronically.
> ⓒ Richard's first and second ideas didn't work at all.
> ⓓ Richard realized what lions were afraid of was a moving light.

➡ _____

**09** 글쓴이가 밑줄 친 (A)와 같이 말한 이유를 우리말로 쓰시오.

➡ _____
_____

[10~11] 다음 글을 읽고 물음에 답하시오.

**Pay It Forward**

Paying it forward means (A)_____ because someone else did something nice for you. It could be as simple as carrying a large bag for an elderly neighbor or holding a door open for someone. It is about spreading the joy of being kind to others.

**The Ice Bucket Challenge**

The Ice Bucket Challenge is a project to inform people about Lou Gehrig's disease and collect donations. People throw a bucket of ice water on their head and make a donation. Then they choose three people to do the same thing.

**10** 주어진 단어를 바르게 배열하여 빈칸 (A)에 들어갈 말을 완성하시오. 필요하다면 단어를 변형하시오.

> (someone / something / do / for / nice)

➡ _____

**11** How many people are chosen to do the challenge after a person carries out the Ice Bucket Challenge? Answer in English with a full sentence.

➡ _____
_____

## 창의사고력 서술형 문제

**01** 주어진 표현을 사용하여 다음 대화를 완성해 봅시다.

> A: _____ (the matter)
> B: I didn't do well on the math test.
> A: That's too bad. I hope _____. (better, next time) (5 words)

**02** 다음 그림을 참고하여 〈조건〉에 맞게 문장을 완성하시오.

(1)     (2)

---
조건

1. 지각동사를 사용하여 과거시제로 쓸 것.
2. (1)에는 hear, talk, Minsu를 사용할 것.
3. (2)에는 see, my little brother를 사용할 것.

➡ (1) I _____ with Mina.
  (2) I _____ on the floor.

**03** 다음 내용을 바탕으로 기부할 물품을 소개하는 글을 써 보시오.

---
조건

Item: a watch
Use: to check time
Characteristic: light and comfortable

---

Item: _____
I have seen students _____ at school. So, I have brought my favorite time, _____, for you. If you want _____, this is exactly what you need. It is very _____. I hope it can be useful for you. Thank you.

## 단원별 모의고사

**01** 다음 짝지어진 두 단어의 관계가 같도록 빈칸에 알맞은 말을 쓰시오.

> dangerous : safe = _____ : sink

**02** 다음 영영풀이에 해당하는 단어로 적절한 것은?

> a machine or tool that does a special job

① device  ② bicycle
③ fence  ④ scarecrow
⑤ community

**03** 다음 문장의 빈칸에 알맞은 것을 〈보기〉에서 찾아 쓰시오.

┌─ 보기 ─┐
with   on   from   up

(1) The book is based _____ personal experience.
(2) How many people have signed _____ for the class?
(3) The rain prevented them _____ eating outdoors.
(4) She came up _____ a new idea for increasing sales.

**04** 다음 빈칸에 들어갈 말로 적절한 것은?

> This can help them _____ away their enemies.

① realize  ② scare
③ press  ④ protect
⑤ ignore

**[05~07]** 다음 대화를 읽고 물음에 답하시오.

B: What's ①the matter, Yura?
G: I'm (A)concerned about this dog. I see it on the street ②every time I go to school. I don't think it has a home.
B: Awww, what a cute dog! I'm ③pleased to hear that it doesn't have a home.
G: I know. ④What should I do with it?
B: Why don't you take it to an animal care center and ⑤ask for help?
G: That's a great idea. Thanks.

**05** 밑줄 친 (A)와 같은 의미의 단어를 주어진 철자로 시작하여 쓰시오.

➡ w_____

**06** 대화의 내용으로 보아 ①~⑤ 중 어색한 것은?

①   ②   ③   ④   ⑤

**07** What will the girl do after the dialogue?

① She will go to school and tell the teacher about the dog.
② She will find a new dog and take care of it.
③ She will take the dog to an animal care center.
④ She will make the dog a new home.
⑤ She will ask the boy to thank the dog and take it to home.

## 08 대화의 빈칸에 들어갈 말로 적절한 것은?

> A: Do you know how to write an English essay? It's too hard for me.
> B: How about reading this book? It will give you some tips.
> A: Thank you so much. I'll try it.
> B: _____

① I'm sorry to hear that.
② I hope you find it helpful.
③ That's what I wanted to do.
④ I like fantasy novels the most.
⑤ My English teacher told me to write it.

### [09~10] 다음 대화를 읽고 물음에 답하시오.

> Henry: You look upset. ( A ) What's (가)_____, Mina?
> Mina: ( B ) A lot of people say there aren't enough fun places to see in our town.
> Henry: That's too bad. ( C ) I'm sorry that they didn't have a chance to visit the nice places here. ( D ) We should do something about that.
> Mina: Why don't we make a video that shows the famous places in our town and put it on the internet? ( E )
> Henry: That's an excellent idea. Let's do that.
> Mina: Sounds good. I (나)_____ they enjoy their time here.

## 09 (A)~(E) 중에서 다음 문장이 들어가기에 적절한 곳은?

> Look at these comments, Henry.

① (A)   ② (B)   ③ (C)   ④ (D)   ⑤ (E)

## 10 (가)와 (나)의 빈칸에 들어가기에 적절한 것은?

|   | (가) | (나) |
|---|------|------|
| ① | the matter | hope |
| ② | wrong | suppose |
| ③ | the occasion | know |
| ④ | your idea | think |
| ⑤ | the problem | believe |

### [11~12] 다음 대화를 읽고 물음에 답하시오.

> G: What's the matter, Mason? Are you hurt?
> B: I fell (A)_____ my bike at Hangang Park this afternoon?
> G: Are you okay? How did it happen?
> B: I'm okay. I just rode (B)_____ a big bump on the bike path.
> G: Weren't there any signs?
> B: No, there weren't.
> G: How (C)_____ writing about the problem (D)_____ the community website?
> B: That's a great idea.

## 11 대화의 빈칸 (A)~(D)에 들어갈 수 없는 것은?

① at        ② off        ③ on
④ about      ⑤ over

## 12 위 대화를 읽고 대답할 수 없는 것은?

① Where was Mason riding a bike?
② What was there on the bike path?
③ When will Mason write about the problem?
④ Were there any signs on the bike path?
⑤ Why did Mason fall off his bike?

**13** 다음 중 밑줄 친 부분의 쓰임이 나머지 넷과 <u>다른</u> 것을 고르시오.

① Do you hear water <u>flowing</u>?
② Sophie felt someone <u>following</u> her in the darkness.
③ There was a baby <u>sleeping</u> on the bed.
④ Mary saw Tom <u>entering</u> the classroom.
⑤ The coach observed the player <u>hitting</u> the punchball.

**14** 다음 빈칸에 들어갈 말을 순서대로 묶은 것은?

> • The movie I saw at the theater is _____ Tony recommended.
> • I have seen students _____ time at school.

① which – checked
② that – to check
③ that – check
④ what – to check
⑤ what – checking

**15** 다음 중 어법상 옳은 문장을 <u>모두</u> 고르시오.

① That I want for my birthday is a backpack.
② I see girls to ride a bike in the park.
③ Did you smell something burning in the house?
④ The book is what she bought it at the bookstore.
⑤ Do you understand what you are reading?

**16** 다음 문장에서 어법상 <u>어색한</u> 것을 바르게 고쳐 다시 쓰시오.

(1) This is exactly that we wanted.
➡ _____

(2) My daughter showed me which she had painted.
➡ _____

(3) If they were successful, the thing what was given to them was some salt.
➡ _____
_____

(4) Tiffany heard a man to answer the phone.
➡ _____

(5) Robert listened to her cried against his shoulder.
➡ _____
_____

**17** 다음 두 문장이 같도록 할 때 빈칸에 알맞은 말을 쓰시오.

> The great pyramids were the things that we saw there.
> = The great pyramids were _____ we saw there.

➡ _____

**[18~21]** 다음 글을 읽고 물음에 답하시오.

At thirteen, I finally made ⓐ_____ I called "lion lights." My father said, "I'm so proud of you, Richard!"
(A) From this experience, I realized that I could make a difference in people's lives even though I am just a young boy. I was also able to prevent lions from being killed.

(B) They thanked me, saying "This is exactly what we wanted, lovely boy!" Surprisingly, my idea is now used all over Kenya to scare away other animals, such as elephants.

(C) Since then, I have set up lights at seven homes in my community and haven't heard anyone complain about lions.

Thanks to my work, I got a scholarship to a great school in Kenya. I am really excited about this. In my new school, I am now teaching my friends how to make and use the lights. I tell my friends, "Our ideas can make a difference in people's lives!"

**18** 다음 중 빈칸 ⓐ에 들어갈 말과 다른 하나는?

① Is that _____ you read last night?

② Tell me _____ he talked about me.

③ I know _____ they bought is cheap.

④ Do you remember _____ you saw?

⑤ The truth is _____ it was my fault.

**19** 자연스러운 글이 되도록 (A)~(C)를 바르게 나열하시오.

➡ _____

**20** 다음 중 위 글의 내용과 일치하지 않는 것은?

① Richard invented "lion lights" when he was just a young boy.

② Lions don't have to be killed because of "lion lights."

③ People's lives were changed because of what Richard had made.

④ Richard set up lights only at his home.

⑤ There aren't any complaints about lions in Richard's community.

**21** 다음 중 Richard의 감정으로 가장 적절한 것은?

① shameful but proud

② proud and excited

③ nervous and anxious

④ relieved but sad

⑤ proud but bored

[22~23] 다음 글을 읽고 물음에 답하시오.

One morning, I woke up and saw our cow lying on the ground. It was dead, and I felt so bad. At first, I thought I couldn't do anything because I was only eleven. Then I realized I shouldn't ignore (A)the problem. I really wanted to help the people in my town in the same situation.

My first idea was to use fire. I thought lions were afraid of it. Sadly, it didn't work. Instead, the fire helped the lions to better watch the cows move. Then I had another idea. It was to use a scarecrow. But the lions were very clever. The first day, they were turned away. On the second day, they jumped in and killed more animals.

**22** 다음 중 밑줄 친 (A)의 의미로 가장 적절한 것은?

① feeling sad about dangerous people

② lions attacking animals

③ cows that are afraid of fire

④ helping lions watch the cows

⑤ lions making their own lives

**23** What were the two ideas that the writer came up with? Answer in English with a full sentence.

➡ _____

_____

# Lesson 2

# Chopsticks or a Fork?

 **의사소통 기능**

- 의견 제시하기
  **It seems to** me that you don't like the food.
- 선호에 대해 묻기
  **Which do you prefer,** fried chicken or chicken salad?

 **언어 형식**

- to부정사의 의미상의 주어
  It was not easy **for** her **to** listen to their arguments.
- 명사의 뒤에서 명사를 수식하는 분사
  They finally found Ms. Disher **sitting** under a huge tree.

# Words & Expressions

## Key Words

- **adventure** [ædvéntʃər] 명 모험
- **allow** [əláu] 동 허용하다
- **argue** [á:rgju:] 동 다투다, 주장하다
- **arrival** [əráivəl] 명 도착
- **ban** [bæn] 동 금지하다
- **boastful** [bóustfəl] 형 자랑하는, 뽐내는
- **celebrate** [séləbrèit] 동 기념하다
- **certainly** [sə́:rtnli] 부 분명히
- **choose** [tʃu:z] 동 선택하다
- **chopsticks** [tʃápstiks] 명 젓가락
- **confused** [kənfjú:zd] 형 혼란스러워하는
- **convenient** [kənví:njənt] 형 편리한
- **disappear** [dìsəpíər] 동 사라지다
- **elegant** [éligənt] 형 우아한
- **focus** [fóukəs] 동 집중하다
- **forgive** [fərgív] 동 용서하다
- **grain** [grein] 명 곡물, 곡식
- **healthy** [hélθi] 형 건강한
- **host** [houst] 동 주최하다 명 주인
- **hurriedly** [hə́:ridli] 부 황급히
- **ignore** [ignó:r] 동 무시하다
- **introduce** [intrədjú:s] 동 소개하다
- **leave** [li:v] 동 떠나다, 남기다
- **manner** [mǽnər] 명 방식
- **manners** [mǽnərz] 명 예의, 예절
- **noodle** [nú:dl] 명 국수
- **patiently** [péiʃəntli] 부 참을성 있게
- **plate** [pleit] 명 접시, 그릇
- **please** [pli:z] 동 원하다, 기쁘게 하다
- **plus** [plʌs] 부 게다가, 더욱이
- **polite** [pəláit] 형 예절 바른, 예의 바른
- **prefer** [prifə́:r] 동 더 좋아하다
- **provide** [prəváid] 동 제공하다
- **raise** [reiz] 동 들어 올리다, 기르다
- **reason** [rí:zn] 명 이유
- **recent** [rí:snt] 형 최근의
- **republic** [ripʌ́blik] 명 공화국
- **salty** [sɔ́:lti] 형 짠
- **save** [seiv] 동 아끼다, 구하다
- **search** [sə:rtʃ] 동 찾다
- **spread** [spred] 동 펼치다
- **suggestion** [səgdʒéstʃən] 명 제안, 의견
- **the Middle Ages** 중세 시대
- **travel** [trǽvəl] 동 여행하다
- **trip** [trip] 명 여행
- **uncooked** [ənkúkt] 형 익히지 않은, 날것의
- **utensil** [ju:ténsəl] 명 기구, 도구
- **wisely** [wáizli] 부 현명하게
- **yet** [jet] 부 그러나

## Key Expressions

- **be eager to** ~하고 싶어 하다
- **every time** ~할 때마다 (= **whenever**)
- **give up** 포기하다
- **go out** 나가다
- **have trouble -ing** ~하는 데 어려움을 겪다
- **make up for** ~을 보상하다
- **no way** 절대로 아니다
- **on time** 정각에
- **raise point** 의견을 내세우다
- **regardless of** ~에 상관없이
- **sense of touch** 촉감
- **stay healthy** 건강을 유지하다
- **take a break** 휴식을 취하다

## Word Power

※ 서로 비슷한 뜻을 가진 어휘

- □ **allow** 허락하다 – **permit** 허락하다
- □ **ban** 금지하다 – **prohibit** 금지하다
- □ **certainly** 확실하게 – **surely** 확실하게
- □ **focus** 집중하다 – **concentrate** 집중하다
- □ **patient** 인내하는 – **tolerant** 참을성 있는

- □ **argue** 주장하다 – **claim** 주장하다
- □ **boastful** 뽐내는 – **arrogant** 거만한
- □ **delicious** 맛있는 – **tasty** 맛있는
- □ **ignore** 무시하다 – **neglect** 무시하다
- □ **provide** 제공하다 – **supply** 공급하다

※ 서로 반대의 뜻을 가진 어휘

- □ **allow** 허락하다 ↔ **forbid** 금지하다
- □ **convenient** 편리한 ↔ **inconvenient** 불편한
- □ **patient** 인내하는 ↔ **impatient** 참을성이 없는
- □ **popular** 인기 있는 ↔ **unpopular** 인기 없는
- □ **wisely** 현명하게 ↔ **foolishly** 어리석게

- □ **arrival** 도착 ↔ **departure** 출발
- □ **disappear** 사라지다 ↔ **appear** 나타나다
- □ **polite** 예절바른 ↔ **impolite** 무례한
- □ **save** 아끼다 ↔ **waste** 낭비하다

※ 동사 – 명사

- □ **allow** 허용하다 – **allowance** 허용, 용돈
- □ **arrive** 도착하다 – **arrival** 도착
- □ **introduce** 소개하다 – **introduction** 소개
- □ **provide** 공급하다 – **provision** 공급

- □ **argue** 주장하다 – **argument** 주장
- □ **ignore** 무시하다 – **ignorance** 무지
- □ **prefer** 더 좋아하다 – **preference** 선호
- □ **suggest** 제안하다 – **suggestion** 제안

※ 명사 – 형용사

- □ **adventure** 모험 – **adventurous** 모험심이 강한
- □ **convenience** 편리함 – **convenient** 편리한
- □ **health** 건강 – **healthy** 건강한
- □ **patience** 참을성 – **patient** 인내하는

- □ **boast** 자랑 – **boastful** 뽐내는
- □ **elegance** 고상함 – **elegant** 고상한
- □ **ignorance** 무지 – **ignorant** 무지한
- □ **pleasure** 즐거움 – **pleasant** 즐거운

## English Dictionary

- □ **adventure** 모험
  → an exciting or dangerous experience
  흥미진진하거나 위험한 경험

- □ **boastful** 자랑하는, 뽐내는
  → talking about yourself in a very proud way
  자랑스럽게 자신에 관해서 말하는

- □ **chopsticks** 젓가락
  → a pair of thin sticks which people in China and the Far East use to eat their food
  중국과 극동 지방에서 음식을 먹기 위하여 사용하는 얇은 막대기 한 쌍

- □ **elegant** 우아한
  → (of people or their behavior) attractive and showing a good sense of style
  사람이나 행동이 매력적이고 훌륭한 스타일 감각을 보여주는

- □ **grain** 곡물
  → the seeds of plants such as wheat, corn, and rice that are used for food
  밀, 옥수수, 쌀 같은 음식으로 사용하는 식물의 씨앗

- □ **noodle** 국수
  → long, thin, curly strips of pasta
  얇고 긴 파스타 가닥

- □ **plate** 접시, 그릇
  → a flat, usually round dish that you put food on
  음식을 올려놓는 얇고 둥근 그릇

- □ **plus** 더욱이, 게다가
  → mentioning an additional item or fact
  추가적인 항목을 언급하는

- □ **prefer** 더 좋아하다, 선호하다
  → to like one thing or person better than another
  어떤 것 또는 어떤 사람을 다른 것 또는 다른 사람보다 더 좋아하다

- □ **utensil** 기구, 도구
  → a tool that is used in the house
  집에서 사용되는 도구

서답형
[01~02] 〈보기〉와 같은 관계가 되도록 빈칸에 알맞은 말을 쓰시오.

**01**

┌─ 보기 ─┐
arrive : arrival

(1) _____ : ignorance
(2) suggest : _____

**02**

┌─ 보기 ─┐
adventure : adventurous

(1) boast : _____
(2) convenience : _____

**03** 다음 중 밑줄 친 부분의 뜻풀이가 바르지 않은 것은?

① In China people use chopsticks to eat food. (젓가락)
② They will raise and argue many points. (기르다)
③ We're sorry we became boastful and ignored you. (뽐내는)
④ I think a fork is more convenient. (편리한)
⑤ Different cultures use different kinds of utensils to eat. (문화)

서답형
**04** 다음 빈칸에 들어갈 적절한 말을 쓰시오.

A _____ is best for grains and soup, and a fork is good for eating meat.

➡ _____

**05** 다음 중 〈보기〉에 있는 단어를 사용하여 자연스러운 문장을 만들 수 없는 것은?

┌─ 보기 ─┐
elegant  adventures  forgive  disappeared

① She is always eager to listen to their _____.
② What can be more _____ than using them to cut meat on a plate!
③ Where is Ms. Disher? She has _____.
④ In the Middle Ages in Europe, a host did not have to _____ his guests with any utensils.
⑤ Please _____ us and come back and join us.

**06** 다음 밑줄 친 부분과 의미가 가장 가까운 것을 고르시오.

Since then, every time they meet, they allow one another to eat in the manner that they please.

① focus         ② forgive
③ suggest       ④ permit
⑤ argue

**07** 다음 빈칸에 공통으로 들어가기에 알맞은 것은?

• She makes _____ for this by hosting a dinner for her friends.
• Nobody wanted to give _____.

① with      ② up      ③ out
④ in       ⑤ for

**01** 주어진 단어를 이용해 빈칸을 완성하시오.

> Forks became popular with the _____ of the Renaissance in Italy.

➡ _____ (arrive)

[02~03] 다음 빈칸에 공통으로 들어갈 단어를 쓰시오.

**02**
> • It seems to me that they are _____ing plates for good luck.
> • We need to take a _____ at this point.

**03**
> • I enjoyed the food. I usually leave some food _____ my plate.
> • If you can't do both, it might be better to focus _____ just one.

**04** 밑줄 친 부분과 의미가 가장 가까운 단어를 주어진 철자로 시작하여 쓰시오.

> The knife is <u>certainly</u> the oldest eating utensil.

➡ s_____

**05** 다음 빈칸에 알맞은 단어를 〈보기〉에서 골라 쓰시오.

┌─── 보기 ───┐
│ raises   regardless   give   trouble │
└──────────────┘

(1) Are you having _____ using your utensils at the dining table?
(2) Food will always be delicious _____ of which utensils they use to eat it with.
(3) After careful consideration, he decided to _____ up the chance.
(4) The book _____ many important questions.

**06** 다음 우리말에 맞게 빈칸에 알맞은 말을 쓰시오.

(1) 그 모든 지체들이 있은 후에 우리는 잃어버린 시간을 만회하기를 간절히 바라고 있었다.
  ➡ After all the delays, we were anxious to _____ up for lost time.
(2) "커피 한 잔 하면서 잠시 쉬면 어떨까요?"라고 그녀가 말했다.
  ➡ She said, "Why don't we _____ a break for coffee?"
(3) 그는 자기 생각을 그 단체 사람들에게 꼭 알리고 싶어 했다.
  ➡ He was _____ to communicate his ideas to the group.
(4) 나는 주중에는 외출을 할 시간이 전혀 없다.
  ➡ I never have time to _____ out in the week.

# Conversation

**1** 의견 제시하기

> **It seems to me** that you don't like the food. 너는 그 음식을 좋아하지 않는 것 같다.

- 동사 seem을 사용하여 "It seems (to me) that ~"이라고 하는 것은 "내 생각은 ~이다"라는 뜻으로 자신의 의견을 완곡하게 이야기할 때 사용하는 표현이다. 또한 "It seems to ~" 혹은 "It seems like ~" 등의 형태로 사용하여 "~인 것처럼 보인다, ~하는 것처럼 보인다"는 의미로 자신의 의견을 나타내기도 한다.

- 자신의 생각이나 의견을 말하고자 할 때 많이 사용하는 표현으로 "In my opinion"이 있다. 우리말로는 "내 (개인적인) 생각은"이라는 뜻으로 문장의 맨 앞에 사용하고 뒤에 콤마(,)를 찍는다. 'In my opinion ~'과 유사 표현으로는 "I think ~, I believe ~, I feel ~" 등이 있고 "It seems to me ~"와 같은 의미이기도 하다.

- "내가 알기로는 ~"이라는 뜻으로 "as far as I know, as far as I'm concerned" 등에 이어서 원하는 내용을 덧붙여 자신의 의견을 표현하는 것도 가능하다.

### 의견 제시하기

- It seems to me that ~. 내 생각은 ~이다.
- I think ~. 나는 ~라고 생각한다.
- I'm convinced that ~. 나는 ~라고 확신한다.
- As far as I know, ~ 내가 알기로는 ~
- In my opinion/view, ~. 내 생각에는 ~
- I believe ~. 나는 ~라고 믿는다.
- I'm sure ~. 분명 ~이다.

## 핵심 Check

1. 다음 밑줄 친 표현 대신 쓰기에 적절하지 <u>않은</u> 것은?

> G: <u>It seems to me that</u> you don't like the food.
> B: No, I enjoyed the food. I usually leave some food on my plate. That's good table manners in my country, China.
> G: Why is that?
> B: We think finishing everything on the plate means that you are still hungry.

① In my opinion,  
② I think that  
③ I believe that  
④ You're sure  
⑤ As far as I know,

**2** 선호에 대해 묻기

**Which do you prefer**, fried chicken or chicken salad? 프라이드 치킨과 치킨 샐러드 중에서 어느 것을 더 좋아하니?

■ A와 B 둘 중에 어떤 것을 더 좋아하는지 상대방의 선호를 물을 때는 "prefer(더 좋아하다)"를 사용하여 "Which do you prefer, A or B?"(너는 … 중에서 어느 것을 더 좋아하니?)라고 표현한다. which는 정해진 범주 내에서 특정 대상의 선호도를 물을 때 사용하는 표현이다.

■ 선호를 물어보는 표현으로 "더 좋아하다"에 해당하는 "prefer, like better"를 사용하여 "Which do you like better[more], A or B?" 또는 "Which one do you like better, A or B?"의 형태로 나타낼 수 있고, "Do you prefer A or B?"라고도 할 수 있다. Which가 뒤에 오는 명사를 수식하는 의문형용사로 쓰이는 경우에는 "Which 명사 + do you prefer, A or B?"라고 할 수도 있다.

■ prefer로 자신이 좋아하는 것을 나타낼 때는 전치사 to를 사용하여 "prefer A to B"(B보다는 A를 더 좋아한다)의 형태로 선호를 표현한다. 이 표현은 "like A better than B"에 해당한다.

선호에 대해 묻기

"A와 B 중에서 어느 것을 더 좋아하니?"

• Which (one) do you prefer, A or B?　　• Which (one) do you like better, A or B?

• Do you prefer A or B?

핵심 Check

2. 다음 우리말에 해당하는 영어 문장을 쓰시오.

> G: What can we do to stay healthy?
> B: I think having healthy food is important.
> G: My brother exercises every day for his health.
> B: Emma야, 건강에 좋은 음식을 먹는 것과 운동하는 것 중에서 어느 것을 더 좋아하니? (prefer)
> G: I prefer to exercise.

➡ _____

3. 다음 대화를 자연스러운 순서로 배열하시오.

> A: Which do you prefer, fruit or ice cream?
> (A) Why do you prefer it?
> (B) I prefer ice cream.
> (C) It seems to me that ice cream is sweeter.

➡ _____

### Listen & Speak 1 A

G: ❶It seems to me that you don't like the food.

B: No, I enjoyed the food. I usually leave some food on my plate. That's good table manners in my country, China.

G: Why is that?

B: ❷We think finishing everything on the plate means that you are still hungry.

G: ❸It is more polite to finish everything on your plate in Korea, though.

B: Different cultures have different rules.

G: 너는 그 음식을 좋아하지 않는 것 같구나.
B: 그렇지 않아. 나는 그 음식을 즐겼어. 나는 보통 접시에 약간의 음식을 남겨. 그것이 우리나라, 중국에서의 올바른 식탁 예절이야.
G: 왜 그러니?
B: 우리는 접시에 있는 음식을 다 먹는 것은 여전히 배가 고프다는 것을 의미한다고 생각해.
G: 하지만, 한국에서는 접시에 있는 모든 것을 다 먹는 것이 더 예절 바르다고 생각해.
B: 문화마다 다른 규칙이 있구나.

❶ "It seems to me that ~"은 "~인 것 같다"는 의미로 자신의 의견을 나타내는 표현이다.
❷ think의 목적어가 되는 명사절을 유도하는 접속사 that이 생략되어 있다. "finishing everything on the plate"는 동명사구로 means의 주어이다.
❸ It은 가주어이고, "to finish ~"가 진주어이다.

**Check(√) True or False**

(1) The boy left some food on his plate because he didn't enjoy the food.  T ☐ F ☐

(2) The girl says that finishing everything on the plate is good table manners in Korea.  T ☐ F ☐

### Real Life Communication

Jinho: Claire, ❶which do you prefer, fish or steak?

Claire: ❷I prefer fish, Jinho.

Jinho: There is fish on the menu.

Claire: That's good. Is it sushi or fried?

Jinho: Both are on the menu.

Claire: Then I will have sushi. ❸It seems to me that fish tastes better when it's uncooked.

Jinho: Okay. Then you get sushi and I'll get fried fish. Let's order.

Jinho: Claire야, 생선과 스테이크 중에서 너는 어느 것을 더 좋아하니?
Claire: 나는 생선을 더 좋아해, 진호야.
Jinho: 메뉴에 생선이 있어.
Claire: 잘됐다. 생선은 스시야, 튀긴 것이야?
Jinho: 두 가지가 모두 있어.
Claire: 그러면 나는 스시를 먹을래. 생선은 익히지 않았을 때 맛이 더 좋은 것 같아.
Jinho: 알았어. 그러면 너는 스시를 먹고 나는 튀긴 생선을 먹을게. 주문하자.

❶ "Which do you prefer, A or B?"는 "A와 B 둘 중에서 어느 것을 더 좋아하니?"라고 상대의 선호를 묻는 말이다.
❷ prefer는 "더 좋아하다, 선호하다"의 의미로 "like better"에 해당한다. "A보다 B를 더 좋아한다"라고 할 때는 than이 아니라 전치사 to를 사용하여 "prefer A to B"라고 한다.
❸ "It seems to me that ~."은 자신의 의견을 나타내는 표현이다.

**Check(√) True or False**

(3) Claire prefers fish to steak.  T ☐ F ☐

(4) Claire thinks that fish tastes better when it's cooked.  T ☐ F ☐

(5) Claire will get sushi and Jinho will get fried fish.  T ☐ F ☐

### Listen & Speak 1 B

W: It seems to me that ❶it's time for dinner. Are you hungry?

B: Yes. Can we order pizza for dinner?

W: I'm going to cook fish, Jacob. ❷Cooking at home is much healthier than ordering pizza.

B: But we can save time ❸by ordering pizza. I'm so hungry.

W: Dinner will be ready soon. So, please be patient.

❶ it's time for ~ = ~할 시간이다
❷ "Cooking at home"이 동명사로 주어이다.
❸ 전치사 by의 목적어로 동명사 ordering이 쓰였다.

### Listen & Speak 2 A

G: ❶What can we do to stay healthy?

B: ❷I think having healthy food is important.

G: My brother exercises every day for his health.

B: ❸Which do you prefer, having healthy food or exercising, Emma?

G: I can't control which food I eat. So, I prefer to exercise.

B: ❹Both of them seem to be important for our health.

G: But if you can't do both, it might be better to focus on just one.

B: I think you are right. I'm going to exercise first.

❶ stay healthy = 건강을 유지하다
❷ I think에 이어지는 명사절의 주어는 동명사 "having healthy food"이다.
❸ "Which do you prefer, ~?"는 선호를 묻는 말이다.
❹ "Both of them"은 "두 가지" 모두를 가리키는 것으로 복수 취급한다.

### Listen & Speak 2 B

W: What time is it now?

M: It's already 8:00 p.m.

W: ❶Why don't we stop now and have a meal?

M: Good idea. ❷We need to take a break at this point.

W: Which do you prefer, having a meal early or late in the evening?

M: I prefer having a meal early.

W: What is the reason?

M: ❸I usually go to bed early, so I eat my last meal early, too. ❹How about you?

W: I have meals late in the evening because I work late at night.

❶ "Why don't we ~?"는 "우리 ~하는 것이 어떠니?"의 의미로 제안하는 표현이다.
❷ take a break = 휴식을 취하다
❸ 앞에서 이유를 물어본 질문에 대한 대답으로 because로 시작할 수 있다.
❹ "How about you?"는 "너는 어떠니?"라는 뜻으로 상대의 의견을 묻는 말이다.

### Real Life Communication B

A: ❶Which do you prefer, fruit or ice cream?

B: I prefer ice cream.

A: ❷Why do you prefer it?

B: It seems to me that ice cream is sweeter.

❶ 상대의 선호를 묻는 말로 "Which do you like better, fruit or ice cream?"이라고 할 수 있다.
❷ 이유를 묻는 말로 대답은 Because로 할 수 있다.

### Let's Check 1

G: Do you like this cap?

B: ❶It seems to me that red does not look good on you.

G: Do you have any suggestion, then?

B: How about this blue cap? ❷Blue looks much better on you than red.

G: That sounds good. I'll take it.

❶ look good on ~ = ~에게 좋아 보이다
❷ much는 비교급을 강조하는 부사이다.

다음 우리말과 일치하도록 빈칸에 알맞은 말을 쓰시오.

### Listen & Speak 1 A

G: It _____ to _____ that you don't _____ the food.

B: No, I _____ the food. I usually _____ some _____ on my _____. That's good table _____ in my country, China.

G: _____ is that?

B: We _____ finishing everything on the _____ means that you are still _____.

G: It is more _____ to finish _____ on your plate in Korea, _____.

B: _____ cultures have different _____.

해석

G: 너는 그 음식을 좋아하지 않는 것 같구나.

B: 그렇지 않아. 나는 그 음식을 즐겼어. 나는 보통 접시에 약간의 음식을 남겨. 그것이 우리나라, 중국에서의 올바른 식탁 예절이야.

G: 왜 그러니?

B: 우리는 접시에 있는 음식을 다 먹는 것은 여전히 배가 고프다는 것을 의미한다고 생각해.

G: 하지만, 한국에서는 접시에 있는 모든 것을 다 먹는 것이 더 예절 바르다고 생각해.

B: 문화마다 다른 규칙이 있구나.

### Listen & Speak 1 B

W: It _____ to _____ that it's _____ for dinner. Are you _____?

B: Yes. _____ we _____ pizza for _____?

W: I'm going to _____ fish, Jacob. _____ at home is _____ healthier than _____ pizza.

B: But we can _____ _____ by _____ pizza. I'm so _____.

W: Dinner will be _____ soon. So, please be _____.

W: 저녁 먹을 시간인 것 같다. 배고프니?

B: 네. 저녁으로 피자 주문해도 돼요?

W: 생선을 요리할 거야, Jacob. 집에서 요리하는 것이 피자를 주문하는 것보다 훨씬 더 건강에 더 좋아.

B: 하지만 피자를 주문하면 시간을 아낄 수 있어요. 너무 배고파요.

W: 저녁이 곧 준비될 거야. 그러니 조금만 참아 줘.

### Listen & Speak 2 A

G: What can we do to _____ _____?

B: I think _____ _____ food is _____.

G: My brother _____ every day for his _____.

B: _____ _____ _____ _____, having healthy food _____ exercising, Emma?

G: I can't _____ _____ food I eat. So, I _____ to exercise.

B: Both of them _____ to be _____ for our _____.

G: But if you _____ do both, it _____ be better to _____ on just one.

B: I think you are _____. I'm going to _____ _____.

G: 건강을 유지하기 위하여 우리는 무엇을 할 수 있을까?

B: 건강에 좋은 음식을 먹는 것이 중요하다고 생각해.

G: 우리 오빠는 매일 건강을 위하여 운동을 해.

B: 건강에 좋은 음식을 먹는 것과 운동을 하는 것 중에서 어느 것을 선호하니, Emma야?

G: 나는 어떤 음식을 먹을지 조절할 수 없어. 그래서 나는 운동을 더 좋아해.

B: 두 가지 모두가 우리의 건강에 중요한 것 같구나.

G: 그러나, 두 가지 모두 할 수 없다면 한 가지에 집중하는 것이 더 나을 거야.

B: 네 말이 맞는 것 같아. 나는 운동을 먼저 할 거야.

## Listen & Speak 2 B

W: _____ time is it _____?

M: It's _____ 8:00 p.m.

W: _____ don't we _____ now and _____ a meal?

M: Good idea. We need to _____ a break at this _____.

W: _____ do you prefer, _____ a meal early or _____ in the evening?

M: I _____ having a meal early.

W: _____ is the reason?

M: I usually go to bed _____, so I eat my last meal _____, too. How about you?

W: I have meals _____ in the evening _____ I _____ late at night.

## Real Life Communication

Jinho: Claire, _____ do you _____, fish or steak?

Claire: I _____ fish, Jinho.

Jinho: There is fish _____ the menu.

Claire: That's good. Is it _____ or _____?

Jinho: Both are on the menu.

Claire: Then I will have sushi. It _____ to me that fish _____ better when it's _____.

Jinho: Okay. Then you get sushi and I'll _____ fried fish. Let's _____.

## Let's Check 1

G: Do you like this _____?

B: It _____ to me that red _____ not _____ good on you.

G: Do you _____ any _____, then?

B: _____ _____ this blue cap? Blue looks _____ _____ on you than red.

G: That _____ good. I'll take it.

## Let's Check 2

A: I'm so _____. Let's get _____ _____ eat.

B: So am I. _____ do you prefer, noodles or rice?

A: I _____ noodles. Do you _____ any good restaurants?

B: There's a good noodle restaurant _____ _____.

해석

W: 지금 몇 시니?
M: 벌써 오후 8시야.
W: 지금 멈추고, 식사하는 것이 어떨까?
M: 좋은 생각이야. 이 시점에서 쉴 필요가 있어.
W: 너는 일찍 식사하는 것과 저녁 늦게 식사하는 것 중에서 어느 것을 더 좋아하니?
M: 나는 일찍 식사하는 것을 더 좋아해.
W: 이유가 뭐야?
M: 나는 보통 일찍 잠자리에 들어, 그래서 마지막 식사도 일찍 먹어. 너는 어떠니?
W: 나는 밤늦게 일하기 때문에 저녁에 늦게 식사를 해.

Jinho: Claire야, 생선과 스테이크 중에서 너는 어느 것을 더 좋아하니?
Claire: 나는 생선을 더 좋아해, 진호야.
Jinho: 메뉴에 생선이 있어.
Claire: 잘됐다. 생선은 스시야, 튀긴 것이야?
Jinho: 두 가지가 모두 있어.
Claire: 그러면 나는 스시를 먹을게. 생선은 익히지 않았을 때 맛이 더 좋은 것 같아.
Jinho: 알았어. 그러면 너는 스시를 먹고, 나는 튀긴 생선을 먹을게. 주문하자.

G: 이 모자 마음에 드니?
B: 내 생각에는 빨간색이 너한테 잘 어울리지 않는 것 같아.
G: 그럼, 추천할 것이 있니?
B: 이 파란색 모자 어때? 빨간색보다 파란색이 너한테 훨씬 더 잘 어울려.
G: 좋은 것 같은데. 그것으로 할게.

A: 배가 너무 고파. 뭐 좀 먹자.
B: 나도 마찬가지야. 국수와 밥 중 어느 것을 더 좋아하니?
A: 난 국수가 좋아. 괜찮은 식당 알고 있니?
B: 저쪽에 괜찮은 국수 식당이 있어.

[01~02] 다음 대화의 빈칸에 들어갈 말로 알맞은 것은?

**01**

> G: It seems to me that you don't like the food.
> B: No, I enjoyed the food. I usually leave some food on my plate. That's good table manners in my country, China.
> G: Why is that?
> B: We think finishing everything on the plate means that you are still hungry.
> G: It is more polite to finish everything on your plate in Korea, though.
> B: Different _____ have different rules.

① cultures      ② families      ③ schools
④ foods      ⑤ manners

**02**

> B: Which do you prefer, having healthy food or exercising, Emma?
> G: I can't control which food I eat. So, I prefer to exercise.
> B: Both of them seem to be important for our health.
> G: But if you can't do both, it might be _____.
> B: I think you are right. I'm going to exercise first.

① better to have healthy food than to exercise
② easy to have healthy food
③ more interesting to exercise after dinner
④ more difficult to exercise
⑤ better to focus on just one

**03** 대화에 이어지기에 순서가 바르게 배열된 것을 고르시오.

> A: Which do you prefer, having a meal early or late in the evening?
> (A) Why is that?
> (B) Because I usually go to bed early, I prefer having my meal early.
> (C) I prefer having a meal early in the evening.

① (A) – (C) – (B)      ② (B) – (A) – (C)
③ (B) – (C) – (A)      ④ (C) – (A) – (B)
⑤ (C) – (B) – (A)

[01~03] 다음 대화를 읽고 물음에 답하시오.

G: It seems to me that you don't like the food. ( A )

B: No, I enjoyed the food. I usually leave some food on my plate. ( B )

G: (가)_____ is that? ( C )

B: We think finishing everything on the plate means that you are still hungry. ( D )

G: It is more polite to finish everything on your plate in Korea, though. ( E )

B: Different cultures have different rules.

**01** ~(A)~(E) 중에서 다음 문장이 들어가기에 가장 적절한 곳은?

> That's good table manners in my country, China.

① (A)  ② (B)  ③ (C)  ④ (D)  ⑤ (E)

**02** 빈칸 (가)에 들어가기에 적절한 것은?

① What  ② Which  ③ Where
④ How  ⑤ Why

**03** 위 대화를 읽고 대답할 수 <u>없는</u> 것은?

① What did the boy said about what the girl thought?
② Why did the boy leave food on his plate?
③ Why did the girl enjoy the food more than the boy?
④ What do they think about finishing everything on the plate in China?
⑤ What is more polite in Korea?

[04~06] 다음 대화를 읽고 물음에 답하시오.

W: (A)It seems to me that it's time for dinner. Are you hungry?

B: Yes. Can we order pizza for dinner?

W: I'm going to cook fish, Jacob. Cooking at home is much healthier than ordering pizza.

B: But we can save time by ordering pizza. I'm so hungry.

W: (B)_____ So, please be patient.

**04** 다음 중 밑줄 친 (A) 대신 쓰기에 적절한 것은?

① You know  ② I think
③ We say  ④ They expect
⑤ I am sure

**05** 빈칸 (B)에 들어가기에 가장 알맞은 말을 고르시오.

① Dinner will be ready soon.
② You will have some pizza.
③ It's time to cook dinner.
④ You'd better exercise before dinner.
⑤ How would you like your pizza?

**06** 위 대화의 내용과 일치하지 <u>않는</u> 것은?

① The woman thinks it's time for dinner.
② Jacob wants to have pizza for dinner.
③ The woman thinks that it's better to make pizza at home.
④ The boy is hungry.
⑤ The woman will cook dinner at home.

[07~09] 다음 대화를 읽고 물음에 답하시오.

G: What can we do to stay healthy?

B: I think having healthy food is important. ( A )

G: My brother exercises every day for his health.

B: ( B ) Which do you prefer, (가)_____ or exercising, Emma?

G: I can't control which food I eat. ( C )

B: Both of them seem to be important for our health. ( D )

G: But if you can't do both, it might be better to focus on just one. ( E )

B: I think you are right. I'm going to exercise first.

**07** 위 대화의 내용으로 보아, 빈칸 (가)에 들어가기에 가장 적절한 것은?

① exercising every day

② to stay healthy

③ focus on the food

④ being right

⑤ having healthy food

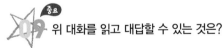 (A)~(E) 중에서 다음 문장이 들어가기에 가장 적절한 곳은?

So, I prefer to exercise.

① (A)　② (B)　③ (C)　④ (D)　⑤ (E)

**09** 위 대화를 읽고 대답할 수 있는 것은?

① What food is good for your health?

② When you can't have healthy food or exercise together, which is better?

③ What kind of exercise is good for your health?

④ Which is more important, having healthy food or exercising?

⑤ What did the girl ask the boy to do?

[10~12] 다음 대화를 읽고 물음에 답하시오.

W: What time is it now?

M: It's already 8:00 p.m.

W: Why don't we stop now and have a meal?

M: Good idea. We need to (A)_____ a break at this point.

W: Which do you prefer, having a meal early or late in the evening?

M: I prefer having a meal early.

W: What is the (B)_____?

M: I usually go to bed early, so I eat my last meal early, too. How about you?

W: I have meals late in the evening because (C) _____.

**10** 다음 중 빈칸 (A)에 들어갈 말과 같은 말이 들어갈 수 있는 것은?

① Who will _____ care of the baby?

② She will _____ up for the lost time.

③ We won't _____ up our plan.

④ They will _____ here on time.

⑤ You will _____ much trouble doing the work.

**11** 빈칸 (B)에 들어가기에 적절한 것은?

① time　② place　③ reason

④ work　⑤ meal

**12** 위 대화의 내용으로 보아 빈칸 (C)에 들어가기에 적절한 것은?

① I get up early in the morning

② I prefer take a break

③ I want to stop the work

④ I want to have dinner with you

⑤ I work late at night

[01~04] 다음 대화를 읽고 물음에 답하시오.

Jinho: Claire, (A)_____ do you prefer, fish or steak?

Claire: I prefer fish, Jinho.

Jinho: There is fish on the menu.

Claire: That's good. Is it sushi or fried?

Jinho: Both are on the menu.

Claire: Then I will have sushi. (B)It seems to me that fish tastes better when it's cooked.

Jinho: Okay. Then you get sushi and I'll get fried fish. Let's order.

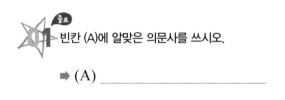

01 빈칸 (A)에 알맞은 의문사를 쓰시오.

➡ (A) _____

02 위 대화에서 다음 설명에 해당하는 단어를 찾아 쓰시오.

to like one thing or person better than another

➡ _____

03 위 대화의 밑줄 친 (B) 대신 들어가기에 적절한 말을 주어진 단어를 포함하여 쓰시오.

➡ _____ (opinion)

04 위 대화에서 흐름상 어색한 것을 찾아 올바르게 고치시오.

➡ _____

[05~07] 다음 대화를 읽고 물음에 답하시오.

G: Do you like this cap?

B: (A)내 생각에는 빨간색이 너한테 잘 어울리지 않는 것 같아. (seem, good)

G: Do you have any suggestion, then?

B: (B)_____ about this blue cap? Blue looks much better on you than red.

G: That sounds good. I'll take it.

05 밑줄 친 (A)의 우리말을 주어진 단어를 이용하여 영어로 옮기시오.

➡ _____

06 빈칸 (B)에 들어가기에 적절한 의문사를 쓰시오.

➡ _____

07 위 대화의 내용에 맞게 다음 빈칸에 적절한 말을 쓰시오.

The boy thinks that a _____ cap looks much better on the girl.

08 다음 (A)에 적절한 말을 쓰시오. (3단어)

A: I'm so hungry. Let's get (A)_____.

B: So am I. Which do you prefer, noodles or rice?

A: I like noodles. Do you know any good restaurants?

B: There's a good noodle restaurant over there.

➡ _____

# Grammar

## ① to부정사의 의미상의 주어

> • It was not easy **for** her **to listen** to their arguments. 그녀가 그들의 논쟁을 듣고 있기는 쉽지 않았습니다.
> • It is very silly **of** him **to say** such a thing. 그런 말을 하다니 그도 아주 바보군.

■ to부정사의 의미상의 주어

to부정사의 동작을 실제로 하는 주체를 to부정사의 의미상의 주어라고 한다. to부정사의 의미상의 주어는 to부정사 바로 앞에 'for+목적격'으로 나타낸다. 이때 문장에 쓰인 형용사가 nice, kind, smart, wise, polite, careful 등과 같이 사람의 성향, 성격을 나타내는 말일 때는 'for+목적격'이 아니라 'of+목적격'으로 쓴다.

• It wasn't easy **for** her **to become** who she is today. 그녀가 오늘날의 그녀가 되기까지는 쉽지 않았다.

• It was very smart **of** him **not to miss** the chance. 그는 아주 약빠르게도 그 기회를 놓치지 않았다.

■ 비교적 긴 to부정사 부분이 문장의 주어로 쓰일 때 보통 그 to부정사 부분을 문장 제일 뒤에 두고 주어 자리에 가주어 it을 넣어준다.

• **It** is important **to use** water carefully. 물을 신중하게 사용하는 것은 중요합니다.
  = **To use** water carefully is important.

• **It** is necessary **for** us **to prepare** the winter. 우리는 겨울을 준비해야 한다.

■ to부정사의 의미상의 주어가 일반적인 사람일 경우에는 보통 생략한다. 또한 to부정사의 부정은 to부정사 앞에 not이나 never를 써서 'not[never]+to부정사'로 나타낸다.

• **It** is exciting **to watch** the soccer game. 축구 경기를 관람하는 것은 흥미진진하다.

• **It** is difficult **not to have** preconceptions. 선입견을 가지지 않기란 어렵다.

---

### 핵심 Check

**1.** 다음 빈칸에 알맞은 말을 어법에 맞게 쓰시오.

(1) It is difficult _____ say how many people use it.

(2) It is important _____ students to do their homework.

(3) It was wise _____ you to keep out of debt.

## ② 명사의 뒤에서 명사를 수식하는 분사

> • They finally found Ms. Disher **sitting** under a huge tree.
> 그들은 마침내 커다란 나무 아래에 앉아 있는 Ms. Disher를 찾았습니다.
>
> • There are two people **named** Mark here. 여기 Mark라는 이름을 가진 사람이 두 명 있어요.

■ 분사는 명사의 앞이나 뒤에서 명사를 꾸며 주는 형용사 역할을 한다. 현재분사는 '능동'이나 '진행'의 의미가 있고, 과거분사는 '수동'이나 '완료'의 의미가 있다.

- She was just a **dancing** girl. (그녀는 단지 춤추는 소녀였다.: 앞에서 수식하는 현재분사 '능동')
- The little girl **dancing** on the stage is Susan. (무대에서 춤추고 있는 작은 소녀는 Susan이다.: 뒤에서 수식하는 현재분사 '능동')
- The **wounded** man walked across the room. (부상을 입은 남자가 방을 가로질러 걸어갔다.: 앞에서 수식하는 과거분사 '수동')
- There was a young man **wounded** in the right knee. (오른쪽 무릎에 부상을 당한 한 젊은 남자가 있었다.: 뒤에서 수식하는 과거분사 '수동')

■ 분사에 다른 어구(목적어나 보어, 수식어구 등)가 함께 있을 때는 뒤에서 명사를 수식한다.

- Do you know the woman **wearing** a pink dress? (너 분홍 옷 입은 여자를 아니?)
- I found the stairs **filled** with smoke. (나는 연기로 꽉 차있는 계단을 보았다.)

■ 명사를 뒤에서 수식하는 경우에는 그 앞에 '주격 관계대명사+be동사'가 생략된 것으로 생각할 수 있다.

- Do you know the woman (who is) **wearing** a pink dress?
- I found the stairs (which was) **filled** with smoke.

■ 분사는 명사를 수식하는 역할 외에도, 주격 보어 또는 목적격 보어로 쓰인다(서술 용법).

- A man stood **waiting** for food. 한 남자가 음식을 기다리며 서 있었다.
- It is rude of me to have kept you **waiting**. 기다리시게 해서 죄송합니다.

---

### 핵심 Check

**2.** 다음 괄호 안에 주어진 어휘를 이용하여 빈칸을 알맞게 채우시오.

(1) The main character is a 10-year-old girl _____ Pucca. (name)

(2) There is a baby _____ next to Mommy. (sleep)

(3) Mr. Park presided the meeting _____ in the conference hall. (hold)

**01** 다음 대화의 빈칸에 알맞은 것을 고르시오.

> A: Is it possible _____?
> B: Of course.

① meet me today at three
② met me today at three
③ to meeting me today at three
④ for you to meet me today at three
⑤ of you to meet me today at three

**02** 다음 괄호 안에서 알맞은 말을 고르시오.

(1) The surgeon operated on my (breaking / broken) leg last week.

(2) What would you like (writing / written) on the greeting card?

(3) The man (carrying / carried) a child just bought a balloon

(4) She carefully laid the (sleeping / slept) baby down on the bed.

**03** 다음 우리말에 맞게 주어진 어휘를 바르게 배열하시오.

> 유명인들은 사생활을 가지기가 어렵다.
> (celebrities, lives, it, difficult, have, is, private, to, for)

➡ _____

**04** 다음 우리말에 맞게 주어진 어휘를 바르게 배열하시오.

(1) 다른 사람들이 우리를 보듯이 우리가 우리 자신을 보는 것은 쉽지 않다.
   (others, ourselves, it, us, us, not, see, see, is, easy, as, for, to)
   ➡ _____

(2) 안전 교육은 아무리 강조해도 지나친 법이 없다.
   (us, it, safety training, impossible, is, overemphasize, for, to)
   ➡ _____

(3) 사랑이란 하늘이 맺어 준 결합이다.
   (a union, love, heaven, made, is, in)
   ➡ _____

**서답형**

**01** 다음 괄호 안에서 알맞은 말을 고르시오.

(1) I think that it is interesting (learn / to learn) a new language.

(2) Sometimes (that / it) is good to bury the differences with others.

(3) The upgrade made it harder (for / of) users to change them.

(4) It would be unwise (for / of) you to attack me.

**02** 밑줄 친 부분의 쓰임이 올바른 것은?

① There is a girl sat under a huge tree.

② The book writing in English is very interesting.

③ The city attacked by the enemy finally surrendered.

④ I accidentally found an old picture taking 15 years ago.

⑤ An actor worn a mask represents a character.

**03** 다음 대화의 빈칸에 들어갈 말로 알맞은 것은?

> M: Do you think it is OK _____ small kids to play with pet dogs?
> W: Sure.

① of      ② for      ③ by

④ at      ⑤ to

**04** 다음 빈칸에 알맞은 말이 바르게 짝지어진 것은?

> • The earth _____ from the space looks like a ball.
> • I have found that it is best _____ me to use a spoon and fork.

① sees – to

② seeing – of

③ seeing – for

④ seen – of

⑤ seen – for

**05** 다음 중 밑줄 친 부분의 쓰임이 다른 하나는?

① Don't you agree that most people like watching TV?

② The girl picking up some trash is Ann.

③ The sleeping baby is really cute.

④ Look at the man talking on the phone.

⑤ When night fell, the only people remaining in the streets were policemen.

**06** 다음 중 어법상 바르지 않은 것은?

① It is natural for her to dislike him.

② It is much better to use a knife and a fork instead.

③ It is advisable for you to start early in the morning.

④ It isn't easy of me to understand.

⑤ It was unwise of him to do so.

**07** Which is suitable for the blank?

> When I went out, there was a lady _____ on the street.

① walk     ② walks     ③ walked

④ walking     ⑤ to walk

**서답형**
**08** 우리말과 일치하도록 빈칸에 알맞은 말을 쓰시오.

> 너무 캄캄해서 나는 아무것도 식별할 수가 없었다.
>
> ➡ It was too dark _____ distinguish anything.

**09** 주어진 우리말을 영어로 바르게 옮긴 것은?

> 그의 집은 파티에 초대된 사람들로 붐비고 있었다.

① His house was crowded with people invite to the party.

② His house was crowded with people who invited to the party.

③ His house was crowded with people were invited to the party.

④ His house was crowded with people inviting to the party.

⑤ His house was crowded with people invited to the party.

**10** 다음 문장의 빈칸에 알맞은 말은?

> It was so rude _____ to forget to call you yesterday.

① for me       ② for my

③ of my       ④ of me

⑤ of mine

**서답형**
**11** 주어진 어휘를 바르게 배열하여 다음 우리말을 영작하시오.

> 그들이 공원을 걷고 있는 동안, 그들 옆을 지나가는 많은 사람들이 매우 공손하게 인사했다.
> (many people, they, them, in the park, bowed, were, passing by, walking, politely, While, very)

➡ _____

_____

**12** 다음 빈칸에 들어갈 말이 나머지와 다른 하나는?

① It was hard _____ me to believe it at first.

② It was easy _____ her to move the boxes.

③ How silly _____ you to tell him such a thing.

④ It's too late _____ me to book anything else for that weekend.

⑤ Don't you think it is easier _____ you to hold a fork in one hand and a knife in the other?

**서답형**
**13** 괄호 안의 단어들을 자연스럽게 배열하시오.

(1) The elderly (a sweater / knitting / lady) hardly notices me coming in.
    ➡ _____

(2) Charles is listing the reasons why he'll never buy (Japan / made / a car / in).
    ➡ _____

(3) On reaching the office, she found (interviewing / him / the applicants).
    ➡ _____

**서답형**

**14** 다음 문장에서 어법상 <u>어색한</u> 것을 바르게 고쳐 다시 쓰시오.

(1) Is there any need of her to stay any longer?

➡ _____

(2) It is most unwise for her to go there alone.

➡ _____

(3) It is quite reasonable for you acting that way.

➡ _____

(4) There is a woman watered the flowers.

➡ _____

(5) Can you believe there is a hotel making out of cake?

➡ _____

(6) Thomas has a building was built in a modern design.

➡ _____
_____

(7) She had her house build.

➡ _____

**서답형**

**15** 다음 문장에서 생략할 수 있는 것을 찾아 쓰시오.

> The man who is swimming against the stream knows the strength of it.

➡ _____

**중요**

**16** 다음 두 문장을 한 문장으로 바르게 연결한 것은?

> • The garden was full of guests.
> • They were enjoying themselves at the party.

① The garden was full of guests enjoy themselves at the party.

② The garden was full of guests who enjoying themselves at the party.

③ The garden was full of guests enjoyed themselves at the party.

④ The garden was full of guests to enjoy themselves at the party.

⑤ The garden was full of guests enjoying themselves at the party.

**17** 다음 문장을 바꾸어 쓸 때 빈칸에 알맞은 말을 쓰시오.

> Can you come to the wedding?
> = Is _____ possible for you _____ to the wedding?

**중요**

**18** 다음 중 어법상 <u>어색한</u> 것을 고르시오. (2개)

① I want to go to a restaurant served delicious noodles.

② Amanda has many books written by Saint Exupery.

③ Picasso was an artist knowing to a lot of people in the world.

④ It was so rude for me to forget to call you yesterday.

⑤ The restaurant had delicious foods for us to enjoy.

**01** 괄호 안의 단어 수대로 주어진 두 문장을 하나의 문장으로
쓰시오.

(1) • The man is Lee Sedol.
• He is playing baduk. (7 단어)
➡ _____

(2) • Many planes were flying in the sky.
• I saw them. (8 단어)
➡ _____

(3) • Kevin bought a small house.
• It was built ten years ago. (9 단어)
➡ _____

**02** 다음 우리말에 맞게 주어진 단어를 바르게 배열하시오.

(1) 두 시까지 오시는 것이 편하시겠어요? (two
o'clock, it, you, convenient, come, is,
for, by, to)
➡ _____

(2) 나에게 자리를 양보해 준 걸 보니 그녀는 예
의 바른 사람이었다. (seat, me, her, her, it,
polite, offer, was, to, of)
➡ _____

(3) 제 잘못된 영어를 교정해 주시기 바랍니다.
(English, I, you, my, broken, correct,
want, to)
➡ _____

(4) 나는 그가 중립적인 태도를 취하는 것이 싫다.
(I, him, a, attitude, like, taking, don't,
neutral)
➡ _____

**03** 그림을 보고, 주어진 어휘를 이용하여 빈칸을 알맞게 채우
시오.

(1) I saw _____.
(on the road, parked, a car, dangerously)

(2) It was _____
the gas stove. (turn off, careless, him,
not)

**04** 다음 괄호 안에 주어진 단어를 이용하여 어법에 맞게 문장을
완성하시오.

(1) It is thoughtful _____
me around. (you, show)

(2) It is necessary _____
the winter. (us, prepare)

**05** 다음 두 문장이 뜻이 비슷하도록 빈칸에 들어갈 알맞은 말을 쓰시오.

(1) You will have difficulty in finding a hotel.

= It will be hard _____ find a hotel.

(2) She kindly explained the process of making a newspaper.

= It was kind _____ explain the process of making a newspaper.

**06** 다음 문장에서 어법상 어색한 것을 바르게 고치시오.

(1) The little wearing glasses girl in the picture is my daughter.

_____ ➡ _____

(2) I read an interesting story book writing in English.

_____ ➡ _____

(3) The child watered the tree is my son.

_____ ➡ _____

(4) Matilda bought a smart phone which made in Korea.

_____ ➡ _____

(5) It's not easy of him to wake up early.

_____ ➡ _____

(6) It is considerate for you not to disturb us.

_____ ➡ _____

(7) It is difficult for the woman climbing a high mountain.

_____ ➡ _____

**07** 다음 문장에서 생략된 것을 넣어 다시 쓰시오.

(1) There are two boys reading a book on the bench.

➡ _____

(2) The most popular landmark in Seoul is N Seoul Tower built in 1975.

➡ _____

(3) It is necessary to prepare for the worst.

➡ _____

**08** 다음 우리말을 괄호 안에 주어진 어휘를 이용하여 영작하시오.

(1) 유명한 작가에 의해 쓰여진 책이 항상 좋은 책인 것은 아니다. (a book, good, writer, not always, 13 단어)

➡ _____

(2) Mel은 편지를 쓰고 있는 그 소녀를 사랑한다. (a letter, write, 7 단어)

➡ _____

(3) 이 구절은 내가 이해하기에는 너무 어렵다. (this passage, difficult, too, 9 단어)

➡ _____

(4) 그가 우리를 오늘 밤 파티에 초대해 준 것은 고마운 일이었다. (it, the party, invite, nice, to, 12 단어)

➡ _____

### Friends from the Dining Republic

Spork, Chopsticks, Knork, Barehands, and Ms. Disher are close
친한(friends 수식)
friends in the Dining Republic. Spork, Chopsticks, Knork, and
Barehands travel a lot with their families, but Ms. Disher's family
많이(부사로 쓰여 travel 수식)
does not travel much. She makes up for this by hosting a dinner for
동명사로 by의 목적어
her friends coming back from their trips. She is always eager to listen
현재분사(friends 수식)
to their adventures. They often talk about what they learned from their
관계대명사 what(~하는 것)
recent trips. The most recent topic was about the best way to eat and
형용사적 용법
Ms. Disher's guests began to argue.

**Spork:** On a recent trip, I have found that it is best to use a spoon and
명사절 접속사 that  가주어 it    진주어 to V
fork. A spoon is best for grains and soup, and a fork is good for
eating meat.
동명사(전치사의 목적어)

**Knork:** No! It is much better to use a knife and a fork instead. Don't you
비교급 강조 부사(much. still. even. far. a lot)
think it is easier for you to hold a fork in one hand and a knife in
to부정사의 의미상 주어(for+목적격)
the other? What can be more elegant than using them to cut meat
chopsticks 지칭  to부정사의 부사적 용법
on a plate!
(목적: ~하기 위해서)

**Chopsticks:** Why do you use two different kinds of utensils when
you can use two of the same utensil? Plus, you can use
chopsticks with just one hand!

close: 가까운, 친한
make up for: ~을 보상하다
host: (행사를) 주최하다
be eager to: ~하고 싶어하다
adventure: 모험
recent: 최근의
argue: 언쟁하다
instead: 대신에
elegant: 우아한
utensil: 식기

---

📎 **확인문제**

- 다음 문장이 본문의 내용과 일치하면 T, 일치하지 <u>않으면</u> F를 쓰시오.

1  Ms. Disher is fond of listening to her friends' adventures. ☐

2  Ms. Disher was invited to her friends' dinner party. ☐

3  Spork thinks using a spoon and fork is best. ☐

4  Knork likes the idea of using chopsticks for eating meat. ☐

5  Two hands are needed to use chopsticks. ☐

**Barehands:** <u>No way!</u> When I eat with my hands, of course I can
절대로 아니야!
see and smell the food, but I can also touch it. <u>Because</u> I use
이유의 접속사(~ 이기 때문에)
my sense of touch when I eat, I <u>get to</u> enjoy my food more.
~하게 되다

They raised and argued many points, and nobody wanted to give up.

<u>It</u> was not easy <u>for their host</u>, Ms. Disher, <u>to listen</u> to their arguments
가주어 It          to부정사의 의미상 주어   their host와 동격   진주어
patiently. So, she hurriedly, <u>yet</u> quietly, left.
접속사(하지만)

**Spork:** Where is Ms. Disher? <u>She has disappeared.</u>
현재완료 결과 용법(사라지고 없다는 의미)

**Knork:** What should we do? <u>Without</u> Ms. Disher, this dinner is not
~이 없으면
complete.

**Chopsticks:** Where did she go?

**Barehands:** Let's go out to find her!

After hours of <u>searching</u> all over the Dining Republic, they finally
동명사
<u>found Ms. Disher sitting</u> under a huge tree.
find+목적어+목적격 보어

**Spork, Knork, Chopsticks, Barehands:** We're sorry we became boastful

and <u>ignored</u> you. Please forgive and come back and join us.
became과 병렬 관계

**Ms. Disher:** It's okay. I forgive you. Let's go back to my home.

Since then, <u>every time</u> they meet, they <u>allow one another to eat</u> in
= whenever                     allow+목적어+to V: 목적어가 V하게 허락하다
the manner that they please. In their hearts they now know <u>that</u> food
명사절 접속사 that
will always be delicious regardless of <u>which utensils they use</u> to eat it
간접의문문(의문사+주어+동사)
with.

**get to+동사원형:** ~하게 되다
**give up:** 포기하다
**argument:** 언쟁
**hurriedly:** 서둘러
**disappear:** 사라지다
**complete:** 완전한
**boastful:** 뽐내는
**ignore:** 무시하다
**forgive:** 용서하다
**please:** 기쁘게 하다
**delicious:** 맛있는
**regardless of:** ~에 상관없이

---

📎 **확인문제**

● 다음 문장이 본문의 내용과 일치하면 T, 일치하지 <u>않으면</u> F를 쓰시오.

1 Barehands can see and smell the food. ☐

2 Nobody wanted to stop arguings. ☐

3 Ms. Disher enjoyed listening to her guests' arguments. ☐

4 They didn't know that Ms. Disher had disappeared. ☐

5 It was difficult for Ms. Disher to forgive her friends. ☐

6 Everyone knows that it doesn't matter which utensils they use to eat food with. ☐

● 우리말을 참고하여 빈칸에 알맞은 말을 쓰시오.

**1** Spork, Chopsticks, Knork, Barehands, and Ms. Disher _____ _____ _____ in the Dining Republic.

**2** Spork, Chopsticks, Knork, and Barehands _____ a lot _____ _____ _____, but Ms. Disher's family does not travel _____.

**3** She _____ _____ _____ this _____ _____ a dinner for her friends _____ _____ _____ their trips.

**4** She _____ always _____ _____ listen _____ their _____.

**5** They often talk about _____ _____ _____ from their recent trips.

**6** The most _____ topic _____ _____ the best way _____ _____ and Ms. Disher's guests began _____ _____.

**7** Spork: _____ a recent trip, I have found _____ it is best _____ _____ a spoon and fork.

**8** A spoon is best _____ _____ and _____, and a fork is good for _____ _____.

**9** Knork: No! It is _____ _____ to use a knife and a fork _____.

**10** Don't you think it is _____ _____ _____ _____ a fork in one hand and a knife in _____ _____?

**11** What can be _____ _____ than _____ _____ to cut meat on a plate!

**12** Chopsticks: Why do you use _____ _____ _____ of utensils when you can use _____ _____ _____ _____ _____?

**13** Plus, you can _____ chopsticks _____ just one hand!

---

**1** Spork와 Chopsticks, Knork, Barehands, Disher 부인은 식탁 공화국의 친구들입니다.

**2** Spork와 Chopsticks, Knork, Barehands는 자신의 가족들과 여행을 많이 다니지만, Ms. Disher의 가족은 여행을 많이 다니지 않습니다.

**3** 그녀는 여행에서 돌아온 친구들을 위해 저녁 식사를 주최함으로써 여행을 많이 하지 않는 것을 보상합니다.

**4** 그녀는 항상 친구들의 모험담을 듣고 싶어 합니다.

**5** 그들은 최근 여행에서 배운 것에 대해 자주 이야기합니다.

**6** 가장 최근 주제는 음식을 먹는 가장 좋은 방법에 대한 것이었고, Ms. Disher의 손님들은 논쟁하기 시작했습니다.

**7** Spork: 최근 여행에서, 나는 숟가락과 포크가 함께 달려 있는 것을 사용하는 것이 가장 좋다는 것을 알았어.

**8** 숟가락은 곡물이나 국을 먹기에 최고이고, 포크는 고기를 먹기에 좋아.

**9** Knork: 아냐! 그 대신에 칼과 포크를 사용하는 것이 훨씬 더 좋아.

**10** 네가 한 손에는 포크를, 다른 손에 칼을 드는 것이 더 쉽다고 생각하지 않니?

**11** 접시 위에 놓인 고기를 자르기 위해 칼과 포크를 사용하는 것보다 더 우아할 수 있는 게 뭐가 있겠어!

**12** Chopsticks: 같은 도구를 두 가지로 사용할 수 있는데 왜 두 종류의 다른 도구를 사용한단 말이야?

**13** 게다가 젓가락은 한 손으로도 사용할 수 있어!

**14** Barehands: _____ _____! When I eat _____ my hands, of course I can _____ and _____ the food, but I can also _____ _____.

**15** Because_____ use my sense of touch when I eat, I _____ _____ _____ my food more.

**16** They _____ and _____ many points, and nobody _____ _____ _____ _____.

**17** _____ was not easy _____ their host, Ms. Disher, _____ _____ _____ _____ _____ patiently.

**18** So, she hurriedly, _____ _____, _____.

**19** Spork: Where is Ms. Disher? She _____ _____.

**20** Knork: What _____ _____ _____? Without Ms. Disher, this dinner is _____ _____.

**21** Chopsticks: _____ did she go?

**22** Barehands: Let's go out _____ _____ _____!

**23** After hours of _____ _____ over the Dining Republic, they finally _____ Ms. Disher _____ _____ a huge tree.

**24** Spork, Knork, Chopsticks, Barehands: We're sorry _____ _____ _____ and _____ you.

**25** Please _____ and come _____ and _____ _____.

**26** Ms. Disher: It's okay. I _____ you. Let's _____ _____ to my home.

**27** _____ then, every time they meet, they _____ one another _____ _____ in the manner _____ _____ _____.

**28** _____ their hearts they now know _____ food will always be _____ _____ _____ _____ utensils they use _____ _____ _____.

● 우리말을 참고하여 본문을 영작하시오.

### Friends from the Dining Republic

**1** ▶ Spork와 Chopsticks, Knork, Barehands, Disher 부인은 식탁 공화국의 친구들입니다.

➡ _____

**2** ▶ Spork와 Chopsticks, Knork, Barehands는 자신의 가족들과 여행을 많이 다니지만, Ms. Disher의 가족은 여행을 많이 다니지 않습니다.

➡ _____

_____

**3** ▶ 그녀는 여행에서 돌아온 친구들을 위해 저녁 식사를 주최함으로써 여행을 많이 하지 않는 것을 보상합니다.

➡ _____

**4** ▶ 그녀는 항상 친구들의 모험담을 듣고 싶어 합니다.

➡ _____

**5** ▶ 그들은 최근 여행에서 배운 것에 대해 자주 이야기합니다.

➡ _____

**6** ▶ 가장 최근 주제는 음식을 먹는 가장 좋은 방법에 대한 것이었고, Ms. Disher의 손님들은 논쟁하기 시작했습니다.

➡ _____

**7** ▶ Spork: 최근 여행에서, 나는 숟가락과 포크가 함께 달려 있는 것을 사용하는 것이 가장 좋다는 것을 알았어.

➡ _____

**8** ▶ 숟가락은 곡물이나 국을 먹기에 최고이고, 포크는 고기를 먹기에 좋아.

➡ _____

**9** ▶ Knork: 아냐! 그 대신에 칼과 포크를 사용하는 것이 훨씬 더 좋아.

➡ _____

**10** ▶ 네가 한 손에는 포크를, 다른 손에 칼을 드는 것이 더 쉽다고 생각하지 않니?

➡ _____

**11** ▶ 접시 위에 놓인 고기를 자르기 위해 칼과 포크를 사용하는 것보다 더 우아할 수 있는 게 뭐가 있겠어!

➡ _____

**12** ▶ Chopsticks: 같은 도구를 두 가지로 사용할 수 있는데 왜 두 종류의 다른 도구를 사용한단 말이야?

➡ _____

**13** ▶ 게다가 젓가락은 한 손으로도 사용할 수 있어!

➡ _____

**14** Barehands: 천만의 말씀! 내가 손으로 음식을 먹으면 당연히 보면서 음식 냄새도 맡을 수 있지만, 음식을 만져 볼 수도 있다고.

➡ _____

_____

**15** 음식을 먹을 때 촉각을 사용하기 때문에 음식을 더 즐기게 돼.

➡ _____

**16** 그들은 여러 의견을 제기하고 논쟁했습니다. 그리고 아무도 포기하고 싶어 하지 않았습니다.

➡ _____

**17** 그들의 주최자인 Ms. Disher가 그들의 언쟁을 참을성 있게 듣고 있는 것은 쉽지 않았습니다.

➡ _____

**18** 그래서 그녀는 서둘러서 그러나 조용히 자리를 떠났습니다.

➡ _____

**19** Spork: Disher 부인은 어디 있지? 그녀가 사라졌어.

➡ _____

**20** Knork: 어떡하지? Disher 부인이 없으면, 저녁 식사는 완전하지 않아.

➡ _____

**21** Chopsticks: 그녀는 어디 갔을까?

➡ _____

**22** Barehands: 나가서 그녀를 찾아보자!

➡ _____

**23** 몇 시간 동안 식탁 공화국을 구석구석 뒤진 끝에, 친구들은 마침내 큰 나무 밑에 앉아 있는 Disher 부인을 찾았습니다.

➡ _____

_____

**24** Spork, Knork, Chopsticks, Barehands: 우리가 자랑스러워하고 너를 무시해서 미안해.

➡ _____

**25** 우리를 용서하고 돌아와서 우리와 함께 있어 줘.

➡ _____

**26** Ms. Disher: 알았어. 용서할게. 우리 집으로 돌아가자.

➡ _____

**27** 그 후로, 그들은 만날 때마다 서로 자신들이 좋아하는 방식으로 음식 먹는 것을 받아들입니다.

➡ _____

**28** 마음속으로 그들은 이제 음식을 먹는 데 어떤 도구를 사용하여 먹는지에 상관없이 음식 맛은 항상 맛있을 거라는 걸 알게 되었습니다.

➡ _____

_____

[01~04] 다음 글을 읽고 물음에 답하시오.

Spork, Chopsticks, Knork, Barehands, and Ms. Disher are close friends in the Dining Republic. Spork, Chopsticks, Knork, and Barehands travel a lot with their families, but Ms. Disher's family does not travel much. She makes (A)_____ for this by hosting a dinner for her friends coming back from their trips. She is always eager to listen to their adventures. They often talk about what they learned from their recent trips. The most recent topic was about the best way to eat and Ms. Disher's guests began to argue.

**01** 다음 중 빈칸 (A)에 들어갈 말과 같은 말이 들어가는 것은?

① Please pay attention _____ his speech.
② Jason looks up _____ Mr. Han.
③ She came up _____ an idea.
④ He put _____ with the hardship.
⑤ Your meaning didn't really come _____ .

**서답형**

**02** 다음과 같이 풀이되는 말을 위 글에서 찾아 쓰시오.

> to speak angrily to each other about something that people disagree about

➡ _____

**서답형**

**03** 위 글의 내용에 맞게 빈칸에 알맞은 말을 쓰시오.

> The following passage will be a debate on _____ _____ _____ _____ _____ between the guests.

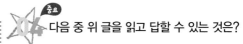 다음 중 위 글을 읽고 답할 수 있는 것은?

① To where do Spork, Chopsticks, Knork, and Barehands usually travel?
② How many family members do Spork, Chopsticks, Knork, and Barehands have?
③ When did Ms. Disher's guests come back from their trips?
④ What do Ms. Disher's guests often talk about?
⑤ How long have Ms. Disher's guests traveled?

[05~07] 다음 글을 읽고 물음에 답하시오.

**Spork:** On a recent trip, I have found that it is best to use a spoon and fork. A spoon is best for grains and soup, and a fork is good for eating meat.

**Knork:** No! It is (A)_____ better to use a knife and a fork instead. Don't you think it is easier for you to hold a fork in one hand and a knife in the other? (B)What can be more elegant than using them to cut meat on a plate!

**05** 다음 중 빈칸 (A)에 들어갈 수 <u>없는</u> 말은?

① a lot      ② much      ③ even
④ far        ⑤ very

**서답형**

**06** What has Spork found on a recent trip? Answer in English with a full sentence.

➡ _____

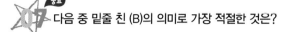

**07** 다음 중 밑줄 친 (B)의 의미로 가장 적절한 것은?

① Using a spoon for grains and soup is good for everyone.

② Holding a fork and a knife at the same time is elegant.

③ A fork is not elegant enough to cut meat.

④ Using a spoon and a fork is uncomfortable.

⑤ Using a knife and a fork is the most elegant way to cut meat.

[08~09] 다음 글을 읽고 물음에 답하시오.

Chopsticks: Why do you use two different kinds of utensils when you can use (A) two of the same utensil? Plus, you can use chopsticks with just one hand!

Barehands: No way! When I eat with my hands, of course I can see and smell the food, but I can also touch it. Because I use my sense of touch when I eat, I get to enjoy my food more.

They raised and argued many points, and nobody wanted to give up.

**서답형**

**08** 밑줄 친 (A)가 의미하는 것을 위 글에서 찾아 쓰시오.

➡ _____

**09** According to the passage, what is the good point of eating with barehands?

① It helps us to see the food better.

② It makes us feel refreshed.

③ It has us use our sense of touch.

④ It helps us cook by ourselves.

⑤ It lets us enjoy making food more.

[10~12] 다음 글을 읽고 물음에 답하시오.

It was not easy for their host, Ms. Disher, to listen to their arguments patiently. So, she hurriedly, yet ①quietly, left.

Spork: Where is Ms. Disher? She ②has disappeared.

Knork: What should we do? Without Ms. Disher, this dinner is not ③complete.

Chopsticks: Where did she go?

Barehands: Let's go out to find her!

After hours of ④searching all over the Dining Republic, they finally found Ms. Disher sitting under a huge tree.

Spork, Knork, Chopsticks, Barehands: We're sorry we became boastful and ⑤respected you. Please forgive and come back and join us.

Ms. Disher: It's okay. I forgive you. Let's go back to my home.

Since (A)then, every time they meet, they allow one another to eat in the manner that they please. In their hearts they now know that food will always be delicious regardless of which utensils they use to eat it with.

**10** 다음 중 밑줄 친 (A)가 의미하는 것은?

① when Ms. Disher invited them

② the time all of them first met

③ when Spork and Knork argued a lot

④ the time Ms. Disher used knork

⑤ when Ms. Disher disappeared and was found

**11** ①~⑤ 중 글의 흐름상 어색한 것은?

①          ②          ③          ④          ⑤

**서답형**

**12** Where did they find Ms. Disher? Answer in English with 8 words.

➡ _____

[13~16] 다음 글을 읽고 물음에 답하시오.

Spork, Chopsticks, Knork, Barehands, and Ms. Disher are close friends in the Dining Republic. Spork, Chopsticks, Knork, and Barehands travel a lot with their families, but Ms. Disher's family does not travel much. She makes up for this by hosting a dinner for her friends coming back from their trips. She is always eager to listen to their adventures. They often talk about what they learned from their recent trips. The most recent topic was about the best way (A)to eat and Ms. Disher's guests began to argue.

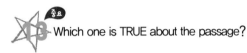 Which one is TRUE about the passage?

① Ms. Disher doesn't know Spork well.
② Ms. Disher is eager to travel much.
③ Ms. Disher is dying to hear her friends' adventures.
④ The friends threw a party for Ms. Disher.
⑤ Ms. Disher's guests argued about the best trip they had had.

**14** What do Ms. Disher's friends often talk about? Answer in English with a full sentence.

➡ _____

_____

**서답형**
**15** 다음 중 위 글의 내용과 틀린 부분을 두 군데 찾아 바르게 고쳐 쓰시오.

Like Ms. Disher, Spork, Chopsticks, Knork, and Barehands travel a lot with their families. So Ms. Disher hosts a dinner for her friends to make up that.

➡ _____

 다음 중 밑줄 친 (A)와 쓰임이 같은 것은?

① It was not easy to see him off.
② He has an ability to memorize everything he reads.
③ He went out to go to church.
④ I was glad to see you there.
⑤ He must be generous to lend you money.

[17~20] 다음 글을 읽고 물음에 답하시오.

**Spork:** On a recent trip, I ①have found that it is best to use a spoon and fork. A spoon is best ②for grains and soup, and a fork is good for eating meat.
**Knork:** No! It is much better ③to use a knife and a fork instead. Don't you think ④that is easier for you to hold a fork in one hand and a knife in the other? What can be more elegant than using them to cut meat on a plate!
**Chopsticks:** Why do you use two different kinds of utensils when you can use two of the same utensil? Plus, you can use chopsticks with just one hand!
**Barehands:** (A)No way! When I eat with my hands, of course I can see and smell the food, but I can also touch it. Because I use my sense of touch when I eat, I get ⑤to enjoy my food more.
They raised and argued many points, and nobody wanted to give up.

 What is 'using a fork' good for?

① It is best for grains.
② It is easy to hold soup with it.
③ It is good for eating meat.
④ It is good to smell food with it.
⑤ It is nice to handle many kinds of vegetables.

**18** 다음 중 밑줄 친 (A)의 의미로 가장 적절한 것은?

① It is not an option.
② There is no other way.
③ I can't agree with you more.
④ I don't think so.
⑤ It is hard to find other ways.

**19** According to the passage, how does Barehands eat? Answer in English with five words.

➡ _____

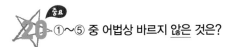

**20** ①~⑤ 중 어법상 바르지 <u>않은</u> 것은?

①　　　②　　　③　　　④　　　⑤

[21~25] 다음 글을 읽고 물음에 답하시오.

It was not easy for their host, Ms. Disher, to listen to their arguments patiently. So, she hurriedly, yet quietly, left.
**Spork:** Where is Ms. Disher? She has disappeared.
**Knork:** What should we do? Without Ms. Disher, this dinner is not complete.
**Chopsticks:** Where did she go?
**Barehands:** Let's go out to find her!
After hours of searching all over the Dining Republic, they finally found Ms. Disher sitting under a huge tree.
**Spork, Knork, Chopsticks, Barehands:** We're sorry we became boastful and ignored you. Please forgive and come back and join us.
**Ms. Disher:** It's okay. I forgive you. Let's go back to my home.
Since then, every time they meet, they allow one another to eat in the manner that they please. In their hearts they now know that food will always be delicious regardless of which utensils they use to eat it with.

**21** According to the passage, what did they argue about?

① when they will have a party
② who invented utensils
③ why they use utensils
④ which utensils are better
⑤ how they use utensils

**22** Write the reason why Ms. Disher left in a hurry. Use the words below.

(it's because / her / her)

➡ _____
_____

**23** 다음 중 위 글에서 반의어를 찾을 수 <u>없는</u> 것은?

① appear　② incomplete　③ noisily
④ blame　⑤ tasty

**24** Which is NOT true about the passage?

① Ms. Disher didn't let her friends know that she went out.
② Spork first noticed that Ms. Disher had disappeared.
③ Her friends wanted to know where Ms. Disher was.
④ Ms. Disher's friends found her after hours of searching.
⑤ Ms. Disher wanted to keep punishing her friends.

**25** What do they allow one another to do?

➡ _____
_____

[01~05] 다음 글을 읽고 물음에 답하시오.

Spork, Chopsticks, Knork, Barehands, and Ms. Disher are close friends in the Dining Republic. Spork, Chopsticks, Knork, and Barehands travel a lot with their families, but Ms. Disher's family does not travel much. She makes up for (A)this by hosting a dinner for her friends coming back from their trips. She is always eager to listen to their adventures. They often talk about what they learned from their recent trips. The most recent topic was about the best way to eat and Ms. Disher's guests began to argue.

**01** 밑줄 친 (A)가 의미하는 것을 우리말로 쓰시오.

➡ _____

**02** Who are Ms. Disher's close friends in the Dining Republic?

➡ _____
_____

**03** What do Ms. Disher's friends do with their families? Answer in English and use the word 'they.'

➡ _____

**04** 위 글의 내용과 일치하도록 빈칸에 알맞은 말을 쓰시오.

Ms. Disher's guests began to argue about _____ _____ _____ _____
_____.

**05** What was the most recent topic of Ms. Disher's friends? Answer in English with a full sentence. (8 words)

➡ _____

[06~09] 다음 글을 읽고 물음에 답하시오.

Spork: On a recent trip, I have found that it is best to use a spoon and fork. A spoon is best for grains and soup, and a fork is good for eating meat.

Knork: No! It is much better to use a knife and a fork instead. Don't you think it is easier for you to hold a fork in one hand and a knife in the other? What can be more elegant than using them to cut meat on a plate!

Chopsticks: Why do you use two different kinds of utensils when you can use two of the same utensil? Plus, you can use chopsticks with just one hand!

Barehands: No way! When I eat with my hands, of course I can see and smell the food, but I can also touch it. Because I use my sense of touch when I eat, I get to enjoy my food more.

They raised and argued many points, and nobody wanted to give up.

**06** 위 글의 내용에 맞게 빈칸에 알맞은 말을 쓰시오.

Knork thinks that _____ _____
_____ _____ _____ _____ is much better than _____ _____
_____ _____.

**07** According to Spork, what is good for eating grains and soup? Answer in English with a full sentence.

➡ _____

**08** According to Chopsticks, what are the two benefits of using chopsticks? Answer in English with a full sentence.

➡ _____

_____

**09** 위 글의 내용에 맞게 빈칸에 알맞은 말을 쓰시오.

> Knork thinks that eating with _____
>
> _____ _____ _____ _____
>
> _____ more elegant than any other way of
> eating.

**[10~14]** 다음 글을 읽고 물음에 답하시오.

It was not easy for their host, Ms. Disher, (A)_____ to their arguments patiently. So, she hurriedly, yet quietly, left.

Spork: Where is Ms. Disher? She has disappeared.

Knork: What should we do? Without Ms. Disher, this dinner is not complete.

Chopsticks: Where did she go?

Barehands: Let's go out to find her!

After hours of searching all over the Dining Republic, they finally found Ms. Disher sitting under a huge tree.

Spork, Knork, Chopsticks, Barehands: We're sorry we became boastful and ignored you. Please forgive and come back and join us.

Ms. Disher: It's okay. I forgive you. Let's go back to my home.

Since then, every time they meet, they allow one another to eat in the manner that they

please. (B)In their hearts they now know that food will always be delicious regardless of which utensils they use to eat it with.

**10** 빈칸 (A)에 listen을 어법에 맞게 쓰시오.

➡ _____

**11** 밑줄 친 (B)와 같은 의미의 문장을 완성하시오.

> In their hearts they now know that no matter
>
> _____ _____ _____ _____
>
> _____ _____ _____ _____ ,
>
> food will always be delicious.

**12** 위 글의 내용에 맞게 빈칸에 알맞은 말을 쓰시오.

> It took _____ to find Ms. Disher _____
> under a huge tree.

**13** What are Spork, Knork, Chopsticks, and Barehands sorry for? Answer in English with a full sentence.

➡ _____

_____

**14** 다음 중 위 글의 내용과 일치하지 않는 것을 찾아 고쳐 쓰시오.

> Ms. Disher didn't want to hear her guest argue, so she left. As soon as they noticed Ms. Disher had disappeared, they realized that their dinner couldn't be complete with Ms. Disher.

➡ _____

### Real Life Communication B

**A:** Which do you prefer, fruit or ice cream?
"어느 것"이라는 의미로 한정된 것에서 선택을 나타낸다.

**B:** I prefer ice cream.
타동사 prefer의 목적어는 명사, 대명사, 동명사를 주로 쓰지만 to부정사를 쓸 수도 있다.

**A:** Why do you prefer it?

**B:** It seems to me that ice cream is sweeter.
"It seems to me that ~"은 자신의 의견을 제시하는 말이다.

구문해설 · seem ~인 것 같다

해석

A: 과일과 아이스크림 중에서 어느 것을 더 좋아하니?

B: 나는 아이스크림을 더 좋아해.

A: 왜 그것을 더 좋아하니?

B: 내 생각에는 아이스크림이 더 달콤한 것 같아.

### Before You Read B

Different cultures use different kinds of utensils to eat. For some people,

chopsticks are easy to use. For another, a fork is more convenient. Other
to부정사의 부사적 용법(형용사 수식)
people might think using a knife and fork is more elegant.
추측의 조동사      동명사 주어

구문해설 · **convenient**: 편리한, 사용하기 좋은 · **elegant**: 기품 있는, (취미·습관·문제 따위가) 우아한, 세련된

다른 문화에서는 음식을 먹는 데 다른 종류의 도구를 사용한다. 어떤 사람들에게 젓가락은 사용하기 쉽다. 또 다른 사람들에게는 포크가 더 편리하다. 다른 사람들은 나이프와 포크를 사용하는 것이 더 우아하다고 생각할지도 모른다.

### Before You Read 1

I think people have bacon and eggs for breakfast in the USA.
think (that) 명사절 접속사 생략
Pho is very popular breakfast in Vietnam. And people in Iran like to eat Naan
to부정사를 목적어로 취하는 동사
for breakfast.

구문해설 · **breakfast**: 아침 · **popular**: 인기 있는 · **Vietnam**: 베트남 · **Iran**: 이란

나는 사람들이 미국에서 아침식사로 베이컨과 계란을 먹는다고 생각합니다. 포는 베트남에서 매우 인기 있는 아침식사입니다. 그리고 이란 사람들은 아침식사로 난을 먹는 것을 좋아합니다.

Words & Expressions

**01** 다음 두 문장에 공통으로 알맞은 것을 고르시오.

> • She is eager _____ his success.
> • He worked hard to make up _____ it.

① to      ② for      ③ with
④ by      ⑤ about

**02** 다음 밑줄 친 단어와 의미가 반대인 단어를 고르시오.

> King Louis XIV of France was not happy with the pointed knives. So, he banned their use.

① allowed      ② prohibited
③ prevented      ④ stayed
⑤ decided

**03** 다음 영영풀이에 해당하는 단어를 고르시오.

> talking about yourself in a very proud way

① boastful      ② wonderful
③ convenient      ④ adventurous
⑤ elegant

**04** 다음 밑줄 친 부분의 우리말 뜻이 알맞지 않은 것은?

① Is it polite in your country? (예절바른)
② We use different kinds of utensils. (도구들)
③ Using a knife and fork is more elegant. (편리한)
④ They often talk about their recent trips. (최근의)
⑤ They provided enough water. (공급하다)

Conversation

**[05~06]** 다음 우리말과 일치하도록 빈칸에 알맞은 말을 쓰시오.

**05**

> A: _____
> _____ (프라이드 치킨을 먹을 때 어느 것을 사용하기를 더 좋아하니), a knife and fork or your hands?
> B: I prefer to use my hands.

**06**

> A: Which do you prefer, fruit or ice cream?
> B: I prefer ice cream.
> A: Why do you prefer it?
> B: _____
> (내 생각에는 아이스크림이 더 달콤한 것 같아.)

**07** 다음 대화의 빈칸에 들어가기에 적절한 말을 쓰시오.

> A: Which do you prefer, having a meal early or late in the evening?
> B: I prefer having a meal _____ in the evening.
> A: Why is that?
> B: Because I usually go to bed early, I prefer having my meal early.

**08** 다음 대화의 빈칸에 들어갈 말로 적절한 것을 고르시오.

> A: I'm so hungry. Let's get something to eat.
>
> B: _____ Which do you prefer, noodles or rice?
>
> A: I like noodles. Do you know any good restaurants?
>
> B: There's a good noodle restaurant over there.

① Me, neither.     ② So you do.

③ It's important.     ④ I like noodles.

⑤ So am I.

**[09~11]** 다음 대화를 읽고 물음에 답하시오.

> G: It seems to me that you don't like the food.
>
> B: No, I enjoyed the food. I usually leave some food on my plate. (A)That's good table manners in my country, China.
>
> G: Why is that?
>
> B: We think (B)_____ everything on the plate means that you are still hungry.
>
> G: It is more polite to finish everything on your plate in Korea, though.
>
> B: Different cultures have different rules.

**09** (A)의 내용을 알 수 있는 문장을 찾아 쓰시오.

➡ _____

**10** 빈칸 (B)에 들어가기에 적절한 것은?

① cooking    ② making    ③ cleaning

④ serving    ⑤ finishing

**11** 위 대화를 통해서 알 수 있는 것이 아닌 것은?

① In China, they think that leaving some food is polite.

② If someone finishes everything on the plate, they think he is still hungry in China.

③ To finish everything on your plate is more polite in Korea.

④ In China, you should not eat much food.

⑤ Every culture has its own rules.

**[12~13]** 다음 대화를 읽고 물음에 답하시오.

> G: What can we do to stay healthy?
>
> B: I think having healthy food is important.
>
> G: My brother exercises every day for his health.
>
> B: (A)_____ do you prefer, having healthy food or exercising, Emma?
>
> G: I can't control which food I eat. So, I prefer to exercise.
>
> B: Both of them seem to be important for our health.
>
> G: But (B)_____, it might be better to focus on just one.
>
> B: I think you are right. I'm going to exercise first.

**12** 위 대화의 빈칸 (A)에 들어가기에 적절한 것은?

① What    ② How    ③ Which

④ Where    ⑤ When

**13** 위 대화의 내용으로 보아 빈칸 (B)에 들어가기에 가장 적절한 것은?

① when you like to exercise

② if you can't do both

③ if you like both of them

④ when you prefer exercising

⑤ if you like to have healthy food better

## Grammar

**14** 다음 괄호 안에서 알맞은 말을 고르시오.

(1) She didn't publish her article (posting / posted) on the website.

(2) The money (spending / spent) overseas by tourists can be considered as an import.

(3) It was nice (to / of) her to encourage him when he was down.

(4) It's necessary (for / of) drivers to carry a driver's license.

**15** 다음 문장의 빈칸에 알맞은 말이 바르게 짝지어진 것은?

> • It was not easy _____ their host, Ms. Disher, to listen to their arguments patiently.
> • I want to see the pictures _____ by Marie Laurencin.

① for – drawing
② for – drawn
③ of – drawn
④ of – drawing
⑤ of – draw

**16** 다음 중 어색한 문장을 모두 고르시오.

① It is difficult for Clare to arrive on time.

② It is quite silly for you to try to force him to consent.

③ It was an interesting experience for the kids to visit the amusement park.

④ He wore dirty shoes covering with dust.

⑤ There were many students standing in line to enter the museum.

⑥ The man bitten by a snake was carried to the hospital.

**17** 그림을 보고, 주어진 어휘를 이용하여 빈칸을 알맞게 채우시오.

➡ It is _____ well-balanced meals. (important, children, eat)

**18** 다음 두 문장의 의미가 같도록 빈칸에 알맞은 말을 쓰시오.

(1) I carelessly made such a wrong guess.
   = It was careless _____ such a wrong guess.

(2) You easily took advantage of them.
   = It was easy _____ advantage of them.

**19** 다음 두 문장의 의미가 같도록 빈칸에 알맞은 말을 쓰시오.

> • The lady is Jane Goodal.
> • She studies chimpanzees in Africa.
> → The lady _____ is Jane Goodal.

Reading

**[20~23]** 다음 글을 읽고 물음에 답하시오.

Spork, Chopsticks, Knork, Barehands, and Mrs. Disher are close friends in the Dining Republic.

(A) She makes up for this by hosting a dinner for her friends coming back from their trips. She is always eager to listen to their adventures. They often talk about ⓐ_____ they learned from their recent trips.

(B) Spork, Chopsticks, Knork, and Barehands travel a lot with their families, but Ms. Disher's family does not travel much.

(C) The most recent topic was about the best way to eat and Ms. Disher's guests began to argue.

**20** 자연스러운 글이 되도록 (A)~(C)를 바르게 나열하시오.

➡ _____

**21** 다음 중 빈칸 ⓐ에 들어갈 말로 가장 적절한 것은?

① that  ② how  ③ which
④ what  ⑤ why

**22** What does Ms. Disher do for her friends coming back from their trips? Answer in English with six words.

➡ _____

**23** 다음 중 위 글의 내용과 일치하는 것은?

① Ms. Disher travels a lot with her family.
② Ms. Disher's friends don't talk about their adventures.
③ Ms. Disher's friends haven't traveled recently.
④ The most recent topic was when the best time to eat is.
⑤ Ms. Disher is very interested in listening to her friends' stories.

**[24~26]** 다음 글을 읽고 물음에 답하시오.

Spork: On a recent trip, I have found that it is best to use a spoon and fork. A spoon is best for grains and soup, and a fork is good for eating meat.

Knork: No! It is much ①better to use a knife and a fork instead. Don't you think it is ② more difficult for you to hold a fork in one hand and a knife in the other? What can be more ③elegant than using them to cut meat on a plate!

Chopsticks: Why do you use two different kinds of utensils when you can use two of the same utensil? Plus, you can use chopsticks with just ④one hand!

Barehands: No way! When I eat with my hands, of course I can see and smell the food, but I can also touch it. Because I use my sense of touch when I eat, I get to enjoy my food ⑤more.

They raised and argued many points, and nobody wanted to give up.

**24** 다음 ①~⑤ 중 글의 흐름상 어색한 것은?

①        ②        ③        ④        ⑤

**25** Which one is NOT true about the passage?

① Spork thinks that using a spoon and fork is the best way to eat.

② Knork disagrees with Spork.

③ Chopsticks uses two hands to eat food.

④ All of them think differently about what the best way to eat is.

⑤ Everyone didn't want to give up.

**26** 위 글의 내용에 맞게 빈칸에 알맞은 말을 쓰시오.

According to Barehands, you can see, smell, and _____ the food when you eat with your _____ .

**[27~29]** 다음 글을 읽고 물음에 답하시오.

**Fork Facts**

Forks were not used by many people about 1,000 years ago. They became popular with the arrival of the Renaissance in Italy. Catherine de Medici introduced the fork to France in 1533. They slowly started to be used in France. By the early 17th century, travelers from all over Europe were spreading their use. People in North America started to use forks in the early 19th century.

**27** 다음 중 위 글의 제목으로 가장 적절한 것은?

① Fun Facts about French People

② The History of Using Forks

③ The Inventor of the Fork

④ Who Introduced Fork to the World

⑤ The History of Fork in Europe

**28** When did Catherine de Medici introduce the fork to France? Answer in English with a full sentence.

➡ _____

_____

**29** 다음 중 위 글을 읽고 답할 수 <u>없는</u> 것은?

① When did forks become popular in Italy?

② Who introduced the fork to France?

③ What did people mainly use to eat about 1,000 years ago?

④ Who spread the use of forks in the early 17th century?

⑤ When did people in North America start to use forks?

출제율 95%

**01** 짝지어진 단어의 관계가 같도록 빈칸에 알맞은 말을 쓰시오.

> ignore : neglect = _____ : supply

출제율 90%

**02** 다음 빈칸에 들어갈 말로 적절한 것은?

> Rachel is very _____ of her son.

① patient      ② boastful
③ pleased      ④ popular
⑤ important

출제율 90%

**03** 다음 빈칸에 공통으로 들어가기에 적절한 것은?

> • I _____ meals late in the evening because I work late at night.
> • Do you _____ trouble using your utensils at the dining table?

① take      ② get
③ have      ④ carry
⑤ allow

출제율 95%

**04** 다음 〈보기〉에 제시된 단어로 자연스러운 문장을 만들 수 없는 것은?

> ┌── 보기 ──┐
> provide   polite   prefer   raise

① His manner was _____ but cool.
② I _____ my coffee black.
③ Can you _____ any proof of identity?
④ How can we _____ standards in schools?
⑤ The most interesting _____ is the hand.

**[05~07]** 다음 대화를 읽고 물음에 답하시오.

W: What time is it now?
M: It's already 8:00 p.m.
W: (A)_____ don't we stop now and have a meal?
M: Good idea. We need to take a break at this point.
W: Which do you prefer, having a meal early or late in the evening?
M: I prefer having a meal early.
W: (B)_____ is the reason?
M: I usually go to bed early, so I eat my last meal early, too. (C)_____
W: I have meals late in the evening because I work late at night.

출제율 95%

**05** 빈칸 (A)와 (B)에 들어가기에 알맞은 것으로 짝지어진 것은?

|   | (A) | (B) |
|---|-----|-----|
| ① | Why | Which |
| ② | How | Why |
| ③ | Why | What |
| ④ | What | Who |
| ⑤ | Which | Where |

출제율 90%

**06** 내용상 빈칸 (C)에 들어가기에 가장 적절한 것은?

① How about you?
② What do you like?
③ Why do you prefer it?
④ When do you have meal?
⑤ What do you like to have?

**07** 위 대화를 읽고 대답할 수 <u>없는</u> 것은?

① What time is it now?

② What will they do?

③ Which does the man prefer, having a meal early or late in the evening?

④ Why does the man prefer having a meal early?

⑤ Where will the woman go to have meals?

---

**[08~10]** 다음 대화를 읽고 물음에 답하시오.

Jinho: Claire, ①<u>which do you prefer, fish or steak?</u>

Claire: ②<u>I prefer fish, Jinho.</u>

Jinho: There is fish on the menu.

Claire: That's good. ③<u>Is it sushi and fried?</u>

Jinho: ④<u>Both are on the menu.</u>

Claire: Then _____ . It seems to me that fish tastes better when it's uncooked.

Jinho: Okay. Then you get sushi and I'll get fried fish. ⑤<u>Let's order.</u>

**08** 빈칸에 들어가기에 가장 적절한 것은?

① I prefer steak

② I like fish better

③ we will order fried

④ I will have sushi

⑤ they don't have cooked fish

**09** 위 대화의 밑줄 ①~⑤ 중 어색한 문장은?

①　　②　　③　　④　　⑤

---

**10** 위 대화를 읽고 알 수 <u>없는</u> 것은?

① They are in a restaurant to have a meal.

② Steak is more expensive than fish.

③ Claire wants to have sushi because it tastes better.

④ Jinho will eat different food than Claire's.

⑤ They will have a meal at the restaurant.

**11** 다음 빈칸에 알맞은 말이 순서대로 짝지어진 것은?

- How foolish _____ the economy to recover so quickly!
- There is a lady _____ on the street.

① of them to expect – running

② for them to expect – running

③ of them expecting – runs

④ for them expecting – to run

⑤ for them to expect – to run

**12** 다음 빈칸에 알맞지 <u>않은</u> 것은?

It was _____ for him to consult the question.

① impossible　　② easy

③ difficult　　④ generous

⑤ boring

출제율 95%

**13** 다음 ⓐ~ⓖ 중 어법상 옳은 것을 <u>모두</u> 고르시오.

> ⓐ Do not use the bread plate and water glass of the person sitting next to you.
> ⓑ Cigarette butts throwing carelessly can cause a fire.
> ⓒ He showed me the photos taken during his trip.
> ⓓ The girl walked her dog is my best friend, Yuna.
> ⓔ It is dangerous for children to ride a bike without a helmet.
> ⓕ It is necessary of her to regularly visit her office.
> ⓖ It is unreasonable of you to expect me to take action immediately.

➡ _____

출제율 90%

**14** 다음 〈보기〉에 주어진 단어를 어법에 맞게 고쳐 쓰시오.

> ┌─ 보기 ┐
> plant

(1) There is a girl _____ trees in the garden.

(2) Look at the trees _____ in the garden.

[15~17] 다음 글을 읽고 물음에 답하시오.

> Spork, Chopsticks, Knork, Barehands, and Ms. Disher are close friends in the Dining Republic. ① Spork, Chopsticks, Knork, and Barehands travel a lot with their families. ② She makes up for this by hosting a dinner for her friends coming back from their trips. ③ She is always eager to listen to their adventures. ④ They often talk about what they learned from their recent trips. ⑤ The most recent topic was about the best way to eat and Ms. Disher's guests began to argue.

출제율 100%

**15** ①~⑤ 중 주어진 문장이 들어가기에 가장 적절한 곳은?

> But Ms. Disher's family does not travel much.

①　　②　　③　　④　　⑤

출제율 95%

**16** What is Ms. Disher always eager to do? Answer in English with 10 words.

➡ _____
_____

출제율 90%

**17** For whom does Ms. Disher host a dinner? Answer in English with a full sentence.

➡ _____
_____

**[18~19]** 다음 글을 읽고 물음에 답하시오.

The knife is most certainly the oldest eating utensil. In the Middle Ages in Europe, a host did not have to provide his guests with any utensils. So guests carried their own knives that were used for both eating and fighting. King Louis XVI of France was not happy with the pointed knives. So, he banned their use.

출제율 100%

**18** What is TRUE about the passage?

① The knife is as old as other utensils.

② There were not many people who used their own knives in the Middle Ages.

③ Guests carried knives only for fighting.

④ King Louis XIV kept people from using the pointed knives.

⑤ Using the pointed knives was encouraged by French government.

출제율 95%

**19** 위 글의 내용에 맞게 빈칸에 알맞은 말을 쓰시오.

In the Middle Ages in Europe, a host didn't have to provide _____ for _____.

**[20~22]** 다음 글을 읽고 물음에 답하시오.

Are you having trouble (A)[using / to use] your utensils at the dining table? Here are some tips. It is important for you to use the utensils on the outside first. Do not use the bread plate and water glass of the person (B)[sitting / seating] next to you. Your bread plate is on the left of the place setting. Your water glass is on the right of the place setting. Try not to become (C) [confusing / confused].

출제율 100%

**20** 다음 중 위 글의 제목으로 가장 적절한 것은?

① How to Make Your Life Better

② Tips for Using a Table Towel

③ How to Wash Utensils Clearly

④ Tips for Using Utensils

⑤ How to Sit When You Are a Guest

출제율 90%

**21** Where is your bread plate on the table?

➡ _____

출제율 95%

**22** (A)~(C)에서 어법상 옳은 것끼리 바르게 짝지어진 것은?

① using – sitting – confusing

② using – seating – confused

③ using – sitting – confused

④ to use – seating – confused

⑤ to use – sitting – confusing

[01~03] 다음 대화를 읽고 물음에 답하시오.

> G: Do you like this cap?
> B: It seems to me that red does not look good on you.
> G: Do you have any suggestion, then?
> B: (A)_____ about this blue cap? (가)빨간색 보다 파란색이 너한테 훨씬 더 잘 어울려. (looks, much, better)
> G: That sounds good. I'll take (B)it.

**01** 빈칸 (A)에 들어가기에 적절한 한 단어를 쓰시오.

➡ _____

**02** (가)의 우리말에 해당하는 영어 문장을 괄호 안의 말을 이용하여 쓰시오.

➡ _____

**03** 밑줄 친 (B)의 it이 가리키는 것을 찾아 3 단어로 쓰시오.

➡ _____

**04** 다음을 it을 사용하여 비슷한 뜻의 문장으로 바꾸어 쓰시오.

(1) The book is interesting and I like to read it.

➡ _____

(2) We need to keep silent in the library.

➡ _____

**05** 주어진 두 문장을 분사를 이용하여 한 문장으로 바꾸어 쓰시오.

(1) • It's good to walk on the leaves.
   • The leaves were fallen on the road.

➡ _____
_____

(2) • I found myself next to a young person.
   • The young person was listening to music.

➡ _____
_____

(3) • That car is very expensive.
   • That car was made in England.

➡ _____
_____

**06** 다음 문장에서 어법상 어색한 것을 바르게 고쳐 다시 쓰시오.

(1) She showed me a letter filling with strange symbols.

➡ _____
_____

(2) The restaurant served delicious food has kind staff.

➡ _____
_____

(3) We ordered rare steak, but it was too rare of all of us to eat.

➡ _____
_____

(4) It is really kind for you to remember my birthday.

➡ _____
_____

(5) It's exciting for me going abroad.

➡ _____

[07~09] 다음 글을 읽고 물음에 답하시오.

**Knife Facts**

The knife is most certainly the oldest eating utensil. In the Middle Ages in Europe, a host did not have to provide his guests with any utensils. So guests carried their own knives that were used for both eating and fighting. King Louis XIV of France was not happy with the pointed knives. So, he banned (A)their use.

**07** Write the reason why guests in the Middle Ages in Europe carried their own knives for eating. Answer in English and use the phrase 'It was because.'

➡ _____

_____

**08** What is the oldest eating utensil? Answer in English with a full sentence.

➡ _____

_____

**09** 밑줄 친 (A)가 가리키는 것을 위 글에서 찾아 쓰시오.

➡ _____

**10** According to the passage, what kinds of utensils are there? Answer in English with a full sentence.

Different cultures use different kinds of utensils to eat. For some people, chopsticks are easy to use. For another, a fork is more convenient. Other people might think using a knife and fork is more elegant.

➡ _____

[11~12] 다음 글을 읽고 물음에 답하시오.

It was not easy for their host, Ms. Disher, to listen to their arguments patiently. So, she hurriedly, yet quietly, left.

**Spork:** Where is Ms. Disher? She has disappeared.

**Knork:** What should we do? Without Ms. Disher, this dinner is not complete.

**Chopsticks:** Where did she go?

**Barehands:** Let's go out to find her!

After hours of searching all over the Dining Republic, they finally found Ms. Disher sitting under a huge tree.

**Spork, Knork, Chopsticks, Barehands:** We're sorry we became boastful and ignored you. Please forgive and come back and join us.

**Ms. Disher:** It's okay. I forgive you. Let's go back to my home.

Since then, every time they meet, they allow one another to eat in the manner that they please. In their hearts they now know that food will always be delicious regardless of which utensils they use to eat it with.

**11** What did Spork, Knork, Chopsticks and Barehands do after they found out Ms. Disher had disappeared? Answer in English with seven words.

➡ _____

**12** 위 글의 내용에 맞게 빈칸에 알맞은 말을 쓰시오.

In the end, they don't care _____ _____ _____ _____ to eat their food with because they know that it doesn't change the taste of the food.

**01** 다음 〈보기〉에서 알맞은 단어를 골라 글을 완성해 봅시다.

┌ 보기 ┐

use   different   utensil   convenient

Different cultures use _____ kinds of _____s to eat. For some people, chopsticks are easy to _____. For another, a fork is more convenient. Other people might think using a knife and fork is more _____.

**02** 다음 그림을 보고, 주어진 조건에 맞게 영작하시오.

┌ 조건 ┐

(1) to부정사를 진주어로 사용할 것
(2) 분사를 활용하여 쓸 것
(3) leg, on, walk, break, very hard를 이용할 것

➡ _____

**03** 다음 조언을 바탕으로 서구식 식사 예절을 설명하는 안내문을 써 보시오.

┌ 조건 ┐

Tip 1. You need to use the utensils on the outside first.
Tip 2. The bread plate is on the left of the place setting.
Tip 3. The water glass is on the right of the place setting.

Are you having trouble using your utensils at the dining table? Here are some tips. It is important for you _____ first. Do not use the bread plate and water glass of the person sitting next to you. Your bread plate is _____. Your water glass is _____. Try not to become confused.

## 단원별 모의고사

**01** 다음 짝지어진 두 단어의 관계가 같도록 빈칸에 알맞은 말을 쓰시오.

argue : argument = arrive : _____

**02** 다음 영영풀이에 해당하는 단어로 적절한 것은?

the seeds of plants such as wheat, corn, and rice that are used for food

① grain
② noodle
③ plate
④ meal
⑤ vegetable

**03** 다음 문장의 빈칸에 알맞은 것을 〈보기〉에서 찾아 쓰시오.

┌─ 보기 ─┐
give   take   regardless   eager

(1) Let's _____ a break under this tree.
(2) Everyone in the class was _____ to learn.
(3) He chose to _____ up the plan.
(4) She always travels first-class _____ of expense.

**04** 다음 빈칸에 들어갈 말로 적절한 것은?

She tried hard to _____ up for her mistake.

① take
② make
③ have
④ get
⑤ grow

**[05~07]** 다음 대화를 읽고 물음에 답하시오.

G: (가)It seems to me that you don't like the food.
B: No, I enjoyed the food. I usually leave some food on my plate. (나)That's good table manners in my country, China.
G: Why is that?
B: We think finishing everything on the plate means that you are still hungry.
G: It is more polite to finish everything on your plate in Korea, though.
B: (A)_____

**05** 밑줄 친 (가)와 바꿔 쓰기에 적절하지 않은 것은?

① I think
② I believe
③ In my opinion,
④ I'm sure
⑤ He is certain

**06** 밑줄 친 (나)That이 가리키는 것은?

① to enjoy the food
② to leave some food on the plate
③ to serve food on the table
④ to finish everything on the plate
⑤ to talk during the dinner

**07** 빈칸 (A)에 들어가기에 가장 적절한 것은?

① Every culture should follow our rule.
② China has more rules about eating.
③ Koreans don't like following rules.
④ We should not leave food on the plate.
⑤ Different cultures have different rules.

[08~09] 다음 대화를 읽고 물음에 답하시오.

G: What can we do to stay healthy?
B: I think (가)_____ is important.
G: My brother exercises every day for his health. ( A )
B: Which do you prefer, having healthy food or exercising, Emma? ( B )
G: I can't control which food I eat. So, I prefer to exercise. ( C )
B: Both of them seem to be important for our health. ( D )
G: But if you can't do both, it might be better to focus on just one.
B: I think you are right. ( E )

**08** (A)~(E) 중에서 다음 문장이 들어가기에 적절한 곳은?

> I'm going to exercise first.

① (A)  ② (B)  ③ (C)  ④ (D)  ⑤ (E)

**09** (가)의 빈칸에 들어가기에 적절한 것은?

① having healthy food
② exercising every day
③ to stay healthy
④ to control the food you eat
⑤ focusing on just one

[10~11] 다음 대화를 읽고 물음에 답하시오.

W: (A)_____ time is it now?
M: It's already 8:00 p.m.
W: Why don't we stop now and have a meal?
M: Good idea. We need to take a break at this point.
W: Which do you prefer, having a meal early or late in the evening?
M: I prefer having a meal early.
W: (B)_____ is the reason?

M: I usually go to bed early, (가)_____ I eat my last meal early, too. How about you?
W: I have meals late in the evening (나)_____ I work late at night.

**10** 대화의 빈칸 (A)와 (B)에 공통으로 들어가기에 적절한 것은?

① What  ② Which  ③ How
④ When  ⑤ Where

**11** (가)와 (나)에 들어가기에 적절한 것으로 짝지어진 것은?

| | (가) | (나) |
|---|---|---|
| ① | so | because |
| ② | and | so |
| ③ | but | while |
| ④ | though | since |
| ⑤ | but | and |

**12** 다음 중 어법상 바르지 <u>않은</u> 것은?

① It is necessary for people to recycle.
② Amy took photos of her house covered with snow.
③ I know the boy walked his dog over there.
④ It is important for you to use your utensils on the outside first.
⑤ She makes up for this by hosting a dinner for her friends coming back from their trips.

**13** 다음 두 문장의 의미가 같도록 빈칸에 알맞은 말을 쓰시오.

> It's important that he should understand the market precisely.
> = It's important _____ the market precisely.

**14** 다음 중 어법상 옳은 문장을 <u>모두</u> 고르시오.

① It isn't easy of the woman to climb a high mountain.

② Seoul is the best place in Korea for many tourists to visit.

③ There is a boy reads a book on the bench.

④ I met the girl swam in the pool.

⑤ The nice car parked on the road side was broken.

**15** 다음 두 문장을 한 문장으로 고쳐 쓰되, 가능한 한 짧게 쓰시오.

(1) • There is a man.

　　• He is watering the flowers.

➡ _____

(2) • Alexis wants to buy the dress.

　　• It is displayed in the shopwindow.

➡ _____

_____

**[16~19]** 다음 글을 읽고 물음에 답하시오.

**Spork:** On a recent trip, I have found that it is best ①<u>to use</u> a spoon and fork. A spoon is best for grains and soup, and a fork is good for eating meat.

**Knork:** No! ②<u>It</u> is much better to use a knife and a fork instead. Don't you think it is easier ③<u>of</u> you to hold a fork in one hand and a knife in ④<u>the other</u>? What can be more elegant than using them to cut meat on a plate!

**Chopsticks:** Why do you use two different kinds of utensils when you can use two of the same utensil? Plus, you can use chopsticks with just one hand!

**Barehands:** No way! When I eat with my hands, of course I can see and smell the food, but I can also touch it. ⑤ <u>Because</u> I use my sense of touch when I eat, I get to enjoy my food more.

They raised and argues many points, and nobody wanted to give (A)_____.

**16** 다음 중 빈칸 (A)에 들어갈 말과 같은 말이 들어가는 것은?

① Pay attention _____ us, please.

② The students look _____ to the man.

③ They walked side _____ side.

④ It turned _____ to be true.

⑤ He kept _____ saying the story.

**17** ①～⑤ 중 어법상 바르지 <u>않은</u> 것은?

①　　②　　③　　④　　⑤

**18** 다음 중 위 글을 읽고 답할 수 있는 것은?

① With whom did Spork take a trip?

② What does Knork use to eat grains?

③ How long did they argue?

④ What does Barehands prefer using to eat?

⑤ Who invited them to dinner?

**19** 위 글의 내용으로 보아 다음 빈칸에 들어갈 말로 가장 적절한 것은?

> The topic is _____ around the world.

① various kinds of food
② how to make the food delicious
③ types of friendship
④ different ways to eat
⑤ what to eat for healthy life

**[20~21]** 다음 글을 읽고 물음에 답하시오.

**Knife Facts**

① The Knife is most certainly the oldest eating utensil. ② In the Middle Ages in Europe, a host did not have to provide his guests with any utensils. ③ So guests carried their own knives that were used for both eating and fighting. ④ King Louis XIV of France was not happy with the pointed knives. ⑤

**20** ①~⑤ 중 주어진 문장이 들어가기에 가장 적절한 곳은?

> So, he banned their use.

①　　　②　　　③　　　④　　　⑤

**21** According to the passage, how were the knives used in the Middle Ages? Answer in English with a full sentence.

➡ _____

**[22~23]** 다음 글을 읽고 물음에 답하시오.

It was not easy for their host, Ms. Disher, to listen to their arguments patiently. So, she hurriedly, yet quietly, left.

**Spork:** Where is Ms. Disher? She has disappeared.

**Knork:** What should we do? Without Ms. Disher, this dinner is not complete.

**Chopsticks:** Where did she go?

**Barehands:** Let's go out to find her!

After hours of searching all over the Dining Republic, they finally found Ms. Disher sitting under a huge tree.

**Spork, Knork, Chopsticks, Barehands:** We're sorry we became boastful and ignored you. Please forgive and come back and join us.

**Ms. Disher:** It's okay. I forgive you. Let's go back to my home.

**22** 다음과 같이 풀이되는 단어를 위 글에서 찾아 쓰시오.

> talking too proudly about something that someone has done or that someone owns

➡ _____

**23** 다음 중 글의 내용을 바르게 이해한 사람은?

① Amelia: Everyone knows that Ms. Disher disappeared because she left saying goodbye.
② Brian: Knork thinks that Ms. Disher is not important to their dinner.
③ Chris: Barehands stays at home in order to wait Ms. Disher.
④ Dick: Ms. Disher was sitting on a huge hill.
⑤ Emily: Ms. Disher suggested going back to her home.

# Lesson 3

# Learning from Nature's Genius

 **의사소통 기능**

- 알고 있는지 묻기
  You know that Leonardo da Vinci painted the *Mona Lisa*, don't you?
- 관심 표현하기
  I'm fascinated by this noodle cooling fan.

**언어 형식**

- not only A but also B
  The fastener was **not only** strong **but also** easy to use.
- 간접의문문
  Do you know **where the key is**?

# Words & Expressions

## Key Words

- **absorb** [æbsɔ́:rb] 동 흡수하다
- **all-purpose** [ɔ:lpə:rpəs] 형 만능의, 다용도의
- **amazing** [əméiziŋ] 형 놀라운
- **apply** [əplái] 동 적용하다
- **article** [á:rtikl] 명 기사, 논문
- **beak** [bi:k] 명 (새의) 부리
- **bite** [bait] 명 물린 상처
- **bug** [bʌg] 명 곤충, 벌레
- **burr** [bə:r] 명 가시 식물
- **cause** [kɔ:z] 동 초래하다
- **closely** [klóusli] 부 자세히
- **contact** [kántækt] 명 접촉
- **cooling fan** 냉각팬
- **creative** [kriéitiv] 형 창의적인
- **decide** [disáid] 동 결심하다
- **design** [dizáin] 동 설계하다, 고안하다
- **dive** [daiv] 동 잠수하다
- **explain** [ikspléin] 동 설명하다
- **explore** [iksplɔ́:r] 동 탐색하다
- **fascinate** [fǽsənèit] 동 매혹하다
- **fastener** [fǽsnər] 명 잠금장치, 고정 장치
- **front** [frʌnt] 명 앞쪽
- **genius** [dʒí:njəs] 명 천재
- **goat** [gout] 명 염소
- **gracefully** [gréisfəli] 부 우아하게
- **hairy** [héəri] 형 털이 많은
- **high-speed** [háispí:d] 형 고속의
- **holder** [hóuldər] 명 받침, 걸이
- **imitate** [ímətèit] 동 모방하다

- **increase** [ínkri:s] 명 증가 동 증가하다
- **inspire** [inspáiər] 동 영감을 불러일으키다
- **inspiration** [inspəréiʃən] 명 영감
- **invention** [invénʃən] 명 발명
- **last** [læst] 동 지속하다
- **length** [leŋkθ] 명 길이
- **material** [mətíərəl] 명 물질, 재료
- **necessity** [nəsésəti] 명 필요성
- **needle** [ní:dl] 명 바늘
- **notice** [nóutis] 동 주목하다
- **observe** [əbzə́:rv] 동 관찰하다
- **painful** [péinfəl] 형 고통스러운
- **polar bear** 북극곰
- **pressure** [préʃər] 명 압력
- **redesign** [rì:dizáin] 동 다시 디자인하다
- **reduce** [ridjú:s] 동 줄이다
- **reflect** [riflékt] 동 반사하다
- **solution** [səlú:ʃən] 명 해결책
- **space** [speis] 명 공간, 우주
- **successful** [səksésfəl] 형 성공적인
- **sudden** [sʌ́dn] 형 갑작스러운
- **surface** [sə́:rfis] 명 표면
- **survivor** [sərváivər] 명 생존자
- **talent** [tǽlənt] 명 타고난 재능
- **tiny** [táini] 형 작은
- **weight** [weit] 명 무게
- **wing** [wiŋ] 명 날개
- **wonder** [wʌ́ndər] 동 궁금해 하다

## Key Expressions

- **as a result** 결과적으로
- **be stuck to** ~에 붙다
- **be good at** ~을 잘하다
- **be covered with** ~로 덮여 있다
- **float away** 떠다니다
- **go -ing** ~하러 가다
- **glide over** 활주하다
- **How come** ~? 어떻게 ~?, 왜 ~?
- **in search of** ~을 찾고 있는

- **keep A from -ing** A가 ~하지 못하게 하다
- **make contact with** ~와 연락하다, 접촉하다
- **make a note of** ~을 메모하다, 기록하다
- **not only A but also B** A뿐만 아니라 B도 역시
- **on one's way to** ~로 가는 길에
- **That's why** ~. 그것이 ~하는 이유이다.
- **try to** ~하기 위해 노력하다, ~하기 위해 애쓰다
- **take a look at** ~을 보다

## Word Power

※ 서로 비슷한 뜻을 가진 어휘

- □ **absorb** 흡수하다 – **soak** 빨아들이다
- □ **beak** (새의) 부리 – **bill** (새의) 부리
- □ **creative** 창의적인 – **inventive** 창의적인
- □ **imitate** 모방하다 – **mimic** 모방하다

- □ **amazing** 놀라운 – **surprising** 놀라운
- □ **bug** 곤충, 벌레 – **insect** 곤충
- □ **fascinate** 매혹하다 – **charm** 매혹하다
- □ **reduce** 줄이다 – **diminish** 줄이다

※ 서로 반대의 뜻을 가진 어휘

- □ **increase** 증가 ↔ **decrease** 감소
- □ **reduce** 줄이다 ↔ **enlarge** 확대하다
- □ **tiny** 작은 ↔ **huge** 거대한

- □ **melt** 녹다 ↔ **freeze** 얼다
- □ **solution** 해결책 ↔ **problem** 문제점

※ 동사 – 명사

- □ **absorb** 흡수하다 – **absorption** 흡수
- □ **decide** 결심하다 – **decision** 결심
- □ **explore** 탐색하다 – **exploration** 탐험
- □ **imitate** 모방하다 – **imitation** 모방
- □ **observe** 관찰하다 – **observation** 관찰
- □ **reflect** 반사하다 – **reflection** 반사

- □ **apply** 적용하다 – **application** 적용
- □ **explain** 설명하다 – **explanation** 설명
- □ **fascinate** 매혹하다 – **fascination** 매혹
- □ **invent** 발명하다 – **invention** 발명
- □ **reduce** 줄이다 – **reduction** 감소

※ 명사 – 형용사

- □ **imitation** 모방 – **imitative** 모방적인
- □ **necessity** 필요성 – **necessary** 필요한
- □ **reflection** 반사 – **reflective** 빛을 반사하는

- □ **invention** 발명 – **inventive** 창의적인
- □ **pain** 고통 – **painful** 고통스러운
- □ **success** 성공 – **successful** 성공적인

## English Dictionary

- □ **all-purpose** 만능의, 다용도의
  - → suitable for many uses 여러 가지 용도에 적절한
- □ **beak** (새의) 부리
  - → the hard usually pointed parts that over a bird's mouth
    새 입 위에 있는 딱딱하고 보통 뾰족한 부분
- □ **dive** 뛰어들다, 잠수하다
  - → to move down through the air at a steep angle
    가파르게 공중에서 아래로 뛰어내리다
- □ **fastener** 잠금장치, 고정 장치
  - → a device used to close a piece of clothing, a window, suitcase, etc. tightly
    옷, 창문, 가방 등을 단단히 닫기 위하여 사용되는 도구
- □ **genius** 천재
  - → a very smart or talented person
    매우 똑똑하거나 재능을 가진 사람
- □ **headache** 두통

- → a pain in your head
  머리에 느끼는 통증
- □ **imitate** 모방하다
  - → to make or do something the same way as something else
    무엇인가를 다른 것과 똑같이 하거나 똑같이 만들다
- □ **narrow** 좁은
  - → long and not wide
    길고 넓지 않은
- □ **redesign** 다시 디자인하다
  - → to change the design of something
    어떤 것의 디자인을 바꾸다
- □ **tunnel** 터널, 굴
  - → a passage that goes under the ground
    지하로 지나가는 통로
- □ **wing** 날개
  - → a part of an animal's body that is used for flying or gliding
    날거나 활공하기 위하여 사용되는 동물의 신체 부위

**서답형**
[01~02] 〈보기〉와 같은 관계가 되도록 빈칸에 알맞은 말을 쓰시오. (주어진 철자로 시작할 것)

**01**
┌─ 보기 ─┐
narrow : wide
└────────┘

(1) m_____ : freeze
(2) t_____ : huge

**02**
┌─ 보기 ─┐
absorb : absorption
└────────┘

(1) apply : _____
(2) decide : _____

**중요**
**03** 다음 중 밑줄 친 부분의 뜻풀이가 바르지 <u>않은</u> 것은?
① This candle holder can make candles <u>last</u> twice as long. (마지막)
② The <u>way</u> nature works fascinates us. (방식)
③ The <u>high-speed</u> train was first made in Japan. (고속의)
④ It often <u>woke</u> people up and caused headaches. (깨웠다)
⑤ He <u>wondered</u> how the bird entered the water so gracefully. (궁금했다)

**서답형**
**04** 다음 빈칸에 들어갈 말로 적절한 말을 쓰시오.

Even though his invention was not successful, he _____d a bird's wings to try to make a flying machine.

➡ _____

**중요**
**05** 다음 중 〈보기〉에 있는 단어를 사용하여 자연스러운 문장을 만들 수 <u>없는</u> 것은?

┌─ 보기 ─┐
apply   amazing   beak   all-purpose
└────────────────────────────────────┘

① This room is used for many purposes. This is an _____ room.
② It's really interesting. That's an _____ story!
③ His theory is so old that it can't _____ to modern society.
④ I'm reading an _____ about a bug robot.
⑤ The gull held the fish in its _____.

**06** 다음 밑줄 친 부분과 의미가 가장 가까운 것을 고르시오.

The aim is to <u>reduce</u> traffic at peak hours.

① absorb        ② forgive
③ decide        ④ diminish
⑤ explore

**07** 다음 빈칸에 공통으로 들어가기에 알맞은 것은?

• Can I take a look _____ your work?
• He's good _____ making things with hands.

① from        ② at        ③ with
④ by          ⑤ during

**01** 다음 주어진 단어를 이용해 빈칸을 완성하시오.

> She has a very _____ mind.

➡ _____ (invent)

**02** 다음 짝지어진 단어의 관계가 같도록 빈칸에 알맞은 말을 쓰시오. (주어진 철자로 시작할 것)

> beak : bill = bug : i_____

[03~04] 다음 빈칸에 공통으로 들어갈 단어를 쓰시오.

**03**
> • They have to _____ contact with the leader.
> • I'll _____ a note of our next meeting in my diary.

**04**
> • I was a little sick. That's _____ I left early.
> • I'd like to know the reason _____ you're so late.

**05** 밑줄 친 부분과 의미가 가장 가까운 단어를 주어진 철자로 시작하여 쓰시오.

> The heavy rain will <u>keep</u> them from going out to play.

➡ s_____

**06** 다음 빈칸에 알맞은 단어를 〈보기〉에서 골라 쓰시오.

> ┤ 보기 ├
> burns　　burrs　　bite　　bug

(1) When you have a mosquito _____, you shouldn't scratch it.

(2) Many people use _____ sprays to keep insects away.

(3) When a candle _____, it melts into the tube below the holder to form a new candle.

(4) On his way home, he saw that _____ were stuck to his clothes and his dog's hair.

**07** 다음 우리말에 맞게 빈칸에 알맞은 말을 쓰시오.

(1) 그녀는 마실 것을 찾아 부엌으로 들어갔다.
➡ She went into the kitchen in _____ of a drink.

(2) 신발에 껌이 달라붙어 있었다.
➡ A piece of chewing gum was _____ to my shoe.

(3) 그 기름이 유출된 결과 많은 바닷새들이 죽었다.
➡ Many seabirds died as a _____ of the oil spill.

(4) 그녀는 이지적일뿐만 아니라 또한 음악성도 대단했다.
➡ She was not _____ intelligent but also very musical.

# Conversation

**1** 알고 있는지 묻기

### You know that Leonardo da Vinci painted the *Mona Lisa*, don't you?
레오나르도 다빈치가 모나리자를 그린 것을 알지, 그렇지 않니?

■ 어떤 사실을 상대방이 알고 있는지 물어보는 말은 know를 사용하여 "Do you know about ~?"(~을 아십니까?) 또는 "You know about ~, don't you?", "Did you know that ~?"이라고 물어볼 수도 있다. "You know ~, don't you?"는 "너는 ~을 알고 있지?"라는 뜻으로 상대방이 이미 알고 있을 법한 소재의 이야기를 꺼낼 때 사용한다.

■ know를 사용하여 직접적으로 물어보는 것보다는 완화된 느낌으로 hear를 사용하여 "Have you (ever) heard about ~?"(~을 들어본 적이 있니?) 또는 "Did you hear about ~?"이라고 하기도 한다. hear를 사용할 때는 know를 사용했을 때보다는 다소 부드러운 느낌을 줄 수 있다.

■ 그 외에 알고 있는지를 물어볼 때는 aware, realize 등을 사용해서 "Are you aware of ~?"(~을 알고 있니?), "Are you aware that ~?" 또는 "Do you realize ~?" 등을 사용하여 상대방이 알고 있는지를 물어볼 수 있다.

### 알고 있는지 묻기

• You know that ~, don't you? 너 ~알지, 그렇지 않니?
• Do you know about/that ~? ~을 아십니까?
• Have you (ever) heard (about) ~? (한번이라도) ~를(에 대해서) 들어본 적이 있습니까?
• Have you been told about ~? ~에 대해 들어본 적 있어?
• Are you aware of/that ~? ~을 알고 있니?
• Do you realize that ~? ~을 알고 있니?

### 핵심 Check

1. 다음 우리말에 해당하는 영어 문장을 빈칸에 쓰시오.

> **B:** _____? (Jian, mosquito needle을 들어본 적이 있니?)
>
> **G:** A mosquito needle? Can you explain it to me?
>
> **B:** Some scientists made this new needle by imitating a mosquito's mouth.
>
> **G:** That's interesting. So how will that help?
>
> **B:** You know mosquito bites are not very painful, don't you? The new needle will also cause less pain.

## ❷ 관심 표현하기

> **I'm fascinated by this noodle cooling fan.** 나는 이 국수 냉각팬에 매료되었어.

- "I'm fascinated by …"는 "나는 …에 매료되었다."라는 뜻으로 "be fascinated by ~"는 관심이 많은 것을 나타내는 표현이다. "fascinate"(마음을 사로잡다) 이외에도 "impress"(인상을 주다)를 사용하여 "… impress(es) me a lot."(…가 나에게는 깊은 인상을 준다.), "… is really impressive"(…은 정말로 인상적이다.), "I'm (really) impressed by …"(나는 정말로 ~에 의해서 인상을 받았다.)라고 할 수도 있다.

- 상대방의 말에 관심을 나타낼 때 사용하는 표현으로는 "interest"를 사용하여 나타낼 수 있다. "interest"는 명사로 "흥미, 관심"이라는 뜻이 있고, 동사로 "관심을 끌다, 관심을 보이다"의 뜻이다. "That interests me a lot."는 글자 그대로 "저것이 나의 관심을 끈다."의 뜻이다. 이 표현은 "그것 참 재미있네요." 또는 "그것 참 흥미롭네요." 정도로 해석할 수 있다.

- 관심을 나타내는 말로 "I am interested in~ "(나는 ~에 관심이 있다.), 또는 "I have an interest in ~ "(나는 ~에 관심이 있다.)라고 할 수 있고, "be into ~" (~에 관심이 있다)와 같은 표현을 사용하여 "I am into ~."(나는 ~에 관심이 있다.)라고 할 수도 있다.

### 관심 표현하기

- I'm fascinated by ~. 나는 ~에 매료되었다.
- That impresses me a lot. 저것은 나에게 깊은 인상을 준다.
- It is really impressive. 그것은 정말로 인상적이다.
- That interests me. 그것 참 흥미롭습니다.
- I am interested in ~. 나는 ~에 관심이 있다.
- I have an interest in ~. 나는 ~에 관심이 있다.
- My main interest is ~. 나의 주된 관심은 ~이다.
- I enjoy/like/love ~ 나는 ~하는 것을 즐긴다. / 좋아한다.

### 핵심 Check

**2.** 다음 밑줄 친 말 대신 쓰기에 적절하지 <u>않은</u> 것은?

> B: <u>I'm fascinated by this noodle cooling fan.</u>
> G: A noodle cooling fan? I've never heard of it.
> B: This little fan will cool noodles when they're very hot.
> G: That looks funny but useful.

① This noodle cooling fan impresses me a lot.

② This noodle cooling fan is really impressive.

③ I'm interested in this noodle cooling fan.

④ I'm eager to use this noodle cooling fan.

⑤ I have an interest in this noodle cooling fan.

### Listen & Speak 1 A

G: ❶You know that Leonardo da Vinci painted the *Mona Lisa*, don't you?

B: Sure. I think he was a really great artist.

G: He was also a great inventor.

B: What did he invent?

G: ❷He dreamed of flying like a bird. ❸So, he drew a flying machine that looked like a bird.

B: Did he also make that machine?

G: No, but his creative idea inspired many other inventors.

소녀: 레오나르도 다빈치가 모나 리자를 그린 것을 알지, 그렇지 않니?
소년: 물론. 그는 정말로 위대한 미술가라고 생각해.
소녀: 그는 또한 위대한 발명가였어.
소년: 그가 무엇을 발명했니?
소녀: 그는 새처럼 나는 것을 꿈꿨어. 그래서 그는 새처럼 보이는 나는 기계를 그렸어.
소년: 그가 그 기계도 만들었니?
소녀: 아니, 하지만 그의 창의적인 생각은 많은 발명가에게 영감을 주었어.

❶ "You know that ~, don't you?"는 "너는 ~을 알지?"라는 뜻으로 상대에게 아는지를 묻는 말이다.
❷ "dream of"는 "~을 꿈꾸다"의 의미이다.
❸ that은 a flying machine을 선행사로 하는 주격 관계 대명사이다.

**Check(√) True or False**

(1) Leonardo da Vinci was a great artist who painted the *Mona Lisa*.    T ☐ F ☐

(2) Leonardo da Vinci was a dreamer who wanted to fly like a bird.    T ☐ F ☐

(3) Leonardo da Vinci was a great inventor who made a flying machine.    T ☐ F ☐

###  Real Life Communication A

Henry: What are you doing, Mina?

Mina: I'm reading an article about a bug robot.

Henry: A bug robot? Is it interesting?

Mina: Yes. ❶I'm really fascinated by this thing.

Henry: Can you tell me more about it?

Mina: ❷You know that some bugs can slip into narrow spaces, don't you?

Henry: Yeah. ❸That's why it's hard to catch them.

Mina: A bug robot can do the same. It can help to find survivors after earthquakes or big fires.

Henry: That's really fascinating!

Henry: 미나야, 뭐 하고 있니?
Mina: 나는 bug robot에 관한 기사를 읽고 있어.
Henry: "bug robot"이라고? 재미있니?
Mina: 응, 나는 이것에 정말로 매료되었어.
Henry: 그것에 대해 좀 더 말해 줄 수 있니?
Mina: 너는 몇몇 곤충이 좁은 공간에 미끄러져 들어갈 수 있는 것을 알지?
Henry: 알아. 그것이 그들을 잡기 어려운 이유이지.
Mina: bug robot이 똑같이 할 수 있어. 그것은 지진이나 대형 화재 이후에 생존자들을 찾는 것을 도와줄 수 있어.
Henry: 그거 정말 흥미롭다!

❶ "I'm really fascinated by ~"는 "나는 정말로 ~에 매료되었다."라는 뜻으로 관심이 많은 것을 나타내는 말이다.
❷ "You know that ~, don't you?"는 "너는 ~을 알지?"라는 뜻으로 상대에게 아는지를 묻는 말이다.
❸ "That's why ~."는 "That's the reason why ~."에서 선행사 the reason을 생략한 형태로 글자 그대로 "그것이 ~한 이유이다."라고 해석할 수 있지만, "그런 이유로 ~하다."라고 해석하기도 한다.

**Check(√) True or False**

(4) A bug robot can slip into narrow spaces like some bugs.    T ☐ F ☐

(5) Some bugs can fly to a distant place with ease.    T ☐ F ☐

(6) A bug robot can help to find survivors during earthquakes or big fires.    T ☐ F ☐

### Listen & Speak 1 B

B: ❶Have you heard of a mosquito needle, Jian?

G: A mosquito needle? Can you explain it to me?

B: Some scientists made this new needle ❷by imitating a mosquito's mouth.

G: That's interesting. So how will that help?

B: You know mosquito bites are not very painful, don't you? The new needle will also cause less pain.

G: That's great. ❸How come it's less painful?

B: Like a mosquito's mouth, it makes less contact with our skin.

G: Wow, I think that there's nothing useless in the world!

❶ "Have you heard of ～?"는 "～을 들어본 적이 있니?"에 해당하는 말로 상대가 알고 있는지를 묻는 말이다.
❷ 전치사 by의 목적어로 동명사가 쓰였다.
❸ "How come ～?"은 "어째서 ～?"라는 뜻으로 이유를 묻는 말이다.

### Listen & Speak 2 A-1

B: ❶I'm fascinated by this noodle cooling fan.

G: A noodle cooling fan? I've never heard of it.

B: This little fan will cool noodles when they're very hot.

G: That looks funny but useful.

❶ "I'm fascinated by ～"는 관심이 있는 것을 나타내는 표현이다.

### Listen & Speak 2 A-2

G: ❶This candle holder can make candles last twice as long.

B: Really? How's that possible?

G: When a candle burns, it melts into the tube below the holder to form a new candle.

B: Wow, ❷I am so fascinated by the idea! Now we can use candles longer.

❶ 동사 make는 사역동사이므로 목적격보어로 원형부정사 last가 쓰였다.
❷ "I am so fascinated by ～"는 "나는 ～에 매우 매료되었다."는 뜻으로 관심을 나타내는 표현이다.

### Listen & Speak 2 A-3

B: You know what? I'm really fascinated by the special door in Juwon's room.

G: ❶What makes the door so special?

B: Juwon and I played table tennis on it.

G: How could you play table tennis on a door?

B: The door ❷can be changed into a table.

G: That's cool!

❶ "What makes ～?"는 "무엇이 ～하게 만드는가?"의 뜻으로 이유를 묻는 말이다.
❷ "can be changed into ～"는 "조동사 can+be+과거분사"의 수동태이다.

### Listen & Speak 2 B

W: Today, we have a special guest, Thomas Thwaites, the Goat Man. Hello, Thomas.

M: Hello, Anna. Great to be here.

W: Thomas, ❶I'm so fascinated by the fact that you lived like a goat in the Alps for three days. Why did you do that?

M: One day, ❷I saw goats playing on the mountain. They looked so peaceful that I wanted to live like them.

W: Didn't you have any problems being a goat?

M: ❸Walking on all four legs was very difficult for me.

W: Do you have any plans to live like a goat again?

M: Sure. I'm planning my second visit to the Alps.

W: I can't wait to hear about your next adventure. Thank you, Thomas, for your time.

❶ "the fact that ～"은 동격을 나타내는 명사절이 사용되었다.
❷ 지각동사 saw의 목적격보어로 현재분사가 쓰였다.
❸ "Walking ～"은 문장의 주어로 쓰인 동명사로 단수 취급한다.

다음 우리말과 일치하도록 빈칸에 알맞은 말을 쓰시오.

### Listen & Speak 1 A

G: You _____ that Leonardo da Vinci _____ the *Mona Lisa*, _____ you?

B: Sure. I _____ he was a really _____ artist.

G: He was _____ a great _____.

B: _____ did he _____?

G: He _____ _____ flying like a bird. So, he _____ a _____ machine that _____ _____ a bird.

B: _____ he _____ _____ that _____?

G: No, but his _____ _____ _____ many other _____.

### Listen & Speak 1 B

B: _____ _____ heard of a mosquito _____, Jian?

G: A mosquito needle? _____ you _____ _____ to me?

B: Some scientists _____ _____ new needle by _____ a mosquito's _____.

G: That's interesting. So _____ _____ that help?

B: You _____ mosquito _____ are not _____ _____, don't you? The new _____ will also _____ _____ _____.

G: That's great. _____ _____ it's less painful?

B: Like a mosquito's mouth, it makes _____ _____ with our skin.

G: Wow, I _____ that there's nothing _____ in the world!

### Listen & Speak 2 A-2

G: This candle _____ can make _____ _____ twice as long.

B: Really? How's that _____?

G: When a candle _____, it _____ into the _____ below the holder to _____ a new candle.

B: Wow, I am so _____ by the idea! Now we can _____ candles _____.

해석

G: 레오나르도 다빈치가 모나리자를 그린 것을 알지, 그렇지 않니?

B: 물론. 그는 정말로 위대한 미술가라고 생각해.

G: 그는 또한 위대한 발명가였어.

B: 그가 무엇을 발명했니?

G: 그는 새처럼 나는 것을 꿈꿨어. 그래서 그는 새처럼 보이는 나는 기계를 그렸어.

B: 그가 그 기계도 만들었니?

G: 아니, 하지만 그의 창의적인 생각은 많은 발명가들에게 영감을 주었어.

B: Jian, mosquito needle을 들어본 적이 있니?

G: mosquito needle이라고? 그것 좀 설명해 줄 수 있니?

B: 몇몇 과학자들이 모기의 입을 모방하여 이 새로운 바늘을 만들었어.

G: 흥미롭군. 그럼 그것이 어떻게 도움이 될까?

B: 모기가 무는 것은 별로 고통스럽지 않다는 건 알지? 이 새로운 주사바늘도 역시 통증을 줄여 줄 거야.

G: 대단한데. 어째서 덜 고통스럽지?

B: 모기의 입처럼 그것은 우리의 피부에 덜 닿아.

G: 와, 세상에 쓸모없는 것은 아무것도 없는 것 같아!

G: 이 양초 받침이 양초를 두 배나 오래 지속되도록 만들 수 있어.

B: 정말? 어떻게 그것이 가능해?

G: 양초가 탈 때 그것은 받침 아래에 있는 관으로 녹아들어 새로운 양초를 만들어.

B: 와, 나는 그 아이디어에 매료되었어! 이제 우리는 양초를 더 오래 사용할 수 있어.

### Listen & Speak 2 A3

B: You know _____? I'm really _____ by the _____ door in Juwon's room.

G: _____ makes the door so _____?

B: Juwon and I _____ table tennis on it.

G: _____ could you play table tennis on a _____?

B: The door can _____ _____ into a _____.

G: That's _____!

### Listen & Speak 2 B

W: Today, we _____ a special _____, Thomas Thwaites, the Goat Man. Hello, Thomas.

M: Hello, Anna. _____ to _____ here.

W: Thomas, I'm so _____ by the _____ that you _____ like a _____ in the Alps for _____ days. _____ did you _____ that?

M: One day, I _____ goats _____ on the mountain. They _____ so _____ that I wanted to _____ like them.

W: Didn't you _____ any _____ being a goat?

M: _____ on all four legs _____ very _____ for me.

W: Do you have _____ plans to live _____ a goat again?

M: Sure. I'm _____ my second _____ to the Alps.

W: I can't _____ to hear about your next _____. Thank you, Thomas, for your time.

### Real Life Communication

Henry: _____ are you _____, Mina?

Mina: I'm reading an _____ about a bug robot.

Henry: A bug robot? Is it _____?

Mina: Yes. I'm _____ fascinated by this thing.

Henry: _____ you tell me _____ about it?

Mina: You _____ that some _____ can _____ into _____ spaces, don't you?

Henry: Yeah. That's _____ it's _____ to catch them.

Mina: A bug robot can do the same. It can _____ to find _____ after earthquakes or big fires.

Henry: That's really _____!

해석

B: 너 그거 알아? 나는 주원이네 방의 특별한 문에 매료되었어.

G: 왜 그 문이 그리 특별하니?

B: 주원이와 내가 그 위에서 탁구를 쳤어.

G: 어떻게 문 위에서 탁구를 칠 수 있어?

B: 문이 탁구대로 바뀔 수 있어.

G: 멋있는데!

W: 오늘 우리는 특별 손님인 염소 인간 Thomas Thwaites를 모시게 되었습니다. 안녕하세요, Thomas.

M: 안녕하세요, Anna. 여기 오게 되어 기쁩니다.

W: Thomas, 나는 당신이 3일 동안 알프스에서 염소처럼 살았다는 사실에 매료되었습니다. 왜 그렇게 했나요?

M: 어느 날, 나는 염소들이 산에서 노는 것을 보았어요. 그들이 너무 평화로워 보여서 나는 그들처럼 살고 싶었습니다.

W: 염소가 되는 데 아무 문제가 없었나요?

M: 네 발로 걷는 것이 나에게는 매우 어려웠어요.

W: 당신은 다시 염소처럼 살 계획이 있나요?

M: 물론이죠. 나는 알프스를 다시 방문할 계획을 하고 있어요.

W: 당신의 다음 모험에 대해 빨리 듣고 싶어요. 시간 내주셔서 감사합니다, Thomas.

Henry: 미나야, 뭐 하고 있니?

Mina: 나는 bug robot에 관한 기사를 읽고 있어.

Henry: "bug robot"라고? 재미있니?

Mina: 응, 나는 이것에 정말로 매료되었어.

Henry: 그것에 대해 좀 더 말해줄 수 있니?

Mina: 너는 몇몇 곤충이 좁은 공간에 미끄러져 들어갈 수 있는 것을 알지?

Henry: 알아. 그것이 그들을 잡기 어려운 이유이지.

Mina: bug robot이 똑같이 할 수 있어. 그것은 지진이나 대형 화재 이후에 생존자들을 찾는 것을 도와줄 수 있어.

Henry: 그거 정말 흥미롭다!

[01~02] 다음 대화의 빈칸에 들어갈 말로 알맞은 것은?

## 01

B: I'm _____ by Sophia, a robot girl.
G: What's so special about her?
B: She is able to show more than 60 facial expressions.
G: That's amazing. What else can she do?
B: She has many other abilities. She looks, talks, and even thinks like a human.
G: That's fascinating!

① fascinated      ② pleased      ③ annoyed
④ disappointed      ⑤ nervous

## 02

B: You know what? I'm really fascinated by the special door in Juwon's room.
G: _____
B: Juwon and I played table tennis on it.
G: How could you play table tennis on a door?
B: The door can be changed into a table.
G: That's cool!

① Where did you play table tennis?
② Who can play table tennis better?
③ What can you make with the door?
④ What makes the door so special?
⑤ Who made the door special?

## 03 다음 대화에 이어지기에 순서가 바르게 배열된 것을 고르시오.

G: This candle holder can make candles last twice as long.
(A) Wow, I am so fascinated by the idea! Now we can use candles longer.
(B) Really? How's that possible?
(C) When a candle burns, it melts into the tube below the holder to form a new candle.

① (A) – (C) – (B)      ② (B) – (A) – (C)
③ (B) – (C) – (A)      ④ (C) – (A) – (B)
⑤ (C) – (B) – (A)

[01~03] 다음 대화를 읽고 물음에 답하시오.

G: You know that Leonardo da Vinci painted the *Mona Lisa*, don't you? ( A )
B: Sure. I think he was a really great artist.
G: He was also a great inventor. ( B )
B: What did he invent? ( C )
G: He dreamed of flying like a bird. ( D )
B: Did he also make that machine? ( E )
G: No, but his (가)_____ idea inspired many other inventors.

 **01** (A)~(E) 중에서 다음 문장이 들어가기에 가장 적절한 곳은?

So, he drew a flying machine that looked like a bird.

① (A)　② (B)　③ (C)　④ (D)　⑤ (E)

**02** 빈칸 (가)에 들어가기에 적절한 것은?

① creative　　② artistic
③ usual　　　④ common
⑤ ordinary

 **03** 위 대화를 읽고 대답할 수 없는 것은?

① What did Leonardo da Vinci paint?
② What did Leonardo da Vinci dream of?
③ How did Leonardo da Vinci make the flying machine?
④ What did the flying machine look like?
⑤ What inspired many other inventors?

[04~05] 다음 대화를 읽고 물음에 답하시오.

B: (A)Have you heard of a mosquito needle, Jian?
G: A mosquito needle? Can you explain it to me?
B: Some scientists made this new needle by imitating a mosquito's mouth.
G: That's interesting. So how will that help?
B: You know mosquito bites are not very painful, don't you? The new needle will also cause less pain.
G: That's great. How come it's less painful?
B: Like a mosquito's mouth, it makes less contact with our skin.
G: Wow, I think that there's nothing useless in the world!

**04** 다음 중 밑줄 친 (A) 대신 쓰기에 적절한 것은?

① You know about a mosquito needle, don't you, Jian?
② Do you know that there's nothing useless in the world, Jian?
③ Jian, you said about a mosquito needle, didn't you?
④ Do you believe scientists are imitating a mosquito's mouth, Jian?
⑤ I know a mosquito needle is useful, Jian.

 **05** 위 대화의 내용과 일치하지 <u>않는</u> 것은?

① The girl hasn't heard of a mosquito needle.
② Some scientists imitated a mosquito's mouth.
③ Mosquito bites are not very painful.
④ The new needle will cause more pain.
⑤ The new needle makes less contact with our skin.

[06~08] 다음 대화를 읽고 물음에 답하시오.

W: Today, we have a special guest, Thomas Thwaites, the Goat Man. Hello, Thomas.

M: Hello, Anna. Great to be here.

W: Thomas, (가)_____ that you lived like a goat in the Alps for three days. ( A )

M: One day, I saw goats playing on the mountain. ( B ) They looked so peaceful that I wanted to live like them. ( C )

W: Didn't you have any problems being a goat? ( D )

M: Walking on all four legs was very difficult for me. ( E )

W: Do you have any plans to live like a goat again?

M: Sure. I'm planning my second visit to the Alps.

W: (나)I can't wait to hear about your next adventure. Thank you, Thomas, for your time.

**06** 대화의 내용으로 보아, 빈칸 (가)에 들어가기에 적절하지 <u>않</u>은 것은?

① I'm so fascinated by the fact
② I'm interested in the fact
③ it is really impressive
④ I have an interest in the fact
⑤ I'm aware of the fact

**07** (A)~(E) 중에서 다음 문장이 들어가기에 가장 적절한 곳은?

> Why did you do that?

① (A)　② (B)　③ (C)　④ (D)　⑤ (E)

**08** 밑줄 친 (나)가 의도하는 것은?

① 감사 표현하기　② 만족 표현하기
③ 관심 표현하기　④ 의무 말하기
⑤ 기대 표현하기

[09~11] 다음 대화를 읽고 물음에 답하시오.

Henry: What are you doing, Mina?

Mina: I'm reading an article about a bug robot.

Henry: A bug robot? Is it interesting?

Mina: Yes. I'm really (A)_____ this thing.

Henry: Can you tell me more about it?

Mina: You know that some bugs can slip into narrow spaces, don't you?

Henry: Yeah. That's (B)_____ it's hard to catch them.

Mina: A bug robot can do the same. It can help to find survivors after earthquakes or big fires.

Henry: That's really (C)_____!

**09** 빈칸 (A)에 들어가기에 적절한 것은?

① worried about
② relieved by
③ wondering about
④ satisfied with
⑤ fascinated by

**10** 다음 중 (B)에 들어갈 말과 같은 말이 들어갈 수 있는 것은?

① I read the book _____ he had written.
② This is the house _____ he designed.
③ Do you know _____ will help her?
④ Tell me _____ you were late for class.
⑤ I know _____ he lives.

**11** 위 대화의 내용으로 보아 (C)에 들어가기에 <u>어색한</u> 것은?

① fascinating　② interesting
③ cool　④ wonderful
⑤ disappointing

[01~03] 다음 대화를 읽고 물음에 답하시오.

B: (A)_____ Sophia, a robot girl.(나는 로봇 소녀, Sophia에 매혹되었어.)

G: (B)_____'s so special about her?

B: She is able to show more than 60 facial expressions.

G: That's amazing. What else can she do?

B: She has no other abilities. She looks, talks, and even thinks like a human.

G: That's fascinating!

**01** 빈칸 (A)를 우리말에 어울리는 영어 표현을 넣어 문장을 완성하시오. (by를 포함할 것)

➡ _____

**02** 빈칸 (B)에 알맞은 의문대명사를 쓰시오.

➡ _____

**03** 위 대화에서 흐름상 어색한 것을 찾아 적절한 것으로 고치시오.

➡ _____

[04~05] 다음 대화를 읽고 물음에 답하시오.

G: (가)너 Leonardo da Vinci가 the *Mona Lisa*를 그린 것을 알지, 그렇지 않니? (do)

B: Sure. I think he was a really great artist.

G: He was also a great inventor.

B: What did he invent?

G: He dreamed of flying like a bird. So, he drew a flying machine that looked like a bird.

B: Did he also make that machine?

G: No, but his creative idea inspired many other inventors.

**04** 밑줄 친 (가)의 우리말을 주어진 단어를 이용하여 영어로 옮기시오.

➡ _____

_____

**05** 위 대화의 내용에 어울리도록 아래 빈칸에 적절한 말을 쓰시오.

Leonardo da Vinci _____ of flying like a bird, but he didn't _____ a flying machine.

[06~07] 다음 대화를 읽고 물음에 답하시오.

B: (A)Have you heard of a mosquito needle, Jian? (aware)

G: A mosquito needle? Can you explain it to me?

B: Some scientists made this new needle by imitating a mosquito's mouth.

G: That's interesting. So how will that help?

B: You know mosquito bites are not very painful, don't you? The new needle will also cause less pain.

G: That's great. (B)_____ _____ it's less painful?

B: Like a mosquito's mouth, it makes less contact with our skin.

G: Wow, I think that there's nothing useless in the world!

**06** 밑줄 친 (A)를 주어진 단어를 이용하여 같은 의미가 되도록 바꿔 쓰시오.

➡ _____

**07** 내용상 빈칸 (B)에 들어가기에 적절한 두 단어를 쓰시오.

➡ _____

# Grammar

## ① not only A but also B

- The fastener was **not only** strong **but also** easy to use. 그 고정 장치는 튼튼할 뿐만 아니라 사용하기도 쉬웠다.
- He is **not only** poor **but also** lazy. 그는 가난할 뿐만 아니라 게으르다.

■ 형태: not only A but also B
  의미: A뿐만 아니라 B도

■ 'not only A but also B'는 'A뿐만 아니라 B도'라는 뜻으로 두 단어가 짝을 이루어 하나의 접속사 역할을 하는 상관접속사로, 두 개의 단어, 구, 절을 연결하며, A와 B의 품사는 같아야 한다.

- She was **not only** intelligent **but also** very musical. 그녀는 이지적일뿐 아니라 음악성도 대단했다.

- She **not only** wrote the text **but also** selected the illustrations.
  그녀는 그 본문을 썼을 뿐만 아니라 삽화들을 선별하기도 했다.

■ 'Not only A but also B'가 주어로 쓰일 경우 수의 일치는 B에 맞춘다.

- **Not only** you **but also** she is pretty. 너뿐만 아니라 그녀도 예뻐.

■ 'not only A but also B'는 'B as well as A'로 바꾸어 쓸 수 있다. 이때도 동사의 수는 B에 맞춘다.

- They sell **not only** newspapers **but also** books.
  = They sell books **as well as** newspapers. 그들은 신문뿐만 아니라 책도 판다.

### 핵심 Check

1. 다음 괄호 안에서 알맞은 것을 고르시오.

  (1) He not only read the book, but also (remembers / remembered) what he had read.

  (2) It makes sense not only politically but also (economical / economically).

  (3) The documentary was not only funny (but / and) also very informative.

## ② 간접의문문

- Do you know **where the key is**? 열쇠가 어디 있는지 아니?
- I'm wondering **what you were talking about**. 네가 무슨 얘기를 하고 있었는지 궁금한데.

■ 형태: 의문사+주어+동사
  의미: ~인지/일지

■ 간접의문문은 의문문이 다른 문장에 포함되어 그 문장의 일부가 되는 것이며 의문사가 있는 경우 '의문사+주어+동사'의 어순이 된다.
  - Do you know? + What did he do today? (의문사+동사+주어)
    = Do you know **what he did today**? (의문사+주어+동사) 오늘 그가 뭘 했는지 알아?

■ 의문사가 주어인 경우에는 의문사 뒤에 바로 동사가 이어진다.
  - Can you tell me? + What happened? (의문사(= 주어)+동사)
    = Can you tell me **what happened**? (의문사(= 주어)+동사) 어떻게 된 건지 말해 줄래?

■ 'how often, how much, how many people, what kind of food'처럼 하나의 의미 단위로 쓰이는 의문사구는 하나의 의문사로 취급한다.
  - Do you know? + How much time did we spend? (의문사구+조동사+주어+동사원형)
    = Do you know **how much time we spent**? (○) 우리가 얼마나 많은 시간을 보냈는지 아니?
    Do you know how time we spent much? (×)

■ 간접의문문이 believe, imagine, suppose, consider, expect, think, guess 등의 목적어로 쓰인 경우 의문사를 맨 앞으로 보낸다.
  - Do you think? + When will you be finished?
    = **When** do you think **you'll be finished**? 언제쯤 끝날 것 같아요?

■ 의문사가 없는 의문문은 의문사 대신 if나 whether를 쓰고 'if[whether]+주어+동사'의 어순이 된다. 이때 'if[whether]'는 '…인지 아닌지'의 뜻을 갖는다.
  - I wonder. + Will there be a pay raise next year? (동사+주어) 내년에 임금이 인상될지 궁금하네.
    = I wonder **if[whether] there will be a pay raise next year**. (접속사+주어+동사)

### 핵심 Check

2. 다음 괄호 안에서 알맞은 것을 고르시오.

(1) Let me know (who is he / who he is) meeting with.

(2) I wonder whether (may I ask you a question / I may ask you a question).

(3) She asked me (how old I was / how I was old).

**01** 다음 두 문장을 하나의 문장으로 만들 때 빈칸에 알맞은 것은?

> • I don't know.
> • Where did she buy this pen?
> → I don't know _____.

① where did she buy this pen
② where she bought this pen
③ did she where buy this pen
④ she bought where this pen
⑤ she bought this pen where

**02** 다음 두 문장을 하나의 문장으로 만들 때 알맞은 것은?

> • He is smart.
> • He is kind, too.

① He is not smart but kind.
② He is only smart also kind.
③ He is not only smart but also kind.
④ He is not smart but also kind.
⑤ He is not only smart also kind.

**03** 다음 우리말에 맞게 괄호 안에 주어진 단어를 바르게 배열하시오.

(1) 난 지금까지 네가 얼마나 많은 책을 읽었는지 궁금해.
   (you, I'm, books, now, many, wondering, read, have, how, until)
   ➡ _____

(2) 왜 코끼리는 긴 코가 있는지 아니?
   (you, trunk, elephant, why, has, know, do, a, an)
   ➡ _____

(3) 소미는 음악 감상뿐만 아니라 그림 그리는 것도 즐긴다.
   (Somi, pictures, music, listening, enjoys, only, painting, also, not, but, to)
   ➡ _____

(4) 그는 개뿐만 아니라 고양이도 있다.
   (he, dog, cat, but, not, a, a, has, also, only)
   ➡ _____

 **01** 다음 중 어법상 어색한 문장을 고르시오.

① Do you know where they were at that time?
② Tell me where are you going to have dinner.
③ There are times when I wonder why I do this job.
④ I'm not sure if I asked you the question before.
⑤ Who do you think gets up the earliest in my family?

**02** 다음 빈칸에 들어갈 말로 적절한 것은?

A seahorse can _____ swim but also change color.

① not only  ② not
③ only  ④ as well
⑤ both

 **03** 다음 두 문장을 한 문장으로 바르게 바꿔 쓴 것을 고르시오.

• They didn't know.
• How could they reduce the noise?

① They didn't know how could they reduce the noise.
② They didn't know if how they could reduce the noise.
③ They didn't know how they could reduce the noise.
④ How they could reduce the noise they didn't know.
⑤ How they didn't know they could reduce the noise.

**04** 다음 두 문장을 한 문장으로 바르게 바꾸지 않은 것은?

• The plants are beautiful.
• The plants are very useful, too.

① The plants are not only beautiful but also very useful.
② The plants are not only beautiful but very useful.
③ The plants are not only beautiful but very useful as well.
④ The plants are not beautiful but very useful.
⑤ The plants are very useful as well as beautiful.

**05** 빈칸에 들어갈 말을 순서대로 바르게 연결한 것은?

• I'm wondering _____ you like sushi.
• Can you tell me _____ you bought yesterday?

① when  –  what
② what  –  where
③ what  –  how
④ if  –  that
⑤ if  –  what

서답형
**06** 다음 문장에서 어색한 것을 찾아 바르게 고쳐 쓰시오.

He enjoys not only playing the guitar but also dance to the music.

➡ _____

_____

**서답형**
**07** 다음 괄호 안에 주어진 어휘를 바르게 배열하여 문장을 완성하시오.

He wondered (the bird, the water, entered, how, gracefully, so).

➡ _____

**08** 다음 두 문장을 한 문장으로 바르게 바꾼 것은?

- His brothers are tall.
- His father is tall, too.

① Either his brothers or his father is tall.
② Neither his brothers nor his father is tall.
③ Not only his brothers but also his father are tall.
④ His father as well as his brothers is tall.
⑤ Both his brothers and his father is tall.

**중요**
**09** 다음 빈칸에 들어갈 수 <u>없는</u> 것을 고르시오.

I don't know _____.

① when she visited the museum
② where you come from
③ how much is it
④ what you are going to do
⑤ if she likes watching movies

**서답형**
**10** 다음 문장에서 어법상 어색한 것을 바르게 고쳐 다시 쓰시오.

Tell me why you did meet her last night.

➡ _____

**서답형**
**11** 다음 괄호 안에서 알맞은 말을 고르시오.

(1) A flying fish can not (merely / rarely) swim but glide over the water.
(2) He is not only a famous chef but a television celebrity (too / as well).
(3) Oliver is not only (heathy / heathily) but also handsome.
(4) The air is not only getting colder, but also (gets / getting) cleaner.
(5) James as well as his brothers (know / knows) me.

**중요**
**12** 다음 중 어법상 알맞은 문장을 고르시오.

① Jake likes not only playing soccer but also jog.
② Dolphins use several different sound frequencies that not only serve to send messages, but also compensate for any interfering noise.
③ Jiho speaks not only Chinese also English.
④ *Harry Potter* as well as *Alita* are very interesting.
⑤ This is a great loss not only for individuals but also our nation.

**서답형**
**13** 다음 우리말을 영작하시오.

그는 축구뿐만 아니라 테니스도 한다.

➡ _____

**14** 주어진 문장의 빈칸에 들어갈 알맞은 말을 고르시오.

> Mike is not only stupid _____ impolite.

① but ② and ③ so
④ that ⑤ also

**15** 다음 중 간접의문문의 사용이 <u>잘못된</u> 것을 고르시오.

① Will you tell me why she got so upset at the party?
② I want to know what I should do to get a good grade.
③ He wondered if he could apply that to make something useful.
④ Can you guess what they are talking about?
⑤ I'm not sure how I paid for the computer much.

**16** 다음 중 어법상 <u>어색한</u> 것을 고르시오.

① I want to know where I can wash my hands.
② Soyeon is not only listening to music but also running.
③ Where do you think he is from?
④ He not only loves but also want to have a date with her.
⑤ I'm worried about whether I can get there on time.

**17** 빈칸에 들어갈 말을 순서대로 바르게 연결한 것은?

> • The boy group is good at not only singing _____ dancing.
> • The man wanted to know _____ her job was.

① but – why ② and – how
③ but – what ④ and – what
⑤ for – why

**18** 다음 중 어법상 <u>어색한</u> 문장을 고르시오.

① Juliet is not only pretty but also healthy.
② Do you believe when you'll become a manager?
③ Now the new train travels not only more quietly but also 10% faster with 15% less electricity.
④ The guest wants to know when his food will be ready.
⑤ You will always have the bad as well as the good in the world.

**서답형**
**19** 다음 문장을 두 문장으로 나누어 쓰시오.

(1) I don't know when this restaurant opens.

➡ _____

(2) I wonder whether this address is correct.

➡ _____

(3) They are a couple in the real world as well as in the movie.

➡ _____

_____

**01** 다음 두 문장을 간접의문을 이용하여 한 문장으로 쓰시오.

(1) • I'm wondering.
  • What is your goal this year?
  ➡ _____

(2) • Can you tell me?
  • Did she call you last night?
  ➡ _____

(3) • Do you know?
  • Who directed the movie?
  ➡ _____

(4) • Do you think?
  • What should I wear?
  ➡ _____

(5) • Can you tell me?
  • What they are talking about?
  ➡ _____

**02** 다음 우리말을 주어진 어휘를 이용하여 영어로 옮기시오.

(1) 그녀는 네가 아픈지를 알고 싶어 한다. (want, sick)
  ➡ _____

(2) 아이들이 수영장에서 무엇을 착용해야 하는지 말해 주시겠습니까? (should, can, wear, the swimming pool)
  ➡ _____
  _____

(3) 이 터널은 좁을 뿐만 아니라 어둡다. (this tunnel, also, not, dark, narrow)
  ➡ _____

**03** 다음 두 문장을 괄호 안의 조건대로 한 문장으로 쓰시오.

(1) • Dolphins can hear sounds clearly.
  • Dolphins can communicate over long distances. (only와 also를 이용하여)
  ➡ _____
  _____

(2) • He has knowledge.
  • Also he has experience, too. (well을 이용하여)
  ➡ _____

**04** 잘못된 부분을 바르게 고쳐 문장을 다시 쓰시오.

(1) It was not only strong but also easily to use.
  ➡ _____

(2) He as well as you are responsible for the problem.
  ➡ _____
  _____

(3) Not only I study a lot, but I also play a lot.
  ➡ _____

(4) Do you think where he might be?
  ➡ _____

(5) I wonder if we have good weather tomorrow.
  ➡ _____

**05** 다음 주어진 빈칸에 괄호 안의 문장을 알맞은 형태로 바꾸어 쓰시오.

> Do you know _____?
> (Why won't this computer turn on?)

**06** 다음 문장을 as well as를 이용하여 바꾸어 쓰시오.

(1) I want to learn not only taekwondo but also tennis.

➡ _____

(2) He treated me not only to lunch but also to cake.

➡ _____

(3) She not only likes playing the guitar but also composes good songs.

➡ _____
_____

(4) Not only Mark but also his brothers want to go to the concert.

➡ _____
_____

**07** 다음 중 어법상 <u>어색한</u> 문장을 찾아 바르게 고쳐 다시 쓰시오.

> a. Do you know what he bought at the store?
> b. I am wondering if I can use your pen.
> c. He wondered how the bird could fly high.
> d. Tell me where the key is.

➡ _____

**08** 다음 문장을 어법에 맞게 고쳐 쓰시오.

(1) The director as well as actors are invited to the party.

➡ _____
_____

(2) He looks not only smart but also friend.

➡ _____

(3) Cathy is not only a smart girl but also has a warm heart.

➡ _____
_____

(4) How do you know old he is?

➡ _____

(5) Do you believe what is causing this symptom?

➡ _____

**09** 다음 문장을 두 문장으로 나누려고 한다. 빈칸에 알맞은 문장을 쓰시오.

(1) Do you know? + _____

➡ Do you know where the key is?

(2) He wants to know. + _____
_____

➡ He wants to know how that happened.

(3) I wonder. + _____

➡ I wonder if we could go there.

(4) Do you think? + _____
_____

➡ What do you think is wrong with the computer?

## Nature's Inspiration

From flying birds to self-cleaning plants, the way nature works
현재분사(birds 수식)                                    = how
fascinates us. Some people not only use nature but also imitate it
not only A but also B 병렬 (use와 병렬 관계)
to find solutions to their problems. Leonardo da Vinci (1452-1519)
was one such person. He wondered how birds could fly. He closely
그러한                 간접의문문(의문사+주어+동사)
watched birds, made notes, and drew pictures of them. Even though his
양보절을 이끄는 부사절 접속사
invention was not successful, he imitated a bird's wings to try to make
to부정사의 부사적 용법 중 목적(~하기 위해서)
a flying machine. Since then, more and more people have successfully
더욱 더 많은
imitated the surprising abilities of nature's genius. Let's explore some
of them.
the surprising abilities of nature's genius

## Learning from a Bird: Moving Fast and Quietly

The high-speed train was first made in Japan. But it had one problem.
When the train entered a tunnel, the sudden increase in air pressure
타동사(전치사 없이 목적어를 취함)
created a very loud sound. It often woke people up and caused
a very loud sound        wake up: ~을 깨우다
headaches. A team of engineers tried to solve the problem, but they
didn't know how they could reduce the noise. One day, one of the
간접의문문(의문사+주어+동사)
engineers was watching a bird in search of a meal. He saw the bird
one of+복수명사: 단수취급              지각동사+목적어+V(ing)(목적어와 목적격 보어가 능동 관계에 있을 때)
quickly and quietly diving into the water. He wondered how the bird
entered the water so gracefully.
간접의문문(의문사+주어+동사)

inspiration: 영감
self-clean: 자정 작용을 하다
work: 작동하다
fascinate: 매료시키다
imitate: 모방하다
closely: 가까이에서, 면밀히
invention: 발명품
suprising: 놀라운
genius: 천재
enter: ~로 들어가다
increase: 증가하다
pressure: 압력
sudden: 갑작스러운
cause: 야기하다
headache: 두통
reduce: 줄이다
in search of: ~을 찾아
gracefully: 우아하게

### 확인문제

● 다음 문장이 본문의 내용과 일치하면 T, 일치하지 않으면 F를 쓰시오.

1  Humans are fascinated by the way nature works. ☐

2  Leonardo da Vinci looked into birds to understand how they flies. ☐

3  The high-speed train that was first made in Japan satisfied all the passengers. ☐

4  Engineers knew how to solve the problem the train had. ☐

So, he studied more about the bird and discovered its long, narrow
beak. He redesigned the front of the train by imitating the bird's beak.
It was successful. Now the new train travels not only more quietly but
also 10% faster with 15% less electricity.

### Learning from Burrs: Inventing an All-Purpose Fastener

One day, a Swiss engineer, George de Mestral, was hiking in the
woods with his dog. On his way home, he saw that burrs were
stuck to his clothes and his dog's hair. He wanted to know how that
happened. He took a closer look at the burrs and noticed that the ends
of the burr needles were not straight. He wondered if he could apply
that to make something useful. After a lot of testing, he finally
invented two new materials. One had many tiny needles like those
of burrs and the other had a hairy surface. When they were pressed
together, they became a very good fastener. It was not only strong but
also easy to use. Since then, many people have used his invention in
many different ways. It is often used for clothing, shoes, and bags.
Some people use it to play a number of different games. In space, it
keeps things from floating away.

There is nothing useless in nature. We just have to become curious
and ask questions.

discover: 발견하다
narrow: 좁은
redesign: 외관을 고치다, 다시 설계하다
beak: 부리
successful: 성공적인
electricity: 전기
burr: 가시 식물
all-purpose: 만능의
on one's way home: 집으로 가는 길에
happen: 발생하다
straight: 곧은
useful: 유용한
hairy: 털이 많은
fastener: 고정 장치
surface: 표면
float away: 떠다니다
useless: 쓸모없는
curious: 호기심 있는

---

### 확인문제

● 다음 문장이 본문의 내용과 일치하면 T, 일치하지 않으면 F를 쓰시오.

1  The train was redesigned like the bird's beak. ☐

2  The new train travels faster than the old one. ☐

3  George de Mestral was interested in burrs because it looked beautiful. ☐

4  The two new materials were easy to use but not strong. ☐

5  Everything in nature is useful. ☐

● 우리말을 참고하여 빈칸에 알맞은 말을 쓰시오.

**Nature's Inspiration**

**1** _____ flying birds _____ self-cleaning plants, the way nature _____ _____ _____.

**2** Some people _____ _____ use nature _____ _____ imitate _____ to find _____ to their problems.

**3** Leonardo da Vinci (1452-1519) was _____ _____ _____.

**4** He wondered _____ _____ _____ _____.

**5** He _____ watched birds, _____ notes, and drew pictures of them.

**6** _____ _____ his invention was not _____, he _____ a bird's wings _____ _____ _____ _____ a flying machine.

**7** _____ then, more and more people _____ successfully _____ the _____ _____ of nature's genius.

**8** _____ _____ some of them.

**Learning from a Bird: Moving Fast and Quietly**

**9** The _____ _____ was first made in Japan. But it _____ one problem.

**10** When the train _____ a tunnel, the _____ _____ in air pressure _____ a very loud sound.

**11** It often _____ _____ _____ and _____ headaches.

**12** A team of engineers tried _____ _____ the problem, but they didn't know _____ _____ _____ the noise.

**13** One day, one of _____ _____ _____ watching a bird _____ _____ _____ a meal.

**14** He _____ the bird quickly and quietly _____ _____ the water.

**15** He wondered _____ _____ _____ _____ the water so gracefully.

1 나는 새에서 자정 작용을 하는 식물까지, 자연이 기능하는 방식은 우리를 매료시킵니다.

2 몇몇 사람들은 그들의 문제에 대한 해결책을 찾기 위해 자연을 이용할 뿐만 아니라 자연을 모방하기까지 합니다.

3 레오나르도 다빈치(1452-1519)가 이러한 사람들 중 한 사람이었습니다.

4 그는 새들이 어떻게 날 수 있는지 궁금했습니다.

5 그는 새를 자세히 관찰했고, 기록했으며, 그림으로 그렸습니다.

6 그의 발명은 비록 성공하지 못했지만, 그는 나는 기계를 만들어 보려고 새의 날개를 모방했습니다.

7 그 후로, 점점 더 많은 사람들이 자연 속 천재의 놀라운 능력을 성공적으로 모방해 오고 있습니다.

8 그들 중 몇 가지를 알아봅시다.

**새에게서 배우기: 빠르고 조용하게 움직이기**

9 고속 열차는 일본에서 처음 만들어졌습니다. 하지만 그것은 한 가지 문제점이 있었습니다.

10 열차가 터널에 들어갔을 때, 갑작스러운 기압의 상승은 매우 시끄러운 소리를 발생시켰습니다.

11 그것은 종종 사람들의 잠을 깨웠고 두통을 일으켰습니다.

12 한 공학자 팀이 그 문제를 해결하려 했지만, 그들은 어떻게 소음을 줄일 수 있을지 몰랐습니다.

13 어느 날, 공학자들 중 한 사람이 먹이를 찾고 있는 새를 관찰하고 있었습니다.

14 그는 새가 빠르고 조용하게 물속으로 뛰어드는 것을 보았습니다.

15 그는 새가 어떻게 그렇게 우아하게 물속으로 들어가는지 궁금했습니다.

**16** So, he _____ _____ about the bird and _____ its long, _____ _____.

**17** He _____ the front of the train _____ _____ the bird's beak.

**18** It was successful. Now the new train travels _____ _____ more quietly _____ _____ 10% faster _____ 15% _____ electricity.

**Learning from Burrs: Inventing an All-Purpose Fastener**

**19** _____ _____, a Swiss engineer, George de Mestral, _____ _____ in the woods _____ his dog.

**20** _____ his way _____, he saw that _____ _____ _____ to his clothes and his dog's _____.

**21** He wanted _____ _____ _____ _____ _____ _____ _____ .

**22** He _____ _____ _____ _____ _____ the burrs and _____ _____ the ends of the burr needles _____ not _____.

**23** He wondered _____ _____ _____ _____ _____ that to make _____ _____.

**24** _____ a lot of _____, he finally _____ two new materials.

**25** One had many _____ _____ like _____ _____ _____ and _____ _____ had a _____ _____.

**26** When they _____ _____ together, they became a very good _____.

**27** It was _____ _____ _____ _____ _____ to use.

**28** _____ then, many people _____ _____ his invention in many _____ _____.

**29** It _____ _____ _____ _____ clothing, shoes, and bags.

**30** Some people use it _____ _____ _____ _____ different games.

**31** In space, it _____ things _____ _____ away.

**32** There is _____ _____ in nature. We just have to become _____ and _____ questions.

16 그래서 그는 그 새에 대해 더 연구했고, 새의 길고 좁은 부리를 발견했습니다.

17 그는 새의 부리를 모방하여 열차의 앞면을 다시 디자인했습니다.

18 그것은 성공이었습니다. 이제 새로운 열차는 더 조용할 뿐만 아니라 전기는 15% 덜 사용하면서 10% 더 빠르게 이동합니다.

**가시 식물들에게서 배우기: 만능 고정 장치 발명하기**

19 어느 날, 스위스 공학자 George de Mestral은 그의 개와 숲에서 하이킹하고 있었습니다.

20 집으로 돌아오는 길에, 그는 가시 식물이 자신의 옷과 개의 털에 붙어 있는 것을 보았습니다.

21 그는 어떻게 그런 일이 일어났는지 알고 싶었습니다.

22 그는 가시 식물들을 자세히 들여다보았고, 가시의 끝이 곧지 않다는 것을 알아챘습니다.

23 그는 유용한 뭔가를 만드는 데 그것을 적용할 수 있을지 궁금했습니다.

24 수많은 실험 후에, 그는 마침내 두 가지 새로운 소재를 발명했습니다.

25 하나는 가시 식물과 같은 조그만 가시들이 많이 있는 것이었고, 다른 하나는 털로 덮인 표면이 있는 것이었습니다.

26 두 소재를 함께 붙이면, 매우 훌륭한 고정 장치가 되었습니다.

27 그것은 튼튼할 뿐만 아니라 사용하기도 쉬웠습니다.

28 그 후로, 많은 사람들이 그의 발명품을 다양한 방법으로 사용해 오고 있습니다.

29 그것은 옷, 신발, 가방에 흔히 사용됩니다.

30 몇몇 사람들은 여러 가지 게임을 하기 위해 그것을 사용합니다.

31 우주에서, 그것은 물건들이 떠다니는 것을 막아줍니다.

32 자연에 쓸모없는 것은 하나도 없습니다. 우리는 그저 호기심을 갖고 질문을 던지면 됩니다.

● 우리말을 참고하여 본문을 영작하시오.

Nature's Inspiration

**1** 나는 새에서 자정 작용을 하는 식물까지, 자연이 기능하는 방식은 우리를 매료시킵니다.

➡ _____

**2** 몇몇 사람들은 그들의 문제에 대한 해결책을 찾기 위해 자연을 이용할 뿐만 아니라 자연을 모방하기까지 합니다.

➡ _____

**3** 레오나르도 다빈치(1452–1519)가 이러한 사람들 중 한 사람이었습니다.

➡ _____

**4** 그는 새들이 어떻게 날 수 있는지 궁금했습니다.

➡ _____

**5** 그는 새를 자세히 관찰했고, 기록했으며, 그림으로 그렸습니다.

➡ _____

**6** 그의 발명은 비록 성공하지 못했지만, 그는 나는 기계를 만들어 보려고 새의 날개를 모방했습니다.

➡ _____

_____

**7** 그 후로, 점점 더 많은 사람들이 자연 속 천재의 놀라운 능력을 성공적으로 모방해 오고 있습니다.

➡ _____

**8** 그들 중 몇 가지를 알아봅시다.

➡ _____

Learning from a bird: Moving Fast and Quietly

**9** 고속 열차는 일본에서 처음 만들어졌습니다. 하지만 그것은 한 가지 문제점이 있었습니다.

➡ _____

**10** 열차가 터널에 들어갔을 때, 갑작스러운 기압의 상승은 매우 시끄러운 소리를 발생시켰습니다.

➡ _____

**11** 그것은 종종 사람들의 잠을 깨웠고 두통을 일으켰습니다.

➡ _____

**12** 한 공학자 팀이 그 문제를 해결하려 했지만, 그들은 어떻게 소음을 줄일 수 있을지 몰랐습니다.

➡ _____

**13** 어느 날, 공학자들 중 한 사람이 먹이를 찾고 있는 새를 관찰하고 있었습니다.

➡ _____

**14** 그는 새가 빠르고 조용하게 물속으로 뛰어드는 것을 보았습니다.

➡ _____

**15** 그는 새가 어떻게 그렇게 우아하게 물속으로 들어가는지 궁금했습니다.

➡ _____

**16** 그래서 그는 그 새에 대해 더 연구했고, 새의 길고 좁은 부리를 발견했습니다.

➡ _____

**17** 그는 새의 부리를 모방하여 열차의 앞면을 다시 디자인했습니다.

➡ _____

**18** 그것은 성공적이었습니다. 이제 새로운 열차는 더 조용할 뿐만 아니라 전기는 15% 덜 사용하면서 10% 더 빠르게 이동합니다.

➡ _____

_____

Learning from Burrs: Inventing an All-Purpose Fastener

**19** 어느 날, 스위스 공학자 George de Mestral은 그의 개와 숲에서 하이킹하고 있었습니다.

➡ _____

**20** 집으로 돌아오는 길에, 그는 가시 식물이 자신의 옷과 개의 털에 붙어 있는 것을 보았습니다.

➡ _____

**21** 그는 어떻게 그런 일이 일어났는지 알고 싶었습니다.

➡ _____

**22** 그는 가시 식물들을 자세히 들여다보았고, 가시의 끝이 곧지 않다는 것을 알아챘습니다.

➡ _____

**23** 그는 유용한 뭔가를 만드는 데 그것을 적용할 수 있을지 궁금했습니다.

➡ _____

**24** 수많은 실험 후에, 그는 마침내 두 가지 새로운 소재를 발명했습니다.

➡ _____

**25** 하나는 가시 식물과 같은 조그만 가시들이 많이 있는 것이었고, 다른 하나는 털로 덮인 표면이 있는 것이었습니다.

➡ _____

**26** 두 소재를 함께 붙이면, 매우 훌륭한 고정 장치가 되었습니다.

➡ _____

**27** 그것은 튼튼할 뿐만 아니라 사용하기도 쉬웠습니다.

➡ _____

**28** 그 후로, 많은 사람들이 그의 발명품을 다양한 방법으로 사용해 오고 있습니다.

➡ _____

**29** 그것은 옷, 신발, 가방에 흔히 사용됩니다.

➡ _____

**30** 몇몇 사람들은 여러 가지 게임을 하기 위해 그것을 사용합니다.

➡ _____

**31** 우주에서, 그것은 물건들이 떠다니는 것을 막아줍니다.

➡ _____

**32** 자연에 쓸모없는 것은 하나도 없습니다. 우리는 그저 호기심을 갖고 질문을 던지면 됩니다.

➡ _____

[01~03] 다음 글을 읽고 물음에 답하시오.

From flying birds to self-cleaning plants, the way nature works fascinates us. Some people not only use nature but also imitate it to find solutions to their problems. Leonardo da Vinci (1452-1519) was one such person.

He wondered how birds could fly. He closely watched birds, made notes, and drew pictures of them. (A)_____ his invention was not successful, he imitated a bird's wings to try to make a flying machine. Since then, more and more people have successfully imitated the surprising abilities of nature's genius. Let's explore some of them.

**01** 다음 중 빈칸 (A)에 들어갈 말로 가장 적절한 것은?

① If      ② Even though   ③ Before
④ Since    ⑤ As soon as

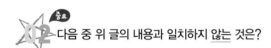

**02** 다음 중 위 글의 내용과 일치하지 <u>않는</u> 것은?

① Leonardo da Vinci tried to imitate nature.
② People are fascinated by the way nature works.
③ Leonardo da Vinci studied birds carefully.
④ What Leonardo da Vinci invented was successful.
⑤ People have succeeded in imitating nature since Leonardo's challenge.

**서답형**
**03** What do some people do in order to find solutions to their problems? Answer in English with a full sentence.

➡ _____

[04~08] 다음 글을 읽고 물음에 답하시오.

**Learning from a Bird: Moving Fast and Quietly**

The high-speed train was first made in Japan. But it had one ①problem. When the train entered a tunnel, the sudden increase in air pressure created a very loud sound. It often woke people up and caused headaches. A team of engineers tried to ②solve the problem, but they didn't know how they could reduce the noise. (A)One day, one of the engineers was watching a bird in search of a meal. He saw the bird quickly and quietly diving into the water. He ③wondered how the bird entered the water so gracefully. So, he studied more about the bird and discovered its long, narrow beak. He redesigned the front of the train by imitating the bird's beak. It was ④unsuccessful. Now the new train travels not only more quietly but also 10% ⑤ faster with 15% less electricity.

**04** ①~⑤ 중 글의 흐름상 어색한 것은?

①      ②      ③      ④      ⑤

**서답형**
**05** What did the engineer do to redesign the front of the train? Answer in English with five words.

➡ _____

**서답형**
**06** 밑줄 친 (A)와 같은 의미의 문장을 완성하시오.

One day, one of the engineers was watching a bird _____ for a meal.

**07** What was the problem of the first high-speed train?

① It made people sit uncomfortably.

② It was not fast enough.

③ It created too much smoke.

④ It was too expensive for people to use.

⑤ It was too noisy when entering a tunnel.

**08** 다음 중 위 글을 읽고 답할 수 있는 것은?

① When was the high-speed train made?

② Who invented the high-speed train?

③ Why did people in the train have headaches?

④ Where did the man see the bird?

⑤ How far did the train travel at a time?

[09~13] 다음 글을 읽고 물음에 답하시오.

**Learning from Burrs: Inventing an All-Purpose Fastener**

(A) One had many tiny needles like those of burrs and the other had a hairy surface. When they were pressed together, they became a very good fastener.

(B) He wanted to know how that happened. He took a closer look at the burrs and noticed ⓐthat the ends of the burr needles were not straight.

(C) One day, a Swiss engineer, George de Mestral, was hiking in the woods with his dog. On his way home, he saw that burrs were stuck to his clothes and his dog's hair.

(D) He wondered if he could apply that to make something useful. After a lot of testing, he finally invented two new materials.

It was not only strong but also easy to use. Since then, many people have used his invention in many different ways. It is often used for clothing, shoes, and bags. Some people use it to play a number of different games. In space, it keeps things from floating away.

There is nothing useless in nature. We just have to become curious and ask questions

**서답형**

**09** 자연스러운 글이 되도록 (A)~(D)를 바르게 나열하시오.

➡ _____

**서답형**

**10** 다음과 같이 풀이되는 말을 위 글에서 찾아 쓰시오.

being interested in something and wanting to know more about it

➡ _____

**서답형**

**11** For what is George's invention often used? Answer in English with a full sentence.

➡ _____

**12** 다음 중 밑줄 친 ⓐ와 쓰임이 같은 것은?

① She made that to make you happy.

② The boy that you met is my brother.

③ The fruit that he bought looks fresh.

④ Did you hear that he stole it?

⑤ Making the pie wasn't that difficult.

**13** 다음 중 위 글의 내용과 일치하는 것은?

① George de Mestral was hiking alone.

② George was a Swiss engineer.

③ Burrs were stuck to George's hair.

④ George failed to invent something new.

⑤ What George invented was strong but hard to use.

[14~17] 다음 글을 읽고 물음에 답하시오.

From flying birds to self-cleaning plants, the way nature works fascinates us. (①) Some people not only use nature but also imitate it to find solutions to their problems. (②) He wondered how birds could fly. He closely watched birds, made notes, and drew pictures of them. (③) Even though his invention was not successful, he imitated a bird's wings to try to make a (A)flying machine. (④) Since then, more and more people have successfully imitated the surprising abilities of nature's genius. (⑤) Let's explore some of them.

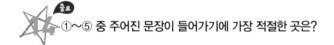

**14** ①~⑤ 중 주어진 문장이 들어가기에 가장 적절한 곳은?

Leonardo da Vinci (1452-1519) was one such person.

①　　　②　　　③　　　④　　　⑤

**15** 다음 중 밑줄 친 (A)와 쓰임이 다른 하나는?

① I need some sleeping pills.
② Please lend me your camping car.
③ Do you see the crying baby over there?
④ I am here in the waiting room.
⑤ Did she buy a washing machine?

**16** 다음 중 위 글에 이어질 내용으로 가장 적절한 것은?

① examples of failed inventions
② what Leonardo da Vinci invented
③ how to draw birds well
④ examples of successful imitation of nature
⑤ some geniuses who destroy nature

**17** 위 글의 내용과 일치하도록 빈칸에 알맞은 말을 쓰시오.

We are _____ by the way nature works.

[18~21] 다음 글을 읽고 물음에 답하시오.

**Learning from a Bird: (A)**_____

The high-speed train was first made in Japan. But it had one problem. When the train entered a tunnel, the sudden increase in air pressure created a very loud sound. It often woke people up and caused headaches. A team of engineers tried to solve the problem, but they didn't know how they could reduce the noise. One day, one of the engineers was watching a bird in search of a meal. He saw the bird quickly and quietly diving into the water. He wondered how the bird entered the water so gracefully. So, he studied more about the bird and discovered its long, narrow beak. He redesigned the front of the train by imitating the bird's beak. It was successful. Now the new train travels not only more quietly but also 10% faster with 15% less electricity.

**18** 다음 중 빈칸 (A)에 들어갈 말로 가장 적절한 것은?

① Moving As Slow As It Can
② Flying Fast and High
③ The Most Grace Animal
④ Flying in Search of Its Meal
⑤ Moving Fast and Quietly

**19** What happened when the high-speed train entered the tunnel? Answer in English with eleven words.

➡ _____

_____

**20** Choose the one that is TRUE about the new train.

① It makes people suffer from headaches.
② Its front looks like a bird tail.
③ The front of the train is long and wide.
④ It uses less electricity than the old one.
⑤ It doesn't travel as fast as the old one.

**서답형**

**21** 위 글의 내용에 맞게 빈칸에 알맞은 말을 쓰시오.

After watching a bird, the engineer studied more about the bird to figure out

_____ .

[22~26] 다음 글을 읽고 물음에 답하시오.

**Learning from Burrs: Inventing an All-Purpose Fastener**

One day, a Swiss engineer, George de Mestral, was hiking in the woods with his dog. On his way home, he saw that burrs were stuck to his clothes and his dog's hair. He wanted to know how that happened. He took a closer look at the burrs and noticed that the ends of the burr needles were not straight. He wondered (A)_____ he could apply that to make something useful. After a lot of testing, he finally invented two new materials. One had many tiny needles like (B)those of burrs and the other had a hairy surface. When they were pressed together, they became a very good fastener. It was not only strong but also easy to use. Since then, many people have used his invention in many different ways. It is often used for clothing, shoes, and bags. Some people use it to play a number of different games. In space, it keeps things from floating away.

There is nothing useless in nature. We just have to become curious and ask questions.

**22** 다음 중 빈칸 (A)에 들어갈 말과 같은 말이 들어가는 것은?

① Can you tell me _____ old you are?
② Do you know _____ invited you?
③ I wonder _____ she came from.
④ Tell me _____ your birthday is.
⑤ Let me know _____ she is hungry.

**서답형**

**23** 밑줄 친 (B)가 가리키는 것을 위 글에서 찾아 쓰시오.

➡ _____

**24** Choose the one that is NOT true about what George de Mestral invented.

① It is divided into two parts.
② One has a hairy surface.
③ It is easy to use but not strong.
④ It has been used in various ways.
⑤ To be used as a fastener, it should be pressed together.

**서답형**

**25** How is the fastener used in space? Answer in English with nine words.

➡ _____

**26** 다음 중 위 글을 읽고 답할 수 있는 것은?

① When did George hike with his dog?
② What did George see when he was hiking?
③ What did burrs' needles look like?
④ How long did it take George to invent a very good fastener?
⑤ How many tests did George take?

[01~04] 다음 글을 읽고 물음에 답하시오.

From flying birds to self-cleaning plants, the way nature works fascinates us. Some people not only use nature but also imitate it to find solutions to their problems. Leonardo da Vinci (1452-1519) was one such person. (A)_____ He closely watched birds, made notes, and drew pictures of them. Even though his invention was not successful, he imitated a bird's wings to try to make a flying machine. Since (B)then, more and more people have successfully imitated the surprising abilities of nature's genius. Let's explore some of them.

**01** 주어진 단어를 바르게 나열하여 빈칸 (A)에 들어갈 말을 쓰시오.

(wondered / fly / birds / could / how / he)

➡ _____

**02** What did Leonard da Vinci do to find out how birds could fly?

➡ _____
_____

**03** 밑줄 친 (B)가 의미하는 것을 위 글에서 찾아 우리말로 쓰시오.

➡ _____
_____

**04** What did Leonardo da Vinci try to make? Answer in English with a full sentence.

➡ _____

[05~09] 다음 글을 읽고 물음에 답하시오.

**Learning from Burrs: Inventing an All-Purpose Fastener**

One day, a Swiss engineer, George de Mestral, was hiking in the woods with his dog. On his way home, he saw that burrs were stuck to his clothes and his dog's hair. He wanted to know how (A)that happened. He took a closer look at the burrs and noticed that the ends of the burr needles were not straight. (B)그는 유용한 무언가를 만드는 데 그것을 적용할 수 있을지 궁금했습니다. After a lot of testing, he finally invented two new materials. One had many tiny needles like those of burrs and the other had a hairy surface. When they were pressed together, they became a very good fastener. It was not only strong but also easy to use. Since then, many people have used his invention in many different ways. It is often used for clothing, shoes, and bags. Some people use it to play a number of different games. In space, (C)it keeps floating away from things.

There is nothing useless in nature. We just have to become curious and ask questions.

**05** 밑줄 친 (A)가 의미하는 것을 우리말로 쓰시오.

➡ _____

**06** 주어진 단어를 바르게 나열하여 밑줄 친 우리말 (B)를 영어로 쓰시오. 하나의 단어를 추가하시오.

(he / he / that / useful / make / wondered / something / could / to / apply)

➡ _____
_____

**07** 밑줄 친 (C)는 문맥상 <u>어색한</u> 문장이다. 단어를 재배열하여 문맥에 맞는 문장으로 고쳐 쓰시오.

➡ _____

**08** When George took a closer look at the burrs, what did he notice? Answer in English with a full sentence.

➡ _____
_____

**09** What do we have to do in order to learn from nature? Answer in English with a full sentence.

➡ _____

[10~14] 다음 글을 읽고 물음에 답하시오.

**Learning from a Bird: Moving Fast and Quietly**

The high-speed train was first made in Japan. But it had one problem. When the train entered a tunnel, the sudden increase in air pressure created a very loud sound. It often woke people up and caused headaches. A team of engineers tried to (A)_____ the problem, but they didn't know how they could (B)_____ the noise. One day, one of the engineers was watching a bird in search of a meal. He saw the bird quickly and quietly diving into the water. He wondered how the bird entered the water so gracefully. So, he studied more about the bird and discovered its long, narrow beak. He redesigned the front of the train by (C)_____ the bird's beak. It was successful. Now the new train travels not only more quietly but also 10% faster with 15% less electricity.

**10** 주어진 단어를 글의 흐름과 어법에 맞게 빈칸 (A)~(C)에 쓰시오.

(imitate / reduce / solve)

➡ (A)_____ (B)_____ (C)_____

**11** What did the engineer wonder when he watched a bird in search of a meal? Answer in English.

➡ _____
_____

**12** What did the bird's beak look like? Answer in English. Use the word 'have.' (6 words)

➡ _____

**13** 다음 물음에 〈조건〉에 맞추어 답하시오.

Q: How does the new train differ from the old train?

┌─ 조건 ─┐
1. 두 개의 문장으로 된 영어로 답할 것.
2. First, Second를 사용하여 답하시오.

➡ _____
_____

**14** 위 글의 내용에 맞게 빈칸에 알맞은 말을 쓰시오.

The high-speed train first made in _____ had one problem. When it entered a tunnel, it made a very loud sound because _____ _____ suddenly _____ in the tunnel.

## Real Life Communication C

You know that some bugs have many eyes, don't you?
부가의문문으로 상대에게 확인하기 위하여 묻는 형식이다.

Some of them have thousands of eyes. I was fascinated by that and designed
"Some of them"은 "그 중의 몇몇"이라는 뜻으로 복수 취급한다.　동사 was와 병렬구조를 이루는 과거 동사이다.

Bug Eye Robot. It has many eyes to see things better. It will help people who
who는 주관 관계대명사로 선행사는 people이다.

can't see well.

구문해설 · thousands of 수천의 · be fascinated by ~에 매료되다. design 디자인하다, 설계하다

너 곤충이 많은 눈을 가지고 있는 것을 알지? 그 중에 몇몇은 수 천 개의 눈을 가지고 있어. 나는 그것에 매료가 되어서 Bug Eye Robot을 만들었어. 그것은 더 잘 보기 위하여 많은 눈을 가지고 있어. 그것은 잘 볼 수 없는 사람을 도와 줄 거야.

## Culture & Life

### Polar Bears, North Pole

Polar bears survive the cold because they have black skin to easily absorb the
the+형용사: 추상명사　　　　　　　형용사적 용법의 to 부정사

heat from the sun. Each of their hairs has an air space. This also helps them
each가 주어일 경우 단수 동사　　　앞 문장의 내용

stay warm.
help의 목적격보어로 동사원형

구문해설 · survive: 생존하다 · absorb: 흡수하다

**북극곰, 북극**
북극곰은 태양열을 쉽게 흡수할 수 있는 검은 피부를 가지고 있기 때문에 추위에서 생존한다. 북극곰 털 하나하나에는 공기층이 있다. 이것 또한 따뜻함을 유지하는 데 도움이 된다.

## Culture & Life

### Sahara Desert Ants, North Africa

The Sahara Desert is not only the driest but also the hottest place on earth. But
not only A but also B: A뿐만 아니라 B도　　　　지구상에서

even at the hottest time of day, Sahara Desert ants go hunting. Do you know
go Ving: V하러 가다

how they survive the heat? Their bodies are covered with unique hairs that
간접의문문(의문사+주어+동사)　　　　　　　　주격 관계대명사(선행사: hairs)

reflect the heat from the sun.

구문해설 · desert: 사막 · dry: 건조한 · survive: 생존하다, 살아남다 · be covered with: ~으로 덮여 있다 · reflect: 반사하다

**사하라 사막 개미들, 북아프리카**
사하라 사막은 지구상에서 가장 건조할 뿐만 아니라 가장 뜨거운 곳이다. 하지만 하루 중 가장 뜨거운 시간에도 사하라 사막 개미들은 사냥을 간다. 그들이 어떻게 그 열기에서 살아남는지 아는가? 개미들의 몸은 태양으로부터의 열기를 반사해내는 독특한 털로 덮여 있다.

## Culture & Life Project

You know horses run very fast, don't you? One of the reasons is that they have
부가의문문　　　　　one of+복수 명사+단수 동사

strong feet. Our group designed shoes by imitating a horse's foot. When you
전치사+동명사

wear them, you will not only run faster but also look taller.
A뿐만 아니라 B도　　　look+형용사 보어

구문해설 · imitate: 모방하다

여러분은 말이 빨리 달리는 것을 알고 있습니다, 그렇죠? 그 이유 중의 하나는 그들이 튼튼한 발을 가지고 있다는 겁니다. 우리 모둠은 말의 발을 모방해서 신발을 만들었습니다. 여러분이 그것을 신으면, 여러분은 빨리 달릴 뿐만 아니라 키가 더 커 보일 겁니다.

**01** 다음 두 문장에 공통으로 알맞은 것을 고르시오.

> • You have to make contact _____ us.
> • The window was covered _____ snow.

① to      ② for      ③ with
④ by      ⑤ about

**02** 다음 주어진 단어의 적절한 형태를 고르시오.

> He will get angry with this _____.
> (decide)

① decisive      ② decided
③ deciding      ④ to decide
⑤ decision

**03** 다음 영영풀이에 해당하는 단어를 고르시오.

> a passage that goes under the ground

① tunnel      ② path
③ subway      ④ transport
⑤ vehicle

**04** 다음 밑줄 친 부분의 우리말 뜻이 알맞지 <u>않은</u> 것은?

① Boys try to <u>imitate</u> stars. (모방하다)
② We will <u>increase</u> the price. (인상하다)
③ His music will <u>inspire</u> children. (관심을 가지다)
④ His speech won't <u>last</u> long. (지속하다)
⑤ She has a very <u>inventive</u> idea. (창의적인)

**[05~06]** 다음 우리말과 일치하도록 빈칸에 알맞은 말을 쓰시오.
(05: 7단어, 06: 11단어)

**05**

> A: _____
> (나는 식물들이 할 수 있는 것에 매혹되었어.)
> B: What do you mean?
> A: For example, some plants never get wet or dirty.
> B: That's interesting!

**06**

> A: _____
> _____
> (북극곰이 수영을 잘하는 거 알지, 그렇지 않니?)
> B: Sure. They can swim more than 60 miles without rest.

**07** 다음 대화의 빈칸에 들어가기에 적절한 것은?

> G: This candle holder can make candles last twice as long.
> B: Really? _____
> G: When a candle burns, it melts into the tube below the holder to form a new candle.
> B: Wow, I am so fascinated by the idea! Now we can use candles longer.

① Where is the holder?
② What's on the holder?
③ How's that possible?
④ Why are you fascinated?
⑤ What's the problem?

[08~10] 다음 대화를 읽고 물음에 답하시오.

B: (A)너는 mosquito needle에 관하여 들어본 적이 있지, Jian?

G: A mosquito needle? Can you explain it to me?

B: Some scientists made this new needle by (B)_____ a mosquito's mouth.

G: That's interesting. So how will that help?

B: You know mosquito bites are not very painful, don't you? The new needle will also cause less pain.

G: That's great. How come it's more painful?

B: Like a mosquito's mouth, it makes less contact with our skin.

G: Wow, I think that there's nothing useless in the world!

**08** 밑줄 친 (A)의 우리말에 해당하는 영어 문장으로 적절한 것은?

① Did you tell about a mosquito needle, Jian?

② Have you studied a mosquito needle, Jian?

③ Will you ask about a mosquito needle, Jian?

④ Did you think about a mosquito needle, Jian?

⑤ Have you heard of a mosquito needle, Jian?

**09** 빈칸 (B)에 들어가기에 적절한 것은?

① drawing      ② making

③ imitating     ④ finding

⑤ increasing

**10** 위 대화에서 내용상 어색한 부분이 있는 문장을 찾아 자연스러운 문장으로 고쳐 쓰시오.

➡ _____

[11~13] 다음 대화를 읽고 물음에 답하시오.

G: (A)You know that Leonardo da Vinci painted the *Mona Lisa*, don't you?

B: Sure. I think he was a really great artist.

G: He was also a great inventor.

B: What did he invent?

G: He dreamed of flying like a bird. So, he drew (B)_____ that looked like a bird.

B: Did he also make that machine?

G: No, but his creative idea inspired many other inventors.

**11** 밑줄 친 (A)와 같은 의미의 문장으로 적절한 것은?

① Did you say that Leonardo da Vinci painted the *Mona Lisa*?

② Have you told Leonardo da Vinci painted the *Mona Lisa*?

③ Are you sure that Leonardo da Vinci painted the *Mona Lisa*?

④ Are you excited that Leonardo da Vinci painted the *Mona Lisa*?

⑤ Are you aware that Leonardo da Vinci painted the *Mona Lisa*?

**12** 빈칸 (B)에 들어가기에 적절한 것은?

① a robot bird      ② a bug robot

③ a cooling fan     ④ a new plane

⑤ a flying machine

**13** 위 대화를 통해서 알 수 있는 것이 아닌 것은?

① Leonardo da Vinci was very inventive.

② Leonardo da Vinci was an artist.

③ Leonardo da Vinci drew a flying machine.

④ Leonardo da Vinci's flying machine looked like a bird.

⑤ He was a great inventor and invented many flying machines.

**14** 다음 중 어법상 <u>어색한</u> 문장을 고르시오.

① Do you think who you're talking to?

② I'm wondering when the library opens.

③ Can you guess where our bananas come from?

④ Can you tell me how the accident came about?

⑤ I don't know if he'll get better soon.

**15** 두 문장의 뜻이 같도록 빈칸에 들어갈 말을 차례대로 바르게 쓴 것은?

> • He works on weekends as well as on weekdays.
> = He works _____ on weekdays _____ on weekends.

① either – or

② neither – nor

③ not – but

④ not only – but also

⑤ as – as

**16** 다음 두 문장을 한 문장으로 바르게 옮긴 것은?

> • I don't know.
> • What was he doing at that time?

① I don't know if he was doing at that time.

② I don't know if what he was doing at that time.

③ I don't know what he was doing at that time.

④ I don't know what was he doing at that time.

⑤ What I don't know he was doing at that time.

**17** 다음 중 어법상 <u>어색한</u> 문장을 고르시오.

① He as well as you has to take part in the meeting.

② Charlotte as well as her sisters like to go hiking.

③ Not only he but also I remember the accident.

④ Not only the teacher but also the students were enjoying the game.

⑤ Not only men but also women want to live long.

**18** 다음 우리말을 주어진 어휘를 이용하여 영작하시오.

(1) 그녀는 얼굴뿐 아니라 마음씨도 곱다. (a pretty face, a warm heart, have, also)

➡ _____

(2) 성공은 재능뿐만 아니라 노력에 의해서도 결정된다. (depend, talent, also, effort, on)

➡ _____
_____

(3) 염소는 나뭇잎뿐만 아니라 과일도 먹는다. (a goat, leaves, fruit, as)

➡ _____

(4) Chris가 점심으로 무엇을 먹었는지 아니? (had, for lunch)

➡ _____

(5) 나는 그가 곧 돌아올지 궁금하다. (wondering, soon, come back)

➡ _____

(6) 그가 언제 집을 나왔다고 생각하니? (think, left home)

➡ _____

**19** 다음 중 어법상 <u>어색한</u> 문장의 개수로 알맞은 것은?

> ⓐ I wonder how much this skirt costs.
> ⓑ Do you know did who make this cake?
> ⓒ Do you think who is suitable for the new project?
> ⓓ Not only my friends but also my teacher like my idea.
> ⓔ A frog can not only jump but also swim.
> ⓕ So he got a good score in not only the English test but also in the math test.

① 1개   ② 2개   ③ 3개   ④ 4개   ⑤ 5개

**Reading**

[20~22] 다음 글을 읽고 물음에 답하시오.

From flying birds to self-cleaning plants, the way nature works fascinates us. Some people not only use nature but also imitate it to find solutions to their problems. Leonardo da Vinci (1452-1519) was one (a)<u>such person</u>.
(A) Even though his invention was not successful, he imitated a bird's wings to try to make a flying machine.
(B) He wondered how birds could fly. He closely watched birds, made notes, and drew pictures of them.
(C) Since then, more and more people have successfully imitated the surprising abilities of nature's genius. Let's explore some of (b)<u>them</u>.

**20** 자연스러운 글이 되도록 (A)~(C)를 바르게 나열하시오.

➡ _____

**21** 다음 중 밑줄 친 (a)가 의미하는 것으로 가장 적절한 것은?

① someone who liked to use technology
② someone who was interested in solving problems
③ someone who was into studying birds
④ someone who fascinated people
⑤ someone who copied nature successfully

**22** 다음 중 밑줄 친 (b)가 의미하는 것으로 가장 적절한 것은?

① some people who invented precious things
② people who have surprising abilities
③ things that have been treated carelessly
④ people who succeeded in their field
⑤ cases that people successfully imitated nature

[23~25] 다음 글을 읽고 물음에 답하시오.

A team of scientists questioned how certain animals climb walls so easily. (①) They have observed what their feet look like and how they stick to walls. (②) "The new material is not only strong but also easy to use," says one of the scientists. (③) In the movie Spider-Man, Spider-Man climbs a tall building with just his hands and feet. (④) Would (A)<u>that</u> ever be possible in the real world? (⑤) It doesn't sound impossible anymore!

## 23 ①~⑤ 중 다음 주어진 문장이 들어가기에 가장 적절한 곳은?

> As a result, they invented a new material that sticks to any surface.

①　　　②　　　③　　　④　　　⑤

## 24 밑줄 친 (A)가 의미하는 것을 10단어의 영어로 쓰시오.

➡ _____

_____

## 25 다음 중 위 글의 내용과 일치하는 것은?

① Some people climb walls with ease.
② Scientists don't care about climbing walls with just hands and feet.
③ The material scientists invented is not strong.
④ Spider-Man uses many gears to climb a tall building.
⑤ It is easy to use the new material scientists invented.

**[26~27]** 다음 글을 읽고 물음에 답하시오.

> Wolves are great hunters. Their wide ①feet help them ②travel a long way in the snow. (A) _____ is also important for their survival. The lead wolf decides ③when the group will travel and hunt. It also ④decides where to go and ⑤know what to do when there is danger.

## 26 다음 중 빈칸 (A)에 들어갈 말로 가장 적절한 것은?

① Friendship　　　② Parentship
③ Leadership　　　④ Ownership
⑤ Citizenship

## 27 ①~⑤ 중 어법상 바르지 <u>않은</u> 것은?

①　　　②　　　③　　　④　　　⑤

**[28~29]** 다음 글을 읽고 물음에 답하시오.

> The high-speed train was first made in Japan. But it had one problem. When the train entered a tunnel, the sudden increase in air pressure created a very loud sound. (A)It often woke people up and caused headaches. A team of engineers tried to solve the problem, but they didn't know how they could reduce the noise. One day, one of the engineers was watching a bird in search of a meal. He saw the bird quickly and quietly diving into the water. He wondered how the bird entered the water so gracefully. So, he studied more about the bird and discovered its long, narrow beak. He redesigned the front of the train by imitating the bird's beak. It was successful. Now the new train travels not only more quietly but also 10% faster with 15% less electricity.

## 28 밑줄 친 (A)가 의미하는 것을 우리말로 쓰시오.

➡ _____

## 29 Choose the one that is NOT true.

① It was in Japan that the first high-speed train was made.
② The first high-speed train couldn't pass a tunnel without making a loud sound.
③ Engineers tried to find out how to decrease the noise.
④ The engineer redesigned the tail of the train by imitating a bird.
⑤ The new train travels faster with less energy.

**출제율 90%**

**01** 짝지어진 단어의 관계가 같도록 빈칸에 알맞은 말을 쓰시오.

creative : inventive = g_____ : graciously

**출제율 90%**

**02** 다음 빈칸에 들어갈 말로 적절한 것은?

The traditions of other cultures often _____ people.

① fascinate
② reduce
③ ignore
④ observe
⑤ reflect

**출제율 95%**

**03** 다음 빈칸에 공통으로 들어가기에 적절한 것은?

• _____ come you are so angry this morning?
• _____ about going for lunch?

① What
② Whether
③ When
④ How
⑤ Which

**출제율 100%**

**04** 다음 〈보기〉의 단어로 자연스러운 문장을 만들 수 없는 것은?

┤ 보기 ├
pressure  redesign  reflect  reduce

① They are trying very hard to _____ the city.
② Let's check your blood _____ first.
③ Dark surface doesn't usually _____ much light.
④ Do you have any creative _____?
⑤ Use ice to _____ the pain.

[05~07] 다음 대화를 읽고 물음에 답하시오.

B: (가)Have you heard of a mosquito needle, Jian?

G: A mosquito needle? Can you explain it to me?

B: Some scientists made this new needle by imitating a mosquito's mouth.

G: That's interesting. So (A)_____ will that help?

B: You know mosquito bites are not very painful, don't you? The new needle will also cause less pain.

G: That's great. (B)_____ come it's less painful?

B: Like a mosquito's mouth, it makes less contact with our skin.

G: Wow, I think that there's nothing useless in the world!

**출제율 90%**

**05** 밑줄 친 (가) 대신 쓰기에 적절하지 않은 것은?

① Do you know about a mosquito needle, Jian?
② Are you aware of a mosquito needle, Jian?
③ Did you ask about a mosquito needle, Jian?
④ Have you been told about a mosquito needle, Jain?
⑤ Jian, you know about a mosquito needle, don't you?

**출제율 95%**

**06** 빈칸 (A)와 (B)에 들어가기에 알맞은 것으로 짝지어진 것은?

|  | (A) | (B) |
|---|---|---|
| ① | what | Why |
| ② | how | What |
| ③ | why | What |
| ④ | how | How |
| ⑤ | which | What |

**07** 위 대화를 읽고 알 수 없는 것은?

① Some scientists made a new needle called a mosquito needle.

② Some scientists imitated a mosquito's mouth to make a new needle.

③ The new needle will cause less pain.

④ The new needle makes less contact with our skin.

⑤ The reason why it causes less pain isn't known to us.

**[08~09]** 다음 대화를 읽고 물음에 답하시오.

W: Today, we have a special guest, Thomas Thwaites, the Goat Man. Hello, Thomas.

M: Hello, Anna. Great to be here.

W: Thomas, I'm so fascinated by the fact (가) that you lived like a goat in the Alps for three days. Why did you do that?

M: One day, I saw goats playing on the mountain. They looked so peaceful that I wanted to live like them.

W: Didn't you have any problems being a goat?

M: Walking on all four legs was very pleasing to me.

W: Do you have any plans to live like a goat again?

M: Sure. I'm planning my second visit to the Alps.

W: I can't wait to hear about your next adventure. Thank you, Thomas, for your time.

**08** 밑줄 친 (가)와 같은 용법으로 쓰인 것은?

① Have you met that boy before?

② The car that he bought is very good.

③ Do you know that was his idea?

④ I agree with his idea that we should delay our picnic.

⑤ Is it the house that he designed?

**09** 위 대화를 읽고 알 수 없는 것은?

① The name of the hostess is Anna.

② The guest is called the Goat Man.

③ Thomas lived like a goat in the Alps.

④ Anna saw goats playing on the mountain.

⑤ Thomas is planning a second visit to the Alps.

**10** 다음 문장에서 어법상 어색한 부분을 찾아 바르게 고쳐 다시 쓰시오.

> Can you explain to me how this machine costs much?

➡ _____

**11** 다음 빈칸에 적절한 말을 주어진 단어를 알맞은 형태로 바꾸어 써 넣으시오.

(1) The baby not only is healthy but also looks very _____. (love)

(2) He works _____ as well as very hard. (efficient)

**12** 다음 우리말을 괄호 안의 어휘를 이용하여 영작하시오.

(1) 너는 학교 축제가 언제 시작됐는지 아니? (your school festival, know, start)

➡ _____

(2) 그녀는 달리기뿐만 아니라 수영하는 것을 즐긴다. (merely, running, also, swimming)

➡ _____

**13** 출제율 90%

다음 주어진 문장을 <u>잘못</u> 바꾼 것을 고르시오.

> Kevin wants to study Greek. He wants to study Latin, too.

① Kevin wants to study Greek and Latin.

② Kevin wants to study Latin as well as Greek.

③ Kevin wants to study not only Greek but also study Latin.

④ Kevin wants to study not only Greek but also Latin.

⑤ Kevin wants to study not only Greek but Latin as well.

**14** 출제율 95%

다음 두 문장을 한 문장으로 고쳐 쓰시오.

(1) • I'm wondering.

   • Have you read the notice about the contest?

   ➡ _____

   _____

(2) • Do you suppose?

   • What will you do?

   ➡ _____

**15** 출제율 90%

다음 빈칸에 공통으로 알맞은 것은?

> • This is _____ she wants to eat.
> • I wonder _____ she wants to eat.

① how        ② when        ③ why

④ that        ⑤ what

**16** 출제율 100%

다음 괄호 안에 주어진 단어의 형태가 바르게 짝지어진 것은?

> Vivian is good at (read) as well as (write) in Korean.

① to read – to write        ② reading – writing

③ to read – writing        ④ reads – writes

⑤ read – write

[17~20] 다음 글을 읽고 물음에 답하시오.

**Learning from Burrs: (A)**_____

One day, a Swiss engineer, George de Mestral, was hiking in the woods with his dog. On his way home, he saw that burrs were stuck to his clothes and his dog's hair. He wanted to know how that happened. He took a closer look at the burrs and noticed that the ends of the burr needles were not straight. He wondered (B) [that / if] he could apply that to make something useful. After a lot of testing, he finally invented two new materials. One had many tiny needles like (C)[that / those] of burrs and (D)[the other / another] had a hairy surface. When they were pressed together, they became a very good fastener. It was not only strong but also easy to use. Since then, many people have used his invention in many different ways. It is often used for clothing, shoes, and bags. Some people use it to play a number of different games. In space, it keeps things from floating away.

There is nothing useless in nature. We just have to become curious and ask questions.

**17** 출제율 90%

빈칸 (A)에 들어갈 말로 가장 적절한 것은?

① Making Lives Difficult

② How It Flies Far Away

③ The Mother of Needs

④ Inventing an All-Purpose Fastener

⑤ Making Invention Easy

출제율 100%

**18** 다음 중 위 글을 읽고 답할 수 있는 것은?

① How often did George hike?
② How old was George?
③ How long did George hike?
④ What was stuck to George's clothes?
⑤ How many times did George test to invent the final material?

출제율 95%

**19** (B)~(D)에서 어법상 옳은 것을 골라 쓰시오.

➡ (B)_____ (C)_____ (D)_____

출제율 90%

**20** What should be done in order for two new materials to be used as a very good fastener? Answer in English with five words.

➡ _____

**[21~22]** 다음 글을 읽고 물음에 답하시오.

The Sahara Desert is not only the driest but also the hottest place on earth. But even at the hottest time of day, Sahara Desert ants go hunting. Do you know (A)(the / how / survive / heat / they)? Their bodies are covered with unique hairs that reflect the heat from the sun.

출제율 90%

**21** 괄호 (A) 안의 단어를 바르게 나열하시오.

➡ _____

출제율 100%

**22** 다음 중 위 글을 읽고 알 수 없는 것은?

① No other desert in the world is drier than the Sahara Desert.
② The Sahara Desert is hotter than any other desert on Earth.
③ Sahara Desert ants go hunting even when it is the hottest time of day.
④ Sahara Desert ants like to go hunting at noon.
⑤ The unique hairs of the ants send back the heat from the sun.

**[23~24]** 다음 글을 읽고 물음에 답하시오.

From flying birds to self-cleaning plants, the way nature works fascinates us. ( ① ) Some people not only use nature but also imitate it to find solutions to their problems. ( ② ) Leonardo da Vinci (1452-1519) was one such person. ( ③ ) He closely watched birds, made notes, and drew pictures of them. ( ④ ) Even though his invention was not successful, he imitated a bird's wings to try to make a flying machine. ( ⑤ ) Since then, more and more people have successfully imitated the surprising abilities of nature's genius. Let's explore some of them.

출제율 95%

**23** ①~⑤ 중 주어진 문장이 들어가기에 가장 적절한 곳은?

He wondered how birds could fly.

①    ②    ③    ④    ⑤

출제율 100%

**24** What is the passage mainly talking about?

① the life of Leonardo da Vinci
② many interesting things in nature
③ fascinating inventions in the world
④ nature's inspiration for people
⑤ surprising abilities of Leonardo da Vinci

**[01~03]** 다음 대화를 읽고 물음에 답하시오.

B: I'm fascinated by Sophia, a robot girl.
G: (가)그녀가 뭐가 그리 특별한데? (so, about)
B: She is able to show more than 60 facial expressions.
G: That's amazing. (A)_____ else can she do?
B: She has many other abilities. She looks, talks, and even thinks like a human.
G: That's (B)(fascinate)!

**01** (가)의 우리말에 해당하는 영어 문장을 괄호 안의 말을 이용하여 쓰시오.

➡ _____

**02** 빈칸 (A)에 들어가기에 적절한 한 단어를 쓰시오.

➡ _____

**03** (B)에 주어진 단어를 적절한 형태로 바꾸어 쓰시오.

➡ _____

**04** 다음 그림을 보고 괄호 안에 주어진 어휘를 이용하여 빈칸을 채우시오.

➡ This fish _____
_____. (swim well, can glide over water, as)

**05** 다음 문장을 두 문장으로 나누려고 한다. 빈칸에 알맞은 문장을 쓰시오.

(1) A team of scientists questioned how certain animals climb walls so easily.
= A team of scientists questioned. +
_____

(2) What do you believe is the most important thing in life?
= Do you believe? + _____
_____

(3) I'm not sure if he was sleepy or drunk.
= I'm not sure. + _____

**06** 다음 문장에서 어색한 부분을 바르게 고쳐 다시 쓰시오.

(1) Do you know why is she crying?
➡ _____

(2) Do you think what she expected to happen as a result of her visit?
➡ _____
_____

(3) They not only made the cake but also eating it a lot.
➡ _____
_____

(4) You as well as your sister has to clean the room.
➡ _____
_____

(A)_____

A team of scientists questioned how certain animals climb walls so easily. They have observed what their feet look like and how they stick to walls. As a result, they invented a new material that sticks to any surface. "(B) The new material is not only strong but also easy to use," says one of the scientists.

In the movie Spider-Man, Spider-Man climbs a tall building with just his hands and feet. Would that ever be possible in the real world? It doesn't sound impossible anymore!

**07** 주어진 단어를 바르게 나열하여 빈칸 (A)에 들어갈 위 글의 제목을 완성하시오.

(Real Life / Spider-Man / in / Possible / is)?

➡ _____

**08** 다음은 밑줄 친 (B)와 같은 의미의 문장이다. 빈칸에 알맞은 말을 쓰시오.

The new material is easy to use _____ _____ _____ strong

[09~11] 다음 글을 읽고 물음에 답하시오.

One day, a Swiss engineer, George de Mestral, was hiking in the woods with his dog. On his way home, he saw that burrs were stuck to his clothes and his dog's hair. He wanted to know how that happened. He took a closer look at the burrs and noticed that the ends of the burr

needles were not straight. He wondered if he could apply (A)that to make something useful. After a lot of testing, he finally invented two new materials. One had many tiny needles like those of burrs and the other had a hairy surface. When they were pressed together, they became a very good fastener. It was not only strong but also easy to use.

**09** What did George see on his way home? Answer in English with a full sentence.

➡ _____
_____

**10** 밑줄 친 (A)가 의미하는 것을 우리말로 쓰시오.

➡ _____

**11** What did the two new materials look like? Use the word 'have.'

➡ _____
_____

# 창의사고력 서술형 문제

**01** 다음 〈보기〉에서 알맞은 단어를 골라 문장을 완성하시오. (필요하면 어형 변화를 할 것.)

보기

imitate   fascinate   redesign   genius   invention

a. The beauty of nature always _____ humans.
b. Necessity is the mother of _____.
c. _____ is 1% talent and 99% hard work.
d. The best way to learn a sport is to watch and _____ a good player.

**02** 다음 그림을 참고하여 빈칸을 채우시오. (괄호 안에 주어진 어휘를 이용할 것.)

We can use the special door in Juwon's room _____ .
(but also, table for table tennis, as)

**03** 다음 연구 노트를 바탕으로 과학 잡지 기사의 일부를 완성하시오.

Question: How do certain animals climb walls so easily?
Observation: what their feet look like and how they stick to walls
Invention: It sticks to any surface. It is strong and easy to use.

A team of scientists questioned _____ . They have observed
_____ and _____ . As a result, they
invented a new material that _____ . "The new material is not only
_____ but also _____," says one of the scientists.

# 단원별 모의고사

**01** 다음 짝지어진 두 단어의 관계가 같도록 빈칸에 알맞은 말을 쓰시오.

> explore : exploration = fascinate : _____

**02** 다음 영영풀이에 해당하는 단어로 적절한 것은?

> the hard usually pointed parts that over a bird's mouth

① robot　　　　② beak
③ burr　　　　④ solution
⑤ needle

**03** 다음 문장의 빈칸에 알맞은 것을 <보기>에서 찾아 쓰시오.

> ┤ 보기 ├
> dive　front　genius　fasteners

(1) He is a great _____ with patience.
(2) Even astronauts use Velcro _____.
(3) Many dolphins can _____ to depths of 200 meters.
(4) He was sitting in _____ of the fire.

**04** 다음 빈칸에 들어갈 말로 적절한 것은?

> The loud noise _____ the baby from sleeping.

① kept　　　　② took
③ made　　　　④ got
⑤ fascinated

**[05~07]** 다음 대회를 읽고 물음에 답하시오.

> Henry: What are you doing, Mina?
> Mina: I'm reading an article about a bug robot.
> Henry: A bug robot? Is it interesting?
> Mina: Yes. I'm really fascinated by this thing.
> Henry: Can you tell me more about it?
> Mina: You know that some bugs can slip into narrow spaces, don't you?
> Henry: Yeah. That's why (A)_____.
> Mina: (B)A bug robot can do the same. It can help to find survivors after earthquakes or big fires.
> Henry: That's really fascinating!

**05** 빈칸 (A)에 적절한 것은?

① it can be a useful machine
② it's hard to catch them
③ it's fascinating us
④ it's very interesting to watch
⑤ it's very difficult to imitate a bug

**06** 밑줄 친 (B)를 다음과 같이 바꾸어 쓸 때 빈칸에 적절한 단어를 쓰시오.

➡ A bug robot can do the same.
= The bug robot can _____ _____ narrow spaces.

**07** 위 대화의 내용과 일치하지 <u>않는</u> 것은?

① Mina is reading an article about a bug robot.
② Mina is fascinated by the bug robot.
③ Henry doesn't know the fact that some bugs can slip into narrow spaces.
④ It is not easy to catch bugs because they can slip into narrow spaces.
⑤ A bug robot can be used to find survivors after earthquakes.

**[08~09]** 다음 대화를 읽고 물음에 답하시오.

B: Have you heard of a mosquito needle, Jian?

G: A mosquito needle? ( A )

B: Some scientists made this new needle by imitating a mosquito's mouth. ( B )

G: That's interesting. ( C ) So how will that help?

B: You know mosquito bites are not very painful, don't you? ( D ) The new needle will also cause less pain.

G: That's great. ( E ) How come it's less painful?

B: Like a mosquito's mouth, it makes less contact with our skin.

G: Wow, I think that there's nothing useless in the world!

**08** (A)~(E) 중에서 다음 문장이 들어가기에 적절한 곳은?

> Can you explain it to me?

① (A)  ② (B)  ③ (C)  ④ (D)  ⑤ (E)

**09** 위 대화의 내용과 일치하는 것은?

① The boy didn't hear of a mosquito needle.
② The girl explains about a mosquito needle.
③ Some scientists imitated a mosquito needle.
④ A mosquito needle causes less pain.
⑤ A mosquito's mouth is useless.

**10** 다음 중 어법상 올바른 문장을 고르시오.

① Do you know what does this mean?
② I wonder you could point me in the right direction for the bus station.
③ What do you suppose I should do?
④ I'm not sure if she is our new leader in the near future.
⑤ Why do you know Jonathan left so early?

**11** 다음 중 어법상 어색한 문장을 고르시오.

① It is not only dirty but also rusty.
② I like not only studying but also go hiking.
③ Mike is a troublemaker not only at the office but also at home.
④ Inho is not only fun but also creative.
⑤ Kate is not only a smart but also a kind girl.

**12** 다음 우리말을 영어로 바르게 옮기지 않은 것은?

> 그 새로운 물질은 튼튼할 뿐만 아니라 사용하기도 쉽습니다.

① The new material is not only strong but also easy to use.
② The new material is not only strong but easy to use.
③ The new material is not only strong but easy to use as well.
④ The new material is easy to use as well as strong.
⑤ The new material is not strong but easy to use.

**13** 우리말과 일치하도록 할 때, 빈칸에 알맞은 것은?

> 내가 올 수 있을시 모르겠지만 노력은 해 볼게.
> → I don't know _____ I can come, but I'll try.

① if  ② that  ③ what
④ which  ⑤ how

**14** 그림을 보고 주어진 어휘를 이용하여 문장을 완성하시오.

➡ Yuna likes _____.
(listen to music, as, running)

**15** 다음 문장에서 'where'가 들어갈 위치로 알맞은 것을 고르시오.

> Do ① you ② know ③ the toilet ④ is ⑤?

①　　②　　③　　④　　⑤

**16** 두 문장이 같은 의미가 되도록, 빈칸에 알맞은 말을 쓰시오.

(1) Siyeong is eating not only salad but also steak.
　= Siyeong is eating steak _____ _____ _____ salad.
(2) Leonardo da Vinci invented not only a moving bridge but also a flying machine.
　= Leonardo da Vinci invented a flying machine _____ _____ _____ a moving bridge.
(3) Please tell me. + _____
　= Please tell me what she does.
(4) I don't know. + Where should I go?
　= _____

**[17~20]** 다음 글을 읽고 물음에 답하시오.

　The high-speed train was first made in Japan.
(A) He saw the bird quickly and quietly ① diving into the water. He wondered how the bird entered the water so gracefully. So, he studied more about the bird and discovered ② its long, narrow beak.
(B) A team of engineers tried to solve the problem, but they didn't know ③how could they reduce the noise. One day, one of the engineers was watching a bird in search of a meal.
(C) He redesigned the front of the train by imitating the bird's beak. It was successful. Now the new train travels not only ④more quietly but also 10% faster with 15% less electricity.
(D) But it had one problem. When the train ⑤entered a tunnel, the sudden increase in air pressure created a very loud sound. It often woke people up and caused headaches.

**17** 자연스러운 글이 되도록 (A)~(D)를 바르게 나열하시오.

➡ _____

**18** 위 글의 내용에 맞게 빈칸에 알맞은 말을 쓰시오.

> Because of a very loud sound, people used to _____ _____ and _____ _____ when the train went into a tunnel.

## 19 ①~⑤ 중 어법상 바르지 <u>않은</u> 것은?

①     ②     ③     ④     ⑤

## 20 다음 중 위 글의 내용과 일치하는 것은?

① Japan was famous for its noisy train.
② The engineers fixed the problem right away as soon as they detected it.
③ The front of the train was redesigned by copying the train of another country.
④ The new train travels as fast as the old one.
⑤ The old train used more electricity than the new one.

**[21~22]** 다음 글을 읽고 물음에 답하시오.

### Is Spider-Man Possible in Real Life?

A team of scientists questioned how ⓐcertain animals climb walls so easily. ⓑThey have observed what ⓒtheir feet look like and how ⓓthey stick to walls. (A)_____, ⓔthey invented a new material that sticks to any surface. "The new material is not only strong but also easy to use," says one of the scientists.

In the movie Spider-Man, Spider-Man climbs a tall building with just his hands and feet. Would that ever be possible in the real world? It doesn't sound impossible anymore!

## 21 빈칸 (A)에 들어갈 말로 가장 적절한 것은?

① On the contrary     ② For example
③ As a result     ④ However
⑤ That is to say

## 22 ⓐ~ⓔ 중 같은 것을 지칭하는 것끼리 바르게 묶으시오.

➡ _____

**[23~24]** 다음 글을 읽고 물음에 답하시오.

From flying birds to self-cleaning plants, the way nature works ①<u>fascinates</u> us. Some people not only use nature but also ②<u>create</u> it to find solutions to their problems. Leonardo da Vinci (1452-1519) was one such person. He wondered how birds could fly. He ③<u>closely</u> watched birds, made notes, and drew pictures of them. Even though his invention was not successful, he imitated a bird's wings to try to make ④<u>a flying machine</u>. Since then, more and more people have ⑤<u>successfully</u> imitated the surprising abilities of nature's genius. Let's explore some of them.

## 23 ①~⑤ 중 글의 흐름상 <u>어색한</u> 것은?

①     ②     ③     ④     ⑤

## 24 다음 중 위 글의 내용과 일치하지 <u>않는</u> 것은?

① There are plants which can self-clean.
② Leonardo da Vinci wanted to know how birds could fly.
③ Leonardo da Vinci studied birds hard.
④ Leonardo da Vinci copied birds' wings to try to make a flying machine.
⑤ People aren't interested in imitating nature's genius.

# Lesson

# 4

# I Don't See It That Way

## 🎙 의사소통 기능

- 만족이나 불만족 묻기
  How do you like the story?
- 이유 묻기
  Why do you think so?

## 🎙 언어 형식

- 과거완료
  The pig **had built** his house of bricks.
- 감정형용사+to부정사
  I'm **sorry to trouble** you.

# Words & Expressions

## Key Words

- **actually** [ǽktʃuəli] 부 실제로
- **advantage** [ədvǽntidʒ] 명 장점
- **apologize** [əpálədʒàiz] 동 사과하다
- **apology** [əpálədʒi] 명 사과
- **artwork** [ártwərk] 명 예술 작품
- **bathroom** [bǽθrùːm] 명 화장실
- **beak** [biːk] 명 부리
- **borrow** [bárou] 동 빌리다
- **bother** [báðər] 동 괴롭히다
- **brick** [brik] 명 벽돌
- **character** [kǽriktər] 명 등장인물
- **compare** [kəmpέər] 동 비교하다
- **complain** [kəmpléin] 동 불평하다
- **completely** [kəmplíːtli] 부 완전하게
- **creative** [kriéitiv] 형 창조적인
- **crime** [kraim] 명 범죄
- **decide** [disáid] 동 결정하다
- **deserve** [dizə́ːrv] 동 ~을 받을 만하다
- **drawing** [drɔ́ːiŋ] 명 그림
- **explain** [ikspléin] 동 설명하다
- **frame** [freim] 동 테를 두르다, 누명을 씌우다
- **frightening** [fráitniŋ] 형 무서운
- **grab** [græb] 동 붙잡다
- **hairy** [hέəri] 형 털이 많은
- **impolite** [impəláit] 형 무례한
- **independent** [indipéndənt] 형 자립심이 강한, 독립적인
- **invite** [inváit] 동 초대하다
- **lend** [lend] 동 빌려주다
- **mean** [miːn] 동 의미하다 형 인색한, 사나운
- **object** [ábdʒikt] 명 물건, 물체
- **original** [ərádʒənl] 형 원래의, 원본의
- **palace** [pǽlis] 명 궁전
- **peacefully** [píːsfəli] 부 평화롭게
- **performance** [pərfɔ́ːrməns] 명 성과, 공연
- **prefer** [prifə́ːr] 동 선호하다
- **response** [rispáns] 명 반응, 응답
- **responsible** [rispánsəbl] 형 책임이 있는
- **retelling** [riːtéliŋ] 명 다시 만든 이야기
- **rude** [ruːd] 형 무례한
- **scared** [skέərd] 형 겁먹은
- **shocked** [ʃɑkt] 형 충격을 받은
- **similar** [símələr] 형 비슷한, 유사한
- **skinny** [skíni] 형 마른
- **sneeze** [sniːz] 동 재채기하다
- **steadily** [stédili] 부 꾸준히
- **stepmother** [stépmʌðər] 명 계모
- **stork** [stɔːrk] 명 황새
- **straw** [strɔː] 명 짚, 지푸라기
- **support** [səpɔ́ːrt] 동 부양하다, 지지하다
- **sweat** [swet] 명 땀 동 땀을 흘리다
- **trouble** [trʌ́bl] 동 귀찮게 하다
- **turtle** [tə́ːrtl] 명 거북이
- **unfortunately** [ʌnfɔ́ːrtʃənətli] 부 불행하게도, 안타깝게도
- **unique** [juːníːk] 형 독특한

## Key Expressions

- **at least** 적어도
- **be afraid of** ~을 두려워하다
- **be made of** ~로 만들어지다
- **be responsible for** ~에 책임이 있다
- **be taken to** 끌려가다
- **blow down** 바람을 불어 넘어뜨리다
- **break into** 침입하다
- **fall in love with** ~와 사랑에 빠지다
- **I can't wait to** ~ 너무 ~하고 싶다
- **instead of** ~ 대신에
- **go perfectly with** 매우 잘 어울리다
- **keep -ing** 계속해서 ~하다
- **look for** ~을 찾다
- **make money** 돈을 벌다
- **make sense** 의미가 통하다, 이해가 되다
- **on one's own** 스스로
- **point of view** 관점, 견해
- **run out of** ~이 다 떨어지다
- **take a look at** ~을 살펴보다

## Word Power

※ 서로 비슷한 뜻을 가진 어휘

- ☐ **actually** 실제로 – **really** 사실은
- ☐ **beak** 부리 – **bill** 부리
- ☐ **decide** 결정하다 – **determine** 결정하다
- ☐ **grab** 붙잡다 – **grasp** 움켜쥐다
- ☐ **performance** 성과 – **achievement** 성취
- ☐ **scared** 겁먹은 – **fearful** 겁먹은

- ☐ **artwork** 예술 작품 – **craft** 공예품
- ☐ **bother** 괴롭히다 – **irritate** 성가시게 하다
- ☐ **explain** 설명하다 – **illustrate** 설명하다
- ☐ **impolite** 무례한 – **rude** 무례한
- ☐ **response** 반응, 응답 – **reply** 응답
- ☐ **unique** 독특한 – **particular** 특별한

※ 서로 반대의 뜻을 가진 어휘

- ☐ **advantage** 장점 ↔ **disadvantage** 단점
- ☐ **complain** 불평하다 ↔ **compliment** 칭찬하다
- ☐ **dependent** 의존적인 ↔ **independent** 독립적인
- ☐ **polite** 예의바른 ↔ **impolite** 무례한
- ☐ **rude** 무례한 ↔ **polite** 예의 바른

- ☐ **borrow** 빌리다 ↔ **lend** 빌려주다
- ☐ **creative** 창조적인 ↔ **uncreative** 창조적이지 않은
- ☐ **fortunately** 다행스럽게 ↔ **unfortunately** 불행하게도
- ☐ **responsible** 책임이 있는 ↔ **irresponsible** 무책임한
- ☐ **similar** 비슷한, 유사한 ↔ **different** 다른

※ 동사 – 명사

- ☐ **apologize** 사과하다 – **apology** 사과
- ☐ **complain** 불평하다 – **complaint** 불평
- ☐ **explain** 설명하다 – **explanation** 설명
- ☐ **perform** 수행하다 – **performance** 수행
- ☐ **respond** 반응하다 – **response** 반응, 응답

- ☐ **compare** 비교하다 – **comparison** 비교
- ☐ **decide** 결정하다 – **decision** 결정
- ☐ **invite** 초대하다 – **invitation** 초대
- ☐ **prefer** 선호하다 – **preference** 선호

※ 명사 – 형용사

- ☐ **advantage** 장점 – **advantageous** 유리한
- ☐ **creation** 창조 – **creative** 창조적인
- ☐ **response** 반응 – **responsive** 반응하는

- ☐ **comparison** 비교 – **comparative** 비교적인
- ☐ **decision** 결정 – **decisive** 결정적인

## English Dictionary

- ☐ **apology** 사과
  - → a statement saying that you are sorry about something 어떤 것에 대해 미안하다고 하는 말
- ☐ **crime** 범죄
  - → an illegal action or activity for which a person can be punished by law
    사람이 법에 의해 처벌받을 수 있는 불법적인 행동이나 행위
- ☐ **deserve** ~을 받을 만하다
  - → be worthy
    가치가 있다
- ☐ **independent** 자립심이 강한, 독립적인
  - → confident and free to do things without needing help from other people
    다른 사람으로부터의 도움 없이 일을 하기에 자신 있고 자유로운
- ☐ **similar** 비슷한, 유사한

  - → having features that are the same
    같은 특징을 가지고 있는
- ☐ **sneeze** 재채기하다
  - → to have air come suddenly and noisily out through your nose and mouth in a way that you cannot control
    통제할 수 없는 방식으로 입과 코를 통해 갑작스럽고 요란하게 공기를 내보내다
- ☐ **straw** 짚, 지푸라기
  - → the dry stems of wheat and other grain plants
    밀과 다른 곡물의 마른 줄기
- ☐ **trouble** 귀찮게 하다
  - → to disturb or bother someone
    어떤 사람을 방해하거나 성가시게 하다
- ☐ **unfortunately** 불행하게도, 안타깝게도
  - → by bad luck
    불운에 의해

**01** 다음 짝지어진 단어의 관계가 같도록 빈칸에 알맞은 말을 쓰시오.

> respond : response = apologize : _____

**02** 다음 영영풀이가 가리키는 것을 고르시오.

> to have air come suddenly and noisily out through your nose and mouth in a way that you cannot control

① sneeze      ② apologize

③ compare      ④ support

⑤ grab

**03** 다음 중 밑줄 친 부분의 뜻풀이가 바르지 <u>않은</u> 것은?

① Going away to a college has made me more <u>independent</u>. (독립적인)

② We carefully <u>compared</u> the first report with the second. (비교했다)

③ They are playing an important <u>match</u> now. (경기, 시합)

④ We're playing <u>against</u> the league champions next week. (또한, 역시)

⑤ She gave me a <u>bright</u> smile. (밝은)

**04** 다음 우리말에 맞게 빈칸을 완성하시오.

(1) 돼지는 그의 집을 벽돌로 지었다.

  ➡ The pig built his house of _____.

(2) 나는 내 동생이 더 자립심이 강해지길 바란다.

  ➡ I want my brother to be more _____.

(3) 나는 느리고 꾸준히 걷는 것을 더 좋아한다.

  ➡ I prefer to walk slowly and _____.

**05** 다음 문장의 빈칸에 들어갈 말을 〈보기〉에서 골라 쓰시오.

> ┤ 보기 ├
>
> fall in love with / goes perfectly with / is made of / broke into / run out of

(1) I'm afraid we've _____ gas.

(2) Somebody _____ our house.

(3) Did you _____ Minsu?

(4) It _____ your hair color.

(5) This food _____ meat and vegetables.

**06** 다음 주어진 문장의 밑줄 친 frame과 같은 의미로 쓰인 것은?

> His family insisted that he was <u>framed</u>.

① John has responsibility for making the <u>frame</u> of a bicycle.

② Stretch the cloth over the <u>frame</u>.

③ It turned out that Jack was <u>framed</u> for the crimes committed by Peter.

④ This <u>frame</u> is made of metal, so it's so strong.

⑤ Susan is standing by the wooden <u>frame</u>.

**07** 다음 문장에 공통으로 들어갈 말은?

> • I'm afraid _____ what will happen if I fail the test.
> • I usually use a coconut oil instead _____ butter when I cook.
> • These clothes are made _____ silk.

① to      ② from      ③ of

④ on      ⑤ by

**01** 다음 짝지어진 단어의 관계가 같도록 빈칸에 알맞은 말을 쓰시오.

> polite : impolite = responsible : _____

➡ _____

**02** 다음 문장의 빈칸에 들어갈 말을 〈보기〉에서 골라 쓰시오.

┌─ 보기 ├─
completely / framed / apology / bricks /
impolite
└─────────────────

(1) It's _____ to talk during the performance.
(2) We received a letter of _____ .
(3) He says he was _____ .
(4) Most of the buildings in the town are made of _____ .
(5) I've _____ forgotten his name.

**03** 다음 우리말에 맞게 빈칸에 알맞은 말을 쓰시오.

(1) 너 혼자 파티에 가는 것은 별로 재미있지 않다.
➡ It's not much fun to go to a party _____ _____ _____ .
(2) 이 예술 작품을 그의 관점에서 보아라.
➡ Look at this artwork from _____ _____ _____ .
(3) 적어도 출발 시간 한 시간 전에 체크인해 주세요.
➡ Please check in _____ _____ one hour before departure time.
(4) 차 대신에 커피를 마실게요.
➡ I'll have coffee _____ _____ tea, please.

**04** 다음 우리말과 일치하도록 주어진 단어를 모두 배열하여 영작하시오.

(1) 활짝 핀 꽃들은 매우 아름답지만, 내가 재채기를 하게 한다.
(flowers / pretty / the / they / sneeze / me / blooming / are / but / very / make)
➡ _____
_____

(2) 그렇게 힘든 일을 했으니 너는 쉴 자격이 있다.
(rest / hard / that / a / all / work / you / after / deserve)
➡ _____

(3) 황새가 부리로 생선을 잡는다.
(its / holds / a fish / beak / a stork / in)
➡ _____

**05** 다음 우리말을 주어진 단어를 이용하여 영작하시오.

(1) 나는 그의 관점에 대해서는 결코 생각해 본 적이 없었다. (about, point)
➡ _____

(2) 나는 설탕이 다 떨어졌다. (ran, of)
➡ _____

(3) 모든 것은 어떤 이유로 일어난다. (happens, reason)
➡ _____

(4) 회사는 어떻게 돈을 버나요? (make, company)
➡ _____

# Conversation

교과서

**1** 만족이나 불만족 묻기

**How do you like the story?** 그 이야기가 어때?

■ 'How do[did] you like ~?'는 '너는 ~이 어때[어땠어]?' 또는 '너는 ~이 좋아[좋았어]/마음에 드니?'라는 뜻으로, 상대방이 어떤 대상에 대해 만족하는지 또는 만족하지 않는지 묻는 표현이다. 이에 대한 응답으로는 주로 만족 여부와 그 이유가 나온다. 'How do you like ~?'는 '(음식 등을) 어떻게 해드릴까요?'의 의미를 나타내기도 한다.

■ 'How do you like ~?'에 대하여 대답할 때는 만족하는지 아닌지를 직접적으로 나타내어 'It is great.', 'It is nice.', 'It wasn't bad.' 등으로 대답하거나 'It isn't easy.', 'It isn't interesting.' 등으로 대답한다.

■ 만족이나 불만족에 대하여 물을 때는 'Are you satisfied with ~?' 또는 'Are you happy with ~?'를 사용하여 '~에 만족하니?'라고 물어보기도 한다. 'Do you like ~?(~을 좋아하니?)'와 'Is this the one that you want(ed)?(이것이 네가 원하는 것이니?)' 같은 표현도 만족이나 불만족을 물어보는 표현이 된다.

### 만족이나 불만족에 관해 묻기

- How do you like it? 그것이 마음에 드니?
- Are you satisfied with it? 그것이 만족스럽니?
  = Are you happy with it?
- Do you like it? 너는 그것을 좋아하니?
- Is this what you wanted? 이것이 네가 원한 것이니?
  = Is this the one that you wanted?

### 만족이나 불만족에 대한 대답

- It is great. = It is nice. 좋아.
- It wasn't bad. 나쁘지 않았어.

### 핵심 Check

1. 다음 우리말에 맞게 빈칸을 채우시오.

> T: Have you seen this movie, *Along with the God?*
>
> Ss: Yes. I have.
>
> T: How _____ _____ _____ the movie? (영화가 어땠어요?)
>
> S1: It was interesting. I'd never thought about what happens after I die.
>
> T: Me, neither. The story was quite unique. Anyone else?
>
> S2: To me, the story was unrealistic. I didn't like it.

## 2 이유 묻기

> **Why do you think so?** 왜 그렇게 생각하니?

- 상대방이 왜 그렇게 말하는지, 혹은 왜 그렇게 생각하는지 등에 대해 이유를 물을 때는 'Why do you think so?(왜 그렇게 생각해?)' 또는 'Why do you say that?(왜 그렇게 말하니?)'과 같은 표현을 사용하여 물을 수 있다.

- 상대방의 생각이나 말의 이유를 물을 때는 'What makes you say that?', 'What makes you think so?'와 같은 표현을 쓸 수도 있다. 이는 '무엇 때문에 그런 말을 하니/그렇게 생각하니?'의 의미로 상대방이 한 말의 이유를 확인하거나 상대방의 생각에 대한 부연 설명을 듣고 싶을 때 쓰는 표현이다. 이런 질문에 대답할 때는 단순히 자기 생각이나 이유를 말하면 되고, Because를 붙여서 말해도 된다.

- 의문사로 시작하는 이유를 묻는 말 앞에 'Can you tell me'나 'I'd like to know', 'I wonder' 등을 붙여, 간접의문문의 형식으로 좀 더 격식을 갖춰 물어볼 수도 있다. 이유를 말할 때에는 문장 앞에 'I think'나 'In my opinion' 등을 덧붙일 수도 있다.

#### 이유 묻기

- Why do you think so? 왜 그렇게 생각하니?
- I wonder what makes you say that. 무엇 때문에 그런 말을 하는지 궁금해.
- Why is that? 왜 그렇지?
- Can you tell me (the reason) why ~? ~한 이유를 설명해 주겠니?

#### 이유 대답하기

- I did it because ~ ~ 때문에 그렇게 했어요.
- (Because) ~ 왜냐하면 ~ 때문이야.
- That's because ~ 그것은 ~ 때문입니다.

### 핵심 Check

2. 다음 밑줄 친 (A)를 대신해서 쓰기에 가장 적절한 것은?

> W: You look worried, Juwon.
> B: I think we will lose the soccer game tomorrow, Ms. Kim.
> W: (A)Why do you think so?
> B: We will have a match against Class 3. They have the strongest players in the school.

① What makes you think so?　② Why do you make so?

③ What do you make?　④ What did you have?

⑤ How do you think so?

**Listen and Speak 1 A**

G: Have you finished the book, Taeho?

B: Yes. I finished ❶it yesterday, Anna.

G: How did you like ❶it?

B: It was interesting.

G: What is the book about?

B: You know the story of Heungbu, right? In the book, Nolbu tells the story from his ❷point of view.

G: What does ❸he say?

B: Well, ❸he says he didn't help Heungbu for a reason. ❸He wanted Heungbu to ❹make money ❺on his own and be independent.

G: Wow, it's a unique story! ❻I can't wait to read the book. Thanks, Taeho.

G: 책 다 읽었니, 태호야?
B: 응. 어제 다 읽었어, Anna.
G: 어땠니?
B: 재미있었어.
G: 그 책은 무슨 내용이니?
B: 너 흥부 이야기 알지, 그렇지? 책에서는 놀부가 자신의 관점에서 이야기해.
G: 놀부가 뭐라고 하는데?
B: 음, 놀부는 이유가 있어서 흥부를 도와주지 않았다고 말하고 있어. 그는 흥부가 스스로 돈을 벌고 자립할 수 있기를 바랐거든.
G: 와, 독특한 이야기구나! 그 책을 빨리 읽고 싶어. 고마워 태호야.

❶ it은 the book을 가리킨다. ❷ point of view: 관점 ❸ he는 모두 'Nolbu'를 가리킨다. ❹ make money: 돈을 벌다 ❺ on one's own: 스스로 ❻ I can't wait to ~: 너무 ~하고 싶다

**Check(√) True or False**

(1) Taeho finished the book about Heungbu yesterday.　　　　　　　　T ☐ F ☐

(2) Taeho wanted Heungbu to make money on his own.　　　　　　　T ☐ F ☐

 **Listen and Speak 2 A**

W: You ❶look worried, Juwon.

B: I think we will lose the soccer game tomorrow, Ms. Kim.

W: ❷Why do you think so?

B: We will have a match ❸against Class 3. They have ❹the strongest players in the school.

W: Look on the bright side. They might have strong players, but your class has the best teamwork.

B: You're right. I didn't think about it that way. I'll go and practice!

W: 걱정스러워 보이는구나, 주원아.
B: 내일 축구 경기에서 질 것 같아요, 김 선생님.
W: 왜 그렇게 생각하니?
B: 저희는 3반과 경기가 있거든요. 3반에는 학교에서 가장 잘하는 선수들이 있어요.
W: 긍정적으로 생각하렴. 3반에 잘하는 선수들이 있을지 모르지만, 너희 반은 팀워크가 가장 좋잖아.
B: 선생님 말씀이 맞아요. 저는 그렇게는 생각하지 못했어요. 가서 연습할게요!

❶ look+형용사: ~하게 보이다 ❷ 이유를 묻는 표현으로 'What makes you say so?' 등으로 바꾸어 표현할 수 있다.
❸ against는 전치사로 '~에 맞서, 반대하여'를 뜻한다. ❹ the+최상급: 가장 ~한

**Check(√) True or False**

(3) Juwon looks worried because his team lost the soccer game.　　　T ☐ F ☐

(4) Juwon is one of the strongest players in his school.　　　　　　T ☐ F ☐

### Listen and Speak 1 B

B: ❶How did you like the movie *Good Friends*, Yura?

G: I liked ❷it. It was fun to ❸compare the movie with the original book.

B: Which did you like better, the movie or the book?

G: Well, I liked the movie, but I think I enjoyed the book more. The book ❹helped me understand the characters better.

B: That's interesting. To me, the movie was better because ❺it was easier to understand the story.

G: That's true. I guess ❻they both have their own advantages.

B: You're right.

❶ How do[did] you like ~?: 너는 ~이 어때[어땠어]?, 너는 ~이 좋아[좋았어]/마음에 드니?
❷ it은 the movie *Good Friends*를 가리킨다.
❸ compare: 비교하다
❹ help는 준사역동사로 목적격보어로 원형부정사를 취할 수 있기 때문에 understand가 이어졌다.
❺ it은 the movie를 가리킨다. ❻ they는 책과 영화를 가리킨다.

### Listen and Speak 2 B

M: What do you think about my drawing, Prince?

B: Wow, this picture is very ❶frightening!

M: Why do you think so?

B: I mean the picture shows a snake ❷that ate an elephant.

M: You're right. Actually, many people thought it was a picture of a hat.

B: Really? That's interesting.

M: I know. ❸That's why I decided to become a pilot ❹instead of a painter.

B: Haha. ❺At least I can understand what you mean.

M: Thank you, Prince.

❶ frightening: 무서운 ❷ 주격 관계대명사로 which로 바꾸어 쓸 수 있다.
❸ That's why ~.: 그것이 ~한 이유이다. ❹ instead of: ~ 대신에
❺ at least: 적어도

### Real Life Communication

Ms. Parker: Now, ❶take a look at this work of art. How do you like ❷it?

Jinho: Well, is it even art?

Henry: To me, it isn't more than a ❸toilet.

Ms. Parker: It is not just art. I think it is the greatest piece of art of the 20th century.

Mina: Why do you think so?

Ms. Parker: It is a perfect example of a different ❹point of view. The artist used ❺real-life objects to create art.

Claire: So, he didn't create something new?

Ms. Parker: That's right. He simply wanted people to look at the objects in a different way.

Mina: Thank you so much, Ms. Parker. I learned a lot today!

❶ take a look at ~을 살펴보다 ❷ it은 the work of art를 가리킨다.
❸ toilet: 변기 ❹ point of view 관점, 견해
❺ real-life object: 실생활 물건

### Let's Check

B: Do you know the story *The Rabbit and the Turtle*?

G: Of course, I do.

B: I think the turtle in the story is ❶mean.

G: Why do you think so?

B: The turtle sees the rabbit ❷sleeping but doesn't wake ❸him up. It is not ❹fair.

G: I don't see it that way. Why should the turtle ❺be responsible for the rabbit? I don't think he should be.

B: That's interesting.

❶ mean: 인색한, 못된 ❷ 현재분사로 동작의 진행을 나타낸다.
❸ him은 the rabbit을 가리킨다. ❹ fair: 공정한
❺ be responsible for: ~에 책임이 있다

● 다음 우리말과 일치하도록 빈칸에 알맞은 말을 쓰시오.

### Listen & Speak 1 A

G: Have you _____ the book, Taeho?

B: Yes. I finished it yesterday, Anna.

G: _____ _____ _____ _____ it?

B: It was _____.

G: _____ is the book _____?

B: You know the story of Heungbu, right? In the book, Nolbu tells the story from his _____ _____ _____.

G: What does he say?

B: Well, he says he didn't help Heungbu for a _____. He wanted Heungbu to _____ _____ on his own and be _____.

G: Wow, it's a _____ story! I _____ _____ _____ read the book. Thanks, Taeho.

### Listen & Speak 1 B

B: _____ did you _____ the movie *Good Friends*, Yura?

G: I liked it. It was fun to _____ the movie _____ the original book.

B: _____ did you like _____, the movie or the book?

G: Well, I liked the movie, but I think I _____ the book _____. The book helped me _____ the _____ better.

B: That's interesting. To me, the movie was _____ because it was _____ to understand the story.

G: That's true. I guess they _____ have their own _____.

B: You're right.

### Listen & Speak 2 A

W: You look worried, Juwon.

B: I think we will _____ _____ _____ _____ tomorrow, Ms. Kim.

W: Why do _____ _____ _____?

B: We will have a _____ _____ Class 3. They have the _____ players in the school.

W: Look on the _____ _____. They might have strong players, but your class has the best _____.

B: You're right. I didn't think about it _____ _____. I'll go and practice!

해석

G: 그 책 다 읽었니, 태호야?

B: 응. 어제 다 읽었어, Anna.

G: 어땠니?

B: 재미있었어.

G: 그 책은 무슨 내용이니?

B: 너 흥부 이야기 알지, 그렇지? 책에서는 놀부가 자신의 관점에서 이야기해.

G: 놀부가 뭐라고 하는데?

B: 음, 놀부는 이유가 있어서 흥부를 도와주지 않았다고 말하고 있어. 그는 흥부가 스스로 돈을 벌고 자립할 수 있기를 바랐거든.

G: 와, 독특한 이야기구나! 그 책을 빨리 읽고 싶어. 고마워, 태호야.

B: 'Good Friends' 영화 어땠니, 유라야?

G: 좋았어. 영화를 원작과 비교하는 게 재미있었어.

B: 너는 영화와 책 중 어떤 것이 더 좋았니?

G: 글쎄, 영화가 좋았지만 책이 더 재미있었던 것 같아. 책이 등장인물을 더 잘 이해하게 해줬거든.

B: 그거 흥미롭구나. 나는 이야기를 이해하기 더 쉬워서 영화가 더 좋았어.

G: 그건 맞아. 책과 영화 둘 다 각각의 장점들이 있는 것 같아.

B: 맞아.

W: 걱정스러워 보이는구나, 주원아.

B: 내일 축구 경기에서 질 것 같아요, 김 선생님.

W: 왜 그렇게 생각하니?

B: 저희는 3반과 경기가 있거든요. 3반에는 학교에서 가장 잘하는 선수들이 있잖아요.

W: 긍정적으로 생각하렴. 3반에 잘하는 선수들이 있을지 모르지만, 너희 반은 팀워크가 가장 좋잖아.

B: 선생님 말씀이 맞아요. 저는 그렇게는 생각하지 못했어요. 가서 연습할게요!

## Listen & Speak 2 B

M: _____ do you _____ about my drawing, Prince?

B: Wow, this picture is very _____!

M: _____ do you _____ _____?

B: I mean the picture shows a _____ that _____ an elephant.

M: You're right. Actually, many people thought it was a picture of a _____.

B: Really? That's _____.

M: I know. That's why I _____ to become a _____ _____ _____ a painter.

B: Haha. _____ I can understand _____ _____ _____.

M: Thank you, Prince.

## Real Life Communication

Ms. Parker: Now, take a look at this work of art. _____ _____ you _____ it?

Jinho: Well, is it even art?

Henry: _____ _____, it isn't more than a _____.

Ms. Parker: It is not just art. I think it is the _____ piece of art of the 20th century.

Mina: _____ do you _____ _____?

Ms. Parker: It is a perfect example of a _____ _____ _____ _____. The artist used _____ _____ to create art.

Claire: So, he didn't create _____ _____?

Ms. Parker: That's _____. He simply wanted people to look at the _____ in a _____ way.

Mina: Thank you so much, Ms. Parker. I learned a lot today!

## Let's Check

B: Do you know the story *The Rabbit and the Turtle*?

G: Of course, I do.

B: I think the _____ in the story is _____.

G: Why do you _____ _____?

B: The turtle sees the rabbit _____ but doesn't _____ _____ _____. It is not _____.

G: I don't see it _____ _____. Why should the turtle _____ _____ _____ the rabbit? I don't think he should be.

B: That's interesting.

해석

M: 왕자님, 제 그림에 대해 어떻게 생각하세요?

B: 우와, 이 그림은 너무 무섭군요!

M: 왜 그렇게 생각하죠?

B: 그림이 코끼리를 먹은 뱀을 보여주잖아요.

M: 왕자님 말이 맞아요. 사실 많은 사람들이 모자 그림이라고 생각했어요.

B: 정말요? 그거 재미있군요.

M: 맞아요. 그래서 제가 화가 대신에 비행사가 되기로 결심했던 거예요.

B: 하하. 적어도 나는 당신이 무엇을 의도한 건지 이해할 수 있어요.

M: 고마워요, 왕자님.

Ms. Parker: 자, 이 예술 작품을 보세요. 어떤가요?

Jinho: 글쎄요, 이것도 예술인가요?

Henry: 저한테는 변기 그 이상은 아닌데요.

Ms. Parker: 이건 그냥 예술이 아니에요. 나는 20세기의 가장 위대한 예술 작품이라고 생각해요.

Mina: 왜 그렇게 생각하세요?

Ms. Parker: 이것은 다른 관점에 대한 완벽한 예시예요. 작가는 작품을 만들기 위해 실생활 물건을 사용했어요.

Claire: 그러면 작가가 새로운 것을 만들지 않았다는 건가요?

Ms. Parker: 맞아요. 그는 그저 사람들이 다른 방식으로 사물을 보기를 원했어요.

Mina: 정말 감사합니다. Parker 선생님. 오늘 많은 걸 배웠어요!

B: 너는 '토끼와 거북이' 이야기를 아니?

G: 물론 알지.

B: 난 그 이야기 속의 거북이가 못됐다고 생각해.

G: 왜 그렇게 생각하니?

B: 거북이는 토끼가 자고 있는 것을 보지만 그를 깨우지 않잖아. 그건 공정하지 않아.

G: 나는 그렇게 보지 않아. 왜 거북이가 토끼에 대해 책임을 져야 해? 그가 그래야 한다고 생각하지 않아.

B: 흥미로운데.

[01~02] 다음 대화를 읽고 물음에 답하시오.

Anna: Have you finished the book, Taeho?

Taeho: Yes. I finished it yesterday, Anna.

Anna: How did you like it?

Taeho: It was interesting.

Anna: What is the book about?

Taeho: You know the story of Heungbu, right? In the book, Nolbu tells the story from his point of view.

Anna: What does he say?

Taeho: Well, he says he didn't help Heungbu for a reason. He wanted Heungbu to make money on his own and be independent.

Anna: Wow, it's a unique story! (A)I can't wait to read the book. (forward) Thanks, Taeho.

**01** 위 대화의 밑줄 친 (A)와 의미가 같도록 주어진 단어를 사용하여 다시 쓰시오.

➡ _____

**02** 위 대화의 내용과 일치하지 <u>않는</u> 것은?

① 태호는 어제 그 책을 다 읽었다.

② 태호는 놀부의 관점에서 이야기하는 책을 읽었다.

③ Anna는 흥부 이야기에 대해 알고 있다.

④ 놀부는 흥부가 스스로 돈을 벌고 자립할 수 있기를 바랐다.

⑤ 놀부는 아무런 이유 없이 흥부를 돕지 않았다.

**03** 다음 대화가 자연스럽게 이어지도록 순서대로 배열하시오.

Jack: Do you know the story *The Rabbit and the Turtle?*

(A) Why do you think so?

(B) I think the turtle in the story is mean.

(C) Of course, I do.

(D) I don't see it that way. Why should the turtle be responsible for the rabbit? I don't think he should be.

(E) The turtle sees the rabbit sleeping but doesn't wake him up. It is not fair.

Jack: That's interesting.

➡ _____

[01~02] 다음 대화를 읽고 물음에 답하시오.

Brian: How did you like the movie *Good Friends*, Yura?

Yura: I liked it. It was fun to compare the movie with the original book. (A)

Brian: Which did you like better, the movie or the book?

Yura: Well, I liked the movie, but I think I enjoyed the book more. (B)

Brian: That's interesting. To me, the movie was better because it was easier to understand the story. (C)

Yura: That's true. I guess they both have their own advantages. (D)

Brian: You're right. (E)

**01** 위 대화의 (A)~(E) 중 주어진 문장이 들어가기에 적절한 곳은?

The book helped me understand the characters better.

① (A)  ② (B)  ③ (C)  ④ (D)  ⑤ (E)

**02** 위 대화의 내용과 일치하지 않는 것은?

① 유라는 영화 'Good Friends'와 원작을 비교하는 게 재미있었다.

② 유라는 영화도 좋았지만 책이 더 재미있었다.

③ 유라는 책이 등장인물을 더 잘 이해하게 해줬다고 생각한다.

④ Brian은 이야기를 이해하기가 더 쉬워서 책이 더 좋았다.

⑤ 유라는 책과 영화 둘 다 각각의 장점이 있다고 생각한다.

[03~05] 다음 대화를 읽고 물음에 답하시오.

Ms. Kim: You look worried, Juwon.

Juwon: I think we will lose the soccer game tomorrow, Ms. Kim. (A)

Ms. Kim: Why do you think so? (B)

Juwon: We will have a match against Class 3. They have the strongest players in the school. (C)

Ms. Kim: Look on the bright side. (D)

Juwon: You're right. I didn't think about it that way. I'll go and practice! (E)

**03** 위 대화의 (A)~(E) 중 주어진 문장이 들어가기에 가장 적절한 곳은?

They might have strong players, but your class has the best teamwork.

① (A)  ② (B)  ③ (C)  ④ (D)  ⑤ (E)

**04** 위 대화에서 주원이의 기분 변화로 적절한 것은?

① anxious → encouraged

② nervous → anxious

③ bored → pleased

④ pleased → encouraged

⑤ satisfied → anxious

**05** 위 대화의 내용과 일치하도록 주원이의 일기를 완성하시오.

I was worried that my team will (A)_____ _____ tomorrow. My team will have a match against (B)_____. They have (C)_____ in the school. But Ms. Kim let me (D)_____ _____. She reminded me of our best teamwork. I think we can beat them. I practiced again with my team members. I'm looking forward to having a match.

[06~07] 다음 대화를 읽고 물음에 답하시오.

Ms. Parker: Now, take a look at this work of art. How do you like it?

Jinho: Well, is it even art?

Henry: To me, it isn't more than a toilet.

Ms. Parker: It is not just art. I think it is the greatest piece of art of the 20th century.

Mina: (A)_____

Ms. Parker: It is a perfect example of a different point of view. The artist used real-life objects to create art.

Claire: So, he didn't create something new?

Ms. Parker: That's right. He simply wanted people to look at the objects in a different way.

Mina: Thank you so much, Ms. Parker. I learned a lot today!

**06** 위 대화의 빈칸 (A)에 들어갈 말로 나머지와 의도가 다른 것은?

① Why do you think so?

② What makes you think so?

③ I wonder what makes you say that.

④ Why is that?

⑤ How do you like it?

**07** 위 대화의 내용과 일치하지 않는 것은?

① Henry에게 그 예술 작품은 변기 그 이상은 아니다.

② Ms. Parker는 그 예술 작품이 20세기의 가장 위대한 예술 작품이라고 생각한다.

③ 그 예술 작품은 다른 관점에 대한 완전한 예시이다.

④ 작가는 그 작품을 만들기 위해 실생활 물건을 사용했다.

⑤ 작가는 새로운 것을 만들어 사람들이 다른 방식으로 사물을 보기를 원했다.

[08~09] 다음 대화를 읽고 물음에 답하시오.

Mike: (A)_____, Prince?

Prince: Wow, this picture is very frightening!

Mike: Why do you think so?

Prince: I mean the picture shows a snake that ate an elephant.

Mike: You're right. Actually, many people thought it was a picture of a hat.

Prince: Really? That's interesting.

Mike: I know. That's why I decided to become a pilot instead of a painter.

Prince: Haha. At least I can understand what you mean.

Mike: Thank you, Prince.

서답형
**08** 위 대화의 빈칸 (A)에 들어갈 말을 〈보기〉에 주어진 단어들을 모두 배열하여 영작하시오.

┌─── 보기 ───┐
think / my / do / what / you / drawing / about
└──────────┘

➡ _____

서답형
**09** 위 대화의 내용과 일치하도록 빈칸을 완성하시오.

Prince: When I looked at Mike's picture, it was so (1)_____ because it showed me a (2)_____ which (3)_____. On the other hand, Mike told me that many people thought it was a (4)_____ _____. It sounded interesting. I thought everyone has their own different points of view.

**[01~03]** 다음 대화를 읽고 물음에 답하시오.

Anna: Have you finished the book, Taeho?

Taeho: Yes. I finished it yesterday, Anna.

Anna: How did you like it?

Taeho: It was interesting.

Anna: What is the book about?

Taeho: You know the story of Heungbu, right? In the book, Nolbu tells the story from his (A)_____.

Anna: What does he say?

Taeho: Well, he says he didn't help Heungbu for a reason. He wanted Heungbu to make money on his own and be independent.

Anna: Wow, it's a unique story! I can't wait to read the book. Thanks, Taeho.

**01** 위 대화의 빈칸 (A)에 '관점'을 나타내는 표현을 3단어로 완성하시오.

➡ _____

**02** What is the book Taeho read about?

➡ It is about the story of _____ written from _____ point of view.

**03** In the book, what did Nolbu want Heungbu to do?

➡ _____

_____

**04** 다음 대화의 내용과 일치하도록 빈칸을 완성하시오.

Jack: Do you know the story *The Rabbit and the Turtle*?

Sora: Of course, I do.

Jack: I think the turtle in the story is mean.

Sora: Why do you think so?

Jack: The turtle sees the rabbit sleeping but doesn't wake him up. It is not fair.

Sora: I don't see it that way. Why should the turtle be responsible for the rabbit? I don't think he should be.

Jack: That's interesting.

⬇

Jack and Sora had a different opinion about the story *The Rabbit and the Turtle*. Jack insisted that the turtle in the story was (A)_____ because (B)_____ _____even though he saw the rabbit (C)_____. On the other hand, Sora claimed that the turtle wasn't (D)_____ for waking him up.

**05** 다음 대화가 자연스럽게 이어지도록 순서대로 배열하시오.

Brian: How did you like the movie *Good Friends*, Yura?

Yura: I liked it. It was fun to compare the movie with the original book.

(A) You're right.

(B) That's true. I guess they both have their own advantages.

(C) Which did you like better, the movie or the book?

(D) That's interesting. To me, the movie was better because it was easier to understand the story.

(E) Well, I liked the movie, but I think I enjoyed the book more. The book helped me understand the characters better.

➡ _____

## 교과서
# Grammar

**1 과거완료시제: had + p.p.**

**The pig had built his house of bricks.** 돼지는 그의 집을 벽돌로 지었다.

■ 과거완료 시제는 특정한 과거 시점보다 더 이전의 과거 시점을 나타낸다.
  • Jay **had gone** out when I arrived at the office. (내가 사무실에 도착했을 때 Jay는 외출하고 없었다.)

■ 완료, 계속, 경험, 결과 등의 용법이 있고, 과거의 어느 시점보다 먼저 일어난 일이나 상태를 나타낼 때도 쓰이며 이것을 보통 '대과거'라고 한다.
  • They **had arrived** at the house before night fell. (그들은 밤이 오기 전에 집에 도착했다.) 〈완료〉
  • He **had lived** there for five years until his girlfriend left him. (그는 여자친구가 그를 떠나기 전까지 그곳에 5년 동안 살아 왔었다.) 〈계속〉
  • She **had thought** very deeply about this problem once. (그녀는 한번은 이 문제에 대해 아주 깊이 생각했었다.) 〈경험〉
  • Spring **had come** by the time she almost forgot him. (그녀가 거의 그를 잊었을 때쯤 봄이 찾아왔다) 〈결과〉
  • He realized that he **had met** her before. (그는 전에 그녀를 만난 적이 있었다는 것을 깨달았다.) 〈대과거〉
  • We were relieved that Jun **had returned** home safely. (Jun이 집에 안전히 돌아와서 우리는 안도했다.) 〈대과거〉

■ 접속사 when, after, before와 같이 시간을 나타내는 말들과 함께 쓰이는 경우가 많다.
  • When I saw her, I realized she **had had** a haircut. 내가 그녀를 봤을 때, 나는 그녀가 머리카락을 잘랐다는 것을 알았다.
  • The train **had just left** when we arrived at the station. 우리가 역에 도착했을 때 기차가 막 떠났다.

■ 한 문장에 두 가지 과거의 일이 나올 때, 두 동작이 거의 동시에 일어났거나 시간차가 거의 없이 연속적으로 일어났을 경우에는 단순과거로 표현한다. 또, 접속사 after나 before가 쓰여 두 동작의 전후 관계가 명백할 때에는 단순과거로 표현하기도 한다.
  • She left **before** her mom got there. 그녀의 어머니가 그곳에 도착하기 전에 그녀는 자리를 떠났다. 〈전후 관계가 명백함〉

**핵심 Check**

**1.** 다음 괄호 안에서 알맞은 말을 고르시오.

   (1) He (hadn't had / has) lunch before we met.

   (2) She remembered everything that (had happened / happens) before.

## ② 감정을 나타내는 형용사+to부정사

> I'm **sorry to** trouble you. 폐를 끼쳐 죄송합니다.

■ '감정을 나타내는 형용사+to부정사'의 형태로 감정을 나타내는 형용사 다음의 to부정사는 감정의 이유나 원인을 나타낸다.
  * 이때 to부정사는 to부정사의 부사 역할이며 감정의 원인(~하여서, ~하니, ~하고)으로 해석한다.
  - I'm **sorry to** hear that. (그것을 듣게 되어 유감입니다.)
  - I was **surprised to** see you at the library. (너를 도서관에서 보고 놀랐다.)

■ 감정을 나타내는 형용사는 anxious, disappointed, glad, happy, pleased, proud, sad, shocked, sorry, surprised, unhappy 등이다.
  - Kay was **surprised to** see me. Kay는 나를 보고 놀랐다.

■ to부정사의 부사적 용법으로 사용된 감정의 이유나 원인을 나타내는 문장은 문장이 나타내는 의미에 따라 부사절(when, that 등)을 사용해서 바꿔 쓸 수 있다.
  - My mother wasn't **shocked to** hear the news. 엄마는 그 소식을 듣고 충격을 받지 않으셨다.
    = My mother wasn't shocked **when** she heard the news.

■ 'must be(~임에 틀림없다)'나 'cannot be(~일 리가 없다)' 뒤에 형용사가 올 때 그 형용사를 수식하는 to부정사는 '판단의 원인, 이유'를 의미한다.
  - He must be **wise to** do such a thing 그렇게 행동하는 것을 보니 그는 틀림없이 현명하군요.
  - He must be **stupid to** break his promise! 그가 약속을 깨다니 어리석음에 틀림없다!
  cf. to부정사의 부사적 용법이 아닌 '감정의 형용사+전치사구' 표현
  - I am interested in English. 나는 영어에 관심이 있다. (be interested in: ~에 관심이 있다)
  - I am tired of the class. 나는 수업에 싫증이 난다. (be tired of: ~에 질리다, 싫증나다)
  - This box is filled with new books. 이 박스는 새 책으로 가득 차 있다. (be filled with = be full of: ~로 가득 차 있다)
  - I was amazed at the news of his death. 나는 그가 죽었다는 소식에 놀랐다. (be amazed at: ~에 놀라다)
  - My dad was pleased with my success. 내 아빠는 나의 성공에 기뻐했다. (be pleased with: ~에 기뻐하다)
  - Don't be angry with him. 그에게 화내지 마. (be angry with: ~에 화나다)

### 핵심 Check

**2.** 다음 괄호 안에서 알맞은 단어를 고르시오.
  (1) I'm glad (meet / to meet) you.
  (2) I was bored (that / to) the lecture was never ending.

**01** 다음 문장에서 어법상 <u>어색한</u> 부분을 바르게 고쳐 쓰시오.

(1) I was very glad see my father.

_____ ➡ _____

(2) I'm happy accept your invitation.

_____ ➡ _____

(3) Was she excited meeting her old friend?

_____ ➡ _____

(4) The client leaves when I arrived at the office.

_____ ➡ _____

(5) I liked the violin that my mom plays when she was young.

_____ ➡ _____

**02** 두 문장의 전후 관계를 고려하여 한 문장으로 쓰시오. (접속사 until을 사용할 것)

> • I played a computer game.
> • My mom told me to stop playing it.

➡ _____

_____

**03** to가 들어갈 곳으로 적절한 곳을 고르시오.

> I'm ①disappointed ②see ③you ④make ⑤the same mistake again.

**04** 다음 우리말에 맞게 주어진 단어를 활용하여 영작하시오.

(1) 그녀가 터미널에 도착했을 때 버스는 떠나고 없었다. (leave, reach) (9 words)

➡ _____

(2) 나는 그녀를 종종 본 적이 있어서 나는 그녀를 잘 알았다. (know, well, see, for) (10 words)

➡ _____

(3) 나는 시계를 잃어버렸다는 것을 알아차렸다. (find, lose) (8 words)

➡ _____

**서답형**

**01** 다음 문장에서 어법상 틀린 부분을 찾아 바르게 고쳐 쓰시오.

> I bought a bag just like the one you bought for me.

_____ ➡ _____

**02** 다음 빈칸에 들어갈 말로 알맞은 것을 고르시오

> I was really shocked _____ read the story.

① with        ② at
③ to          ④ in
⑤ of

**서답형**

**03** 〈보기〉처럼 과거완료의 쓰임이 경험이면 (경), 완료면 (완), 계속이면 (계), 결과이면 (결), 대과거면 (대)라고 쓰시오.

> ┤ 보기 ├
> The train had already gone when I got to the station. ___(완)___

(1) When Suji arrived at the party, Eric had already gone home. ➡ _____

(2) Had she heard about the rumor before you told her? ➡ _____

(3) I realized that he had lied to me the previous day. ➡ _____

**서답형**

**04** 괄호 안의 어구와 조건을 참고하여 우리말을 영작하시오.

(1) 그녀는 그가 실패했다는 것을 듣고 놀랐다. (surprise, of)
   ➡ (to부정사를 이용) _____
   _____
   ➡ (부사절 that을 이용) _____
   _____

(2) 그가 그렇게 행동하는 것을 보니 그는 틀림없이 미쳤다. (mad, do, such)
   ➡ (must be 이용) _____
   _____

(3) 그녀는 문을 활짝 열어 놓았었다. (leave, wide)
   ➡ (과거완료 이용) _____
   _____

(4) 내 친구 모두는 그녀가 무슨 말을 했었는지 곰곰이 생각했다. (all of, think carefully)
   ➡ (전후 관계를 따져 과거완료 이용) _____
   _____

**서답형**

**05** 우리말에 맞게 괄호 안의 단어를 활용하여 빈칸을 채우시오.

(1) 그가 내게 신문에서 그것을 읽게 된 경위를 말해 주었다.
   ➡ He told me how he _____ _____ about it in the paper. (read)

(2) 그 오케스트라는 심포니를 연주했다. (대과거로 표현할 것.)
   ➡ The orchestra _____ _____ a symphony. (play)

(3) 자취가 이미 사라져 버린 상태였다.
   ➡ The trail _____ _____ cold. (go)

**06** 다음 빈칸에 들어갈 말로 알맞은 것을 고르시오

> I was amazed _____ her ability to deal with the difficult situation.

① to        ② at
③ of        ④ in
⑤ on

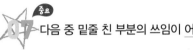 **07** 다음 중 밑줄 친 부분의 쓰임이 <u>어색한</u> 것을 고르시오

① Kay was surprised <u>to meet</u> his friend in Paris.
② Jadon was shocked <u>that</u> he heard the bad news.
③ Cathy was excited <u>to win</u> the badminton match.
④ Tom is sad <u>that</u> he lost the soccer game.
⑤ Jenny was bored <u>studying</u> math for 3 hours.

**08** 다음 우리말을 옮긴 것으로 알맞은 것을 <u>모두</u> 고르시오.

> 우리 가족은 어려운 문제를 해결해서 기뻤다.

① My family was happy to solve the difficult problem.
② My family was happy that we solved the difficult problem.
③ My family was happy that we solve the difficult problem.
④ My family was happy to solved the difficult problem.
⑤ My family was happy solved the difficult problem.

 **09** 빈칸에 들어갈 말로 올바른 것은?

> Ann had _____ skating for three hours before she got tired out.

① be        ② is        ③ been
④ was       ⑤ being

**서답형**
**10** 다음 문장을 괄호 안의 단어를 활용하여 영작하시오.

(1) 나는 집에 도착했을 때, 누군가가 몰래 나의 집에 잠입했었다는 것을 알아차렸다. (when, home, somebody, break)
➡ _____
_____

(2) Rachel은 전에 그녀를 본 적이 없었다고 말했다. (say, that, see)
➡ _____

(3) 그는 다리를 다쳐서 축구를 할 수 없었다. (injure, so, soccer)
➡ _____
_____

(4) 그는 프랑스로 가기 전에 3년 동안 불어를 공부했었다. (study, go)
➡ _____
_____

**서답형**
**11** 우리말에 맞게 괄호 안의 어휘들을 배열하여 영작할 때, 주어진 지시에 따라 쓰시오.

(1) 4번째 단어를 쓰시오.
• 그들은 그가 이미 떠났다는 것을 알고 놀랐다. (surprised, were, to, that, had, find, they, he, already, left) ➡ _____

(2) 2번째 단어를 쓰시오.
• 집에 도착하면 기쁠 것 같다. (I'll, home, be, get, glad, to) ➡ _____

(3) 5번째 단어를 쓰시오.
• 나는 그들이 가는 것을 보고 슬펐다. (was, I, them, see, go, sad, to) ➡ _____

**서답형**

**12** 다음 문장에서 어법상 어색한 부분을 찾아 바르게 고치시오.

(1) Alice knew that Ted picked strawberries with Jane before.

_____ ➡ _____

(2) I'm sorry that say bad news.

_____ ➡ _____

**중요**

**13** 다음 중 어색한 것을 고르시오.

① I'll be sad to hear the news that they got married.

② She was anxious to be a doctor.

③ He was anxious knowing the results of her blood test.

④ I'd be proud to have you as my guest.

⑤ I would be pleased to do so.

**중요**

**14** 빈칸에 들어갈 말로 적절한 것을 모두 고르시오.

My dad _____ my secret before I told it to him.

① know          ② knows

③ knew          ④ has known

⑤ had known

**서답형**

**15** that을 사용하여 주어진 문장과 같은 뜻이 되도록 쓰시오.

(1) She was disappointed to get a bad grade.

➡ _____

(2) I was glad to hear you're alive and well.

➡ _____

(3) She felt unhappy to see the accident.

➡ _____

(4) I feel very proud to be a part of the team.

➡ _____

(5) I was somewhat surprised to see him.

➡ _____

**16** 다음 빈칸에 들어갈 말로 알맞은 것을 고르시오

When Rachel went to get some money from her wallet, she discovered that someone _____ it.

① had taken          ② takes

③ take               ④ took

⑤ taken

**서답형**

**17** 두 문장을 한 문장으로 연결할 때 과거완료 시제를 사용해야 하는 문장을 고르시오. 또한, 과거완료 시제를 써야 할 부분을 찾아 고쳐 쓰시오.

① The house was dirty.

② They didn't cleaned it for weeks.

(1) 과거완료 시제를 써야 할 문장: _____

(2) 과거완료 시제를 쓸 부분: _____

➡ _____

**01** 우리말에 맞게 괄호 안의 단어를 활용하여 영작하시오.

(1) 그녀는 내 옷을 입기 전에 그것을 나에게 말하지 않았다. (tell, it, wear)

➡ _____

_____

_____

(2) 나는 Jane을 만나기 전에는 그렇게 아름다운 소녀를 만난 적이 없었다. (such, before)

➡ _____

_____

_____

(3) 내가 표를 사러 website에 들어갔을 때 이미 표가 모두 매진되어 있었다. (all, sold out, enter)

➡ _____

_____

(4) 그들은 그가 전화했을 때 출근하고 없었다. (go, call)

➡ _____

**02** 괄호 안의 단어와 주어진 조건대로 영작하시오.

(1) 너는 너 자신이 정말 자랑스럽겠다. (proud, must를 쓸 것.)

➡ _____

(2) 그들은 한국인인 것을 매우 자랑스러워한다. (proud, to부정사를 사용할 것.)

➡ _____

**03** 다음 〈보기〉의 짝지어진 단어를 활용하여 빈칸을 채우시오.

┌─ 보기 ─────────────────────┐
proud–support   glad–be   sad–hear
anxious–finish   eat–leave   be–interest
└────────────────────────────┘

(1) The trip has been exhausting and I'll be _____ home.

(2) I'm _____ their work.

(3) She was _____ school and get a job.

(4) I _____ Math.

(5) We are _____ that you are leaving.

(6) The monkeys ate the bananas the tourists _____ for them.

**04** 괄호 안의 단어를 활용하여 우리말에 맞게 빈칸을 채우시오.

(1) 그녀는 대통령을 만났던 것을 자랑한다.

➡ She _____(proud) have met the President.

(2) 그는 그들을 기다리는 것에 지친 것처럼 보였다.

➡ He seemed to _____(tire) waiting for them.

(3) 너는 분명 그 사람에 대한 존경심이 대단하구나.

➡ You must _____(full) respect for him.

➡ You must _____(fill) respect for him.

**05** (A)와 (B)의 문장을 as를 이용하여 알맞게 연결하여 한 문장으로 쓰시오. (문장 연결시 사건의 전후 관계를 판단하여 이전 사건은 과거완료를 사용하여 작성할 것.)

> (A)
> • I was very proud of myself.
> • I had no money.
> • My mother scolded my sister.
> *scold 혼내다

> (B)
> • My sister bothered me.
> • I won the prize at the contest.
> • I lost my wallet.

➡ (1) _____

_____

(2) _____

(3) _____

_____

**06** 그림을 참고하여, 과거에 했던 경험을 표현하고자 한다. 괄호 안의 단어를 활용하여 우리말에 맞게 빈칸을 채우시오.

> 그는 2010년쯤까지 방과 후 매일 축구를 했었다고 말했다. (around, play)

➡ He said that until _____

_____ .

**07** 그림을 참고하여 괄호 안의 단어를 이용하여 어법에 맞게 빈칸에 쓰시오.

(1) He _____ (diligent, clean, enough) the soccer field by himself.

(2) This picture _____ (creative, make, enough) its engines out of cups.

**08** 다음 그림을 참고하고 괄호 안의 단어를 사용하여, 문장을 완성하시오.

➡ I'm _____ .

(happy, my friend, with)

**The Three Little Pigs: Its True Story**

**Reporter:** Welcome to Animal World News. Last Sunday, a wolf <u>was taken to</u> the police station for blowing down pigs' houses.
<small>~로 연행되었다(take A to B: A를 B로 데려가다)</small>

Today, we have the third little pig and the wolf with us. Mr. Pig, could you explain <u>what happened to you and your brothers</u>?
<small>간접의문문(의문대명사+동사)</small>

**Pig:** Yes. My brothers and I thought <u>it was time to build</u> our own
<small>it was time to V: V할 시간이었다</small>
houses, so we <u>built</u> houses <u>with</u> straw, sticks, and bricks. <u>One day,</u>
<small>build A with B: B로 A를 짓다</small> <small>(과거의) 어느 날</small>
the wolf came and completely blew down my brothers' houses.

He almost blew down my house, but it <u>was made of</u> bricks, so he
<small>~으로 만들어졌다</small>
couldn't.
<small>= couldn't blow down my house</small>

**Reporter:** How are your brothers doing now?

**Pig:** They are shocked <u>to lose</u> their houses. They are resting in my
<small>감정의 원인을 나타내는 to부정사</small>
house.

**Reporter:** Thank you, Mr. Pig. Now, <u>let's</u> meet our second guest, the
<small>제안하는 말(let's+동사원형)</small>
wolf. Mr. Wolf, could you tell us <u>what happened</u>?
<small>간접의문문(tell의 직접목적어)</small>

**Wolf:** This whole "Big Bad Wolf" thing is wrong. The real story is about a sneeze from a terrible cold and a cup of sugar.

**Reporter:** What do you mean?

---

**be taken to**: ~에 끌려가다, 연행되다
**blow down**: 바람을 불어 넘어뜨리다
**explain**: 설명하다
**straw**: 짚, 지푸라기
**brick**: 벽돌
**completely**: 완전히
**almost**: 거의
**shocked**: 충격을 받은
**rest**: 쉬다
**whole**: 모든, 전체의
**terrible**: 지독한
**sneeze**: 재채기; 재채기하다

---

### 확인문제

● 다음 문장이 본문의 내용과 일치하면 T, 일치하지 않으면 F를 쓰시오.

1  Straw, sticks, and bricks were used to make the three pigs' houses. ☐

2  The wolf blew down all the houses in the town. ☐

3  All the pigs were there except the third pig. ☐

4  The first and second pigs are resting in the house made of bricks. ☐

5  The wolf considers himself to be a Big Bad Wolf. ☐

**Wolf:** Back then, I was making a birthday cake for my dear old grandmother. I ran out of sugar. I walked down the street to ask
<sub>목적을 나타내는 to부정사(~하기 위해서)</sub>
my neighbor for a cup of sugar. When I knocked on the door, it fell down. Then I called, "Little pig, are you in?" I had just grabbed
<sub>과거완료(재채기가 나오려던 시점보다 앞서 일어난 일)</sub>
the broken door when I felt a sneeze coming on. I sneezed a great
<sub>지각동사+목적어+Ving</sub>
sneeze and you know what? The whole straw house fell down. I
<sub>그거 아세요</sub>
was very surprised by what had happened. Unfortunately, the same
<sub>충격을 느낀 것이므로 과거분사</sub> <sub>과거완료(내가 놀란 것보다 먼저 일어난 일)</sub> <sub>재채기를 하자 집이 무너져버린 것</sub>
thing happened to the second little pig's house.

**Reporter:** Then why did you go to the third little pig's house?

**Wolf:** I still needed that cup of sugar, so I went to the next house.
<sub>지시형용사</sub> <sub>결과를 이끄는 접속사</sub>
The third little pig had built his house of bricks. I called out, "I'm
<sub>과거보다 먼저 일어난 일이므로 과거완료</sub>
sorry to trouble you, but are you in?" And do you know what he
<sub>간접의문문</sub>
answered? "Go away. Don't bother me again!" How impolite! I
<sub>감탄문(How+형용사/부사)</sub>
thought I deserved an apology, so I kept knocking. When the police
<sub>keep+Ving: 계속해서 V하다</sub>
came, of course they thought I was breaking into this pig's house.

**Reporter:** Do you think you were framed?

**Wolf:** Yes. The news reporters of the town thought a sick wolf going to
<sub>현재분사</sub>
borrow a cup of sugar didn't sound very exciting. So, they made
<sub>아픈 늑대의 이야기가 흥미를 유발하지 않는다는 의미이므로 현재분사</sub>
me the "Big Bad Wolf." Could you maybe lend me a cup of sugar?
<sub>lend+사람+사물: ~에게 …을 빌려주다</sub>

**Reporter:** Thank you for your time. Everyone, which do you think is
<sub>간접의문문(동사 believe. think. guess 등이 간접의문문을 목적어로 취할 때 의문사를 문두에 배치)</sub>
the true story, the pig's or the wolf's?

---

run out of: ~이 다 떨어지다
grab: 잡다
fall down: 무너지다
unfortunately: 불행하게도
trouble: 귀찮게 하다
bother: 괴롭히다
impolite: 무례한
deserve: ~을 받을 만하다
apology: 사과
break into: 침입하다
frame: 죄를 뒤집어씌우다

---

**확인문제**

● 다음 문장이 본문의 내용과 일치하면 T, 일치하지 않으면 F를 쓰시오.

1 The wolf just wanted his neighbor to give him some sugar. ☐

2 A terrible cold made the wolf sneeze. ☐

3 The wolf didn't go to the second pig's house because he was sick. ☐

4 The wolf thinks the reporters framed him. ☐

5 The news reporters made their news exciting by making the wolf a victim. ☐

• 우리말을 참고하여 빈칸에 알맞은 말을 쓰시오.

**The Three Little Pigs: Its True Story**

**1**  Reporter: _____ _____ Animal World News. Last Sunday, a wolf _____ _____ _____ the police station _____ _____ _____ pigs' houses.

**2**  Today, we have _____ _____ _____ _____ and the wolf with us.

**3**  Mr. Pig, could you explain _____ _____ _____ you and your brothers?

**4**  Pig: Yes. My brothers and I thought it was _____ _____ _____ _____ own houses, so we built houses _____ _____, _____, and _____.

**5**  One day, the wolf came and _____ _____ my brothers' houses.

**6**  He almost _____ _____ my house, but it was _____ _____ bricks, so he _____.

**7**  Reporter: _____ are your brothers _____ _____?

**8**  Pig: They are _____ _____ _____ their houses. They are _____ _____ my house.

**9**  Reporter: Thank you, Mr. Pig. Now, _____ _____ our second guest, the wolf. Mr. Wolf, could you _____ _____ _____?

**10**  Wolf: This whole "Big Bad Wolf" thing _____ _____.

**11**  The real story is _____ _____ _____ from _____ _____ and a cup of sugar.

**12**  Reporter: _____ do you _____?

**13**  Wolf: Back then, I _____ _____ a birthday cake _____ my dear old grandmother.

**14**  I _____ _____ _____ sugar. I walked down the street _____ my neighbor _____ a cup of sugar.

---

아기 돼지 삼 형제: 그것의 진짜 이야기

**1**  리포터: 'Animal World News'에 오신 것을 환영합니다. 지난 일요일, 돼지들의 집들을 바람을 불어 넘어뜨린 늑대가 경찰서로 연행되었습니다.

**2**  오늘, 우리는 셋째 아기 돼지와 늑대를 모셨습니다.

**3**  Pig씨, 당신과 당신 형제들에게 무슨 일이 일어났는지 설명해 주시겠어요?

**4**  돼지: 네. 제 형제들과 저는 각자의 집들을 지을 때라고 생각했어요. 그래서 우리는 짚, 나무 막대기, 그리고 벽돌로 집을 지었어요.

**5**  어느 날, 늑대가 와서 제 형들의 집들을 바람을 불어 완전히 날려 버렸어요.

**6**  그는 제 집도 거의 날려 버릴 뻔했는데, 벽돌로 만들어져서 그럴 수가 없었죠.

**7**  리포터: 당신의 형제들은 지금 어떻게 지내고 있나요?

**8**  돼지: 그들은 집을 잃어서 충격을 받았어요. 그들은 제 집에서 쉬고 있어요.

**9**  리포터: 감사합니다, Pig씨. 이제 두 번째 손님인 늑대를 만나 보시죠. Wolf씨, 무슨 일이 있었는지 말씀해 주시겠어요?

**10**  늑대: 이 모든 '덩치 크고 못된 늑대' 사건은 잘못된 거예요.

**11**  진짜 이야기는 지독한 감기로 인한 재채기와 설탕 한 컵에 관한 거예요.

**12**  리포터: 무슨 말씀인가요?

**13**  늑대: 그때, 저는 사랑하는 할머니를 위해 생일 케이크를 만들고 있었어요.

**14**  설탕이 다 떨어졌더라고요. 저는 이웃에게 설탕 한 컵을 달라고 부탁하기 위해 길을 걸어갔어요.

**15** When I _____ _____ the door, it _____ _____.

**16** Then I _____, "Little pig, are you in?"

**17** I _____ _____ _____ the broken door when I felt a sneeze _____ _____.

**18** I _____ a great _____ and you know what? The whole straw house _____ _____.

**19** I was very surprised _____ _____ _____ _____.

**20** Unfortunately, the same thing _____ _____ the second little pig's house.

**21** Reporter: Then _____ _____ _____ _____ _____ the third little pig's house?

**22** Wolf: I still needed _____ _____ _____ _____, so I went to the next house.

**23** The third little pig _____ _____ his house _____ bricks.

**24** I _____ _____, "I'm sorry _____ _____ _____, but are you _____?"

**25** And do you know _____ _____ _____? "Go away. Don't _____ _____ again!"

**26** _____ _____! I thought I _____ an apology, so I kept _____.

**27** _____ the police _____, of course they thought I was _____ _____ this pig's house.

**28** Reporter: Do you think you _____ _____?

**29** Wolf: Yes. The news reporters of the town thought a sick wolf _____ _____ _____ a cup of sugar didn't sound very _____.

**30** So, they made me the "Big Bad Wolf." _____ you maybe _____ _____ a cup of sugar?

**31** Reporter: Thank you for your time. Everyone, _____ _____ _____ _____ _____ the true story, the pig's or the wolf's?

| | |
|---|---|
| **15** | 제가 이웃집 분을 두드렸을 때, 문이 떨어졌어요. |
| **16** | 그다음에 저는 "아기 돼지 씨, 안에 계신가요?"라고 불렀어요. |
| **17** | 제가 부서진 문을 막 움켜잡았을 때 재채기가 나오는 걸 느꼈어요. |
| **18** | 저는 재채기를 아주 크게 했고, 그거 아세요? 짚으로 만든 집 전체가 무너졌어요. |
| **19** | 저는 일어난 일에 매우 놀랐어요. |
| **20** | 안타깝게도, 둘째 아기 돼지의 집에서도 같은 일이 일어나고 말았어요. |
| **21** | 리포터: 그렇다면 셋째 아기 돼지의 집에 왜 갔죠? |
| **22** | 늑대: 저는 여전히 설탕 한 컵이 필요했어요, 그래서 옆집으로 갔어요. |
| **23** | 셋째 아기 돼지는 벽돌로 집을 지었더라고요. |
| **24** | 제가 소리쳤어요, "귀찮게 해드려 죄송하지만, 안에 계신가요?" |
| **25** | 그리고 그가 뭐라고 대답했는지 아세요? "가버려, 다신 귀찮게 하지 마!" |
| **26** | 얼마나 무례한가요! 저는 사과를 받아 마땅하다고 생각했기 때문에 계속 문을 두드렸어요. |
| **27** | 경찰이 왔을 때, 물론 그들은 제가 이 돼지의 집에 침입하고 있다고 생각했죠. |
| **28** | 리포터: 당신은 당신이 누명을 썼다고 생각하나요? |
| **29** | 늑대: 네. 마을의 신문 기자들은 설탕 한 컵을 빌리러 간 아픈 늑대가 별로 흥미롭지 않다고 생각했겠죠. |
| **30** | 그래서 그들은 저를 '덩치 크고 못된 늑대'로 만든 거예요. 당신은 아마 제게 설탕 한 컵쯤은 빌려 줄 수 있으시겠죠? |
| **31** | 리포터: 시간 내 주셔서 감사합니다. 여러분, 어떤 이야기가 진짜 이야기라고 생각하시나요, 돼지의 이야기일까요, 아니면 늑대의 이야기일까요? |

● 우리말을 참고하여 본문을 영작하시오.

**The Three Little Pigs: Its True Story**

**1** 리포터: 'Animal World News'에 오신 것을 환영합니다. 지난 일요일, 돼지들의 집들을 바람을 불어 넘어뜨린 늑대가 경찰서로 연행되었습니다.

➡ _____

_____

**2** 오늘, 우리는 셋째 아기 돼지와 늑대를 모셨습니다.

➡ _____

**3** Pig씨, 당신과 당신 형제들에게 무슨 일이 일어났는지 설명해 주시겠어요?

➡ _____

**4** 돼지: 네. 제 형제들과 저는 각자의 집들을 지을 때라고 생각했어요. 그래서 우리는 짚, 나무 막대기, 그리고 벽돌로 집을 지었어요.

➡ _____

_____

**5** 어느 날, 늑대가 와서 제 형들의 집들을 바람을 불어 완전히 날려 버렸어요.

➡ _____

**6** 그는 제 집도 거의 날려 버릴 뻔했는데, 벽돌로 만들어져서 그럴 수가 없었죠.

➡ _____

**7** 리포터: 당신의 형제들은 지금 어떻게 지내고 있나요?

➡ _____

**8** 돼지: 그들은 집을 잃어서 충격을 받았어요. 그들은 제 집에서 쉬고 있어요.

➡ _____

**9** 리포터: 감사합니다, Pig씨. 이제 두 번째 손님인 늑대를 만나 보시죠. Wolf씨, 무슨 일이 있었는지 말씀해 주시겠어요?

➡ _____

_____

**10** 늑대: 이 모든 '덩치 크고 못된 늑대' 사건은 잘못된 거예요.

➡ _____

**11** 진짜 이야기는 지독한 감기로 인한 재채기와 설탕 한 컵에 관한 거예요.

➡ _____

**12** 리포터: 무슨 말씀인가요?

➡ _____

**13** 늑대: 그때, 저는 사랑하는 할머니를 위해 생일 케이크를 만들고 있었어요.

➡ _____

**14** 설탕이 다 떨어졌더라고요. 저는 이웃에게 설탕 한 컵을 달라고 부탁하기 위해 길을 걸어갔어요.

➡ _____

**15** 제가 이웃집 문을 두드렸을 때, 문이 떨어졌어요.

➡ _____

**16** 그다음에 저는 "아기 돼지 씨, 안에 계신가요?"라고 불렀어요.

➡ _____

**17** 제가 부서진 문을 막 움켜잡았을 때 재채기가 나오는 걸 느꼈어요.

➡ _____

**18** 저는 재채기를 아주 크게 했고, 그거 아세요? 짚으로 만든 집 전체가 무너졌어요.

➡ _____

**19** 저는 일어난 일에 매우 놀랐어요.

➡ _____

**20** 안타깝게도, 둘째 아기 돼지의 집에서도 같은 일이 일어나고 말았어요.

➡ _____

**21** 리포터: 그렇다면 셋째 아기 돼지의 집에 왜 갔죠?

➡ _____

**22** 늑대: 저는 여전히 설탕 한 컵이 필요했어요, 그래서 옆집으로 갔어요.

➡ _____

**23** 셋째 아기 돼지는 벽돌로 집을 지었더라고요.

➡ _____

**24** 제가 소리쳤어요, "귀찮게 해 드려 죄송하지만, 안에 계신가요?"

➡ _____

**25** 그리고 그가 뭐라고 대답했는지 아세요? "가버려, 다신 귀찮게 하지 마!"

➡ _____

**26** 얼마나 무례한가요! 저는 사과를 받아 마땅하다고 생각했기 때문에 계속 문을 두드렸어요.

➡ _____

**27** 경찰이 왔을 때, 물론 그들은 제가 이 돼지의 집에 침입하고 있다고 생각했죠.

➡ _____

**28** 리포터: 당신은 당신이 누명을 썼다고 생각하나요?

➡ _____

**29** 늑대: 네. 마을의 신문 기자들은 설탕 한 컵을 빌리러 간 아픈 늑대가 별로 흥미롭지 않다고 생각했겠죠.

➡ _____

**30** 그래서 그들은 저를 '덩치 크고 못된 늑대'로 만든 거예요. 당신은 아마 제게 설탕 한 컵쯤은 빌려 줄 수 있으시겠죠?

➡ _____

**31** 리포터: 시간 내 주셔서 감사합니다. 여러분, 어떤 이야기가 진짜 이야기라고 생각하시나요, 돼지의 이야기일까요, 아니면 늑대의 이야기일까요?

➡ _____

_____

[01~04] 다음 글을 읽고 물음에 답하시오.

**Reporter:** Welcome to Animal World News. Last Sunday, a wolf was taken to the police station for blowing down pigs' houses. Today, we have the third little pig and the wolf with us. Mr. Pig, could you explain what happened to you and your brothers?

**Pig:** Yes. My brothers and I thought it was time to build our own houses, so we built houses with straw, sticks, and bricks. One day, the wolf came and completely blew down my brothers' houses. He almost blew down my house, but it was made of bricks, so he couldn't.

**Reporter:** (A)_____

**Pig:** They are shocked to lose their houses. They are resting in my house.

**1** 다음 중 빈칸 (A)에 들어갈 말로 적절한 것은?

① What do your brothers do?
② What do you usually do at home?
③ How are your brothers doing now?
④ What brought your brothers here?
⑤ How long did they build the house?

**02** 다음 중 위 글의 내용과 일치하는 것은?

① The police took a wolf to the police station today.
② All the three pigs will appear on the news.
③ A wolf blew down the houses of the three pigs.
④ The three pigs built their houses with straw, sticks, and bricks.
⑤ The third pig doesn't know what happened to his brothers.

**03** Write the reason why the three pigs built houses. Use the phrase 'It's because.'

➡ _____

_____

**04** 다음 중 위 글을 읽고 답할 수 있는 것은?

① What is the reporter's name?
② How many guests are there?
③ When did the pigs build their houses?
④ Why did the wolf blow down the pigs' houses?
⑤ How many bricks were needed to build a house?

[05~08] 다음 글을 읽고 물음에 답하시오.

**Reporter:** Thank you, Mr. Pig. Now, let's meet our second guest, the wolf. Mr. Wolf, could you tell us ①what happened?

**Wolf:** This whole "Big Bad Wolf" thing is wrong. The real story is about a (A)_____ from a terrible cold and a cup of sugar.

**Reporter:** What do you mean?

**Wolf:** Back then, I was making a birthday cake ②for my dear old grandmother. I ran out of sugar. I walked down the street ③to ask my neighbor for a cup of sugar. When I knocked on the door, it fell down. Then I called, "Little pig, are you in?" I had just grabbed the broken door when I felt a sneeze ④to come on. I sneezed a great sneeze and you know what? The whole straw house fell down. I was very ⑤surprised by what had happened. (B)_____, the same thing happened to the second little pig's house.

서답형
**05** 빈칸 (A)에 들어갈 말로 가장 적절한 것을 위 글에서 찾아 쓰시오.

➡ _____

**06** 다음 중 빈칸 (B)에 들어갈 말로 가장 적절한 것은?

① Luckily ② Therefore
③ That is ④ Unfortunately
⑤ On the contrary

**07** 밑줄 친 ①~⑤ 중 어법상 어색한 것은?

①          ②          ③          ④          ⑤

서답형
**08** According to what the wolf said, what was the first neighbor's house made of? Answer in English with five words.

➡ _____

[09~12] 다음 글을 읽고 물음에 답하시오.

> Reporter: Then why did you go to the third little pig's house?
> Wolf: I still needed that cup of sugar, so I went to the next house. The third little pig had built his house of bricks. I called out, "I'm sorry to trouble you, but are you in?" And do you know what he answered? "Go away. Don't bother me again!" How (A)_____! I thought I deserved an apology, so I kept knocking. When the police came, of course they thought I was breaking into this pig's house.
> Reporter: Do you think you were framed?

> Wolf: Yes. The news reporters of the town thought a sick wolf going to borrow a cup of sugar didn't sound very (B)_____. So, they made me the "Big Bad Wolf." Could you maybe lend me a cup of sugar?
> Reporter: Thank you for your time. Everyone, which do you think is the true story, the pig's or the wolf's?.

**09** 빈칸 (A)에 들어갈 말로 가장 적절한 것은?

① interesting ② delightful ③ normal
④ typical ⑤ impolite

서답형
**10** 단어 excite를 어법에 맞게 빈칸 (B)에 쓰시오.

➡ _____

**11** According to the dialogue, why did the wolf go to the third little pig's house?

① to get some advice from him
② to make friends with him
③ to learn how to buy sugar
④ to get some sugar from him
⑤ to have a conversation with him

**12** 다음 중 위 글의 내용과 일치하지 않는 것은?

① The wolf visited the third little pig's house to get some sugar.
② The third little pig had a house made of bricks.
③ The wolf intended to break into the pig's house.
④ The third pig was very rude to the wolf.
⑤ The wolf wanted to get an apology.

**[13~16]** 다음 글을 읽고 물음에 답하시오.

Reporter: Welcome to Animal World News. Last Sunday, a wolf was taken to the police station (A)_____ blowing down pigs' houses. Today, we have the third little pig and the wolf with us. Mr. Pig, could you explain what happened to you and your brothers?

Pig: Yes. My brothers and I thought it was time to build our own houses, so we built houses with straw, sticks, and bricks. One day, the wolf came and completely blew down my brothers' houses. He almost blew down my house, but it was made of bricks, so he couldn't.

Reporter: How are your brothers doing now?

Pig: They are shocked to lose their houses. They are resting in my house.

**13** 다음 중 빈칸 (A)에 들어갈 말과 같은 말이 들어가는 것은?

① Who did you take care _____?

② Is there anyone you can rely _____?

③ Amie died _____ a cancer.

④ I had nothing except _____ a pencil.

⑤ I knew the elevator broke _____.

**14** 위 글의 종류로 가장 적절한 것은?

① survey          ② journal

③ interview       ④ advertisement

⑤ documentary

**15** 다음과 같이 풀이되는 말을 위 글에서 찾아 쓰시오.

> to make something clear or easy to understand

➡ _____

**16** 위 글의 내용에 맞게 빈칸에 알맞은 말을 쓰시오.

> In order to _____ _____ _____ _____, the three pigs used _____ _____, and _____.

**[17~20]** 다음 글을 읽고 물음에 답하시오.

Reporter: Thank you, Mr. Pig. Now, let's meet our second guest, the wolf. Mr. Wolf, could you tell us ⓐ무슨 일이 있었는지?

Wolf: This whole "Big Bad Wolf" thing is wrong. The real story is about a sneeze from a terrible cold and a cup of sugar.

Reporter: What do you mean?

Wolf: Back then, I was making a birthday cake for my dear old grandmother.

(A) When I knocked on the door, it fell down. Then I called, "Little pig, are you in?" I had just grabbed the broken door when I felt a sneeze coming on.

(B) I ran out of sugar. I walked down the street to ask my neighbor for a cup of sugar.

(C) I sneezed a great sneeze and you know what? The whole straw house fell down. I was very surprised by what had happened.

Unfortunately, ⓑthe same thing happened to the second little pig's house.

**17** 밑줄 친 우리말 ⓐ를 영어로 옮기시오.

➡ _____

**18** 자연스러운 흐름이 되도록 (A)~(C)를 바르게 나열하시오.

➡ _____

**19** 밑줄 친 ⓑ의 의미로 가장 적절한 것은?

① running out of sugar

② the fact that Mr. Wolf couldn't borrow some sugar

③ feeling a great sneeze coming

④ the fact that a house was destroyed by his sneeze

⑤ the fact that Mr. Wolf was surprised by what people say

 Which is TRUE about the passage?

① The reporter didn't interview Mr. Pig.

② The wolf is the only guest.

③ The wolf doesn't know how to make a cake.

④ The wolf didn't visit the second little pig's house.

⑤ The wolf didn't intend to blow down the little pigs' houses.

[21~24] 다음 글을 읽고 물음에 답하시오.

**Reporter:** Then why did you go to the third little pig's house?

**Wolf:** I still needed that cup of sugar, so I went to the next house. (①) The third little pig had built his house of bricks. (②) I called out, "I'm sorry to trouble you, but are you in?" (③) And do you know what he answered? "Go away. Don't bother me again!" (④) I thought I deserved an apology, so I kept knocking. (⑤) When the police came, of course they thought I was breaking into this pig's house.

**Reporter:** Do you think you were framed?

**Wolf:** Yes. The news reporters of the town thought a sick wolf going to borrow a cup of sugar didn't sound very exciting. So, they made me the "Big Bad Wolf." Could you maybe lend me a cup of sugar?

**Reporter:** Thank you for your time. Everyone, which (A)_____ is the true story, the pig's or the wolf's?

**21** 빈칸 (A)에 들어갈 말로 적절하지 <u>않은</u> 것은?

① do you think     ② do you know

③ do you believe     ④ do you guess

⑤ do you suppose

**서답형**

**22** ①~⑤ 중 주어진 문장이 들어가기에 가장 적절한 곳은?

| How impolite! |
| :---: |

①     ②     ③     ④     ⑤

**23** 다음 중 위 글의 내용과 일치하지 <u>않는</u> 것은?

① The wolf had visited the other two pigs' houses to get some sugar.

② The wolf felt sorry to trouble the third little pig.

③ The wolf still needed a cup of sugar.

④ The third little pig welcomed the wolf with a warm heart.

⑤ The wolf was sick when he wanted to borrow some sugar.

**서답형**

**24** Why does the wolf think he was framed? Answer in English by beginning with 'The wolf thinks that', and use the word 'because'.

➡ _____

_____

_____

_____

[01~04] 다음 글을 읽고 물음에 답하시오.

> **Reporter:** Welcome to Animal World News. Last Sunday, a wolf was taken to the police station for blowing down pigs' houses. Today, we have the third little pig and the wolf with us. Mr. Pig, could you explain what happened to you and your brothers?
>
> **Pig:** Yes. My brothers and I thought it was time to build our own houses, so we built houses with straw, sticks, and bricks. One day, the wolf came and completely blew down my brothers' houses. He almost blew down my house, but it was made of bricks, so he couldn't.
>
> **Reporter:** How are your brothers doing now?
>
> **Pig:** They are shocked to lose their houses. They are resting in my house.

**01** Write the reason why a wolf was taken to the police station. Answer in English with using the words 'because', and 'he.'

➡ _____

**02** According to what the third pig said, what is his house made of? Answer in English.

➡ _____

**03** How are the first and second little pigs doing? Answer in English.

➡ _____
_____

**04** Who are there as guests of Animal World News? Answer in English.

➡ _____
_____

[05~09] 다음 글을 읽고 물음에 답하시오.

> **Reporter:** Thank you, Mr. Pig. Now, let's meet our second guest, the wolf. Mr. Wolf, could you tell us what happened?
>
> **Wolf:** This whole "Big Bad Wolf" thing is wrong. The real story is about a sneeze from a terrible cold and a cup of sugar.
>
> **Reporter:** (A)무슨 의미인가요?
>
> **Wolf:** Back then, I was making a birthday cake for my dear old grandmother. I ran out of sugar. I walked down the street to ask my neighbor for a cup of sugar. When I knocked on the door, it fell down. Then I called, "Little pig, are you in?" I had just grabbed the broken door when I felt a sneeze coming on. I sneezed a great sneeze and you know what? The whole straw house fell down. I was very surprised by what had happened. Unfortunately, the same thing happened to the second little pig's house.

**05** 밑줄 친 우리말 (A)를 4단어로 이루어진 한 문장의 영어로 쓰시오.

➡ _____

**06** What was the wolf doing for his grandmother? Answer in English.

➡ _____

**07** Write the reason why the wolf walked down the street. Answer with a full sentence and use the phrase 'in order to.'

➡ _____

_____

**08** What happened when the wolf knocked on his neighbor's door? Answer in English.

➡ _____

**09** Write the reason why the whole straw house fell down. Use the phrase 'It's because.'

➡ _____

**[10~14]** 다음 글을 읽고 물음에 답하시오.

> **Reporter:** Then why did you go to the third little pig's house?
>
> **Wolf:** (A)I still needed that cup of sugar, so I went to the next house. The third little pig had built his house of bricks. I called out, "I'm sorry to ①trouble you, but are you in?" And do you know what he answered? "Go away. Don't ②bother me again!" How impolite! I thought I ③deserved an apology, so I kept knocking. When the police came, of course they thought I was breaking into this pig's house.
>
> **Reporter:** Do you think you were framed?
>
> **Wolf:** Yes. The news reporters of the town thought a sick wolf going to ④lend a cup of sugar didn't sound very ⑤exciting. So, they made me the "Big Bad Wolf." Could you maybe lend me a cup of sugar?
>
> **Reporter:** Thank you for your time. Everyone, which do you think is the true story, the pig's or the wolf's?

**10** 다음은 밑줄 친 (A)를 통해 유추할 수 있는 내용이다. 빈칸에 알맞은 말을 쓰시오.

> To get some sugar, the wolf _____ _____ other houses before he went to the third little pig's house.

**서답형**

**11** 위 글의 내용에 맞게 빈칸에 알맞은 말을 쓰시오.

> Q: How did the wolf feel about what the third pig had said?
>
> A: He felt that _____ _____ _____.

**12** 다음과 같이 풀이되는 말을 위 글에서 찾아 쓰시오.

> a statement saying that you are sorry about something

➡ _____

**13** 밑줄 친 ①~⑤ 중 글의 흐름상 어색한 것을 찾아 바르게 고쳐 쓰시오.

➡ _____

**14** 위 글의 내용에 맞게 빈칸에 알맞은 말을 쓰시오.

> The wolf says that the police thought he was _____ _____ the pig's house but that in fact he was just _____. He also argues that he _____ _____.

## Real Life Communication – C Communication Task

A: Can anyone guess the title of the story?

B: I think it is *Sleeping Beauty*.

A: Why do you think so?
= What makes you think so?

B: I think Semi is the princess who is sleeping peacefully and Minsu is the
= that (주격 관계대명사)
prince who is looking for the princess.

A: Sorry, but that's not the answer.

구문해설 • title: 제목 • peacefully: 평화롭게 • look for: ~을 찾다

해석

A: 그 이야기의 제목을 추측 해 볼 수 있나요?

B: 제 생각에 '잠자는 숲속의 공주' 같아요.

A: 왜 그렇게 생각하니?

B: 세미는 평화롭게 잠을 자 고 있는 공주이고 민수는 공주를 찾고 있는 왕자예 요.

A: 미안하지만 정답이 아니 에요.

## Before You Read

Everyone deserves a fun story like this. – *Book Weekly*
단수 취급 전치사(~와 같은)

I think I should make an apology to the wolf. I'd never thought about his point
make an apology: 사과하다
of view. – *The Book Times*

I still don't know whose story is true, but I learned that everyone can be
간접의문문(의문사+주어+동사) 명사절 접속사
framed for a crime. – *Library & Paper*

구문해설 • deserve: ~할 자격이 있다 • apology: 사과 • point of view: 관점 • frame: 함정에 빠뜨리다

모든 사람이 이와 같은 재미 있는 이야기를 읽을 자격이 있다. – Book Weekly
내 생각에 나는 늑대에게 사 과해야 할 것 같다. 나는 그 의 관점에 대해 생각해 본 적 이 없었다. – The Book Times
나는 여전히 누구의 이야기 가 진실인지 모르겠지만, 누 구든지 범죄에 누명을 쓸 수 있다는 것을 알게 되었다. – Library & Paper

## After You Read

**The Pig's Story**

The three little pigs decided to build their own houses. So, they built houses
목적어로 쓰인 부정사 소유격 강조
with different things. One day, the wolf came and blew down the first and the
[도구 · 수단] ~으로, ~을 사용하여 came과 병렬
second little pigs' houses completely. But the wolf couldn't blow down the
complete(X)
third pig's house because it was made of bricks.
이유를 나타내는 접속사 ~로 만들어지다

구문해설 • completely: 완전히 • blow down: 바람을 불어 넘어뜨리다

돼지 이야기
세 마리의 아기 돼지들은 자 신들의 집을 짓기로 결정했 다. 그래서 그들은 다른 재료 들로 집을 지었다. 어느 날, 늑대가 와서 첫째와 둘째 아 기 돼지의 집을 바람을 불어 완전히 무너뜨렸다. 하지만 늑대는 셋째 돼지의 집은 무 너뜨릴 수 없었는데, 왜냐하 면 그것은 벽돌로 만들어졌기 때문이었다.

**01** 다음 짝지어진 단어의 관계가 같도록 빈칸에 알맞은 말을 쓰시오.

comparison : _____ = decision : decide

**02** 다음 우리말에 맞게 빈칸에 알맞은 말을 쓰시오.

(1) 나는 내가 사과를 받아 마땅하다고 생각해서 계속 문을 두드렸다.
➡ I thought I deserved an _____, so I _____ knocking on the door.

(2) 나를 다시는 괴롭히지 마!
➡ Don't _____ me again!

(3) 나는 누구든지 범죄에 대해 누명을 쓸 수 있다는 것을 알았다.
➡ I learned that everybody can be _____ for a _____.

(4) 당신은 아마도 제게 설탕 한 컵을 빌려 줄 수 있으시겠죠?
➡ Could you maybe _____ me a cup of sugar?

**03** 다음 영영풀이가 가리키는 것을 고르시오.

an illegal action or activity for which a person can be punished by law

① right           ② character
③ crime          ④ response
⑤ palace

**04** 다음 문장의 (A)와 (B)에 공통으로 들어갈 말을 고르시오.

- I can't wait (A)_____ meet you.
- He was taken (A)_____ the police station.
- We need to drop by the grocery store because we ran out (B)_____ salt.
- The book is written from my mother's point (B)_____ view.

        (A)   (B)                    (A)   (B)
① of – to                ② by – from
③ to – of                ④ from – on
⑤ by – of

[05~07] 다음 대화를 읽고 물음에 답하시오.

Jack: Do you know the story *The Rabbit and the Turtle*?
Sora: Of course, I do.
Jack: I think the turtle in the story is (A) mean.
Sora: Why do you think so?
Jack: The turtle sees the rabbit sleeping but doesn't wake ⓐhim up. It is not fair.
Sora: I don't see it that way. Why should the turtle be responsible for the rabbit? I don't think ⓑhe should be.
Jack: That's interesting.

**05** 위 대화의 밑줄 친 (A)와 같은 의미로 쓰인 것을 고르시오.

① Don't be so <u>mean</u> to your little sister.
② What does this sentence <u>mean</u>?
③ I know what you <u>mean</u>.
④ What do you <u>mean</u> by that?
⑤ You <u>mean</u> that we should leave earlier, right?

**06** 위 대화의 밑줄 친 ⓐ, ⓑ가 가리키는 것을 찾아 쓰시오.

➡ ⓐ _____ , ⓑ _____

**07** 위 대화의 내용으로 보아 알 수 <u>없는</u> 것은?

① Jack은 '토끼와 거북이' 이야기 속의 거북이 못 됐다고 생각한다.

② Jack은 거북이 토끼를 깨우지 않은 것이 공정하지 않다고 생각한다.

③ 소라는 Jack과 다른 의견을 갖고 있다.

④ 소라는 거북이 토끼에 대해 책임을 져야 한다고 생각하지 않는다.

⑤ Jack은 거북과 토끼의 경주가 공정하지 않다고 생각한다.

**[08~09]** 다음 대화를 읽고 물음에 답하시오.

Mike: What do you think about my drawing, Prince?

Prince: Wow, this picture is very frightening!

Mike: Why do you think so?

Prince: I mean the picture shows a snake (A)[what / that] ate an elephant.

Mike: You're right. Actually, many people thought it was a picture of a hat.

Prince: Really? That's interesting.

Mike: I know. That's why I decided to become a pilot (B)[instead / instead of] a painter.

Prince: Haha. At least I can understand (C)[which / what] you mean.

Mike: Thank you, Prince.

**08** 위 대화의 괄호 (A)~(C)에 알맞은 말이 바르게 짝지어진 것은?

| | (A) | (B) | (C) |
|---|---|---|---|
| ① | what | instead | which |
| ② | what | instead of | what |
| ③ | that | instead of | which |
| ④ | that | instead of | what |
| ⑤ | that | instead | which |

**09** 위 대화를 읽고 대답할 수 <u>없는</u> 것은?

① What does Prince think about Mike's drawing?

② What do many people think about Mike's drawing?

③ Why is the picture frightening to Prince?

④ Why did Mike decide to become a pilot?

⑤ What kind of a hat did Mike draw?

**[10~11]** 다음 대화를 읽고 물음에 답하시오.

Ms. Kim: You look worried, Juwon.

Juwon: I think we will lose the soccer game tomorrow, Ms. Kim.

Ms. Kim: Why do you think so?

Juwon: We will have a match against Class 3. They have the strongest players in the school.

Ms. Kim: Look on the bright side. They might have strong players, but your class has the best teamwork.

Juwon: You're right. I didn't think about it that way. I'll go and practice!

**10** Why was Juwon worried about the soccer game against Class 3?

➡ _____

_____

**11** What is the strong point of Juwon's class?

➡ _____

**12** 다음 짝지어진 대화가 <u>어색한</u> 것을 고르시오.

① A: How do you like the shoes?
　B: I like them. They are too small and difficult to wear.
② A: How did you like the movie?
　B: It was interesting. I'd never thought about what happens after I die.
③ A: Is this what you wanted?
　B: Actually it's not. I wanted a bigger one.
④ A: What makes you think so?
　B: It's because he helps the poor.
⑤ A: I don't think Robin Hood is a good character.
　B: Why do you think so?

Grammar

**13** 다음 문장에서 어법상 <u>어색한</u> 부분을 찾아 올바른 문장으로 고쳐 쓰시오.

(1) They will be excited teaching you again.
　➡ _____
(2) I was scared being left home alone.
　➡ _____
(3) She answered that she would be happy coming.
　➡ _____

**14** 다음 중 어법상 올바른 문장을 <u>모두</u> 고르시오.

① I was proud to succeed in our experiment on Covid-19.
② I had never been sick until then.
③ She didn't know that her brother had wanted to go there.
④ I was proud to my father.
⑤ He was angry to his brother.

**15** 괄호 안의 단어와 과거완료 시제를 사용하여 우리말을 영작하시오.

내가 공항에 도착했을 때 그는 이미 떠나고 없었다. (leave, get)

➡ _____

**16** 괄호 안의 단어를 배열하여 우리말과 같은 뜻이 되도록 영작하시오.

제가 기꺼이 공항으로 모시러 가겠습니다.
(pick, I, to, would, glad, be, up, you, the, at, airport)

➡ _____

**17** 괄호 안의 단어를 활용하여 우리말에 맞게 영작하시오.

(1) 나는 여동생이 내 옷을 더럽힌 것을 보고 싸웠다. (fight, when, see, that, make)

➡ _____

_____

(2) 우리는 우리의 차가 사라졌다는 것을 알았을 때 당황했다. (embarrass, know, that, go)

➡ _____

_____

(3) 나는 남자친구가 우리의 기념일을 잊어버렸던 것이 떠올랐을 때 울었다. (cry, bring to mind, that, forget, anniversary)

➡ _____

_____

**18** 다음 중 어법상 어색한 것은?

① I was happy that see him again.

② She was glad to hear the news that her sister would be back soon.

③ My teacher was tired of preparing her class using remote lecture.

④ My younger brother was bored to stay at home during two weeks.

⑤ Kidson was upset that she didn't know how to use this machine.

**19** 괄호 안의 단어를 사용하여 우리말에 맞게 영작하시오.

> 그녀는 그를 떠나보내게 되어 슬펐다. (let, leave)

➡ _____

**20** 〈보기〉의 단어를 활용하여 그림의 내용에 맞게 빈칸을 채우시오.

┌─── 보기 ───┐
lose   win   happy   take a nap
└──────────┘

(1) The rabbit _____

_____ .

(2) The turtle _____ .

---

**Reading**

[21~22] 다음 글을 읽고 물음에 답하시오.

Reporter: Welcome to Animal World News. Last Sunday, a wolf was taken to the police station for blowing down pigs' houses. Today, we have the third little pig and the wolf with us. Mr. Pig, could you explain what happened to you and your brothers?

**21** What is likely to follow after the passage?

① the reason why the wolf was so upset

② interviews with the third little pig and the wolf

③ how the third little pig built his house

④ exciting news about raising animals

⑤ how to blow down pigs houses

## 22 What is TRUE about the passage?

① The news is about food chain.

② The wolf is resting in his house now.

③ The reporter is talking on the news.

④ The wolf wasn't arrested by the police yet.

⑤ The wolf will explain what happened to the pigs.

**[23~24]** 다음 글을 읽고 물음에 답하시오.

> Pig: Yes. My brothers and I thought it was time to build our own houses, so we built houses with straw, sticks, and bricks. One day, the wolf came and completely blew down my brothers' houses. He almost blew down my house, but it was made of bricks, so he couldn't.
>
> Reporter: How are your brothers doing now?
>
> Pig: They are shocked (A)to lose their houses. They are resting in my house.

## 23 다음 중 밑줄 친 (A)와 쓰임이 다른 하나는?

① David was sad to hear the news.

② Yumi was excited to see them dancing.

③ Nora was glad to speak in front of so many people.

④ June felt bored to read the book so long.

⑤ Julian must be diligent to wake up early in the morning.

## 24 What is the pig mainly talking about?

① how he made his house with bricks

② why he wants to make his own house

③ how long it took to build his own house

④ the accident the wolf blew down his brothers' houses

⑤ the friendship between him and the wolf

**[25~26]** 다음 글을 읽고 물음에 답하시오.

> Reporter: Thank you, Mr. Pig. Now, let's ①meet our second guest, the wolf. Mr. Wolf, could you tell us what happened?
>
> Wolf: This whole "Big Bad Wolf" thing is ②right. The real story is about a sneeze from a terrible cold and a cup of sugar.
>
> Reporter: What do you mean?
>
> Wolf: Back then, I was making a birthday cake for my dear old grandmother. I ran out of sugar. I walked down the street to ③ask my neighbor for a cup of sugar. When I knocked on the door, it ④fell down. Then I called, "Little pig, are you in?" I had just grabbed the broken door when I felt a sneeze coming on. I ⑤sneezed a great sneeze and you know what? The whole straw house fell down. I was very surprised by what had happened. Unfortunately, the same thing happened to the second little pig's house.

## 25 ①~⑤ 중 글의 흐름상 어색한 것은?

①       ②       ③       ④       ⑤

## 26 다음 중 위 글을 읽고 답할 수 없는 것은?

① Who is the second guest?

② What did the wolf need to make the cake?

③ For what did the wolf want to ask his neighbor?

④ What happened when the wolf knocked on the door?

⑤ When was the wolf making the cake?

**01** 주어진 우리말에 맞게 빈칸을 채우시오. (철자가 주어진 경우 그 철자로 시작할 것)

(1) 그 미술가는 작품을 만들기 위해 실생활 물건을 사용했다.

➡ The artist used real-life o_____ to create art.

(2) 왜 거북이 토끼에 대해 책임을 져야 하지?

➡ Why should the turtle be _____ for the rabbit?

(3) 나는 느리고 꾸준히 걷는 것을 더 좋아한다.

➡ I prefer to walk slowly and _____.

(4) Ward는 7살 때 그의 아빠와 계모로부터 도망쳤다.

➡ Ward ran away from his father and _____ when he was seven years old.

**02** 다음 문장의 빈칸에 들어갈 말을 〈보기〉에서 골라 쓰시오.

┌─ 보기 ─┐
framed / straw / grabbed / trouble / sneeze
└────────┘

(1) I had just _____ the broken door when I felt a sneeze coming on.

(2) We built houses with _____, sticks, and bricks.

(3) Do you think you were _____?

(4) The real story is about a _____ from a terrible cold and a cup of sugar.

(5) I'm sorry to _____ you.

**03** 다음 우리말과 일치하도록 주어진 단어를 모두 배열하여 영작하시오.

(1) 나의 집은 너무 약해서 늑대가 날려버릴 수 있었다.

(for / to / was / house / my / weak / too / down / wolf / the / blow)

➡ _____

(2) 함께 이 사진을 봅시다.

(a / look / together / let's / this / take / picture / at)

➡ _____

(3) 제 생각에 그것은 당신의 치마와 매우 잘 어울리네요.

(with / I / it / your / skirt / think / goes / perfectly)

➡ _____

[04~05] 다음 대화를 읽고 물음에 답하시오.

Jack: Do you know the story *The Rabbit and the Turtle*?
Sora: Of course, I do.
Jack: I think the turtle in the story is ⓐmean.
Sora: Why do you think so?
Jack: The turtle sees the rabbit ⓑsleeping but doesn't ⓒwake up him. It is not fair.
Sora: I don't see it ⓓthat way. Why should the turtle be ⓔresponsible for the rabbit? I don't think he should be.
Jack: That's interesting.

**04** 위 대화의 밑줄 친 ⓐ~ⓔ 중 어법상 틀린 것을 찾아 바르게 고치시오.

➡ _____

**05** 위 대화를 읽고 대답할 수 <u>없는</u> 것은?

① What does Jack think about Sora's view on *The Rabbit and the Turtle*?

② Why does Jack think the turtle in the story is mean?

③ Who doesn't wake up the rabbit in the story?

④ Does Sora think the turtle should be responsible for the rabbit?

⑤ Who is fair in the story *The Rabbit and the Turtle*?

**[06~07]** 다음 대화를 읽고 물음에 답하시오.

Mike: What do you think about my drawing, Prince?

Prince: Wow, this picture is very ⓐ<u>frightened</u>!

Mike: Why do you think so?

Prince: I mean the picture shows a snake ⓑ<u>that</u> ate an elephant.

Mike: You're right. Actually, many people thought it was a picture of a hat.

Prince: Really? That's ⓒ<u>interesting</u>.

Mike: I know. That's why I decided to become a pilot ⓓ<u>instead of</u> a painter.

Prince: Haha. At least I can understand ⓔ<u>what</u> you mean.

Mike: Thank you, Prince.

**06** 위 대화의 밑줄 친 ⓐ~ⓔ 중 어법상 어색한 것을 찾아 바르게 고치시오.

➡ _____

**07** 위 대화의 내용과 일치하지 <u>않는</u> 것은?

① 왕자는 Mike의 그림이 매우 무섭다고 생각한다.

② 왕자는 Mike의 그림이 코끼리를 먹은 뱀을 보여 준다고 생각한다.

③ 많은 사람들은 Mike의 그림이 모자를 그린 그림이라고 생각했다.

④ Mike는 화가 대신에 비행사가 되기로 결심했다.

⑤ 왕자는 Mike의 그림을 이해하기가 어려웠다.

**[08~10]** 다음 대화를 읽고 물음에 답하시오.

Brian: How did you like the movie *Good Friends*, Yura?

Yura: I liked it. It was fun ⓐ<u>to compare</u> the movie with the original book.

Brian: ⓑ<u>Which</u> did you like better, the movie or the book?

Yura: Well, I liked the movie, but I think I enjoyed the book more. The book helped me ⓒ<u>understanding</u> the characters better.

Brian: That's ⓓ<u>interesting</u>. To me, the movie was better ⓔ<u>because</u> it was easier to understand the story.

Yura: That's true. I guess they both have their own advantages.

Brian: You're right.

**08** 위 대화의 밑줄 친 ⓐ~ⓔ 중 어법상 어색한 것을 찾아 바르게 고치시오.

➡ _____

**09** 위 대화의 내용과 일치하도록 빈칸을 완성하시오.

Brian and Yura talked about the movie *Good Friends*. They had different opinion about it. Yura preferred (A)_____ to (B)_____ because (C)_____. On the other hand, Brian liked (D)_____ better because it was easier for him (E)_____. They agreed that both of them had their own advantages.

**10** 위 대화를 읽고 대답할 수 없는 것은?

① What movie did Yura watch?

② What did Yura compare with the movie?

③ Why did Yura enjoy the book more than the movie?

④ Why did Brian think the movie was better?

⑤ What did Yura think the movie's disadvantage was?

**11** 다음 그림을 참고하고, 괄호 안의 단어를 활용하여 빈칸을 알맞게 채우시오.

(1)　　　　(2)　　　　(3)

(1) I _____ my father. (enjoy, help)

(2) I made a plan about her idea that she _____ during our meeting. (tell)

(3) I _____ teach my grandmother how to use a cell phone. (happy)

**12** 괄호 안의 단어를 활용하여 우리말에 맞게 영작하시오.

(1) 나는 엄마에게 숙제를 끝냈다고 말했다. (tell, mother, finish)

➡ _____

_____

(2) 이모가 그녀의 딸에게 인형을 주고 싶었다고 쓰여 있었다. (it, that, my aunt, write, give, to)

➡ _____

_____

(3) 그는 맨체스터에서 뛰고 싶었다고 나에게 말했다. (tell, want)

➡ _____

_____

**13** 다음 중 어색한 문장을 고르시오.

① The Prince was happy to find Cinderella.

② I'm glad to meet you here.

③ I was shocked that see the building on fire.

④ My friends were sorry to hear the news.

⑤ I was excited to be invited to the party.

**14** 괄호 안의 단어를 활용하여 우리말에 맞게 영작하시오.

> 우리가 그 게임에서 진 것은 운이 없었다. (unfortunate, lose)

➡ _____

**[15~17]** 다음 글을 읽고 물음에 답하시오.

Reporter: Thank you, Mr. Pig. Now, let's meet our second guest, the wolf. Mr. Wolf, could you tell us what happened?

Wolf: This whole "Big Bad Wolf" thing is wrong. The real story is about (A)_____.

Reporter: What do you mean?

Wolf: Back then, I was making a birthday cake for my dear old grandmother. I ran out of sugar. I walked down the street to ask my neighbor for a cup of sugar. When I knocked on the door, it fell down. Then I called, "Little pig, are you in?" I had just grabbed the broken door when I felt a sneeze coming on. I sneezed a great sneeze and you know what? The whole straw house fell down. I was very surprised by (B)what had happened. Unfortunately, the same thing happened to the second little pig's house.

**15** 다음 중 빈칸 (A)에 들어갈 말로 가장 적절한 것은?

① a sneeze from three pigs and my grandmother
② throwing a dinner party for my grandmother
③ making a birthday cake for the three little pigs
④ a cup of sugar and learning how to make a strong house
⑤ a sneeze from a terrible cold and a cup of sugar

출제율 90%

**16** 밑줄 친 (B)가 의미하는 것을 우리말로 쓰시오.

➡ _____

출제율 100%

**17** 다음 중 위 글을 읽고 답할 수 있는 것은?

① What is the name of the reporter?
② How many animals is the reporter going to interview?
③ Why did the wolf's neighbor build his house with straw?
④ What happened when the wolf grabbed the broken door?
⑤ When was the wolf's grandmother's birthday?

[18~20] 다음 글을 읽고 물음에 답하시오.

Reporter: Then why did you go to the third little pig's house?

Wolf: I still needed that cup of sugar, so I went to the next house. The third little pig ① had built his house of bricks. I called out, "I'm sorry to trouble you, but are you in?" And do you know ②what he answered? "Go away. Don't bother me again!" ③How impolite! I thought I deserved an apology,

so I kept knocking. When the police came, of course they thought I was breaking into this pig's house.

Reporter: Do you think you were ④framed?

Wolf: Yes. The news reporters of the town thought a sick wolf going to borrow a cup of sugar didn't sound very exciting. So, they made me the "Big Bad Wolf." Could you maybe lend me a cup of sugar?

Reporter: Thank you for your time. Everyone, which do you think is the true story, ⑤ the pig or the wolf?

출제율 95%

**18** ①~⑤ 중 어법상 바르지 않은 것은?

①        ②        ③        ④        ⑤

출제율 90%

**19** What did the wolf do to get an apology from the third little pig? Answer in English with a full sentence.

➡ _____

출제율 100%

**20** 다음 중 위 글의 내용으로 보아 알 수 없는 것은?

① The wolf wanted the pig to give him an apology.
② The police thought the wolf was breaking into the pig's house.
③ The news reporters wanted to make their news sound exciting.
④ The reporter interviewing the wolf believes what the wolf is saying.
⑤ The wolf was made the "Big Bad Wolf" by the news reporters.

[01~03] 다음 대화를 읽고 물음에 답하시오.

Ms. Parker: Now, take a look at this work of art. How do you like it?

Mina: Well, is it even art?

Henry: To me, it isn't more than a toilet.

Ms. Parker: It is not just art. I think it is the greatest piece of art of the 20th century.

Mina: Why do you think so?

Ms. Parker: It is a perfect example of a different point of view. The artist used real-life objects to create art.

Claire: So, he didn't create something new?

Ms. Parker: That's right. He simply wanted people to look at the objects in a different way.

Mina: Thank you so much, Ms. Parker. I learned a lot today!

**01** What does Ms. Parker think about the work of art?

➡ _____

_____

**02** What did the artist use to create the work of art?

➡ _____

**03** What did the artist want people to do?

➡ _____

_____

**04** 다음은 Suji에 대한 이야기이다. 주어진 〈Feeling〉과 〈Reason〉을 조합하여 문장을 완성하시오. (〈Feeling〉과 〈Reason〉에 나오는 단어 또는 어구는 한번 씩만 사용할 것.)

<Feeling>
bored   happy   excited   surprised

<Reason>
• receive a present that she hadn't think ever
• see her brother enjoy the party
• read a boring book
• join a popular club in her school

(1) _____

(2) _____

_____

(3) _____

_____

(4) _____

_____

**05** 다음 그림을 보고 괄호 안의 단어를 사용하여 빈칸을 채우시오.

Last weekend I _____(go) to the souvenir shop. I _____(glad) see my new classmate there. He _____(tell) me that he _____(know) about me because he _____(see) me before.

Reporter: Welcome to Animal World News. Last Sunday, a wolf was taken to the police station for blowing down pigs' houses. Today, we have the third little pig and the wolf with us. Mr. Pig, (A) 당신과 당신 형제들에게 무슨 일이 일어났는지 설명해 주시겠어요?

Pig: Yes. My brothers and I thought it was time to build our own houses, so we built houses with straw, sticks, and bricks. One day, the wolf came and completely blew down my brothers' houses. He almost blew down my house, but it was made of bricks, so he couldn't.

Reporter: How are your brothers doing now?

Pig: They are shocked to lose their houses. They are resting in my house.

Reporter: Thank you, Mr. Pig. Now, let's meet our second guest, the wolf. Mr. Wolf, could you tell us what happened?

**06** According to the dialogue, why were the pigs shocked? Answer in English and use the words 'they', and 'due to.'

➡ _____

**07** 주어진 단어를 활용하여 밑줄 친 (A)를 영어로 쓰시오.

| (could / explain / to) |
| --- |

➡ _____
_____

Reporter: Then why did you go to the third little pig's house?

Wolf: I still needed that cup of sugar, so I went to the next house. The third little pig had built his house of bricks. I called out, "I'm sorry to trouble you, but are you in?" And do you know what he answered? "Go away. Don't bother me again!" How impolite! I thought I (A)_____ an apology, so I kept (B)_____. When the police came, of course they thought I was (C)_____ into this pig's house.

Reporter: Do you think you were framed?

Wolf: Yes. The news reporters of the town thought a sick wolf going to borrow a cup of sugar didn't sound very exciting. So, they made me the "Big Bad Wolf." Could you maybe lend me a cup of sugar?

**08** 주어진 단어를 내용과 어법에 맞게 빈칸 (A)~(C)에 쓰시오.

| knock / break / deserve |
| --- |

➡ (A)_____ (B)_____ (C)_____

**09** According to the passage, why did the wolf visit pigs' houses? Use the phrase 'in order to.'

➡ _____
_____

## 창의사고력 서술형 문제

**01** 다음 그림을 보고 대화의 내용과 일치하도록 빈칸을 완성하시오.

> Ms. Parker: Now, take a look at this work of art. How do you like it?
>
> Jinho: Well, is it even art?
>
> Henry: To me, it isn't more than a toilet.
>
> Ms. Parker: It is not just art. I think it is the greatest piece of art of the 20th century.
>
> Mina: Why do you think so?
>
> Ms. Parker: It is a perfect example of a different point of view. The artist used real-life objects to create art.
>
> Claire: So, he didn't create something new?
>
> Ms. Parker: That's right. He simply wanted people to look at the objects in a different way.
>
> Mina: Thank you so much, Ms. Parker. I learned a lot today!

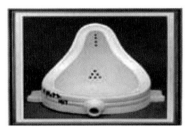

Title: Fountain

Artist: Marcel Duchamp

Special Point:

1) The artist used _____ _____ _____ to create art.

2) The artist wanted people to look at the objects _____ _____ _____ _____.

**02** 다음 내용을 바탕으로 재판에서 배심원에게 낭독할 글을 완성하시오.

> The wolf says, "I blew down the first and the second pigs' houses because of a sneeze from a terrible cold." And according to the wolf's friend, he had seen the wolf going to a hospital that day.

> What the wolf said is true.
>
> The wolf said he (A)_____ the first and the second pigs' houses because of (B)_____. I think what he said is (C)_____. His (D)_____ said that he had seen (E)_____. I would be glad to hear your wise decision. Thank you.

## 단원별 모의고사

**01** 다음 영영풀이가 가리키는 것을 고르시오.

> by bad luck

① impolitely　　　② uniquely
③ steadily　　　　④ unfortunately
⑤ peacefully

**02** 다음 중 밑줄 친 부분의 뜻풀이가 바르지 <u>않은</u> 것은?

① The noise was <u>frightening</u>. (무서운)
② If he continues to bother you, <u>simply</u> ignore him. (단순히)
③ I bought a <u>straw</u> hat at the market. (짚, 지푸라기)
④ Most of the buildings in the town are made of <u>bricks</u>. (벽돌)
⑤ I have to go back to the house and <u>grab</u> the car keys. (빌리다)

**03** 다음 우리말을 주어진 단어를 이용하여 영작하시오.

(1) 지난 일요일, 한 늑대가 경찰서에 끌려갔다. (take)
　➡ Last Sunday, a wolf _____ _____ _____ the police station.

(2) 늑대는 돼지들의 집들을 바람을 불어 넘어뜨렸다. (blow)
　➡ The wolf _____ _____ the pigs' houses.

(3) 그들은 내가 이 돼지의 집에 침입하고 있다고 생각했다. (break)
　➡ They thought I was _____ _____ this pig's house.

(4) 당신은 늑대의 이야기가 이해가 되나요? (make)
　➡ Does the wolf's story _____ _____ to you?

**[04~06]** 다음 대화를 읽고 물음에 답하시오.

> Anna: Have you finished the book, Taeho?
> Taeho: Yes. I finished it yesterday, Anna.
> Anna: (A)[What / How] did you like it?
> Taeho: It was interesting.
> Anna: What is the book about?
> Taeho: You know the story of Heungbu, right? In the book, Nolbu tells the story from his point of view.
> Anna: What does he say?
> Taeho: Well, he says he didn't help Heungbu for a reason. He wanted Heungbu to make money on his own and be (B)[dependent / independent].
> Anna: Wow, it's a (C)[common / unique] story! I can't wait to read the book. Thanks, Taeho.

**04** 위 대화의 괄호 (A)~(C)에 알맞은 말이 바르게 짝지어진 것은?

|   | (A) | (B) | (C) |
|---|---|---|---|
| ① | What | dependent | common |
| ② | What | independent | unique |
| ③ | How | independent | common |
| ④ | How | independent | unique |
| ⑤ | How | dependent | common |

**05** 위 대화를 읽고 대답할 수 <u>없는</u> 것은?

① What is the book Taeho read about?
② From whose point of view is the story in the book told?
③ Why didn't Nolbu help Heungbu in the book?
④ What did Nolbu want Heungbu to do in the book?
⑤ Did Heungbu want to make money for himself?

**06** 위 대화의 내용과 일치하도록 Anna의 일기를 완성하시오.

> Today, Taeho introduced an interesting book for me. He finished the book (A)_____ and explained the story. The book was about the story of Heungbu written from Nolbu's (B)_____ . Taeho told me that Nolbu didn't help Heungbu (C)_____ . Nolbu wanted Heungbu to (D)_____ on his own and be independent. It sounded so unique and interesting. I'm looking forward to (E)_____

**[07~08]** 다음 대화를 읽고 물음에 답하시오.

> **Brian:** How did you like the movie *Good Friends*, Yura?
> **Yura:** I liked it. It was fun to compare the movie with the original book.
> **Brian:** Which did you like better, the movie or the book?
> **Yura:** Well, I liked the movie, but I think I enjoyed the book more. The book helped me understand the characters better.
> **Brian:** That's interesting. To me, the movie was better because it was easier to understand the story.
> **Yura:** That's true. I guess they both have their own advantages.
> **Brian:** You're right.

**07** Which did Brian like better, the movie or the book and why?

➡ _____

_____

**08** Why did Yura prefer the book?

➡ _____

_____

**[09~10]** 다음 대화를 읽고 물음에 답하시오.

> **Ms. Kim:** You look worried, Juwon.
> **Juwon:** I think we will lose the soccer game tomorrow, Ms. Kim.
> **Ms. Kim:** (A)왜 그렇게 생각해?
> **Juwon:** We will have a match against Class 3. They have the strongest players in the school.
> **Ms. Kim:** Look on the bright side. They might have strong players, but your class has the best teamwork.
> **Juwon:** You're right. I didn't think about it that way. I'll go and practice!

**09** 위 대화의 밑줄 친 (A)의 우리말을 주어진 말을 써서 영작하시오. (why, so)

➡ _____

**10** 위 대화의 내용과 일치하지 <u>않는</u> 것은?

① 주원이는 내일 축구 경기에 질 것 같다고 생각한다.
② 주원이네 반은 내일 3반과 축구 경기를 할 예정이다.
③ 3반에는 학교에서 가장 잘하는 선수들이 있다.
④ 주원이네 반은 팀워크가 가장 좋다.
⑤ 주원이는 자기네 반의 팀워크가 좋다고 생각하지 않는다.

**[11~12]** 다음 대화를 읽고 물음에 답하시오.

> **Ms. Parker:** Now, take a look at this work of art. How do you like it?
> **Jinho:** Well, is it even art?
> **Henry:** To me, it isn't more than a toilet.

Ms. Parker: (A) It is not just art. I think it is the greatest piece of art of the 20th century.

Mina: (B) Why do you think so?

Ms. Parker: (C) The artist used real-life objects to create art.

Claire: (D) So, he didn't create something new?

Ms. Parker: (E) That's right. He simply wanted people to look at the objects in a different way.

Mina: Thank you so much, Ms. Parker. I learned a lot today!

## 11 위 대화의 (A)~(E) 중 주어진 문장이 들어가기에 적절한 곳은?

It is a perfect example of a different point of view.

① (A)  ② (B)  ③ (C)  ④ (D)  ⑤ (E)

## 12 위 대화를 읽고 대답할 수 없는 것은?

① What are they looking at now?

② What does Ms. Parker think about the work of art?

③ According to Ms. Parker, why is the work of art a perfect example of a different point of view?

④ What did the artist want people to do?

⑤ How did the artist use real-life objects to create art?

## 13 괄호 안의 단어를 활용하여 우리말에 맞게 영작하시오.

(1) 그들은 집을 잃어 충격에 빠졌다. (lose, shock)

➡ _____

(2) 재채기가 나오려 할 때 나는 부서진 문을 막 움켜잡았었다. (grab, sneeze)

➡ _____

_____

## 14 다음 빈칸에 공통으로 들어갈 단어를 고르시오

- It is surprising _____ he should do such a thing.
- It is lucky _____ I live in Korea.
- I was happy _____ you will go to study abroad.

① to        ② for        ③ at
④ that      ⑤ in

## 15 다음 중 어법상 어색한 것은?

① I'm glad that you won the first prize.

② It is strange for your friend to come here.

③ Were you surprised to receive the news?

④ We are afraid that go to the hospital tomorrow.

⑤ She is proud of you.

## 16 다음 그림을 보고 〈보기〉에 있는 표현 중 적절한 것을 골라 빈칸을 알맞게 채우시오.

보기
be sad to     be surprised to
be happy to     be sorry to

➡ He _____ think that he will go on safari this summer vacation.

**17** 다음 그림은 Suji의 블로그에 올라온 Suji의 가족 사진으로 2년 전에 찍은 것이다. 각 문제에 알맞게 답하시오.

(1) 빈칸에 공통으로 들어갈 알맞은 것을 고르시오. (시간의 차이가 나도록 할 것.)

> I remembered that
> • I _____ the guitar, sitting on a chair beside the sofa.
> • my mom and my brother _____ Baduk.

① play       ② playing
③ played     ④ had played
⑤ to play

(2) 괄호 안의 단어를 사용하여 빈칸을 채우시오. (시간의 차이가 나도록 할 것.)

> I remembered that my lovely cat _____ (sit) on my grandmother's knee.

(3) 우리말에 맞게 괄호 안의 단어를 배열하시오.

> 나는 가족과 즐거운 시간을 보내서 행복했다.

(family, great, a, my, with, happy, was, to, I, have, time)

➡ _____

[18~21] 다음 글을 읽고 물음에 답하시오.

Pig: Yes. My brothers and I thought it was time to build our own houses, so we built houses with straw, sticks, and bricks. One day, the wolf came and completely blew down my brothers' houses. He almost blew down my house, but it was made of bricks, so he couldn't.

Reporter: How are your brothers doing Mnow?

Pig: They are shocked to lose their houses. They are resting in my house.

Reporter: Thank you, Mr. Pig. Now, let's meet our second guest, the wolf. Mr. Wolf, could you tell us what happened?

Wolf: This whole "Big Bad Wolf" thing is wrong. The real story is about a sneeze from a terrible cold and a cup of sugar.

Reporter: What do you mean?

Wolf: Back then, I was making a birthday cake for my dear old grandmother. I ran out of sugar. I walked down the street to ask my neighbor for a cup of sugar. When I knocked on the door, it fell down. Then I called, "Little pig, are you in?" I had just grabbed the broken door when I felt a sneeze coming on. I sneezed a great sneeze and you know what? The whole straw house fell down. I was very surprised by what had happened. Unfortunately, the same thing happened to the second little pig's house.

**18** 다음 중 위 글의 내용과 일치하지 <u>않는</u> 것은?

① The three pigs built their own houses.
② The reporter wonders what happened to both the pigs and the wolf.
③ The wolf sneezed because of a cold.
④ The wolf broke down the door on purpose.
⑤ The pig blames the wolf for destroying his brothers' houses.

**19** Write the reason why the wolf couldn't blow down the third little pig's house. Answer in English and use the phrase 'It's because.'

➡ _____

**20** 다음은 위 글의 내용을 요약한 것이다. 빈칸에 알맞은 말을 쓰시오.

> The pig says the wolf came and completely _____ _____ _____ _____ _____. On the other hand, the wolf says the houses fell down because of _____ _____ _____ _____ _____.

**21** What did the wolf run out of when he was making a birthday cake for his grandmother? Answer in English with five words.

➡ _____

**[22~25]** 다음 글을 읽고 물음에 답하시오.

**Reporter:** Then why did you go to the third little pig's house?

**Wolf:** I still needed that ①cup of sugar, so I went to the next house.

(A) And do you know what he answered? "Go away. Don't bother me again!" How impolite!

(B) The third little pig had built his house ②of bricks. I called out, "I'm sorry ③to trouble you, but are you in?"

(C) I thought I deserved an apology, ④so I kept knocking. When the police came, of course they thought I was breaking into this pig's house.

**Reporter:** Do you think you were ⓐ_____?

**Wolf:** Yes. The news reporters of the town thought a sick wolf going to borrow a cup of sugar didn't sound very ⑤excited. So, they made me the "Big Bad Wolf." Could you maybe lend me a cup of sugar?

**22** ①~⑤ 중 어법상 바르지 <u>않은</u> 것은?

①     ②     ③     ④     ⑤

**23** 자연스러운 글이 되도록 (A)~(C)를 바르게 나열한 것은?

① (A)–(C)–(B)     ② (B)–(A)–(C)
③ (B)–(C)–(A)     ④ (C)–(A)–(B)
⑤ (C)–(B)–(A)

**24** 다음 중 빈칸 ⓐ에 들어갈 말로 가장 적절한 것은?

① guilty     ② desperate
③ wrong     ④ depressed
⑤ framed

**25** 다음 빈칸에 들어갈 말이 바르게 짝지어진 것은?

> Q: Why did the police think the wolf was breaking into the third pig's house?
> A: It's because he kept _____ on the pig's door. He thought he deserved a(n) _____ for the pig's _____ response.

① kicking – apology – rude
② knocking – forgiveness – impolite
③ kicking – forgiveness – polite
④ knocking – apology – rude
⑤ knocking – manners – impolite

# MEMO

MEMO

중간+기말 plus⁺

영어 기출문제집

영어 중 3

지학 | 민찬규

*Best Collection*

내용문의 중등영어발전소 적중100 편집부  TEL 070-7707-0457
인터넷 서비스 www.jj100.co.kr

# INSIGHT
## on the textbook

교과서 파헤치기

영어 기출 문제집

적중 100 plus
1학기 전과정

영어 중 3

지학 | 민찬규

# INSIGHT
## on the textbook

교과서 파헤치기

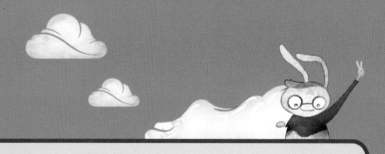

※ 다음 영어를 우리말로 쓰시오.

| | | | |
|---|---|---|---|
| 01 accept | | 22 elderly | |
| 02 comfortable | | 23 invent | |
| 03 electronically | | 24 exactly | |
| 04 scholarship | | 25 trash bin | |
| 05 device | | 26 fence | |
| 06 useful | | 27 finally | |
| 07 sort | | 28 work | |
| 08 freely | | 29 ignore | |
| 09 community | | 30 lie | |
| 10 protect | | 31 discover | |
| 11 situation | | 32 realize | |
| 12 raise | | 33 float | |
| 13 complain | | 34 scarecrow | |
| 14 hallway | | 35 be afraid of | |
| 15 need | | 36 sign up for | |
| 16 surprisingly | | 37 scare away | |
| 17 inform | | 38 take the place of | |
| 18 excellent | | 39 prevent A from -ing | |
| 19 instead | | 40 thanks to | |
| 20 path | | 41 such as | |
| 21 press | | 42 be proud of | |
| | | 43 as a result | |

※ 다음 우리말을 영어로 쓰시오.

| | | | |
|---|---|---|---|
| 01 | 분류하다 | 22 | 허수아비 |
| 02 | 편안한 | 23 | 뜨다 |
| 03 | 위험한 | 24 | 전자적으로 |
| 04 | 장학금 | 25 | 울타리 |
| 05 | 언론 | 26 | 연세가 드신 |
| 06 | 불평하다, 항의하다 | 27 | 눕다, 놓여 있다 |
| 07 | 발견하다 | 28 | 훌륭한 |
| 08 | 쓰레기통 | 29 | 작동하다, 효과가 있다 |
| 09 | 질병 | 30 | 자유롭게 |
| 10 | 놀랍게도 | 31 | 지역 사회, 공동체 |
| 11 | 보호하다 | 32 | 복도 |
| 12 | 기르다 | 33 | 기분이 상한 |
| 13 | 정확하게 | 34 | 결정하다 |
| 14 | 무시하다 | 35 | ~에 바탕을 두다 |
| 15 | 작은 길 | 36 | ~을 신청하다 |
| 16 | 깨닫다 | 37 | 우울해 보이다 |
| 17 | 알려주다 | 38 | ~을 대신하다 |
| 18 | 대신에 | 39 | 결과적으로 |
| 19 | 경험 | 40 | ~을 자랑스러워하다 |
| 20 | 받아들이다 | 41 | ~을 생각해 내다 |
| 21 | 마침내 | 42 | 돌려보내다 |
| | | 43 | A가 ~하지 못하게 막다 |

※ 다음 영영풀이에 알맞은 단어를 <보기>에서 골라 쓴 후, 우리말 뜻을 쓰시오.

1 _____ : making you feel physically relaxed: _____

2 _____ : to taste food or drink to find out what it is like: _____

3 _____ : a small raised area on a surface: _____

4 _____ : to stay on or near the surface of a liquid and not sink: _____

5 _____ : a track that is specially made for people to walk or ride on: _____

6 _____ : a machine or tool that does a special job: _____

7 _____ : to refuse to show that you hear or see something or someone:
_____

8 _____ : to separate and put people or things in a particular order: _____

9 _____ : newspapers, magazines, and radio and television news reports:
_____

10 _____ : to say or write that you are unhappy, sick, uncomfortable, etc.:
_____

11 _____ : a space or passage inside the entrance or front door of a building::
_____

12 _____ : an illness affecting humans, animals or plants, often caused by infection:
_____

13 _____ : an event at which things are sold to raise money for people or an
organization: _____

14 _____ : a structure like a wall built outdoors usually of wood or metal that
separates two areas: _____

15 _____ : a figure made to look like a person, that is dressed in old clothes and put
in a field to frighten birds away: _____

16 _____ : an amount of money that is given by a school, an organization, etc.:
_____

| 보기 | | | |
|---|---|---|---|
| float | comfortable | complain | bazaar |
| try | sort | fence | scholarship |
| path | ignore | disease | press |
| bump | device | scarecrow | hallway |

※ 다음 우리말과 일치하도록 빈칸에 알맞은 말을 쓰시오.

### Listen & Speak 1 A

**B:** What's the _____, Yura?

**G:** I'm _____ _____ this dog. I _____ it _____ the _____ _____ _____ I go to school. I don't _____ it _____ a home.

**B:** Awww, _____ a _____ _____! I'm _____ to _____ that it doesn't _____ a home.

**G:** I know. _____ _____ I do _____ it?

**B:** _____ _____ you _____ it to an _____ care center and _____ _____ _____?

**G:** _____ a great idea. Thanks.

### Listen & Speak 1 B

**G:** What's the _____, Mason? Are you _____?

**B:** I _____ _____ my bike at Hangang Park this afternoon.

**G:** Are you okay? _____ did it _____?

**B:** I'm okay. I just _____ over a big _____ on the _____ _____.

**G:** _____ there any _____?

**B:** No, there weren't.

**G:** How _____ _____ _____ the _____ on the community _____?

**B:** That's a great _____.

### Listen & Speak 1 C

**A:** You _____ _____. What's the _____?

**B:** I _____ _____ _____ my textbook.

**A:** Oh, no. I'm _____ _____ _____ that.

### Listen & Speak 2 A

**G:** I love our _____!

**B:** Me, too! I _____ these stickers will be _____.

**G:** I'm _____ they will help people _____ their _____ for _____.

B: Let's _____ back _____ to _____ _____ they work.

G: Sounds good.

B: 그것들이 효과가 있는지 내일 다시 와 보자.
G: 좋아.

---

### Listen & Speak 2 B

G: Hi, my name is Malala Yousafzai. I'm _____ Pakistan. In my country, there _____ some people _____ _____ _____ girls do not _____ _____ go to school. So they started to _____ _____ some _____ _____. I _____ so bad. I _____ _____ _____ _____ _____ about it and _____ many talks. _____ _____ the support from many people, an _____ _____ was finally _____ in my country. Now I have a _____ dream. I _____ every _____ in the world can _____ an education.

소녀: 안녕하세요. 제 이름은 Malala Yousafzai입니다. 저는 파키스탄에서 왔습니다. 우리나라에서는 여자들은 학교에 갈 필요가 없다고 믿는 사람들이 있었습니다. 그래서 그들은 몇몇 여학교를 폐쇄하기 시작했습니다. 저는 매우 기분이 좋지 않았습니다. 그래서 그것에 관하여 언론에 글을 썼고, 많은 대화를 했습니다. 많은 사람들의 지지 덕택에 우리나라에서 교육법이 마침내 통과되었습니다. 이제 저는 더 큰 꿈이 있습니다. 나는 세계의 모든 아이들이 교육을 받을 수 있기를 희망합니다.

---

### Real Life Communication

Henry: You _____ upset. What's the _____, Mina?

Mina: _____ _____ these _____, Henry. _____ _____ _____ people say there aren't _____ _____ places to _____ in our town.

Henry: That's too bad. I'm _____ that they didn't _____ a _____ to _____ the nice places here. We should do _____ about that.

Mina: Why _____ we make a video that _____ the _____ in our _____ and _____ it on the internet?

Henry: That's an _____ idea. _____ do that.

Mina: Sounds good. I _____ they _____ their time here.

Henry: 너 속상해 보여. 미나야, 무슨 일 있니?
Mina: Henry야, 이 댓글들을 봐. 많은 사람들이 우리 마을에 재미있는 장소가 충분하지 않다고 말해.
Henry: 그것 참 안됐다. 그들이 여기서 멋있는 장소를 방문할 기회를 가지지 못했다는 것이 유감이야. 우리가 무엇인가를 해야 해.
Mina: 우리 마을의 유명한 장소를 보여주는 비디오를 만들어 인터넷에 게시하는 것은 어떨까?
Henry: 그거 좋은 생각이야. 그렇게 하자.
Mina: 좋아. 그들이 여기서 즐거운 시간을 보냈으면 좋겠어.

---

### Let's Check 1

G: You _____ _____. What's the _____?

B: I _____ _____ for the soccer team, but I couldn't _____.

G: Why not?

B: There were _____ too many students _____ the team, so the coach won't _____ any new students _____ _____.

G: That's too bad. I _____ you find _____ _____ club.

B: Thanks.

G: 너 우울해 보인다. 무슨 일 있니?
B: 나는 축구팀에 지원했어. 그런데 가입할 수가 없어.
G: 왜 안 돼?
B: 이미 팀에 선수가 너무 많아, 그래서 코치가 올해는 새로운 학생을 받지 않을 거야.
G: 그거 참 안됐다. 나는 네가 다른 재미있는 동아리를 찾기를 바라.
B: 고마워.

※ 다음 우리말에 맞도록 대화를 영어로 쓰시오.

### Listen & Speak 1 A

B: _____

G: _____

_____

B: _____

G: _____

B: _____

G: _____

B: 유라야, 무슨 문제가 있니?

G: 이 개가 걱정이 돼. 학교에 갈 때마다 길에서 봐. 집이 없는 것 같아.

B: 어이구, 정말 귀여운 개구나! 집이 없다는 말을 들으니 유감이다.

G: 알아. 어떻게 해야 할까?

B: 동물 보호센터에 데리고 가서 도움을 요청하면 어떨까?

G: 좋은 생각이야. 고마워.

### Listen & Speak 1 B

G: _____

B: _____

G: _____

B: _____

G: _____

B: _____

G: _____

B: _____

G: Mason, 무슨 일 있니? 너 다쳤니?

B: 오늘 오후 한강 공원에서 자전거에서 떨어졌어.

G: 괜찮니? 어떻게 하다 그런 일이 벌어졌니?

B: 괜찮아. 나는 단지 자전거 도로에 있는 큰 요철을 타고 넘었을 뿐이야.

G: 표지판이 없었어?

B: 아니, 없었어.

G: 동네 웹 사이트에 그 문제에 관하여 글을 쓰는 것이 어떠니?

B: 그거 좋은 생각이다.

### Listen & Speak 1 C

A: _____

B: _____

A: _____

A: 너 걱정스러워 보인다. 무슨 일 있니?

B: 나는 교과서를 안 가져왔어.

A: 오, 저런. 그 말을 들으니 안됐다.

### Listen & Speak 2 A

G: _____

B: _____

G: _____

G: 나는 우리 스티커가 아주 좋아!

B: 나도 그래! 나는 이 스티커들이 도움이 되기를 희망해.

G: 그것이 사람들에게 재활용 쓰레기를 분류하도록 도움을 줄 거라고 확신해.

B: _____

G: _____

B: 그것들이 효과가 있는지 내일 다시 와 보자.

G: 좋아.

### Listen & Speak 2 B

G: _____

_____

_____

_____

_____

_____

소녀: 안녕하세요. 제 이름은 Malala Yousafzai입니다. 저는 파키스탄에서 왔습니다. 우리나라에서는 여자들은 학교에 갈 필요가 없다고 믿는 사람들이 있었습니다. 그래서 그들은 몇몇 여학교를 폐쇄하기 시작했습니다. 저는 매우 기분이 좋지 않았습니다. 그래서 그것에 관하여 언론에 글을 썼고, 많은 대화를 했습니다. 많은 사람들의 지지 덕택에 우리나라에서 교육법이 마침내 통과되었습니다. 이제 저는 더 큰 꿈이 있습니다. 나는 세계의 모든 아이들이 교육을 받을 수 있기를 희망합니다.

### Real Life Communication

Henry: _____

Mina: _____

_____

Henry: _____

_____

Mina: _____

_____

Henry: _____

Mina: _____

Henry: 너 속상해 보여. 미나야, 무슨 일 있니?

Mina: Henry야, 이 댓글들을 봐. 많은 사람들이 우리 마을에 재미있는 장소가 충분하지 않다고 말해.

Henry: 그것 참 안됐다. 그들이 여기서 멋있는 장소를 방문할 기회를 가지지 못했다는 것이 유감이야. 우리가 무엇인가를 해야 해.

Mina: 우리 마을의 유명한 장소를 보여주는 비디오를 만들어 인터넷에 게시하는 것은 어떨까?

Henry: 그거 좋은 생각이야. 그렇게 하자.

Mina: 좋아. 그들이 여기서 즐거운 시간을 보냈으면 좋겠어.

### Let's Check 1

G: _____

B: _____

G: _____

B: _____

G: _____

B: _____

G: _____

B: _____

G: 너 우울해 보인다. 무슨 일 있니?

B: 나는 축구팀에 지원했어. 그런데 가입할 수가 없어.

G: 왜 안 돼?

B: 이미 팀에 선수가 너무 많아, 그래서 코치가 올해는 새로운 학생을 받지 않을 거야.

G: 그거 참 안됐다. 나는 네가 다른 재미있는 동아리를 찾기를 바라.

B: 고마워.

※ 다음 우리말과 일치하도록 빈칸에 알맞은 것을 골라 쓰시오.

**The Idea That Brought Peace to My Town**

**1** My name is Richard Turere. I _____ _____ Kenya in the _____ _____ of Nairobi National Park.

    A. southern      B. in      C. part      D. live

**2** The southern part of the park does not have a _____, so wild animals _____ lions move _____ of the park _____.

    A. out      B. fence      C. freely      D. like

**3** They _____ the animals that _____ _____ _____.

    A. farmers      B. kill      C. raising      D. are

**4** _____ a result, farmers try to _____ the lions _____ they want to _____ their animals.

    A. because      B. as      C. protect      D. kill

**5** One morning, I _____ _____ and saw our cow _____ on the _____.

    A. up      B. woke      C. ground      D. lying

**6** It was _____, and I felt _____ _____.

    A. so      B. dead      C. bad

**7** At first, I thought I couldn't _____ _____ _____ I was _____ eleven.

    A. only      B. anything      C. because      D. do

**8** Then I _____ I shouldn't _____ the _____.

    A. ignore      B. realized      C. problem

**9** I really _____ to _____ the people in my town in the _____ _____.

    A. help      B. same      C. situation      D. wanted

**10** My first _____ was to _____ _____.

    A. idea      B. fire      C. use

---

**1** 내 이름은 Richard Turere야. 나는 케냐의 나이로비 국립공원의 남쪽 지역에 살고 있어.

**2** 공원의 남쪽 지역은 울타리가 없어서 사자와 같은 야생 동물들이 공원 밖으로 자유롭게 나가.

**3** 그들은 농부들이 키우고 있는 동물들을 죽여.

**4** 그 결과, 농부들은 그들의 동물들을 보호하기를 원하기 때문에 사자들을 죽이려고 해.

**5** 어느 날 아침, 나는 일어나서 우리 소가 바닥에 누워 있는 것을 보았어.

**6** 소는 죽어 있었고, 나는 아주 기분이 좋지 않았어.

**7** 처음에는, 내가 겨우 열한 살이었기 때문에 아무것도 할 수 없을 거라고 생각했어.

**8** 그러고 나서 나는 이 문제를 무시하지 않아야 한다는 걸 깨달았어.

**9** 나는 같은 상황에 있는 우리 마을 사람들을 정말로 돕고 싶었어.

**10** 나의 첫 번째 아이디어는 불을 사용하는 것이었어.

**11** I thought lions were _____ _____ it. _____, it didn't _____.

A. of          B. work          C. afraid          D. sadly

**12** _____, the fire helped the lions to _____ _____ the cows _____.

A. move          B. better          C. instead          D. watch

**13** Then I had _____ _____. It was _____ use a _____.

A. idea          B. scarecrow          C. another          D. to

**14** But the lions _____ _____ _____.

A. clever          B. very          C. were

**15** The _____ _____, they were _____ _____.

A. away          B. day          C. turned          D. first

**16** _____ the second day, they _____ _____ and _____ more animals.

A. in          B. killed          C. on          D. jumped

**17** One night, I was _____ _____ the cows _____ a _____, and the lions didn't come.

A. around          B. light          C. with          D. walking

**18** I _____ that lions were _____ _____ a _____ light.

A. afraid          B. discovered          C. moving          D. of

**19** So I came _____ _____ an idea. I decided to _____ lights that _____ electronically.

A. invent          B. up          C. move          D. with

**20** _____ I like machines, I could find _____ I _____ to make the _____.

A. needed          B. because          C. lights          D. what

**21** I _____ an old car battery, a small _____ from a motorcycle, a switch, and a _____ electronic _____.

A. broken          B. device          C. light          D. found

---

나는 사자들이 불을 무서워 할 거라고 생각했어. 슬프게도 그것은 효과가 없었어.

**12** 대신에 불은 사자들이 소들이 움직이는 것을 더욱 잘 볼 수 있도록 도왔어.

**13** 그리고 나서 나는 다른 아이디어를 생각해 냈어. 그것은 허수아비를 사용하는 거였어.

**14** 하지만 사자들은 매우 영리했어.

**15** 첫날에는 사자들이 돌아갔어.

**16** 둘째 날에는 사자들이 뛰어 들어와서 더 많은 동물들을 죽였어.

**17** 어느 날 밤, 나는 전등을 들고 소들의 주위를 걷고 있었는데 사자들은 오지 않았어.

**18** 나는 사자들이 움직이는 불빛을 두려워한다는 것을 발견했어.

**19** 그래서 나는 생각해 냈지. 나는 전자적으로 움직이는 전등들을 발명하기로 결심했어.

**20** 나는 기계들을 좋아했기 때문에 전등들을 만들기 위해 내가 필요한 것들을 찾을 수 있었어.

**21** 나는 오래된 자동차 배터리, 오토바이에서 찾은 작은 장치, 스위치, 그리고 부서진 전등을 찾았어.

**10** Lesson 1. We Can Make a Difference

**22** _____ thirteen, I finally made _____ _____ _____ "lion lights."

    A. called          B. what          C. at          D. I

**23** My father said, "I'm _____ _____ _____ you, Richard!"

    A. of          B. proud          C. so

**24** Since then, I have _____ _____ lights at seven homes in my community and haven't _____ anyone _____ about lions.

    A. complain          B. up          C. set          D. heard

**25** They thanked me, _____ "This is exactly _____ we _____, _____ boy!"

    A. wanted          B. saying          C. what          D. lovely

**26** _____, my idea is now used all over Kenya to _____ other animals, _____ as elephants.

    A. such          B. scare          C. surprisingly      D. away

**27** _____ this experience, I realized that I could _____ a _____ in people's lives even _____ I am just a young boy.

    A. difference          B. though          C. from          D. make

**28** I was also _____ _____ _____ lions _____ being killed.

    A. from          B. to          C. able          D. prevent

**29** _____ _____ my _____, I got a _____ to a great school in Kenya.

    A. to          B. scholarship          C. thanks          D. work

**30** I am _____ _____ _____ this.

    A. excited          B. really          C. about

**31** In my new school, I am now _____ my friends _____ to _____ and _____ the lights.

    A. how          B. teaching          C. use          D. make

**32** I tell my friends, "Our ideas can _____ a _____ in _____!"

    A. lives          B. make          C. people's          D. difference

**22** 열세 살에 나는 내가 '사자 전등'이라고 불렀던 것을 마침내 만들었어.

**23** 나의 아버지께서는 말씀하셨어. "정말 자랑스럽구나, Richard!"

**24** 그때 이후로, 나는 우리 동네 일곱 가구의 집에 전등을 설치했고. 어느 누구도 사자들에 대해 불평하는 것을 듣지 못했어.

**25** "이것이 바로 우리가 원했던 거야, 사랑스러운 소년아!"라고 말하면서 그들은 나에게 감사를 표했어.

**26** 놀랍게도 나의 아이디어는 이제 코끼리와 같은 다른 동물들을 쫓기 위해서 케냐 전역에 걸쳐 사용되고 있어.

**27** 이 경험을 통해 나는 내가 어린 소년이지만 사람들의 삶에 변화를 일으킬 수 있다는 것을 깨달았어.

**28** 나는 사자들이 죽임을 당하는 것 또한 막을 수 있었어.

**29** 나의 작업 덕분에, 나는 케냐 최고의 학교에 장학금을 받고 입학하게 되었어.

**30** 나는 정말 기분이 좋아.

**31** 나의 새 학교에서 나는 지금 나의 친구들에게 어떻게 전등들을 만들고 사용하는지 가르쳐 주고 있어.

**32** 나는 친구들에게 "우리의 아이디어가 사람들의 삶에 변화를 일으킬 수 있어!"라고 이야기해.

※ 다음 우리말과 일치하도록 빈칸에 알맞은 것을 골라 쓰시오.

**The Idea That Brought Peace to My Town**

**1** My name _____ Richard Turere. I _____ _____ Kenya _____ _____ _____ _____ of Nairobi National Park.

**2** The _____ _____ of the park _____ not _____ _____, so wild animals _____ lions move _____ _____ the park _____.

**3** They kill the animals _____ farmers _____ _____.

**4** _____ _____ _____, farmers _____ _____ the lions _____ they want to _____ their animals.

**5** One morning, I _____ and saw our cow _____ _____ the ground.

**6** It was _____, and I _____ so _____.

**7** At first, I thought I couldn't _____ _____ _____ I was _____ _____.

**8** Then I _____ I _____ _____ the problem.

**9** I really _____ _____ _____ the people in my town in _____ _____ _____.

**10** My first idea was _____ _____ _____.

**11** I thought lions _____ _____ _____ _____. Sadly, it didn't _____.

**12** _____, the fire helped the lions _____ _____ _____ the cows _____.

**13** Then I had _____ _____. It was to use _____ _____.

**14** But the lions _____ very _____.

**15** _____ _____ _____, they were _____ _____.

**16** On the second day, they _____ _____ and _____ more animals.

**17** One night, I was _____ _____ the cows _____ _____, and the lions didn't come.

**1** 내 이름은 Richard Turere야. 나는 케냐의 나이로비 국립공원의 남쪽 지역에 살고 있어.

**2** 공원의 남쪽 지역은 울타리가 없어서 사자와 같은 야생 동물들이 공원 밖으로 자유롭게 나가.

**3** 그들은 농부들이 키우고 있는 동물들을 죽여.

**4** 그 결과, 농부들은 그들의 동물들을 보호하기를 원하기 때문에 사자들을 죽이려고 해.

**5** 어느 날 아침, 나는 일어나서 우리 소가 바닥에 누워 있는 것을 보았어.

**6** 소는 죽어 있었고, 나는 아주 기분이 좋지 않았어.

**7** 처음에는, 내가 겨우 열한 살이었기 때문에 아무것도 할 수 없을 거라고 생각했어.

**8** 그리고 나서 나는 이 문제를 무시하지 않아야 한다는 걸 깨달았어.

**9** 나는 같은 상황에 있는 우리 마을 사람들을 정말로 돕고 싶었어.

**10** 나의 첫 번째 아이디어는 불을 사용하는 것이었어.

**11** 나는 사자들이 불을 무서워 할 거라고 생각했어. 슬프게도 그것은 효과가 없었어.

**12** 대신에 불은 사자들이 소들이 움직이는 것을 더욱 잘 볼 수 있도록 도왔어.

**13** 그리고 나서 나는 다른 아이디어를 생각해 냈어. 그것은 허수아비를 사용하는 거였어.

**14** 하지만 사자들은 매우 영리했어.

**15** 첫날에는 사자들이 돌아갔어.

**16** 둘째 날에는 사자들이 뛰어 들어와서 더 많은 동물들을 죽였어.

**17** 어느 날 밤, 나는 전등을 들고 소들의 주위를 걷고 있었는데 사자들은 오지 않았어.

**18** I _____ _____ l i o n s _____ _____ _____ a _____ light.

**19** So I _____ _____ _____ an idea. I _____ _____ _____ lights that _____ _____.

**20** _____ I like machines, I could find _____ _____ _____ _____ _____ the lights.

**21** I found an old car battery, _____ _____ from a motorcycle, a switch, and a _____ _____ _____.

**22** _____ _____, I finally made _____ _____ _____ "lion lights."

**23** My father said, "I'm _____ _____ _____ you, Richard!"

**24** _____ then, I _____ _____ _____ lights _____ seven homes in my _____ and _____ _____ anyone _____ _____ lions.

**25** They thanked me, _____ "This is _____ _____, _____ boy!"

**26** _____, my idea is now _____ all over Kenya _____ _____ _____ _____ other animals, _____ _____ elephants.

**27** _____ this experience, I _____ _____ I could _____ _____ _____ in people's lives _____ _____ I am just a young boy.

**28** I was also _____ _____ _____ lions _____ _____.

**29** _____ _____ my work, I got _____ _____ to a great school in Kenya.

**30** I am really _____ _____ this.

**31** In my new school, I am now _____ my friends _____ _____ _____ and _____ the lights.

**32** I tell my friends, "Our ideas can _____ _____ _____ in _____ _____!"

---

18 나는 사자들이 움직이는 불빛을 두려워한다는 것을 발견했어.

19 그래서 나는 생각해 냈지. 나는 전자적으로 움직이는 전등들을 발명하기로 결심했어.

20 나는 기계들을 좋아했기 때문에 전등들을 만들기 위해 내가 필요한 것들을 찾을 수 있었어.

21 나는 오래된 자동차 배터리, 오토바이에서 찾은 작은 장치, 스위치, 그리고 부서진 전등을 찾았어.

22 열세 살에 나는 내가 '사자 전등'이라고 불렀던 것을 마침내 만들었어.

23 나의 아버지께서는 말씀하셨어. "정말 자랑스럽구나, Richard!"

24 그때 이후로, 나는 우리 동네 일곱 가구의 집에 전등을 설치했고, 어느 누구도 사자들에 대해 불평하는 것을 듣지 못했어.

25 "이것이 바로 우리가 원했던 거야, 사랑스러운 소년아!"라고 말하면서 그들은 나에게 감사를 표했어.

26 놀랍게도 나의 아이디어는 이제 코끼리와 같은 다른 동물들을 쫓기 위해서 케냐 전역에 걸쳐 사용되고 있어.

27 이 경험을 통해 나는 내가 어린 소년이지만 사람들의 삶에 변화를 일으킬 수 있다는 것을 깨달았어.

28 나는 사자들이 죽임을 당하는 것 또한 막을 수 있었어.

29 나의 작업 덕분에, 나는 케냐 최고의 학교에 장학금을 받고 입학하게 되었어.

30 나는 정말 기분이 좋아.

31 나의 새 학교에서 나는 지금 나의 친구들에게 어떻게 전등들을 만들고 사용하는지 가르쳐 주고 있어.

32 나는 친구들에게 "우리의 아이디어가 사람들의 삶에 변화를 일으킬 수 있어!"라고 이야기해.

※ 다음 문장을 우리말로 쓰시오.

**The Idea That Brought Peace to My Town**

**1** My name is Richard Turere. I live in Kenya in the southern part of Nairobi National Park.
➡ _____

**2** The southern part of the park does not have a fence, so wild animals like lions move out of the park freely.
➡ _____

**3** They kill the animals that farmers are raising.
➡ _____

**4** As a result, farmers try to kill the lions because they want to protect their animals.
➡ _____

**5** One morning, I woke up and saw our cow lying on the ground.
➡ _____

**6** It was dead, and I felt so bad.
➡ _____

**7** At first, I thought I couldn't do anything because I was only eleven.
➡ _____

**8** Then I realized I shouldn't ignore the problem.
➡ _____

**9** I really wanted to help the people in my town in the same situation.
➡ _____

**10** My first idea was to use fire.
➡ _____

**11** I thought lions were afraid of it. Sadly, it didn't work.
➡ _____

**12** Instead, the fire helped the lions to better watch the cows move.
➡ _____

**13** Then I had another idea. It was to use a scarecrow.
➡ _____

**14** But the lions were very clever.
➡ _____

**15** The first day, they were turned away.
➡ _____

**16** On the second day, they jumped in and killed more animals.
➡ _____

**17** One night, I was walking around the cows with a light, and the lions didn't come.
➡ _____

**18** I discovered that lions were afraid of a moving light.

➡ _____

**19** So I came up with an idea. I decided to invent lights that move electronically.

➡ _____

**20** Because I like machines, I could find what I needed to make the lights.

➡ _____

**21** I found an old car battery, a small device from a motorcycle, a switch, and a broken electronic light.

➡ _____

**22** At thirteen, I finally made what I called "lion lights."

➡ _____

**23** My father said, "I'm so proud of you, Richard!"

➡ _____

**24** Since then, I have set up lights at seven homes in my community and haven't heard anyone complain about lions.

➡ _____

**25** They thanked me, saying "This is exactly what we wanted, lovely boy!"

➡ _____

**26** Surprisingly, my idea is now used all over Kenya to scare away other animals, such as elephants.

➡ _____

**27** From this experience, I realized that I could make a difference in people's lives even though I am just a young boy.

➡ _____

**28** I was also able to prevent lions from being killed.

➡ _____

**29** Thanks to my work, I got a scholarship to a great school in Kenya.

➡ _____

**30** I am really excited about this.

➡ _____

**31** In my new school, I am now teaching my friends how to make and use the lights.

➡ _____

**32** I tell my friends, "Our ideas can make a difference in people's lives!"

➡ _____

※ 다음 괄호 안의 단어들을 우리말에 맞도록 바르게 배열하시오.

**The Idea That Brought Peace to My Town**

**1** (name / my / is / Turere. / Richard // live / I / Kenya / in / the / in / southern / of / part / Nairobi / Park. / National)

➡ _____

_____

**2** (southern / the / of / part / the / does / park / have / not / fence, / a / wild / so / like / animals / lions / out / move / of / park / the / freely.)

➡ _____

_____

**3** (kill / they / animals / the / farmers / that / raising. / are)

➡ _____

**4** (a / as / result, / try / farmers / kill / to / the / because / lions / they / to / want / their / protect / animals.)

➡ _____

_____

**5** (morning, / one / woke / I / up / and / our / saw / lying / cow / the / on / ground.)

➡ _____

**6** (was / it / dead, / I / and / felt / bad. / so)

➡ _____

**7** (first, / at / thought / I / couldn't / I / anything / do / because / was / I / eleven. / only)

➡ _____

**8** (I / then / realized / shouldn't / I / ignore / problem. / the)

➡ _____

**9** (really / I / to / wanted / help / people / the / my / in / town / the / in / situation. / same)

➡ _____

**10** (first / my / was / idea / to / fire. / use)

➡ _____

---

**1** 내 이름은 Richard Turere야. 나는 케냐의 나이로비 국립공원의 남쪽 지역에 살고 있어.

**2** 공원의 남쪽 지역은 울타리가 없어서 사자와 같은 야생 동물들이 공원 밖으로 자유롭게 나가.

**3** 그들은 농부들이 키우고 있는 동물들을 죽여.

**4** 그 결과, 농부들은 그들의 동물들을 보호하기를 원하기 때문에 사자들을 죽이려고 해.

**5** 어느 날 아침, 나는 일어나서 우리 소가 바닥에 누워 있는 것을 보았어.

**6** 소는 죽어 있었고, 나는 아주 기분이 좋지 않았어.

**7** 처음에는, 내가 겨우 열한 살이었기 때문에 아무것도 할 수 없을 거라고 생각했어.

**8** 그리고 나서 나는 이 문제를 무시하지 않아야 한다는 걸 깨달았어.

**9** 나는 같은 상황에 있는 우리 마을 사람들을 정말로 돕고 싶었어.

**10** 나의 첫 번째 아이디어는 불을 사용하는 것이었어.

**11** (thought / I / were / lions / afraid / it. / of // / it / sadly, / work. / didn't)

➡ _____

**12** (the / instead, / fire / the / helped / lions / better / to / the / watch / move. / cows)

➡ _____

**13** (I / then / another / had / idea. // was / it / use / to / scarecrow. / a)

➡ _____

**14** (the / but / were / lions / clever. / very)

➡ _____

**15** (first / the / day, / were / they / away. / turned)

➡ _____

**16** (the / on / day, / second / jumped / they / and / in / more / killed / animals.)

➡ _____

**17** (night, / one / was / I / around / walking / cows / the / a / with / light, / the / and / didn't / lions / come.)

➡ _____
_____

**18** (discovered / I / lions / that / afraid / were / a / of / light. / moving)

➡ _____

**19** (I / so / up / came / with / idea. / an // decided / I / invent / to / that / lights / electronically. / move)

➡ _____
_____

**20** (I / because / machines, / like / could / I / what / find / needed / I / make / to / lights. / the)

➡ _____

**21** (found / I / old / an / battery, / car / small / a / from / device / motorcycle / a / switch, / a / and / broken / a / light. / electronic)

➡ _____
_____

**11** 나는 사자들이 불을 무서워 할 거라고 생각했어. 슬프게도 그것은 효과가 없었어.

**12** 대신에 불은 사자들이 소들이 움직이는 것을 더욱 잘 볼 수 있도록 도왔어.

**13** 그러고 나서 나는 다른 아이디어를 생각해 냈어. 그것은 허수아비를 사용하는 거였어.

**14** 하지만 사자들은 매우 영리했어.

**15** 첫날에는 사자들이 돌아갔어.

**16** 둘째 날에는 사자들이 뛰어 들어와서 더 많은 동물들을 죽였어.

**17** 어느 날 밤, 나는 전등을 들고 소들의 주위를 걷고 있었는데 사자들은 오지 않았어.

**18** 나는 사자들이 움직이는 불빛을 두려워한다는 것을 발견했어.

**19** 그래서 나는 생각해 냈지. 나는 전자적으로 움직이는 전등들을 발명하기로 결심했어.

**20** 나는 기계들을 좋아했기 때문에 전등들을 만들기 위해 내가 필요한 것들을 찾을 수 있었어.

**21** 나는 오래된 자동차 배터리, 오토바이에서 찾은 작은 장치, 스위치, 그리고 부서진 전등을 찾았어.

**22** (thirteen, / at / finally / I / what / made / called / I / lights." / "lion)

➡ _____

**23** (father / my / said, / so / "I'm / proud / you, / of / Richard!")

➡ _____

**24** (then, / since / have / I / up / set / lights / seven / at / in / homes / my / and / community / heard / haven't / complain / anyone / lions. / about)

➡ _____

_____

**25** (thanked / they / saying / me, / is / "this / what / exactly / wanted, / we / boy!" / lovely)

➡ _____

**26** (my / surprisingly, / idea / now / is / all / used / over / to / Kenya / away / scare / animals, / other / such / elephants. / as)

➡ _____

**27** (this / from / experience, / realized / I / that / could / I / a / make / in / difference / lives / people's / though / even / am / I / just / young / a / boy.)

➡ _____

_____

**28** (was / I / able / also / prevent / to / from / lions / killed. / being)

➡ _____

**29** (to / thanks / work, / my / got / I / scholarship / a / to / great / a / school / Kenya. / in)

➡ _____

**30** (am / I / really / about / excited / this.)

➡ _____

**31** (my / in / school, / new / am / I / now / my / teaching / friends / to / how / and / make / use / lights. / the)

➡ _____

**32** (tell / I / friends, / my / "our / can / ideas / make / difference / a / in / lives!" / people's)

➡ _____

**22** 열세 살에 나는 내가 '사자 전등'이라고 불렀던 것을 마침내 만들었어.

**23** 나의 아버지께서는 말씀하셨어, "정말 자랑스럽구나, Richard!"

**24** 그때 이후로, 나는 우리 동네 일곱 가구의 집에 전등을 설치했고, 어느 누구도 사자들에 대해 불평하는 것을 듣지 못했어.

**25** "이것이 바로 우리가 원했던 거야, 사랑스러운 소년아!"라고 말하면서 그들은 나에게 감사를 표했어.

**26** 놀랍게도 나의 아이디어는 이제 코끼리와 같은 다른 동물들을 쫓기 위해서 케냐 전역에 걸쳐 사용되고 있어.

**27** 이 경험을 통해 나는 내가 어린 소년이지만 사람들의 삶에 변화를 일으킬 수 있다는 것을 깨달았어.

**28** 나는 사자들이 죽임을 당하는 것 또한 막을 수 있었어.

**29** 나의 작업 덕분에, 나는 케냐 최고의 학교에 장학금을 받고 입학하게 되었어.

**30** 나는 정말 기분이 좋아.

**31** 나의 새 학교에서 나는 지금 나의 친구들에게 어떻게 전등들을 만들고 사용하는지 가르쳐 주고 있어.

**32** 나는 친구들에게 "우리의 아이디어가 사람들의 삶에 변화를 일으킬 수 있어!"라고 이야기해.

※ **다음 우리말을 영어로 쓰시오.**

The Idea That Brought Peace to My Town

**1** 내 이름은 Richard Turere야. 나는 케냐의 나이로비 국립공원의 남쪽 지역에 살고 있어.
➡ _____

**2** 공원의 남쪽 지역은 울타리가 없어서 사자와 같은 야생 동물들이 공원 밖으로 자유롭게 나가.
➡ _____

**3** 그들은 농부들이 키우고 있는 동물들을 죽여.
➡ _____

**4** 그 결과, 농부들은 그들의 동물들을 보호하기를 원하기 때문에 사자들을 죽이려고 해..
➡ _____

**5** 어느 날 아침, 나는 일어나서 우리 소가 바닥에 누워 있는 것을 보았어.
➡ _____

**6** 소는 죽어 있었고, 나는 아주 기분이 좋지 않았어.
➡ _____

**7** 처음에는, 내가 겨우 열한 살이었기 때문에 아무것도 할 수 없을 거라고 생각했어.
➡ _____

**8** 그러고 나서 나는 이 문제를 무시하지 않아야 한다는 걸 깨달았어.
➡ _____

**9** 나는 같은 상황에 있는 우리 마을 사람들을 정말로 돕고 싶었어.
➡ _____

**10** 나의 첫 번째 아이디어는 불을 사용하는 것이었어.
➡ _____

**11** 나는 사자들이 불을 무서워 할 거라고 생각했어. 슬프게도 그것은 효과가 없었어.
➡ _____

**12** 대신에 불은 사자들이 소들이 움직이는 것을 더욱 잘 볼 수 있도록 도왔어.
➡ _____

**13** 그러고 나서 나는 다른 아이디어를 생각해 냈어. 그것은 허수아비를 사용하는 거였어.
➡ _____

**14** 하지만 사자들은 매우 영리했어.
➡ _____

**15** 첫날에는 사자들이 돌아갔어.
➡ _____

**16** 둘째 날에는 사자들이 뛰어 들어와서 더 많은 동물들을 죽였어.
➡ _____

**17** 어느 날 밤, 나는 전등을 들고 소들의 주위를 걷고 있었는데 사자들은 오지 않았어.
➡ _____

**18** 나는 사자들이 움직이는 불빛을 두려워한다는 것을 발견했어.

  ➡ _____

**19** 그래서 나는 생각해 냈지. 나는 전자적으로 움직이는 전등들을 발명하기로 결심했어.

  ➡ _____

**20** 나는 기계들을 좋아했기 때문에 전등들을 만들기 위해 내가 필요한 것들을 찾을 수 있었어.

  ➡ _____

**21** 나는 오래된 자동차 배터리, 오토바이에서 찾은 작은 장치, 스위치, 그리고 부서진 전등을 찾았어.

  ➡ _____

_____

**22** 열세 살에 나는 내가 '사자 전등'이라고 불렀던 것을 마침내 만들었어.

  ➡ _____

**23** 나의 아버지께서는 말씀하셨어, "정말 자랑스럽구나, Richard!"

  ➡ _____

**24** 그때 이후로, 나는 우리 동네 일곱 가구의 집에 전등을 설치했고. 어느 누구도 사자들에 대해 불평하는 것을 듣지 못했어.

  ➡ _____

**25** "이것이 바로 우리가 원했던 거야, 사랑스러운 소년아!"라고 말하면서 그들은 나에게 감사를 표했어.

  ➡ _____

**26** 놀랍게도 나의 아이디어는 이제 코끼리와 같은 다른 동물들을 쫓기 위해서 케냐 전역에 걸쳐 사용되고 있어.

  ➡ _____

**27** 이 경험을 통해 나는 내가 어린 소년이지만 사람들의 삶에 변화를 일으킬 수 있다는 것을 깨달았어.

  ➡ _____

_____

**28** 나는 사자들이 죽임을 당하는 것 또한 막을 수 있었어.

  ➡ _____

**29** 나의 작업 덕분에, 나는 케냐 최고의 학교에 장학금을 받고 입학하게 되었어.

  ➡ _____

**30** 나는 정말 기분이 좋아.

  ➡ _____

**31** 나의 새 학교에서 나는 지금 나의 친구들에게 어떻게 전등들을 만들고 사용하는지 가르쳐 주고 있어.

  ➡ _____

**32** 나는 친구들에게 "우리의 아이디어가 사람들의 삶에 변화를 일으킬 수 있어!"라고 이야기해.

  ➡ _____

※ 다음 우리말과 일치하도록 빈칸에 알맞은 말을 쓰시오.

## Communication Task Step 2

1. A: _____ the _____, Minsu?

2. B: _____ _____ _____ _____ in our community. _____ _____ we can have _____ _____.

3. A: Me, _____. That _____ _____ _____.

1. A: 민수야, 무슨 일 있니?
2. B: 우리 동네에 공원이 많지 않아. 나는 좀 더 많은 공원이 있으면 좋겠어.
3. A: 나도 그래. 그러면 좋겠다.

## Before You Read

1. _____ is Jessica's _____ _____ on a _____.

2. She _____ _____ the _____.

3. Her mother _____ _____ _____ the _____.

4. Her father _____ _____ _____ the market _____ a motorcycle.

5. They are _____ _____ _____!

1. Jessica의 농장에서의 첫 날이다.
2. 그녀는 울타리를 칠하고 있다.
3. 그녀의 엄마는 허수아비를 설치하고 있다.
4. 그녀의 아빠는 오토바이를 타고 시장에 가고 있다.
5. 그들은 좋은 팀이다!

## Let's Write

1. I _____ _____ students _____ many things at school.

2. _____, I _____ _____ my favorite _____, _____ _____, for you.

3. _____ you want _____ _____ many things, this bag is exactly _____ you _____.

4. It is very _____ and _____.

5. I hope _____ can _____ _____ _____ you. Thank you.

1. 저는 학생들이 학교에서 많은 것들을 가지고 다니는 것을 봤습니다.
2. 그래서 저는 제가 가장 좋아하는 물건인 가방을 여러분을 위해 가지고 왔습니다.
3. 만약 여러분이 많은 것들을 가지고 다니고 싶다면, 이 가방은 정확히 여러분이 필요로 하는 것입니다.
4. 이것은 매우 가볍고 편합니다.
5. 저는 이것이 여러분에게 쓸모가 있기를 바랍니다. 감사합니다.

## 구석구석 지문 Test

※ 다음 우리말을 영어로 쓰시오.

### Communication Task Step 2

1. A: 민수야, 무슨 일 있니?

➡ _____

2. B: 우리 동네에 공원이 많지 않아. 나는 좀 더 많은 공원이 있으면 좋겠어.

➡ _____

3. A: 나도 그래. 그러면 좋겠다.

➡ _____

### Before You Read

1. Jessica의 농장에서의 첫 날이다.

➡ _____

2. 그녀는 울타리를 칠하고 있다.

➡ _____

3. 그녀의 엄마는 허수아비를 설치하고 있다.

➡ _____

4. 그녀의 아빠는 오토바이를 타고 시장에 가고 있다.

➡ _____

5. 그들은 좋은 팀이다!

➡ _____

### Let's Write

1. 저는 학생들이 학교에서 많은 것들을 가지고 다니는 것을 봤습니다.

➡ _____

2. 그래서 저는 제가 가장 좋아하는 물건인 가방을 여러분을 위해 가지고 왔습니다.

➡ _____

3. 만약 여러분이 많은 것들을 가지고 다니고 싶다면, 이 가방은 정확히 여러분이 필요로 하는 것입니다.

➡ _____

4. 이것은 매우 가볍고 편합니다.

➡ _____

5. 저는 이것이 여러분에게 쓸모가 있기를 바랍니다. 감사합니다.

➡ _____

※ 다음 영어를 우리말로 쓰시오.

| | | | | |
|---|---|---|---|---|
| 01 | argue | _____ | 22 | focus | _____ |
| 02 | disappear | _____ | 23 | forgive | _____ |
| 03 | grain | _____ | 24 | wisely | _____ |
| 04 | adventure | _____ | 25 | raise | _____ |
| 05 | confused | _____ | 26 | reason | _____ |
| 06 | uncooked | _____ | 27 | spread | _____ |
| 07 | polite | _____ | 28 | suggestion | _____ |
| 08 | salty | _____ | 29 | celebrate | _____ |
| 09 | ban | _____ | 30 | certainly | _____ |
| 10 | ignore | _____ | 31 | host | _____ |
| 11 | convenient | _____ | 32 | prefer | _____ |
| 12 | arrival | _____ | 33 | choose | _____ |
| 13 | hurriedly | _____ | 34 | manners | _____ |
| 14 | provide | _____ | 35 | give up | _____ |
| 15 | utensil | _____ | 36 | regardless of | _____ |
| 16 | recent | _____ | 37 | raise point | _____ |
| 17 | republic | _____ | 38 | be eager to | _____ |
| 18 | patiently | _____ | 39 | take a break | _____ |
| 19 | plate | _____ | 40 | make up for | _____ |
| 20 | boastful | _____ | 41 | have trouble -ing | _____ |
| 21 | elegant | _____ | 42 | on time | _____ |
| | | | 43 | stay healthy | _____ |

※ 다음 우리말을 영어로 쓰시오.

| 01 | 모험 | |
| 02 | 예절 바른, 예의 바른 | |
| 03 | 기념하다 | |
| 04 | 분명히 | |
| 05 | 익히지 않은, 날것의 | |
| 06 | 최근의 | |
| 07 | 혼란스러워하는 | |
| 08 | 이유 | |
| 09 | 편리한 | |
| 10 | 사라지다 | |
| 11 | 기구, 도구 | |
| 12 | 공화국 | |
| 13 | 현명하게 | |
| 14 | 우아한 | |
| 15 | 집중하다 | |
| 16 | 제공하다 | |
| 17 | 주최하다; 주인 | |
| 18 | 제안, 의견 | |
| 19 | 황급히 | |
| 20 | 펼치다 | |
| 21 | 다투다, 주장하다 | |

| 22 | 금지하다 | |
| 23 | 보호하다 | |
| 24 | 예의, 예절 | |
| 25 | 무시하다 | |
| 26 | 참을성 있게 | |
| 27 | 선택하다 | |
| 28 | 도착 | |
| 29 | 용서하다 | |
| 30 | 곡물, 곡식 | |
| 31 | 더 좋아하다 | |
| 32 | 아끼다, 구하다 | |
| 33 | 찾다 | |
| 34 | 짠 | |
| 35 | 정각에 | |
| 36 | ~을 보상하다 | |
| 37 | ~하고 싶어 하다 | |
| 38 | 포기하다 | |
| 39 | ~에 상관없이 | |
| 40 | 촉감 | |
| 41 | 건강을 유지하다 | |
| 42 | ~하는 데 어려움을 겪다 | |
| 43 | ~할 때마다 | |

※ 다음 영영풀이에 알맞은 단어를 <보기>에서 골라 쓴 후, 우리말 뜻을 쓰시오.

1 _____ : social conduct: _____

2 _____ : long, thin, curly strips of pasta: _____

3 _____ : an exciting or dangerous experience: _____

4 _____ : a tool that is used in the house: _____

5 _____ : mentioning an additional item or fact: _____

6 _____ : talking about yourself in a very proud way: _____

7 _____ : to disagree or fight by using angry words: _____

8 _____ : a flat, usually round dish that you put food on: _____

9 _____ : to open, arrange, or place something over a large area: _____

10 _____ : to like one thing or person better than another: _____

11 _____ : to keep something available for use in the future: _____

12 _____ : to decide that a particular person or thing is the one that you want: _____

13 _____ : (of people or their behavior) attractive and showing a good sense of style: _____

14 _____ : the seeds of plants such as wheat, corn, and rice that are used for food: _____

15 _____ : to do something special or enjoyable for an important event, occasion, holiday, etc.: _____

16 _____ : a pair of thin sticks which people in China and the Far East use to eat their food: _____

| 보기 | | | |
|---|---|---|---|
| plus | argue | celebrate | grain |
| manners | noodle | spread | save |
| plate | boastful | utensil | elegant |
| chopsticks | adventure | prefer | choose |

※ 다음 우리말에 맞도록 대화를 영어로 쓰시오.

### Listen & Speak 1 A

G: It _____ to _____ that you don't _____ the food.

B: No, I _____ the food. I usually _____ some _____ _____ my _____. That's good _____ _____ in my country, China.

G: _____ is that?

B: We _____ _____ everything on the _____ means _____ you are still _____.

G: _____ is more _____ _____ finish _____ on your plate in Korea, _____.

B: _____ _____ have different _____.

G: 너는 그 음식을 좋아하지 않는 것 같구나.
B: 그렇지 않아. 나는 그 음식을 즐겼어. 나는 보통 접시에 약간의 음식을 남겨. 그것이 우리나라, 중국에서의 올바른 식탁 예절이야.
G: 왜 그러니?
B: 우리는 접시에 있는 음식을 다 먹는 것은 여전히 배가 고프다는 것을 의미한다고 생각해.
G: 하지만, 한국에서는 접시에 있는 모든 것을 다 먹는 것이 더 예절 바르다고 생각해.
B: 문화마다 다른 규칙이 있구나.

### Listen & Speak 1 B

W: It _____ to _____ that it's _____ for dinner. Are you _____?

B: Yes. _____ we _____ pizza _____ _____?

W: I'm going to _____ fish, Jacob. _____ at home is _____ _____ _____ _____ pizza.

B: But we can _____ _____ _____ _____ pizza. I'm so _____.

W: Dinner will be _____ soon. So, please be _____.

W: 저녁 먹을 시간인 것 같다. 배고프니?
B: 네. 저녁으로 피자 주문해도 돼요?
W: 생선을 요리할 거야, Jacob. 집에서 요리하는 것이 피자를 주문하는 것보다 훨씬 더 건강에 좋아.
B: 하지만 피자를 주문하면 시간을 아낄 수 있어요. 너무 배고파요.
W: 저녁이 곧 준비될 거야. 그러니 조금만 참아 줘.

### Listen & Speak 2 A

G: What can we do _____ _____ _____?

B: I think _____ _____ food is _____.

G: My brother _____ _____ _____ for his _____.

B: _____ _____ _____ _____ _____, having healthy food _____ _____, Emma?

G: I can't _____ _____ food I eat. So, I _____ _____ exercise.

B: _____ of them _____ to be _____ for our _____.

G: But if you _____ do both, it _____ be better _____ on just one.

B: I think you are _____. I'm going to _____ _____.

G: 건강을 유지하기 위하여 우리는 무엇을 할 수 있을까?
B: 건강에 좋은 음식을 먹는 것이 중요하다고 생각해.
G: 우리 오빠는 매일 건강을 위하여 운동을 해.
B: 건강에 좋은 음식을 먹는 것과 운동을 하는 것 중에서 어느 것을 선호하니, Emma야?
G: 나는 어떤 음식을 먹을지 조절할 수 없어. 그래서 나는 운동을 더 좋아해.
B: 두 가지 모두가 우리의 건강에 중요한 것 같구나.
G: 그러나, 두 가지 모두 할 수 없다면 한 가지에 집중하는 것이 더 나을 거야.
B: 네 말이 맞는 것 같다. 나는 운동을 먼저 할 거야.

### Listen & Speak 2 B

W: _____ time is it _____?

M: It's _____ 8:00 p.m.

W: _____ don't we _____ now and _____ a _____?

M: Good idea. We need to _____ _____ _____ at this _____.

W: _____ do you _____, _____ a meal early or _____ in the evening?

M: I _____ having a meal _____.

W: _____ is the reason?

M: I usually _____ _____ _____ _____, so I eat my last meal _____, too. How about you?

W: I have meals _____ in the evening _____ I _____ _____ at night.

### Real Life Communication

Jinho: Claire, _____ do you _____, fish or steak?

Claire: I _____ fish, Jinho.

Jinho: There is fish _____ the menu.

Claire: That's good. Is it _____ or _____?

Jinho: _____ are on the menu.

Claire: Then I will have sushi. It _____ _____ _____ that fish _____ better when it's _____.

Jinho: Okay. Then you get sushi and I'll _____ fried fish. Let's _____.

### Let's Check 1

G: Do you like this _____?

B: It _____ to me that red _____ not _____ good on you.

G: Do you _____ any _____, then?

B: _____ _____ this blue cap? Blue looks _____ _____ on you _____ red.

G: That _____ good. I'll take it.

### Let's Check 2

A: I'm so _____. _____ get _____ _____ eat.

B: So am I. _____ do you _____, noodles or rice?

A: I _____ noodles. Do you _____ any good restaurants?

B: There's a good noodle restaurant _____ _____.

W: 지금 몇 시니?
M: 벌써 오후 8시야.
W: 지금 멈추고, 식사하는 것이 어떨까?
M: 좋은 생각이야. 이 시점에서 쉴 필요가 있어.
W: 너는 일찍 식사하는 것과 저녁 늦게 식사하는 것 중에서 어느 것을 더 좋아하니?
M: 나는 일찍 식사하는 것을 더 좋아해.
W: 이유가 뭐야?
M: 나는 보통 일찍 잠자리에 들어, 그래서 마지막 식사도 일찍 먹어. 너는 어떠니?
W: 나는 밤늦게 일하기 때문에 저녁에 늦게 식사를 해.

Jinho: Claire야, 생선과 스테이크 중에서 너는 어느 것을 더 좋아하니?
Claire: 나는 생선을 더 좋아해, 진호야.
Jinho: 메뉴에 생선이 있어.
Claire: 잘됐다. 생선은 스시야, 튀긴 것이야?
Jinho: 두 가지가 모두 있어.
Claire: 그러면 나는 스시를 먹을게. 생선은 익히지 않았을 때 맛이 더 좋은 것 같아.
Jinho: 알았어. 그러면 너는 스시를 먹고, 나는 튀긴 생선을 먹을게. 주문하자.

G: 이 모자 마음에 드니?
B: 내 생각에는 빨간색이 너한테 잘 어울리지 않는 것 같아.
G: 그럼, 추천할 것이 있니?
B: 이 파란색 모자 어때? 빨간색보다 파란색이 너한테 훨씬 더 잘 어울려.
G: 좋은 것 같은데. 그것으로 할게.

A: 배가 너무 고파. 뭐 좀 먹자.
B: 나도 마찬가지야. 국수와 밥 중 어느 것을 더 좋아하니?
A: 난 국수가 좋아. 괜찮은 식당 알고 있니?
B: 저쪽에 괜찮은 국수 식당이 있어.

※ 다음 우리말과 일치하도록 빈칸에 알맞은 말을 쓰시오.

### Listen & Speak 1 A

G: _____

B: _____

　 _____

G: _____

B: _____

G: _____

B: _____

G: 너는 그 음식을 좋아하지 않는 것 같구나.
B: 그렇지 않아. 나는 그 음식을 즐겼어. 나는 보통 접시에 약간의 음식을 남겨. 그것이 우리나라, 중국에서의 올바른 식탁 예절이야.
G: 왜 그러니?
B: 우리는 접시에 있는 음식을 다 먹는 것은 여전히 배가 고프다는 것을 의미한다고 생각해.
G: 하지만, 한국에서는 접시에 있는 모든 것을 다 먹는 것이 더 예절 바르다고 생각해.
B: 문화마다 다른 규칙이 있구나.

### Listen & Speak 1 B

W: _____

B: _____

W: _____

　 _____

B: _____

W: _____

W: 저녁 먹을 시간인 것 같다. 배고프니?
B: 네. 저녁으로 피자 주문해도 돼요?
W: 생선을 요리할 거야, Jacob. 집에서 요리하는 것이 피자를 주문하는 것보다 훨씬 더 건강에 더 좋아.
B: 하지만 피자를 주문하면 시간을 아낄 수 있어요. 너무 배고파요.
W: 저녁이 곧 준비될 거야. 그러니 조금만 참아 줘.

### Listen & Speak 2 A

G: _____

B: _____

G: _____

B: _____

G: _____

B: _____

G: _____

B: _____

G: 건강을 유지하기 위하여 우리는 무엇을 할 수 있을까?
B: 건강에 좋은 음식을 먹는 것이 중요하다고 생각해.
G: 우리 오빠는 매일 건강을 위하여 운동을 해.
B: 건강에 좋은 음식을 먹는 것과 운동을 하는 것 중에서 어느 것을 선호하니, Emma야?
G: 나는 어떤 음식을 먹을지 조절할 수 없어. 그래서 나는 운동을 더 좋아해.
B: 두 가지 모두가 우리의 건강에 중요한 것 같구나.
G: 그러나, 두 가지 모두 할 수 없다면 한 가지에 집중하는 것이 더 나을 거야.
B: 네 말이 맞는 것 같다. 나는 운동을 먼저 할 거야.

## Listen & Speak 2 B

W: _____

M: _____

W: _____

M: _____

W: _____

M: _____

W: _____

M: _____

W: _____

## Real Life Communication

Jinho: _____

Claire: _____

Jinho: _____

Claire: _____

Jinho: _____

Claire: _____

Jinho: _____

## Let's Check 1

G: _____

B: _____

G: _____

B: _____

G: _____

## Let's Check 2

A: _____

B: _____

A: _____

B: _____

W: 지금 몇 시니?

M: 벌써 오후 8시야.

W: 지금 멈추고, 식사하는 것이 어떨까?

M: 좋은 생각이야. 이 시점에서 쉴 필요가 있어.

W: 너는 일찍 식사하는 것과 저녁 늦게 식사하는 것 중에서 어느 것을 더 좋아하니?

M: 나는 일찍 식사하는 것을 더 좋아해.

W: 이유가 뭐야?

M: 나는 보통 일찍 잠자리에 들어. 그래서 마지막 식사도 일찍 먹어. 너는 어떠니?

W: 나는 밤늦게 일하기 때문에 저녁에 늦게 식사를 해.

Jinho: Claire야, 생선과 스테이크 중에서 너는 어느 것을 더 좋아하니?

Claire: 나는 생선을 더 좋아해, 진호야.

Jinho: 메뉴에 생선이 있어.

Claire: 잘됐다. 생선은 스시야, 튀긴 것이야?

Jinho: 두 가지가 모두 있어.

Claire: 그러면 나는 스시를 먹을게. 생선은 익히지 않았을 때 맛이 더 좋은 것 같아.

Jinho: 알았어. 그러면 너는 스시를 먹고, 나는 튀긴 생선을 먹을게. 주문하자.

G: 이 모자 마음에 드니?

B: 내 생각에는 빨간색이 너한테 잘 어울리지 않는 것 같아.

G: 그럼, 추천할 것이 있니?

B: 이 파란색 모자 어때? 빨간색보다 파란색이 너한테 훨씬 더 잘 어울려.

G: 좋은 것 같은데. 그것으로 할게.

A: 배가 너무 고파. 뭐 좀 먹자.

B: 나도 마찬가지야. 국수와 밥 중 어느 것을 더 좋아하니?

A: 난 국수가 좋아. 괜찮은 식당 알고 있니?

B: 저쪽에 괜찮은 국수 식당이 있어.

※ 다음 우리말과 일치하도록 빈칸에 알맞은 것을 골라 쓰시오.

**1** Spork, Chopsticks, Knork, Barehands, and Ms. Disher _____ _____ _____ in the Dining _____.

A. close          B. Republic          C. friends          D. are

**2** Spork, Chopsticks, Knork, and Barehands _____ a lot _____ their _____, but Ms. Disher's family does not travel _____.

A. with          B. much          C. families          D. travel

**3** She makes _____ _____ this by _____ a dinner for her friends coming _____ from their trips.

A. hosting          B. for          C. up          D. back

**4** She _____ always _____ _____ listen to their _____.

A. to          B. adventures          C. eagar          D. is

**5** They often talk about _____ _____ _____ from their _____ trips.

A. recent          B. what          C. learned          D. they

**6** The most _____ topic was _____ the best _____ to eat and Ms. Disher's guests began to _____.

A. argue          B. about          C. recent          D. way

**7** Spork: _____ a recent trip, I have found _____ it is best _____ _____ a spoon and fork.

A. to          B. on          C. use          D. that

**8** A spoon is best _____ _____ and soup, and a fork is good for _____ _____.

A. grains          B. meat          C. eating          D. for

**9** Knork: No! It is _____ _____ to _____ a knife and a fork _____.

A. instead          B. much          C. use          D. better

**10** Don't you think it is _____ _____ you to _____ a fork in one hand and a knife in the _____?

A. other          B. for          C. hold          D. easier

**1** Spork와 Chopsticks, Knork, Barehands, Disher 부인은 식탁 공화국의 친구들입니다.

**2** Spork와 Chopsticks, Knork, Barehands는 자신의 가족들과 여행을 많이 다니지만, Ms. Disher의 가족은 여행을 많이 다니지 않습니다.

**3** 그녀는 여행에서 돌아온 친구들을 위해 저녁 식사를 주최함으로써 여행을 많이 하지 않는 것을 보상합니다.

**4** 그녀는 항상 친구들의 모험담을 듣고 싶어 합니다.

**5** 그들은 최근 여행에서 배운 것에 대해 자주 이야기합니다.

**6** 가장 최근 주제는 음식을 먹는 가장 좋은 방법에 대한 것이었고, Ms. Disher의 손님들은 논쟁하기 시작했습니다.

**7** Spork: 최근 여행에서, 나는 숟가락과 포크가 함께 달려 있는 것을 사용하는 것이 가장 좋다는 것을 알았어.

**8** 숟가락은 곡물이나 국을 먹기에 최고이고, 포크는 고기를 먹기에 좋아.

**9** Knork: 아냐! 그 대신에 칼과 포크를 사용하는 것이 훨씬 더 좋아.

**11** What can be _____ _____ than _____ them to cut meat on a _____!

A. plate　　　　B. elegant　　　　C. using　　　　D. more

**12** Chopsticks: Why do you use two _____ _____ of utensils when you can use two of the _____ _____?

A. same　　　　B. different　　　　C. kinds　　　　D. utensil

**13** Plus, you can _____ chopsticks _____ just _____ hand!

A. with　　　　B. use　　　　C. one

**14** Barehands: No _____! When I eat _____ my hands, of course I can see and _____ the food, but I can also _____ it.

A. smell　　　　B. touch　　　　C. with　　　　D. way

**15** _____ I use my sense of _____ when I eat, I _____ to _____ my food more.

A. touch　　　　B. because　　　　C. enjoy　　　　D. get

**16** They _____ and _____ many points, and nobody wanted to _____ _____.

A. up　　　　B. argued　　　　C. give　　　　D. raised

**17** _____ was not easy _____ their host, Ms. Disher, _____ listen to their _____ patiently.

A. arguments　　　　B. for　　　　C. it　　　　D. to

**18** So, she _____, _____ quietly, _____.

A. left　　　　B. yet　　　　C. hurriedly

**19** Spork: _____ is Ms. Disher? She _____ _____.

A. disappeared　　　　B. has　　　　C. where

**20** Knork: What _____ we do? _____ Ms. Disher, this dinner is _____ _____.

A. without          B. complete          C. should          D. not

**21** Chopsticks: _____ did she _____?

A. go                    B. where

**22** Barehands: _____ go out _____ _____ her!

A. to                    B. let's                    C. find

**23** After hours of _____ all over the Dining Republic, they finally _____ Ms. Disher _____ _____ a huge tree.

A. sitting          B. found          C. under          D. searching

**24** Spork, Knork, Chopsticks, Barehands: We're _____ we _____ _____ and _____ you.

A. boastful          B. sorry          C. ignored          D. became

**25** Please _____ and come _____ and _____ _____.

A. back                    B. forgive                    C. us                    D. join

**26** Ms. Disher: It's okay. I _____ you. Let's _____ _____ to my home.

A. go                    B. back                    C. forgive

**27** _____ then, every time they meet, they _____ one _____ to eat in the manner that they _____.

A. please          B. allow          C. since          D. another

**28** In their hearts they now know _____ food will always be delicious _____ of _____ utensils they use to eat it _____.

A. regardless          B. with          C. which          D. that

**20** Knork: 어떡하지? Disher 부인이 없으면, 저녁 식사는 완전하지 않아.

**21** Chopsticks: 그녀는 어디 갔을까?

**22** Barehands: 나가서 그녀를 찾아보자!

**23** 몇 시간 동안 식탁 공화국을 구석구석 뒤진 끝에, 친구들은 마침내 큰 나무 밑에 앉아 있는 Disher 부인을 찾았습니다.

**24** Spork, Knork, Chopsticks, Barehands: 우리가 자랑스러워하고 너를 무시해서 미안해.

**25** 우리를 용서하고 돌아와서 우리와 함께 있어 줘.

**26** Ms. Disher: 알았어. 용서할게. 우리 집으로 돌아가자.

**27** 그 후로, 그들은 만날 때마다 서로 자신들이 좋아하는 방식으로 음식 먹는 것을 받아들입니다.

**28** 마음속으로 그들은 이제 음식을 먹는 데 어떤 도구를 사용하여 먹는지에 상관없이 음식 맛은 항상 맛있을 거라는 걸 알게 되었습니다.

※ 다음 우리말과 일치하도록 빈칸에 알맞은 말을 쓰시오.

**1** Spork, Chopsticks, Knork, Barehands, and Ms. Disher _____ _____ _____ in the _____ _____.

**2** Spork, Chopsticks, Knork, and Barehands _____ a lot _____ _____ _____, but Ms. Disher's family does not _____ _____.

**3** She _____ _____ _____ this _____ _____ a dinner for her friends _____ _____ _____ their trips.

**4** She _____ always _____ _____ listen _____ their _____.

**5** They often talk about _____ _____ _____ from their _____ _____.

**6** The most _____ topic _____ _____ _____ the best way _____ _____ and Ms. Disher's guests began _____ _____.

**7** Spork: _____ a recent trip, I _____ _____ _____ it is best _____ _____ a spoon and fork.

**8** A spoon is best _____ _____ and _____, and a fork is _____ _____ _____ _____.

**9** Knork: No! It is _____ _____ _____ _____ a knife and a fork _____.

**10** Don't you think it is _____ _____ _____ _____ a fork in one hand and a knife in _____ _____?

**11** What can be _____ _____ than _____ _____ _____ _____ meat on a plate!

**12** Chopsticks: Why do you use _____ _____ _____ of _____ when you can use _____ _____ _____ _____?

**13** Plus, you can _____ chopsticks _____ just one hand!

---

1 Spork와 Chopsticks, Knork, Barehands, Disher 부인은 식탁 공화국의 친구들입니다.

2 Spork와 Chopsticks, Knork, Barehands는 자신의 가족들과 여행을 많이 다니지만, Ms. Disher의 가족은 여행을 많이 다니지 않습니다.

3 그녀는 여행에서 돌아온 친구들을 위해 저녁 식사를 주최함으로써 여행을 많이 하지 않는 것을 보상합니다.

4 그녀는 항상 친구들의 모험담을 듣고 싶어 합니다.

5 그들은 최근 여행에서 배운 것에 대해 자주 이야기합니다.

6 가장 최근 주제는 음식을 먹는 가장 좋은 방법에 대한 것이었고, Ms. Disher의 손님들은 논쟁하기 시작했습니다.

7 Spork: 최근 여행에서. 나는 숟가락과 포크가 함께 달려 있는 것을 사용하는 것이 가장 좋다는 것을 알았어.

8 숟가락은 곡물이나 국을 먹기에 최고이고, 포크는 고기를 먹기에 좋아.

9 Knork: 아냐! 그 대신에 칼과 포크를 사용하는 것이 훨씬 더 좋아.

10 네가 한 손에는 포크를, 다른 손에 칼을 드는 것이 더 쉽다고 생각하지 않니?

11 접시 위에 놓인 고기를 자르기 위해 칼과 포크를 사용하는 것보다 더 우아할 수 있는 게 뭐가 있겠어!

12 Chopsticks: 같은 도구를 두 가지로 사용할 수 있는데 왜 두 종류의 다른 도구를 사용한단 말이야?

13 게다가 젓가락은 한 손으로도 사용할 수 있어!

**Step2**

**14** Barehands: _____ _____! When I eat _____ my hands, _____ _____ I can _____ and _____ the food, but I can also _____ _____.

**15** Because _____ use my _____ of _____ when I eat, I _____ _____ _____ my food more.

**16** They _____ and _____ many points, and nobody _____ _____ _____ _____.

**17** _____ was not easy _____ their host, Ms. Disher, _____ _____ _____ _____ _____ _____.

**18** So, she _____, _____ _____, _____.

**19** Spork: Where is Ms. Disher? She _____ _____.

**20** Knork: What _____ _____ _____? _____ Ms. Disher, this dinner is _____ _____.

**21** Chopsticks: _____ did she _____?

**22** Barehands: Let's go out _____ _____ _____!

**23** After hours of _____ _____ over the Dining Republic, they finally _____ Ms. Disher _____ _____ a huge tree.

**24** Spork, Knork, Chopsticks, Barehands: We're sorry _____ _____ _____ and _____ you.

**25** Please _____ and come _____ and _____ _____.

**26** Ms. Disher: It's okay. I _____ you. Let's _____ _____ to my home.

**27** _____ then, every time they meet, they _____ one another _____ _____ in the manner _____ _____ _____.

**28** _____ their hearts they now know _____ food will always be _____ _____ _____ _____ they use _____ _____ _____ _____.

**14** Barehands: 천만의 말씀! 내가 손으로 음식을 먹으면 당연히 보면서 음식 냄새도 맡을 수 있지만, 음식을 만져 볼 수도 있다고.

**15** 음식을 먹을 때 촉각을 사용하기 때문에 음식을 더 즐기게 돼.

**16** 그들은 여러 의견을 제기하고 논쟁했습니다. 그리고 아무도 포기하고 싶어 하지 않았습니다.

**17** 그들의 주최자인 Ms. Disher가 그들의 언쟁을 참을성 있게 듣고 있는 것은 쉽지 않았습니다.

**18** 그래서 그녀는 서둘러서 그러나 조용히 자리를 떠났습니다.

**19** Spork: Disher 부인은 어디 있지? 그녀가 사라졌어.

**20** Knork: 어떡하지? Disher 부인이 없으면, 저녁 식사는 완전하지 않아.

**21** Chopsticks: 그녀는 어디 갔을까?

**22** Barehands: 나가서 그녀를 찾아보자!

**23** 몇 시간 동안 식탁 공화국을 구석구석 뒤진 끝에, 친구들은 마침내 큰 나무 밑에 앉아 있는 Disher 부인을 찾았습니다.

**24** Spork, Knork, Chopsticks, Barehands: 우리가 자랑스러워하고 너를 무시해서 미안해.

**25** 우리를 용서하고 돌아와서 우리와 함께 있어 줘.

**26** Ms. Disher: 알았어. 용서할게. 우리 집으로 돌아가자.

**27** 그 후로, 그들은 만날 때마다 서로 자신들이 좋아하는 방식으로 음식 먹는 것을 받아들입니다.

**28** 마음속으로 그들은 이제 음식을 먹는 데 어떤 도구를 사용하여 먹는지에 상관없이 음식 맛은 항상 맛있을 거라는 걸 알게 되었습니다.

※ 다음 문장을 우리말로 쓰시오.

Friends from the Dining Republic

**1** ▸ Spork, Chopsticks, Knork, Barehands, and Ms. Disher are close friends in the Dining Republic.

➡ _____

**2** ▸ Spork, Chopsticks, Knork, and Barehands travel a lot with their families, but Ms. Disher's family does not travel much.

➡ _____

_____

**3** ▸ She makes up for this by hosting a dinner for her friends coming back from their trips.

➡ _____

**4** ▸ She is always eager to listen to their adventures.

➡ _____

**5** ▸ They often talk about what they learned from their recent trips.

➡ _____

**6** ▸ The most recent topic was about the best way to eat and Ms. Disher's guests began to argue.

➡ _____

**7** ▸ Spork: On a recent trip, I have found that it is best to use a spoon and fork.

➡ _____

**8** ▸ A spoon is best for grains and soup, and a fork is good for eating meat.

➡ _____

**9** ▸ Knork: No! It is much better to use a knife and a fork instead.

➡ _____

**10** ▸ Don't you think it is easier for you to hold a fork in one hand and a knife in the other?

➡ _____

**11** ▸ What can be more elegant than using them to cut meat on a plate!

➡ _____

**12** ▸ Chopsticks: Why do you use two different kinds of utensils when you can use two of the same utensil?

➡ _____

**13** ▸ Plus, you can use chopsticks with just one hand!

➡ _____

**14**  Barehands: No way! When I eat with my hands, of course I can see and smell the food, but I can also touch it.

➡ _____

**15**  Because I use my sense of touch when I eat, I get to enjoy my food more.

➡ _____

**16**  They raised and argued many points, and nobody wanted to give up.

➡ _____

**17**  It was not easy for their host, Ms. Disher, to listen to their arguments patiently.

➡ _____

**18**  So, she hurriedly, yet quietly, left.

➡ _____

**19**  Spork: Where is Ms. Disher? She has disappeared.

➡ _____

**20**  Knork: What should we do? Without Ms. Disher, this dinner is not complete.

➡ _____

**21**  Chopsticks: Where did she go?

➡ _____

**22**  Barehands: Let's go out to find her!

➡ _____

**23**  After hours of searching all over the Dining Republic, they finally found Ms. Disher sitting under a huge tree.

➡ _____

**24**  Spork, Knork, Chopsticks, Barehands: We're sorry we became boastful and ignored you.

➡ _____

**25**  Please forgive and come back and join us.

➡ _____

**26**  Ms. Disher: It's okay. I forgive you. Let's go back to my home.

➡ _____

**27**  Since then, every time they meet, they allow one another to eat in the manner that they please.

➡ _____

**28**  In their hearts they now know that food will always be delicious regardless of which utensils they use to eat it with.

➡ _____

_____

※ 다음 괄호 안의 단어들을 우리말에 맞도록 바르게 배열하시오.

**1** Friends from the Dining Republic
(Chopsticks, / Spork, / Barehands, / Knork, / and / Disher / Ms. / close / are / in / friends / the / Republic. / Dining)
➡ _____
_____

**2** (Chopsticks, / Spork, / Knork, / and / travel / Barehands / a / with / lot / families / their / Ms. / but / Disher's / does / family / not / much. / travel)
➡ _____

**3** (makes / she / for / up / by / this / hostinig / dinner / a / for / friends / her / back / coming / their / from / trips.)
➡ _____

**4** (is / she / eager / always / listen / to / adventures. / to / their)
➡ _____

**5** (often / they / about / talk / they / what / from / learned / recent / their / trips.)
➡ _____

**6** (most / the / topic / recent / about / was / best / the / to / way / eat / and / Disher's / Ms. / began / guests / argue. / to)
➡ _____

**7** (Spork: / a / on / trip, / recent / have / I / that / found / is / it / to / best / a / use / spoon / fork. / and)
➡ _____

**8** (spoon / a / best / is / for / and / grains / soup, / and / fork / a / good / is / eating / for / meat.)
➡ _____

**9** (Knork: / no! // is / it / better / much / use / to / knife / a / and / fork / a / instead.)
➡ _____

**10** (you / don't / it / think / easier / is / you / for / hold / to / a / in / fork / one / hand / a / and / knife / in / other? / the)
➡ _____

**11** (can / what / more / be / than / elegant / them / using / cut / to / meat / on / plate! / a)
➡ _____

**12** (Chopsticks: / do / why / use / you / different / two / of / kinds / when / utensils / can / you / two / use / of / utensil? / same / the)
➡ _____

**13** (you / plus, / use / can / with / chopsticks / just / hand! / one)
➡ _____

**1** Spork와 Chopsticks, Knork, Barehands, Disher 부인은 식탁 공화국의 친구들입니다.

**2** Spork와 Chopsticks, Knork, Barehands는 자신의 가족들과 여행을 많이 다니지만, Ms. Disher의 가족은 여행을 많이 다니지 않습니다.

**3** 그녀는 여행에서 돌아온 친구들을 위해 저녁 식사를 주최함으로써 여행을 많이 하지 않는 것을 보상합니다.

**4** 그녀는 항상 친구들의 모험담을 듣고 싶어 합니다.

**5** 그들은 최근 여행에서 배운 것에 대해 자주 이야기합니다.

**6** 가장 최근 주제는 음식을 먹는 가장 좋은 방법에 대한 것이었고, Ms. Disher의 손님들은 논쟁하기 시작했습니다.

**7** Spork: 최근 여행에서, 나는 숟가락과 포크가 함께 달려 있는 것을 사용하는 것이 가장 좋다는 것을 알았어.

**8** 숟가락은 곡물이나 국을 먹기에 최고이고, 포크는 고기를 먹기에 좋아.

**9** Knork: 아냐! 그 대신에 칼과 포크를 사용하는 것이 훨씬 더 좋아.

**10** 네가 한 손에는 포크를, 다른 손에 칼을 드는 것이 더 쉽다고 생각하지 않니?

**11** 접시 위에 놓인 고기를 자르기 위해 칼과 포크를 사용하는 것보다 더 우아할 수 있는 게 뭐가 있겠어!

**12** Chopsticks: 같은 도구를 두 가지로 사용할 수 있는데 왜 두 종류의 다른 도구를 사용한단 말이야?

**13** 게다가 젓가락은 한 손으로도 사용할 수 있어!

**14** (Barehands: / way! / no // I / when / with / eat / hands / my / course, / of / I / see / can / smell / and / food, / the / but / can / I / touch / it. / also)

➡ _____

**15** (I / beause / my / use / sense / of / when / touch / eat, / I / get / to / enjoy / food / my / more.)

➡ _____

**16** (raised / they / argued / and / points, / many / and / wanted / nobody / give / to / up.)

➡ _____

**17** (was / it / easy / for / not / host, / their / Disher, / Ms. / listen / to / their / to / patiently. / arguments)

➡ _____

**18** (she / so, / hurriedly, / quietly, / yet / left.)

➡ _____

**19** (Spork: / is / where / Disher? / Ms. // has / she / disappeared.)

➡ _____

**20** (Knork: / should / what / do? / we // Ms. / without / Disher, / dinner / this / not / complete. / is)

➡ _____

**21** (Chopsticks: / did / where / go? / she)

➡ _____

**22** (Barehands: / go / let's / to / out / her! / find)

➡ _____

**23** (hours / after / searching / of / over / all / Dining / the / Republic, / finally / they / Ms. / found / Disher / under / sitting / a / tree. / huge)

➡ _____

**24** (Knork, / Spork, / Barenhands: / Chopsticks, / sorry / we're / became / we / ignored / and / boastful / you.)

➡ _____

**25** (forgive / please / and / back / come / and / us. / join)

➡ _____

**26** (Disher: / Ms. / okay. / it's // forgive / I / you. // go / let's / to / back / home. / my)

➡ _____

**27** (then, / since / time / every / meet, / they / allow / they / another / one / eat / to / the / in / that / manner / please. / they)

➡ _____

**28** (their / in / they / hearts / know / now / food / that / will / be / always / regardless / delicious / which / of / they / utensils / to / use / it / eat / with.)

➡ _____

---

**14** Barehands: 천만의 말씀! 내가 손으로 음식을 먹으면 당연히 보면서 음식 냄새도 맡을 수 있지만, 음식을 만져 볼 수도 있다고.

**15** 음식을 먹을 때 촉각을 사용하기 때문에 음식을 더 즐기게 돼.

**16** 그들은 여러 의견을 제기하고 논쟁했습니다. 그리고 아무도 포기하고 싶어 하지 않았습니다.

**17** 그들의 주최자인 Ms. Disher가 그들의 언쟁을 참을성 있게 듣고 있는 것은 쉽지 않았습니다.

**18** 그래서 그녀는 서둘러서 그러나 조용히 자리를 떠났습니다.

**19** Spork: Disher 부인은 어디 있지? 그녀가 사라졌어.

**20** Knork: 어떡하지? Disher 부인이 없으면, 저녁 식사는 완전하지 않아.

**21** Chopsticks: 그녀는 어디 갔을까?

**22** Barehands: 나가서 그녀를 찾아보자!

**23** 몇 시간 동안 식탁 공화국을 구석구석 뒤진 끝에, 친구들은 마침내 큰 나무 밑에 앉아 있는 Disher 부인을 찾았습니다.

**24** Spork, Knork, Chopsticks, Barehands: 우리가 자랑스러워하고 너를 무시해서 미안해.

**25** 우리를 용서하고 돌아와서 우리와 함께 있어 줘.

**26** Ms. Disher: 알았어. 용서할게. 우리 집으로 돌아가자.

**27** 그 후로, 그들은 만날 때마다 서로 자신들이 좋아하는 방식으로 음식 먹는 것을 받아들입니다.

**28** 마음속으로 그들은 이제 음식을 먹는 데 어떤 도구를 사용하여 먹는지에 상관없이 음식 맛은 항상 맛있을 거라는 걸 알게 되었습니다.

※ 다음 우리말을 영어로 쓰시오.

Friends from the Dining Republic

**1** Spork와 Chopsticks, Knork, Barehands, Disher 부인은 식탁 공화국의 친구들입니다.

➡ _____

**2** Spork와 Chopsticks, Knork, Barehands는 자신의 가족들과 여행을 많이 다니지만, Ms. Disher의 가족은 여행을 많이 다니지 않습니다.

➡ _____

_____

**3** 그녀는 여행에서 돌아온 친구들을 위해 저녁 식사를 주최함으로써 여행을 많이 하지 않는 것을 보상합니다.

➡ _____

**4** 그녀는 항상 친구들의 모험담을 듣고 싶어 합니다.

➡ _____

**5** 그들은 최근 여행에서 배운 것에 대해 자주 이야기합니다.

➡ _____

**6** 가장 최근 주제는 음식을 먹는 가장 좋은 방법에 대한 것이었고, Ms. Disher의 손님들은 논쟁하기 시작했습니다.

➡ _____

**7** Spork: 최근 여행에서, 나는 숟가락과 포크가 함께 달려 있는 것을 사용하는 것이 가장 좋다는 것을 알았어.

➡ _____

**8** 숟가락은 곡물이나 국을 먹기에 최고이고, 포크는 고기를 먹기에 좋아.

➡ _____

**9** Knork: 아냐! 그 대신에 칼과 포크를 사용하는 것이 훨씬 더 좋아.

➡ _____

**10** 네가 한 손에는 포크를, 다른 손에 칼을 드는 것이 더 쉽다고 생각하지 않니?

➡ _____

**11** 접시 위에 놓인 고기를 자르기 위해 칼과 포크를 사용하는 것보다 더 우아할 수 있는 게 뭐가 있겠어!

➡ _____

**12** Chopsticks: 같은 도구를 두 가지로 사용할 수 있는데 왜 두 종류의 다른 도구를 사용한단 말이야?

➡ _____

**13** 게다가 젓가락은 한 손으로도 사용할 수 있어!

➡ _____

**14** Barehands: 천만의 말씀! 내가 손으로 음식을 먹으면 당연히 보면서 음식 냄새도 맡을 수 있지만, 음식을 만져 볼 수도 있다고.

➡ _____

_____

**15** 음식을 먹을 때 촉각을 사용하기 때문에 음식을 더 즐기게 돼.

➡ _____

**16** 그들은 여러 의견을 제기하고 논쟁했습니다. 그리고 아무도 포기하고 싶어 하지 않았습니다.

➡ _____

**17** 그들의 주최자인 Ms. Disher가 그들의 언쟁을 참을성 있게 듣고 있는 것은 쉽지 않았습니다.

➡ _____

**18** 그래서 그녀는 서둘러서 그러나 조용히 자리를 떠났습니다.

➡ _____

**19** Spork: Disher 부인은 어디 있지? 그녀가 사라졌어.

➡ _____

**20** Knork: 어떡하지? Disher 부인이 없으면, 저녁 식사는 완전하지 않아.

➡ _____

**21** Chopsticks: 그녀는 어디 갔을까?

➡ _____

**22** Barehands: 나가서 그녀를 찾아보자!

➡ _____

**23** 몇 시간 동안 식탁 공화국을 구석구석 뒤진 끝에, 친구들은 마침내 큰 나무 밑에 앉아 있는 Disher 부인을 찾았습니다.

➡ _____

**24** Spork, Knork, Chopsticks, Barehands: 우리가 자랑스러워하고 너를 무시해서 미안해.

➡ _____

**25** 우리를 용서하고 돌아와서 우리와 함께 있어 줘.

➡ _____

**26** Ms. Disher: 알았어. 용서할게. 우리 집으로 돌아가자.

➡ _____

**27** 그 후로, 그들은 만날 때마다 서로 자신들이 좋아하는 방식으로 음식 먹는 것을 받아들입니다.

➡ _____

**28** 마음속으로 그들은 이제 음식을 먹는 데 어떤 도구를 사용하여 먹는지에 상관없이 음식 맛은 항상 맛있을 거라는 걸 알게 되었습니다.

➡ _____

_____

※ 다음 우리말과 일치하도록 빈칸에 알맞은 말을 쓰시오.

### Real Life Communication B

1. A: _____ do you _____, fruit _____ ice cream?

2. B: I _____ _____.

3. A: _____ do you _____ _____?

4. B: _____ _____ _____ _____ _____ ice cream is sweeter.

1. A: 과일과 아이스크림 중에서 어느 것을 더 좋아하니?
2. B: 나는 아이스크림을 더 좋아해.
3. A: 왜 그것을 더 좋아하니?
4. B: 내 생각에는 아이스크림이 더 달콤한 것 같아.

### Before You Read B

1. _____ cultures use _____ _____ _____ utensils _____ _____.

2. For some people, chopsticks _____ _____ _____ _____.

3. _____ _____, a fork is _____ _____.

4. Other people _____ _____ _____ a knife and fork is _____ _____.

1. 다른 문화에서는 음식을 먹는 데 다른 종류의 도구를 사용한다.
2. 어떤 사람들에게 젓가락은 사용하기 쉽다.
3. 또 다른 사람들에게는 포크가 더 편리하다.
4. 다른 사람들은 나이프와 포크를 사용하는 것이 더 우아하다고 생각할지도 모른다.

### Before You Read 1

1. I _____ people have bacon and eggs _____ _____ in the USA.

2. Pho is very _____ _____ _____ Vietnam.

3. And people in Iran _____ _____ _____ Naan _____ _____.

1. 나는 사람들이 미국에서 아침식사로 베이컨과 계란을 먹는다고 생각합니다.
2. 포는 베트남에서 매우 인기 있는 아침식사입니다.
3. 그리고 이란 사람들은 아침식사로 난을 먹는 것을 좋아합니다.

※ 다음 우리말을 영어로 쓰시오.

**Real Life Communication B**

1. A: 과일과 아이스크림 중에서 어느 것을 더 좋아하니?

➡ _____

2. B: 나는 아이스크림을 더 좋아해.

➡ _____

3. A: 왜 그것을 더 좋아하니?

➡ _____

4. B: 내 생각에는 아이스크림이 더 달콤한 것 같아.

➡ _____


**Before You Read B**

1. 다른 문화에서는 음식을 먹는 데 다른 종류의 도구를 사용한다.

➡ _____

2. 어떤 사람들에게 젓가락은 사용하기 쉽다.

➡ _____

3. 또 다른 사람들에게는 포크가 더 편리하다.

➡ _____

4. 다른 사람들은 나이프와 포크를 사용하는 것이 더 우아하다고 생각할지도 모른다.

➡ _____


**Before You Read 1**

1. 나는 사람들이 미국에서 아침식사로 베이컨과 계란을 먹는다고 생각합니다.

➡ _____

2. 포는 베트남에서 매우 인기 있는 아침식사입니다.

➡ _____

3. 그리고 이란 사람들은 아침식사로 난을 먹는 것을 좋아합니다.

➡ _____

※ 다음 영어를 우리말로 쓰시오.

| | | | |
|---|---|---|---|
| 01 high-speed | _____ | 22 solution | _____ |
| 02 burr | _____ | 23 painful | _____ |
| 03 explain | _____ | 24 inspire | _____ |
| 04 imitate | _____ | 25 successful | _____ |
| 05 absorb | _____ | 26 cause | _____ |
| 06 all-purpose | _____ | 27 gracefully | _____ |
| 07 fascinate | _____ | 28 sudden | _____ |
| 08 holder | _____ | 29 surface | _____ |
| 09 fastener | _____ | 30 reduce | _____ |
| 10 article | _____ | 31 reflect | _____ |
| 11 beak | _____ | 32 survivor | _____ |
| 12 contact | _____ | 33 length | _____ |
| 13 bite | _____ | 34 necessity | _____ |
| 14 pressure | _____ | 35 glide over | _____ |
| 15 redesign | _____ | 36 make contact with | _____ |
| 16 apply | _____ | 37 float away | _____ |
| 17 explore | _____ | 38 keep A from -ing | _____ |
| 18 genius | _____ | 39 on one's way to | _____ |
| 19 hairy | _____ | 40 be stuck to | _____ |
| 20 increase | _____ | 41 not only A but also B | _____ |
| 21 notice | _____ | 42 as a result | _____ |
| | | 43 That's why ~. | _____ |

※ 다음 우리말을 영어로 쓰시오.

| | | | |
|---|---|---|---|
| 01 흡수하다 | | 22 생존자 | |
| 02 곤충, 벌레 | | 23 발명 | |
| 03 창의적인 | | 24 자세히 | |
| 04 적용하다 | | 25 접촉 | |
| 05 길이 | | 26 필요성 | |
| 06 (새의) 부리 | | 27 매혹하다 | |
| 07 물린 상처 | | 28 천재 | |
| 08 만능의, 다용도의 | | 29 주목하다 | |
| 09 탐색하다 | | 30 압력 | |
| 10 우아하게 | | 31 다시 디자인하다 | |
| 11 관찰하다 | | 32 표면 | |
| 12 고통스러운 | | 33 줄이다 | |
| 13 성공적인 | | 34 갑작스러운 | |
| 14 모방하다 | | 35 ~을 찾고 있는 | |
| 15 증가; 증가하다 | | 36 ~와 연락하다, 접촉하다 | |
| 16 가시 식물 | | 37 ~에 붙다 | |
| 17 기사, 논문 | | 38 ~로 덮여 있다 | |
| 18 초래하다 | | 39 A가 ~하지 못하게 하다 | |
| 19 무게 | | 40 떠다니다 | |
| 20 영감을 불러일으키다 | | 41 결과적으로 | |
| 21 고속의 | | 42 ~로 가는 길에 | |
| | | 43 A뿐만 아니라 B도 역시 | |

※ 다음 영영풀이에 알맞은 단어를 <보기>에서 골라 쓴 후, 우리말 뜻을 쓰시오.

1 _____ : pain in your head: _____

2 _____ : long and not wide: _____

3 _____ : suitable for many uses: _____

4 _____ : the act of inventing something: _____

5 _____ : a natural ability to do something well: _____

6 _____ : covered with a lot of hair: _____

7 _____ : to see or notice somebody/something: _____

8 _____ : a passage that goes under the ground: _____

9 _____ : a very smart or talented person: _____

10 _____ : the hard usually pointed parts that over a bird's mouth: _____

11 _____ : to move down through the air at a steep angle: _____

12 _____ : to make or do something the same way as something else: _____

13 _____ : to change the design of something: _____

14 _____ : a part of an animal's body that is used for flying or gliding: _____

15 _____ : a device used to close a piece of clothing, a window, suitcase, etc. tightly:

_____

16 _____ : a person who continues to live, especially despite being nearly killed or

experiencing great danger or difficulty: _____

| 보기 | | | |
|---|---|---|---|
| talent | hairy | dive | wing |
| narrow | headache | fastener | imitate |
| tunnel | observe | genius | redesign |
| invention | all-purpose | survivor | beak |

※ 다음 우리말과 일치하도록 빈칸에 알맞은 말을 쓰시오.

### Listen & Speak 1 A

G: You _____ that Leonardo da Vinci _____ the *Mona Lisa*, _____ you?

B: Sure. I _____ he was a really _____ _____ .

G: He was _____ a _____ _____ .

B: _____ did he _____ ?

G: He _____ _____ _____ _____ a bird. So, he _____ a _____ machine that _____ _____ a bird.

B: _____ he _____ _____ that _____ ?

G: No, but his _____ _____ _____ many _____ _____ .

### Listen & Speak 1 B

B: _____ _____ _____ of a mosquito _____ , Jian?

G: A mosquito needle? _____ you _____ _____ to me?

B: Some scientists _____ _____ new needle by _____ a _____ _____ .

G: That's interesting. So _____ _____ that help?

B: You _____ mosquito _____ are not _____ _____ , _____ _____ ? The new _____ will also _____ _____ _____ .

G: That's great. _____ _____ it's _____ _____ ?

B: _____ a mosquito's mouth, it makes _____ _____ _____ our skin.

G: Wow, I _____ that there's _____ _____ in the world!

### Listen & Speak 2 A-2

G: This candle _____ can make _____ _____ _____ as long.

B: Really? How's that _____ ?

G: _____ a candle _____ , it _____ _____ the _____ _____ the holder to _____ a new candle.

B: Wow, I am so _____ by the idea! Now we can _____ candles _____ .

해석

G: 레오나르도 다빈치가 모나리자를 그린 것을 알지, 그렇지 않니?
B: 몰론. 그는 정말로 위대한 미술가라고 생각해.
G: 그는 또한 위대한 발명가였어.
B: 그가 무엇을 발명했니?
G: 그는 새처럼 나는 것을 꿈꿨어. 그래서 그는 새처럼 보이는 나는 기계를 그렸어.
B: 그가 그 기계도 만들었니?
G: 아니, 하지만 그의 창의적인 생각은 많은 발명가들에게 영감을 주었어.

B: Jian, mosquito needle을 들어본 적이 있니?
G: mosquito needle이라고? 그것 좀 설명해 줄 수 있니?
B: 몇몇 과학자들이 모기의 입을 모방하여 이 새로운 바늘을 만들었어.
G: 흥미롭군. 그럼 그것이 어떻게 도움이 될까?
B: 모기가 무는 것은 별로 고통스럽지 않다는 건 알지? 이 새로운 주사바늘도 역시 통증을 줄여 줄 거야.
G: 대단한데. 어째서 덜 고통스럽지?
B: 모기의 입처럼 그것은 우리의 피부에 덜 닿아.
G: 와, 세상에 쓸모없는 것은 아무것도 없는 것 같아!

G: 이 양초 받침이 양초를 두 배나 오래 지속되도록 만들 수 있어.
B: 정말? 어떻게 그것이 가능해?
G: 양초가 탈 때 그것은 받침 아래에 있는 관으로 녹아들어 새로운 양초를 만들어.
B: 와, 나는 그 아이디어에 매료되었어! 이제 우리는 양초를 더 오래 사용할 수 있어.

### Listen & Speak 2 A-3

B: You know _____? I'm really _____ _____ the _____
door in Juwon's room.

G: _____ _____ the door so _____?

B: Juwon and I _____ _____ _____ on it.

G: _____ could you play table tennis on a _____?

B: The door can _____ _____ _____ a _____.

G: That's _____!

B: 너 그거 알아? 나는 주원이네 방의 특별한 문에 매료되었어.
G: 왜 그 문이 그리 특별하니?
B: 주원이와 내가 그 위에서 탁구를 쳤어.
G: 어떻게 문 위에서 탁구를 칠 수 있어?
B: 문이 탁구대로 바뀔 수 있어.
G: 멋있는데!

### Listen & Speak 2 B

W: Today, we _____ a special _____, Thomas Thwaites, the Goat
Man. Hello, Thomas.

M: Hello, Anna. _____ to _____ here.

W: Thomas, I'm so _____ by the _____ that you _____
_____ a _____ in the Alps _____ _____ _____.
_____ did you _____ that?

M: One day, I _____ _____ _____ on the mountain. They
_____ so _____ that I wanted to _____ _____ them.

W: _____ you _____ any _____ being a goat?

M: _____ _____ all four legs _____ very _____ for me.

W: Do you have _____ plans _____ _____ _____ a goat
again?

M: Sure. I'm _____ my second _____ to the Alps.

W: I _____ _____ _____ hear about your next _____. Thank
you, Thomas, for your time.

W: 오늘 우리는 특별 손님인 염소 인간 Thomas Thwaites를 모시게 되었습니다. 안녕하세요, Thomas.
M: 안녕하세요, Anna. 여기 오게 되어 기쁩니다.
W: Thomas, 나는 당신이 3일 동안 알프스에서 염소처럼 살았다는 사실에 매료되었습니다. 왜 그렇게 했나요?
M: 어느 날, 나는 염소들이 산에서 노는 것을 보았어요. 그들이 너무 평화로워 보여서 나는 그들처럼 살고 싶었습니다.
W: 염소가 되는 데 아무 문제가 없었나요?
M: 네 발로 걷는 것이 나에게는 매우 어려웠어요.
W: 당신은 다시 염소처럼 살 계획이 있나요?
M: 물론이죠. 나는 알프스를 다시 방문할 계획을 하고 있어요.
W: 당신의 다음 모험에 대해 빨리 듣고 싶어요. 시간 내주셔서 감사합니다, Thomas.

### Real Life Communication

Henry: _____ are you _____, Mina?

Mina: I'm _____ _____ _____ about a bug robot.

Henry: A bug robot? Is it _____?

Mina: Yes. I'm _____ _____ _____ this thing.

Henry: _____ you tell me _____ about it?

Mina: You _____ that some _____ can _____ _____
_____, don't you?

Henry: Yeah. That's _____ it's _____ to catch them.

Mina: A bug robot can do the same. It can _____ to find _____ after
_____ or _____ _____.

Henry: That's really _____!

Henry: 미나야, 뭐 하고 있니?
Mina: 나는 bug robot에 관한 기사를 읽고 있어.
Henry: "bug robot"라고? 재미있니?
Mina: 응, 나는 이것에 정말로 매료되었어.
Henry: 그것에 대해 좀 더 말해줄 수 있니?
Mina: 너는 몇몇 곤충이 좁은 공간에 미끄러져 들어갈 수 있는 것을 알지?
Henry: 알아. 그것이 그들을 잡기 어려운 이유이지.
Mina: bug robot이 똑같이 할 수 있어. 그것은 지진이나 대형 화재 이후에 생존자들을 찾는 것을 도와줄 수 있어.
Henry: 그거 정말 흥미롭다!

## 대화문 Test

※ 다음 우리말에 맞도록 대화를 영어로 쓰시오.

### Listen & Speak 1 A

G: _____

B: _____

G: _____

B: _____

G: _____

_____

B: _____

G: _____

G: 레오나르도 다빈치가 모나리자를 그린 것을 알지, 그렇지 않니?

B: 몰론. 그는 정말로 위대한 미술가라고 생각해.

G: 그는 또한 위대한 발명가였어.

B: 그가 무엇을 발명했니?

G: 그는 새처럼 나는 것을 꿈꿨어. 그래서 그는 새처럼 보이는 나는 기계를 그렸어.

B: 그가 그 기계도 만들었니?

G: 아니, 하지만 그의 창의적인 생각은 많은 발명가들에게 영감을 주었어.

### Listen & Speak 1 B

B: _____

G: _____

B: _____

G: _____

B: _____

_____

G: _____

B: _____

G: _____

B: Jian, mosquito needle을 들어본 적이 있니?

G: mosquito needle이라고? 그것 좀 설명해 줄 수 있니?

B: 몇몇 과학자들이 모기의 입을 모방하여 이 새로운 바늘을 만들었어.

G: 흥미롭군. 그럼 그것이 어떻게 도움이 될까?

B: 모기가 무는 것은 별로 고통스럽지 않다는 건 알지? 이 새로운 주사바늘도 역시 통증을 줄여 줄 거야.

G: 대단한데. 어째서 덜 고통스럽지?

B: 모기의 입처럼 그것은 우리의 피부에 덜 닿아.

G: 와, 세상에 쓸모없는 것은 아무것도 없는 것 같아!

### Listen & Speak 2 A-2

G: _____

B: _____

G: _____

_____

B: _____

G: 이 양초 받침이 양초를 두 배나 오래 지속되도록 만들 수 있어.

B: 정말? 어떻게 그것이 가능해?

G: 양초가 탈 때 그것은 받침 아래에 있는 관으로 녹아들어 새로운 양초를 만들어.

B: 와, 나는 그 아이디어에 매료되었어! 이제 우리는 양초를 더 오래 사용할 수 있어.

## Listen & Speak 2 A-3

B: _____

G: _____

B: _____

G: _____

B: _____

G: _____

B: 너 그거 알아? 나는 주원이네 방의 특별한 문에 매료되었어.
G: 왜 그 문이 그리 특별하니?
B: 주원이와 내가 그 위에서 탁구를 쳤어.
G: 어떻게 문 위에서 탁구를 칠 수 있어?
B: 문이 탁구대로 바뀔 수 있어.
G: 멋있는데!

## Listen & Speak 2 B

W: _____

M: _____

W: _____

_____

M: _____

_____

W: _____

M: _____

W: _____

M: _____

W: _____

W: 오늘 우리는 특별 손님인 염소 인간 Thomas Thwaites를 모시게 되었습니다. 안녕하세요, Thomas.
M: 안녕하세요, Anna. 여기 오게 되어 기쁩니다.
W: Thomas, 나는 당신이 3일 동안 알프스에서 염소처럼 살았다는 사실에 매료되었습니다. 왜 그렇게 했나요?
M: 어느 날, 나는 염소들이 산에서 노는 것을 보았어요. 그들이 너무 평화로워 보여서 나는 그들처럼 살고 싶었습니다.
W: 염소가 되는 데 아무 문제가 없었나요?
M: 네 발로 걷는 것이 나에게는 매우 어려웠어요.
W: 당신은 다시 염소처럼 살 계획이 있나요?
M: 물론이죠. 나는 알프스를 다시 방문할 계획을 하고 있어요.
W: 당신의 다음 모험에 대해 빨리 듣고 싶어요. 시간 내주셔서 감사합니다, Thomas.

## Real Life Communication

Henry: _____

Mina: _____

Henry: _____

Mina: _____

Henry: _____

Mina: _____

Henry: _____

Mina: _____

_____

Henry: _____

Henry: 미나야, 뭐 하고 있니?
Mina: 나는 bug robot에 관한 기사를 읽고 있어.
Henry: "bug robot"라고? 재미있니?
Mina: 응, 나는 이것에 정말로 매료되었어.
Henry: 그것에 대해 좀 더 말해줄 수 있니?
Mina: 너는 몇몇 곤충이 좁은 공간에 미끄러져 들어갈 수 있는 것을 알지?
Henry: 알아. 그것이 그들을 잡기 어려운 이유이지.
Mina: bug robot이 똑같이 할 수 있어. 그것은 지진이나 대형 화재 이후에 생존자들을 찾는 것을 도와줄 수 있어.
Henry: 그거 정말 흥미롭다!

※ 다음 우리말과 일치하도록 빈칸에 알맞은 것을 골라 쓰시오.

**Nature's Inspiration**

**1** From _____ birds to _____ plants, the _____ nature works _____ us.

A. fascinates     B. self-cleaning     C. flying     D. way

**2** Some people not _____ use nature but _____ imitate _____ to find _____ to their problems.

A. also     B. solutions     C. only     D. it

**3** Leonardo da Vinci (1452-1519) was _____ _____ _____.

A. such     B. one     C. person

**4** He wondered _____ _____ _____ _____.

A. could     B. how     C. fly     D. birds

**5** He _____ watched birds, _____ notes, and _____ pictures _____ them.

A. drew     B. closely     C. made     D. of

**6** Even _____ his invention was not _____, he _____ a bird's wings to _____ to make a flying machine.

A. imitated     B. try     C. though     D. successful

**7** _____ then, more and more people _____ successfully _____ the surprising _____ of nature's genius.

A. abilities     B. since     C. imitated     D. have

**8** _____ _____ some _____ them.

A. explore     B. let's     C. of

**Learning from a Bird: Moving Fast and Quietly**

**9** The _____ _____ was first _____ in Japan. But it _____ one problem.

A. train     B. had     C. high-speed     D. made

**10** When the train _____ a tunnel, the _____ _____ in air pressure created a very _____ sound.

A. loud     B. sudden     C. entered     D. increase

**11** It often _____ _____ and _____ headaches.

A. caused     B. people     C. up     D. woke

**12** A team of engineers tried to _____ the problem, but they didn't know _____ they _____ _____ the noise.

A. reduce     B. solve     C. how     D. could

---

**1** 나는 새에서 자정 작용을 하는 식물까지, 자연이 기능하는 방식은 우리를 매료시킵니다.

**2** 몇몇 사람들은 그들의 문제에 대한 해결책을 찾기 위해 자연을 이용할 뿐만 아니라 자연을 모방하기까지 합니다.

**3** 레오나르도 다빈치(1452-1519)가 이러한 사람들 중 한 사람이었습니다.

**4** 그는 새들이 어떻게 날 수 있는지 궁금했습니다.

**5** 그는 새를 자세히 관찰했고, 기록했으며, 그림으로 그렸습니다.

**6** 그의 발명은 비록 성공하지 못했지만, 그는 나는 기계를 만들어 보려고 새의 날개를 모방했습니다.

**7** 그 후로, 점점 더 많은 사람들이 자연 속 천재의 놀라운 능력을 성공적으로 모방해 오고 있습니다.

**8** 그들 중 몇 가지를 알아봅시다.

**새에게서 배우기: 빠르고 조용하게 움직이기**

**9** 고속 열차는 일본에서 처음 만들어졌습니다. 하지만 그것은 한 가지 문제점이 있었습니다.

**10** 열차가 터널에 들어갔을 때, 갑작스러운 기압의 상승은 매우 시끄러운 소리를 발생시켰습니다.

**11** 그것은 종종 사람들의 잠을 깨웠고 두통을 일으켰습니다.

**12** 한 공학자 팀이 그 문제를 해결하려 했지만, 그들은 어떻게 소음을 줄일 수 있을지 몰랐습니다.

**13** One day, one of the _____ was watching a bird _____ _____ _____ a meal.

    A. search        B. engineers      C. of        D. in

**14** He _____ the bird quickly and _____ _____ _____ the water.

    A. diving        B. saw        C. quietly     D. into

**15** He wondered _____ the _____ _____ the water so _____.

    A. entered      B. gracefully    C. bird      D. how

**16** So, he studied _____ about the bird and _____ its long, _____ _____.

    A. discovered    B. more       C. beak      D. narrow

**17** He _____ the _____ of the train _____ _____ the bird's beak.

    A. front        B. imitating     C. redesigned    D. by

**18** It was successful. Now the new train travels _____ only more quietly _____ also 10% faster _____ 15% _____ electricity.

    A. with        B. but        C. less      D. not

**Learning from Burrs: Inventing an All-Purpose Fastener**

**19** _____ day, a Swiss engineer, George de Mestral, _____ _____ in the woods _____ his dog.

    A. was        B. with       C. one       D. hiking

**20** _____ his way _____, he saw that _____ were _____ to his clothes and his dog's hair.

    A. burrs       B. home      C. on       D. stuck

**21** He wanted to _____ _____ _____ _____.

    A. how        B. happened     C. know      D. that

**22** He _____ a _____ look at the burrs and _____ that the ends of the burr needles were not _____.

    A. noticed      B. straight     C. closer     D. took

**23** He wondered _____ he could _____ that to make _____ _____.

    A. apply       B. useful     C. if       D. something

**13** 어느 날, 공학자들 중 한 사람이 먹이를 찾고 있는 새를 관찰하고 있었습니다.

**14** 그는 새가 빠르고 조용하게 물속으로 뛰어드는 것을 보았습니다.

**15** 그는 새가 어떻게 그렇게 우아하게 물속으로 들어가는지 궁금했습니다.

**16** 그래서 그는 그 새에 대해 더 연구했고, 새의 길고 좁은 부리를 발견했습니다.

**17** 그는 새의 부리를 모방하여 열차의 앞면을 다시 디자인했습니다.

**18** 그것은 성공이었습니다. 이제 새로운 열차는 더 조용할 뿐만 아니라 전기는 15% 덜 사용하면서 10% 더 빠르게 이동합니다.

**가시 식물들에게서 배우기: 만능 고정 장치 발명하기**

**19** 어느 날, 스위스 공학자 George de Mestral은 그의 개와 숲에서 하이킹하고 있었습니다.

**20** 집으로 돌아오는 길에, 그는 가시 식물이 자신의 옷과 개의 털에 붙어 있는 것을 보았습니다.

**21** 그는 어떻게 그런 일이 일어났는지 알고 싶었습니다.

**22** 그는 가시 식물들을 자세히 들여다보았고, 가시의 끝이 곧지 않다는 것을 알아챘습니다.

**23** 그는 유용한 뭔가를 만드는 데 그것을 적용할 수 있을지 궁금했습니다.

**24** _____ a lot of _____, he finally _____ two new _____.

A. materials       B. after       C. invented       D. testing

**25** One had many _____ needles like those of _____ and the _____ had a hairy _____.

A. other       B. tiny       C. surface       D. burrs

**26** When they _____ _____ together, they _____ a very good _____.

A. pressed       B. became       C. were       D. fastener

**27** It was not _____ _____ _____ also _____ to use.

A. strong       B. but       C. easy       D. only

**28** _____ then, many people have _____ his invention in many _____ _____.

A. different       B. since       C. ways       D. used

**29** It _____ _____ _____ _____ clothing, shoes, and bags.

A. used       B. is       C. for       D. often

**30** Some people _____ it to _____ a _____ of _____ games.

A. number       B. different       C. use       D. play

**31** In space, it _____ things _____ _____ _____.

A. away       B. keeps       C. floating       D. from

**32** There is _____ _____ in nature. We just have to become _____ and _____ questions.

A. curious       B. nothing       C. ask       D. useless

---

**24** 수많은 실험 후에, 그는 마침내 두 가지 새로운 소재를 발명했습니다.

**25** 하나는 가시 식물과 같은 조그만 가시들이 많이 있는 것이었고, 다른 하나는 털로 덮인 표면이 있는 것이었습니다.

**26** 두 소재를 함께 붙이면, 매우 훌륭한 고정 장치가 되었습니다.

**27** 그것은 튼튼할 뿐만 아니라 사용하기도 쉬웠습니다.

**28** 그 후로, 많은 사람들이 그의 발명품을 다양한 방법으로 사용해 오고 있습니다.

**29** 그것은 옷, 신발, 가방에 흔히 사용됩니다.

**30** 몇몇 사람들은 여러 가지 게임을 하기 위해 그것을 사용합니다.

**31** 우주에서, 그것은 물건들이 떠다니는 것을 막아줍니다.

**32** 자연에 쓸모없는 것은 하나도 없습니다. 우리는 그저 호기심을 갖고 질문을 던지면 됩니다.

※ 다음 우리말과 일치하도록 빈칸에 알맞은 말을 쓰시오.

## Nature's Inspiration

**1** _____ flying birds _____ _____ plants, the way nature _____ _____ _____.

**2** Some people _____ _____ use nature _____ _____ _____ _____ to find _____ to their problems.

**3** Leonardo da Vinci (1452-1519) was _____ _____ _____.

**4** He wondered _____ _____ _____ _____ _____.

**5** He _____ watched birds, _____ _____, and drew pictures of them.

**6** _____ _____ his invention was not _____, he _____ a bird's wings _____ _____ _____ _____ _____ a _____ _____.

**7** _____ then, more and more people _____ successfully _____ the _____ _____ of _____ _____.

**8** _____ _____ some of them.

## Learning from a Bird: Moving Fast and Quietly

**9** The _____ _____ was first made in Japan. But it _____ one problem.

**10** When the train _____ a tunnel, the _____ _____ in air pressure _____ a very _____ _____.

**11** It often _____ and _____ headaches.

**12** A team of engineers _____ _____ _____ the problem, but they didn't know _____ _____ _____ _____ _____ the noise.

**13** One day, one of _____ _____ _____ watching a bird _____ _____ _____ a meal.

**14** He _____ the bird _____ and _____ the water.

**15** He wondered _____ _____ _____ _____ _____ the water so _____.

**1** 나는 새에서 자정 작용을 하는 식물까지, 자연이 기능하는 방식은 우리를 매료시킵니다.

**2** 몇몇 사람들은 그들의 문제에 대한 해결책을 찾기 위해 자연을 이용할 뿐만 아니라 자연을 모방하기까지 합니다.

**3** 레오나르도 다빈치(1452-1519)가 이러한 사람들 중 한 사람이었습니다.

**4** 그는 새들이 어떻게 날 수 있는지 궁금했습니다.

**5** 그는 새를 자세히 관찰했고, 기록했으며, 그림으로 그렸습니다.

**6** 그의 발명은 비록 성공하지 못했지만, 그는 나는 기계를 만들어 보려고 새의 날개를 모방했습니다.

**7** 그 후로, 점점 더 많은 사람들이 자연 속 천재의 놀라운 능력을 성공적으로 모방해 오고 있습니다.

**8** 그들 중 몇 가지를 알아봅시다.

**새에게서 배우기: 빠르고 조용하게 움직이기**

**9** 고속 열차는 일본에서 처음 만들어졌습니다. 하지만 그것은 한 가지 문제점이 있었습니다.

**10** 열차가 터널에 들어갔을 때, 갑작스러운 기압의 상승은 매우 시끄러운 소리를 발생시켰습니다.

**11** 그것은 종종 사람들의 잠을 깨웠고 두통을 일으켰습니다.

**12** 한 공학자 팀이 그 문제를 해결하려 했지만, 그들은 어떻게 소음을 줄일 수 있을지 몰랐습니다.

**13** 어느 날, 공학자들 중 한 사람이 먹이를 찾고 있는 새를 관찰하고 있었습니다.

**14** 그는 새가 빠르고 조용하게 물속으로 뛰어드는 것을 보았습니다.

**15** 그는 새가 어떻게 그렇게 우아하게 물속으로 들어가는지 궁금했습니다.

**16** So, he _____ _____ about the bird and _____ its long, _____ _____.

**17** He _____ the _____ of the train _____ _____ the bird's _____.

**18** It was successful. Now the new train travels _____ _____ more quietly _____ _____ 10% faster _____ 15% _____ _____.

**Learning from Burrs: Inventing an All-Purpose Fastener**

**19** _____ _____, a Swiss engineer, George de Mestral, _____ _____ in the woods _____ his dog.

**20** _____ his _____ _____, he saw that _____ _____ _____ _____ his clothes and his dog's _____.

**21** He wanted _____ _____ _____ _____ _____ _____ _____ _____.

**22** He _____ _____ _____ _____ _____ the burrs and _____ _____ the ends of the burr needles _____ not _____.

**23** He wondered _____ _____ _____ _____ that to make _____ _____.

**24** _____ a _____ of _____, he finally _____ two new materials.

**25** One had many _____ _____ like _____ _____ and _____ _____ had a _____ _____.

**26** When they _____ _____ _____, they became a very good _____.

**27** It was _____ _____ _____ _____ _____ _____ to use.

**28** _____ then, many people _____ _____ his invention in _____ _____.

**29** It _____ _____ _____ _____ clothing, shoes, and bags.

**30** Some people use it _____ _____ _____ _____ _____ games.

**31** In space, it _____ things _____ _____ _____.

**32** There is _____ _____ in nature. We just have to become _____ and _____ questions.

**16** 그래서 그는 그 새에 대해 더 연구했고, 새의 길고 좁은 부리를 발견했습니다.

**17** 그는 새의 부리를 모방하여 열차의 앞면을 다시 디자인했습니다.

**18** 그것은 성공이었습니다. 이제 새로운 열차는 더 조용할 뿐만 아니라 전기는 15% 덜 사용하면서 10% 더 빠르게 이동합니다.

**가시 식물들에게서 배우기: 만능 고정 장치 발명하기**

**19** 어느 날, 스위스 공학자 George de Mestral은 그의 개와 숲에서 하이킹하고 있었습니다.

**20** 집으로 돌아오는 길에, 그는 가시 식물이 자신의 옷과 개의 털에 붙어 있는 것을 보았습니다.

**21** 그는 어떻게 그런 일이 일어났는지 알고 싶었습니다.

**22** 그는 가시 식물들을 자세히 들여다보았고, 가시의 끝이 곧지 않다는 것을 알아챘습니다.

**23** 그는 유용한 뭔가를 만드는 데 그것을 적용할 수 있을지 궁금했습니다.

**24** 수많은 실험 후에, 그는 마침내 두 가지 새로운 소재를 발명했습니다.

**25** 하나는 가시 식물과 같은 조그만 가시들이 많이 있는 것이었고, 다른 하나는 털로 덮인 표면이 있는 것이었습니다.

**26** 두 소재를 함께 붙이면, 매우 훌륭한 고정 장치가 되었습니다.

**27** 그것은 튼튼할 뿐만 아니라 사용하기도 쉬웠습니다.

**28** 그 후로, 많은 사람들이 그의 발명품을 다양한 방법으로 사용해 오고 있습니다.

**29** 그것은 옷, 신발, 가방에 흔히 사용됩니다.

**30** 몇몇 사람들은 여러 가지 게임을 하기 위해 그것을 사용합니다.

**31** 우주에서, 그것은 물건들이 떠다니는 것을 막아줍니다.

**32** 자연에 쓸모없는 것은 하나도 없습니다. 우리는 그저 호기심을 갖고 질문을 던지면 됩니다.

※ 다음 문장을 우리말로 쓰시오.

Nature's Inspiration

**1** From flying birds to self-cleaning plants, the way nature works fascinates us.

➡ _____

**2** Some people not only use nature but also imitate it to find solutions to their problems.

➡ _____

**3** Leonardo da Vinci (1452-1519) was one such person.

➡ _____

**4** He wondered how birds could fly.

➡ _____

**5** He closely watched birds, made notes, and drew pictures of them.

➡ _____

**6** Even though his invention was not successful, he imitated a bird's wings to try to make a flying machine.

➡ _____

**7** Since then, more and more people have successfully imitated the surprising abilities of nature's genius.

➡ _____

**8** Let's explore some of them.

➡ _____

Learning from a bird: Moving Fast and Quietly

**9** The high-speed train was first made in Japan. But it had one problem.

➡ _____

**10** When the train entered a tunnel, the sudden increase in air pressure created a very loud sound.

➡ _____

**11** It often woke people up and caused headaches.

➡ _____

**12** A team of engineers tried to solve the problem, but they didn't know how they could reduce the noise.

➡ _____

**13** One day, one of the engineers was watching a bird in search of a meal.

➡ _____

**14** He saw the bird quickly and quietly diving into the water.

➡ _____

**15** He wondered how the bird entered the water so gracefully.

➡ _____

**16** So, he studied more about the bird and discovered its long, narrow beak.

➡ _____

**17** He redesigned the front of the train by imitating the bird's beak.

➡ _____

**18** It was successful. Now the new train travels not only more quietly but also 10% faster with 15% less electricity.

➡ _____

_____


Learning from Burrs: Inventing an All-Purpose Fastener

**19** One day, a Swiss engineer, George de Mestral, was hiking in the woods with his dog.

➡ _____

**20** On his way home, he saw that burrs were stuck to his clothes and his dog's hair.

➡ _____

**21** He wanted to know how that happened.

➡ _____

**22** He took a closer look at the burrs and noticed that the ends of the burr needles were not straight.

➡ _____

**23** He wondered if he could apply that to make something useful.

➡ _____

**24** After a lot of testing, he finally invented two new materials.

➡ _____

**25** One had many tiny needles like those of burrs and the other had a hairy surface.

➡ _____

**26** When they were pressed together, they became a very good fastener.

➡ _____

**27** It was not only strong but also easy to use.

➡ _____

**28** Since then, many people have used his invention in many different ways.

➡ _____

**29** It is often used for clothing, shoes, and bags.

➡ _____

**30** Some people use it to play a number of different games.

➡ _____

**31** In space, it keeps things from floating away.

➡ _____

**32** There is nothing useless in nature. We just have to become curious and ask questions.

➡ _____

※ 다음 괄호 안의 단어들을 우리말에 맞도록 바르게 배열하시오.

**Nature's Inspiration**

**1** (flying / from / to / birds / plants, / self-cleaning / way / the / works / nature / us. / fascinates)

➡ _____

**2** (people / some / only / not / nature / use / also / but / it / imitate / find / to / solutions / their / to / problems.)

➡ _____

**3** (da / Leonardo / Vinci / (1452-1519) / one / was / person. / such)

➡ _____

**4** (wondered / he / birds / how / fly. / could)

➡ _____

**5** (closely / he / birds, / watched / notes, / made / drew / and / of / them. / pictures)

➡ _____

**6** (though / even / invention / his / not / was / successful, / imitated / he / birds's / a / wings / try / to / make / to / flying / a / machine.)

➡ _____

**7** (then, / since / more / more / and / people / have / successfully / the / imitated / abilities / surprising / nature's / of / genius.)

➡ _____

**8** (explore / let's / of / some / them.)

➡ _____

**Learning from a bird: Moving Fast and Quietly**

**9** (high-speed / the / was / train / made / first / Japan. / in // but / had / it / problem. / one)

➡ _____

**10** (the / when / entered / train / tunnel, / a / sudden / the / in / increase / pressure / air / created / very / a / sound. / loud)

➡ _____

**11** (often / it / people / woke / up / and / headaches. / caused)

➡ _____

새에게서 배우기: 빠르고 조용하게 움직이기

1 나는 새에서 자정 작용을 하는 식물까지, 자연이 기능하는 방식은 우리를 매료시킵니다.

2 몇몇 사람들은 그들의 문제에 대한 해결책을 찾기 위해 자연을 이용할 뿐만 아니라 자연을 모방하기까지 합니다.

3 레오나르도 다빈치(1452-1519)가 이러한 사람들 중 한 사람이었습니다.

4 그는 새들이 어떻게 날 수 있는지 궁금했습니다.

5 그는 새를 자세히 관찰했고, 기록했으며, 그림으로 그렸습니다.

6 그의 발명은 비록 성공하지 못했지만, 그는 나는 기계를 만들어 보려고 새의 날개를 모방했습니다.

7 그 후로, 점점 더 많은 사람들이 자연 속 천재의 놀라운 능력을 성공적으로 모방해 오고 있습니다.

8 그들 중 몇 가지를 알아봅시다.

**새에게서 배우기: 빠르고 조용하게 움직이기**

9 고속 열차는 일본에서 처음 만들어졌습니다. 하지만 그것은 한 가지 문제점이 있었습니다.

10 열차가 터널에 들어갔을 때, 갑작스러운 기압의 상승은 매우 시끄러운 소리를 발생시켰습니다.

11 그것은 종종 사람들의 잠을 깨웠고 두통을 일으켰습니다.

**12** (team / a / engineers / of / to / tried / the / solve / problem, / they / but / know / didn't / they / how / reduce / could / noise. / the)

➡ _____

**13** (day, / one / of / one / engineers / the / was / a / watching / bird / search / in / a / of / meal.)

➡ _____

**14** (saw / he / the / quickly / bird / and / diving / quietly / into / water. / the)

➡ _____

**15** (wondered / he / the / how / bird / the / entered / water / gracefully. / so)

➡ _____

**16** (he / so, / studied / about / more / bird / the / and / its / discovered / long, / beak. / narrow)

➡ _____

**17** (redesigned / he / the / of / front / the / by / train / imitating / bird's / the / beak.)

➡ _____

**18** (was / it / successful. // the / now / train / new / not / travels / more / only / quietly / also / but / 10% / with / faster / 15% / electricity. / less)

➡ _____

**Learning from Burrs: Inventing an All-Purpose Fastener**

**19** (day, / one / Swiss / a / engineer, / de / George / Mestral, / hiking / was / the / in / woods / his / dog. / with)

➡ _____

**20** (his / way / on / home, / saw / he / burrs / that / stuck / were / his / to / clothes / and / dog's / his / hair.)

➡ _____

**21** (wanted / he / know / to / how / happened. / that)

➡ _____

**22** (took / he / closer / a / at / look / burrs / the / and / that / noticed / ends / the / of / burr / the / were / needles / straight. / not)

➡ _____

**12** 한 공학자 팀이 그 문제를 해결하려 했지만, 그들은 어떻게 소음을 줄일 수 있을지 몰랐습니다.

**13** 어느 날, 공학자들 중 한 사람이 먹이를 찾고 있는 새를 관찰하고 있었습니다.

**14** 그는 새가 빠르고 조용하게 물속으로 뛰어드는 것을 보았습니다.

**15** 그는 새가 어떻게 그렇게 우아하게 물속으로 들어가는지 궁금했습니다.

**16** 그래서 그는 그 새에 대해 더 연구했고, 새의 길고 좁은 부리를 발견했습니다.

**17** 그는 새의 부리를 모방하여 열차의 앞면을 다시 디자인했습니다.

**18** 그것은 성공이었습니다. 이제 새로운 열차는 더 조용할 뿐만 아니라 전기는 15% 덜 사용하면서 10% 더 빠르게 이동합니다.

**가시 식물들에게서 배우기: 만능 고정 장치 발명하기**

**19** 어느 날, 스위스 공학자 George de Mestral은 그의 개와 숲에서 하이킹하고 있었습니다.

**20** 집으로 돌아오는 길에, 그는 가시 식물이 자신의 옷과 개의 털에 붙어 있는 것을 보았습니다.

**21** 그는 어떻게 그런 일이 일어났는지 알고 싶었습니다.

**22** 그는 가시 식물들을 자세히 들여다보았고, 가시의 끝이 곧지 않다는 것을 알아챘습니다.

**23** (wondered / he / if / could / he / that / apply / to / something / make / useful.)

➡ _____

**24** (a / after / of / lot / testing, / finally / he / two / invented / materials. / new)

➡ _____

**25** (had / one / tiny / many / needles / those / like / burrs / of / the / and / had / other / a / surface. / hairy)

➡ _____
_____

**26** (they / when / pressed / were / together, / became / they / very / a / fastener. / good)

➡ _____

**27** (was / it / only / not / strong / also / but / to / easy / use.)

➡ _____

**28** (then, / since / people / many / have / his / used / invention / many / in / ways. / different)

➡ _____
_____

**29** (it / it / often / for / used / clothing, / and / shoes, / bags.)

➡ _____

**30** (people / some / it / use / play / to / a / of / number / games. / different)

➡ _____

**31** (space, / in / keeps / it / from / things / away. / floating)

➡ _____

**32** (is / there / useless / nothing / nature. / in // just / we / to / have / curious / become / and / questions. / ask)

➡ _____
_____

**23** 그는 유용한 뭔가를 만드는 데 그것을 적용할 수 있을지 궁금했습니다.

**24** 수많은 실험 후에, 그는 마침내 두 가지 새로운 소재를 발명했습니다.

**25** 하나는 가시 식물과 같은 조그만 가시들이 많이 있는 것이었고, 다른 하나는 털로 덮인 표면이 있는 것이었습니다.

**26** 두 소재를 함께 붙이면, 매우 훌륭한 고정 장치가 되었습니다.

**27** 그것은 튼튼할 뿐만 아니라 사용하기도 쉬웠습니다.

**28** 그 후로, 많은 사람들이 그의 발명품을 다양한 방법으로 사용해 오고 있습니다.

**29** 그것은 옷, 신발, 가방에 흔히 사용됩니다.

**30** 몇몇 사람들은 여러 가지 게임을 하기 위해 그것을 사용합니다.

**31** 우주에서, 그것은 물건들이 떠다니는 것을 막아줍니다.

**32** 자연에 쓸모없는 것은 하나도 없습니다. 우리는 그저 호기심을 갖고 질문을 던지면 됩니다.

※ 다음 우리말을 영어로 쓰시오.

Nature's Inspiration

**1** 나는 새에서 자정 작용을 하는 식물까지, 자연이 기능하는 방식은 우리를 매료시킵니다.

➡ _____

**2** 몇몇 사람들은 그들의 문제에 대한 해결책을 찾기 위해 자연을 이용할 뿐만 아니라 자연을 모방하기까지 합니다.

➡ _____

**3** 레오나르도 다빈치(1452–1519)가 이러한 사람들 중 한 사람이었습니다.

➡ _____

**4** 그는 새들이 어떻게 날 수 있는지 궁금했습니다.

➡ _____

**5** 그는 새를 자세히 관찰했고, 기록했으며, 그림으로 그렸습니다.

➡ _____

**6** 그의 발명은 비록 성공하지 못했지만, 그는 나는 기계를 만들어 보려고 새의 날개를 모방했습니다.

➡ _____

_____

**7** 그 후로, 점점 더 많은 사람들이 자연 속 천재의 놀라운 능력을 성공적으로 모방해 오고 있습니다.

➡ _____

_____

**8** 그들 중 몇 가지를 알아봅시다.

➡ _____

Learning from a bird: Moving Fast and Quietly

**9** 고속 열차는 일본에서 처음 만들어졌습니다. 하지만 그것은 한 가지 문제점이 있었습니다.

➡ _____

**10** 열차가 터널에 들어갔을 때, 갑작스러운 기압의 상승은 매우 시끄러운 소리를 발생시켰습니다.

➡ _____

**11** 그것은 종종 사람들의 잠을 깨웠고 두통을 일으켰습니다.

➡ _____

**12** 한 공학자 팀이 그 문제를 해결하려 했지만, 그들은 어떻게 소음을 줄일 수 있을지 몰랐습니다.

➡ _____

**13** 어느 날, 공학자들 중 한 사람이 먹이를 찾고 있는 새를 관찰하고 있었습니다.

➡ _____

**14** 그는 새가 빠르고 조용하게 물속으로 뛰어드는 것을 보았습니다.

➡ _____

**15** 그는 새가 어떻게 그렇게 우아하게 물속으로 들어가는지 궁금했습니다.
➡ _____

**16** 그래서 그는 그 새에 대해 더 연구했고, 새의 길고 좁은 부리를 발견했습니다.
➡ _____

**17** 그는 새의 부리를 모방하여 열차의 앞면을 다시 디자인했습니다.
➡ _____

**18** 그것은 성공적이었습니다. 이제 새로운 열차는 더 조용할 뿐만 아니라 전기는 15% 덜 사용하면서 10% 더 빠르게 이동합니다.
➡ _____
_____

Learning from Burrs: Inventing an All-Purpose Fastener

**19** 어느 날, 스위스 공학자 George de Mestral은 그의 개와 숲에서 하이킹하고 있었습니다.
➡ _____

**20** 집으로 돌아오는 길에, 그는 가시 식물이 자신의 옷과 개의 털에 붙어 있는 것을 보았습니다.
➡ _____

**21** 그는 어떻게 그런 일이 일어났는지 알고 싶었습니다.
➡ _____

**22** 그는 가시 식물들을 자세히 들여다보았고, 가시의 끝이 곧지 않다는 것을 알아챘습니다.
➡ _____

**23** 그는 유용한 뭔가를 만드는 데 그것을 적용할 수 있을지 궁금했습니다.
➡ _____

**24** 수많은 실험 후에, 그는 마침내 두 가지 새로운 소재를 발명했습니다.
➡ _____

**25** 하나는 가시 식물과 같은 조그만 가시들이 많이 있는 것이었고, 다른 하나는 털로 덮인 표면이 있는 것이었습니다.
➡ _____

**26** 두 소재를 함께 붙이면, 매우 훌륭한 고정 장치가 되었습니다.
➡ _____

**27** 그것은 튼튼할 뿐만 아니라 사용하기도 쉬웠습니다.
➡ _____

**28** 그 후로, 많은 사람들이 그의 발명품을 다양한 방법으로 사용해 오고 있습니다.
➡ _____

**29** 그것은 옷, 신발, 가방에 흔히 사용됩니다.
➡ _____

**30** 몇몇 사람들은 여러 가지 게임을 하기 위해 그것을 사용합니다.
➡ _____

**31** 우주에서, 그것은 물건들이 떠다니는 것을 막아줍니다.
➡ _____

**32** 자연에 쓸모없는 것은 하나도 없습니다. 우리는 그저 호기심을 갖고 질문을 던지면 됩니다.
➡ _____

※ 다음 우리말과 일치하도록 빈칸에 알맞은 말을 쓰시오.

### Culture & Life

1. Polar Bears, _____ _____

2. Polar bears _____ _____ _____ because they have _____ _____ _____ _____ _____ the heat from the sun.

3. _____ _____ their hairs _____ an _____ _____.

4. This also _____ them _____ _____.

1. 북극곰, 북극
2. 북극곰은 태양열을 쉽게 흡수할 수 있는 검은 피부를 가지고 있기 때문에 추위에서 생존한다.
3. 북극곰 털 하나하나에는 공기층이 있다.
4. 이것 또한 따뜻함을 유지하는 데 도움이 된다.

### Culture & Life

1. Sahara Desert _____, _____ _____ _____

2. The Sahara Desert is _____ _____ the driest but also the _____ _____ _____ _____.

3. But even at _____ _____ _____ of day, Sahara Desert ants _____ _____.

4. Do you know _____ _____ _____ _____ _____?

5. Their bodies _____ _____ _____ unique hairs _____ _____ _____ _____ _____ the sun.

1. 사하라 사막 개미들, 북아프리카
2. 사하라 사막은 지구상에서 가장 건조할 뿐만 아니라 가장 뜨거운 곳이다.
3. 하지만 하루 중 가장 뜨거운 시간에도 사하라 사막 개미들은 사냥을 간다.
4. 그들이 어떻게 그 열기에서 살아남는지 아는가?
5. 개미들의 몸은 태양으로부터의 열기를 반사해내는 독특한 털로 덮여 있다.

### Culture & Life Project

1. You know horses _____ _____ _____, _____ _____?

2. _____ _____ _____ _____ is that they have _____ _____.

3. Our group designed shoes _____ _____ a _____ _____.

4. _____ you _____ them, you will _____ _____ run faster _____ _____ _____ _____.

1. 여러분은 말이 빨리 달리는 것을 알고 있습니다, 그렇죠?
2. 그 이유 중의 하나는 그들이 튼튼한 발을 가지고 있다는 겁니다.
3. 우리 모둠은 말의 발을 모방해서 신발을 만들었습니다.
4. 여러분이 그것을 신으면, 여러분은 빨리 달릴 뿐만 아니라 키가 더 커 보일 겁니다.

※ **다음 우리말을 영어로 쓰시오.**

### Culture & Life

1. 북극곰, 북극

   ➡ _____

2. 북극곰은 태양열을 쉽게 흡수할 수 있는 검은 피부를 가지고 있기 때문에 추위에서 생존한다.

   ➡ _____

3. 북극곰 털 하나하나에는 공기층이 있다.

   ➡ _____

4. 이것 또한 따뜻함을 유지하는 데 도움이 된다.

   ➡ _____

### Culture & Life

1. 사하라 사막 개미들, 북아프리카

   ➡ _____

2. 사하라 사막은 지구상에서 가장 건조할 뿐만 아니라 가장 뜨거운 곳이다.

   ➡ _____

3. 하지만 하루 중 가장 뜨거운 시간에도 사하라 사막 개미들은 사냥을 간다.

   ➡ _____

4. 그들이 어떻게 그 열기에서 살아남는지 아는가?

   ➡ _____

5. 개미들의 몸은 태양으로부터의 열기를 반사해내는 독특한 털로 덮여 있다.

   ➡ _____

### Culture & Life Project

1. 여러분은 말이 빨리 달리는 것을 알고 있습니다, 그렇죠?

   ➡ _____

2. 그 이유 중의 하나는 그들이 튼튼한 발을 가지고 있다는 겁니다.

   ➡ _____

3. 우리 모둠은 말의 발을 모방해서 신발을 만들었습니다.

   ➡ _____

4. 여러분이 그것을 신으면, 여러분은 빨리 달릴 뿐만 아니라 키가 더 커 보일 겁니다.

   ➡ _____

※ 다음 영어를 우리말로 쓰시오.

01 apologize _____

02 trouble _____

03 unique _____

04 response _____

05 creative _____

06 responsible _____

07 beak _____

08 sneeze _____

09 compare _____

10 actually _____

11 crime _____

12 retelling _____

13 unfortunately _____

14 steadily _____

15 advantage _____

16 straw _____

17 deserve _____

18 stepmother _____

19 borrow _____

20 stork _____

21 complain _____

22 frame _____

23 bother _____

24 support _____

25 grab _____

26 hairy _____

27 impolite _____

28 independent _____

29 skinny _____

30 peacefully _____

31 shocked _____

32 completely _____

33 artwork _____

34 rude _____

35 break into _____

36 be made of _____

37 instead of _____

38 point of view _____

39 be taken to _____

40 run out of _____

41 fall in love with _____

42 on one's own _____

43 make sense _____

※ 다음 우리말을 영어로 쓰시오.

01 부리 _____

02 등장인물 _____

03 범죄 _____

04 꾸준히 _____

05 계모 _____

06 벽돌 _____

07 붙잡다 _____

08 불행하게도, 안타깝게도 _____

09 털이 많은 _____

10 무례한 _____

11 완전하게 _____

12 무례한 _____

13 짚, 지푸라기 _____

14 예술 작품 _____

15 누명을 씌우다 _____

16 자립심이 강한, 독립적인 _____

17 사과 _____

18 부양하다, 지지하다 _____

19 땀; 땀을 흘리다 _____

20 비교하다 _____

21 비슷한, 유사한 _____

22 실제로 _____

23 불평하다 _____

24 반응, 응답 _____

25 ~을 받을 만하다 _____

26 궁전 _____

27 장점 _____

28 사과하다 _____

29 책임이 있는 _____

30 마른 _____

31 선호하다 _____

32 괴롭히다 _____

33 재채기하다 _____

34 귀찮게 하다 _____

35 침입하다 _____

36 스스로 _____

37 관점, 견해 _____

38 ~ 대신에 _____

39 ~로 만들어지다 _____

40 ~이 다 떨어지다 _____

41 끌려가다 _____

42 적어도 _____

43 ~와 사랑에 빠지다 _____

※ 다음 영영풀이에 알맞은 단어를 <보기>에서 골라 쓴 후, 우리말 뜻을 쓰시오.

1 _____ : not polite: _____

2 _____ : covered with a lot of hair: _____

3 _____ : by bad luck: _____

4 _____ : very thin or too thin: _____

5 _____ : be worthy: _____

6 _____ : to disturb or bother someone: _____

7 _____ : the hard usually pointed parts that cover a bird's mouth: _____

8 _____ : a large bird that has long legs and a long bill and neck: _____

9 _____ : having features that are the same: _____

10 _____ : a statement saying that you are sorry about something: _____

11 _____ : the dry stems of wheat and other grain plants: _____

12 _____ : an illegal action or activity for which a person can be punished by law: _____

13 _____ : to produce a clear liquid from your skin when you are hot or nervous: _____

14 _____ : to have air come suddenly and noisily out through your nose and mouth in a way that you cannot control: _____

15 _____ : confident and free to do things without needing help from other people: _____

16 _____ : to say or write that you are unhappy, sick, uncomfortable, etc., or that you do not like something: _____

보기

| | | | |
|---|---|---|---|
| skinny | hairy | apology | straw |
| trouble | stork | sneeze | independent |
| unfortunately | rude | similar | crime |
| deserve | beak | complain | sweat |

※ 다음 우리말과 일치하도록 빈칸에 알맞은 말을 쓰시오.

### Listen & Speak 1 A

G: _____ you _____ the book, Taeho?

B: Yes. I finished it yesterday, Anna.

G: _____ _____ _____ _____ it?

B: It was _____ .

G: _____ is the book _____ ?

B: You know the story of Heungbu, _____ ? In the book, Nolbu tells the story from his _____ _____ _____ .

G: What does he _____ ?

B: Well, he says he didn't help Heungbu for a _____ . He wanted Heungbu to _____ _____ on his own and be _____ .

G: Wow, it's a _____ story! I _____ _____ _____ _____ the book. Thanks, Taeho.

G: 그 책 다 읽었니, 태호야?
B: 응. 어제 다 읽었어, Anna.
G: 어땠니?
B: 재미있었어.
G: 그 책은 무슨 내용이니?
B: 너 흥부 이야기 알지, 그렇지? 책에서는 놀부가 자신의 관점에서 이야기해.
G: 놀부가 뭐라고 하는데?
B: 음, 놀부는 이유가 있어서 흥부를 도와주지 않았다고 말하고 있어. 그는 흥부가 스스로 돈을 벌고 자립할 수 있기를 바랐거든.
G: 와, 독특한 이야기구나! 그 책을 빨리 읽고 싶어. 고마워, 태호야.

### Listen & Speak 1 B

B: _____ did you _____ the movie *Good Friends*, Yura?

G: I liked it. It was fun to _____ the movie _____ the original book.

B: _____ did you like _____ , the movie or the book?

G: Well, I liked the movie, but I think I _____ the book _____ . The book _____ _____ _____ the _____ better.

B: That's interesting. To me, the movie was _____ because it was _____ _____ _____ the story.

G: That's true. I guess they _____ have their own _____ .

B: You're _____ .

B: 'Good Friends' 영화 어땠니, 유라야?
G: 좋았어. 영화를 원작과 비교하는 게 재미있었어.
B: 너는 영화와 책 중 어떤 것이 더 좋았니?
G: 글쎄, 영화가 좋았지만 책이 더 재미있었던 것 같아. 책이 등장인물을 더 잘 이해하게 해줬거든.
B: 그거 흥미롭구나. 나는 이야기를 이해하기 더 쉬워서 영화가 더 좋았어.
G: 그건 맞아. 책과 영화 둘 다 각각의 장점들이 있는 것 같아.
B: 맞아.

### Listen & Speak 2 A

W: You look _____ , Juwon.

B: I think we will _____ _____ _____ _____ tomorrow, Ms. Kim.

W: Why do _____ _____ _____ ?

B: We will have a _____ _____ Class 3. They have _____ _____ _____ in the school.

W: Look on the _____ _____ . They might have strong players, but your class has _____ _____ _____ .

B: You're right. I didn't think about it _____ _____ . I'll go and practice!

W: 걱정스러워 보이는구나, 주원아.
B: 내일 축구 경기에서 질 것 같아요, 김 선생님.
W: 왜 그렇게 생각하니?
B: 저희는 3반과 경기가 있거든요. 3반에는 학교에서 가장 잘하는 선수들이 있잖아요.
W: 긍정적으로 생각하렴. 3반에 잘하는 선수들이 있을지 모르지만, 너희 반은 팀워크가 가장 좋잖아.
B: 선생님 말씀이 맞아요. 저는 그렇게는 생각하지 못했어요. 가서 연습할게요!

### Listen & Speak 2 B

M: _____ do you _____ about my drawing, Prince?

B: Wow, this picture is very _____!

M: _____ do you _____ _____?

B: I mean the picture shows a _____ that _____ an elephant.

M: You're right. Actually, many people thought it was a picture of a _____.

B: Really? That's _____.

M: I know. That's _____ I _____ to become a _____ _____ a painter.

B: Haha. _____ _____ I can understand _____ _____ _____.

M: Thank you, Prince.

M: 왕자님, 제 그림에 대해 어떻게 생각하세요?
B: 우와, 이 그림은 너무 무섭군요!
M: 왜 그렇게 생각하죠?
B: 그림이 코끼리를 먹은 뱀을 보여주잖아요.
M: 왕자님 말이 맞아요. 사실 많은 사람들이 모자 그림이라고 생각했어요.
B: 정말요? 그거 재미있군요.
M: 맞아요. 그래서 제가 화가 대신에 비행사가 되기로 결심했던 거예요.
B: 하하. 적어도 나는 당신이 무엇을 의도한 건지 이해할 수 있어요.
M: 고마워요, 왕자님.

### Real Life Communication

Ms. Parker: Now, _____ _____ _____ _____ this work of art. _____ _____ you _____ it?

Jinho: Well, is it even art?

Henry: _____ _____, it isn't _____ _____ a _____.

Ms. Parker: It is not just art. I think it is the _____ _____ of the 20th century.

Mina: _____ do you _____ _____?

Ms. Parker: It is a perfect example of a _____ _____ _____. The artist used _____ _____ to create art.

Claire: So, he didn't create _____ _____?

Ms. Parker: That's _____. He simply wanted people to look at the _____ _____ _____ _____ _____ _____.

Mina: Thank you so much, Ms. Parker. I _____ _____ _____ today!

Ms. Parker: 자, 이 예술 작품을 보세요. 어떤가요?
Jinho: 글쎄요, 이것도 예술인가요?
Henry: 저한테는 변기 그 이상은 아닌데요.
Ms. Parker: 이건 그냥 예술이 아니에요. 나는 20세기의 가장 위대한 예술 작품이라고 생각해요.
Mina: 왜 그렇게 생각하세요?
Ms. Parker: 이것은 다른 관점에 대한 완벽한 예시예요. 작가는 작품을 만들기 위해 실생활 물건을 사용했어요.
Claire: 그러면 작가가 새로운 것을 만들지 않았다는 건가요?
Ms. Parker: 맞아요. 그는 그저 사람들이 다른 방식으로 사물을 보기를 원했어요.
Mina: 정말 감사합니다. Parker 선생님. 오늘 많은 걸 배웠어요!

### Let's Check

B: Do you know the story *The Rabbit and the Turtle*?

G: Of _____, I do.

B: I think the _____ in the story is _____.

G: _____ do you _____ _____?

B: The turtle sees the rabbit _____ but doesn't _____ _____ _____. It is not _____.

G: I don't see it _____ _____. Why should the turtle _____ _____ _____ the rabbit? I don't think he _____ be.

B: That's _____.

B: 너는 '토끼와 거북이' 이야기를 아니?
G: 물론 알지.
B: 난 그 이야기 속의 거북이가 못됐다고 생각해.
G: 왜 그렇게 생각하니?
B: 거북이는 토끼가 자고 있는 것을 보지만 그를 깨우지 않잖아. 그건 공정하지 않아.
G: 나는 그렇게 보지 않아. 왜 거북이가 토끼에 대해 책임을 져야 해? 그가 그래야 한다고 생각하지 않아.
B: 흥미로운데.

# 대화문 Test

※ 다음 우리말에 맞도록 대화를 영어로 쓰시오.

## Listen & Speak 1 A

G: _____

B: _____

G: _____

B: _____

G: _____

B: _____

G: _____

B: _____

G: _____

G: 그 책 다 읽었니, 태호야?

B: 응. 어제 다 읽었어, Anna.

G: 어땠니?

B: 재미있었어.

G: 그 책은 무슨 내용이니?

B: 너 흥부 이야기 알지, 그렇지? 책에서는 놀부가 자신의 관점에서 이야기해.

G: 놀부가 뭐라고 하는데?

B: 음, 놀부는 이유가 있어서 흥부를 도와주지 않았다고 말하고 있어. 그는 흥부가 스스로 돈을 벌고 자립할 수 있기를 바랐거든.

G: 와, 독특한 이야기구나! 그 책을 빨리 읽고 싶어. 고마워, 태호야.

## Listen & Speak 1 B

B: _____

G: _____

B: _____

G: _____

B: _____

G: _____

B: _____

B: 'Good Friends' 영화 어땠니, 유라야?

G: 좋았어. 영화를 원작과 비교하는 게 재미있었어.

B: 너는 영화와 책 중 어떤 것이 더 좋았니?

G: 글쎄, 영화가 좋았지만 책이 더 재미있었던 것 같아. 책이 등장인물을 더 잘 이해하게 해줬거든.

B: 그거 흥미롭구나. 나는 이야기를 이해하기 더 쉬워서 영화가 더 좋았어.

G: 그건 맞아. 책과 영화 둘 다 각각의 장점들이 있는 것 같아.

B: 맞아.

## Listen & Speak 2 A

W: _____

B: _____

W: _____

B: _____

W: _____

B: _____

W: 걱정스러워 보이는구나, 주원아.

B: 내일 축구 경기에서 질 것 같아요, 김 선생님.

W: 왜 그렇게 생각하니?

B: 저희는 3반과 경기가 있거든요. 3반에는 학교에서 가장 잘하는 선수들이 있잖아요.

W: 긍정적으로 생각하렴. 3반에 잘하는 선수들이 있을지 모르지만, 너희 반은 팀워크가 가장 좋잖아.

B: 선생님 말씀이 맞아요. 저는 그렇게는 생각하지 못했어요. 가서 연습할게요!

## Listen & Speak 2 B

M: _____

B: _____

M: _____

B: _____

M: _____

B: _____

M: _____

B: _____

M: _____

M: 왕자님, 제 그림에 대해 어떻게 생각하세요?

B: 우와, 이 그림은 너무 무섭군요!

M: 왜 그렇게 생각하죠?

B: 그림이 코끼리를 먹은 뱀을 보여주잖아요.

M: 왕자님 말이 맞아요. 사실 많은 사람들이 모자 그림이라고 생각했어요.

B: 정말요? 그거 재미있군요.

M: 맞아요. 그래서 제가 화가 대신에 비행사가 되기로 결심했던 거예요.

B: 하하. 적어도 나는 당신이 무엇을 의도한 건지 이해할 수 있어요.

M: 고마워요, 왕자님.

## Real Life Communication

Ms. Parker: _____

Jinho: _____

Henry: _____

Ms. Parker: _____

Mina: _____

Ms. Parker: _____

_____

Claire: _____

Ms. Parker: _____

_____

Mina: _____

Ms. Parker: 자, 이 예술 작품을 보세요. 어떤가요?

Jinho: 글쎄요, 이것도 예술인가요?

Henry: 저한테는 변기 그 이상은 아닌데요.

Ms. Parker: 이건 그냥 예술이 아니에요. 나는 20세기의 가장 위대한 예술 작품이라고 생각해요.

Mina: 왜 그렇게 생각하세요?

Ms. Parker: 이것은 다른 관점에 대한 완벽한 예시예요. 작가는 작품을 만들기 위해 실생활 물건을 사용했어요.

Claire: 그러면 작가가 새로운 것을 만들지 않았다는 건가요?

Ms. Parker: 맞아요. 그는 그저 사람들이 다른 방식으로 사물을 보기를 원했어요.

Mina: 정말 감사합니다. Parker 선생님. 오늘 많은 걸 배웠어요!

## Let's Check

B: _____

G: _____

B: _____

G: _____

B: _____

G: _____

B: _____

B: 너는 '토끼와 거북이' 이야기를 아니?

G: 물론 알지.

B: 난 그 이야기 속의 거북이가 못됐다고 생각해.

G: 왜 그렇게 생각하니?

B: 거북이는 토끼가 자고 있는 것을 보지만 그를 깨우지 않잖아. 그건 공정하지 않아.

G: 나는 그렇게 보지 않아. 왜 거북이가 토끼에 대해 책임을 져야 해? 그가 그래야 한다고 생각하지 않아.

B: 흥미로운데.

※ 다음 우리말과 일치하도록 빈칸에 알맞은 것을 골라 쓰시오.

**The Three Little Pigs: Its True Story**

**1** Reporter: _____ to Animal World News. Last Sunday, a wolf was _____ to the police station for _____ _____ pigs' houses.

    A. blowing        B. taken        C. down        D. welcome

**2** Today, we have the _____ _____ _____ and the wolf _____ us.

    A. little        B. with        C. third        D. pig

**3** Mr. Pig, could you _____ _____ _____ you and your brothers?

    A. what        B. to        C. explain        D. happened

**4** Pig: Yes. My brothers and I thought it was time to _____ our own houses, so we _____ houses with _____, sticks, and _____.

    A. build        B. bricks        C. built        D. straw

**5** _____ day, the wolf came and _____ _____ my brothers' houses.

    A. blew        B. completely        C. down        D. one

**6** He almost _____ _____ my house, but it was _____ _____ bricks, so he couldn't.

    A. of        B. blew        C. made        D. down

**7** Reporter: _____ are your brothers _____ _____?

    A. doing        B. how        C. now

**8** Pig: They are _____ _____ _____ their houses. They are _____ in my house.

    A. resting        B. to        C. shocked        D. lose

**9** Reporter: Thank you, Mr. Pig. Now, _____ meet our second _____, the wolf. Mr. Wolf, could you tell us _____ _____?

    A. happened        B. guest        C. what        D. let's

**10** Wolf: This _____ "Big Bad Wolf" _____ is _____.

    A. wrong        B. whole        C. thing

**11** The _____ story is about a _____ from a _____ and a cup of sugar.

    A. terrible        B. sneeze        C. cold        D. real

**12** Reporter: _____ you _____?

    A. mean        B. do        C. what

**13** Wolf: _____ then, I _____ _____ a birthday cake _____ my dear old grandmother.

    A. for        B. was        C. back        D. making

**14** I _____ _____ of sugar. I _____ the street to ask my neighbor for a cup of sugar.

    A. out        B. down        C. ran        D. walked

**아기 돼지 삼 형제: 그것의 진짜 이야기**

**1** 리포터: 'Animal World News'에 오신 것을 환영합니다. 지난 일요일, 돼지들의 집들을 바람을 불어 넘어뜨린 늑대가 경찰서로 연행되었습니다.

**2** 오늘, 우리는 셋째 아기 돼지와 늑대를 모셨습니다.

**3** Pig씨, 당신과 당신 형제들에게 무슨 일이 일어났는지 설명해 주시겠어요?

**4** 돼지: 네. 제 형제들과 저는 각자의 집들을 지을 때라고 생각했어요. 그래서 우리는 짚, 나무 막대기, 그리고 벽돌로 집을 지었어요.

**5** 어느 날, 늑대가 와서 제 형들의 집들을 바람을 불어 완전히 날려 버렸어요.

**6** 그는 제 집도 거의 날려 버릴 뻔했는데, 벽돌로 만들어져서 그럴 수가 없었죠.

**7** 리포터: 당신의 형제들은 지금 어떻게 지내고 있나요?

**8** 돼지: 그들은 집을 잃어서 충격을 받았어요. 그들은 제 집에서 쉬고 있어요.

**9** 리포터: 감사합니다, Pig씨. 이제 두 번째 손님인 늑대를 만나 보시죠. Wolf씨, 무슨 일이 있었는지 말씀해 주시겠어요?

**10** 늑대: 이 모든 '덩치 크고 못된 늑대' 사건은 잘못된 거예요.

**11** 진짜 이야기는 지독한 감기로 인한 재채기와 설탕 한 컵에 관한 거예요.

**12** 리포터: 무슨 말씀인가요?

**13** 늑대: 그때, 저는 사랑하는 할머니를 위해 생일 케이크를 만들고 있었어요.

**14** 설탕이 다 떨어졌더라고요. 저는 이웃에게 설탕 한 컵을 달라고 부탁하기 위해 길을 걸어갔어요.

**15** When I _____ _____ the door, it _____ _____.
A. on　　　　　B. down　　　　C. fell　　　　D. knocked

**16** Then I _____, "_____ pig, are you _____?"
A. little　　　　B. in　　　　C. called

**17** I _____ just _____ the broken door when I felt a sneeze _____ _____.
A. coming　　　B. grabbed　　C. on　　　　D. had

**18** I _____ a great _____ and you know what? The whole straw house _____ _____.
A. fell　　　　B. sneeze　　　C. down　　　D. sneezed

**19** I was very surprised _____ _____ _____ _____.
A. had　　　　B. by　　　　C. happened　　D. what

**20** _____, the _____ thing _____ _____ the second little pig's house.
A. to　　　　B. unfortunately　C. happened　D. same

**21** Reporter: Then _____ _____ _____ _____ to the third little pig's house?
A. you　　　　B. why　　　　C. go　　　　D. did

**22** Wolf: I still _____ that _____ of _____, so I went to the _____ house.
A. next　　　　B. needed　　　C. sugar　　　D. cup

**23** The _____ little pig _____ _____ his house _____ bricks.
A. of　　　　B. had　　　　C. third　　　D. built

**24** I _____ _____, "I'm sorry to _____ you, but are you _____?"
A. trouble　　　B. in　　　　C. out　　　　D. called

**25** And do you know _____ he _____? "Go _____. Don't _____ me again!"
A. bother　　　B. answered　　C. what　　　D. away

**26** How _____! I thought I _____ an _____, so I kept _____.
A. apology　　　B. knocking　　C. deserved　　D. impolite

**27** When the police _____, of _____ they thought I was _____ _____ this pig's house.
A. into　　　　B. came　　　　C. breaking　　D. course

**28** Reporter: Do you _____ you _____ _____ _____?
A. were　　　　B. think　　　C. framed

**29** Wolf: Yes. The news reporters of the town thought a sick wolf _____ _____ _____ a cup of sugar didn't sound very _____.
A. exciting　　B. to　　　　C. going　　　D. borrow

**30** So, they _____ me the "Big Bad Wolf." _____ you maybe _____ me a _____ of sugar?
A. could　　　B. lend　　　C. made　　　D. cup

**31** Reporter: Thank you for your time. Everyone, _____ _____ _____ is the true story, the pig's or the wolf's?
A. think　　　　B. do　　　　C. which　　　D. you

**15** 제가 이웃집 문을 두드렸을 때, 문이 떨어졌어요.

**16** 그다음에 저는 "아기 돼지 씨, 안에 계신가요?"라고 불렀어요.

**17** 제가 부서진 문을 막 움켜잡았을 때 재채기가 나오는 걸 느꼈어요.

**18** 저는 재채기를 아주 크게 했고, 그거 아세요? 짚으로 만든 집 전체가 무너졌어요.

**19** 저는 일어난 일에 매우 놀랐어요.

**20** 안타깝게도, 둘째 아기 돼지의 집에서도 같은 일이 일어나고 말았어요.

**21** 리포터: 그렇다면 셋째 아기 돼지의 집에 왜 갔죠?

**22** 늑대: 저는 여전히 설탕 한 컵이 필요했어요. 그래서 옆집으로 갔어요.

**23** 셋째 아기 돼지는 벽돌로 집을 지었더라고요.

**24** 제가 소리쳤어요. "귀찮게 해 드려 죄송하지만, 안에 계신가요?"

**25** 그리고 그가 뭐라고 대답했는지 아세요? "가버려, 다신 귀찮게 하지 마!"

**26** 얼마나 무례한가요! 저는 사과를 받아 마땅하다고 생각했기 때문에 계속 문을 두드렸죠.

**27** 경찰이 왔을 때, 물론 그들은 제가 이 돼지의 집에 침입하고 있다고 생각했죠.

**28** 리포터: 당신은 당신이 누명을 썼다고 생각하나요?

**29** 늑대: 네. 마을의 신문 기자들은 설탕 한 컵을 빌리러 간 아픈 늑대가 별로 흥미롭지 않다고 생각했겠죠.

**30** 그래서 그들은 저를 '덩치 크고 못된 늑대'로 만든 거예요. 당신은 아마 제게 설탕 한 컵쯤은 빌려 줄 수 있으시겠죠?

**31** 리포터: 시간 내 주셔서 감사합니다. 여러분, 어떤 이야기가 진짜 이야기라고 생각하시나요, 돼지의 이야기일까요, 아니면 늑대의 이야기일까요?

※ 다음 우리말과 일치하도록 빈칸에 알맞은 것을 골라 쓰시오.

**The Three Little Pigs: Its True Story**

1  Reporter: _____ _____ Animal World News. Last Sunday, a wolf _____ _____ _____ the police station _____ _____ _____ _____ _____ .

2  Today, we have _____ _____ _____ _____ and the wolf _____ us.

3  Mr. Pig, could you _____ _____ _____ _____ you and your brothers?

4  Pig: Yes. My brothers and I thought it was _____ _____ _____ _____ own houses, _____ we built houses _____ _____ , _____ , and _____ .

5  One day, the wolf came and _____ _____ my _____ _____ .

6  He _____ _____ _____ my house, but it was _____ _____ bricks, _____ he _____ .

7  Reporter: _____ are your brothers _____ _____ ?

8  Pig: They are _____ _____ _____ their houses. They are _____ _____ my house.

9  Reporter: Thank you, Mr. Pig. Now, _____ _____ our second guest, the wolf. Mr. Wolf, could you _____ _____ _____ _____ ?

10  Wolf: This _____ "Big Bad Wolf" thing _____ _____ .

11  The _____ _____ is _____ _____ _____ from _____ _____ _____ and a cup of sugar.

12  Reporter: _____ do you _____ ?

13  Wolf: Back then, I _____ _____ a birthday cake _____ my dear old grandmother.

14  I _____ _____ _____ sugar. I _____ _____ the street _____ _____ my neighbor _____ a cup of sugar.

1  리포터: 'Animal World News'에 오신 것을 환영합니다. 지난 일요일, 돼지들의 집들을 바람을 불어 넘어뜨린 늑대가 경찰서로 연행되었습니다.

2  오늘, 우리는 셋째 아기 돼지와 늑대를 모셨습니다.

3  Pig씨, 당신과 당신 형제들에게 무슨 일이 일어났는지 설명해 주시겠어요?

4  돼지: 네. 제 형제들과 저는 각자의 집들을 지을 때라고 생각했어요. 그래서 우리는 짚, 나무 막대기, 그리고 벽돌로 집을 지었어요.

5  어느 날, 늑대가 와서 제 형들의 집들을 바람을 불어 완전히 날려 버렸어요.

6  그는 제 집도 거의 날려 버릴 뻔했는데, 벽돌로 만들어져서 그럴 수가 없었죠.

7  리포터: 당신의 형제들은 지금 어떻게 지내고 있나요?

8  돼지: 그들은 집을 잃어서 충격을 받았어요. 그들은 제 집에서 쉬고 있어요.

9  리포터: 감사합니다. Pig씨. 이제 두 번째 손님인 늑대를 만나 보시죠. Wolf씨, 무슨 일이 있었는지 말씀해 주시겠어요?

10  늑대: 이 모든 '덩치 크고 못된 늑대' 사건은 잘못된 거예요.

11  진짜 이야기는 지독한 감기로 인한 재채기와 설탕 한 컵에 관한 거예요.

12  리포터: 무슨 말씀인가요?

13  늑대: 그때, 저는 사랑하는 할머니를 위해 생일 케이크를 만들고 있었어요.

14  설탕이 다 떨어졌더라고요. 저는 이웃에게 설탕 한 컵을 달라고 부탁하기 위해 길을 걸어갔어요.

**15** When I _____ _____ the door, it _____ _____.

**16** Then I _____, "Little pig, are you _____?"

**17** I _____ _____ _____ the broken door when I felt a _____ _____ _____.

**18** I _____ a great _____ and you know what? The whole _____ house _____ _____.

**19** I was very surprised _____ _____ _____ _____.

**20** _____, the same thing _____ _____ the second little pig's house.

**21** Reporter: Then _____ _____ _____ _____ _____ the third little pig's house?

**22** Wolf: I still needed _____ _____ _____ _____, so I went to the next house.

**23** The third little pig _____ _____ his house _____ bricks.

**24** I _____ _____, "I'm sorry _____ _____ _____, but are you _____?"

**25** And do you know _____ _____ _____? " _____ _____. Don't _____ _____ again!"

**26** _____ _____! I thought I _____ an _____, _____ I _____ _____.

**27** _____ the police _____, _____ _____ they thought I was _____ _____ this pig's house.

**28** Reporter: Do you think you _____ _____?

**29** Wolf: Yes. The news reporters of the town _____ a sick wolf _____ _____ _____ a cup of sugar didn't sound very _____.

**30** So, they made me the "Big Bad Wolf." _____ you maybe _____ _____ a cup of sugar?

**31** Reporter: Thank you for your time. Everyone, _____ _____ _____ _____ the true story, the pig's or the wolf's?

**15** 제가 이웃집 문을 두드렸을 때, 문이 떨어졌어요.

**16** 그다음에 저는 "아기 돼지 씨, 안에 계신가요?"라고 불렀어요.

**17** 제가 부서진 문을 막 움켜잡았을 때 재채기가 나오는 걸 느꼈어요.

**18** 저는 재채기를 아주 크게 했고, 그거 아세요? 짚으로 만든 집 전체가 무너졌어요.

**19** 저는 일어난 일에 매우 놀랐어요.

**20** 안타깝게도, 둘째 아기 돼지의 집에서도 같은 일이 일어나고 말았어요.

**21** 리포터: 그렇다면 셋째 아기 돼지의 집에 왜 갔죠?

**22** 늑대: 저는 여전히 설탕 한 컵이 필요했어요, 그래서 옆집으로 갔어요.

**23** 셋째 아기 돼지는 벽돌로 집을 지었더라고요.

**24** 제가 소리쳤어요, "귀찮게 해 드려 죄송하지만, 안에 계신가요?"

**25** 그리고 그가 뭐라고 대답했는지 아세요? "가버려, 다신 귀찮게 하지 마!"

**26** 얼마나 무례한가요! 저는 사과를 받아 마땅하다고 생각했기 때문에 계속 문을 두드렸어요.

**27** 경찰이 왔을 때, 물론 그들은 제가 이 돼지의 집에 침입하고 있다고 생각했죠.

**28** 리포터: 당신은 당신이 누명을 썼다고 생각하나요?

**29** 늑대: 네. 마을의 신문 기자들은 설탕 한 컵을 빌리러 간 아픈 늑대가 별로 흥미롭지 않다고 생각했겠죠.

**30** 그래서 그들은 저를 '덩치 크고 못된 늑대'로 만든 거예요. 당신은 아마 제게 설탕 한 컵쯤은 빌려 줄 수 있으시겠죠?

**31** 리포터: 시간 내 주셔서 감사합니다. 여러분, 어떤 이야기가 진짜 이야기라고 생각하시나요, 돼지의 이야기일까요, 아니면 늑대의 이야기일까요?

※ 다음 문장을 우리말로 쓰시오.

**The Three Little Pigs: Its True Story**

**1** Reporter: Welcome to Animal World News. Last Sunday, a wolf was taken to the police station for blowing down pigs' houses.

➡ _____

_____

**2** Today, we have the third little pig and the wolf with us.

➡ _____

**3** Mr. Pig, could you explain what happened to you and your brothers?

➡ _____

**4** Pig: Yes. My brothers and I thought it was time to build our own houses, so we built houses with straw, sticks, and bricks.

➡ _____

_____

**5** One day, the wolf came and completely blew down my brothers' houses.

➡ _____

**6** He almost blew down my house, but it was made of bricks, so he couldn't.

➡ _____

**7** Reporter: How are your brothers doing now?

➡ _____

**8** Pig: They are shocked to lose their houses. They are resting in my house.

➡ _____

**9** Reporter: Thank you, Mr. Pig. Now, let's meet our second guest, the wolf. Mr. Wolf, could you tell us what happened?

➡ _____

**10** Wolf: This whole "Big Bad Wolf" thing is wrong.

➡ _____

**11** The real story is about a sneeze from a terrible cold and a cup of sugar.

➡ _____

**12** Reporter: What do you mean?

➡ _____

**13** Wolf: Back then, I was making a birthday cake for my dear old grandmother.

➡ _____

**14** I ran out of sugar. I walked down the street to ask my neighbor for a cup of sugar.

➡ _____

**15** When I knocked on the door, it fell down.

➡ _____

**16** Then I called, "Little pig, are you in?"

➡ _____

**17** I had just grabbed the broken door when I felt a sneeze coming on.

➡ _____

**18** I sneezed a great sneeze and you know what? The whole straw house fell down.

➡ _____

**19** I was very surprised by what had happened.

➡ _____

**20** Unfortunately, the same thing happened to the second little pig's house.

➡ _____

**21** Reporter: Then why did you go to the third little pig's house?

➡ _____

**22** Wolf: I still needed that cup of sugar, so I went to the next house.

➡ _____

**23** The third little pig had built his house of bricks.

➡ _____

**24** I called out, "I'm sorry to trouble you, but are you in?"

➡ _____

**25** And do you know what he answered? "Go away. Don't bother me again!"

➡ _____

**26** How impolite! I thought I deserved an apology, so I kept knocking.

➡ _____

**27** When the police came, of course they thought I was breaking into this pig's house.

➡ _____

**28** Reporter: Do you think you were framed?

➡ _____

**29** Wolf: Yes. The news reporters of the town thought a sick wolf going to borrow a cup of sugar didn't sound very exciting.

➡ _____

**30** So, they made me the "Big Bad Wolf." Could you maybe lend me a cup of sugar?

➡ _____

**31** Reporter: Thank you for your time. Everyone, which do you think is the true story, the pig's or the wolf's?

➡ _____

_____

※ 다음 괄호 안의 단어들을 우리말에 맞도록 바르게 배열하시오.

### The Three Little Pigs: Its True Story

**1** (Reporter: / to / welcome / World / Animal / News. // Sunday, / last / wolf / a / was / to / taken / the / station / police / blowing / for / pigs' / down / houses.)
➡ _____
_____

**2** (we / today, / the / have / third / pig / little / and / wolf / the / us. / with)
➡ _____

**3** (Pig, / Mr. / you / could / what / explain / to / happened / you / your / and / brothers?)
➡ _____

**4** (Pig: / yes. // brothers / my / and / thought / I / was / it / to / time / build / own / our / houses, / we / so / houses / built / straw, / with / sticks, / bricks. / and)
➡ _____

**5** (day, / one / wolf / the / came / and / blew / completely / down / brothers' / my / houses.)
➡ _____

**6** (almost / he / down / blew / house, / my / it / but / was / of / made / bricks, / he / so / couldn't.)
➡ _____

**7** (Reporter: / are / how / brothers / your / now? / doing)
➡ _____

**8** (Pig: / are / they / to / shocked / lose / houses. / their // are / they / in / resting / house. / my)
➡ _____

**9** (Reporter: / you, / thank / Pig. / Mr. // now, / meet / let's / second / our / guest, / wolf. / the // Wolf, / Mr. / you / could / us / tell / happened? / what)
➡ _____

**10** (Wolf: / whole / this / Bad / "Big / thing / Wolf" / wrong. / is)
➡ _____

**11** (real / the / is / story / about / sneeze / a / from / a / cold / terrible / and / cup / a / sugar. / of)
➡ _____

**12** (Reporter: / do / what / mean? / you)
➡ _____

**13** (Wolf: / then, / back / was / I / making / birthday / a / for / cake / dear / my / grandmother. / old)
➡ _____

**14** (ran / I / of / out / sugar. // walked / I / down / street / the / ask / to / neighbor / my / a / for / of / cup / sugar.)
➡ _____
_____

아기 돼지 삼 형제: 그것의 진짜 이야기

**1** 리포터: 'Animal World News'에 오신 것을 환영합니다. 지난 일요일, 돼지들의 집들을 바람을 불어 넘어뜨린 늑대가 경찰서로 연행되었습니다.

**2** 오늘, 우리는 셋째 아기 돼지와 늑대를 모셨습니다.

**3** Pig씨, 당신과 당신 형제들에게 무슨 일이 일어났는지 설명해 주시겠어요?

**4** 돼지: 네. 제 형제들과 저는 각자의 집들을 지을 때라고 생각했어요. 그래서 우리는 짚, 나무 막대기, 그리고 벽돌로 집을 지었어요.

**5** 어느 날, 늑대가 와서 제 형들의 집들을 바람을 불어 완전히 날려 버렸어요.

**6** 그는 제 집도 거의 날려 버릴 뻔했는데, 벽돌로 만들어져서 그럴 수가 없었죠.

**7** 리포터: 당신의 형제들은 지금 어떻게 지내고 있나요?

**8** 돼지: 그들은 집을 잃어서 충격을 받았어요. 그들은 제 집에서 쉬고 있어요.

**9** 리포터: 감사합니다, Pig씨. 이제 두 번째 손님인 늑대를 만나 보시죠. Wolf씨, 무슨 일이 있었는지 말씀해 주시겠어요?

**10** 늑대: 이 모든 '덩치 크고 못된 늑대' 사건은 잘못된 거예요.

**11** 진짜 이야기는 지독한 감기로 인한 재채기와 설탕 한 컵에 관한 거예요.

**12** 리포터: 무슨 말씀인가요?

**13** 늑대: 그때, 저는 사랑하는 할머니를 위해 생일 케이크를 만들고 있었어요.

**14** 설탕이 다 떨어졌더라고요. 저는 이웃에게 설탕 한 컵을 달라고 부탁하기 위해 길을 걸어갔어요.

**15** (I / when / knocked / the / on / door, / fell / it / down.)
➡ _____

**16** (I / then / called, / pig, / "little / are / in?" / you)
➡ _____

**17** (had / I / just / the / grabbed / door / broken / when / felt / I / a / sneeze / on. / coming)
➡ _____

**18** (sneezed / I / great / a / sneeze / you / and / what? / know // whole / the / straw / fell / house / down.)
➡ _____

**19** (was / I / surprised / very / what / by / happened. / had)
➡ _____

**20** (the / unfortunately, / same / happended / thing / the / to / little / second / house. / pig's)
➡ _____

**21** (Reporter: / why / then / you / did / to / go / third / the / pig's / little / house?)
➡ _____

**22** (Wolf: / still / I / that / needed / cup / sugar, / of / so / went / I / the / to / house. / next)
➡ _____

**23** (third / the / pig / little / built / had / house / his / bricks. / of)
➡ _____

**24** (called / I / out, / sorry / "I'm / to / you, / trouble / are / but / in?" / you)
➡ _____

**25** (do / and / know / you / he / what / answered? // away. / "go // bother / don't / again!" / me)
➡ _____

**26** (impolite! / how // thought / I / deserved / I / apology, / an / I / so / knocking. / kept)
➡ _____

**27** (the / when / police / of / came, / course / thought / they / was / I / breaking / into / pig's / this / house.)
➡ _____

**28** (Reporter: / you / do / you / think / framed? / were)
➡ _____

**29** (Wolf: / yes. // news / the / of / reporters / town / the / thought / a / wolf / sick / to / going / borrow / cup / a / of / didn't / sugar / sound / exciting. / very)
➡ _____

**30** (they / so, / me / made / the / Bad / "Big / Wolf." // you / could / lend / maybe / me / cup / a / sugar? / of)
➡ _____

**31** (Reporter: / you / thank / for / time. / your // which / everyone, / you / do / think / the / is / story, / true / pig's / the / the / or / wolf's?)
➡ _____
_____

**15** 제가 이웃집 문을 두드렸을 때, 문이 떨어졌어요.

**16** 그다음에 저는 "아기 돼지 씨, 안에 계신가요?"라고 불렀어요.

**17** 제가 부서진 문을 막 움켜잡았을 때 재채기가 나오는 걸 느꼈어요.

**18** 저는 재채기를 아주 크게 했고, 그거 아세요? 짚으로 만든 집 전체가 무너졌어요.

**19** 저는 일어난 일에 매우 놀랐어요.

**20** 안타깝게도, 둘째 아기 돼지의 집에서도 같은 일이 일어나고 말았어요.

**21** 리포터: 그렇다면 셋째 아기 돼지의 집에 왜 갔죠?

**22** 늑대: 저는 여전히 설탕 한 컵이 필요했어요. 그래서 옆집으로 갔어요.

**23** 셋째 아기 돼지는 벽돌로 집을 지었더라고요.

**24** 제가 소리쳤어요, "귀찮게 해 드려 죄송하지만, 안에 계신가요?"

**25** 그리고 그가 뭐라고 대답했는지 아세요? "가버려, 다신 귀찮게 하지 마!"

**26** 얼마나 무례한가요! 저는 사과를 받아 마땅하다고 생각했기 때문에 계속 문을 두드렸어요.

**27** 경찰이 왔을 때, 물론 그들은 제가 이 돼지의 집에 침입하고 있다고 생각했죠.

**28** 리포터: 당신은 당신이 누명을 썼다고 생각하나요?

**29** 늑대: 네. 마을의 신문 기자들은 설탕 한 컵을 빌리러 간 아픈 늑대가 **별로** 흥미롭지 않다고 **생각했**겠죠.

**30** 그래서 그들은 저를 '덩치 크고 못된 늑대'로 만든 거예요. 당신은 아마 제게 설탕 한 컵쯤은 빌려 줄 수 있으시겠죠?

**31** 리포터: 시간 내 주셔서 감사합니다. 여러분, 어떤 이야기가 진짜 이야기라고 생각하시나요, 돼지의 이야기일까요, 아니면 늑대의 이야기일까요?

※ 다음 우리말을 영어로 쓰시오.

**The Three Little Pigs: Its True Story**

**1** 리포터: 'Animal World News'에 오신 것을 환영합니다. 지난 일요일, 돼지들의 집들을 바람을 불어 넘어뜨린 늑대가 경찰서로 연행되었습니다.

➡ _____

_____

**2** 오늘, 우리는 셋째 아기 돼지와 늑대를 모셨습니다.

➡ _____

**3** Pig씨, 당신과 당신 형제들에게 무슨 일이 일어났는지 설명해 주시겠어요?

➡ _____

**4** 돼지: 네. 제 형제들과 저는 각자의 집들을 지을 때라고 생각했어요. 그래서 우리는 짚, 나무 막대기, 그리고 벽돌로 집을 지었어요.

➡ _____

_____

**5** 어느 날, 늑대가 와서 제 형들의 집들을 바람을 불어 완전히 날려 버렸어요.

➡ _____

**6** 그는 제 집도 거의 날려 버릴 뻔했는데, 벽돌로 만들어져서 그럴 수가 없었죠.

➡ _____

**7** 리포터: 당신의 형제들은 지금 어떻게 지내고 있나요?

➡ _____

**8** 돼지: 그들은 집을 잃어서 충격을 받았어요. 그들은 제 집에서 쉬고 있어요.

➡ _____

**9** 리포터: 감사합니다, Pig씨. 이제 두 번째 손님인 늑대를 만나 보시죠. Wolf씨, 무슨 일이 있었는지 말씀해 주시겠어요?

➡ _____

_____

**10** 늑대: 이 모든 '덩치 크고 못된 늑대' 사건은 잘못된 거예요.

➡ _____

**11** 진짜 이야기는 지독한 감기로 인한 재채기와 설탕 한 컵에 관한 거예요.

➡ _____

**12** 리포터: 무슨 말씀인가요?

➡ _____

**13** 늑대: 그때, 저는 사랑하는 할머니를 위해 생일 케이크를 만들고 있었어요.

➡ _____

**14** 설탕이 다 떨어졌더라고요. 저는 이웃에게 설탕 한 컵을 달라고 부탁하기 위해 길을 걸어갔어요.

➡ _____

**15** 제가 이웃집 문을 두드렸을 때, 문이 떨어졌어요.

➡ _____

**16** 그다음에 저는 "아기 돼지 씨, 안에 계신가요?"라고 불렀어요.

➡ _____

**17** 제가 부서진 문을 막 움켜잡았을 때 재채기가 나오는 걸 느꼈어요.

➡ _____

**18** 저는 재채기를 아주 크게 했고, 그거 아세요? 짚으로 만든 집 전체가 무너졌어요.

➡ _____

**19** 저는 일어난 일에 매우 놀랐어요.

➡ _____

**20** 안타깝게도, 둘째 아기 돼지의 집에서도 같은 일이 일어나고 말았어요.

➡ _____

**21** 리포터: 그렇다면 셋째 아기 돼지의 집에 왜 갔죠?

➡ _____

**22** 늑대: 저는 여전히 설탕 한 컵이 필요했어요, 그래서 옆집으로 갔어요.

➡ _____

**23** 셋째 아기 돼지는 벽돌로 집을 지었더라고요.

➡ _____

**24** 제가 소리쳤어요, "귀찮게 해 드려 죄송하지만, 안에 계신가요?"

➡ _____

**25** 그리고 그가 뭐라고 대답했는지 아세요? "가버려, 다신 귀찮게 하지 마!"

➡ _____

**26** 얼마나 무례한가요! 저는 사과를 받아 마땅하다고 생각했기 때문에 계속 문을 두드렸어요.

➡ _____

**27** 경찰이 왔을 때, 물론 그들은 제가 이 돼지의 집에 침입하고 있다고 생각했죠.

➡ _____

**28** 리포터: 당신은 당신이 누명을 썼다고 생각하나요?

➡ _____

**29** 늑대: 네. 마을의 신문 기자들은 설탕 한 컵을 빌리러 간 아픈 늑대가 별로 흥미롭지 않다고 생각했겠죠.

➡ _____

_____

**30** 그래서 그들은 저를 '덩치 크고 못된 늑대'로 만든 거예요. 당신은 아마 제게 설탕 한 컵쯤은 빌려 줄 수 있으시겠죠?

➡ _____

**31** 리포터: 시간 내 주셔서 감사합니다. 여러분, 어떤 이야기가 진짜 이야기라고 생각하시나요, 돼지의 이야기일까요, 아니면 늑대의 이야기일까요?

➡ _____

_____

※ 다음 우리말과 일치하도록 빈칸에 알맞은 말을 쓰시오.

## Communication Task

1. A: Can anyone _____ the _____ _____ _____ _____?

2. B: _____ _____ it is *Sleeping Beauty*.

3. A: _____ do you _____ _____?

4. B: I think Semi is the princess _____ _____ _____ _____
   and Minsu is the _____ _____ _____ _____ _____
   the princess.

5. A: Sorry, but that's _____ _____ _____.

1. A: 이야기의 제목을 추측해 볼 수 있나요?
2. B: 제 생각에 '잠자는 숲속의 공주' 같아요.
3. A: 왜 그렇게 생각하니?
4. B: 세미는 평화롭게 잠을 자고 있는 공주이고 민수는 공주를 찾고 있는 왕자예요.
5. A: 미안하지만 정답이 아니에요.

## Before You Read

1. _____ _____ a fun story _____ this. - *Book Weekly*

2. I think I should _____ _____ _____ to the wolf. I'd _____
   _____ about _____ _____ _____ _____ _____. - *The Book
   Times*

3. I still don't know _____ _____ _____ _____, but I
   learned _____ everyone _____ _____ _____ _____ a
   crime. - *Library & Paper*

1. 모든 사람이 이와 같은 재미있는 이야기를 읽을 자격이 있다. - Book Weekly
2. 내 생각에 나는 늑대에게 사과해야 할 것 같다. 나는 그의 관점에 대해 생각해 본 적이 없었다. - The Book Times
3. 나는 여전히 누구의 이야기가 진실인지 모르겠지만, 누구든지 범죄에 누명을 쓸 수 있다는 것을 알게 되었다. - Library & Paper

## After You Read

1. The _____ _____

2. The _____ _____ _____ decided _____ _____ _____
   _____ _____.

3. So, they _____ houses _____ _____ _____.

4. _____ _____, the wolf _____ _____ _____ _____ _____
   the first and the _____ _____ _____ _____ _____.

5. But the wolf _____ _____ _____ the third pig's house _____
   it _____ _____ _____ _____ bricks.

1. 돼지 이야기
2. 세 마리의 아기 돼지들은 자신들의 집을 짓기로 결정했다.
3. 그래서 그들은 다른 재료들로 집을 지었다.
4. 어느 날, 늑대가 와서 첫째와 둘째 아기 돼지의 집을 바람을 불어 완전히 무너뜨렸다.
5. 하지만 늑대는 셋째 돼지의 집은 무너뜨릴 수 없었는데, 왜냐하면 그것은 벽돌로 만들어졌기 때문이었다.

※ 다음 우리말을 영어로 쓰시오.

## Communication Task

1. A: 이야기의 제목을 추측해 볼 수 있나요?

➡ _____

2. B: 제 생각에 '잠자는 숲속의 공주' 같아요.

➡ _____

3. A: 왜 그렇게 생각하니?

➡ _____

4. B: 세미는 평화롭게 잠을 자고 있는 공주이고 민수는 공주를 찾고 있는 왕자예요.

➡ _____

➡ _____

5. A: 미안하지만 정답이 아니에요.

➡ _____

## Before You Read

1. 모든 사람이 이와 같은 재미있는 이야기를 읽을 자격이 있다. – *Book Weekly*

➡ _____

2. 내 생각에 나는 늑대에게 사과해야 할 것 같다. 나는 그의 관점에 대해 생각해 본 적이 없었다. – *The Book Times*

➡ _____

3. 나는 여전히 누구의 이야기가 진실인지 모르겠지만, 누구든지 범죄에 누명을 쓸 수 있다는 것을 알게 되었다. – *Library & Paper*

➡ _____

## After You Read

1. 돼지 이야기

➡ _____

2. 세 마리의 아기 돼지들은 자신들의 집을 짓기로 결정했다.

➡ _____

3. 그래서 그들은 다른 재료들로 집을 지었다.

➡ _____

4. 어느 날, 늑대가 와서 첫째와 둘째 아기 돼지의 집을 바람을 불어 완전히 무너뜨렸다.

➡ _____

5. 하지만 늑대는 셋째 돼지의 집은 무너뜨릴 수 없었는데, 왜냐하면 그것은 벽돌로 만들어졌기 때문이었다.

➡ _____

MEMO

# MEMO

영어 기출 문제집

적중100 plus
1학기 전과정

1학기

# 정답 및 해설

지학 | 민찬규

중 3

적중100

영어 기출 문제집

적중100 plus

1학기 전과정

1학기

# 정답 및 해설

지학 | 민찬규

중3

적중100

# We Can Make a Difference

01 자전거를 타다가 떨어진 이유를 묻는 말에 자전거 통행로에 큰 요철 모양을 넘다가 넘어졌다고 이야기하는 상황이다. bump 도로의 튀어나온 부분, 요철

02 ~을 신청하다 = sign up for ~ / 우울해 보여서 무슨 일이 있는지 묻는 말에 축구팀에 지원했지만 가입할 수 없기 때문이라고 대답하고 있다. look down = 우울해 보이다. join = 가입하다

03 comfortable 편안한 / 그것은 정말 편안한 침대입니다.

04 scarecrow: 허수아비 / 들판 한가운데에 허수아비가 서 있다.

05 ① 그들은 농부가 기르는 동물을 죽인다. ② 처음에 나는 내가 겨우 11살이기 때문에 아무것도 할 수 없다고 생각했다. ③ 나는 사자가 불을 두려워한다고 생각했다. 그러나 그것은 효과가 없었다. work: 효과가 있다. 작동하다 ④ 그때 나는 내가 그 문제를 무시하지 말아야 한다는 것을 깨달았다. ⑤ 13살에 나는 마침내 내가 "lion lights"라고 부르는 것을 만들었다.

06 ① trash bin: 쓰레기통 / 남은 것을 쓰레기통에 버려 줄래? ② try to: ~하기 위해 애쓰다 / 너는 물을 아끼기 위해 애써야 한다. ③ upset: 화난 / 그가 나를 무시했을 때 화가 났어요. ④ useful: 유익한 / 그가 나에게 유익한 충고를 좀 해 주었다. ⑤ visitors: 방문객들 / 박물관 문이 열리자 방문객들이 들어오기 시작했다.

07 당신 관리자에게 항의를 하겠어요. complain 항의하다, 불평하다 – grumble 불평하다

**서술형 시험대비**    p.09

01 realization
02 (f)loat
03 prevent
04 up
05 (i)llness
06 (1) donation   (2) result   (3) set   (4) protect
07 (1) difference   (2) away   (3) proud   (4) complained

01 realization: 깨달음 realize: 깨닫다 / 이 깨달음은 그가 그의 상황을 받아들이도록 만들었다.

02 주어진 단어는 반의어 관계이다. dangerous 위험한 safe 안전

한 float 뜨다 sink 가라앉다

03 prevent A from -ing A가 ~하지 못하게 막다 / 경찰은 그들이 건물에 들어가지 못하게 할 것이다. prevent weight gain 체중 증가를 막다 / 규칙적인 운동은 체중 증가를 막는 데 도움이 된다.

04 sign up for: ~을 신청하다 / 그는 농구부에 신청했지만 가입할 수 없었다. come up with: ~을 생각해 내다 / 그녀가 학급 현장학습을 위한 새로운 아이디어를 내놓았다.

05 disease: 질병 illness: 질병 / 그들은 그 질병의 원인을 찾을 수 없었다.

06 (1) make a donation: 기부하다 / 나는 지난달에 적십자에 돈을 조금 기부했다. (2) as a result: 결과적으로 / 그녀는 병에 걸리고 그 결과로 사망했다. (3) set up: 세우다 / 그녀의 어머니는 어제 들판에 허수아비를 세웠다. (4) protect: 보호하다 / 그녀는 폭우로부터 아이들을 보호하려고 애썼다.

07 (1) make a difference: 차별을 두다, 차이를 만들어 내다 (2) scare away: 겁주어 쫓아보내다 (3) be proud of: ~을 자랑스러워하다 (4) complain: 불평하다

## 교과서 Conversation

01 상대에게 걱정이 있어 보일 때 걱정이나 염려를 묻는 표현으로 "무슨 일 있니?"라는 의미의 What's the matter?, What's wrong?, Is there anything wrong?, What happened? 등을 사용한다.

02 다른 사람에게 좋은 일이 있기를 기원하는 표현은 "I hope + 주어 +동사 ~"이다.

03 상대가 속상해 보이는 이유를 묻는 것에 대하여 (B) 학생들이 복도에서 뛰는 것 때문이라는 대답을 듣고 (A) 학생들이 뛰지 않기를 희망한다는 말을 하자 (C) 동의 한다는 말을 하는 순서이다.

## 교과서 대화문 익히기

**Listen & Speak 1 A**

matter / worried about, see, on, street every time, think, has / what, sorry, hear, have / What, with / Why, take, animal, ask / That's

**Listen & Speak 1 B**

matter, hurt / fell / How, happen / rode, bump / signs / about, problem, website / idea

**Listen & Speak 1 C**

look, matter / forgot / sorry

**Listen & Speak 2 A**

stickers / hope, helpful / sure, sort, recycling / come, tomorrow , see if

**Listen & Speak 2 B**

from, were, who believed, need, close down, felt, press, gave, Thanks to, education, passed, bigger, hope, child, get

**Real Life Communication**

look, matter / comments, enough fun, see / sorry, have, chance, visit, something / don't, shows, town, put / excellent / hope, enjoy

**Let's Check 1**

down, matter / signed up, join / already, on, accept / hope, fun

---

**시험대비 기본평가**     p.16

01 ②     02 ⑤     03 ④

01 개가 집이 없는 것 같다는 말을 듣고 동정심이 생기는 상황에서 "집이 없다니 안됐다."가 들어가는 것이 적절하다.

02 자전거 도로 요철에 대하여 안내판이 없어서 사고가 난 것에 대하여 지역 웹 사이트에 그 문제를 알리자는 의미의 질문이 되도록 하는 ⑤가 가장 적절하다.

03 (C) 그 스티커들이 사람들에게 재활용 쓰레기 분류를 도와 줄 것이라고 확신해. (A) 그것들이 효과가 있는지 내일 다시 와 보자. (B) 좋은 생각이야.

---

**시험대비 실력평가**     p.17~18

01 ⑤     02 ①     03 ②     04 ⑤
05 ⑤     06 ⑤
**07 마을의 유명한 장소들을 보여주는 비디오를 만들어서 인터넷에 올리는 것.**
08 ④     09 ②     10 ③

---

01 페스티벌에서 사람들에게 차를 맛보도록 제공할 계획이라는 말에 이어지기에 적절한 것은 그 사람들이 재미있기를 기원하는 것이다

02 ① "What's the matter (with you)?"는 상대방의 걱정이나 염려를 묻는 표현이므로 이어지는 내용이 좋은 내용이 나오면 어색하다.

03 빈칸 다음에 이어지는 내용이 soccer team에 들어갈 수 없는 이유이기 때문에 빈칸에는 soccer team에 가입할 수 없는 이유를 묻는 질문이 적절하다.

04 축구팀에는 이미 학생이 너무 많아서 새로운 회원을 뽑지 않기로 했다고 나와 있는 것으로 보아 소년을 새 회원으로 뽑을 것이라는 ⑤의 내용은 대화와 일치하지 않는다.

05 상대방의 걱정이나 염려를 묻는 질문은 "What's the matter?", "What's wrong?", "Is there anything wrong?", "What's the problem?" "What happened?" 등이 있다.

06 상대에게 권하거나 제안하는 표현은 "Why don't you+동사원형 ~?", "How about -ing?", "What about -ing?", "Let's+동사원형 ~." 등이 있다.

07 That은 지시대명사로 앞 문장의 내용을 받는다.

08 그들의 마을에 유명한 장소가 얼마나 있는지는 알 수 없다.

09 우울해 보이는 이유로, 축구부에 지원했지만 가입할 수 없었다는 내용이다.

10 축구 동아리에 가입하지 못해서 우울한 학생에게 위로해 줄 수 있는 말로 재미있는 다른 동아리를 찾기를 바란다는 ③이 적절하다.

---

**서술형 시험대비**     p.19

01 to bring
02 (A) What   (B) Why
03 a chance to visit the nice places here
04 shows the famous places in our town and put it on the internet
05 in
06 Thanks to the support from many people
07 child, education

---

01 "~할 것을 잊다"의 의미는 "forget+to부정사"이다.

02 (A) 무슨 문제가 있니? = What's the matter? (B) ~하는 것이 어떠니? = Why don't we ~?

03 주어진 우리말에 해당하는 영어 표현은 to부정사가 명사를 수식하는 형태이다.

04 (나) 앞에 있는 주격 관계대명사 that은 선행사가 단수이기 때

3

문에 단수동사인 shows가 와야 하고 이어서 show의 목적어인 the famous places in our town이 온다. 접속사 and에 이어지는 동사 put은 make와 병렬구조이다.

05 (A), (B) 우리나라에서 = in my country, (C) 전 세계에 = in the world

06 ~ 덕택에 = thanks to, 많은 사람들의 후원 = the support from many people

07 본문에 소개된 Malala의 희망은 "I hope every child in the world can get an education."에서 찾을 수 있다.

교과서
# Grammar

---

핵심 Check                                    p.20~21

1 (1) What  (2) what  (3) what  (4) what
2 (1) playing  (2) sing  (3) done  (4) washed

---

### 시험대비 기본평가                          p.22

01 ⑤
02 (1) burning  (2) answer  (3) what  (4) what
03 ①, ③
04 (1) What he proposed was different from what he really thought.
   (2) Do not forget what I told you.
   (3) I watched her walking across the field.

01 the thing(s) that[which]은 선행사를 포함하는 관계대명사 what으로 바꿔 쓸 수 있다.

02 (1), (2) 지각동사의 목적격보어로 원형부정사나 현재분사를 쓰는 것이 적절하다. (3) is의 보어와 do의 목적어 역할을 할 수 있는 what이 적절하다. (4) believe와 was telling의 목적어 역할을 할 수 있는 what이 적절하다.

03 지각동사 saw의 목적격보어로 원형부정사나 현재분사를 쓰는 것이 적절하나 의미상 그 동작이 진행 중인 것을 나타낼 때에는 주로 현재분사를 사용한다.

04 (1), (2) the thing(s) which[that]로 쓰일 수 있는 선행사를 포함하는 관계대명사 what을 이용한다. (3) 목적격보어로 현재분사를 쓰는 지각동사를 이용한다.

---

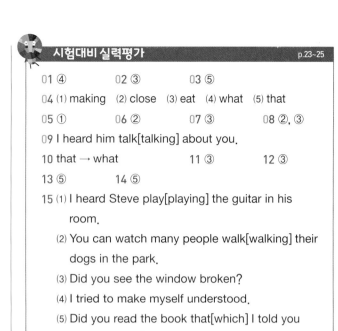

### 시험대비 실력평가                          p.23~25

01 ④           02 ③           03 ⑤
04 (1) making  (2) close  (3) eat  (4) what  (5) that
05 ①           06 ②           07 ③           08 ②, ③
09 I heard him talk[talking] about you.
10 that → what           11 ③           12 ③
13 ⑤           14 ⑤
15 (1) I heard Steve play[playing] the guitar in his room.
   (2) You can watch many people walk[walking] their dogs in the park.
   (3) Did you see the window broken?
   (4) I tried to make myself understood.
   (5) Did you read the book that[which] I told you the other day?
   (6) Learning how to play the game is what I want to do now.
16 ①, ④           17 ③           18 ⑤

01 ① Last night, I heard the dog barking fiercely. ② I saw our cow lying on the ground. ③ She watched her sister doing the dishes. ⑤ She made him do his homework right away.

02 believe와 told의 직접목적어 역할을 할 수 있도록 that을 what으로 고쳐야 한다.

03 지각동사의 목적격보어로 목적어와의 관계가 능동이므로 원형부정사나 현재분사를 쓰는 것이 적절하다. 동사 is의 보어와 bought의 목적어 역할을 할 수 있는 것은 what이다.

04 (1), (2) 지각동사의 목적격보어로 목적어와의 관계가 능동이므로 원형부정사나 현재분사를 쓰는 것이 적절하다. (3) 사역동사의 목적격보어로 목적어와 능동의 관계일 경우 동사원형이 나온다. (4) is의 보어와 for의 목적어 역할을 할 수 있는 what이 적절하다. (5) 선행사로 the last thing이 있으므로 관계대명사 that이 적절하다.

05 do의 목적어와 is의 주어 역할을 할 수 있는 What이 적절하다.

06 지각동사 hear의 목적격보어로 목적어와의 관계가 능동이므로 원형부정사나 현재분사를 쓰는 것이 적절하다.

07 지각동사의 목적격보어로 목적어와의 관계가 능동이면 원형부정사나 현재분사를 쓰고 수동이면 과거분사를 쓰는 것이 적절하다.

08 what이 관계대명사인지 의문대명사인지 구분하는 문제로 보통 의문사 what은 '무엇이 ~인(한)지'로, 관계대명사 what은 '~하는 것'으로 해석한다. ①, ④, ⑤ 의문대명사 ②, ③ 관계대명사

09 '지각동사+목적어+원형부정사/현재분사'

10 what is called: 소위, 이른바

11 지각동사의 목적격보어로 목적어와의 관계가 능동이면 원형부정사나 현재분사를 쓰는 것이 적절하다.

12 ③번은 information과 it is possible을 동격으로 연결하는 접속사 that이 들어가야 하고, 나머지는 선행사가 없는 관계대명사 what이 적절하다.

13 the food which[that]의 역할을 하는 what을 이용하여 나타내도록 한다.

14 'David이 하는 것'을 선행사를 포함한 관계대명사 what을 이용한다.

15 (1) 지각동사 heard의 목적격보어로 목적어와의 관계가 능동이므로 원형부정사나 현재분사를 쓰는 것이 적절하다. (2) 지각동사 watch의 목적격보어로 목적어와의 관계가 능동이므로 원형부정사나 현재분사를 쓰는 것이 적절하다. (3) 지각동사 see의 목적격보어로 목적어와의 관계가 수동이므로 과거분사를 쓰는 것이 적절하다. (4) 사역동사의 목적격보어로 목적어와 수동의 관계이므로 과거분사를 쓰는 것이 적절하다. (5) the book이 선행사로 나왔으므로 what이 아니라 which나 that을 써야 한다. (6) is의 주어와 do의 목적어 역할을 할 수 있도록 that을 what으로 고쳐야 한다.

16 ① 지각동사의 목적격보어로 목적어와의 관계가 능동이므로 원형부정사나 현재분사를 쓰는 것이 적절하다. ④ the ring이라는 선행사가 있으므로 what을 that으로 고쳐야 한다.

17 ③번은 앞에 있는 the girl을 수식하는 현재분사이고 나머지는 다 목적격 보어로 쓰인 현재분사이다.

18 what = the thing(s) that[which]

## 서술형 시험대비
p.26~27

01 (1) woke up and saw our cow lying on the ground.
　(2) I saw Marianne studying in the library.
　(3) He heard the girl walk out of the house.
02 (1) If you don't understand what I say, please ask me.
　(2) She can remember what she did at that time.
　(3) Rebecca felt someone touch her hand.
03 (1) What she is watching
　(2) what she wanted
04 (1) shake[shaking]　(2) called
　(3) answer[answering]　(4) run[running]
05 (1) Let's review what you learned.
　(2) I think what keeps me young is the work.
　(3) What you did made me look like a fool.
　(4) Don't spend too much time doing what is trash.
06 (1) to carry → carry[carrying]
　(2) arrives → arrive[arriving]
　(3) walked → walk[walking]

　(4) lift → lifted
　(5) tells you that → tell you what
　(6) what → that
　(7) that → what
07 (1) who are
　(2) who were
08 (1) I heard them making a noise in the house.
　(2) I watched a girl smell[smelling] flowers.
　(3) When did you last have your hair cut?
　(4) Don't put off what you can do today until tomorrow.
　(5) She was impressed with what he did to her.

01 지각동사의 목적격보어로 목적어와의 관계가 능동이므로 원형부정사나 현재분사를 쓰는 것이 적절하다.

02 (1)~(2) 선행사를 포함하는 관계대명사 what을 이용하여 배열한다. what이 선행사를 포함하므로 문장에서 두 가지의 역할을 함에 유의한다. (3) 지각동사의 목적격보어로 목적어와의 관계가 능동이면 원형부정사나 현재분사를 쓰는 것에 유의한다.

03 선행사를 포함하는 관계대명사 what을 이용한다.

04 지각동사의 목적격보어로 목적어와의 관계가 능동이면 원형부정사나 현재분사를 쓰고 수동이면 과거분사를 쓰는 것이 적절하다.

05 선행사를 포함하여 the thing(s) which[that]의 역할을 하는 what을 이용하여 하나의 문장으로 쓴다.

06 (1)~(4) 지각동사의 목적격보어로 목적어와의 관계가 능동이면 원형부정사나 현재분사를 쓰고 수동이면 과거분사를 쓰는 것이 적절하다. (5) 사역동사 let의 목적격보어로 동사원형 tell이 나와야 하고 tell의 직접목적어와 means의 목적어 역할을 할 수 있도록 that을 what으로 고친다. (6) the shirt라는 선행사가 있으므로 what을 that으로 고친다. (7) did와 imagine의 목적어 역할을 해야 하므로 that을 what으로 고친다.

07 명사를 뒤에서 수식하는 현재분사이므로 그 앞에 '관계대명사+be동사'가 생략된 것으로 볼 수 있다. ordinarily: 보통은, 대개는

08 (1)~(2) 지각동사의 목적격보어로 목적어와의 관계가 능동이면 원형부정사나 현재분사를 쓰는 것이 적절하며 의미상 그 동작이 진행 중인 것을 나타낼 때에는 주로 현재분사를 사용한다. (3) 사역동사의 목적격보어로 목적어와 수동의 관계일 경우 과거분사가 나온다. (4) put off와 do의 목적어 역할을 할 수 있는 what을 이용한다. (5) 전치사 with의 목적어와 동사 did의 목적어 역할을 할 수 있는 what을 이용한다.

## Reading

확인문제                                   p.28

1 F   2 F   3 F   4 T   5 T

확인문제                                   p.29

1 F   2 T   3 T   4 F   5 F   6 T

### 교과서 확인학습 A                        p.30~31

01 is, live in, southern part

02 southern part, does, have a fence, like, out of, freely

03 that, are raising

04 As a result, to kill, because, protect

05 woke up, lying

06 dead, felt

07 do anything because

08 realized, ignore

09 wanted to help, the same

10 to use fire

11 were afraid of it, work

12 Instead, to better watch

13 another idea, a scarecrow

14 were, clever

15 The first day

16 jumped in, killed

17 walking around, with a light

18 discovered that, were afraid of, moving

19 came up with, to invent, move

20 Because, what I needed

21 a small device, broken electronic light

22 At, what I called

23 so proud of

24 have set up, at, haven't heard, complain about

25 saying, what we wanted

26 Surprisingly, used, to scare away, such as

27 From, that, make a difference, even though

28 able to prevent, from

29 Thanks to, a scholarship

30 excited about

31 teaching, how to make, use

32 make a difference, lives

### 교과서 확인학습 B                        p.32~33

1 My name is Richard Turere. I live in Kenya in the southern part of Nairobi National Park.

2 The southern part of the park does not have a fence, so wild animals like lions move out of the park freely.

3 They kill the animals that farmers are raising.

4 As a result, farmers try to kill the lions because they want to protect their animals.

5 One morning, I woke up and saw our cow lying on the ground.

6 It was dead, and I felt so bad.

7 At first, I thought I couldn't do anything because I was only eleven.

8 Then I realized I shouldn't ignore the problem.

9 I really wanted to help the people in my town in the same situation.

10 My first idea was to use fire.

11 I thought lions were afraid of it. Sadly, it didn't work.

12 Instead, the fire helped the lions to better watch the cows move.

13 Then I had another idea. It was to use a scarecrow.

14 But the lions were very clever.

15 The first day, they were turned away.

16 On the second day, they jumped in and killed more animals.

17 One night, I was walking around the cows with a light, and the lions didn't come.

18 I discovered that lions were afraid of a moving light.

19 So I came up with an idea. I decided to invent lights that move electronically.

20 Because I like machines, I could find what I needed to make the lights.

21 I found an old car battery, a small device from a motorcycle, a switch, and a broken electronic light.

22 At thirteen, I finally made what I called "lion lights."

23 My father said, "I'm so proud of you, Richard!"

24 Since then, I have set up lights at seven homes in my community and haven't heard anyone complain about lions.

25 They thanked me, saying "This is exactly what we wanted, lovely boy!"

26 Surprisingly, my idea is now used all over Kenya to scare away other animals, such as elephants.

27 From this experience, I realized that I could make a difference in people's lives even though I am just a young boy.

28 I was also able to prevent lions from being killed.

29 Thanks to my work, I got a scholarship to a great school in Kenya.

30 I am really excited about this.

31 In my new school, I am now teaching my friends how to make and use the lights.

32 I tell my friends, "Our ideas can make a difference in people's lives!"

## 시험대비 실력평가
p.34~37

01 ignore

02 Because he found his cow dead.

03 ③  04 ③  05 ④  06 ③

07 fire  08 ⑤  09 ③  10 ⑤

11 lions, other animals, such as elephants

12 ④  13 The writer likes machines.

14 ⑤  15 ③  16 ④  17 ⑤

18 It's because the southern part of the park does not have a fence.  19 ④  20 ③

21 The writer used fire and a scarecrow to turn lions away.

22 He was walking around the cows with a light.

23 ④  24 ④  25 ④  26 ③

27 lions, other animals, such as elephants

28 He is now teaching his friends how to make and use the lights.

01 어떠한 것에 관심을 기울이지 않다는 '무시하다(ignore)'이다.

02 글쓴이가 슬펐던 이유는 자신의 소가 죽어 있는 것을 발견했기 때문이다.

03 자신이 겨우 열한 살밖에 되지 않았기 때문에 어떠한 것도 할 수 없다고 생각했다고 하였으므로 ③번이 가장 적절하다.

04 ⓐ는 사자를 가리키는 말이며, 나머지는 모두 농부를 가리키는 말이다.

05 농부들이 키우는 것은 야생동물이 아니며, 야생동물들이 농부들이 키우는 동물을 죽인다고 하였다.

06 ③번 뒤에 나오는 It이 가리키는 것은 글쓴이가 떠올린 또 다른 생각(another idea)을 가리키는 말이다.

07 앞 문장의 '불'을 가리키는 말이다.

08 허수아비를 세운 둘째 날에 사자들은 더 많은 동물들을 죽였다고 하였다.

09 어린 소년일지라도 사람들의 삶에 차이를 만들 수 있다는 의미가

자연스러우므로 양보절 접속사 even though가 적절하다.

10 글의 내용으로 보아 'lion lights'의 쓰임은 사자들을 쫓아내는 것임을 알 수 있다.

11 해석: 사자 전등은 사자뿐만 아니라 코끼리 같은 다른 동물들도 쫓아낸다.

12 이어지는 글의 내용으로 보아 사자는 움직이는 불빛을 두려워한다는 것이 적절하다.

13 글쓴이는 기계를 좋아한다고 하였다.

14 전자적으로 움직이는 전등을 만드는 데 사용되지 않은 것은 ⑤번이다.

15 사자들이 농부들이 기르는 동물들을 죽였기 때문에 그 결과 농부들이 사자를 죽이려 했다는 것이 자연스럽다.

16 농부들에 의해 길러지던 동물들을 사자가 죽였다고 하였다.

17 어느 날 아침, 잠에서 깬 글쓴이는 자신의 소가 죽은 것을 발견하고는 기분이 좋지 않았다고 하였다.

18 공원의 남쪽 지역에 울타리가 없기 때문에 야생동물들이 자유롭게 공원 밖으로 나간다고 하였다.

19 밑줄 친 (A)는 '효과가 있다'는 의미로 쓰였다. ① 일하다 ② 직장에 다니다 ③ (기계 장치 등이) 작동되다 ④ 효과가 있다 ⑤ 직장, 일자리

20 불빛을 들고 소 주변을 걸었을 때 사자가 오지 않는 것을 본 후 (C) 사자가 움직이는 불빛을 두려워한다는 사실을 깨닫고 (B) 전기로 움직이는 전등을 만들기로 결정함 (D) 필요한 재료 나열

21 글쓴이는 사자들을 돌려보내기 위해서 불과 허수아비를 사용하였다.

22 글쓴이는 불을 들고 소 주변을 걷고 있었다고 하였다.

23 글쓴이가 사자 전등을 만든 것은 사자나 코끼리 같은 동물들을 쫓아내기 위함임을 유추할 수 있다.

24 사자들이 죽임을 당하지 않게 할 수 있었다고 하였으므로 사자들이 예전에는 죽임을 당했음을 알 수 있다.

25 모두 글쓴이가 만든 "lion lights"를 의미하지만 ⓓ는 글쓴이가 장학금을 받고 케냐에 있는 훌륭한 학교에 간 것을 의미한다.

26 글쓴이가 "lion light"를 만들기 위해서 몇 년을 노력해 왔는지는 위 글을 읽고 답할 수 없다.

27 lion light는 사자뿐만 아니라 코끼리와 같은 다른 동물들도 쫓아낸다.

28 글쓴이는 지금 학교에서 친구들에게 사자 전등을 어떻게 만들고 사용하는지를 가르쳐주고 있다고 하였다.

## 서술형 시험대비
p.38~39

01 (A) so  (B) because  (C) because

02 killed

03 Farmers want to protect their animals from lions.

04 afternoon → morning

05 another idea

06 He thought lions were afraid of it.

07 Lions were turned away.

08 The writer decided to invent lights that move electronically.

09 He discovered that lions were afraid of a moving light.

10 An old car battery, a small device from a motorcycle, a switch, and a broken electronic light were needed.

11 He called what he made at thirteen "lion lights."

12 lion lights

13 He realized that he could make a difference in people's lives even though he is just a young boy.

14 He got a scholarship to a great school in Kenya.

15 lions from being killed

---

01 because는 이유를 이끄는 접속사이고, so는 결과를 이끄는 접속사이다. (A) 울타리가 없는 것이 원인이 되어 그 결과 야생 동물들이 공원 밖으로 자유롭게 이동하는 것이고 (B)와 (C)는 '농부들이 동물들을 보호하기를 원하기 때문에', '내가 열 한 살이기 때문에'라고 말하는 것이 자연스럽다.

02 글쓴이는 같은 상황에 있는 마을 사람들을 돕기를 원했고, 이것은 사자에 의해 동물이 죽임을 당하는 상황을 의미한다.

03 농부들은 사자로부터 그들의 동물을 보호하기를 원한다고 하였다.

04 글쓴이가 자신의 소가 죽어 있는 것을 발견한 것은 어느 날 아침이라고 하였다.

05 글쓴이가 떠올린 또 다른 아이디어를 가리키는 말이다.

06 글쓴이가 불을 사용하기로 했을 때 사자들이 불을 무서워한다고 생각했다.

07 허수아비를 설치한 첫날 사자들은 돌아갔다고 하였다.

08 글쓴이는 전자적으로 움직이는 전등을 발명하기로 결정했다.

09 글쓴이는 사자들이 움직이는 불빛을 두려워한다는 것을 발견하였다.

10 글쓴이가 발명하기를 원하는 전등을 만들기 위하여 오래된 자동차 배터리, 오토바이에서 찾은 작은 장치들, 스위치, 그리고 부서진 전등이 필요했다.

11 글쓴이는 자신이 열세 살에 만든 것을 "사자 전등"이라고 불렀다.

12 'lion lights'를 가리키는 말이다.

13 그 경험으로부터 Richard는 자신이 비록 어린 소년이라 할지라도 사람들의 삶에 차이를 가져다 줄 수 있다는 것을 깨달았다.

14 그는 자신의 발명 덕분에 케냐의 좋은 학교에 장학금을 받고 입

학하게 되었다.

15 사람들의 삶에 차이를 만든 것에 더해서, Richard는 또한 사자들이 죽임을 당하는 것을 멈추게 할 수 있었다. prevent A from B = stop A from B: A가 B하는 것을 못하게 막다

---

### 영역별 핵심문제 p.41~45

| | | | |
|---|---|---|---|
| 01 ② | 02 ① | 03 ① | 04 ⑤ |
| 05 ④ | 06 running | 07 ⑤ | 08 ④ |
| 09 ①, ⑤ | 10 ③ | 11 ④ | 12 for |
| 13 ② | 14 ③ | 15 eat[eating] | |
| 16 ③, ④ | 17 ⑤ | 18 ② | 19 ④ |
| 20 ② | | | |

21 getting a scholarship to a great school in Kenya

22 He made it at thirteen.　23 ①, ⑤

24 spreading the joy of being kind to others

25 throw a bucket of ice water on their head and make a donation

| | | |
|---|---|---|
| 26 ② | 27 ③ | 28 ③ |

29 It means doing something nice for someone because someone else did something nice for you.

30 ④

---

01 • 나는 그들이 복도에서 뛰어다니는 것을 멈추기를 희망해. stop -ing = ~하기를 멈추다 • 우리는 간식을 사기 위해 멈춰야 했다. stop to ~ = ~하기 위해 멈추다 • 비는 그들이 밖에 나가지 못하게 할 것이다. stop A from -ing = A가 ~하지 못하게 하다

02 나는 데이터를 분류해야 한다. sort = 분류하다, classify = 분류하다, complain = 불평하다, decide = 결심하다

03 "새를 겁주어 쫓아 보내기 위하여 사람처럼 옷을 입혀서 들판에 세워놓은 형상"은 "scarecrow 허수아비"를 나타낸다.

04 ignorant 무지한, helpful 도움이 되는

05 (A) ~을 맛보다 = try (B) 즐겁게 보내다 = have a great time

06 "나는 그들이 복도에서 뛰는 것을 중단하기를 희망해." ~하기를 중단하다 = stop -ing

07 "What's the matter?"는 주로 걱정이나 염려를 나타내는 상황을 보고 사용하는 표현이므로 ⑤는 어색하다. pleased = 즐거운, disappointed = 실망한, upset = 기분이 상한

08 ⓐ 지시대명사 ⓑ 접속사 ⓒ 관계대명사 ⓓ 지시대명사 ⓔ 접속사

09 상대에게 제안하거나 권유하는 의미로 쓰는 표현은 "Let's ~", "How about -ing?", "What about -ing?", "Shall we ~?" 등이다.

10 ③ "I'm sorry that they didn't have a chance to visit the nice places here."를 보면 그의 마을에 아름다운 장소들이 있다는 것을 알 수 있다.

11 (A)의 "down"은 "우울한"이라는 뜻이다. ① ~ 아래로 ② 아래에 ③ 작동하지 않는 ④ 우울한 ⑤ ~ 아래로

12 ~을 신청하다 = sign up for

13 상대에게 좋지 않은 일이 있을 때 유감을 나타내는 말로 "I am sorry to hear that."이 적절하다.

14 Jim looked at her play[playing] on the floor.

15 지각동사 saw의 목적격보어로 John이 많이 먹는 '능동'이므로 원형부정사나 현재분사를 쓰는 것이 적절하다.

16 ③ I watched him enter[entering] the room. ④ I never thought that we could love each other more.

17 이어지는 내용으로 보아 울타리가 없기 때문에 야생 동물들이 공원 밖으로 자유롭게 이동한다는 내용이 가장 적절하다.

18 밑줄 친 (B)는 want의 목적어로 쓰인 to부정사이다. ① 부사적 용법(목적) ② decided의 목적어 ③ something을 수식하는 형용사 ④ 진주어 ⑤ 부사적 용법(감정의 원인)

19 위 글을 통해 나이로비 국립공원은 케냐에 있음을 알 수 있다.

20 사람들이 사자에 관해 '칭찬하는' 것이 아니라 '불평하는' 말을 들어본 적이 없다고 말하는 것이 자연스럽다. compliment: 칭찬하다

21 Richard는 케냐에 있는 훌륭한 학교의 장학금을 받는 것에 대해 신이 난다고 하였다.

22 Richard가 사자 전등을 만든 때는 그가 13세 때였다.

23 문맥상 이유를 나타내는 접속사가 와야 한다.

24 타인에게 친절을 베푸는 즐거움을 널리 퍼트린다는 의미가 적절하다.

25 한 양동이의 얼음물을 머리 위로 끼얹고 기부를 하는 것을 의미한다.

26 문맥상 동격을 나타내는 접속사 that이 와야 한다.

27 ⓐ 이어지는 예시는 친절을 베푸는 간단한 방법이다. ⓑ 내용상 루게릭병을 사람들에게 알리는 프로젝트이다. ⓒ 서비스에 대한 비용을 지불하지 않고 타인을 돕기 위해 자신의 기술이나 재능을 사용할 수 있다고 하였으므로 work가 적절하다.

28 기부를 한 후 Ice Bucket Challenge에 도전할 세 사람을 선택한다고 하였다.

29 'Paying it forward'란 누군가가 당신에게 좋은 일을 했기 때문에 당신도 누군가를 위해서 좋은 일을 하는 것을 의미한다.

30 밑줄 친 (A)는 타인을 위해 단순한 친절을 베푸는 것을 의미한다. 반 친구에게 '안녕'이라고 인사한 것은 이에 해당하지 않는다.

---

단원별 예상문제 p.46~49

01 (c)omplain  02 ②
03 (1) (c)ommunity  (2) (i)nform  04 ②
05 ③  06 ①  07 ⑤  08 ⑤
09 ①  10 ②  11 ④  12 ②
13 ⑤  14 ③
15 (1) shake  (2) what looked like a fish  (3) what we choose
16 ③  17 It's because he likes machines.
18 better watch the cows move  19 ③
20 ④
21 Because the writer has seen students carrying many things at school.
22 ③
23 It's because they want to protect their animals.

01 주어진 단어는 동사와 명사의 관계이다. accept: 받아들이다 acceptance: 수용 complain: 불평하다 complaint: 불평

02 float 뜨다 / 수면[물] 위에는 나뭇잎들이 떠 있었다. discover 발견하다, decide 결심하다, accept 받아들이다, ignore 무시하다

03 (1) community: 지역 사회, 공동체 (2) inform A of B: A에게 B를 알려주다

04 화가 난 이유를 묻는 말에 (B) 학생들이 새치기를 한다고 말하자 (A) 끼어들지 말고 자기 차례를 기다리면 좋겠다고 하고 (C) 거기에 동의하는 순서이다.

05 (A) 떨어지다, 넘어지다 = fell off (B) 자전거 길에 = on the bike path (C) 지역 웹 사이트에 = on the community website

06 이어지는 설명의 내용이 사고가 일어나게 된 과정이므로 어떻게 사고가 일어나게 되었는지를 묻는 ①이 가장 적절하다.

07 대화 속에서 "G: Weren't there any signs? B: No, there weren't."를 보면 자전거 도로에는 sign이 없었다는 것을 알 수 있다.

08 'What's the matter?'는 '무슨 일이야?' 또는 '괜찮아?'라는 뜻으로 상대방에 대한 염려를 묻는 표현이다. (가)의 앞에는 염려를 나타내는 ⑤가 적절하다.

10 ⓐ 주격 관계대명사 that에 이어지는 동사로 선행사가 단수이기 때문에 단수동사 shows가 적절하다. ⓑ 동사 hope의 목적어인 명사절에서 주어 they에 이어지는 복수동사 enjoy가 적절하다.

11 뒤에 목적격보어로 동사원형이 나오므로 사역동사나 지각동사가 나와야 한다. ask는 to부정사가 나온다.

12 ②에는 something이라는 선행사가 있으므로 that[which]이 적절하다. 나머지는 모두 what[What]이 적절하다.

13 observe의 목적격보어로 목적어와의 관계가 능동이므로 원형부정사나 현재분사를 쓰는 것이 적절하다.

**14** ① This isn't what I expected! ② The movie that I saw last night was fantastic. ④ What my friend cooked for me yesterday was really yummy. ⑤ You should learn the things that you have to do.

**15** (1) 지각동사의 목적격보어로 원형부정사나 현재분사를 쓰는 것이 적절하다. (2) something that을 선행사를 포함한 관계대명사 what으로 바꿔 쓸 수 있다. (3) the food 다음에 목적격 관계대명사 that이 생략되어 있는 형태이므로 the food that을 관계대명사 what으로 바꿔 쓸 수 있다.

**16** 사자들이 영리했다고 말한 이유는 허수아비를 설치한 첫 날은 돌아갔지만 둘째 날부터 다시 동물들을 죽이기 시작했기 때문이다. 따라서 ③번에 들어가는 것이 가장 자연스럽다.

**17** Richard는 기계를 좋아하기 때문에 자신이 그 불을 만들기 위해 필요한 것을 발견할 수 있었다고 하였다.

**18** Richard가 사용한 불 때문에 사자들은 소들이 움직이는 것을 더 잘 볼 수 있었다.

**19** 허수아비를 세운 첫 날은 사자들이 돌아갔다고 하였으므로 '첫 날부터 효과가 없었다'는 말은 적절하지 않다.

**20** '네가 필요한 것'이라는 의미이므로 관계대명사 what이 적절하다.

**21** 글쓴이가 학급 바자회에 가방을 가지고 온 이유는 학생들이 학교에서 많은 것들을 가지고 다니는 것을 보았기 때문이다.

**22** Richard는 자신과 같은 상황에 있는 사람들을 돕기를 원했다.

**23** 농부들이 사자를 죽이려고 한 이유는 그들이 기르는 동물을 보호하고 싶어서이다.

### 서술형 실전문제
p.50~51

**01** (A) bike   (B) bump   (C) signs

**02** path

**03** ⑤ the occasion → the matter

**04** (1) What I want to do for the community is to pick up trash.
(2) I liked what Yuna gave to me last month.
(3) Did you enjoy what we saw at the theater last night?

**05** I saw the airplane flying low from south to north.

**06** (1) You will be surprised by what you can find.
(2) What's worse, it started raining.
(3) Samuel heard his name called.
(4) I saw Ann walking[walk] her dog.

**07** what

**08** ⓒ-ⓐ-ⓓ-ⓑ

**09** 허수아비를 설치한 첫째 날은 돌아갔지만 둘째 날 더 많은 동물들을 죽였기 때문이다.

**10** doing something nice for someone

**11** Three people are chosen to do the Ice Bucket Challenge.

**01** (A) 자전거를 타다 넘어졌다. (B) 요철이 있었다. (C) 표지판이 없었다.

**02** 특히 사람이 걷거나 뭔가를 타고 다니기 위해 만든 'path 길'을 나타낸다.

**03** "What's the occasion?"(무슨 날이니?)은 평소와 달리 좋아 보일 때 주로 쓰는 말이고, 걱정이나 염려를 나타내는 말은 "What't the matter?"이다.

**04** what은 선행사를 포함한 관계대명사로 '~하는 것'으로 해석하며, the thing(s) which[that]를 나타낸다.

**05** 지각동사의 목적격보어로 목적어와의 관계가 능동이면 원형부정사나 현재분사를 쓰고 수동이면 과거분사를 쓰는 것이 적절하다.

**06** (1) 선행사를 포함한 관계대명사 what을 이용한다. what you can find: 당신이 찾을 수 있는 것 (2) what's worse: 설상가상으로 (3) 지각동사의 목적격보어로 목적어와의 관계가 수동이므로 과거분사를 쓰는 것이 적절하다. (4) 지각동사의 목적격보어로 목적어와의 관계가 능동이므로 원형부정사나 현재분사를 쓰는 것이 적절하며 의미상 그 동작이 진행 중인 것을 나타낼 때에는 주로 현재분사를 사용한다.

**07** '전등들을 만들기 위해 내가 필요했던 것'이라는 의미이므로 관계대명사 what을 쓰는 것이 적절하다.

**08** ⓒ 불과 허수아비로 사자를 쫓아내려던 Richard의 첫 번째와 두 번째 아이디어가 모두 효과가 없었다. 그러던 어느 날 ⓐ Richard가 전등을 들고 소들 주위를 걸었을 때 사자가 오지 않았다. ⓓ Richard는 사자들이 두려워하는 것이 움직이는 불빛이라는 사실을 깨닫고 ⓑ 전자적으로 움직이는 전등을 발명하기로 결정했다.

**09** 사자를 돌려보내기 위해 설치한 허수아비를 본 첫 날은 사자들이 그냥 돌아갔지만 둘째 날은 다시 동물들을 죽이기 시작했기 때문이다.

**10** 글의 내용상 Paying it forward는 '누군가를 위해 어떤 좋은 일을 하는 것'을 의미한다. -thing으로 끝나는 부정대명사는 형용사의 수식을 뒤에서 받는다.

**11** 세 명의 사람들이 선택된다고 하였다.

### 창의사고력 서술형 문제
p.52

|모범답안|

**01** What's the matter? / you do better next time

**02** (1) heard Minsu talk(talking)
(2) saw my little brother dance(dancing)

**03** A watch / checking time, a watch, to check time, light and comfortable

01 float       02 ①

03 (1) on   (2) up   (3) from   (4) with

04 ②        05 (w)orried   06 ③      07 ③

08 ②        09 ②       10 ①       11 ①

12 ③        13 ③       14 ⑤       15 ③, ⑤

16 (1) This is exactly what we wanted.

   (2) My daughter showed me what she had painted.

   (3) If they were successful, the thing that was given to them was some salt. 또는 If they were successful, what was given to them was some salt.

   (4) Tiffany heard a man answer[answering] the phone.

   (5) Robert listened to her cry[crying] against his shoulder.

17 what       18 ⑤       19 (C)–(B)–(A)

20 ④        21 ②       22 ②

23 The first idea was to use fire and the second idea was to use a scarecrow.

01 두 단어의 관계는 반의어이다. dangerous 위험한, safe 안전한, float 뜨다 sink 가라앉다

02 "특정한 작업을 위한 기계나 도구"는 "device 도구, 장치"를 나타낸다.

03 (1) be based on: ~에 바탕을 두다 (2) sign up for: ~에 신청하다 (3) prevent A from -ing: A가 ~하지 못하게 하다 (4) come up with: ~을 생각해 내다

04 scare away: 겁주어 쫓아보내다./ 이것은 그들이 적을 겁주어 쫓아보낼 수 있게 도와줘요.

05 be concerned about ~ = be worried about ~ (~에 대하여 걱정하다)

06 안 좋은 일을 듣고 유감을 나타내는 말은 "I am sorry to hear ~."이다. "pleased"는 "즐거운"이라는 뜻으로 적절하지 않다.

07 소년이 "Why don't you take it to an animal care center and ask for help?"라고 제안했으므로 소녀는 개를 동물 보호 센터로 데리고 갈 것이다.

08 상대에게 책을 읽도록 추천해 주고 그것이 도움이 되기를 바라는 말은 "I hope ~."가 적절하다.

09 주어진 문장은 Mina가 댓글을 Henry에게 소개하는 말로 좋지 않은 내용이 나오기 시작하는 (B)가 적절한 위치이다.

10 (가) 걱정이나 염려를 나타내는 말은 "What's the matter?", "What's wrong?" 등이다. (나) 기원을 나타낼 때 쓰는 표현은 'I hope 주어+동사'(나는 …을 바란다.)이다.

11 (A) fall off: 떨어지다, 넘어지다 (B) over ~: ~을 넘어서 (C) How about -ing?: ~하는 것이 어떠니? (D) on the

website: 웹 사이트에

12 Mason이 그 문제를 웹 사이트에 쓰는 것이 좋겠다고 했지만 언제 쓸지는 알 수 없다.

13 ③번은 앞에 있는 a baby를 수식하는 현재분사이고, 나머지는 다 목적격 보어로 쓰인 현재분사이다.

14 첫 번째 빈칸에는 is의 보어와 recommended의 목적어 역할을 할 수 있는 what이 적절하고, 두 번째 빈칸에는 지각동사의 목적격보어로 목적어와의 관계가 능동이므로 원형부정사나 현재분사를 쓰는 것이 적절하다.

15 ① What I want for my birthday is a backpack. ② I see girls riding a bike in the park. ④ The book is what she bought at the bookstore.

16 (1) that을 is의 보어와 wanted의 목적어 역할을 할 수 있는 what으로 고치는 것이 적절하다. (2) which를 showed의 직접목적어와 painted의 목적어 역할을 할 수 있는 what으로 고치는 것이 적절하다. (3) what = the thing that[which] (4), (5) 지각동사의 목적격보어로 목적어와의 관계가 능동이므로 원형부정사나 현재분사를 쓰는 것이 적절하다.

17 관계대명사 what은 선행사를 포함한 관계대명사로 the thing(s) which[that]를 나타낸다.

18 빈칸 ⓐ에는 관계대명사 what이 들어간다. 모두 관계대명사 what이 쓰이지만, ⑤번에는 완전한 절을 이끄는 명사절 접속사가 쓰인다.

19 (C) then이 의미하는 것은 Richard가 사자 전등을 만들었을 때이며 (B)에서 they가 지칭하는 것은 Richard가 사자 전등을 설치해 준 일곱 가구의 사람들이다. (A) this experience는 자신의 발명으로 사람들의 삶을 바꾼 경험을 의미하므로 가장 마지막에 오는 것이 적절하다.

20 Richard는 사자 전등을 일곱 가구에 설치하였다.

21 자신이 발명한 것으로 사람들의 삶에 차이를 만들었고 장학금까지 받았다고 하였으므로 ②번이 적절하다.

22 이어지는 글의 내용으로 보아 사자가 동물들을 공격하는 것이 문제이다.

23 첫 번째 아이디어는 불을 사용하는 것이었고, 두 번째 아이디어는 허수아비를 사용하는 것이었다.

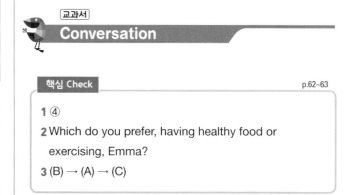

계없이 = regardless of (3) give up 포기하다 (4) raise a question 질문을 제기하다

06 (1) make up for = 만회하다, 보상하다 (2) take a break 휴식을 취하다 (3) be eager to = ~하고 싶어 하다 (4) go out = 외출하다, 나가다

## Lesson 2

# Chopsticks or a Fork?

---

### 시험대비 실력평가 p.60

01 (1) ignore  (2) suggestion

02 (1) boastful  (2) convenient  03 ②

04 spoon  05 ④  06 ④  07 ②

---

01 주어진 보기의 단어는 동사-명사의 관계이다. arrive 도착하다, arrival 도착, ignore 무시하다, ignorance 무지, suggest 제안하다, suggestion 제안

02 보기에 주어진 단어는 명사-형용사의 관계이다. adventure 모험, adventurous 모험심이 강한, boast 자랑 : boastful 뽐내는, convenience 편리함 : convenient 편리한

03 ② "raise"는 "기르다, 들어 올리다, (문제를) 제기하다" 등의 뜻을 가진다. 여기서는 "문제를 제기하다"의 의미이다.

04 곡물이나 수프를 먹기에 좋은 식사 도구는 spoon이다.

05 ① adventures ② elegant ③ disappeared ⑤ forgive ④ "중세 유럽에서는, 주인이 손님에게 자신의 도구를 제공할 필요가 없었다."는 의미로 "provide"가 적절하다.

06 "allow 허용하다"와 비슷한 말은 "permit 허용하다"이다.

07 make up for = 보상하다, give up 포기하다

---

### 서술형 시험대비 p.61

01 arrival

02 break

03 on

04 (s)urely

05 (1) trouble  (2) regardless  (3) give  (4) raises

06 (1) make  (2) take  (3) eager  (4) go

---

01 arrival: 도착, 출현

02 • 그들은 행운을 위하여 접시를 깨는 것 같다. break plates 접시를 깨다 • 이 시점에 우리는 휴식을 취할 필요가 있다. take a break 휴식을 취하다

03 • 나는 음식을 즐겼다. 나는 보통 접시에 음식을 남긴다. "접시에 = on my plate • 만약 네가 두 가지를 모두 할 수 없다면, 단지 한 가지에 집중하는 것이 더 나을지도 모른다. "집중하다 = focus on"

04 확실하게 = certainly, surely

05 (1) ~하는 데 어려움을 겪다 = have trouble -ing (2) ~와 관

---

### 교과서 Conversation

#### 핵심 Check p.62~63

1 ④

2 Which do you prefer, having healthy food or exercising, Emma?

3 (B) → (A) → (C)

---

01 "It seems to me that"은 자신의 의견을 나타내는 말로, in my opinion, I think, I believe, as far as I know 등을 사용할 수 있다.

02 "~ 중에서 어느 것을 더 좋아하니?"는 "Which do you prefer, A or B?"이다.

03 상대가 선호하는 것을 묻자 (B) ice cream을 선호 한다고 대답한다. (A) 왜 그런지 이유를 묻고 (C) icecream이 더 달다는 자신의 의견을 덧붙여 대답한다.

---

### 교과서 대화문 익히기

#### Check(√) True or False p.64

1 F  2 T  3 T  4 F  5 T

---

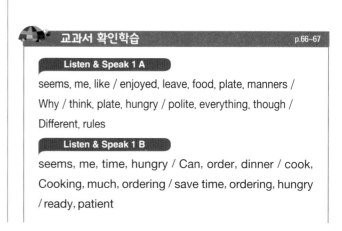

### 교과서 확인학습 p.66~67

**Listen & Speak 1 A**

seems, me, like / enjoyed, leave, food, plate, manners / Why / think, plate, hungry / polite, everything, though / Different, rules

**Listen & Speak 1 B**

seems, me, time, hungry / Can, order, dinner / cook, Cooking, much, ordering / save time, ordering, hungry / ready, patient

---

**12** 정답 및 해설

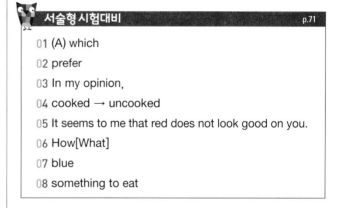

## 시험대비 기본평가                                p.68

01 ①          02 ⑤          03 ④

01 중국에서는 음식을 남기는 것이 예절이라고 하자 한국에서는 다 먹는 것이 예절 바른 것이라는 말에 대한 응답은 문화마다 규칙이 다르다가 되어야 한다.

02 대화의 흐름상 한 가지에 집중하는 것이 더 좋다는 말이 와야 한다.

03 (C) 일찍 저녁을 먹는 것과 늦게 먹는 것 중에서 어느 것을 선호하느냐는 질문에 일찍 식사하는 것을 선호한다고 대답한다. (A) 왜 그러냐고 묻자 (B) 일찍 자기 때문이라고 대답한다.

## 시험대비 실력평가                               p.69~70

01 ②     02 ⑤     03 ③     04 ②
05 ①     06 ③     07 ⑤     08 ③
09 ②     10 ①     11 ③     12 ⑤

01 주어진 문장에서 설명하는 것은 음식을 남기는 것이 예를 지키는 것이라는 중국의 문화를 설명하는 것으로 (B)가 적절하다.

02 "We think finishing everything on the plate means that you are still hungry."가 음식을 남기는 이유이므로 이유를 묻는 Why가 적절하다.

03 이 글에서 음식을 남기는 것과 음식을 남기지 않는 것이 각자의 문화에서 예의를 지키는 것이라는 설명을 했지만 왜 소녀가 음식을 더 즐겼는지에 대한 말은 언급되지 않았다.

04 "It seems to me that ~"은 자신의 생각을 나타내는 말로 "I think ~"에 해당한다.

05 빈칸 뒤에 이어지는 인내심을 가지라는 말은 배가 고파도 조금 참으면 식사를 할 수 있다는 의미로 Jacob에게 하는 말이라고 보아야 한다.

06 여자는 생선을 요리할 것이라고 언급했다.

07 앞에서 나눈 대화에 등장한 건강에 좋은 음식을 먹는 것과 운동을 하는 것 둘 중에서 어느 것을 더 좋아하는지를 묻는 말이 되어야 한다.

08 어느 음식을 먹을지 조절할 수 없기 때문에 운동을 더 좋아한다는 것으로 (C)가 적절한 위치이다.

09 이 대화를 통해서 알 수 있는 것은 건강한 음식을 먹는 것과 운동을 하는 것을 모두 할 수 없을 때는 한 가지에 집중하는 것이 더 좋다는 것이다.

10 (A)는 "휴식을 취하다"는 의미로 "take a break"가 되어야 한다. ① take care of ~을 돌보다 ② make up for ~을 보충하다 ③ give up ~을 포기하다 ④ arrive 도착하다 ⑤ have trouble -ing ~하는 데 어려움을 겪다

11 보통 일찍 잔다는 것이 앞에 나온 "I prefer having a meal early."에 대한 이유이다.

12 "I have meals late in the evening"에 대한 이유는 늦게 일하기 때문이라고 해야 한다.

## 서술형 시험대비                                p.71

01 (A) which
02 prefer
03 In my opinion,
04 cooked → uncooked
05 It seems to me that red does not look good on you.
06 How[What]
07 blue
08 something to eat

01 (A) 선호를 물어볼 때는 "Which do you prefer, A or B?"라고 한다.

02 "다른 것 또는 다른 사람보다 어떤 것 또는 어떤 사람을 더 좋아하다"는 "prefer – 선호하다"에 해당한다.

03 "It seems to me that"은 자신의 의견을 제시하는 말로 "In my opinion"에 해당한다.

04 Claire는 "Then I will have sushi."라고 했기 때문에 익히지 않은 생선을 더 좋아한다고 해야 자연스러운 흐름이다.

05 내 생각에는 ~인 것 같다 = It seems to me that ~, 빨간색이 너한테 잘 어울리지 않는다 = red does not look good on

you

06 상대에게 제안하는 말은 "What about ~?" 또는 "How about ~?"이다.

07 "Blue looks much better on you than red."를 보면 소년은 파란색 모자가 훨씬 더 잘 어울린다고 생각하는 것을 알 수 있다.

08 배가 고프다고 했으므로 "먹을 것 something to eat"이 적절하다.

## Grammar
교과서

핵심 Check                                    p.72~73

1 (1) to   (2) for   (3) of
2 (1) named   (2) sleeping   (3) held

### 시험대비 기본평가                          p.74

01 ④

02 (1) broken   (2) written   (3) carrying   (4) sleeping

03 It is difficult for celebrities to have private lives.

04 (1) It is not easy for us to see ourselves as others see us.
   (2) It is impossible for us to overemphasize safety training.
   (3) Love is a union made in heaven.

01 it을 가주어로 하고 to부정사를 진주어로 하며 의미상의 주어로 'for you'를 쓰고 있는 ④번이 적절하다.

02 (1) 다리가 부러진 것이므로 수동의 의미를 갖는 과거분사가 적절하다. (2) 무엇이 씌여지는 것이므로 수동의 의미를 갖는 과거분사가 적절하다. (3) 아이를 데리고 있는 것이므로 능동의 의미를 갖는 현재분사가 적절하다. (4) 아기가 잠을 자는 것이므로 능동의 의미를 갖는 현재분사가 적절하다.

03 it을 가주어로 하고 to부정사를 진주어로 하는 구문을 이용한다. 의미상의 주어로 'for+목적격'을 쓴다.

04 (1), (2) it을 가주어로 하고 to부정사를 진주어로 하는 구문을 이용한다. 의미상의 주어로 'for+목적격'을 쓴다. (3) 결합이 맺어지는 것이므로 수동의 의미를 갖는 과거분사를 이용한다.

### 시험대비 실력평가                          p.75~77

01 (1) to learn   (2) it   (3) for   (4) of      02 ③
03 ②          04 ⑤          05 ①          06 ④
07 ④          08 for me to   09 ⑤          10 ④
11 While they were walking in the park, many people passing by them bowed politely.      12 ③
13 (1) lady knitting a sweater
   (2) a car made in Japan
   (3) him interviewing the applicants
14 (1) Is there any need for her to stay any longer?
   (2) It is most unwise of her to go there alone.
   (3) It is quite reasonable for you to act that way.
   (4) There is a woman watering the flowers.
   (5) Can you believe there is a hotel made out of cake?
   (6) Thomas has a building built in a modern design. 또는 Thomas has a building which[that] was built in a modern design.
   (7) She had her house built.
15 who is      16 ⑤          17 it, to come
18 ①, ③, ④

01 (1) 진주어로 to부정사가 적절하다. (2) 가주어로는 that이 아니라 it을 쓴다. (3) to부정사의 의미상의 주어는 to부정사 바로 앞에 'for+목적격'으로 나타낸다. (4) 문장에 쓰인 형용사가 nice, kind, smart, wise 등과 같이 사람의 성향, 성격을 나타내는 말일 때는 'of+목적격'으로 쓴다.

02 ① sat → sitting ② writing → written ④ taking → taken ⑤ worn → wearing. accidentally: 우연히 surrender: 항복[굴복]하다

03 to부정사의 의미상의 주어로 'for+목적격'이 적절하다.

04 첫 번째 문장에서는 지구가 우주에서 '보이는' 것이므로 수동의 의미를 갖는 과거분사가 적절하다. 두 번째 문장에서는 to부정사의 의미상의 주어로 'for+목적격'이 적절하다.

05 ①번은 like의 목적어로 쓰인 동명사이고, 나머지는 모두 명사를 앞이나 뒤에서 수식해 주는 현재분사이다.

06 문장에 쓰인 형용사가 사람의 성향, 성격을 나타내는 말이 아니므로 to부정사의 의미상의 주어로 'for+목적격'을 써야 한다.

07 사람이 걸어가는 것이므로 능동의 뜻을 갖는 현재분사가 적절하다.

08 to부정사의 의미상의 주어로 'for+목적격'이 적절하다.

09 '초대된' 것이므로 수동의 뜻을 갖는 과거분사가 적절하다. 분사가 명사를 뒤에서 수식하는 경우 그 앞에 '주격 관계대명사+be동사'가 생략된 것으로 생각할 수 있다.

10 문장에 사람의 성격을 나타내는 형용사가 있는 경우 의미상의 주어로 'of+목적격'을 쓴다.

11 '그들 옆을 지나가는 사람들'을 '진행'의 의미를 갖는 현재분사를 이

용하여 'people passing by them'으로 쓴다.

12 ③번은 사람의 성향, 성격을 나타내는 형용사 silly가 있으므로 of를 써야 한다. 나머지는 모두 for를 써야 한다.

13 분사에 다른 어구(목적어나 보어, 수식어구 등)가 함께 있을 때는 뒤에서 명사를 수식한다.

14 (1) to부정사의 의미상의 주어는 'for+목적격'으로 나타낸다. (2) 문장에 쓰인 형용사가 사람의 성향, 성격을 나타내는 말이므로 'of+목적격'으로 쓰는 것이 적절하다. (3) 의미상의 주어로 'for+목적격'이 나왔으므로 진주어로 to부정사를 쓴다. (4) 여자가 '물을 주는' 것이므로 능동의 의미를 갖는 현재분사 watering이 되어야 한다. (5) '케이크로 만들어진' 호텔이므로 수동의 의미를 갖는 과거분사 made가 되어야 한다. (6) 분사가 명사를 뒤에서 수식하는 경우에는 그 앞에 '주격 관계대명사 +be 동사'가 생략된 것으로 생각할 수 있다. was를 삭제하거나 was 앞에 주격 관계대명사 which[that]를 넣어 주어야 한다. (7) 사역동사 had의 목적격보어로 her house가 지어지는 것이므로 built가 적절하다.

15 분사가 명사 뒤에서 명사를 꾸며줄 때, 분사 앞에는 '주격 관계대명사+ be동사'가 생략되었다고 볼 수 있다.

16 분사에 다른 어구(목적어나 보어, 수식어구 등)가 함께 있을 때는 뒤에서 명사를 수식하는 것을 이용하여 나타낸다. guests가 즐기는 것이므로(능동) enjoying이 적절하다.

17 to부정사와 의미상의 주어로 'for+you'가 나왔으므로 가주어로 it을 쓰고 진주어로 to부정사를 쓴다.

18 ① 식당에서 음식을 '제공하는' 것이므로 능동의 의미를 갖는 현재분사 serving이 되어야 한다. ③ Picasso가 '알려진' 것이므로 수동의 의미를 갖는 과거분사 known이 되어야 한다. ④ 사람의 성향, 성격을 나타내는 형용사(rude)가 나왔으므로 'of you'가 적절하다.

### 서술형 시험대비   p.78~79

01 (1) The man playing baduk is Lee Sedol.
  (2) I saw many planes flying in the sky.
  (3) Kevin bought a small house built ten years ago.

02 (1) Is it convenient for you to come by two o'clock?
  (2) It was polite of her to offer me her seat.
  (3) I want you to correct my broken English.
  (4) I don't like him taking a neutral attitude.

03 (1) a car dangerously parked on the road
  (2) careless of him not to turn off

04 (1) of you to show   (2) for us to prepare

05 (1) for you to   (2) of her to

06 (1) wearing glasses girl → girl wearing glasses
  (2) writing → written

  (3) watered → watering
  (4) which made → which was made, 또는 which 생략
  (5) of → for
  (6) for → of
  (7) climbing → to climb

07 (1) There are two boys who[that] are reading a book on the bench.
  (2) The most popular landmark in Seoul is N Seoul Tower which[that] was built in 1975.
  (3) It is necessary for people to prepare for the worst.

08 (1) A book written by a famous writer is not always a good book.
  (2) Mel loves the girl writing a letter.
  (3) This passage is too difficult for me to understand.
  (4) It was nice of him to invite us to the party tonight.

01 단어 수에 맞추려면 관계대명사를 이용하면 안 된다. (1) 그가 바둑을 '두고 있는' 것이므로 진행의 의미를 갖는 현재분사를 이용한다. (2) 비행기가 '날고 있는' 것이므로 진행의 의미를 갖는 현재분사를 이용한다. (3) 집이 '지어진' 것이므로 수동의 의미를 갖는 과거분사를 이용한다.

02 (1)~(2) to부정사의 의미상의 주어는 'for+목적격'으로 나타내지만 문장에 쓰인 형용사가 사람의 성향, 성격을 나타내는 말일 때는 'of+목적격'으로 쓴다. (3) '잘못된 영어'이므로 수동의 의미를 갖는 과거분사를 이용한다. (4) '태도를 취하는' 것이므로 능동의 의미를 갖는 현재분사를 이용한다.

03 (1) 차가 위험하게 주차되어 있으므로 과거분사가 뒤에서 수식하도록 한다. (2) 진주어로 to부정사를 쓰고 careless가 사람의 성격을 나타내는 말이므로 'of+목적격'으로 쓴다. to부정사의 부정으로 'not+to부정사'를 쓴다.

04 의미상의 주어는 'for+목적격'으로 나타내지만 문장에 쓰인 형용사가 사람의 성향, 성격을 나타내는 말일 때는 'of+목적격'으로 쓴다.

05 '가주어(it) ~ for[of] ...(의미상의 주어) 진주어(to부정사)' 구문을 이용한다. 이때 to부정사의 의미상의 주어는 'for+목적격'으로 나타내지만, 문장에 쓰인 형용사가 사람의 성향, 성격을 나타내는 말일 때는 'of+목적격'으로 쓴다.

06 (1) 분사에 다른 어구(목적어나 보어, 수식어구 등)가 함께 있을 때는 뒤에서 명사를 수식한다. (2) '씌여진' 책이므로 수동의 의미를 갖는 과거분사를 이용한다. (3) 물을 '주는' 것이므로 능동의 의미를 갖는 현재분사를 이용한다. (4) 분사가 명사를 뒤에서 수식하는 경우에는 그 앞에 '주격 관계대명사+be 동사'가 생략된

것으로 생각할 수 있으므로 which was made로 쓰거나 which 를 생략한다. (5), (6) to부정사의 의미상의 주어는 'for+목적격' 으로 나타내지만, 문장에 쓰인 형용사가 사람의 성향, 성격을 나타내는 말일 때는 'of+목적격'으로 쓴다. (7) 의미상의 주어로 'for the woman'이 나와 있으므로 climbing을 to climb으로 고친다.

07 (1), (2) 분사가 명사를 뒤에서 수식하는 경우에는 그 앞에 '주격 관계대명사+be 동사'가 생략된 것으로 생각할 수 있다. (3) to부정사의 의미상의 주어가 일반적인 사람일 경우에는 보통 생략한다.

08 (1) 책이 '쓰여진' 것이므로 수동의 의미를 갖는 과거분사를 이용한다. (2) 편지를 '쓰고 있는' 것이므로 진행의 의미를 갖는 현재분사를 이용한다. (3) to부정사의 의미상의 주어는 'for+목적격'으로 나타낸다. (4) it을 가주어로 하고 to invite를 진주어로 하여, nice가 있으므로 'of him'을 의미상의 주어로 쓴다.

## 교과서 Reading

### 확인문제 p.80
1 T  2 F  3 T  4 F  5 F

### 확인문제 p.81
1 T  2 T  3 F  4 F  5 F  6 T

### 교과서 확인학습 A  p.82~83

01 are close friends
02 travel, with their families, much
03 makes up for, by hosting, coming back from
04 is, eager to, to, adventures
05 what they learned
06 recent, was about, to eat, to argue
07 On, that, to use
08 for grains, soup, eating meat
09 much better, instead
10 easier for you to hold, the other
11 more elegant, using them
12 two different kinds, two of the same utensil
13 use, with
14 No way, with, see, smell, touch it
15 I, get to enjoy
16 raised, argued, wanted to give up

17 It, for, to listen to their arguments
18 yet quietly, left
19 has disappeared
20 should we do, not complete
21 Where
22 to find her
23 searching all, found, sitting under
24 we became boastful, ignored
25 forgive, back, join us
26 forgive, go back
27 Since, allow, to eat, that they please
28 In, that, delicious regardless of which, to eat it with

### 교과서 확인학습 B  p.84~85

01 Spork, Chopsticks, Knork, Barehands, and Ms. Disher are close friends in the Dining Republic.
02 Spork, Chopsticks, Knork, and Barehands travel a lot with their families, but Ms. Disher's family does not travel much.
03 She makes up for this by hosting a dinner for her friends coming back from their trips.
04 She is always eager to listen to their adventures.
05 They often talk about what they learned from their recent trips.
06 The most recent topic was about the best way to eat and Ms. Disher's guests began to argue.
07 Spork: On a recent trip, I have found that it is best to use a spoon and fork.
08 A spoon is best for grains and soup, and a fork is good for eating meat.
09 Knork: No! It is much better to use a knife and a fork instead.
10 Don't you think it is easier for you to hold a fork in one hand and a knife in the other?
11 What can be more elegant than using them to cut meat on a plate!
12 Chopsticks: Why do you use two different kinds of utensils when you can use two of the same utensil?
13 Plus, you can use chopsticks with just one hand!
14 Barehands: No way! When I eat with my hands, of course I can see and smell the food, but I can also touch it.
15 Because I use my sense of touch when I eat, I get to enjoy my food more.

16 They raised and argued many points, and nobody wanted to give up.

17 It was not easy for their host, Ms. Disher, to listen to their arguments patiently.

18 So, she hurriedly, yet quietly, left.

19 Spork: Where is Ms. Disher? She has disappeared.

20 Knork: What should we do? Without Ms. Disher, this dinner is not complete.

21 Chopsticks: Where did she go?

22 Barehands: Let's go out to find her!

23 After hours of searching all over the Dining Republic, they finally found Ms. Disher sitting under a huge tree.

24 Spork, Knork, Chopsticks, Barehands: We're sorry we became boastful and ignored you.

25 Please forgive and come back and join us.

26 Ms. Disher: It's okay. I forgive you. Let's go back to my home.

27 Since then, every time they meet, they allow one another to eat in the manner that they please.

28 In their hearts they now know that food will always be delicious regardless of which utensils they use to eat it with.

### 시험대비 실력평가
p.86~89

01 ④　　　　　　02 argue

03 the best way to eat　　04 ④　　　05 ⑤

06 It has found that it is best to use a spoon and fork.

07 ⑤　　　　08 chopsticks　09 ③　　　10 ⑤

11 ⑤

12 They found Ms. Disher under a huge tree.

13 ③

14 They often talk about what they learned from their recent trips.

15 Like → Unlike, make up → make up for

16 ②　　　　17 ③　　　　18 ④

19 Barehands eats with its hands.　　　20 ④

21 ④

22 It's because it was not easy for her to listen to her friends' arguments patiently.

23 ⑤　　　　24 ⑤

25 They allow one another to eat in the manner that they please.

---

01 빈칸 (A)에는 '~을 보상하다'라는 의미를 완성하는 부사 up이 들어간다. ① pay attention to: ~에 주의를 기울이다 ② look up to: ~를 존경하다 ③ come up with: ~을 떠올리다 ④ put up with: ~을 참다, 견디다 ⑤ come across: 이해되다

02 사람들이 동의하지 않는 어떠한 것에 대해서 서로 화내어 말하다는 '논쟁하다(argue)'이다.

03 먹기에 가장 좋은 방법에 관한 것이 최근 주제였고 손님들이 논쟁하기 시작했다고 하였으므로 the best way to eat이 가장 적절하다.

04 Ms. Disher의 손님들이 종종 말하는 것은 그들이 최근 여행으로부터 배운 것이라고 하였다.

05 빈칸 (A)에는 비교급을 강조하는 부사(구)가 쓰여야 한다. 따라서 very는 적절하지 않다.

06 Spork는 최근 여행에서 숟가락과 포크가 함께 달려 있는 것을 사용하는 것이 가장 좋다는 것을 발견했다고 하였다.

07 (B)의 의미는 포크와 나이프를 사용하는 것이 가장 우아하다는 의미이다.

08 젓가락을 의미하는 말이다.

09 손으로 음식을 먹는 것은 촉각을 사용하므로 음식을 더 즐길 수 있게 되는 장점이 있다고 하였다.

10 모두의 언쟁으로 Ms. Disher가 사라지고, 친구들에 의해 그녀가 다시 발견되었을 때를 의미한다.

11 내용상 Spork, Knork, Chopsticks, Barehands가 Ms. Disher를 무시했다고 말하는 것이 자연스럽다.

12 그들은 Ms. Disher를 큰 나무 아래에서 찾았다고 하였다.

13 Ms. Disher는 친구들의 모험담을 듣고 싶어 한다고 하였다. be eager[dying] to V: 매우 ~하고 싶어 하다

14 Ms. Disher의 친구들은 그들의 최근 여행으로부터 배운 것에 관하여 종종 이야기한다고 하였다.

15 Ms. Disher의 가족은 다른 친구들만큼 여행을 다니지 않는다고 하였으므로 '~와는 달리'라는 의미의 전치사 Unlike가 적절하다. 친구들을 위한 저녁 식사 자리를 마련하면서 이것을 보상한다고 하였으므로 make up for가 적절하다. make up: ~을 이루다, 형성하다, ~와 화해하다

16 (A)는 to부정사의 형용사적 용법으로 쓰였다. ① 진주어 ② 형용사적 용법 ③ 부사적 용법(목적) ④ 부사적 용법(감정의 원인) ⑤ 부사적 용법(판단의 이유)

17 Spork에 따르면 포크는 고기를 먹기에 좋다고 하였다.

18 밑줄 친 (A)는 '아니야!'라는 의미로 상대방의 말에 동의하지 않을 때 쓰는 말이다. 따라서 ④번이 가장 적절하다.

19 Barehands는 손으로 식사한다고 하였다.

20 가주어로 쓰이는 것은 it이다. that은 가주어로 쓰일 수 없다.

21 서로 자신들이 좋아하는 방식으로 음식 먹는 것을 받아들이고 어떤 식기를 사용하여 먹는지에 상관없이 음식 맛은 언제나 좋을 거라는 것을 깨닫게 되었다고 하였으므로 '어떤 식기가 더 나은지'

에 관하여 논쟁하였음을 알 수 있다.

22 Ms. Disher가 서둘러서 떠난 이유는 친구들의 논쟁을 인내심을 가지고 듣는 것이 쉽지 않았기 때문이다.

23 각각 ① disappear ② complete ③ quietly ④ forgive의 반의어이며 tasty는 delicious의 동의어이다.

24 Ms. Disher는 그녀의 친구들을 용서하였으므로 계속 벌주고 싶어 했다는 것은 글의 내용과 맞지 않는다.

25 그들은 서로 자신들이 좋아하는 방식으로 음식 먹는 것을 받아들인다고 하였다.

---

## 서술형 시험대비　　　　　　p.90~91

01 친구들과 달리 Disher 부인의 가족은 여행을 자주 다니지 않는 것

02 Spork, Chopsticks, Knork, Barehands are close friends in the Dining Republic.

03 They travel a lot with their families.

04 the best way to eat

05 It was about the best way to eat.

06 using a knife and a fork, using a spoon and fork

07 A spoon is good for eating grains and soup.

08 You can use two of the same utensil and you can use them with just one hand.

09 a knife and a fork is

10 to listen

11 which utensils they use to eat it with

12 hours, sitting

13 They are sorry for becoming boastful and ignoring Ms. Disher.

14 with → without

---

01 앞 문장의 내용을 가리키는 말이다.

02 Ms. Disher의 친한 친구는 Spork, Chopsticks, Knork, Barehands라고 하였다.

03 Ms. Disher의 친구들은 그들의 가족들과 함께 여행을 많이 한다고 하였다.

04 Ms. Disher의 손님들은 음식을 먹는 가장 좋은 방법에 관해 논쟁하기 시작하였다.

05 가장 최근의 주제는 음식을 먹는 가장 좋은 방법에 관한 것이라고 하였다.

06 Knork는 숟가락과 포크가 함께 달려 있는 것을 사용하는 것보다 나이프와 포크를 사용하는 것이 훨씬 더 좋다고 생각한다.

07 Spork에 따르면 곡물과 국을 먹기에 좋은 것은 스푼이다.

08 Chopsticks에 따르면 젓가락은 같은 도구 두 개를 사용할 수 있다는 것과 한 손으로 사용할 수 있다는 장점을 가지고 있다.

---

09 Knork는 나이프와 포크를 들고 식사하는 것이 다른 식사 방법보다 더 우아하다고 생각한다.

10 가주어 It과 의미상의 주어 ‘for+목적격’이 있으므로 진주어 to부정사를 쓰는 것이 적절하다.

11 먹을 때 어떤 식기를 사용하여 먹는지에 상관없이 음식은 항상 맛있을 것이라는 것을 마음속으로 알고 있다는 의미이다. no matter which+명사 ~: 어떤 명사를 ~하든지

12 Ms. Disher가 커다란 나무 아래에 앉아 있는 것을 발견하는데 몇 시간이 걸렸다. It takes 시간 to V: V하는 데 ~만큼의 시간이 걸리다

13 Spork, Knork, Chopsticks, and Barehands는 자랑스러워하고 Ms. Disher를 무시한 것에 대해 미안해 한다.

14 위 글에 따르면 Ms. Disher의 손님들은 그녀가 없이는 저녁 식사가 완전해질 수 없다고 생각했으므로 with를 without으로 고치는 것이 적절하다. 혹은 couldn’t를 could로 고쳐도 좋다.

---

## 영역별 핵심문제　　　　　　p.93~97

| 01 ② | 02 ① | 03 ① | 04 ③ |

05 Which do you prefer to use when you eat fried chicken

06 It seems to me that ice cream is sweeter.

07 early　　08 ⑤

09 I usually leave some food on my plate.　10 ⑤

| 11 ④ | 12 ③ | 13 ② |

14 (1) posted　(2) spent　(3) of　(4) for　　15 ②

16 ②, ④　　17 important for children to eat

18 (1) of me to make　(2) for you to take

19 studying chimpanzees in Africa

20 (B)-(A)-(C)　　　　21 ④

22 She hosts a dinner for them.　　23 ⑤

24 ②　　25 ③　　26 touch, hands

27 ②

28 Catherine de Medici introduced the fork to France in 1533.

29 ③

---

01 be eager to+동사원형/for+명사 = ~을 열망하다, make up for = ~을 보상하다, ~을 보충하다

02 “ban”은 “금지하다”는 뜻으로 반대가 되는 것은 “allow”이다.

03 “아주 자랑스럽게 자신에 대하여 말하는”에 해당하는 것은 “뽐내는 boastful”이다.

04 “elegant”는 “우아한, 고상한”에 해당한다.

07 일찍 자기 때문에 일찍 식사를 한다는 것으로 보아 early가 적절하다.

08 배가 고파서 식사를 하자는 제안에 같이 식사를 하러 가자는 상

황이므로 상대의 말에 동의하는 "나도 그래. = So am I."가 적절하다.

09 밑줄 친 (A)의 내용은 앞에 나온 음식을 남긴다는 내용이다.

10 "you are still hungry"를 보면 배가 고파서 음식을 다 먹는다고 생각하는 것이므로 "finishing"이 적절하다.

11 중국에서 많은 음식을 먹지 말아야 한다는 것은 본문의 내용과는 다르다.

12 선호를 물어보는 의문사는 Which이다.

13 뒤에 이어지는 내용이 한 가지에 집중하는 것이 더 좋다는 것이므로 두 가지를 모두 할 수 없을 때에 해당하는 조건이 들어가는 것이 적절하다.

14 (1) '게시된' 것이므로 수동의 의미를 갖는 과거분사가 적절하다. (2) 돈이 '사용되는' 것이므로 수동의 의미를 갖는 과거분사가 적절하다. (3), (4) to부정사의 의미상의 주어는 'for+목적격'으로 나타낸다. 이때 문장에 쓰인 형용사가 사람의 성향, 성격을 나타내는 말일 때는 'of+목적격'으로 쓴다.

15 첫 번째 문장에서 to부정사의 의미상의 주어는 to부정사 바로 앞에 'for+목적격'으로 나타낸다. 두 번째 문장에서 그림이 '그려지는' 것이므로 수동의 의미를 갖는 과거분사가 적절하다.

16 ② It is quite silly of you to try to force him to consent.
④ He wore dirty shoes covered with dust.

17 진주어로 to부정사를 쓰고 의미상의 주어로 to부정사 바로 앞에 'for+목적격'으로 쓴다.

18 to부정사의 의미상의 주어는 'for+목적격'으로 나타내지만, 문장에 쓰인 형용사가 사람의 성향, 성격을 나타내는 말일 때는 'of+목적격'으로 쓴다.

19 분사에 다른 어구(목적어나 보어, 수식어구 등)가 함께 있을 때는 뒤에서 명사를 수식한다.

20 (B) Ms. Disher와 달리 그녀의 친구들은 가족들과 함께 여행을 많이 다님 - (A) Ms. Disher는 저녁 식사 자리를 마련함으로써 이것을 보상함. 친구들은 그들이 최근 여행에서 배운 것에 관해 말하고 - (C) 가장 최근의 주제는 음식을 먹는 가장 좋은 방법에 관한 것이었음

21 '~하는 것'이라는 의미의 관계대명사 what이 가장 적절하다.

22 Ms. Disher는 여행에서 돌아오는 친구들을 위하여 저녁 식사 자리를 마련한다고 하였다.

23 Ms. Disher는 친구들의 이야기를 기꺼이 들으려 한다고 하였다. 따라서 ⑤번이 가장 적절하다.

24 Knork는 나이프와 포크를 쓰는 것이 훨씬 더 좋다고 하였으므로 easier라고 쓰는 것이 적절하다.

25 젓가락은 한 손으로 잡고 쓰는 식기이다.

26 Barehands에 따르면, 손으로 먹을 때 음식을 보고, 냄새 맡고, 만질 수 있다.

27 위 글은 포크 사용의 역사에 관한 글이라고 보는 것이 가장 적절하다.

28 메디치가 프랑스에 포크를 도입한 것은 1533년이라고 하였다.

29 1000년 전에 많은 사람들에 의해 포크가 사용되지 않았다고 했을 뿐, 사람들이 주로 무엇으로 식사했는지는 위 글을 읽고 답할 수 없다.

---

### 단원별 예상문제 p.98~101

01 provide  02 ②  03 ③  04 ⑤
05 ③  06 ①  07 ⑤  08 ④
09 ③  10 ②  11 ①  12 ④
13 ⓐ, ⓒ, ⓔ, ⓖ
14 (1) planting  (2) planted  15 ②
16 She is always eager to listen to her friends' adventures.
17 She hosts a dinner for her friends coming back from their trips.
18 ④    19 any utensils, his guests  20 ④
21 It is on the left of the place setting.  22 ③

---

01 주어진 단어는 유의어 관계이다. ignore 무시하다, neglect 무시하다, provide 제공하다, supply 공급하다

02 "Rachel은 그녀의 아들을 매우 자랑한다." 자랑하는 = boastful

03 "have a meal 식사하다", "have trouble -ing ~하는 데 어려움을 겪다"

04 ① 그의 태도는 정중했지만 냉정했다. polite ② 나는 커피가 블랙인 것이 더 좋다 prefer ③ 당신의 신분을 증명할 뭔가를 제시할 수 있습니까? provide ④ 우리가 어떻게 학교의 수준을 높일 것인가 raise ⑤ 가장 흥미로운 도구는 손이에요. utensil

05 (A) 우리 ~하는 것이 어떠니? = Why don't we ~? ( B) 이유가 무엇이니? What is the reason?

06 자신이 선호하는 것에 대하여 그 이유를 설명하고 상대의 의견을 묻는 것으로 권유, 제안, 의견을 나타내는 "How about you?"가 적절하다.

07 이 대화에서는 저녁을 일찍 먹는 것과 늦게 먹는 것을 좋아하는 이유가 소개되어 있지만 식사하는 장소에 대한 언급은 없다.

08 "It seems to me that fish tastes better when it's uncooked."를 보면 Claire는 스시를 좋아하는 것을 알 수 있다.

09 ③ 둘 중에서 더 좋아하는 것을 고르는 경우에는 둘 중에 하나를 나타내는 "A or B"의 형태가 되어야 한다.

10 서로 좋아하는 음식에 대하여 선택을 하지만 음식의 가격에 대하여서는 언급되지 않았다.

11 첫 번째 문장에서는 foolish가 사람의 성향, 성격을 나타내는 말이므로 'of+목적격'이 적절하며 진주어로는 to부정사가 적절

19

하다. 두 번째 문장에서는 여자가 '뛰고 있는' 것이므로 진행의 의미를 갖는 현재분사가 적절하다.

12 의미상의 주어 앞에 전치사 for가 있으므로 빈칸에 사람의 성격을 나타내는 형용사인 generous는 알맞지 않다.

13 ⓑ throwing → thrown ⓓ walked → walking ⓕ of → for. cigarette butt: 담배꽁초

14 (1) 소녀가 나무를 '심고 있는' 것이므로 진행의 의미를 갖는 현재분사가 적절하다. (2) 나무가 '심겨져 있는' 것이므로 수동의 의미를 갖는 과거분사가 적절하다.

15 주어진 문장은 ①번의 내용과 대조를 이루며, ②번이 이끄는 문장의 지시대명사 this가 가리키는 것은 Ms. Disher의 가족들이 여행을 많이 하지 않는 것이다. 따라서 ②번이 가장 적절하다.

16 Ms. Disher는 항상 친구들의 모험을 듣고자 한다.

17 Ms. Disher는 여행에서 돌아오는 그녀의 친구들을 위하여 저녁 식사 자리를 마련한다고 하였다.

18 루이 14세는 뾰족한 칼을 사용하지 못하게 하였다. 따라서 ④번이 적절하다. keep A from Ving: A가 V하지 못하게 막다

19 provide A with B = provide B for A: A에게 B를 제공하다

20 위 글은 식기를 사용하는 방법을 조언하는 글이다.

21 빵 접시는 개인별 식기 세트의 왼쪽에 있다고 하였다.

22 (A) have trouble (in) Ving: V하는 데 어려움이 있다 (B) sit: (자동사) 앉다, seat(타동사) ~을 앉히다 (C) 혼란을 느낄 때는 과거분사

## 서술형 실전문제 p.102~103

01 How[What]

02 Blue looks much better on you than red.

03 the blue cap

04 (1) It is interesting for me to read the book.
  (2) It is necessary (for us) to keep silent in the library.

05 (1) It's good to walk on the leaves fallen on the road.
  (2) I found myself next to a young person listening to music.
  (3) That car made in England is very expensive.

06 (1) She showed me a letter filled with strange symbols.
  (2) The restaurant serving delicious food has kind staff.
  (3) We ordered rare steak, but it was too rare for all of us to eat.
  (4) It is really kind of you to remember my birthday.
  (5) It's exciting for me to go abroad.

07 It was because a host did not have to provide his guests with any utensils.

08 The knife is 'most certainly' the oldest eating utensil.

09 the pointed knives

10 There are chopsticks, a fork, and a knife and fork.

11 They searched all over the Dining Republic.

12 which utensils they use

01 "Do you have any suggestion?"에 대한 대답이기 때문에 제안을 나타내는 "How[What] about ~?"가 적절하다.

02 파란색이 너한테 훨씬 더 잘 어울려 = Blue looks much better on you, 빨간색보다 = than red

03 소년이 권하는 것은 파란 모자이므로 it이 가리키는 것은 the blue cap이다.

04 가주어 it을 사용하고 to부정사를 진주어로 쓴다. 의미상의 주어를 빠뜨리지 말아야 한다. 의미상의 주어가 일반적인 사람일 경우에는 보통 생략한다.

05 분사가 명사를 뒤에서 수식하는 경우에는 그 앞에 '주격 관계대명사+be 동사'가 생략된 것으로 생각할 수 있다.

06 (1) 이상한 기호로 '가득 채워진' 것이므로 수동의 의미를 갖는 과거분사가 적절하다. (2) 식당에서 맛있는 음식을 '제공하는' 것이므로 능동의 의미를 갖는 현재분사를 이용한다. (3), (4) to부정사의 의미상의 주어는 'for+목적격'으로 나타낸다. 이때 문장에 쓰인 형용사가 사람의 성향, 성격을 나타내는 말일 때는 'of+목적격'으로 쓴다. (5) 의미상의 주어로 'for+목적격'이 나왔으므로 진주어로 to부정사를 쓴다.

07 집주인이 손님들에게 어떠한 식기도 제공할 필요가 없었으므로 손님들은 자신의 칼을 가지고 다녔다고 하였다.

08 가장 오래된 식기는 칼이라고 하였다.

09 뾰족한 칼들을 가리키는 말이다.

10 식기류에는 젓가락, 포크, 그리고 나이프와 포크가 나와 있다.

11 Spork, Knork, Chopsticks, Barehands는 Ms. Disher가 사라진 것을 알고 식탁 공화국을 구석구석 뒤졌다.

12 결국 모든 친구들은 어떤 식기를 사용하여 식사를 하는지 신경 쓰지 않게 되었다.

## 창의사고력 서술형 문제 p.104

|모범답안|

01 different, utensil(s), use, convenient

02 It is very hard for him to walk on his broken leg.

03 to use the utensils on the outside, on the left of the place setting, on the right of the place setting

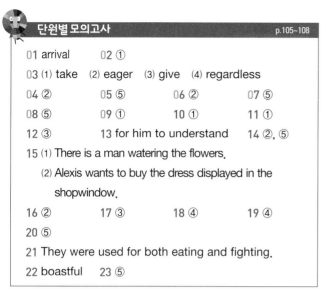

01 arrival　　　02 ①

03 (1) take　(2) eager　(3) give　(4) regardless

04 ②　　　　05 ⑤　　　　06 ②　　　　07 ⑤

08 ⑤　　　　09 ①　　　　10 ①　　　　11 ①

12 ③　　　　13 for him to understand　　14 ②, ⑤

15 (1) There is a man watering the flowers.

　　(2) Alexis wants to buy the dress displayed in the
　　　 shopwindow.

16 ②　　　　17 ③　　　　18 ④　　　　19 ④

20 ⑤

21 They were used for both eating and fighting.

22 boastful　　23 ⑤

01 두 단어의 관계는 동사-명사의 관계이다. argue 주장하다,
　 argument 주장, arrive 도착하다, arrival 도착

02 "식품으로 사용되는 밀, 옥수수, 쌀 같은 식물의 씨앗"은 "grain
　 곡식, 곡물"이다.

03 (1) take a break 휴식을 취하다 (2) be eager to ~하고 싶어
　 하다 (3) give up 포기하다 (4) regardless of ~에 관계없이

04 make up for 보상하다, 보충하다. / 그녀는 그녀의 실수를 보
　 상하기 위하여 열심히 노력했다.

05 자신의 의견을 나타내는 말은 "I think/believe ~", "In my
　 opinion,", "I'm sure ~" 등이다.

06 밑줄 친 that이 가리키는 것은 "I usually leave some food
　 on my plate."에 나온 내용이다.

07 중국과 한국에서 서로 예의 바르다고 생각하는 행동이 다른 것
　 에 대한 적절한 말은 ⑤이다.

08 주어진 문장은 어느 것을 먼저 해야 할지에 대한 조언을 듣고 마
　 지막에 결정한 사실이기 때문에 (E)에 들어가는 것이 적절하다.

09 뒤에 나오는 "Which do you prefer, having healthy food
　 or exercising, Emma?"를 보면 앞에서 having healthy
　 food와 exercising에 대한 언급이 있었음을 알 수 있다.

10 (A) 시간을 묻는 말은 "What time ~?"이다 (B) 이유가 무엇
　 인가? = What's the reason?

11 (가) 앞에 나온 원인에 이어지는 결과를 유도하는 so가 적절하
　 다. (나) 이유를 나타내는 부사절의 접속사 because가 적절하
　 다.

12 개를 '산책시키는' 것이므로 진행의 의미를 갖는 현재분사
　 walking으로 써야 한다.

13 to부정사의 의미상의 주어는 to부정사 바로 앞에 'for+목적격'
　 으로 나타낸다.

14 ① It isn't easy for the woman to climb a high
　 mountain. ③ There is a boy reading a book on the
　 bench. ④ I met the girl swimming in the pool.

15 가능한 한 짧게 쓰라고 했으므로 '주격 관계대명사+be동사'를

생략하고 분사가 뒤에서 수식하는 문장으로 쓴다.

16 빈칸 (A)에는 up이 쓰인다. ① pay attention to: ~에 주의를
　 기울이다 ② look up to: ~를 존경하다 ③ side by side: 나란
　 히 ④ turn out to be: ~으로 판명이 나다 ⑤ keep on Ving:
　 계속해서 V하다

17 easier는 사람의 성질에 해당하는 형용사가 아니므로 to부정사
　 의 의미상 주어로 'for+목적격'을 쓰는 것이 적절하다.

18 Barehands는 식사하기 위해서 식기를 쓰지 않고 맨손을 사용
　 하는 것을 선호한다.

19 등장인물들은 다양한 먹는 방법에 관해 이야기하고 있다. 따라
　 서 ④번이 가장 적절하다.

20 he가 지칭하는 것은 루이 14세 왕이며, 그는 뾰족한 칼을 좋아
　 하지 않았기 때문에 그것들의 사용을 금지하였다고 말하는 것이
　 자연스럽다.

21 중세 시대에 칼은 먹고 싸우기 위해 사용되었다.

22 누군가가 한 일이나 가진 것에 대해 아주 자랑스럽게 말하는 것은
　 '자랑하는(boastful)'이다.

23 Ms. Disher는 자신의 집으로 돌아가자고 제안했다. 따라서 ⑤
　 번이 적절하다.

# Lesson 3

# Learning from Nature's Genius

## 시험대비 실력평가
p.112

01 (1) (m)elt  (2) (t)iny

02 (1) application  (2) decision   03 ①

04 imitate   05 ④    06 ④    07 ②

01 주어진 보기의 단어는 반의어 관계이다. narrow 좁은, wide 넓은, melt 녹다, freeze 얼다, tiny 아주 작은, huge 거대한

02 보기에 주어진 단어는 동사–명사의 관계이다. absorb 흡수하다, absorption 흡수, apply 적용하다, application 적용, decide 결심하다, decision 결심

03 ①의 last는 "지속하다"의 뜻으로 동사로 쓰였다.

04 나는 기계를 발명하기 위하여 새의 날개를 모방하였기 때문에 "imitated"가 적절하다.

05 ① 다용도실 = an all-purpose room ② 놀라운 이야기 = an amazing story ③ 적용하다 = apply ④ 곤충 로봇에 관한 논문 = an article about a bug robot ⑤ 부리 = beak

06 "줄이다"는 뜻으로 "reduce"와 비슷한 말은 "diminish"이다. absorb 흡수하다, forgive 용서하다, decide 결심하다, explore 탐색하다

07 take a look at = 살펴보다, be good at = ~을 잘하다, 능숙하다

## 서술형 시험대비
p.113

01 inventive

02 (i)nsect

03 make

04 why

05 (s)top

06 (1) bite  (2) bug  (3) burns  (4) burrs

07 (1) search  (2) stuck  (3) result  (4) only

01 "그녀는 매우 창의적인 생각을 가지고 있다." / invent 발명하다, inventive 창의적인

02 주어진 단어는 유의어 관계이다. beak (새의) 부리, bill 부리, bug 곤충, 벌레, insect 곤충

03 • 그들은 지도자와 연락을 해야 한다. • 나는 일기장에 다음 회의를 메모해 놓을 것이다. make contact with = 연락하다, make

a note of = ~을 메모하다, 기록하다

04 • 나는 몸이 좀 아팠다. 그것이 내가 일찍 떠난 이유이다. • 나는 네가 그토록 늦은 이유를 알고 싶다. That's why ~. = 그것이 ~한 이유이다, the reason why = ~한 이유

05 keep A from -ing (A가 ~하지 못하게 하다) = stop A from -ing

06 (1) 모기에 물린 자리 = a mosquito bite (2) bug spray = 방충제 (3) 타다 = burn (4) burr = 가시 식물

07 (1) in search of = ~을 찾아서 (2) be stuck to = ~에 달라붙다 (3) as a result of ~ = ~의 결과로 (4) not only ... but also ~ = ...뿐만 아니라 또한 ~인

**교과서**
## Conversation

### 핵심 Check
p.114~115

1 Have you heard of a mosquito needle, Jian  2 ④

01 "~을 들어본 적이 있니?"는 "Have you heard of ~?"라고 한다.

## 교과서 대화문 익히기

### Check(√) True or False
p.116

1 T  2 T  3 F  4 T  5 F  6 F

## 교과서 확인학습
p.118~119

**Listen & Speak 1 A**

know, painted, don't / think, great / also, inventor / What, invent / dreamed of, drew, flying, looked like / Did, also make, machine / creative idea inspired, inventors

**Listen & Speak 1 B**

Have you, needle / Can, explain it / made this, imitating, mouth / how will / know, bites, very painful, needle, cause less pain / How come / less contact / think, useless

## 시험대비 기본평가  p.120

01 ①        02 ④        03 ③

01 로봇 소녀 Sophia가 60가지가 넘는 얼굴 표정을 보여 줄 수 있다는 것에 대하여 관심을 나타내는 말로 "be fascinated by"가 되어야 한다.

02 주원이의 방문이 특별하다는 말을 듣고 왜 그 방문이 그렇게 특별하다고 생각하는지 이유를 묻는 의미 "What makes ~?"가 들어가는 것이 적절하다.

03 (B) 양초 받침이 초를 오래 타도록 만들어 준다는 말에 대한 이유를 묻는다. (C) 양초가 녹을 때 받침대 아래 관에서 새로운 양초로 만들어진다는 설명을 하자 (A) 그 설명에 대한 관심을 표시한다.

## 시험대비 실력평가  p.121~122

01 ④      02 ①      03 ③      04 ①
05 ④      06 ⑤      07 ①      08 ⑤
09 ⑤      10 ④      11 ⑤

01 주어진 문장의 So는 결과를 유도하는 접속사이다. 다빈치가 새처럼 나는 기계를 꿈꾸었다는 문장 다음인 (D)가 적절한 위치이다.

02 많은 발명가들에게 영감을 주는 다빈치의 아이디어는 창의적이었다고 해야 자연스럽다. artistic 예술적인, usual 일상적인, common 평범한, ordinary 평범한

03 위 대화에서 모나리자를 그린 Leonardo da Vinci가 나는 것

을 꿈꾸어서 나는 기계를 발명하려고 했다는 것을 소개하지만 실제로 그 기계를 만들지는 못했기 때문에 ③은 이 대화를 통해 대답할 수 없다.

04 "Have you heard of a mosquito needle, Jian?"은 아는지를 묻는 말로 "You know ~, don't you?"에 해당한다.

05 새로운 "a mosquito needle"은 통증을 줄인다고 하였으므로 ④는 대화의 내용과 다르다.

06 주어진 빈칸에 들어가기에 적절한 말은 관심을 표현하는 말이지만, ⑤는 알고 있다는 의미로 빈칸에 적절하지 않다.

07 주어진 문장은 이유를 묻는 말로 3일 동안 염소처럼 산 것에 대한 이유를 묻는 의미로 (A)가 적절한 위치이다.

08 "I can't wait"는 매우 기대가 된다는 의미로 말하는 사람의 기대를 나타낸다.

09 a bug robot에 대한 관심을 표현하는 말로 "~에 매료되다"에 해당하는 "be fascinated by"가 적절하다.

10 빈칸에 들어가기에 적절한 말은 why이다. 이유를 말할 때는 why를 쓴다. ① which/that ② which/that ③ who ④ why ⑤ where

11 빈칸에 들어가는 것은 상대의 관심에 대하여 놀라움이나 흥미를 표현하는 말이 적절하다.

## 서술형 시험대비  p.123

01 I'm fascinated by
02 What
03 no → many
04 You know (that) Leonardo da Vinci painted the *Mona Lisa*, don't you?
05 dreamed, make
06 Are you aware of a mosquito needle, Jian?
07 How come

01 "~에 매료[매혹]되다"는 "be fascinated by"이다.

02 (B) 특별한 것이 무엇인지 물어보는 말로 문장의 주어 역할을 하는 의문대명사 what이 적절하다.

03 "She looks, talks, and even thinks like a human."을 보면 그 외에도 다른 능력이 많다고 하여야 한다.

04 "~에 대해서 알지?"라는 의미로 아는지 묻는 말은 "You know (that) ~, don't you?"이다.

06 아는지를 묻는 말로 aware를 포함하여 "Are you aware of ~?"가 적절하다.

07 빈칸에는 "어째서, 왜"의 뜻으로 이유를 묻는 "How come"이 적절하다.

**핵심 Check**                                    p.124~125

**1** (1) remembered   (2) economically   (3) but

**2** (1) who he is   (2) I may ask you a question

(3) how old I was

### 시험대비 기본평가                              p.126

01 ②            02 ③

03 (1) I'm wondering how many books you have read
until now.

(2) Do you know why an elephant has a trunk?

(3) Somi enjoys not only listening to music but
also painting pictures.

(4) He has not only a dog but also a cat.

01 간접의문문은 '의문사+주어+동사'의 순서로 쓰고, 의문사를 제
외한 문장의 주어와 동사는 평서문의 형태가 되어야 한다.

02 'not only A but also B'는 'A뿐만 아니라 B도'라는 뜻으로 두
개의 단어, 구, 절을 연결한다.

03 (1), (2) 간접의문문은 '의문사+주어+동사'의 순서로 쓴다. (3),
(4) 'A뿐 아니라 B도 역시'의 문장은 'not only A but also B'
의 형태로 쓴다.

### 시험대비 실력평가                              p.127~129

01 ②       02 ①       03 ③       04 ④

05 ⑤

06 He enjoys not only playing the guitar but also
dancing to the music.

07 how the bird entered the water so gracefully

08 ④            09 ③

10 Tell me why you met her last night.

11 (1) merely   (2) as well   (3) heathy   (4) getting

(5) knows   12 ②

13 He plays not only soccer but also tennis.

14 ①       15 ⑤       16 ④       17 ③

18 ②

19 (1) I don't know. When does this restaurant open?

(2) I wonder. Is this address correct?

(3) They are a couple in the movie. They are a
couple in the real world, too.

01 간접의문문은 '의문사+주어+동사'의 순서로 쓰므로 'Tell me
where you are going to have dinner.'로 쓰는 것이 적절하
다.

02 not only A but also B: A뿐 아니라 B도

03 'They didn't know' 다음에 의문사절 'how they could
reduce the noise'를 평서문의 형태로 바꿔 써야 한다.

04 not only A but also B = not only A but B = not only A
but B ~ as well. = B as well as A ④ not A but B: A가
아니라 B

05 첫 번째 문장에서는 빈칸 뒤에 완전한 절이 나오므로 what은
적절하지 않고 when 또한 어색하다. 두 번째 문장에서는 동사
bought의 목적어가 필요하므로 what이 적절하다.

06 'not only A but also B'에서 A와 B는 문법적으로 같은 형태
여야 하며, enjoy는 동명사를 목적어로 취하므로 sing을 동명사
dancing으로 써야 한다.

07 간접의문문이므로 '의문사+주어+동사'의 어순으로 쓴다.

08 'not only A but also B'는 'B as well as A'로 바꾸어 쓸 수
있으며 이때 동사의 수는 B에 맞춘다. ① Either A or B: A 또
는 B ② Neither A nor B: A도 B도 아니다

09 know의 목적어로 간접의문문이 나오는 경우이다. 의문사가 있
는 경우에는 '의문사+주어+동사'로 쓰고, 의문사가 없는 경우에
는 'if[whether]+주어+동사'의 어순으로 쓴다.

10 간접의문문에서 의문사가 주어인 경우에는 의문사 뒤에 바로 동
사가 이어진다.

11 (1), (2) not only A but also B = not merely A but also B
= not just A but also B = not simply A but also B = not
only A but B as well = B as well as A (3), (4) 'not only A
but also B'에서 A와 B는 문법적으로 같은 형태여야 한다. (4)에
서 is 다음에 not only가 나왔으므로 is에 대응하는 gets가 아니
라 getting에 대응하는 getting을 써야 함에 주의한다. (5) 'B as
well as A'에서 동사의 수는 B에 맞춘다.

12 ① jog → jogging ③ also → but also ④ are → is ⑤
our nation → for our nation

13 not only A but also B: A뿐만 아니라 B도

14 not only A but (also) B: A뿐만 아니라 B도

15 ⑤ 의문사구(how much)는 함께 붙여 써야 한다. ④번의 경우
동사가 guess이지만 Yes나 No로 답할 수 있으므로 의문사를 문
두에 쓰지 않았다.

16 'not only A but also B'에서 A와 B는 문법적으로 같은 형태여
야 하므로, loves에 맞추어 wants로 써야 한다.

17 첫 번째 문장에서는 'not only A but (also) B' 구문의 but이
적절하다. 두 번째 문장에서는 her job을 묻는 의문사 what이
적절하다.

18 believe 동사가 있으므로 의문사를 문두에 써야 한다. When do you believe you'll become a manager?

19 (1) '의문사+주어+동사' 순서의 간접의문문을 직접의문문의 어순인 '의문사+동사+주어'로 바꾼다. (2) 'whether+주어+동사'의 어순을 의문문의 어순으로 바꾼다. (3) 'B as well as A'를 A(in the movie)와 B(in the real world)로 따로 쓴다.

## 서술형 시험대비                                        p.130~131

01 (1) I'm wondering what your goal is this year.
   (2) Can you tell me if[whether] she called you last night?
   (3) Do you know who directed the movie?
   (4) What do you think I should wear?
   (5) Can you tell me what they are talking about?

02 (1) She wants to know if[whether] you are sick.
   (2) Can you tell me what children should wear in the swimming pool?
   (3) This tunnel is not only narrow but also dark.

03 (1) Dolphins can not only hear sounds clearly but also communicate over long distances.
   (2) He has experience as well as knowledge.

04 (1) It was not only strong but also easy to use.
   (2) He as well as you is responsible for the problem.
   (3) Not only do I study a lot, but I also play a lot.
   (4) Where do you think he might be?
   (5) I wonder if we will have good weather tomorrow.

05 why this computer won't turn on

06 (1) I want to learn tennis as well as taekwondo.
   (2) He treated me to cake as well as to lunch.
   (3) She composes good songs as well as likes playing the guitar.
   (4) His brothers as well as Mark want to go to the concert.

07 c. He wondered how high the bird could fly.

08 (1) The director as well as actors is invited to the party.
   (2) He looks not only smart but also friendly.
   (3) Cathy not only is a smart girl but also has a warm heart.
   (4) Do you know how old he is?
   (5) What do you believe is causing this symptom?

09 (1) Where is the key?
   (2) How did that happen?
   (3) Could we go there?
   (4) What is wrong with the computer?

01 (1), (5) 주절 뒤에 간접의문문을 '의문사+주어+동사'의 어순으로 쓴다. (2) 주절 뒤에 간접의문문을 'if[whether]+주어+동사'의 어순으로 쓴다. (3) 의문사가 주어인 경우에는 의문사 뒤에 바로 동사가 이어진다. (4) 주절에 think 동사가 있으므로 의문사를 문두로 보내야 한다.

02 (1), (2) 간접의문문은 '의문사 또는 if[whether]+주어+동사'의 순서로 쓴다. (3) not only A but (also) B: A뿐만 아니라 B도

03 not only A but also B = B as well as A: A뿐만 아니라 B도. B에 강조의 초점이 맞춰져 있다.

04 (1) 'not only A but also B'에서 A와 B는 문법적으로 같은 형태여야 하므로, strong에 맞추어 easy로 써야 한다. (2) 'B as well as A'에서 동사의 수는 B에 맞춘다. (3) 'Not only'가 문두에 나오면, 주어와 동사를 의문문 형식으로 도치시킨다. (4) 주절에 think 동사가 있으므로 의문사를 문두로 보내야 한다. (5) if가 이끄는 절이 wonder의 목적어로 쓰인 간접의문문(명사절)이므로 미래시제는 will을 써서 나타내야 한다.

05 직접의문문이 간접의문문이 될 때 '의문사+주어+동사'의 어순으로 쓴다.

06 (1)~(3) 'not only A but also B'는 'B as well as A'로 바꾸어 쓸 수 있다. (4) 'not only A but also B'와 'B as well as A'는 B에 동사의 수를 일치시킨다.

07 c. 하나의 의미 단위로 쓰이는 의문사구는 하나의 의문사로 취급하므로, '의문사구(how high)+주어(the bird)+동사(could fly)'의 어순으로 써야 한다.

08 (1) 'B as well as A'는 B에 동사의 수를 일치시킨다. (2) 'not only A but also B'에서 A와 B에는 대등한 형태의 말이 와야 한다. (3) 'not only A but also B'에서 A와 B에는 대등한 형태의 말이 와야 하므로 A와 B에 동사구가 오도록 고쳐야 한다. (4) 주절에 know 동사가 있는 간접의문문은 의문사를 문두로 보내지 않는다. (5) 주절에 believe 동사가 있는 간접의문문은 의문사를 문두로 보내야 한다.

09 간접의문문은 '의문사+주어+동사'의 어순으로 쓴다. 의문사가 없는 경우 의문사 대신 if나 whether를 쓰고, 의문사가 주어인 경우에는 의문사 뒤에 바로 동사가 이어진다. 이때 주절의 동사로 believe가 쓰인 경우 의문사를 맨 앞에 써야 한다.

교과서
## Reading

### 확인문제                                             p.132

1 T  2 T  3 F  4 F

### 확인문제                                             p.133

1 T  2 T  3 F  4 F  5 T

01 From, to, works fascinates us

02 not only, but also, it, solutions

03 one such person

04 how birds could fly

05 closely, made

06 Even though, successful, imitated, to try to make

07 Since, have, imitated, surprising abilities

08 Let's explore

09 high-speed train, had

10 entered, sudden increase, created

11 woke people up, caused

12 to solve, how they could reduce

13 the engineers was, in search of

14 saw, diving into

15 how the bird entered

16 studied more, discovered, narrow beak

17 redesigned, by imitating

18 not only, but also, with, less

19 One day, was hiking, with

20 On, home, burrs were stuck, hair

21 to know how that happened

22 took a closer look at, noticed that, were, straight

23 if he could apply, something useful

24 After, testing, invented

25 tiny needles, those of burrs, the other, hairy surface

26 were pressed, fastener

27 not only strong but also easy

28 Since, have used, different ways

29 is often used for

30 to play a number of

31 keeps, from floating

32 nothing useless, curious, ask

1 From flying birds to self-cleaning plants, the way nature works fascinates us.

2 Some people not only use nature but also imitate it to find solutions to their problems.

3 Leonardo da Vinci (1452–1519) was one such person.

4 He wondered how birds could fly.

5 He closely watched birds, made notes, and drew pictures of them.

6 Even though his invention was not successful, he imitated a bird's wings to try to make a flying machine.

7 Since then, more and more people have successfully imitated the surprising abilities of nature's genius.

8 Let's explore some of them.

9 The high-speed train was first made in Japan. But it had one problem.

10 When the train entered a tunnel, the sudden increase in air pressure created a very loud sound.

11 It often woke people up and caused headaches.

12 A team of engineers tried to solve the problem, but they didn't know how they could reduce the noise.

13 One day, one of the engineers was watching a bird in search of a meal.

14 He saw the bird quickly and quietly diving into the water.

15 He wondered how the bird entered the water so gracefully.

16 So, he studied more about the bird and discovered its long, narrow beak.

17 He redesigned the front of the train by imitating the bird's beak.

18 It was successful. Now the new train travels not only more quietly but also 10% faster with 15% less electricity.

19 One day, a Swiss engineer, George de Mestral, was hiking in the woods with his dog.

20 On his way home, he saw that burrs were stuck to his clothes and his dog's hair.

21 He wanted to know how that happened.

22 He took a closer look at the burrs and noticed that the ends of the burr needles were not straight.

23 He wondered if he could apply that to make something useful.

24 After a lot of testing, he finally invented two new materials.

25 One had many tiny needles like those of burrs and the other had a hairy surface.

26 When they were pressed together, they became a very good fastener.

27 It was not only strong but also easy to use.

28 Since then, many people have used his invention in many different ways.

29 It is often used for clothing, shoes, and bags.

30 Some people use it to play a number of different games.

31 In space, it keeps things from floating away.

32 There is nothing useless in nature. We just have to become curious and ask questions.

01 ②　　　　　02 ④

03 They not only use nature but also imitate it.

04 ④　　　　　05 He imitated the bird's beak.

06 searching　07 ⑤　　　　08 ③

09 (C)–(B)–(D)–(A)　　　　10 curious

11 It is often used for clothing, shoes, and bags.

12 ④　　　　13 ②　　　　14 ②　　　　15 ③

16 ④　　　　17 fascinated　18 ⑤

19 The sudden increase in air pressure created a very loud sound.

20 ④

21 how the bird entered the water so gracefully

22 ⑤　　　　23 needles　　24 ③

25 It is used to keep things from floating away.

26 ③

---

01 발명이 성공하진 못했지만 나는 기계를 만들기 위하여 새의 날개를 모방했다는 의미가 자연스럽다. 따라서 양보절 접속사 Even though가 적절하다.

02 레오나르도 다빈치의 발명은 성공적이지 않았다고 하였다.

03 어떤 사람들은 문제 해결을 위하여 자연을 이용할 뿐만 아니라 모방하기도 한다.

04 기존 기차의 문제점을 해결하였으므로 '성공적'이었다고 말하는 것이 적절하다.

05 공학자는 새의 부리를 모방하여 기차의 전면부를 다시 디자인하였다.

06 지각동사의 목적격 보어로 현재분사를 사용하여 (A)와 같은 의미의 문장을 완성할 수 있다.

07 최초의 초고속 열차는 터널에 들어갔을 때 기압의 상승으로 인해 매우 시끄러운 소리를 내는 것이 문제였다.

08 기차가 터널에 들어갈 때 갑작스러운 기압의 상승으로 인해 시끄러운 소음을 만들어내고, 이 소리에 사람들이 두통을 느낀다고 하였다.

09 (C) 개와 함께 하이킹을 하고 집으로 돌아오던 George de Mestral은 그의 옷과 개의 털에 가시식물이 붙어 있는 것을 봄 (B) 그 가시식물을 유심히 살펴봄 (D) 가시의 모양을 적용하여 유용한 것을 만들려고 하였고 두 개의 새로운 재료를 발명함 (A) 두 개의 재료 소개

10 무언가에 흥미를 가지고 더 알기를 원하는 것은 '호기심 많은(curious)'이다.

11 George가 발명한 것은 옷, 신발, 가방을 위해 사용된다고 하였다.

12 ⓐ는 완전한 절을 이끄는 명사절 접속사이다. ① 지시대명사

②, ③ 관계대명사 ④ 명사절 접속사 ⑤ 지시 부사

13 George de Mestral은 스위스 공학자라고 하였다.

14 주어진 문장의 one such person은 문제를 해결하기 위하여 자연을 모방하는 사람을 가리키며, ②번에 이어지는 문장의 대명사 He가 가리키는 것은 주어진 문장의 레오나르도 다빈치이다.

15 (A)는 동명사이다. 따라서 명사를 수식하는 현재분사 ③번이 답이다.

16 자연의 놀라운 능력을 성공적으로 모방한 사례를 살펴보자고 하였으므로 ④번이 가장 적절하다.

17 자연이 작동하는 방식은 우리를 매료시킨다는 문장의 수동태이므로 fascinate의 과거분사 형태를 쓰는 것이 적절하다.

18 이어지는 내용은 새에게서 빠르고 조용하게 이동하는 방법을 배웠다는 것이므로 ⑤번이 가장 적절하다.

19 기차가 터널로 들어갈 때 갑작스러운 기압의 상승으로 인해 시끄러운 소리를 낸다고 하였다.

20 다시 디자인한 기차는 예전 기차보다 10 퍼센트만큼 더 빠르게 달리고, 전기는 15 퍼센트만큼 덜 사용한다고 하였다.

21 새를 관찰한 후에, 공학자는 어떻게 새가 물에 그렇게 우아하게 들어가는지를 알아내기 위해 새에 관하여 더 연구했다고 하였다.

22 빈칸 (A)에는 '~인지 아닌지'라는 의미의 명사절 접속사 if[whether]가 쓰인다. 의문사가 없는 문장의 간접의문문을 만들 때 사용된다. ① how ② who ③ where ④ when ⑤ if[whether]

23 those는 복수명사 needles를 가리키는 말이다.

24 George de Mestral이 발명한 것은 튼튼하고 사용하기 편리하다.

25 George de Mestral이 발명한 고정 장치는 우주에서 물건이 떠다니지 않도록 하는 데 쓰이고 있다.

26 가시 식물의 가시는 끝이 곧지 않다고 하였다.

---

01 He wondered how birds could fly.

02 He closely watched birds, made notes, and drew pictures of them.

03 레오나르도 다빈치가 나는 기계를 만들기 위해서 새의 날개를 모방했을 때

04 He tried to make a flying machine.

05 가시가 자신의 옷과 개의 털에 들러붙은 것

06 He wondered if[whether] he could apply that to make something useful.

07 it keeps things from floating away

08 He noticed that the ends of the burr needles were not straight.

09 We have to become curious and ask questions.

10 (A) solve   (B) reduce   (C) imitating

11 He wondered how the bird entered the water so gracefully.

12 It had a long, narrow beak.

13 First, it travels more quietly. Second, it travels 10% faster with 15% less electricity.

14 Japan, air pressure, increased

01 wonder라는 동사의 목적어로 '의문사+주어+동사' 어순의 간접의문이 쓰이는 것에 유의하자.

02 레오나르도 다빈치는 새가 어떻게 날 수 있는지 궁금해서 새를 관찰하고 기록하고 새의 그림을 그렸다.

03 비록 성공적이지는 못했지만, 레오나르도 다빈치는 새의 날개를 모방하여 나는 기계를 만들었다고 하였다.

04 레오나르도 다빈치는 나는 기계를 만들려고 노력했다.

05 that은 앞 문장의 'burrs were stuck to his clothes and his dog's hair'를 가리키는 말이다.

06 '~인지 아닌지'라는 의미로 쓰이는 명사절 접속사 if 혹은 whether를 추가하여 문장을 완성할 수 있다.

07 fastener의 쓰임으로 보아 우주에서도 물건이 떠다니지 않게 하는 데 쓰인다고 말하는 것이 적절하다. keep Ving: 계속해서 V하다, keep A from Ving: A가 V하지 못하게 막다

08 George가 가시를 자세히 살펴보았을 때, 가시의 끝이 곧지 않은 것을 알아차렸다.

09 자연으로부터 배우기 위해서 우리는 호기심을 가지고 질문해야만 한다.

10 (A) 기차가 가진 소음 문제를 해결하려고 노력했다, (B) 하지만 소음을 줄이는 방법을 알 수 없었다, (C) 새의 부리를 모방함으로써 기차를 다시 디자인했다고 말하는 것이 가장 자연스럽다. by+Ving: V함으로써

11 공학자는 어떻게 새가 그렇게 우아하게 물속으로 들어가는지 궁금했다고 하였다.

12 공학자 중 한 명이 관찰한 새의 부리 모양은 길고 좁았다고 하였다.

13 다시 디자인한 기차는 예전 기차보다 더 조용히 달린다. 또한 15% 더 적은 전기를 사용하여 10%를 더 빠르게 달린다고 하였다.

14 일본에서 처음 만들어진 고속 열차가 가진 문제는 터널 안으로 들어갈 때 갑작스러운 기압 상승의 상승으로 인해 시끄러운 소리를 내는 것이었다.

p.145~149

영역별 핵심문제

01 ③          02 ⑤          03 ①          04 ③

05 I'm fascinated by what plants can do.

06 You know that polar bears are good at swimming, don't you?     07 ③

08 ⑤          09 ③

10 How come it's less painful?

11 ⑤          12 ⑤          13 ⑤          14 ①

15 ④          16 ③          17 ②

18 (1) She has not only a pretty face but also a warm heart.

(2) Success depends not only on talent, but also on effort.

(3) A goat eats fruit as well as leaves.

(4) Do you know what Chris had for lunch?

(5) I'm wondering if[whether] he will come back soon.

(6) When do you think he left home?

19 ④          20 (B)-(A)-(C)          21 ⑤

22 ⑤          23 ②

24 climbing a tall building with just one's hands and feet

25 ⑤          26 ③          27 ⑤

28 기차가 터널 안으로 들어가면 시끄러운 소리를 내는 것

29 ④

01 make contact with ~와 연락하다, be covered with ~로 덮여 있다

02 동사 decide의 명사형인 decision이 적절하다.

03 "지하로 지나가는 통로"는 "tunnel 터널, 굴"을 가리킨다. path 길, subway 지하철, transport 운송하다, vehicle 탈것

04 inspire는 "영감을 불어넣다"의 의미이다.

05 "~에 매혹되다"는 "be fascinated by"로 나타낸다.

06 "~을 잘 알지, 그렇지 않니?"는 "You know ~, don't you?"이다.

07 이어지는 설명을 보면, 주어진 빈칸에는 어떻게 그것이 가능한지를 묻는 "How's that possible?"이 적절하다.

08 상대가 아는지를 물어보는 말로 "~을 들어본 적이 있니?"에 해당하는 것은 "Have you heard of/about ~?"이다.

09 내용상 모기의 입을 모방하여 새로운 주사 바늘을 만들었다는 의미로 "모방하다"에 해당하는 "imitate"의 동명사 "imitating"이 적절하다.

10 모기의 입을 모방해서 새로 만든 주사 바늘은 이전보다 더 나은 것으로 "You know mosquito bites are not very painful, don't you?"를 보면 통증이 더 적다는 것을 알 수 있다.

11 상대에게 알고 있는지를 묻는 말은 "You know ~, don't you?", "Have you heard ~?", "Are you aware that ~?"

**12** "He dreamed of flying like a bird."를 보면 다빈치가 만들려고 한 것은 날 수 있는 기계였을 것이라고 생각할 수 있다.

**13** 다빈치는 나는 기계를 그림으로 남겼지만 직접 그 기계를 만들지는 못했다.

**14** ① 주절의 동사로 think가 쓰인 경우 의문사를 맨 앞에 써야 한다. ③ 주절의 동사로 guess가 쓰일 때는 의문사가 문두에 올 수도 있고 동사 뒤에 올 수도 있다.

**15** not only A but also B = B as well as A

**16** 간접의문문은 의문사가 있는 경우 '의문사+주어+동사'의 순서로 써야 한다.

**17** 'not only A but also B'나 'B as well as A'가 주어로 쓰일 경우 동사의 수는 B에 일치시켜야 하므로 ②의 동사 'like'를 'likes'로 쓰는 것이 적절하다.

**18** (1) not only A but (also) B: A뿐만 아니라 B도 (2) 'not only A but also B'에서 A와 B에는 대등한 형태의 말이 와야 한다. (3) not only A but also B = B as well as A (4) 간접의문문의 어순은 '의문사+주어+동사'이다. (5) if[whether]이 목적어로 쓰인 명사절이므로 미래는 미래시제로 나타낸다. (6) 주절의 동사로 think가 쓰인 경우 의문사를 맨 앞에 써야 한다.

**19** ⓑ 의문사가 주어인 간접의문문이므로 주어인 의문사 다음에 바로 동사를 평서문의 어순으로 쓴다. Do you know who made this cake? ⓒ 주절의 동사로 think가 있으므로 간접의문문의 의문사를 맨 앞으로 보내야 한다. Who do you think is suitable for the new project? ⓓ 'not only A but also B'가 주어로 쓰일 경우 동사의 수는 B에 일치시킨다. Not only my friends but also my teacher likes my idea. ⓕ 'not only A but also B'에서 A와 B에는 같은 성격의 말이 와야 한다. So he got a good score not only in the English test but also in the math test.

**20** (B) 레오나르도 다빈치는 새가 어떻게 날 수 있는지 궁금해서 새를 연구함 (A) 비록 그의 발명은 실패했지만 날 수 있는 기계를 만들기 위해 새의 날개를 모방했고 (C) 그때 이후로 점점 더 많은 사람들이 새의 날아다니는 능력을 성공적으로 모방해 왔음

**21** 자신의 문제에 대한 해결책을 발견하기 위해 자연을 모방하는 사람을 가리키는 말이다.

**22** 사람들이 성공적으로 자연을 모방한 사례를 의미하는 말이다.

**23** ②번에 이어지는 문장의 the new material은 주어진 문장에서 과학자들이 발명한 a new material이다..

**24** 단지 손과 발만을 이용해서 높은 건물을 올라가는 것을 의미한다.

**25** 과학자들이 만든 새로운 물질은 강할 뿐만 아니라 사용하기 쉽다고 하였다.

**26** 언제 무리가 떠나고 사냥할지를 결정하고 어디로 갈지 결정하고 위험이 있을 때 무엇을 할지 아는 것은 모두 지도력

(leadership)과 관련이 있다.

**27** decides에 병렬 연결되므로 knows라고 쓰는 것이 적절하다.

**28** 기차가 터널 안으로 들어가면 갑작스러운 기압의 상승으로 인해 시끄러운 소리를 내고, 이것이 승객들의 잠을 깨우고 두통을 야기한다고 하였다.

**29** 기차의 앞면을 다시 디자인하였다.

---

### 단원별 예상문제
p.150~153

| | | | |
|---|---|---|---|
| 01 (g)racefully | 02 ① | 03 ④ | 04 ④ |
| 05 ③ | 06 ④ | 07 ⑤ | 08 ④ |
| 09 ④ | | | |

10 Can you explain to me how much this machine costs?

11 (1) lovely (2) efficiently

12 (1) Do you know when your school festival started?
(2) She enjoys not merely running but also swimming.

13 ③

14 (1) I'm wondering if[whether] you have read the notice about the contest.
(2) What do you suppose you will do?

| 15 ⑤ | 16 ② | 17 ④ | 18 ④ |
|---|---|---|---|

19 (B) if (C) those (D) the other

20 They should be pressed together.

21 how they survive the heat

| 22 ④ | 23 ③ | 24 ④ |
|---|---|---|

---

**01** 주어진 단어는 유의어 관계이다. creative 창의적인, inventive 창의적인, gracefully 우아하게, graciously 우아하게

**02** "사람들은 다른 문화권의 전통에 끌리는 경우가 많다."는 의미로 "fascinate"가 적절하다.

**03** "어째서 ~인가?"는 "How come ~?"이다. "~는 어때?"에 해당하는 제안은 "How about ~?"이다.

**04** ① redesign ② pressure ③ reflect ④ solutions ⑤ reduce

**05** 이미 알고 있는지를 묻는 말은 know, hear, be aware 등으로 나타낼 수 있다.

**06** (A) 그것이 어떻게 도움이 되니? = how will that help? (B) 어째서 ~이니? = How come ~?

**07** 새로운 주사 바늘이 통증을 덜 초래하는 이유는 이미 밝혀진 상태이므로 어울리지 않는 것은 ⑤이다.

**08** (가)의 that은 동격의 명사절을 유도하는 접속사 that이다. ① 지시형용사 ② 관계대명사 ③ 지시대명사 ④ 접속사 ⑤ 관계대명사

09 염소가 산에서 뛰어노는 것을 본 것은 Thomas이다.

10 의문사구 'how much'를 함께 써야 한다.

11 'not only A but also B'에서 A와 B에는 대등한 형태의 말이 와야 한다. (1) healthy와 같은 형용사인 lovely가 적절하고, (2) 부사 hard에 맞춰 부사인 efficiently로 쓰는 것이 적절하다.

12 (1) Do you know의 목적어로 간접의문문을 '의문사+주어+동사'의 어순으로 쓴다. (2) not merely A but (also) B: A뿐만 아니라 B도

13 'not only A but also B'에서 A와 B에는 대등한 형태의 말이 와야 한다. study Latin의 study가 빠져야 한다.

14 (1) 의문사가 없으므로 주절 다음에 'if[whether]+주어+동사'의 어순으로 쓴다. (2) 주절의 동사로 suppose가 있으므로 간접의문문의 의문사를 맨 앞으로 보내야 한다.

15 첫 번째 문장에는 관계대명사 what, 두 번째 문장에는 간접의문문의 의문사로 eat의 목적어 what이 들어가야 한다.

16 'not only A but also B'에서 A와 B는 어법상 같은 성질의 것이어야 한다. at의 목적어로 동명사를 쓰는 것이 적절하다.

17 글의 내용으로 보아 ④번이 가장 적절하다.

18 George의 옷에 달라붙어 있던 것은 가시였다.

19 (B) '~인지 아닌지'라는 의미로 쓰이고 있으므로 if, (C) many tiny needles를 지칭하는 것이므로 those, (D) 둘 중 남은 하나를 가리키는 말은 the other이다.

20 아주 좋은 고정 장치로 쓰이기 위해서는 두 소재가 함께 붙어야 한다.

21 간접의문문의 어순은 '의문사+주어+동사'임에 유의한다.

22 사하라 사막의 개미들이 정오에 사냥하러 가는 것을 좋아한다는 말은 나와 있지 않다.

23 ③번 다음 문장의 them이 지칭하는 것은 주어진 문장의 birds이다.

24 위 글은 자연이 인간에게 영감을 주는 존재라는 것에 대하여 주로 말하고 있다.

### 서술형 실전문제
p.154~155

01 What's so special about her?

02 What

03 fascinating

04 can glide over water as well as swim well

05 (1) How do certain animals climb walls so easily?
   (2) What is the most important thing in life?
   (3) Was he sleepy or drunk?

06 (1) Do you know why she is crying?
   (2) What do you think she expected to happen as a result of her visit?
   (3) They not only made the cake but also ate it a lot.
   (4) You as well as your sister have to clean the room.

07 Is Spider-Man Possible in Real Life?

08 as well as

09 He saw that burrs were stuck to his clothes and his dog's hair.

10 가시의 끝 부분이 곧지 않은 것

11 One had many tiny needles like those of burrs and the other had a hairy surface.

01 무엇이 그리 특별한데? = What's so special?

02 그 외에 무엇인지를 묻는 말은 "What else ~?"이다.

03 사람을 매혹하는 의미로 사물이 사람의 감정을 생기게 할 때는 현재분사를 쓴다.

04 수영을 잘할 수 있을 뿐만 아니라 물 위로 활공할 수 있으므로 'as well as' 구문을 이용한다.

05 (1) 간접의문문으로 쓰인 문장을 '의문사+조동사+주어'의 의문문의 어순으로 바꾼다. (2) 주절의 동사 believe로 인해 의문사가 맨 앞으로 나간 것이므로 간접의문문을 '의문사+be동사+주어'의 의문문의 어순으로 바꾼다. (3) 의문사 없이 'if+주어+동사'의 간접의문문이므로 'be동사+주어'의 의문문의 어순으로 바꾼다.

06 (1) '의문사+주어+동사'의 어순으로 쓴다. (2) 주절의 동사로 think가 있으므로 간접의문문의 의문사를 맨 앞으로 보내야 한다. (3) 'not only A but also B'에서 A와 B에는 대등한 형태의 말이 와야 한다. (4) 'B as well as A'가 주어로 쓰일 경우 동사의 수는 B에 일치시킨다.

07 현실에서 스파이더맨이 가능한지에 관한 글이다.

08 not only A but also B = B as well as A: A뿐만 아니라 B도

09 집으로 오는 길에 George는 가시가 자신의 옷과 개의 털에 붙어 있는 것을 보았다.

10 가시가 자신의 옷과 개의 털에 붙은 이유가 가시의 끝 부분이 곧지 않은 것 때문이라고 생각하여, 이것을 유용한 무언가를 만들기 위해 사용할 수 있는지 궁금해 했다는 의미이다.

11 두 개의 새로운 재료 중 하나는 가시 식물과 같은 조그만 가시들이 많이 있는 것이었고, 다른 하나는 털로 덮인 표면이 있다고 하였다.

|모범답안|

01 fascinates / invention / Genius / imitate

02 not only as a door but also as a table for table tennis

03 how certain animals climb walls so easily / what their feet look like / how they stick to walls / sticks to any surface / strong / easy to use

01 imitate 모방하다, fascinate 매혹하다, redesign 다시 디자인 하다, genius 천재, invention 발명

02 이 문은 문으로도 쓰일 수 있고 탁구대로도 쓰일 수 있으므로 'not only A but also B' 구문을 이용한다.

01 fascination    02 ②

03 (1) genius   (2) fasteners   (3) dive   (4) front

04 ①     05 ②     06 slip into

07 ③     08 ①     09 ④     10 ③

11 ②     12 ⑤     13 ①

14 listening to music as well as running    15 ③

16 (1) as well as   (2) as well as

   (3) What does she do?

   (4) I don't know where I should go.

17 (D)─(B)─(A)─(C)

18 woke up, have headaches

19 ③     20 ⑤     21 ③

22 ⓐ, ⓒ, ⓓ - ⓑ, ⓔ     23 ②     24 ⑤

01 두 단어의 관계는 동사-명사의 관계이다. explore 탐험하다, exploration 탐험, fascinate 매혹하다, fascination 매혹

02 "새 입 위에 있는 딱딱하고 보통 뾰족한 부분"은 "새의 부리", 즉 beak이다.

03 (1) genius 천재 (2) fastener 잠금장치, 접착포 (3) dive 잠수 하다 (4) front 앞쪽

04 keep A from -ing = A가 ~하지 못하게 하다 / 그 요란한 소음 은 아기가 잠을 자지 못하게 했다.

05 "That's why"는 결과를 유도하는 표현이다. 좁은 틈으로 도망 가는 것의 결과는 잡기가 어렵다는 것이다.

06 "A bug robot can do the same"은 "some bugs can slip into narrow spaces"의 내용을 가리킨다.

07 "Yeah. That's why it's hard to catch them."이라는 대답 을 보면 Henry는 벌레가 좁은 틈으로 도망가는 것을 알고 있었 다.

08 주어진 문장은 처음 듣는 a mosquito needle에 대한 설명을 요청하는 문장으로 구체적인 설명이 시작되기 전인 (A)가 적절 한 위치이다.

09 ① a mosquito needle에 대해서 들은 적이 없는 것은 소녀이 다. ② 설명을 하는 사람은 소년이다. ③ 과학자들이 모방한 것 은 모기의 입이다. ⑤ 세상에 쓸모없는 것은 없다고 했다.

10 ① Do you know what this means? ② I wonder if[whether] you could point me in the right direction for the bus station. ④ I'm not sure if she will be our new leader in the near future. ⑤ Do you know why Jonathan left so early?

11 'not only A but also B'에서 A와 B에는 대등한 형태의 말 이 와야 한다. I like not only studying but also going hiking.

12 not A but B: A가 아니라 B

13 '~인지 아닌지'의 의미를 가진 의문사가 없는 간접의문문이므로 'if나 whether'가 적절하다.

14 B as well as A: A뿐만 아니라 B도. running이 나와 있으므 로 listen도 listening으로 써야 한다.

15 know의 목적어로 간접의문문을 이끄는 것이 자연스럽다.

16 (1), (2) not only A but also B = B as well as A (3), (4) 간접의문문의 어순은 '의문사+주어+동사'이다.

17 (D) 초고속 열차의 문제점 제시 (B) 이 문제점을 해결하려고 노 력하던 어느 날 먹이를 찾는 새를 관찰함 (A) 새가 빠르고 조용 히 물속으로 뛰어드는 것을 보고 새를 연구함 (C) 새의 부리를 모방함으로써 기차를 다시 디자인하여 기존 기차의 문제를 해결 함

18 기차가 터널에 들어가면 시끄러운 소리가 사람들의 잠을 깨우고 두통을 일으켰다고 하였다.

19 know의 목적어로 쓰이는 간접의문문이므로 how they could reduce라고 쓰는 것이 적절하다.

20 다시 디자인한 기차는 예전 기차보다 15 퍼센트 더 적은 전기로 10 퍼센트 더 빨리 이동한다고 하였으므로 ⑤번이 글의 내용과 일치한다.

21 이어지는 문장이 앞 문장의 결과를 이끌고 있으므로 ③번이 가 장 적절하다.

22 ⓐ, ⓒ, ⓓ는 벽을 쉽게 오르는 동물들을, ⓑ, ⓔ는 과학자들을 가리키는 말이다.

23 자연을 창조하는 것이 아니라 모방하는 것이므로 imitate라고 쓰 는 것이 적절하다.

24 점점 더 많은 사람들이 자연 속 천재의 능력을 성공적으로 모방해 왔다고 하였으므로 ⑤번은 글의 내용과 일치하지 않는다.는 것이 적절하다.

# I Don't See It That Way

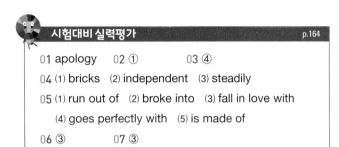

### 시험대비 실력평가    p.164

01 apology    02 ①      03 ④
04 (1) bricks   (2) independent   (3) steadily
05 (1) run out of   (2) broke into   (3) fall in love with
     (4) goes perfectly with   (5) is made of
06 ③        07 ③

01 주어진 단어는 동사와 명사의 관계를 나타낸다. apologize: 사
과하다, apology: 사과

02 '통제할 수 없는 방식으로 입과 코를 통해 갑작스럽고 요란하게
공기를 내보내다'를 의미하는 말은 sneeze(재채기하다)이다.

03 against: ~에 맞서, 반대하여

04 brick: 벽돌, independent: 독립적인, steadily: 꾸준히

05 fall in love with: ~와 사랑에 빠지다, go perfectly with: ~
와 잘 어울리다, be made of: ~로 만들어지다, break into: 침
입하다, run out of: ~이 다 떨어지다

06 주어진 문장에서 frame은 '누명을 씌우다'를 의미하며 이와 같은
의미로 쓰인 것은 ③번이다. 나머지는 모두 '틀'을 의미한다.

07 be afraid of: ~을 두려워하다, instead of: ~ 대신에, be made
of: ~로 만들어지다

### 서술형 시험대비    p.165

01 irresponsible
02 (1) impolite   (2) apology   (3) framed   (4) bricks
     (5) completely
03 (1) on your own   (2) his point of view
     (3) at least   (4) instead of
04 (1) The blooming flowers are very pretty, but they
     make me sneeze.
     (2) You deserve a rest after all that hard work.
     (3) A stork holds a fish in its beak.
05 (1) I never thought about his point of view.
     (2) I ran out of sugar.
     (3) Everything happens for a reason.
     (4) How does the company make money?

01 주어진 단어는 반의어 관계를 나타낸다. responsible: 책임감이
있는, irresponsible: 책임감이 없는

02 completely: 완전하게, frame: 누명을 씌우다, apology: 사
과, brick: 벽돌, impolite: 무례한

03 on one's own: 혼자서, point of view: 관점, 견해, at least: 적
어도, instead of: ~ 대신에

04 sneeze: 재채기하다, deserve: ~을 받을 만하다, beak: 부리,
stork: 황새

05 point of view: 관점, 견해, run out of: ~이 다 떨어지다,
make money: 돈을 벌다

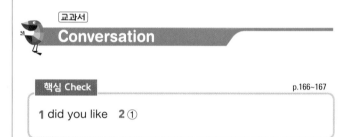

### 교과서 Conversation

#### 핵심 Check    p.166~167

1 did you like   2 ①

### 교과서 대화문 익히기

#### Check(√) True or False    p.168

1 T   2 F   3 F   4 F

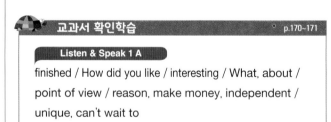

### 교과서 확인학습    p.170~171

##### Listen & Speak 1 A
finished / How did you like / interesting / What, about /
point of view / reason, make money, independent /
unique, can't wait to

##### Listen & Speak 1 B
How, like / compare, with / Which, better / enjoyed,
more, understand, characters / better, easier / both,
advantages

##### Listen & Speak 2 A
lose the soccer game / you think so / match against,
strongest / bright side, teamwork, that way

##### Listen & Speak 2 B
What, think / frightening / Why, think so / snake, ate
/ hat / interesting / decided, pilot instead of / At
least, what you mean

## 시험대비 기본평가     p.172

01 I'm looking forward to reading the book.
02 ⑤        03 (C) → (B) → (A) → (E) → (D)

01 I can't wait to ~ = I'm looking forward to ~ing: ~이 몹시 기대되다

03 (C) 이야기를 알고 있음을 대답 → (B) 거북이에 대한 의견 표현 → (A) 이유 질문 → (E) 거북이에 대한 이유 설명 → (D) 반대하는 의견 표현

## 시험대비 실력평가     p.173~174

01 ②     02 ④     03 ④     04 ①
05 (A) lose the soccer game   (B) Class 3
    (C) the strongest players
    (D) look on the bright side
06 ⑤       07 ⑤
08 What do you think about my drawing
09 (1) frightening   (2) snake   (3) ate an elephant
    (4) picture of a hat

01 주어진 문장은 책이 더 좋은 이유를 설명해 주고 있으므로 (B)에 들어가는 것이 적절하다.

02 ④ Brian은 이야기를 이해하기가 더 쉬워서 영화가 더 좋았다.

03 주어진 문장이 앞 문장의 the bright side를 설명해 주고 있으므로 (D)에 들어가는 것이 적절하다.

04 주원이는 축구 경기를 질까봐 걱정했다가 김 선생님과의 대화를 통해 용기를 얻었음을 알 수 있다.

05 나는 내일 우리 팀이 축구 경기에서 질까봐 걱정이 되었다. 나의 팀은 3반과 경기를 가질 것이다. 그들은 학교에서 가장 강한 선수들을 지녔다. 하지만 김 선생님은 내가 밝은 면을 보도록 하셨다. 그녀는 내게 우리의 강한 팀워크를 상기시키셨다. 나는 우리가 그들을 이길 수 있을 것이라고 생각한다. 나는 우리 팀원들과 다시 연습을 했다. 나는 경기를 기대하고 있다.

06 ⑤번을 제외한 나머지는 모두 이유를 묻는 표현이다.

07 'So, he didn't create something new?'라는 물음에 Ms. Parker는 'That's right.'라고 답하고 있다.

09 내가 Mike의 그림을 보았을 때, 매우 무시웠다. 왜냐하면 그것은 내게 코끼리를 먹은 뱀을 보여 주었기 때문이다. 반면에 Mike는 내게 많은 사람들이 그것을 모자 그림이라고 생각한다고 말했다. 그것은 매우 흥미로웠다. 나는 모든 사람들이 다른 관점들을 갖고 있다고 생각했다.

## 서술형 시험대비     p.175

01 point of view
02 Heungbu, Nolbu's
03 He wanted Heungbu to make money on his own and be independent.
04 (A) mean   (B) he didn't wake up the rabbit
    (C) sleeping   (D) responsible
05 (C) → (E) → (D) → (B) → (A)

02 태호가 읽은 책은 놀부의 관점에서 쓰인 흥부의 이야기이다.

03 그 책에서 놀부는 흥부가 스스로 돈을 벌고 자립할 수 있기를 바랐다.

04 Jack과 Sora는 '토끼와 거북이' 이야기에 대해 다른 의견을 갖고 있었다. Jack은 이야기에서 거북이가 못됐다고 주장했다. 왜냐하면 거북이는 토끼가 자고 있는 것을 보았지만 토끼를 깨우지 않았기 때문이다. 반면에 소라는 거북이가 그를 깨워야 할 책임이 없다고 주장했다.

05 (C) 영화와 책 중 선호하는 것 질문 → (E) 선호하는 것 대답 및 이유 설명 → (D) 반응 및 의견 표현 → (B) 반응 및 추측 표현 → (A) 동의 표현

**교과서**
# Grammar

## 핵심 Check     p.176~177

1 (1) hadn't had   (2) had happened
2 (1) to meet   (2) that

01 (1) see → to see   (2) accept → to accept

(3) meeting → to meet   (4) leave → left 또는 had left

(5) plays → played 또는 had played

02 I had played a computer game until my mom told me to stop playing it.

03 ②

04 (1) The bus had left when she reached the terminal.

(2) I knew her well, for I had often seen her.

(3) I found that I had lost my watch.

---

01 (1), (2), (3) 감정형용사 뒤에 to부정사가 쓰여 이유나 원인을 나타내는 문장. '주어+동사+감정형용사+to부정사' 어순이다. (4) 고객이 떠난 것은 내가 사무실에 도착했던 것보다 먼저 일어난 일이므로 leaves를 had left나 과거형 left로 고치는 것이 적절하다. (5) 엄마가 어렸을 때 연주했던 바이올린이므로 plays를 played나 had played로 쓰는 것이 적절하다.

02 엄마가 컴퓨터 게임을 그만하라고 하실 때까지 계속 컴퓨터 게임을 한 것이므로 계속 용법의 과거완료가 적절하다.

03 (1) 그녀가 터미널에 도착한 것보다 버스가 떠난 것이 앞선 사건이므로 had left가 적절하다. (2) 내가 그녀를 아는 이유는 이전에 종종 그녀를 보았다는 앞선 사건이 있기 때문이므로 had seen으로 쓰는 것이 적절하다. (3) 시계를 잃어버린 것이 알아차린 것보다 앞선 사건이므로 had lost로 쓰는 것이 적절하다.

01 뒤의 bought → had bought      02 ③

03 (1) (완)   (2) (경)   (3) (대)

04 (1) (to부정사를 이용) She was surprised to hear of his failure.

(부사절 that을 이용) She was surprised that she heard of his failure.

(2) (must be 이용) He must be mad to do such a thing.

(3) (과거완료 이용) She had left the door wide open.

(4) (전후 관계를 따져 과거완료 이용) All of my friends thought carefully what she had said.

05 (1) had read   (2) had played   (3) had gone

06 ②      07 ⑤      08 ①, ②      09 ③

10 (1) When I arrived home, I found someone had broken into my house.

(2) Rachel said that she had not seen her before.

(3) He had injured his leg so he couldn't play soccer.

(4) He had studied French for three years before he went to France.

11 (1) to   (2) be   (3) see

12 (1) picked → had picked   (2) that → to

13 ③      14 ③, ⑤

15 (1) She was disappointed that she got a bad grade.

(2) I was glad that I heard you're alive and well.

(3) She felt unhappy that she saw the accident.

(4) I feel very proud that I am a part of the team.

(5) I was somewhat surprised that I saw him.

16 ①

17 (1) ②   (2) didn't cleaned → hadn't cleaned

---

01 '네가 전에 사줬던 가방과 꼭 같은 가방을 산 것'으로 you가 산 것이 앞선 시제이므로 bought를 had bought로 고쳐야 한다.

02 나는 그 이야기를 읽고 정말로 충격 받았다. '감정 형용사+to부정사'로 to부정사 뒤에 오는 내용은 원인이나 이유를 나타낸다.

03 (1) 수지가 파티에 도착했을 때, Eric은 이미 집에 가고 없었다. (2) 그녀는 네가 그녀에게 말하기 전에 그 소문에 대해 들었던 적이 있니? (3) 나는 그가 그 전날 내게 거짓말을 한 것을 깨달았다.

04 (1) '감정 형용사+to부정사'로 to부정사 뒤에 오는 내용은 원인이나 이유를 나타낸다. to부정사 뒤에 오는 내용은 부사절 that을 이용하여 쓸 수도 있다. (2) 'must be 감정형용사 to부정사'이며 to부정사 뒤에 나오는 내용은 원인이나 이유를 나타낸다. (3) 과거완료는 'had+p.p.'로 'had left'를 쓴 5형식 문장이다. (4) 그녀가 말했던 것이 곰곰이 생각하는 것보다 앞선 사건이므로 had said로 쓴다.

05 (1) 경위를 설명하는 것보다 신문에서 읽은 것이 더 이전 상황이므로 had+p.p.로 쓴다. (2) 대과거로 표현하라는 지시에 따라 had played로 쓴다. (3) 이미 사라져 없어진 것이므로 had p.p.로 쓴다.

06 나는 어려운 상황에 대처하는 그녀의 능력에 놀랐다. 빈칸 뒤에 명사가 왔으므로 to부정사 자리가 아니다. be amazed at: ~에 놀라다

07 ⑤ Jenny was bored to study math for 3 hours. Jenny는 3시간 동안 수학 공부를 해서 지겨웠다.

08 ① '감정형용사+to부정사'로 to부정사 뒤에 오는 말은 원인이나 이유를 나타낸다. ② '감정형용사+to부정사'를 '감정형용사 that S+V'로 바꿔 쓸 수 있다. ③ solve →solved ④ solved → solve ⑤ solved → to solve

09 과거완료는 'had+p.p.'이므로 been이 들어가야 한다.

10 과거보다 앞선 시제를 과거완료로 나타내고 과거완료는 'had+ p.p.'로 쓰고 부정은 'had+not+p.p.'로 쓴다.

11 어법에 맞게 배열하면, (1) They were surprised to find that he had already left. (2) I'll be glad to get home. (3) I was sad to see them go.이다.

12 (1) Alice는 Ted가 전에 Jane과 딸기를 땄다는 것을 알고 있었다. 딸기를 같이 딴 것이 알고 있는 것보다 이전 상황이므로 had picked가 적절하다. (2) 나쁜 소식을 전해서 유감이에요. '감정 형용사+to부정사'이다. to부정사 뒤의 내용은 이유나 원인을 나타낸다.

13 ③ be anxious to부정사: ~하기를 열망하다. knowing을 to know로 바꾸어야 적절하다. ① 그들이 결혼했다는 소식을 들으면 슬플 거예요. ② 그녀는 의사가 되길 간절히 열망했다. ③ 그녀는 혈액검사 결과를 알고 싶어 했다. ④ 당신을 손님으로 맞게 되어 영광입니다. ⑤ 나는 그렇게 하면 기쁠 것이다.

14 아빠는 내가 비밀을 이야기하기 전에 그것을 알고 있었다. 과거완료는 had+p.p.로 쓰며 전후 관계를 명확하게 하는 부사절이 올 경우에는 주절에 과거 동사를 쓸 수 있다.

15 (1) 그녀는 나쁜 성적을 받아 실망했다. (2) 나는 네가 무사히 살아 있다는 소식을 듣고 기뻤어. (3) 그녀는 사고를 목격하고 매우 마음 아프게 생각했다. (4) 나는 이 팀의 일원이 된 것이 정말 자랑스럽습니다. (5) 나는 그를 보게 되어 약간 놀랐다.

16 Rachel이 지갑에서 돈을 꺼내러 갔을 때, 그는 누군가가 지갑을 가져간 것을 알았다. Rachel이 간 것보다 누군가가 지갑을 가져간 것이 앞서므로 앞선 것을 과거완료로 나타내는 것이 적절하다.

17 몇 주 동안 집을 치우지 않아서 집이 더러운 것이므로 치우지 않은 것이 이전 상황에 속한다. 그러므로 hadn't cleaned로 쓰는 것이 적절하다.

## 서술형 시험대비
p.182~183

01 (1) She had not told me it before she wore my clothes. 또는 She did not tell me it before she wore my clothes.

(2) I had never met such a beautiful girl before I met Jane. 또는 I didn't meet such a beautiful girl before I met Jane.

(3) All the tickets had been sold out when I entered the website.

(4) They had gone to work when he called.

02 (1) You must be proud of yourself.

(2) They are very proud to be Korean.

03 (1) glad to be  (2) proud to support

(3) anxious to finish  (4) am interested in

(5) very sad to hear  (6) had left

04 (1) is proud to  (2) be tired of

(3) be full of / be filled with

05 (1) I was very proud of myself as I had won the prize at the contest.

(2) I had no money as I had lost my wallet.

(3) My mother scolded my sister as my sister had bothered me.

06 around 2010, he had played soccer every day after school

07 (1) is diligent enough to clean

(2) is creative enough to make

08 happy to be with my friend

01 (1), (2)의 경우 before로 시간의 전후 관계가 명백하므로 과거 시제로도 쓸 수 있다. (3) 표를 사러 웹 사이트에 들어간 것보다 표가 매진된 것이 이전 상황이므로 과거완료 시제를 사용한다. (4) 그가 전화한 것보다 출근하고 없는 것이 이전 상황이므로 과거완료 시제를 사용한다.

02 be proud of+명사[대명사], be proud to부정사: ~을 자랑스러워하다

03 (1) 여행이 너무 힘들어서 난 집에 가면 기쁠 거야. (2) 나는 그들의 일을 지원해 줄 수 있어 자랑스럽다. (3) 그녀는 학교를 마치고 취직하기를 열망했다. (4) 나는 수학에 관심이 있다. (5) 우리는 네가 떠난다는 소식을 들어서 매우 슬퍼. (6) 그 원숭이들은 여행객들이 그들을 위해 남겨 둔 바나나를 먹었다.

04 (1) be proud to be+명사 (2) be tired of: ~에 지치다 (3) be full of = be filled with: ~로 가득 차 있다

05 (1) 나는 대회에서 상을 타서 내 자신이 매우 자랑스러웠다. (2) 나는 지갑을 잃어버려서 돈이 없었다. (3) 언니가 나를 괴롭혀서 엄마는 언니를 혼냈다.

06 '2010년쯤까지 방과 후 축구를 매일 했었다'를 경험을 나타내는 had p.p.를 사용한다.

07 (1) 그는 혼자서 축구장 청소를 할 만큼 부지런하다. (2) 두 컵으로 엔진을 만들 만큼 이 사진은 창의적이다.

08 나는 내 친구와 함께여서 행복하다. '감정형용사+to부정사'이며 to부정사 뒤에 나오는 내용은 감정에 대한 원인이나 이유가 된다.

35

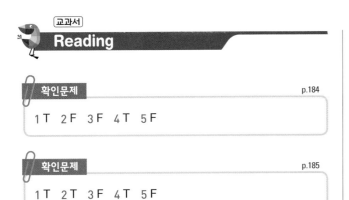

## Reading

p.184

**확인문제**

1 T  2 F  3 F  4 T  5 F

p.185

**확인문제**

1 T  2 T  3 F  4 T  5 F

### 교과서 확인학습 A
p.186~187

01 Welcome to, was taken to, for blowing down

02 the third little pig

03 what happened to

04 time to build our, with straw, sticks, bricks

05 completely blew down

06 blew down, made of, couldn't

07 How, doing now

08 shocked to lose, resting in

09 let's meet, tell us what happened

10 is wrong

11 about a sneeze, a terrible cold

12 What, mean

13 was making, for

14 ran out of, to ask, for

15 knocked on, fell down

16 called

17 had just grabbed, coming on

18 sneezed, sneeze, fell down

19 by what had happened

20 happened to

21 why did you go to

22 that cup of sugar

23 had built, of

24 called out, to trouble you, in

25 what he answered, bother me

26 How impolite, deserved, knocking

27 When, came, breaking into

28 were framed

29 going to borrow, exciting

30 Could, lend me

31 which do you think is

### 교과서 확인학습 B
p.188~189

1 Reporter: Welcome to Animal World News. Last Sunday, a wolf was taken to the police station for blowing down pigs' houses.

2 Today, we have the third little pig and the wolf with us.

3 Mr. Pig, could you explain what happened to you and your brothers?

4 Pig: Yes. My brothers and I thought it was time to build our own houses, so we built houses with straw, sticks, and bricks.

5 One day, the wolf came and completely blew down my brothers' houses.

6 He almost blew down my house, but it was made of bricks, so he couldn't.

7 Reporter: How are your brothers doing now?

8 Pig: They are shocked to lose their houses. They are resting in my house.

9 Reporter: Thank you, Mr. Pig. Now, let's meet our second guest, the wolf. Mr. Wolf, could you tell us what happened?

10 Wolf: This whole "Big Bad Wolf" thing is wrong.

11 The real story is about a sneeze from a terrible cold and a cup of sugar.

12 Reporter: What do you mean?

13 Wolf: Back then, I was making a birthday cake for my dear old grandmother.

14 I ran out of sugar. I walked down the street to ask my neighbor for a cup of sugar.

15 When I knocked on the door, it fell down.

16 Then I called, "Little pig, are you in?"

17 I had just grabbed the broken door when I felt a sneeze coming on.

18 I sneezed a great sneeze and you know what? The whole straw house fell down.

19 I was very surprised by what had happened.

20 Unfortunately, the same thing happened to the second little pig's house.

21 Reporter: Then why did you go to the third little pig's house?

22 Wolf: I still needed that cup of sugar, so I went to the next house.

23 The third little pig had built his house of bricks.

24 I called out, "I'm sorry to trouble you, but are you in?"

25 And do you know what he answered? "Go away. Don't bother me again!"

26 How impolite! I thought I deserved an apology, so I kept knocking.

27 When the police came, of course they thought I was breaking into this pig's house.

28 Reporter: Do you think you were framed?

29 Wolf: Yes. The news reporters of the town thought a sick wolf going to borrow a cup of sugar didn't sound very exciting.

30 So, they made me the "Big Bad Wolf." Could you maybe lend me a cup of sugar?

31 Reporter: Thank you for your time. Everyone, which do you think is the true story, the pig's or the wolf's?

## 시험대비 실력평가
p.190~193

01 ③         02 ④

03 It's because they thought it was time to build their own houses.

04 ②         05 sneeze      06 ④        07 ④

08 It was made of straw.      09 ⑤

10 exciting    11 ④         12 ③        13 ④

14 ③         15 explain

16 build their own houses, straw sticks, bricks

17 what happened          18 (B)—(A)—(C)

19 ④         20 ⑤         21 ②        22 ④

23 ④

24 The wolf thinks that the news reporters of the town made him the "Big Bad Wolf" because they thought a sick wolf going to borrow a cup of sugar didn't sound very exciting.

01 대답으로 미루어 보아 형제들의 현재 상태를 묻는 말이 들어가는 것이 가장 자연스럽다.

02 돼지 삼형제는 지푸라기, 막대, 벽돌로 집을 지었다고 하였다.

03 돼지 삼형제가 집을 지은 이유는 자신들의 집을 지을 때라고 생각했기 때문이다.

04 인터뷰 손님으로 셋째 돼지와 늑대가 왔다고 하였다.

05 늑대의 답변으로 보아 모든 사건은 늑대의 재채기와 설탕 한 컵으로 인한 것이었음을 알 수 있다.

06 늑대의 입장에서는 '불행히도' 두 번째 집에서도 똑같은 일이 발생했다고 말하는 것이 가장 자연스럽다.

07 지각동사 feel의 목적격보어로 동사원형, 현재분사, 과거분사가 쓰일 수 있으며, 재채기를 할 것 같았다는 의미이므로 coming이나 come을 쓰는 것이 적절하다.

08 늑대의 말에 따르면 첫 번째 이웃의 집은 지푸라기로 만들어졌다.

09 사과를 받을 만하다고 생각했다고 하였으므로 무례하다고 말하

는 것이 적절하다.

10 감정을 유발하는 것은 현재분사형 형용사를 쓴다.

11 여전히 설탕이 필요했기 때문에 세 번째 돼지의 집으로 갔다고 하였으므로, 늑대가 세 번째 돼지의 집으로 산 이유는 ④번이 가장 적절하다.

12 늑대는 돼지의 집을 침입할 의도가 아니었다.

13 빈칸 (A)에는 '이유'를 나타내는 전치사 for가 들어간다. ① take care of: ~을 돌보다 ② rely on: ~에 의존하다 ③ die of: ~으로 죽다 ④ except for: ~을 제외하고 ⑤ break down: 고장나다

14 위 글은 뉴스 진행자가 돼지와 늑대를 인터뷰하는 글이다.

15 무언가를 분명하고 이해하기 쉽게 만드는 것은 '설명하다(explain)'이다.

16 그들의 집을 짓기 위해서 세 마리의 돼지는 짚, 나무 막대기, 벽돌을 사용했다.

17 의문대명사 what을 이용하여 간접의문문 문장을 만들 수 있다.

18 (B) 할머니 생일 케이크를 만들던 중 설탕이 다 떨어져 이웃집 문을 두드림 → (A) 문이 떨어졌고, 부서진 문을 움켜잡았을 때 재채기가 나오는 걸 느낌 → (C) 재채기를 아주 크게 함

19 '같은 일'이라는 것은 '그의 재채기로 인하여 집이 무너진 것'을 의미한다.

20 글의 내용으로 보아 늑대는 돼지들의 집을 무너지게 할 의도가 없었음을 알 수 있다.

21 간접의문문은 '의문사+주어+동사+'의 어순으로 쓰지만, 생각 동사 think, believe, guess, suppose 등은 의문사를 문두로 보낸다. 따라서 ②번은 적절하지 않다.

22 돼지의 응답이 무례하다고 생각했기 때문에 사과를 받아 마땅하다고 말하는 것이 적절하다.

23 셋째 아기 돼지는 늑대에게 다시는 귀찮게 하지 말라며 무례하게 대했다.

24 마을의 신문 기자들은 설탕 한 컵을 빌리려는 아픈 늑대가 별로 흥미롭지 않다고 생각했기 때문에 늑대를 '덩치 크고 못된 늑대'로 만든 것이라고 늑대는 생각한다.

## 서술형 시험대비
p.194~195

01 Because he blew down pigs' houses.

02 It is made of bricks.

03 They are so shocked to lose their houses and they are resting at the third little pig's house.

04 There are the third little pig and the wolf as guests

of Animal World News.

05 What do you mean?

06 He was making a birthday cake for his grandmother.

07 He walked down the street in order to ask his neighbor for a cup of sugar.

08 It fell down.

09 It's because the wolf sneezed a great sneeze.

10 had visited

11 it was impolite

12 apology

13 ④번 → borrow

14 breaking into, knocking, was framed

01 늑대가 경찰에 잡혀간 이유는 돼지들의 집을 불어 넘어뜨렸기 때문이다.

02 셋째 돼지의 말에 따르면 그의 집은 벽돌로 만들어졌다.

03 첫째 아기 돼지와 둘째 아기 돼지는 집을 잃고 충격을 받아서 셋째 아기 돼지의 집에서 쉬고 있다고 하였다.

04 Animal World News에 셋째 아기 돼지와 늑대가 손님으로 왔다.

05 mean: 의미하다

06 늑대는 할머니를 위한 생일 케이크를 만들던 중이었다.

07 늑대는 이웃에게 설탕 한 컵을 달라고 하기 위해 길을 걸어갔다고 하였다.

08 늑대가 이웃의 문을 두드렸을 때 문이 떨어졌다고 하였다.

09 늑대가 재채기를 아주 크게 했기 때문에 짚으로 만든 집 전체가 무너졌다.

10 설탕을 얻기 위해 셋째 아기 돼지의 집으로 가기 전 다른 집들을 방문했었다는 사실을 유추할 수 있다.

11 늑대는 돼지의 말이 무례하다고 생각했다.

12 당신이 무언가에 관해 미안하다고 말하는 것은 '사과(apology)'이다.

13 글의 내용상 늑대는 설탕을 빌려주려던 것이 아니라 빌리려던 것이다. 따라서 lend가 아닌 borrow를 쓰는 것이 적절하다.

14 해석: 경찰은 늑대가 돼지의 집을 침입하고 있다고 생각했지만 사실 늑대는 문을 두드리고 있던 중이었다고 말한다. 늑대는 또한 자신이 누명을 썼다고 주장한다.

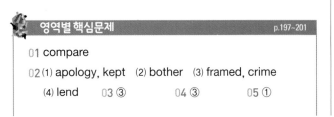

**영역별 핵심문제**            p.197~201

01 compare

02 (1) apology, kept (2) bother (3) framed, crime
(4) lend    03 ③      04 ③      05 ①

06 ⓐ the rabbit, ⓑ the turtle      07 ⑤

08 ④          09 ⑤

10 He was worried because Class 3 has the strongest players in the school.

11 It is the best teamwork.    12 ①

13 (1) They will be excited to teach you again.
(2) I was scared to be left home alone.
(3) She answered that she would be happy to come.

14 ①, ②, ③

15 He had already left when I got to the airport.

16 I would be glad to pick you up at the airport.

17 (1) I fought with my sister when I saw that she had made my clothes dirty.
(2) We were embarrassed when we knew that our car had gone.
(3) I cried when I brought to mind that my boyfriend had forgotten our anniversary.

18 ①

19 She was sad to let him leave.

20 (1) lost in the race because he had taken a nap during the race
(2) was happy to win the race

21 ②      22 ③      23 ⑤      24 ④

25 ②      26 ⑤

01 주어진 단어는 명사와 동사의 관계를 나타낸다. comparison: 비교, compare: 비교하다

02 apology: 사과, keep ~ing: 계속 ~하다, bother: 괴롭히다, frame: 누명을 씌우다, crime: 범죄, lend: 빌려주다

03 '사람이 법에 의해 처벌받을 수 있는 불법적인 행동이나 행위'를 가리키는 말은 crime(범죄)이다.

04 I can't wait to ~: 너무 ~하고 싶다, be taken to: ~에 끌려가다, run out of: ~이 다 떨어지다, point of view: 관점, 견해

05 밑줄 친 (A)는 '못된, 나쁜'을 의미하며 이와 같은 의미로 쓰인 것은 ①번이다. 나머지는 모두 '의미하다'를 뜻한다.

07 ⑤ Jack이 거북과 토끼의 경주가 공정하지 않다고 생각하는지는 알 수 없다.

08 (A) 선행사 a snake에 대한 주격 관계대명사로 that, (B) 뒤에 명사가 이어지므로 instead of, (C) 선행사를 포함하는 관계대명사 what이 적절하다.

09 위 대화를 통해 Mike가 무슨 모자를 그렸는지 알 수 없다.

10 그는 학교에서 가장 강한 선수들이 3반에 있기 때문에 걱정했다.

11 주원이네 반의 강점은 팀워크가 가장 좋다는 것이다.

12 이어지는 설명에서 너무 작고 신기가 어렵다는 불편함을 나타내고 있으므로 좋아한다는 대답과 어울리지 않는다.

13 (1) 그들은 너희를 다시 가르치게 되어 신이 날 것이다. (2) 나는 집에 홀로 남겨져서 무서웠다. (3) 그녀가 기꺼이 오겠다고 대답했다.

14 나는 우리가 코로나 19에 대한 실험이 성공했기 때문에 기뻤다. ② 나는 그때까지는 아픈 적이 없었다. ③ 그녀는 그녀의 오빠가 거기에 가고 싶어 한다는 것을 몰랐다. ④ '감정형용사+to부정사' 구문으로 to부정사 뒤에는 동사원형이 와야 한다. 명사가 올 경우에 proud는 to를 of로 고치는 것이 적절하다. ⑤ 그는 그의 남동생에게 화났다. be angry with를 써야 하므로 to를 with로 고치는 것이 적절하다.

15 과거완료는 had+p.p.로 쓰기 때문에 내가 공항에 도착한 것보다 그가 떠난 것이 이전 상황이므로 떠나고 없었다는 내용에 과거완료시제를 사용한다.

16 '감정형용사+to부정사'로 to부정사 뒤에 나오는 내용은 감정의 원인이나 이유를 나타낸다.

17 3개 문장 모두 과거에 있었던 일을 쓴 것이다. 과거 상황에서도 사건의 전후 관계가 있는 것으로 앞서 일어난 상황에는 had p.p.를 써서 영작하는 것이 적절하다.

18 ① 나는 그를 다시 보게 되어 기뻤다. '감정형용사+to부정사' 문장으로 that을 to로 고치는 것이 적절하다.

19 감정형용사+to부정사'로 to부정사 뒤에 나오는 내용은 감정의 원인이나 이유를 나타낸다.

20 (1) 토끼는 경기 도중 낮잠을 잤기 때문에 경기에서 졌다. (2) 거북이는 경기에서 이겨 기뻤다.

21 뉴스에서 셋째 아기 돼지와 늑대를 모셨다고 하였으므로 돼지와 늑대의 인터뷰가 이어진다고 보는 것이 가장 적절하다.

22 Reporter는 뉴스에서 이야기를 하고 있는 중이다.

23 밑줄 친 (A)는 감정의 원인을 나타내는 to부정사이다. ⑤번은 판단의 근거를 나타내고 있다.

24 돼지는 늑대가 자신의 형제들의 집을 날려버린 사건에 대해 주로 이야기하고 있다.

25 늑대는 자신의 이야기가 진짜 이야기라며 이에 관하여 서술하고 있으므로 "덩치 크고 못된 늑대" 사건은 옳지 않다고 말하는 것이 적절하다. right→wrong

26 늑대가 케이크를 언제 만들고 있었는지는 위 글을 읽고 답할 수 없다.

### 단원별 예상문제
p.202~205

01 (1) (o)bjects  (2) responsible  (3) steadily  (4) stepmother

02 (1) grabbed  (2) straw  (3) framed  (4) sneeze
   (5) trouble

03 (1) My house was too weak for the wolf to blow down.
   (2) Let's take a look at this picture together.

---

(3) I think it goes perfectly with your skirt.

04 ⓒ → wake him up    05 ⑤

06 ⓐ → frightening    07 ⑤

08 ⓒ → (to) understand

09 (A) the book  (B) the movie  (C) the book helped her understand the characters better
   (D) the movie  (E) to understand the story

10 ⑤

11 (1) enjoyed helping  (2) had told  (3) was happy to

12 (1) I told my mother that I had finished my homework.
   (2) It was written that my aunt had wanted to give a doll to her daughter.
   (3) He told me that he had wanted to play in Manchester.

13 ③

14 We were unfortunate to lose the game.

15 ⑤

**16 재채기를 하자 짚으로 만든 집이 무너진 것**  17 ④

18 ⑤            19 He kept knocking.    20 ④

---

01 object: 물체, 물건, responsible: 책임이 있는, steadily: 꾸준히, stepmother: 계모

02 frame: 누명을 씌우다, straw: 짚, 지푸라기, grab: 붙잡다, trouble: 귀찮게 하다, sneeze: 재채기하다

03 blow down: 바람을 불어 넘어뜨리다, take a look at: ~을 살펴보다, go perfectly with: ~와 매우 잘 어울리다

04 이어동사의 목적어가 인칭대명사일 때 대명사는 동사와 부사 사이에 위치한다.

05 '토끼와 거북이' 이야기에서 누가 공정한지 알 수 없다.

06 frightening: 무서운

08 help는 목적격보어로 동명사를 취하지 않는다.

09 Brian과 Yura는 영화 'Good Friends'에 대해 이야기했다. 그들은 그것에 대해 다른 의견을 갖고 있었다. Yura는 영화보다 책을 선호했다. 왜냐하면 책은 그녀가 인물들을 이해하는 데 도움이 되었기 때문이다. 반면에 Brian은 영화를 더 좋아했다. 왜냐하면 그가 이야기를 이해하는 것이 더 쉬웠기 때문이다. 그들은 그것들 둘 다 각각의 장점이 있다는데 동의했다.

10 위 대화를 통해 유라가 생각하는 영화의 단점은 알 수 없다.

11 (1) 나는 아빠를 도와서 즐거웠다. (2) 나는 그녀가 회의 중 말했던 아이디어에 대해 계획을 만들었다. (3) 나는 할머니에게 핸드폰 사용에 대해 알려드려 기뻤다.

12 대과거는 had+p.p.로 쓴다.

13 ③ 나는 불에 타고 있는 빌딩을 보고 충격 받았다. that → to ①

왕자는 신데렐라를 찾아서 행복했다. ② 너를 여기서 만나 반가워. ④ 내 친구들은 그 소식을 듣고 유감스러웠다. ⑤ 나는 파티에 초대되어 흥분했다.

14 '감정형용사+to부정사' 구문으로 to부정사는 부사적 용법으로 사용되었다.

15 늑대의 말로 보아 지독한 감기로 인한 재채기와 설탕 한 컵에 관한 것임을 알 수 있다.

16 재채기를 하자 짚으로 만든 집이 무너져 늑대가 놀란 것이다.

17 늑대가 부서진 문을 막 움켜잡았을 때 재채기가 나오는 것을 느꼈다고 하였다.

18 돼지와 늑대의 이야기라는 의미이므로 the pig's or the wolf's 가 적절하다.

19 사과 받기를 원했던 늑대는 셋째 아기 돼지의 집 문을 계속 두드렸다고 하였다.

20 늑대를 인터뷰하고 있는 Reporter가 늑대의 말을 믿는다는 말은 위 글에 나와 있지 않다.

## 서술형 실전문제 p.206~207

01 She thinks it is the greatest piece of art of the 20th century.

02 He used real-life objects to create art.

03 He simply wanted people to look at the objects in a different way.

04 (1) Suji was bored to read a boring book.
(2) Suji was happy to see her brother enjoy the party.
(3) Suji was excited to join a popular club in her school.
(4) Suji was surprised to receive a present that she hadn't think ever.

05 went, was glad to, told, knew, had seen

06 Because they lost their houses due to the wolf.

07 could you explain what happened to you and your brothers?

08 (A) deserved   (B) knocking   (C) breaking

09 He visited pigs' houses in order to borrow a cup of sugar.

01 그녀는 그것이 20세기의 가장 위대한 예술 작품이라고 생각한다.

02 미술가는 작품을 만들기 위해 실생활 물건을 사용했다.

03 미술가는 그저 사람들이 다른 방식으로 사물을 바라보기를 원했

04 (1) 수지는 지루한 책을 읽어 지루해 했다. (2) 수지는 남동생이 파티를 즐기는 것을 보고 기뻤다. (3) 수지는 학교에서 인기 있는 동아리에 가입하여 즐거웠다. (4) 수지는 그녀가 생각지 못한 선물을 받아 놀랐다.

05 지난 주 나는 기념품 가게에 갔다. 나는 거기에서 새 학급 친구를 만나 반가웠다. 그는 나를 전에 봤기 때문에 나에 대해 알고 있다고 말했다.

06 돼지들이 충격을 받은 이유는 늑대 때문에 집을 잃어서였다.

07 요청하는 말에 could를 쓸 수 있으며, '무슨 일이 일어났는지'는 간접의문문을 활용하여 답할 수 있다.

08 (A) 사과를 받아 마땅하다고 생각했다는 의미이므로 deserve이며, 주절의 시제가 과거이므로 deserved라고 쓰는 것이 적절하다. (B) keep+Ving: 계속해서 V하다 (C) break into: ~에 침입하다

09 글의 내용으로 미루어 보아, 늑대는 설탕 한 컵을 빌리기 위해 돼지들의 집을 방문했음을 알 수 있다.

## 창의사고력 서술형 문제 p.208

|모범답안|

01 (1) the real-life objects   (2) in a different way

02 (A) blew down   (B) a sneeze from a terrible cold
(C) true   (D) friend
(E) the wolf going to a hospital that day

01 미술 작품의 특별한 점은 미술가가 작품을 만들기 위해 실생활 물건을 사용했다는 것과 미술가가 사람들이 다른 방식으로 사물을 바라보기를 원했다는 것이다.

## 단원별 모의고사 p.209~213

01 ④          02 ⑤

03 (1) was taken to   (2) blew down   (3) breaking into
(4) make sense

04 ④          05 ⑤

06 (A) yesterday   (B) point of view   (C) for a reason
(D) make money   (E) reading the book

07 He liked the movie better because it was easier to understand the story.

08 She preferred the book because it helped her understand the characters better.

09 Why do you think so?   10 ⑤

11 ③          12 ⑤

13 (1) They were shocked to lose their houses.

01 '불운에 의해'를 가리키는 말은 unfortunately(불행하게도)이다.

02 grab: 잡다

03 be taken to: ~에 끌려가다, blow down: 바람을 불어 넘어뜨리다, break into: ~에 침입하다, make sense: 이해가 되다

04 (A) How did you like it?: 그것은 어땠니?, (B) dependent: 의존적인, independent: 독립적인, (C) common: 흔한, unique: 독특한

05 위 대화를 통해 흥부가 스스로 돈을 벌기를 원했는지는 알 수 없다.

06 오늘 태호는 내게 재미있는 책을 소개해 줬다. 그는 책을 어제 다 읽고 내용을 설명했다. 책은 놀부의 관점에서 쓰인 흥부에 대한 이야기였다. 태호는 내게 놀부는 이유가 있어서 흥부를 도와주지 않았다고 이야기했다. 놀부는 흥부가 스스로 돈을 벌고 자립하기를 바랐다. 매우 독특하고 재미있게 들렸다. 나는 이 책을 읽기가 기대된다.

07 Brian은 영화를 더 좋아했다. 왜냐하면 영화가 이야기를 이해하는 데 더 쉬웠기 때문이다.

08 유라는 책이 등장인물을 더 잘 이해하도록 도와줬기 때문에 책을 더 선호했다.

10 주원이는 자기네 반의 팀워크가 가장 좋다는 김선생님의 말에 동의한다.

11 주어진 문장은 20세기의 가장 위대한 작품이라는 설명에 대한 이유로 적절하므로 (C)가 적절하다.

12 위 대화를 통해 미술가가 작품을 만들기 위해 실생활 물건을 어떻게 사용했는지는 알 수 없다.

13 (1) '감정형용사+to부정사' 구문으로 to부정사에 이어지는 내용은 감정의 원인이나 이유가 된다. (2) 과거에 완료된 상황을 설명한 문장으로 재채기가 나오려 할 때 막 부서진 문을 잡았다는 상황을 묘사한 것이다.

14 It is surprising that he should do such a thing. 그가 그러한 것을 해야 한다는 사실이 참으로 놀랍다. It is lucky that I live in Korea. 내가 한국에 살아서 다행이다. I was happy that you will go to study abroad. 네가 해외에 가 공부하게 되어 기쁘다.

15 ④ that을 to로 바꾸는 것이 적절하다. ① 네가 1등을 해서 기쁘구나. ② 너의 친구가 여기에 오다니 이상하다. ③ 너는 뉴스를 듣고 놀랐니? ④ We are afraid to go to the hospital tomorrow. 우리는 내일 병원에 가야 해서 두렵다. ⑤ 그녀는 너를 자랑스러워한다.

16 그는 이번 여름 방학에 사파리 여행을 갈 생각을 해서 기뻤다.

17 (1) 나는 기억했다 • 소파 옆 의자에 앉아 기타를 연주했었던 것을 • 나의 엄마와 내 남동생이 바둑을 두었던 것을
(2) 나는 나의 사랑스러운 고양이가 할머니 무릎 위에 앉아 있었던 것을 기억했다.

18 늑대가 문을 고의로 부순 것은 아니었다. on purpose: 고의로, 일부러

19 늑대가 셋째 아기 돼지의 집을 날려버릴 수 없었던 이유는 그의 집이 벽돌로 만들어져서이다.

20 돼지는 늑대가 와서 형들의 집을 완전히 날려버렸다고 말한다. 반면에, 늑대는 지독한 감기로 인한 재채기 때문에 집이 무너졌다고 말한다.

21 늑대는 할머니를 위한 생일 케이크를 만들던 중 설탕이 다 떨어졌다고 하였다.

22 아픈 늑대의 이야기가 흥미를 유발하지 않는다는 의미이므로 현재분사형 형용사 exciting을 쓰는 것이 적절하다.

23 (B) 셋째 아기 돼지의 집으로 가서 그를 부름 → (A) 돼지가 무례하게 행동함 → (C) 늑대는 돼지의 행동에 대한 사과를 원함

24 이어지는 늑대의 말로 보아 늑대는 자신이 누명을 썼다고 생각함을 알 수 있다.

25 늑대가 돼지의 문을 계속해서 두드린 이유는 그가 돼지의 무례한 응답에 대해 사과를 받아 마땅하다고 생각했기 때문이다.

# 교과서 파헤치기

**Lesson 1**

단어 TEST Step 1     p.02

| | | |
|---|---|---|
| 01 받아들이다 | 02 편안한 | 03 전자적으로 |
| 04 장학금 | 05 도구, 장치 | 06 유용한 |
| 07 분류하다 | 08 자유롭게 | 09 지역 사회, 공동체 |
| 10 보호하다 | 11 상황 | 12 기르다 |
| 13 불평하다, 항의하다 | | 14 복도 |
| 15 욕구, 요구 | 16 놀랍게도 | 17 알려주다 |
| 18 훌륭한 | 19 대신에 | 20 작은 길 |
| 21 언론 | 22 연세가 드신 | 23 발명하다 |
| 24 정확하게 | 25 쓰레기통 | 26 울타리 |
| 27 마침내 | 28 작동하다, 효과가 있다 | |
| 29 무시하다 | 30 눕다, 놓여 있다 | 31 발견하다 |
| 32 깨닫다 | 33 뜨다 | 34 허수아비 |
| 35 ~을 두려워하다 | 36 ~에 신청하다 | |
| 37 겁주어 쫓아보내다 | | 38 ~을 대신하다 |
| 39 A가 ~하지 못하게 막다 | | 40 ~ 덕택에 |
| 41 ~와 같은 | 42 ~을 자랑스러워하다 | |
| 43 결과적으로 | | |

단어 TEST Step 2     p.03

| | | |
|---|---|---|
| 01 sort | 02 comfortable | 03 dangerous |
| 04 scholarship | 05 press | 06 complain |
| 07 discover | 08 trash bin | 09 disease |
| 10 surprisingly | 11 protect | 12 raise |
| 13 exactly | 14 ignore | 15 path |
| 16 realize | 17 inform | 18 instead |
| 19 experience | 20 accept | 21 finally |
| 22 scarecrow | 23 float | 24 electronically |
| 25 fence | 26 elderly | 27 lie |
| 28 excellent | 29 work | 30 freely |
| 31 community | 32 hallway | 33 upset |
| 34 decide | 35 be based on | 36 sign up for |
| 37 look down | 38 take the place of | |
| 39 as a result | 40 be proud of | 41 come up with |
| 42 turn away | 43 prevent A from -ing | |

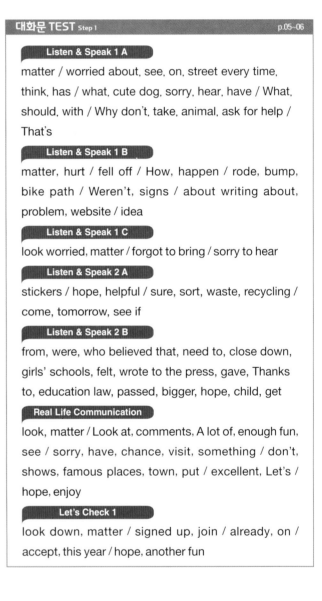

단어 TEST Step 3     p.04

1 comfortable, 편안한   2 try, 맛보다
3 bump, 요철, 고르지 못한 노면   4 float, 뜨다
5 path, 길   6 device, 도구, 장치   7 ignore, 무시하다
8 sort, 분류하다   9 press, 언론
10 complain, 불평하다, 항의하다   11 hallway, 복도
12 disease, 질병   13 bazaar, 바자회
14 fence, 울타리   15 scarecrow, 허수아비
16 scholarship, 장학금

대화문 TEST Step 1     p.05~06

**Listen & Speak 1 A**

matter / worried about, see, on, street every time, think, has / what, cute dog, sorry, hear, have / What, should, with / Why don't, take, animal, ask for help / That's

**Listen & Speak 1 B**

matter, hurt / fell off / How, happen / rode, bump, bike path / Weren't, signs / about writing about, problem, website / idea

**Listen & Speak 1 C**

look worried, matter / forgot to bring / sorry to hear

**Listen & Speak 2 A**

stickers / hope, helpful / sure, sort, waste, recycling / come, tomorrow, see if

**Listen & Speak 2 B**

from, were, who believed that, need to, close down, girls' schools, felt, wrote to the press, gave, Thanks to, education law, passed, bigger, hope, child, get

**Real Life Communication**

look, matter / Look at, comments, A lot of, enough fun, see / sorry, have, chance, visit, something / don't, shows, famous places, town, put / excellent, Let's / hope, enjoy

**Let's Check 1**

look down, matter / signed up, join / already, on / accept, this year / hope, another fun

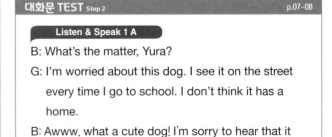

대화문 TEST Step 2     p.07~08

**Listen & Speak 1 A**

B: What's the matter, Yura?

G: I'm worried about this dog. I see it on the street every time I go to school. I don't think it has a home.

B: Awww, what a cute dog! I'm sorry to hear that it

doesn't have a home.

G: I know. What should I do with it?

B: Why don't you take it to an animal care center and ask for help?

G: That's a great idea. Thanks.

G: What's the matter, Mason? Are you hurt?

B: I fell off my bike at Hangang Park this afternoon.

G: Are you okay? How did it happen?

B: I'm okay. I just rode over a big bump on the bike path.

G: Weren't there any signs?

B: No, there weren't.

G: How about writing about the problem on the community website?

B: That's a great idea.

A: You look worried. What's the matter?

B: I forgot to bring my textbook.

A: Oh, no. I'm sorry to hear that.

G: I love our stickers!

B: Me, too! I hope these stickers will be helpful.

G: I'm sure they will help people sort their waste for recycling.

B: Let's come back tomorrow to see if they work.

G: Sounds good.

G: Hi, my name is Malala Yousafzai. I'm from Pakistan. In my country, there were some people who believed that girls do not need to go to school. So they started to close down some girls' schools. I felt so bad. I wrote to the press about it and gave many talks. Thanks to the support from many people, an education law was finally passed in my country. Now I have a bigger dream. I hope every child in the world can get an education.

Henry: You look upset. What's the matter, Mina?

Mina: Look at these comments, Henry. A lot of people say there aren't enough fun places to see in our town.

Henry: That's too bad. I'm sorry that they didn't have a chance to visit the nice places here. We should do something about that.

Mina: Why don't we make a video that shows the famous places in our town and put it on the internet?

Henry: That's an excellent idea. Let's do that.

Mina: Sounds good. I hope they enjoy their time here.

G: You look down. What's the matter?

B: I signed up for the soccer team, but I couldn't join.

G: Why not?

B: There were already too many students on the team, so the coach won't accept any new students this year.

G: That's too bad. I hope you find another fun club.

B: Thanks.

01 live in, southern part

02 fence, like, out, freely

03 kill, farmers are raising

04 As, kill, because, protect

05 woke up, lying, ground

06 dead, so bad

07 do anything because, only

08 realized, ignore, problem

09 wanted, help, same situation

10 idea, use fire

11 afraid of, Sadly, work

12 Instead, better watch, move

13 another idea, to, scarecrow

14 were very clever

15 first day, turned away

16 On, jumped in, killed

17 walking around, with, light

18 discovered, afraid of, moving

19 up with, invent, move

20 Because, what, needed, lights

21 found, device, broken, light

22 At, what I called

23 so proud of

24 set up, heard, complain

25 saying, what, wanted, lovely

26 Surprisingly, scare away, such

27 From, make, difference, though

28 able to prevent, from

29 Thanks to, work, scholarship

30 really excited about

31 teaching, how, make, use

32 make, difference, people's lives

43

01 is, live in, in the southern part

02 southern part, does, have a fence, like, out of, freely

03 that, are raising

04 As a result, try to kill, because, protect

05 woke up, lying on

06 dead, felt, bad

07 do anything because, only eleven

08 realized, shouldn't ignore

09 wanted to help, the same situation

10 to use fire      11 were afraid of it, work

12 Instead, to better watch, move

13 another idea, a scarecrow

14 were, clever      15 The first day, turned away

16 jumped in, killed

17 walking around, with a light

18 discovered that, were afraid of, moving

19 came up with, decided to invent, move electronically

20 Because, what I needed to make

21 a small device, broken electronic light

22 At thirteen, what I called      23 so proud of

24 Since, have set up, at, community, haven't heard, complain about

25 saying, exactly what we wanted, lovely

26 Surprisingly, used, to scare away, such as

27 From, realized that, make a difference, even though

28 able to prevent, from being killed

29 Thanks to, a scholarship      30 excited about

31 teaching, how to make, use

32 make a difference, people's lives

1 내 이름은 Richard Turere야. 나는 케냐의 나이로비 국립공원의 남쪽 지역에 살고 있어.

2 공원의 남쪽 지역은 울타리가 없어서 사자와 같은 야생 동물들이 공원 밖으로 자유롭게 나가.

3 그들은 농부들이 키우고 있는 동물들을 죽여.

4 그 결과, 농부들은 그들의 동물들을 보호하기를 원하기 때문에 사자들을 죽이려고 해.

5 어느 날 아침, 나는 일어나서 우리 소가 바닥에 누워 있는 것을 보았어.

6 소는 죽어 있었고, 나는 아주 기분이 좋지 않았어.

7 처음에는, 내가 겨우 열한 살이었기 때문에 아무것도 할 수 없을 거라고 생각했어.

8 그리고 나서 나는 이 문제를 무시하지 않아야 한다는 걸 깨달았어.

9 나는 같은 상황에 있는 우리 마을 사람들을 정말로 돕고 싶었어.

10 나의 첫 번째 아이디어는 불을 사용하는 것이었어.

11 나는 사자들이 불을 무서워 할 거라고 생각했어. 슬프게도 그것은 효과가 없었어.

12 대신에 불은 사자들이 소들이 움직이는 것을 더욱 잘 볼 수 있도록 도왔어.

13 그리고 나서 나는 다른 아이디어를 생각해 냈어. 그것은 허수아비를 사용하는 거였어.

14 하지만 사자들은 매우 영리했어.

15 첫날에는 사자들이 돌아갔어.

16 둘째 날에는 사자들이 뛰어 들어와서 더 많은 동물들을 죽였어.

17 어느 날 밤, 나는 전등을 들고 소들의 주위를 걷고 있었는데 사자들은 오지 않았어.

18 나는 사자들이 움직이는 불빛을 두려워한다는 것을 발견했어.

19 그래서 나는 생각해 냈지. 나는 전자적으로 움직이는 전등들을 발명하기로 결심했어.

20 나는 기계들을 좋아했기 때문에 전등들을 만들기 위해 내가 필요한 것들을 찾을 수 있었어.

21 나는 오래된 자동차 배터리, 오토바이에서 찾은 작은 장치, 스위치, 그리고 부서진 전등을 찾았어.

22 열세 살에 나는 내가 '사자 전등'이라고 불렀던 것을 마침내 만들었어.

23 나의 아버지께서는 말씀하셨어, "정말 자랑스럽구나, Richard!"

24 그때 이후로, 나는 우리 동네 일곱 가구의 집에 전등을 설치했고, 어느 누구도 사자들에 대해 불평하는 것을 듣지 못했어.

25 "이것이 바로 우리가 원했던 거야, 사랑스러운 소년아!"라고 말하면서 그들은 나에게 감사를 표했어.

26 놀랍게도 나의 아이디어는 이제 코끼리와 같은 다른 동물들을 쫓기 위해서 케냐 전역에 걸쳐 사용되고 있어.

27 이 경험을 통해 나는 내가 어린 소년이지만 사람들의 삶에 변화를 일으킬 수 있다는 것을 깨달았어.

28 나는 사자들이 죽임을 당하는 것 또한 막을 수 있었어.

29 나의 작업 덕분에, 나는 케냐 최고의 학교에 장학금을 받고 입학하게 되었어.

30 나는 정말 기분이 좋아.

31 나의 새 학교에서 나는 지금 나의 친구들에게 어떻게 전등들을 만들고 사용하는지 가르쳐 주고 있어.

32 나는 친구들에게 "우리의 아이디어가 사람들의 삶에 변화를 일으킬 수 있어!"라고 이야기해.

1 My name is Richard Turere. I live in Kenya in the southern part of Nairobi National Park.

2 The southern part of the park does not have a fence, so wild animals like lions move out of the park freely.

3 They kill the animals that farmers are raising.

4 As a result, farmers try to kill the lions because they want to protect their animals.

5 One morning, I woke up and saw our cow lying on the ground.

6 It was dead, and I felt so bad.

7 At first, I thought I couldn't do anything because I was only eleven.

8 Then I realized I shouldn't ignore the problem.

9 I really wanted to help the people in my town in the same situation.

10 My first idea was to use fire.

11 I thought lions were afraid of it. Sadly, it didn't work.

12 Instead, the fire helped the lions to better watch the cows move.

13 Then I had another idea. It was to use a scarecrow.

14 But the lions were very clever.

15 The first day, they were turned away.

16 On the second day, they jumped in and killed more animals.

17 One night, I was walking around the cows with a light, and the lions didn't come.

18 I discovered that lions were afraid of a moving light.

19 So I came up with an idea. I decided to invent lights that move electronically.

20 Because I like machines, I could find what I needed to make the lights.

21 I found an old car battery, a small device from a motorcycle, a switch, and a broken electronic light.

22 At thirteen, I finally made what I called "lion lights."

23 My father said, "I'm so proud of you, Richard!"

24 Since then, I have set up lights at seven homes in my community and haven't heard anyone complain about lions.

25 They thanked me, saying "This is exactly what we wanted, lovely boy!"

26 Surprisingly, my idea is now used all over Kenya to scare away other animals, such as elephants.

27 From this experience, I realized that I could make a difference in people's lives even though I am just a young boy.

28 I was also able to prevent lions from being killed.

29 Thanks to my work, I got a scholarship to a great school in Kenya.

30 I am really excited about this.

31 In my new school, I am now teaching my friends how to make and use the lights.

32 I tell my friends, "Our ideas can make a difference in people's lives!"

**Communication Task Step 2**

1. What's, matter
2. There aren't many parks, I hope, some more
3. too, would be nice

**Before You Read**

1. It, first day, farm
2. is painting, fence
3. is setting up, scarecrow
4. is going to, on
5. a good time

**Let's Write**

1. have seen, carrying
2. So, have brought, item, a bag
3. If, to carry, what, need
4. light, comfortable
5. it, be useful for

**Communication Task Step 2**

1. A: What's the matter, Minsu?
2. B: There aren't many parks in our community. I hope we can have some more.
3. A: Me, too. That would be nice.

**Before You Read**

1. It is Jessica's first day on a farm.
2. She is painting the fence.
3. Her mother is setting up the scarecrow.
4. Her father is going to the market on a motorcycle.
5. They are a good team!

**Let's Write**

1. I have seen students carrying many things at school.
2. So, I have brought my favorite item, a bag, for you.

3. If you want to carry many things, this bag is exactly what you need.

4. It is very light and comfortable.

5. I hope it can be useful for you. Thank you.

## 단어 TEST Step 1          p.23

01 다투다, 주장하다    02 사라지다      03 곡물, 곡식

04 모험             05 혼란스러워하는

06 익히지 않은, 날것의

07 예절 바른, 예의 바른            08 짠

09 금지하다      10 무시하다      11 편리한

12 도착           13 황급히        14 제공하다

15 기구, 도구     16 최근의        17 공화국

18 참을성 있게    19 접시, 그릇     20 자랑하는, 뽐내는

21 우아한         22 집중하다      23 용서하다

24 현명하게      25 들어 올리다, 기르다

26 이유           27 펼치다        28 제안, 의견

29 기념하다      30 분명히        31 주최하다; 주인

32 더 좋아하다    33 선택하다      34 예의, 예절

35 포기하다      36 ~에 상관없이    37 의견을 내세우다

38 ~하고 싶어 하다 39 휴식을 취하다    40 ~을 보상하다

41 ~하는 데 어려움을 겪다      42 정각에

43 건강을 유지하다

## 단어 TEST Step 2          p.24

01 adventure    02 polite       03 celebrate

04 certainly      05 uncooked    06 recent

07 confused      08 reason       09 convenient

10 disappear     11 utensil      12 republic

13 wisely        14 elegant     15 focus

16 provide       17 host         18 suggestion

19 hurriedly      20 spread      21 argue

22 ban          23 boastful     24 manners

25 ignore       26 patiently    27 choose

28 arrival        29 forgive      30 grain

31 prefer        32 save         33 search

34 salty         35 on time      36 make up for

37 be eager to    38 give up      39 regardless of

40 sense of touch            41 stay healthy

42 have trouble -ing         43 every time

## 단어 TEST Step 3          p.25

1 manners, 예의, 예절    2 noodle, 국수

3 adventure, 모험    4 utensil, 기구, 도구

5 plus, 더욱이, 게다가    6 boastful, 자랑하는, 뽐내는

7 argue, 다투다    8 plate, 접시, 그릇    9 spread, 펼치다

10 prefer, 더 좋아하다, 선호하다　11 save, 아끼다

12 choose, 선택하다　13 elegant, 우아한

14 grain, 곡물　15 celebrate, 기념하다

16 chopsticks, 젓가락

**Listen & Speak 1 A**

seems, me, like / enjoyed, leave, food on, plate, table manners / Why / think finishing, plate, that, hungry / It, polite to, everything, though / Different cultures, rules

**Listen & Speak 1 B**

seems, me, time, hungry / Can, order, for dinner / cook, Cooking, much healthier than ordering / save time by ordering, hungry / ready, patient

**Listen & Speak 2 A**

to stay healthy / having healthy, important / exercises every day, health / Which do you prefer, or exercising / control which, prefer to / Both, seem, important, health / can't, might, to focus / right, exercise first

**Listen & Speak 2 B**

What, now / already / Why, stop, have, meal / take a break, point / Which, prefer, having, late / prefer, early / What / go to bed early, early / late, because, work late

**Real Life Communication**

which, prefer / prefer / on / sushi, fried / Both / seems to me, tastes, uncooked / get, order

**Let's Check 1**

cap / seems, does, look / have, suggestion / How about, much better, than / sounds

**Let's Check 2**

hungry, Let's, something to / Which, prefer / like, know / over there

**Listen & Speak 1 A**

G: It seems to me that you don't like the food.

B: No, I enjoyed the food. I usually leave some food on my plate. That's good table manners in my country, China.

G: Why is that?

B: We think finishing everything on the plate means that you are still hungry.

G: It is more polite to finish everything on your plate in Korea, though.

B: Different cultures have different rules.

**Listen & Speak 1 B**

W: It seems to me that it's time for dinner. Are you hungry?

B: Yes. Can we order pizza for dinner?

W: I'm going to cook fish, Jacob. Cooking at home is much healthier than ordering pizza.

B: But we can save time by ordering pizza. I'm so hungry.

W: Dinner will be ready soon. So, please be patient.

**Listen & Speak 2 A**

G: What can we do to stay healthy?

B: I think having healthy food is important.

G: My brother exercises every day for his health.

B: Which do you prefer, having healthy food or exercising, Emma?

G: I can't control which food I eat. So, I prefer to exercise.

B: Both of them seem to be important for our health.

G: But if you can't do both, it might be better to focus on just one.

B: I think you are right. I'm going to exercise first.

**Listen & Speak 2 B**

W: What time is it now?

M: It's already 8:00 p.m.

W: Why don't we stop now and have a meal?

M: Good idea. We need to take a break at this point.

W: Which do you prefer, having a meal early or late in the evening?

M: I prefer having a meal early.

W: What is the reason?

M: I usually go to bed early, so I eat my last meal early, too. How about you?

W: I have meals late in the evening because I work late at night.

**Real Life Communication**

Jinho: Claire, which do you prefer, fish or steak?

Claire: I prefer fish, Jinho.

Jinho: There is fish on the menu.

Claire: That's good. Is it sushi or fried?

Jinho: Both are on the menu.

Claire: Then I will have sushi. It seems to me that fish tastes better when it's uncooked.

Jinho: Okay. Then you get sushi and I'll get fried fish. Let's order.

**Let's Check 1**

G: Do you like this cap?

B: It seems to me that red does not look good on you.

G: Do you have any suggestion, then?

B: How about this blue cap? Blue looks much better on you than red.

G: That sounds good. I'll take it.

**Let's Check 2**

A: I'm so hungry. Let's get something to eat.

B: So am I. Which do you prefer, noodles or rice?

A: I like noodles. Do you know any good restaurants?

B: There's a good noodle restaurant over there.

## 본문 TEST Step 1 p.30~32

01 are close friends, Republic

02 travel, with, families, much

03 up for, hosting, back

04 is, eager to, adventures

05 what they learned, recent

06 recent, about, way, argue

07 On, that, to use

08 for grains, eating meat

09 much better, use, instead

10 easier for, hold, other

11 more elegant, using, plate

12 different kinds, same utensil

13 use, with, one

14 way, with, smell, touch

15 Because, touch, get, enjoy

16 raised, argued, give up

17 It, for, to, arguments

18 hurriedly, yet, left

19 Where, has disappeared

20 should, Without, not complete

21 Where, go

22 Let's, to find

23 searching, found, sitting under

24 sorry, became boastful, ignored

25 forgive, back, join us

26 forgive, go back

27 Since, allow, another, please

28 that, regardless, which, with

## 본문 TEST Step 2 p.33~34

01 are close friends, Dining Republic

02 travel, with their families, travel much

03 makes up for, by hosting, coming back from

04 is, eager to, to, adventures

05 what they learned, recent trips

06 recent, was about, to eat, to argue

07 On, have found that, to use

08 for grains, soup, good for eating meat

09 much better to use, instead

10 easier for you to hold, the other

11 more elegant, using them to cut

12 two different kinds, utensils, two of the same utensil

13 use, with

14 No way, with, of course, see, smell, touch it

15 I, sense, touch, get to enjoy

16 raised, argued, wanted to give up

17 It, for, to listen to their arguments patiently

18 hurriedly, yet quietly, left

19 has disappeared

20 should we do, Without, not complete

21 Where, go

22 to find her

23 searching all, found, sitting under

24 we became boastful, ignored

25 forgive, back, join us

26 forgive, go back

27 Since, allow, to eat, that they please

28 In, that, delicious regardless of which utensils, to eat it with

## 본문 TEST Step 3 p.35~36

1 Spork와 Chopsticks, Knork, Barehands, Disher 부인은 식탁 공화국의 친구들입니다.

2 Spork와 Chopsticks, Knork, Barehands는 자신의 가족들과 여행을 많이 다니지만, Ms. Disher의 가족은 여행을 많이 다니지 않습니다.

3 그녀는 여행에서 돌아온 친구들을 위해 저녁 식사를 주최함으로써 여행을 많이 하지 않는 것을 보상합니다.

4 그녀는 항상 친구들의 모험담을 듣고 싶어 합니다.

5 그들은 최근 여행에서 배운 것에 대해 자주 이야기합니다.

6 가장 최근 주제는 음식을 먹는 가장 좋은 방법에 대한 것이었고, Ms. Disher의 손님들은 논쟁하기 시작했습니다.

7 Spork: 최근 여행에서, 나는 숟가락과 포크가 함께 달려 있는 것을 사용하는 것이 가장 좋다는 것을 알았어.

8 숟가락은 곡물이나 국을 먹기에 최고이고, 포크는 고기를 먹기에 좋아.

9 Knork: 아냐! 그 대신에 칼과 포크를 사용하는 것이 훨씬 더 좋아.

10 네가 한 손에는 포크를, 다른 손에 칼을 드는 것이 더 쉽다고 생각하지 않니?

11 접시 위에 놓인 고기를 자르기 위해 칼과 포크를 사용하는 것보다 더 우아할 수 있는 게 뭐가 있겠어!

12 Chopsticks: 같은 도구를 두 가지로 사용할 수 있는데 왜 두 종류의 다른 도구를 사용한단 말이야?

13 게다가 젓가락은 한 손으로도 사용할 수 있어!

14 Barehands: 천만의 말씀! 내가 손으로 음식을 먹으면 당연히 보면서 음식 냄새도 맡을 수 있지만, 음식을 만져 볼 수도 있다고.

15 음식을 먹을 때 촉각을 사용하기 때문에 음식을 더 즐기게 돼.

16 그들은 여러 의견을 제기하고 논쟁했습니다. 그리고 아무도 포기하고 싶어 하지 않았습니다.

17 그들의 주최자인 Ms. Disher가 그들의 언쟁을 참으성 있게 듣고 있는 것은 쉽지 않았습니다.

18 그래서 그녀는 서둘러서 그러나 조용히 자리를 떠났습니다.

19 Spork: Disher 부인은 어디 있지? 그녀가 사라졌어.

20 Knork: 어떡하지? Disher 부인이 없으면, 저녁 식사는 완전하지 않아.

21 Chopsticks: 그녀는 어디 갔을까?

22 Barehands: 나가서 그녀를 찾아보자!

23 몇 시간 동안 식탁 공화국을 구석구석 뒤진 끝에, 친구들은 마침내 큰 나무 밑에 앉아 있는 Disher 부인을 찾았습니다.

24 Spork, Knork, Chopsticks, Barehands: 우리가 자랑스러워하고 너를 무시해서 미안해.

25 우리를 용서하고 돌아와서 우리와 함께 있어 줘.

26 Ms. Disher: 알았어. 용서할게. 우리 집으로 돌아가자.

27 그 후로, 그들은 만날 때마다 서로 자신들이 좋아하는 방식으로 음식 먹는 것을 받아들입니다.

28 마음속으로 그들은 이제 음식을 먹는 데 어떤 도구를 사용하여 먹는지에 상관없이 음식 맛은 항상 맛있을 거라는 걸 알게 되었습니다.

01 Spork, Chopsticks, Knork, Barehands, and Ms. Disher are close friends in the Dining Republic.

02 Spork, Chopsticks, Knork, and Barehands travel a lot with their families, but Ms. Disher's family does not travel much.

03 She makes up for this by hosting a dinner for her friends coming back from their trips.

04 She is always eager to listen to their adventures.

05 They often talk about what they learned from their recent trips.

06 The most recent topic was about the best way to eat and Ms. Disher's guests began to argue.

07 Spork: On a recent trip, I have found that it is best to use a spoon and fork.

08 A spoon is best for grains and soup, and a fork is good for eating meat.

09 Knork: No! It is much better to use a knife and a fork instead.

10 Don't you think it is easier for you to hold a fork in one hand and a knife in the other?

11 What can be more elegant than using them to cut meat on a plate!

12 Chopsticks: Why do you use two different kinds of utensils when you can use two of the same utensil?

13 Plus, you can use chopsticks with just one hand!

14 Barehands: No way! When I eat with my hands, of course I can see and smell the food, but I can also touch it.

15 Because I use my sense of touch when I eat, I get to enjoy my food more.

16 They raised and argued many points, and nobody wanted to give up.

17 It was not easy for their host, Ms. Disher, to listen to their arguments patiently.

18 So, she hurriedly, yet quietly, left.

19 Spork: Where is Ms. Disher? She has disappeared.

20 Knork: What should we do? Without Ms. Disher, this dinner is not complete.

21 Chopsticks: Where did she go?

22 Barehands: Let's go out to find her!

23 After hours of searching all over the Dining Republic, they finally found Ms. Disher sitting under a huge tree.

24 Spork, Knork, Chopsticks, Barehands: We're sorry we became boastful and ignored you.

25 Please forgive and come back and join us.

26 Ms. Disher: It's okay. I forgive you. Let's go back to my home.

27 Since then, every time they meet, they allow one another to eat in the manner that they please.

28 In their hearts they now know that food will always be delicious regardless of which utensils they use to eat it with.

**Real Life Communication B**

1. Which, prefer, or
2. prefer ice cream
3. Why, prefer it
4. It seems to me that

**Before You Read B**

1. Different, different kinds of, to eat
2. are easy to use
3. For another, more convenient
4. might think using, more elegant

**Before You Read 1**

1. think, for breakfast
2. popular breakfast in
3. like to eat, for breakfast

**Real Life Communication B**

1. A: Which do you prefer, fruit or ice cream?
2. B: I prefer ice cream.
3. A: Why do you prefer it?
4. B: It seems to me that ice cream is sweeter.

**Before You Read B**

1. Different cultures use different kinds of utensils to eat.
2. For some people, chopsticks are easy to use.
3. For another, a fork is more convenient.
4. Other people might think using a knife and fork is more elegant.

**Before You Read 1**

1. I think people have bacon and eggs for breakfast in the USA.
2. Pho is very popular breakfast in Vietnam.
3. And people in Iran like to eat Naan for breakfast.

**Lesson 3**

| 01 고속의 | 02 가시 식물 | 03 설명하다 |
| 04 모방하다 | 05 흡수하다 | 06 만능의, 다용도의 |
| 07 매혹하다 | 08 받침, 걸이 | |
| 09 잠금장치, 고정 장치 | | 10 기사, 논문 |
| 11 (새의) 부리 | 12 접촉 | 13 물린 상처 |
| 14 압력 | 15 다시 디자인하다 | 16 적용하다 |
| 17 탐색하다 | 18 천재 | 19 털이 많은 |
| 20 증가; 증가하다 | 21 주목하다 | 22 해결책 |
| 23 고통스러운 | 24 영감을 불러일으키다 | |
| 25 성공적인 | 26 초래하다 | 27 우아하게 |
| 28 갑작스러운 | 29 표면 | 30 줄이다 |
| 31 반사하다 | 32 생존자 | 33 길이 |
| 34 필요성 | 35 활주하다 | |
| 36 ~와 연락하다, 접촉하다 | | 37 떠다니다 |
| 38 A가 ~하지 못하게 하다 | | 39 ~로 가는 길에 |
| 40 ~에 붙다 | 41 A뿐만 아니라 B도 역시 | |
| 42 결과적으로 | 43 그것이 ~하는 이유이다. | |

| 01 absorb | 02 bug | 03 creative |
| 04 apply | 05 length | 06 beak |
| 07 bite | 08 all-purpose | 09 explore |
| 10 gracefully | 11 observe | 12 painful |
| 13 successful | 14 imitate | 15 increase |
| 16 burr | 17 article | 18 cause |
| 19 weight | 20 inspire | 21 high-speed |
| 22 survivor | 23 invention | 24 closely |
| 25 contact | 26 necessity | 27 fascinate |
| 28 genius | 29 notice | 30 pressure |
| 31 redesign | 32 surface | 33 reduce |
| 34 sudden | 35 in search of | |
| 36 make contact with | | 37 be stuck to |
| 38 be covered with | | |
| 39 keep A from -ing | | 40 float away |
| 41 as a result | 42 on one's way to | |
| 43 not only A but also B | | |

1 headache, 두통　2 narrow, 좁은
3 all-purpose, 만능의, 다용도의　4 invention, 발명

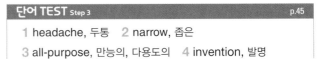

5 talent, 타고난 재능　6 hairy, 털이 많은

7 observe, 관찰하다　8 tunnel, 터널, 굴

9 genius, 천재　10 beak, (새의) 부리

11 dive, 뛰어들다, 잠수하다　12 imitate, 모방하다

13 redesign, 다시 디자인하다　14 wing, 날개

15 fastener, 잠금장치, 고정 장치　16 survivor, 생존자

## 대화문 TEST Step 1　　　p.46~47

### Listen & Speak 1 A

know, painted, don't / think, great artist / also, great inventor / What, invent / dreamed of flying like, drew, flying, looked like / Did, also make, machine / creative idea inspired, other inventors

### Listen & Speak 1 B

Have you heard, needle / Can, explain it / made this, imitating, mosquito's mouth / how will / know, bites, very painful, don't you, needle, cause less pain / How come, less painful / Like, less contact with / think, nothing useless

### Listen & Speak 2 A2

holder, candles last twice / possible / When, burns, melts into, tube below, form / fascinated, use, longer

### Listen & Speak 2 A3

what, fascinated by, special / What makes, special / played table tennis / How, door / be changed into, table / cool

### Listen & Speak 2 B

have, guest / Great, be / fascinated, fact, lived like, goat, for three days, Why, do / saw goats playing, looked, peaceful, live like / Didn't, have, problems / Walking on, was, difficult / any, to live like / planning, visit / can't wait to, adventure

### Real Life Communication

What, doing / reading an article / interesting / really fascinated by / Can, more / know, bugs, slip into narrow spaces / why, hard / help, survivors, earthquakes, big fires / fascinating

## 대화문 TEST Step 2　　　p.48~49

### Listen & Speak 1 A

G: You know that Leonardo da Vinci painted the *Mona Lisa*, don't you?

B: Sure. I think he was a really great artist.

G: He was also a great inventor.

B: What did he invent?

G: He dreamed of flying like a bird. So, he drew a flying machine that looked like a bird.

B: Did he also make that machine?

G: No, but his creative idea inspired many other inventors.

### Listen & Speak 1B

B: Have you heard of a mosquito needle, Jian?

G: A mosquito needle? Can you explain it to me?

B: Some scientists made this new needle by imitating a mosquito's mouth.

G: That's interesting. So how will that help?

B: You know mosquito bites are not very painful, don't you? The new needle will also cause less pain.

G: That's great. How come it's less painful?

B: Like a mosquito's mouth, it makes less contact with our skin.

G: Wow, I think that there's nothing useless in the world!

### Listen & Talk 2 A-2

G: This candle holder can make candles last twice as long.

B: Really? How's that possible?

G: When a candle burns, it melts into the tube below the holder to form a new candle.

B: Wow, I am so fascinated by the idea! Now we can use candles longer.

### Listen & Speak 2 A3

B: You know what? I'm really fascinated by the special door in Juwon's room.

G: What makes the door so special?

B: Juwon and I played table tennis on it.

G: How could you play table tennis on a door?

B: The door can be changed into a table.

G: That's cool!

### Listen & Speak 2 B

W: Today, we have a special guest, Thomas Thwaites, the Goat Man. Hello, Thomas.

M: Hello, Anna. Great to be here.

W: Thomas, I'm so fascinated by the fact that you lived like a goat in the Alps for three days. Why did you do that?

M: One day, I saw goats playing on the mountain. They looked so peaceful that I wanted to live like them.

W: Didn't you have any problems being a goat?

M: Walking on all four legs was very difficult for me.

W: Do you have any plans to live like a goat again?

M: Sure. I'm planning my second visit to the Alps.

W: I can't wait to hear about your next adventure. Thank you, Thomas, for your time.

**Real Life Communication**

Henry: What are you doing, Mina?

Mina: I'm reading an article about a bug robot.

Henry: A bug robot? Is it interesting?

Mina: Yes. I'm really fascinated by this thing.

Henry: Can you tell me more about it?

Mina: You know that some bugs can slip into narrow spaces, don't you?

Henry: Yeah. That's why it's hard to catch them.

Mina: A bug robot can do the same. It can help to find survivors after earthquakes or big fires.

Henry: That's really fascinating!

## 본문 TEST Step 1                                          p.50~52

01 flying, self-cleaning, way, fascinates

02 only, also, it, solutions

03 one such person

04 how birds could fly

05 closely, made, drew, of

06 though, successful, imitated, try

07 Since, have, imitated, abilities

08 Let's explore, of

09 high-speed train, made, had

10 entered, sudden increase, loud

11 woke people up, caused

12 solve, how, could reduce

13 engineers, in search of

14 saw, quietly diving into

15 how, bird entered, gracefully

16 more, discovered, narrow beak

17 redesigned, front, by imitating

18 not, but, with, less

19 One, was hiking, with

20 On, home, burrs, stuck

21 know how that happened

22 took, closer, noticed, straight

23 if, apply, something useful

24 After, testing, invented, materials

25 tiny, burrs, other, surface

26 were pressed, became, fastener

27 only strong but, easy

28 Since, used, different ways

29 is often used for

30 use, play, number, different

31 keeps, from floating away

32 nothing useless, curious, ask

## 본문 TEST Step 2                                          p.53~54

01 From, to self-cleaning, works fascinates us

02 not only, but also, imitate it, solutions

03 one such person

04 how birds could fly

05 closely, made notes

06 Even though, successful, imitated, to try to make, flying machine

07 Since, have, imitated, surprising abilities, nature's genius

08 Let's explore

09 high-speed train, had

10 entered, sudden increase, created, loud sound

11 woke people up, caused

12 tried to solve, how they could reduce

13 the engineers was, in search of

14 saw, quickly, quietly diving into

15 how the bird entered, gracefully

16 studied more, discovered, narrow beak

17 redesigned, front, by imitating, break

18 not only, but also, with, less electricity

19 One day, was hiking, with

20 On, way home, burrs were stuck to, hair

21 to know how that happened

22 took a closer look at, noticed that, were, straight

23 if he could apply, something useful

24 After, lot, testing, invented

25 tiny needles, those of burrs, the other, hairy surface

26 were pressed together, fastener

27 not only strong but also easy

28 Since, have used, many different ways

29 is often used for

30 to play a number of different

31 keeps, from floating away

32 nothing useless, curious, ask

1 나는 새에서 자정 작용을 하는 식물까지, 자연이 기능하는 방식은 우리를 매료시킵니다.

2 몇몇 사람들은 그들의 문제에 대한 해결책을 찾기 위해 자연을 이용할 뿐만 아니라 자연을 모방하기까지 합니다.

3 레오나르도 다빈치(1452-1519)가 이러한 사람들 중 한 사람이었습니다.

4 그는 새들이 어떻게 날 수 있는지 궁금했습니다.

5 그는 새를 자세히 관찰했고, 기록했으며, 그림으로 그렸습니다.

6 그의 발명은 비록 성공하지 못했지만, 그는 나는 기계를 만들어 보려고 새의 날개를 모방했습니다.

7 그 후로, 점점 더 많은 사람들이 자연 속 천재의 놀라운 능력을 성공적으로 모방해 오고 있습니다.

8 그들 중 몇 가지를 알아봅시다.

9 고속 열차는 일본에서 처음 만들어졌습니다. 하지만 그것은 한 가지 문제점이 있었습니다.

10 열차가 터널에 들어갔을 때, 갑작스러운 기압의 상승은 매우 시끄러운 소리를 발생시켰습니다.

11 그것은 종종 사람들의 잠을 깨웠고 두통을 일으켰습니다.

12 한 공학자 팀이 그 문제를 해결하려 했지만, 그들은 어떻게 소음을 줄일 수 있을지 몰랐습니다.

13 어느 날, 공학자들 중 한 사람이 먹이를 찾고 있는 새를 관찰하고 있었습니다.

14 그는 새가 빠르고 조용하게 물속으로 뛰어드는 것을 보았습니다.

15 그는 새가 어떻게 그렇게 우아하게 물속으로 들어가는지 궁금했습니다.

16 그래서 그는 그 새에 대해 더 연구했고, 새의 길고 좁은 부리를 발견했습니다.

17 그는 새의 부리를 모방하여 열차의 앞면을 다시 디자인했습니다.

18 그것은 성공적이었습니다. 이제 새로운 열차는 더 조용할 뿐만 아니라 전기는 15% 덜 사용하면서 10% 더 빠르게 이동합니다.

19 어느 날, 스위스 공학자 George de Mestral은 그의 개와 숲에서 하이킹하고 있었습니다.

20 집으로 돌아오는 길에, 그는 가시 식물이 자신의 옷과 개의 털에 붙어 있는 것을 보았습니다.

21 그는 어떻게 그런 일이 일어났는지 알고 싶었습니다.

22 그는 가시 식물들을 자세히 들여다보았고, 가시의 끝이 곧지 않다는 것을 알아챘습니다.

23 그는 유용한 뭔가를 만드는 데 그것을 적용할 수 있을지 궁금했습니다.

24 수많은 실험 후에, 그는 마침내 두 가지 새로운 소재를 발명했습니다.

25 하나는 가시 식물과 같은 조그만 가시들이 많이 있는 것이었고, 다른 하나는 털로 덮인 표면이 있는 것이었습니다.

26 두 소재를 함께 붙이면, 매우 훌륭한 고정 장치가 되었습니다.

27 그것은 튼튼할 뿐만 아니라 사용하기도 쉬웠습니다.

28 그 후로, 많은 사람들이 그의 발명품을 다양한 방법으로 사용해 오고 있습니다.

29 그것은 옷, 신발, 가방에 흔히 사용됩니다.

30 몇몇 사람들은 여러 가지 게임을 하기 위해 그것을 사용합니다.

31 우주에서, 그것은 물건들이 떠다니는 것을 막아줍니다.

32 자연에 쓸모없는 것은 하나도 없습니다. 우리는 그저 호기심을 갖고 질문을 던지면 됩니다.

1 From flying birds to self-cleaning plants, the way nature works fascinates us.

2 Some people not only use nature but also imitate it to find solutions to their problems.

3 Leonardo da Vinci (1452–1519) was one such person.

4 He wondered how birds could fly.

5 He closely watched birds, made notes, and drew pictures of them.

6 Even though his invention was not successful, he imitated a bird's wings to try to make a flying machine.

7 Since then, more and more people have successfully imitated the surprising abilities of nature's genius.

8 Let's explore some of them.

9 The high-speed train was first made in Japan. But it had one problem.

10 When the train entered a tunnel, the sudden increase in air pressure created a very loud sound.

11 It often woke people up and caused headaches.

12 A team of engineers tried to solve the problem, but they didn't know how they could reduce the noise.

13 One day, one of the engineers was watching a bird in search of a meal.

14 He saw the bird quickly and quietly diving into the water.

15 He wondered how the bird entered the water so gracefully.

16 So, he studied more about the bird and discovered its long, narrow beak.

17 He redesigned the front of the train by imitating the bird's beak.

18 It was successful. Now the new train travels not only more quietly but also 10% faster with 15% less electricity.

19 One day, a Swiss engineer, George de Mestral, was hiking in the woods with his dog.

20 On his way home, he saw that burrs were stuck to his clothes and his dog's hair.

21 He wanted to know how that happened.

22 He took a closer look at the burrs and noticed that the ends of the burr needles were not straight.

23 He wondered if he could apply that to make something useful.

24 After a lot of testing, he finally invented two new materials.

25 One had many tiny needles like those of burrs and the other had a hairy surface.

26 When they were pressed together, they became a very good fastener.

27 It was not only strong but also easy to use.

28 Since then, many people have used his invention in many different ways.

29 It is often used for clothing, shoes, and bags.

30 Some people use it to play a number of different games.

31 In space, it keeps things from floating away.

32 There is nothing useless in nature. We just have to become curious and ask questions.

### Culture & Life

1. North Pole
2. survive the cold, black skin to easily absorb
3. Each of, has, air space
4. helps, stay warm

### Culture & Life

1. Ants, North Africa
2. not only, hottest place on earth
3. the hottest time, go hunting
4. how they survive the heat
5. are covered with, that reflect the heat from

### Culture & Life Project

1. run very fast, don't you
2. One of the reasons, strong feet
3. by imitating, horse's foot
4. When, wear, not only, but also look taller

### Culture & Life

1. Polar Bears, North Pole
2. Polar bears survive the cold because they have black skin to easily absorb the heat from the sun.
3. Each of their hairs has an air space.
4. This also helps them stay warm.

### Culture & Life

1. Sahara Desert Ants, North Africa
2. The Sahara Desert is not only the driest but also the hottest place on earth.
3. But even at the hottest time of day, Sahara Desert ants go hunting.
4. Do you know how they survive the heat?
5. Their bodies are covered with unique hairs that reflect the heat from the sun.

### Culture & Life Project

1. You know horses run very fast, don't you?
2. Our group designed shoes by imitating a horse's foot.
3. One of the reasons is that they have strong feet.
4. When you wear them, you will not only run faster but also look taller.

## Lesson 4

### 단어 TEST Step 1

p.64

| | | |
|---|---|---|
| 01 사과하다 | 02 귀찮게 하다 | 03 독특한 |
| 04 반응, 응답 | 05 창조적인 | 06 책임이 있는 |
| 07 부리 | 08 재채기하다 | 09 비교하다 |
| 10 실제로 | 11 범죄 | 12 다시 만든 이야기 |
| 13 불행하게도, 안타깝게도 | | 14 꾸준히 |
| 15 장점 | 16 짚, 지푸라기 | 17 ~을 받을 만하다 |
| 18 계모 | 19 빌리다 | 20 황새 |
| 21 불평하다 | 22 누명을 씌우다, 테를 두르다 | |
| 23 괴롭히다 | 24 부양하다, 지지하다 | |
| 25 붙잡다 | 26 털이 많은 | 27 무례한 |
| 28 자립심이 강한, 독립적인 | | 29 마른 |
| 30 평화롭게 | 31 충격을 받은 | 32 완전하게 |
| 33 예술 작품 | 34 무례한 | 35 침입하다 |
| 36 ~로 만들어지다 | 37 ~ 대신에 | 38 관점, 견해 |
| 39 끌려가다 | 40 ~이 다 떨어지다 | |
| 41 ~와 사랑에 빠지다 | | 42 스스로 |
| 43 의미가 통하다, 이해가 되다 | | |

### 단어 TEST Step 2

p.65

| | | |
|---|---|---|
| 01 beak | 02 character | 03 crime |
| 04 steadily | 05 stepmother | 06 brick |
| 07 grab | 08 unfortunately | 09 hairy |
| 10 impolite | 11 completely | 12 rude |
| 13 straw | 14 artwork | 15 frame |
| 16 independent | 17 apology | 18 support |
| 19 sweat | 20 compare | 21 similar |
| 22 actually | 23 complain | 24 response |
| 25 deserve | 26 palace | 27 advantage |
| 28 apologize | 29 responsible | 30 skinny |
| 31 prefer | 32 bother | 33 sneeze |
| 34 trouble | 35 break into | 36 on one's own |
| 37 point of view | 38 instead of | 39 be made of |
| 40 run out of | 41 be taken to | 42 at least |
| 43 fall in love with | | |

### 단어 TEST Step 3

p.66

1 rude, 무례한    2 hairy, 털이 많은

3 unfortunately, 불행하게도, 안타깝게도

4 skinny, 바싹 마른, 너무 마른    5 deserve, ~을 받을 만하다

6 trouble, 귀찮게 하다    7 beak, 부리    8 stork, 황새

9 similar, 비슷한, 유사한    10 apology, 사과

11 straw, 짚, 지푸라기    12 crime, 범죄

13 sweat, 땀을 흘리다    14 sneeze, 재채기하다

15 independent, 자립심이 강한, 독립적인

16 complain, 불평하다

### 대화문 TEST Step 1

p.67~68

**Listen & Speak 1 A**

Have, finished / How did you like / interesting / What, about / right / point of view / say / reason, make money, independent / unique, can't wait to read

**Listen & Speak 1 B**

How, like / compare, with / Which, better / enjoyed, more, helped me understand, characters / better, easier to understand / both, advantages / right

**Listen & Speak 2 A**

worried / lose the soccer game / you think so / match against, the strongest players / bright side, the best teamwork / that way

**Listen & Speak 2 B**

What, think / frightening / Why, think so / snake, ate / hat / interesting / why, decided, pilot instead of / At least, what you mean

**Real Life Communication**

take a look at, How do, like / To me, more than, toilet / greatest piece of art / Why, think so / different point of view, real-life objects / something new / right, objects in a different way / learned a lot

**Let's Check**

course / turtle, mean / Why, think so / sleeping, wake him up, fair / that way, be responsible for, should / interesting

### 대화문 TEST Step 2

p.69~70

**Listen & Speak 1 A**

G: Have you finished the book, Taeho?

B: Yes, I finished it yesterday, Anna.

G: How did you like it?

B: It was interesting.

G: What is the book about?

B: You know the story of Heungbu, right? In the book, Nolbu tells the story from his point of view.

G: What does he say?

B: Well, he says he didn't help Heungbu for a reason. He wanted Heungbu to make money on his own and be independent.

G: Wow, it's a unique story! I can't wait to read the book. Thanks, Taeho.

**Listen & Speak 1 B**

B: How did you like the movie *Good Friends*, Yura?

G: I liked it. It was fun to compare the movie with the original book.

B: Which did you like better, the movie or the book?

G: Well, I liked the movie, but I think I enjoyed the book more. The book helped me understand the characters better.

B: That's interesting. To me, the movie was better because it was easier to understand the story.

G: That's true. I guess they both have their own advantages.

B: You're right.

**Listen & Speak 2 A**

W: You look worried, Juwon.

B: I think we will lose the soccer game tomorrow, Ms. Kim.

W: Why do you think so?

B: We will have a match against Class 3. They have the strongest players in the school.

W: Look on the bright side. They might have strong players, but your class has the best teamwork.

B: You're right. I didn't think about it that way. I'll go and practice!

**Listen & Speak 2 B**

M: What do you think about my drawing, Prince?

B: Wow, this picture is very frightening!

M: Why do you think so?

B: I mean the picture shows a snake that ate an elephant.

M: You're right. Actually, many people thought it was a picture of a hat.

B: Really? That's interesting.

M: I know. That's why I decided to become a pilot instead of a painter.

B: Haha. At least I can understand what you mean.

M: Thank you, Prince.

**Real Life Communication**

Ms. Parker: Now, take a look at this work of art. How do you like it?

Jinho: Well, is it even art?

Henry: To me, it isn't more than a toilet.

Ms. Parker: It is not just art. I think it is the greatest piece of art of the 20th century.

Mina: Why do you think so?

Ms. Parker: It is a perfect example of a different point of view. The artist used real-life objects to create art.

Claire: So, he didn't create something new?

Ms. Parker: That's right. He simply wanted people to look at the objects in a different way.

Mina: Thank you so much, Ms. Parker. I learned a lot today!

**Let's Check**

B: Do you know the story *The Rabbit and the Turtle*?

G: Of course, I do.

B: I think the turtle in the story is mean.

G: Why do you think so?

B: The turtle sees the rabbit sleeping but doesn't wake him up. It is not fair.

G: I don't see it that way. Why should the turtle be responsible for the rabbit? I don't think he should be.

B: That's interesting.

**본문 TEST Step 1** p.71~72

01 Welcome, taken, blowing down
02 third little pig, with
03 explain what happened to
04 build, built, straw, bricks
05 One, completely blew down
06 blew down, made of
07 How, doing now
08 shocked to lose, resting
09 let's, guest, what happened
10 whole, thing, wrong
11 real, sneeze, terrible cold
12 What do, mean
13 Back, was making, for
14 ran out, walked down
15 knocked on, fell down
16 called, Little, in
17 had, grabbed, coming on
18 sneezed, sneeze, fell down
19 by what had happened
20 Unfortunately, same, happened to
21 why did you go
22 needed, cup, sugar, next
23 third, had built, of

24 called out, trouble, in

25 what, answered, away, bother

26 impolite, deserved, apology, knocking

27 came, course, breaking into

28 think, were framed

29 going to borrow, exciting

30 made, Could, lend, cup

31 which do you think

1 리포터: 'Animal World News'에 오신 것을 환영합니다. 지난 일요일, 돼지들의 집들을 바람을 불어 넘어뜨린 늑대가 경찰서로 연행되었습니다.

2 오늘, 우리는 셋째 아기 돼지와 늑대를 모셨습니다.

3 Pig씨, 당신과 당신 형제들에게 무슨 일이 일어났는지 설명해 주시겠어요?

4 돼지: 네. 제 형제들과 저는 각자의 집들을 지을 때라고 생각했어요. 그래서 우리는 짚, 나무 막대기, 그리고 벽돌로 집을 지었어요.

5 어느 날, 늑대가 와서 제 형들의 집들을 바람을 불어 완전히 날려 버렸어요.

6 그는 제 집도 거의 날려 버릴 뻔했는데, 벽돌로 만들어져서 그럴 수가 없었죠.

7 리포터: 당신의 형제들은 지금 어떻게 지내고 있나요?

8 돼지: 그들은 집을 잃어서 충격을 받았어요. 그들은 제 집에서 쉬고 있어요.

9 리포터: 감사합니다. Pig씨. 이제 두 번째 손님인 늑대를 만나보시죠. Wolf씨, 무슨 일이 있었는지 말씀해 주시겠어요?

10 늑대: 이 모든 '덩치 크고 못된 늑대' 사건은 잘못된 거예요.

11 진짜 이야기는 지독한 감기로 인한 재채기와 설탕 한 컵에 관한 거예요.

12 리포터: 무슨 말씀인가요?

13 늑대: 그때, 저는 사랑하는 할머니를 위해 생일 케이크를 만들고 있었어요.

14 설탕이 다 떨어졌더라고요. 저는 이웃에게 설탕 한 컵을 달라고 부탁하기 위해 길을 걸어갔어요.

15 제가 이웃집 문을 두드렸을 때, 문이 떨어졌어요.

16 그다음에 저는 "아기 돼지 씨, 안에 계신가요?"라고 불렀어요.

17 제가 부서진 문을 막 움켜잡았을 때 재채기가 나오는 걸 느꼈어요.

18 저는 재채기를 아주 크게 했고, 그거 아세요? 짚으로 만든 집 전체가 무너졌어요.

19 저는 일어난 일에 매우 놀랐어요.

20 안타깝게도, 둘째 아기 돼지의 집에서도 같은 일이 일어나고 말았어요.

21 리포터: 그렇다면 셋째 아기 돼지의 집에 왜 갔죠?

22 늑대: 저는 여전히 설탕 한 컵이 필요했어요. 그래서 옆집으로 갔어요.

23 셋째 아기 돼지는 벽돌로 집을 지었더라고요.

24 제가 소리쳤어요. "귀찮게 해 드려 죄송하지만, 안에 계신가요?"

25 그리고 그가 뭐라고 대답했는지 아세요? "가버려, 다신 귀찮게 하지 마!"

26 얼마나 무례한가요! 저는 사과를 받아 마땅하다고 생각했기 때문에 계속 문을 두드렸어요.

27 경찰이 왔을 때, 물론 그들은 제가 이 돼지의 집에 침입하고 있다고 생각했죠.

01 Welcome to, was taken to, for blowing down pigs' houses

02 the third little pig, with

03 explain what happened to

04 time to build our, so, with straw, sticks, bricks

05 completely blew down, brothers' houses

06 almost blew down, made of, so, couldn't

07 How, doing now

08 shocked to lose, resting in

09 let's meet, tell us what happened

10 whole, is wrong

11 real story, about a sneeze, a terrible cold

12 What, mean

13 was making, for

14 ran out of, walked down, to ask, for

15 knocked on, fell down

16 called, in

17 had just grabbed, sneeze coming on

18 sneezed, sneeze, straw, fell down

19 by what had happened

20 Unfortunately, happened to

21 why did you go to

22 that cup of sugar

23 had built, of

24 called out, to trouble you, in

25 what he answered, Go away, bother me

26 How impolite, deserved, apology, so, kept knocking

27 When, came, of course, breaking into

28 were framed

29 thought, going to borrow, exciting

30 Could, lend me

31 which do you think is

28 리포터: 당신은 당신이 누명을 썼다고 생각하나요?

29 늑대: 네. 마을의 신문 기자들은 설탕 한 컵을 빌리러 간 아픈 늑대가 별로 흥미롭지 않다고 생각했겠죠.

30 그래서 그들은 저를 '덩치 크고 못된 늑대'로 만든 거예요. 당신은 아마 제게 설탕 한 컵쯤은 빌려 줄 수 있으시겠죠?

31 리포터: 시간 내 주셔서 감사합니다. 여러분, 어떤 이야기가 진짜 이야기라고 생각하시나요, 돼지의 이야기일까요, 아니면 늑대의 이야기일까요?

---

1 Reporter: Welcome to Animal World News. Last Sunday, a wolf was taken to the police station for blowing down pigs' houses.

2 Today, we have the third little pig and the wolf with us.

3 Mr. Pig, could you explain what happened to you and your brothers?

4 Pig: Yes. My brothers and I thought it was time to build our own houses, so we built houses with straw, sticks, and bricks.

5 One day, the wolf came and completely blew down my brothers' houses.

6 He almost blew down my house, but it was made of bricks, so he couldn't.

7 Reporter: How are your brothers doing now?

8 Pig: They are shocked to lose their houses. They are resting in my house.

9 Reporter: Thank you, Mr. Pig. Now, let's meet our second guest, the wolf. Mr. Wolf, could you tell us what happened?

10 Wolf: This whole "Big Bad Wolf" thing is wrong.

11 The real story is about a sneeze from a terrible cold and a cup of sugar.

12 Reporter: What do you mean?

13 Wolf: Back then, I was making a birthday cake for my dear old grandmother.

14 I ran out of sugar. I walked down the street to ask my neighbor for a cup of sugar.

15 When I knocked on the door, it fell down.

16 Then I called, "Little pig, are you in?"

17 I had just grabbed the broken door when I felt a sneeze coming on.

18 I sneezed a great sneeze and you know what? The whole straw house fell down.

19 I was very surprised by what had happened.

20 Unfortunately, the same thing happened to the second little pig's house.

21 Reporter: Then why did you go to the third little pig's house?

22 Wolf: I still needed that cup of sugar, so I went to the next house.

23 The third little pig had built his house of bricks.

24 I called out, "I'm sorry to trouble you, but are you in?"

25 And do you know what he answered? "Go away. Don't bother me again!"

26 How impolite! I thought I deserved an apology, so I kept knocking.

27 When the police came, of course they thought I was breaking into this pig's house.

28 Reporter: Do you think you were framed?

29 Wolf: Yes. The news reporters of the town thought a sick wolf going to borrow a cup of sugar didn't sound very exciting.

30 So, they made me the "Big Bad Wolf." Could you maybe lend me a cup of sugar?

31 Reporter: Thank you for your time. Everyone, which do you think is the true story, the pig's or the wolf's?

---

**Communication Task**

1. guess, title of the story

2. I think

3. Why, think so

4. who is sleeping peacefully, prince who is looking for

5. not the answer

**Before You Read**

1. Everyone deserves, like

2. make an apology, never thought, his point of view

3. whose story is true, that, can be framed for

**After You Read**

1. Pig's Story

2. three little pigs, to build their own houses

3. built, with different things

4. One day, came and blew down, second little pigs' houses completely

5. couldn't blow down, because, was made of

---

**Communication Task**

1. A: Can anyone guess the title of the story?

2. B: I think it is *Sleeping Beauty*.

3. A: Why do you think so?

4. B: I think Semi is the princess who is sleeping

---

peacefully and Minsu is the prince who is looking for the princess.

5. A: Sorry, but that's not the answer.

**Before You Read**

1. Everyone deserves a fun story like this. - *Book Weekly*

2. I think I should make an apology to the wolf. I'd never thought about his point of view. - *The Book Times*

3. I still don't know whose story is true, but I learned that everyone can be framed for a crime. - *Library & Paper*

**After You Read**

1. The Pig's Story

2. The three little pigs decided to build their own houses.

3. So, they built houses with different things.

4. One day, the wolf came and blew down the first and the second little pigs' houses completely.

5. But the wolf couldn't blow down the third pig's house because it was made of bricks.

# MEMO

적중100 plus
1학기 전과정
영어 기출 문제집
정답 및 해설

지학 | 민찬규

적중 1◐◐ + 특별부록

# Plan B

# 우리학교
# 최신기출

지학 · 민찬규 교과서를 배우는

학교 시험문제 분석 · 모음 · 해설집

전국단위 학교 시험문제 수집 및 분석
출제 빈도가 높은 문제 위주로 선별
문제 풀이에 필요한 상세한 해설

중3-1
영어

지학 · 민찬규

◎ 선택형 문항의 답안은 컴퓨터용 수정 싸인펜을 사용하여 OMR 답안지에 바르게 표기하시오.
◎ 서술형 문제는 답을 답안지에 반드시 검정 볼펜으로 쓰시오.
◎ 총 28문항 100점 만점입니다. 문항별 배점은 각 문항에 표시되어 있습니다.

[충북 ○○중]

**1. 다음 밑줄 친 부분의 뜻풀이가 바르지 않은 것은?** (3점)

① Let's come back tomorrow to see if they work. (~인지 아닌지)
② The traffic jam prevented them from arriving in time. (막았다)
③ I gave him some advice, but he decided to ignore it. (무시하다)
④ The coach won't accept any new students this year. (받아들이다)
⑤ Stickers help people sort their waste for recycling. (버리다)

|정답| ⑤
|해설| sort: 분류하다, 구분하다

[영등포구 ○○중]

**2. 다음 대화의 빈칸에 들어갈 말을 순서대로 나열한 것은?** (4점)

A: What's the matter, Manson? Are you hurt?
B: I fell (A)_____ my bike at Hangang Park this afternoon.
A: Are you OK? How did it happen?
B: I'm OK. I rode over a big (B)_____ on the bike path.
A: Weren't there any signs?
B: No, there weren't.
A: How about (C)_____ about the problem on the community website?
B: That's a great idea.

| | (A) | (B) | (C) |
|---|---|---|---|
| ① | of | bump | riding |
| ② | of | care | writing |
| ③ | off | bump | riding |
| ④ | off | care | riding |
| ⑤ | off | bump | writing |

|정답| ⑤
|해설| (A) fall off: ~에서 떨어지다 (B) bump: (도로의) 튀어나온 부분[요철] (C) 그 문제에 대해 '쓰는 것'이 적절하다.

[울산 ○○중]

**3. 다음 대화의 순서가 바르게 나열된 것은?** (4점)

(A) I love our stickers!
(B) Sounds good.
(C) Me, too! I hope these stickers will be helpful.
(D) Let's come back tomorrow to see if they work.
(E) I'm sure they will help people sort their waste for recycling.

① (A)–(B)–(C)–(D)–(E)
② (A)–(C)–(B)–(D)–(E)
③ (A)–(C)–(E)–(D)–(B)
④ (B)–(D)–(A)–(C)–(E)
⑤ (B)–(E)–(D)–(C)–(A)

|정답| ③
|해설| (A)에서 스티커가 아주 좋다고 하자 (C)에서 스티커가 도움이 되길 바란다고 하고 (E)에서 도움이 될 거라고 확신한다고 하자 (D)에서 효과가 있는지 내일 다시 오자고 하고 (B)에서 좋다고 하는 순서가 자연스럽다.

|정답| ⑤
|해설| 'Why don' you ~?'는 '~하는 게 어때?'라는 의미로 권유할 때 쓰인다.

**4. 다음 대화의 밑줄 친 (A)~(E)의 우리말을 영작한 것 중에 표현이 옳지 않은 것은?** (4점)

> B: (A)무슨 일이야?
>
> G: I'm worried about this dog. (B)내가 학교 갈 때마다 그것을 길에서 봐. I don't think it has a home.
>
> B: Awww, what a cute dog! (C)그것이 집이 없다는 말을 들으니 유감이다.
>
> G: I know. (D)내가 그 개에게 무엇을 해야만 할까?
>
> B: (E)동물보호센터에 데려가서 도움을 요청하는 건 어떨까?
>
> G: That's a great idea. Thanks.

① What's wrong?

② I see it on the street every time I go to school.

③ I'm sorry to hear that it doesn't have a home.

④ What should I do with it?

⑤ Why didn't you take it to an animal care center and ask for help?

**[5~6]** 다음 대화를 읽고 물음에 답하시오.

> Henry: You look upset. ⓐWhat's the matter?
>
> Mina: Look at these comments, Henry. A lot of people say there aren't enough fun places to see in our town.
>
> Henry: That's too bad. I'm sorry that they didn't have a chance to visit the nice places here. We should do something about that.
>
> Mina: Why don't we make a video that shows the famous places in our town and put it on the Internet?
>
> Henry: That's an excellent idea. Let's do that.
>
> Mina: Sounds good. I hope they enjoy their time here.

**5. 위 대화의 밑줄 친 ⓐ와 바꿔 쓸 수 없는 것은?** (3점)

① What's wrong?

② What's going on?

③ What's the problem?

④ What about going on?

⑤ Is there something wrong?

|정답| ④
|해설| ④번은 '계속하는 게 어때?'라는 의미로 상대방의 걱정 또는 염려를 묻는 표현인 'What's the matter?'와는 다르다.

**6. 위 대화의 내용과 일치하지 않는 것은?** (4점)

① Mina is upset about some comments.

② Mina and Henry read some comments from the visitors of their town.

③ Henry feels sorry that the visitors didn't have a chance to visit the nice places in his town.

④ Mina and Henry will put some pictures of famous places in their town on the Internet.

⑤ Mina hopes the visitors enjoy their time in her town.

|정답| ④
|해설| 'Why don't we make a video that shows the famous places in our town and put it on the Internet?'이라고 했다.

**7. 다음 대화의 빈칸에 들어갈 문장으로 가장 적절한 것은?** (4점)

A: What can we do to stay healthy?

B: I think having healthy food is important.

A: My brother exercises every day for his health.

B: Which do you prefer, having healthy food or exercising, Emma?

A: I can't control which food I eat. So, I prefer to exercise.

B: Both of them seem to be important for our health.

A: _____

B: I think you are right. I'm going to exercise first.

① That's right. We should always work on both of them at the same time.

② I don't think so. Eating healthy food is much more important than exercising

③ It's very hard to keep exercising for a long time.

④ You shouldn't eat food while exercising.

⑤ But if you can't do both, it might be better to focus on just one.

|정답| ⑤

|해설| 앞에서 'Both of them seem to be important for our health.'라고 했고 뒤에서는 'I think you are right. I'm going to exercise first.'라고 했으므로 ⑤번이 적절하다.

**8. 다음 중 어법상 올바른 것은?** (3점)

① She heard the doorbell rang.

② The things what he said was true.

③ We watched them to run back and forth.

④ Many people watched the singer danced on the stage.

⑤ He was upset about what his son did yesterday.

|정답| ⑤

|해설| ① rang → ring[ringing] ② The things what → What, 또는 The things what he said was true. → The things that he said were true. ③ to run → run[running] ④ danced → dance[dancing]

G: (가)너 우울해 보여. What's the matter?

B: (나)나는 가입 신청했어 for the soccer team, but I couldn't join.

G: Why not?

B: There were already too many students on the team, so the coach won't accept any new students this year.

G: That's too bad. I hope you find another fun club.

B: Thanks.

**9. 밑줄 친 (가)의 표현을 영어 두 단어를 추가하여 쓰시오.** (3점)

정답: You _____ d_____. (두 번째 빈칸의 단어는 d로 시작함)

|정답| look down

|해설| look down: 우울해 보이다

**10. 밑줄 친 (나)의 표현을 영어 두 단어를 추가하여 쓰시오.** (3점)

정답: I s_____ _____ (첫 번째 빈칸의 단어는 s로 시작함)

|정답| signed up

|해설| sign up for: ~에 신청(가입)하다, ~에 등록하다

**11. 다음 빈칸에 what[What]이 들어가기에 적절하지 않은 것은?** (4점)

① I can't believe _____ he said.

② Tom gave me _____ he had in his pocket.

③ Can you guess _____ I want for my birthday?

④ I saw the movie _____ you recommended.

⑤ _____ he likes to do after school is dancing.

|정답| ④

|해설| what은 선행사를 포함하고 있는 관계대명사이므로 선행사가 나와 있는 ④번은 어색하다.

**12. 다음 우리말에 맞도록 주어진 단어를 사용하여 알맞은 영어 문장을 쓰시오. (필요하면 어형 변화를 할 것.)** (3점)

> 그는 그 아기가 우는 것을 들었다.
> (he, hear, cry)

정답: _____

|정답| He heard the baby crying.
|해설| 지각동사 heard의 목적격 보어로 동사원형이나 현재분사를 쓴다.

**13. 다음 (1), (2)의 우리말을 주어진 단어를 이용하여 영작하시오.** (4점)

> (1) 무슨 일이야? (the matter)

> (2) 나는 네가 다른 재미있는 동아리를 찾기를 바라. (hope / another fun club)

(1) _____
(2) _____

|정답| (1) What's the matter? (2) I hope you find another fun club.
|해설| (1) What's the matter?: 무슨 일이니? (2) 'I hope'로 '소망'을 나타낼 수 있다.

**14. 다음 빈칸에 들어갈 단어의 형태로 알맞은 것은?** (3점)

> Look at the birds _____ on the tree.

① sings  ② sang  ③ are singing
④ singing  ⑤ sung

|정답| ④
|해설| 지각동사 look at의 목적격 보어로 동사원형이나 현재분사를 쓴다.

**15. 다음 우리말에 맞도록 주어진 단어를 배열하여 문장을 완성하시오.** (4점)

> I hope (they, have, parks, can, more).
> 나는 그들이 더 많은 공원을 가질 수 있기를 바라.

정답: I hope _____.

|정답| they can have more parks
|해설| 'I hope'로 '소망'을 나타낼 수 있다.

---

**[16~21] 다음 글을 읽고 물음에 답하시오.**

My name is Richard Turere. I live in Kenya in the southern part of Nairobi National Park. The southern part of the park does not have a fence, so wild animals like lions move out of the park freely. They kill the animals that farmers are raising. ⓐAs a result, farmers try to kill the lions because they want protecting their animals.

(A) My first idea was to use fire. I thought lions were afraid of it. Sadly, it didn't work. ⓑInstead, the fire helped the lions to better watch the cows to move. Then I had another idea. It was to use a scarecrow. But the lions were very clever. The first day, ⓒthey turned away. On the second day, they jumped in and killed more animals.

(B) ⓓAt thirteen, I finally made that I called "lion lights." My father said, "I'm so proud of you, Richard!" Since then, I have set up lights at seven homes in my community and haven't heard anyone (가)_____ about lions. They thanked me, saying "This is exactly what we wanted, lovely boy!" ㉠Surprisingly, my idea is now used all over Kenya to scare away other animals, such as elephants. From this experience, I realized that I could make a difference in people's lives even though I am just a young boy. ⓔI was also able to prevent lions of being killed.

(C) One night, I was walking around the cows with a light, and the lions didn't come. I discovered that lions were afraid of a moving light. So I came up with an idea. ⓕI decided to invent lights that move electronic. Because I like machines, I could find what I needed to make the lights. I found an old car battery, a small device from a motorcycle, a switch, and a broken electronic light.

(D) ⓖOne morning, I woke up and saw our cow to lie on the ground. It was dead, and I felt so bad. At first, I thought I couldn't do anything because I was only eleven. Then I realized I shouldn't ignore the problem. I really wanted to help the people in my town in the same situation.

Thanks to my work, I got a scholarship to a great school in Kenya. I am really excited about this. ⓗIn my new school, I am now teaching my friends how to make and use the lights. I tell my friends, "Our ideas can make a difference in people's lives!"

**16.** 위 글의 흐름에 맞게 (A)~(D)를 옳게 배열한 것은? (4점)

① (A)–(B)–(C)–(D)  ② (B)–(C)–(D)–(A)
③ (C)–(B)–(A)–(D)  ④ (D)–(B)–(C)–(A)
⑤ (D)–(A)–(C)–(B)

|정답| ⑤
|해설| (D)에서 소가 죽어 있는 것을 보고 문제를 무시하면 안 된다는 것을 깨닫고 (A)에서 첫 번째 아이디어로 실패하고 (C)에서 사자들이 움직이는 불빛을 두려워한다는 것을 발견하고 (B)에서 마침내 '사자 전등'을 만들게 되는 순서가 적절하다.

**17.** 위 글의 내용과 일치하는 것은? (4점)

① Lions easily move out of the park because there's no fence in the northern part of the park.
② Richard thought ignoring the lion problem was bad.
③ Richard came up with an idea with his father's help.
④ Nobody in Richard's community liked his idea.
⑤ Richard believed that our ideas cannot help people.

|정답| ②
|해설| 'I realized I shouldn't ignore the problem.'이라고 했다.

**18.** 위 글의 밑줄 친 ⓐ~ⓗ 중 어법상 자연스러운 문장의 개수는? (3점)

① 0개  ② 1개  ③ 2개  ④ 3개  ⑤ 4개

|정답| ②
|해설| ⓐ to protect ⓑ cows move ⓒ were turned away ⓓ made what ⓔ from being ⓕ electronically ⓖ cow lie[lying]

**19.** 위 글을 읽고 대답할 수 없는 질문은? (3점)

① What was Richard's first idea?
② What did Richard decide to invent?
③ What did Richard finally make at fifteen?
④ What did Richard realize from his experience?
⑤ How did Richard's idea to use a scarecrow go?

|정답| ③
|해설| Richard가 15살에 무엇을 만들었는지는 알 수 없다.

20. 위 글의 빈칸 (가)에 들어갈 단어의 영영 풀이로 옳은 것은? (3점)

① to think of it or make something for the first time

② to stop feeling angry with somebody who has done something to harm, annoy or upset you

③ to say or write that you are unhappy, sick, uncomfortable, etc.

④ to breed a particular type of animal or grow that type of crop

⑤ to ask people for money which you collect

|정답| ③

|해설| (가)에는 complain(당신이 불행하거나, 아프거나, 불편하다는 것 등을 말하거나 쓰다)이 들어간다.

21. 위 글의 밑줄 친 문장 ㉠에서 'to scare away'와 같은 용법으로 쓰인 것은? (정답 2개) (4점)

① Let's go out to find her!

② I wanted to use a scarecrow.

③ My first idea was to use fire.

④ It is much better to use a knife and a fork instead.

⑤ I went to the library to borrow some books.

|정답| ①, ⑤

|해설| ㉠, ①, ⑤: to부정사의 부사적 용법 ②, ③, ④: 명사적 용법

---

**[22~23] 다음 글을 읽고 물음에 답하시오.**

(A) At thirteen, ⓐI finally made that I called "lion lights." My father said, "I'm so proud of you, Richard!" (B) They thanked me, saying "ⓑThis is exactly which we wanted, lovely boy!" (C) Surprisingly, my idea is now used all over Kenya to scare away other animals, such as elephants. (D) From this experience, I realized that I could make a difference in people's lives even though I am just a young boy. (E) I was also able to prevent lions from being killed.

Thanks to my work, I got a scholarship to a great school in Kenya. I am really excited about this. In my new school, I am now teaching my friends how to make and use the lights. I tell my friends, "Our ideas can make a difference in people's lives!"

22. 위 글을 읽고 다음 주어진 문장이 들어갈 위치로 가장 적절한 곳은? (3점)

Since then, I have set up lights at seven homes in my community and haven't heard anyone complain about lions.

① (A)　② (B)　③ (C)　④ (D)　⑤ (E)

|정답| ②

|해설| 주어진 문장의 then이 (B) 앞에서 '사자 전등'이라고 불렀던 것을 만든 때를 말하므로 (B)가 적절하다.

23. 위 글의 밑줄 친 ⓐ와 ⓑ의 문장에서 어법상 어색한 곳을 찾아 바르게 고쳐 문장을 다시 쓰시오. (4점)

ⓐ I finally made that I called "lion lights."

→ _____

ⓑ This is exactly which we wanted.

→ _____

|정답| ⓐ I finally made what I called "lion lights." ⓑ This is exactly what we wanted,

|해설| ⓐ made와 called의 목적어 역할을 하도록 that을 what으로 고쳐야 한다. ⓑ is의 보어와 wanted의 목적어 역할을 하도록 that을 what으로 고쳐야 한다.

**[24~26]** 다음 글을 읽고 물음에 답하시오.

My first idea was to use fire. I thought lions were afraid of it. ⓐ_____, it didn't work. Instead, the fire helped the lions to better watch the cows move. Then I had another idea. It was to use a scarecrow. But the lions were very clever. The first day, they were turned away. On the second day, they jumped in and killed more animals.

One night, I was walking around the cows with a light, and the lions didn't come. I discovered that lions were afraid of a moving light. So I came up with an idea. I decided to invent lights that move electronically. Because I like machines, 나는 전등을 만들기 위해 내가 필요했던 것들을 찾을 수 있었다. I found an old car battery, a small device from a motorcycle.

**24.** 위 글의 빈칸 ⓐ에 들어갈 말로 가장 적절한 것은? (4점)

① Sadly
② Thus
③ Therefore
④ So
⑤ Luckily

|정답| ①
|해설| 기대했던 결과가 안 나왔으므로 Sadly가 적절하다.

**25.** 위 글의 내용과 일치하는 것은? (4점)

① 소들은 불을 무서워했다.
② '나'는 기계를 좋아하지 않는다.
③ 사자들은 움직이는 전등을 두려워했다.
④ '나'는 수동으로 움직이는 전등을 발명하기로 결심했다.
⑤ '나'는 새로운 부품을 사서 전등을 만들었다.

|정답| ③
|해설| 'I discovered that lions were afraid of a moving light.'라고 했다.

**26.** 위 글의 밑줄 친 우리말과 일치하도록 괄호 안의 주어진 단어를 모두 배열하여 문장을 완성하시오. (4점)

> 나는 전등을 만들기 위해 내가 필요했던 것들을 찾을 수 있었다.

> I / needed / what / to / the / could / find / I / make / lights

→ _____

|정답| I could find what I needed to make the lights.
|해설| 나는 찾을 수 있었다: I could find 내가 필요했던 것들: what I needed 전등을 만들기 위해: to make the lights

**[27~28]** 다음 글을 읽고 물음에 답하시오.

My name is Richard Turere. I live in Kenya in the southern part of Nairobi National Park. The southern part of the park does not have a fence, (가)_____ wild animals like lions move out of the park freely. They kill the animals that farmers are raising. As a result, farmers try to kill the lions because they want to protect their animals.

One morning, (나)I wake up and saw our cow laying on the ground. It was dead, and I felt so bad.

**27.** 위 글의 빈칸 (가)에 알맞은 접속사를 쓰시오. (3점)

정답: _____

|정답| so
|해설| 문맥상 결과를 나타내는 so가 적절하다.

**28.** 위 글의 밑줄 친 (나)에서 틀린 두 곳을 고쳐 쓰시오. (4점)

정답: _____

|정답| I woke up and saw our cow lying
|해설| 과거의 일이므로 woke이며 saw의 목적격 보어로 lie의 현재분사 lying이 적절하다.

# 3학년 영어 1학기 중간고사(1과) 2회

문항수 : 선택형(17문항)   서술형(13문항)   |   20 .   .   .

◎ 선택형 문항의 답안은 컴퓨터용 수정 싸인펜을 사용하여 OMR 답안지에 바르게 표기하시오.
◎ 서술형 문제는 답을 답안지에 반드시 검정 볼펜으로 쓰시오.
◎ 총 30문항 100점 만점입니다. 문항별 배점은 각 문항에 표시되어 있습니다.

[영등포구 ○○중]

**1.** 다음 대화의 빈칸에 들어갈 말을 바르게 짝지은 것은?   (4점)

A: You look upset. What's the (A)_____, Mina?
B: Look at these comments, Henry. A lot of people say there aren't enough fun places to see in our town.
A: That's too bad. I'm (B)_____ that they didn't have a chance to visit the nice places here. We should do something about that.
B: Why don't we make a video that shows the famous places in our town and put it on the Internet?
A: That's an excellent idea. Let's do that.
B: Sounds good. I (C)_____ they enjoy their time here.

| | (A) | (B) | (C) |
|---|---|---|---|
| ① | good | hope | matter |
| ② | sorry | matter | hope |
| ③ | matter | sure | sorry |
| ④ | matter | sorry | hope |
| ⑤ | sorry | sure | good |

|정답| ④
|해설| (A) What's the matter?: 무슨 일이니? (B) 유감을 나타내는 sorry (C) 소망하는 것을 나타내는 hope가 적절하다.

[울산 ○○중]

**2.** 다음 대화의 빈칸에 우리말에 해당하는 영어 문장을 쓰시오. (3점)

A: _____ _____ _____? (무슨 일이니?)
  Are you hurt?
B: I fell off my bike at Hangang Park this afternoon.

정답: _____

|정답| What's the matter?
|해설| What's the matter?: 무슨 일이니?

[충북 ○○중]

**3.** 다음 대화의 빈칸에 들어갈 말로 적절한 표현은?   (3점)

A: What are you going to do for the festival, Sophia?
B: I'm going to help people try flower tea.
  _____
A: You are very kind.

① I hope they will stop using the trash bin.
② I hope they will cut in line.
③ I hope they will have a great time.
④ I hope they will run in the hallway.
⑤ I hope they will leave trash on the floor.

|정답| ③
|해설| 앞에서 'I'm going to help people try flower tea.'라고 했으므로 ③번이 적절하다.

**[4~5]** 빈칸 (가), (나)에 적합한 표현을 보기에서 찾아 쓰시오.(4점)

B: (가)_____
G: I'm worried about this dog. I see it on the street every time I go to school. I don't think it has a home.
B: Awww, what a cute dog!
  (나)_____
G: What should I do with it?
B: Why don't you take it to an animal care center and ask for help?
G: That's a great idea. Thanks.

- What's the matter?
- Where do you live?
- I'm sorry to hear that.
- I'm so happy.

4. (가): _____

5. (나): _____

|정답| (가) What's the matter? (나) I'm sorry to hear that.
|해설| (가) 뒤에서 'I'm worried about this dog.'이라고 했으므로 'What's the matter?' (나) 앞에서 'I don't think it has a home.'이라고 했으므로 'I'm sorry to hear that.'이 적절하다.

**[6~7] 다음 대화를 읽고 물음에 답하시오.**

G: What's the matter, Mason? Are you hurt?

B: I fell off my bike at Hangang Park this afternoon.

G: Are you okay? How did it happen?

B: I'm okay. I just rode over a big bump on the bike path.

G: Weren't there any signs?

B: No, there weren't.

G: (가)How about wrote about the problem on the community website?

B: That's a great idea.

**6. 다음 질문에 대한 답을 위 대화를 참고하여 쓰시오.** (4점)

Q: Why was Mason hurt?

A: _____

|정답| Because he fell off his bike at Hangang Park this afternoon.
|해설| 'I fell off my bike at Hangang Park this afternoon.'이라고 했다.

**7. 밑줄 친 (가)를 어법에 맞게 고쳐 쓰시오** (3점)

정답: _____

|정답| How about writing about the problem on the community website?
|해설| about의 목적어로 동명사 writing이 되어야 한다.

**8. 다음 대화의 내용을 요약할 때 빈칸 (A), (B)에 들어갈 말로 가장 적절한 것은?** (4점)

Henry: You look upset. What's wrong, Mina?

Mina: Look at these comments, Henry. A lot of people say there aren't enough fun places to see in our town.

Henry: That's too bad. I'm sorry that they didn't have a chance to visit the nice places here. We should do something about that.

Mina: Why don't we make a video that shows the famous places in our town and put it on the Internet?

Henry: That's an excellent idea. Let's do that.

Mina: Sounds good. I hope they enjoy their time here.

Mina and Henry read some (A)_____ from the visitors of their town. They felt sorry that many people didn't have a chance to visit the nice places in their town. So they decided to make (B)_____ of famous places in their town.

| | (A) | (B) |
|---|---|---|
| ① | comments | a video |
| ② | comments | posters |
| ③ | places | posters |
| ④ | articles | a video |
| ⑤ | articles | comments |

|정답| ①
|해설| (A) 'Look at these comments, Henry.' (B) 'Why don't we make a video that shows the famous places in our town and put it on the Internet?'이라고 했다.

9. 다음 문장을 우리말로 해석하시오.                (5점)

> ⓐ I forgot to bring my textbook.
> ⓑ Please be patient.
> ⓒ What can we do to stay healthy?
> ⓓ We should do something about that.
> ⓔ I am sorry to hear that.

ⓐ _____

ⓑ _____

ⓒ _____

ⓓ _____

ⓔ _____

|정답| ⓐ 나는 나의 교과서를 가져오는 것을 잊어버렸다. ⓑ 제발 인내심이 있어라. ⓒ 건강을 유지하기 위해서 우리는 무엇을 할 수 있을까? ⓓ 우리는 그것에 대해 무언가를 해야 한다. ⓔ 그 말을 들으니 유감이다.

|해설| ⓐ forget+to부정사: ~할 것을 잊다 ⓑ patient: 인내심 있는 ⓒ stay healthy: 건강을 유지하다 ⓓ should do something: 무언가를 해야 한다 ⓔ I am sorry ~: 유감의 표현

11. 다음 빈칸 (A)~(D) 중 어디에도 들어갈 수 <u>없는</u> 것은?        (3점)

> G: (A)_____
> B: I fell off my bike at Hangang Park this afternoon.
> G: (B)_____
> B: I'm okay. I just rode over a big bump on the bike path.
> G: (C)_____
> B: No, there weren't.
> G: (D)_____
> B: That's a great idea.

① Weren't there any signs?

② Are you okay? How did it happen?

③ What's the problem? Are you hurt?

④ How about writing about the problem on the community website?

⑤ What are you going to do to solve the problem?

|정답| ⑤

|해설| 각각 (A) ③ (B) ② (C) ① (D) ④가 들어간다.

10. 다음 우리말에 맞도록 관계대명사 'what'을 사용하여 영어 문장을 완성하시오.                (3점)

> This is _____.
> 이것은 그들이 필요로 하는 것이다.

This is _____.

|정답| what they need

|해설| 관계대명사 'what'은 선행사를 포함하는 것으로 the thing(s) that/which로 바꿔 쓸 수 있다.

12. 다음 주어진 단어를 우리말에 맞도록 순서대로 배열할 때 세 번째로 오는 말은?                (3점)

> I'm / this / worried / dog / about
> 나는 이 개가 걱정이 돼.

① I'm        ② this        ③ worried

④ dog        ⑤ about

|정답| ⑤

|해설| 영작하면 'I'm worried about this dog'이다.

|정답| ①

|해설| 이어지는 내용으로 보아 ⓐ는 'there were some people who believed that girls do not need to go to school'이 적절하다.

[경남 ㅇㅇ중]

**13. 다음 빈칸에 공통으로 들어갈 알맞은 말은?** (3점)

> • _____ kind of sports do you like?
>
> • _____ I want for my birthday is a guitar.

① Which    ② What    ③ Who

④ That    ⑤ Whom

|정답| ②

|해설| 첫 번째 빈칸: 의문형용사 What, 두 번째 빈칸: 관계대명사 What이 적절하다.

**16. 다음 글의 흐름상 어색한 문장은?** (3점)

> Hi, my name is Malala Yousafzai. I'm from Pakistan. ⓐIn my country, there were some people who believed that girls need to go to school. ⓑSo they started to close down some girls' schools. I felt so bad. ⓒI wrote to the press about it and gave many talks. ⓓThanks to the support from many people, an education law was finally passed in my country. Now I have a bigger dream. ⓔI hope every child in the world can get an education.

① ⓐ    ② ⓑ    ③ ⓒ    ④ ⓓ    ⑤ ⓔ

[영등포구 ㅇㅇ중]

**14. 다음 중 밑줄 친 부분의 용법이 나머지 넷과 다른 것은?** (3점)

① I'll do <u>what</u> I want to do!

② She can't believe <u>what</u> she just saw.

③ His kindness is <u>what</u> really made her fall in love with him.

④ He looked at <u>what</u> Mary brought.

⑤ My mother unwrapped <u>what</u> I bought her.

|정답| ③

|해설| ③번은 what이 보어가 되는 명사절을 이끌고, 나머지는 목적어가 되는 명사절을 이끈다.

**[17~18] 다음 글을 읽고 물음에 답하시오.**

> A: Hi. My name is Malala Yousafzai. I'm from Pakistan. In my country, there were some people who believed that girls do not need to go to school. So they started to close down some girls' schools. I felt so bad. I wrote to the press about it and gave many talks. Thanks to the support from many people, an education law was finally passed in my country. Now I have a bigger dream. (A)저는 세상의 모든 아이들이 교육을 받을 수 있기를 바랍니다.

[울산 ㅇㅇ중]

**15. 다음 빈칸에 들어갈 단어의 형태로 알맞은 것은?** (3점)

> I saw you _____ on the street.

① walks    ② walked

③ have walked    ④ walking

⑤ to walk

|정답| ④

|해설| 지각동사 saw의 목적격 보어로 동사원형이나 현재분사를 쓴다.

[영등포구 ㅇㅇ중]

**17. 위 글의 밑줄 친 문장 (A)를 아래 조건에 맞게 영어로 쓰시오.** (3점)

┌─ 조건 ┄
1. hope, every, child, an education을 반드시 사용할 것.
2. 12단어로 쓸 것.
└

→ _____

|정답| I hope that every child in the world can get an education.

|해설| 저는 바랍니다: I hope 세상의 모든 아이들: every child in the world 교육을 받을 수 있다: can get an education

**18. 위 글의 내용과 일치하는 것은?**                    (4점)

① Malala는 파키스탄으로 이민을 갔다.
② Malala의 나라에서는 여학교들이 항상 문을 열었다.
③ Malala는 자기 나라의 교육 문제에 대해 관심이 없었다.
④ Malala는 교육 문제에 관해 많은 토론을 했다.
⑤ 많은 사람들의 지원 덕분에 Malala의 나라에서 교육법이 통과되었다.

**19. 다음 글의 내용과 일치하지 <u>않는</u> 것은?**            (4점)

My name is Richard Turere. I live in Kenya in the southern part of Nairobi National Park. The southern part of the park does not have a fence, so wild animals like lions move out of the park freely. They kill the animals that farmers are raising. As a result, farmers try to kill the lions because they want to protect their animals.

One morning, I woke up and saw our cow lying on the ground. It was dead, and I felt so bad. At first, I thought I couldn't do anything because I was only eleven. Then I realized I shouldn't ignore the problem. I really wanted to help the people in my town in the same situation.

① Richard는 케냐의 나이로비 국립 공원의 남쪽 지역에 살고 있다.
② 국립 공원 남쪽 지역에는 울타리가 없어서 야생 동물들이 공원 밖으로 자유롭게 나가서 가축을 죽인다.
③ Richard는 어느 날 아침 자기 집의 소가 바닥에 누워 있는 것을 보았다.
④ Richard는 처음부터 이 문제를 무시해서는 안 된다고 생각했다.
⑤ Richard는 같은 상황에 있는 마을 사람들을 돕고 싶어 했다.

**20. 다음 글을 읽고 흐름상 가장 자연스럽게 나열한 것은?**      (3점)

My first idea was to use fire. I thought lions were afraid of it. Sadly, it didn't work.
(A) Then I had another idea. It was to use a scarecrow. But the lions were very clever.
(B) Instead, the fire helped the lions to better watch the cows move.
(C) The first day, they were turned away. On the second day, they jumped in and killed more animals.

① (A) – (B) – (C)    ② (A) – (C) – (B)
③ (B) – (A) – (C)    ④ (B) – (C) – (A)
⑤ (C) – (A) – (B)

**[21~23]** 다음 글을 읽고 물음에 답하시오.

My name is Richard Turere. I live in Kenya in the southern part of Nairobi National Park. The southern part of the park does not have a fence, so wild animals like lions move out of the park freely. They kill the animals that farmers are ⓐ_____. As a result, farmers try to kill the lions because they want to protect their animals.

One morning, I woke up and <u>우리 소가 바닥에 누워 있는 것을 보았어</u>. It was dead, and I felt so bad. At first, I thought I couldn't do anything because I was only eleven. Then I realized I shouldn't ignore the problem. I really wanted to help the people in my town in the same situation.

**21. 위 글의 빈칸 @에 들어갈 단어의 형태로 올바른 것은?** (3점)

① raising ② raise ③ to raise

④ raised ⑤ raises

|정답| ①

|해설| be동사 다음에 진행형을 만드는 현재분사가 적절하다.

**22. 위 글을 읽고 대답할 수 없는 질문은?** (3점)

① Where does Richard live?

② What animals do lions kill?

③ How many domestic animals did lions kill?

④ Who did Richard want to hclp?

⑤ Why can wild animals move out of the park?

|정답| ③

|해설| 야생 동물들이 얼마나 많은 가축들을 죽였는지는 알 수 없다.

**23. 위 글의 밑줄 친 우리말을 〈조건〉에 맞도록 문장을 완성하시오.** (4점)

┌─ 조건 ─┐

• lie, see, the ground를 사용하되, 필요시 어형을 바꿀 것.

• 소가 누워 있는 동작의 진행의 의미를 강조할 것

→ I woke up and _____.

|정답| saw our cow lying on the ground

|해설| saw의 목적격 보어로 현재분사 lying을 쓴다.

**[24~25] 다음 글을 읽고 물음에 답하시오.**

At thirteen, I finally made (가)that I called "lion lights." My father said, "I'm so proud of you, Richard!" Since then, I have set up lights at seven homes in my community and haven't heard anyone complain about lions. They thanked me, saying "This is exactly (나) that we wanted, lovely boy!" Surprisingly, my idea is now used all over Kenya to scare away other animals, such as elephants. From this experience, I realized that I could make a difference in people's lives even though I am just a young boy. (다)I could _____.

**24. 위 글의 밑줄 친 (가), (나)에서 공통으로 틀린 곳을 고치시오.** (4점)

(가) _____

(나) _____

|정답| that → what

|해설| (가) made와 called의 목적어 역할을 하도록 that을 what으로 고쳐야 한다. (나) is의 보어와 wanted의 목적어 역할을 하도록 that을 what으로 고쳐야 한다.

**25. 위 글의 빈칸 (다)를 주어진 조건에 맞게 쓰시오.** (4점)

┌─ 조건 ─┐

• 해석: 나는 사자들이 죽임을 당하는 것을 막을 수 있었다.

• prevent, from을 사용할 것.

• 적절한 단어를 추가할 것.

→ I could _____.

|정답| prevent lions from being killed

|해설| prevent ... from -ing: …을 ~하는 것으로부터 막다. 죽임을 당하는 것: being killed

**26. 다음 주어진 단어를 사용하여 우리말에 맞는 영어 문장을 쓰시오.** (4점)

can / in / a / lives / people's

우리의 생각들이 사람들의 생활에서 차이점을 만들 수 있다.

정답: _____

|정답| Our ideas can make a difference in people's lives.

|해설| make a difference: 변화를 가져오다, 차이를 만들다

**[27~28]** 다음 글을 읽고 물음에 답하시오.

My name is Richard Turere. I live in Kenya in the southern part of Nairobi National Park. ⓐThe southern part of the park does not have a fence, so wild animals like lions move out of the park free. (A)They kill the animals that farmers are raising. As a result, farmers try to kill the lions because (B)they want to protect their animals.

ⓑOne morning, I woke up and saw our cow to lie on the ground. ⓒIt was dead, and I felt so badly. ⓓAt first, I thought I couldn't do anything because I was only eleven. Then I realized I shouldn't ignore the problem. ⓔI really wanted helping the people in my town in the same situation.

**27.** 위 글의 밑줄 친 ⓐ~ⓔ 중 어법상 자연스러운 문장은? (3점)

① ⓐ  ② ⓑ  ③ ⓒ  ④ ⓓ  ⑤ ⓔ

|정답| ④
|해설| ⓐ free → freely ⓑ to lie → lying ⓒ badly → bad ⓔ helping → to help

**28.** 위 글의 밑줄 친 (A)와 (B)가 가리키는 대상이 바르게 연결된 것은? (3점)

① (A)They – cows

② (A)They – farmers

③ (A)They – wild animals

④ (B)they – wild animals

⑤ (B)they – cows

|정답| ③
|해설| (A)는 wild animals (B)는 farmers를 가리킨다.

**29.** 다음 글의 밑줄 친 ⓐ~ⓔ 중 흐름상 어색한 것은? (3점)

G: Hi, my name is Malala Yousafzai. I'm from Pakistan. ⓐIn my country, there were some people who believed that girls do not need to go to school. ⓑSo they started to close down some girls' schools. ⓒI felt so bad. I wrote to the press about it and gave many talks. ⓓThanks to the support from many people, an education law was finally passed in my country. Now I have a bigger dream. ⓔI hope every child in the world can not get an education.

① ⓐ  ② ⓑ  ③ ⓒ  ④ ⓓ  ⑤ ⓔ

|정답| ⑤
|해설| ⓔ는 'I hope every child in the world can get an education.'으로 쓰는 것이 적절하다.

**30.** 보기의 문장이 들어가기에 가장 적절한 곳의 바로 앞 문장을 쓰시오. (4점)

┌─ 보기 ├─

It was to use scarecrow.

My first idea was to use fire. I thought lions were afraid of it. Sadly, it didn't work. Instead, the fire helped the lions to better watch the cows move. Then I had another idea. But the lions were very clever. The first day, they were turned away. On the second day, they jumped in and killed more animals.

정답: _____

|정답| Then I had another idea.
|해설| 보기의 It이 가리키는 것이 'another idea'이다.

# 3학년 영어 1학기 중간고사(2과) 1회

| 반 | | 점수 |
|---|---|---|
| 이름 | | |

문항수 : 선택형(16문항) 서술형(10문항)      20 . . .

◎ 선택형 문항의 답안은 컴퓨터용 수정 싸인펜을 사용하여 OMR 답안지에 바르게 표기하시오.

◎ 서술형 문제는 답을 답안지에 반드시 검정 볼펜으로 쓰시오.

◎ 총 26문항 100점 만점입니다. 문항별 배점은 각 문항에 표시되어 있습니다.

[울산 ○○중]

**1. 다음 영영 풀이에 해당하는 단어는?** (4점)

> a cereal crop, especially wheat, corn or rice

① device ② grain
③ fence ④ farm
⑤ vegetable

**[2~3] 다음 대화를 읽고 물음에 답하시오.**

> G: It seems to me that you don't like the food.
> B: No, I enjoyed the food. I usually ⓐ_____ some food on my plate. That's good table manners in my country, China.
> G: Why is that?
> B: We think finishing everything on the plate means that you are still hungry.
> G: It is more polite to finish everything on your plate in Korea, though.
> B: Different ⓑ_____ have different rules.

[울산 ○○중]

**2. 위 대화의 빈칸 ⓐ에 들어갈 가장 알맞은 말은?** (3점)

① finish ② wash ③ leave
④ mix ⑤ throw away

[대전 ○○중]

**3. 위 대화의 빈칸 ⓑ에 들어갈 가장 알맞은 말은?** (4점)

① houses ② foods
③ utensils ④ clothings
⑤ cultures

[울산 ○○중]

**4. 다음 대화의 내용과 일치하지 않는 것은?** (4점)

> W: What time is it now?
> M: It's already 8:00 p.m.
> W: Why don't we stop now and have a meal?
> M: Good idea. We need to take a break at this point.
> W: Which do you prefer, having a meal early or late in the evening?
> M: I prefer having a meal early.
> W: What is the reason?
> M: I go to bed early, so I eat my last meal early, too. How about you?
> W: I have meals late in the evening because I work late at night.

① 지금 시각은 오후 8시이다.
② W는 잠깐 멈추고 식사를 하자고 제안하였다.
③ M은 저녁 식사를 일찍 먹는 것을 선호한다.
④ M은 일찍 잠자리에 들기 때문에 첫 식사를 일찍 한다.
⑤ W는 밤 늦게까지 일을 하므로 저녁 식사를 늦게 한다.

5. 다음 주어진 어구를 이용하여 대화를 완성하시오. (단, 현재분사
구문을 활용할 것)                                        (4점)

> A: I can't find Suji and Tom in the picture.
> Who is Suji in this picture?
> B: She is the girl (A)_____.
>   (water the flowers)
> A: Who is Tom in this picture?
> B: He is the boy (B)_____.
>   (read a book on the bench)

(A) _____

(B) _____

**[6~7]** 다음 대화를 읽고 물음에 답하시오.          (6점)

> W: It seems to me that it's time for dinner.
>   (가)_____
> B: Yes. Can we order pizza for dinner?
> W: I'm going to cook fish, Jacob. Cooking
>   at home is much healthier than ordering
>   pizza.
> B: But we can save time by ordering pizza.
>   I'm so hungry.
> W: Dinner will be ready soon. So, please
>   (나)_____.
> B: Okay.

┌─ 보기 ┐
• Are you hungry?
• Are you full?
• be patient
• go out now
└─────────┘

6. (가): _____

7. (나): _____

8. 다음 밑줄 친 우리말 표현에 맞게 주어진 단어를 모두 나열하여
문장을 완성하시오.                                        (4점)

> A: <u>나에게는 당신이 그 음식을 좋아하지 않는 것 같군
> 요.</u>
> B: No, I enjoyed the food. I usually leave
>   some food on my plate. That's good table
>   manners in my country, China.
> A: Why is that?
> B: We think finishing everything on the plate
>   means that you are still hungry.

> seems / to me / you / don't like
> / it / that / the food

정답: _____

9. 다음 대화를 구성할 때, 흐름상 가장 자연스럽게 순서대로 나열
한 것은?                                                (4점)

> (A) I'm so hungry. Let's get something to eat.
> (B) I like noodles. Do you know any good
>   restaurant?
> (C) So am I. Which do you prefer, noodles or
>   rice?
> (D) There's a good noodle restaurant over
>   there.

① (A)–(C)–(D)–(B)     ② (A)–(C)–(B)–(D)

③ (B)–(C)–(A)–(D)     ④ (C)–(A)–(B)–(D)

⑤ (C)–(A)–(D)–(B)

**10.** 다음 대화의 내용과 일치하는 것은? (3점)

> G: It seems to me that you don't like the food.
>
> B: No, I enjoyed the food. I usually leave some food on my plate. That's good table manners in my country, China.
>
> G: Why is that?
>
> B: We think finishing everything on the plate means that you are still hungry.
>
> G: It is more polite to finish everything on your plate in Korea, though.
>
> B: Different cultures have different rules.
>
> *G: girl, B: boy

① The girl didn't think that the boy enjoyed the food at first.

② People leave some food on a plate when they are hungry in China.

③ Finishing everything on a plate is good table manners in China.

④ Leaving some food on a plate is good table manners in Korea.

⑤ The boy didn't enjoy the food.

**11.** 다음 대화의 흐름상 (A), (B)에 가장 알맞은 표현을 〈보기〉에서 골라 바르게 짝지은 것은? (4점)

> W: What time is it now?
>
> M: It's already 8:00 p.m.
>
> W: Why don't we stop now and have a meal?
>
> M: Good idea. We need to take a break at this point.
>
> W: (A)_____
>
> M: I prefer having a meal early.
>
> W: (B)_____
>
> M: I usually go to bed early, so I eat my last meal early, too. How about you?
>
> W: I have meals late in the evening because I work late at night.

┤ 보기 ├

ⓐ Why do you prefer that?

ⓑ Which do you prefer, having a meal early or late in the evening?

ⓒ What is the reason?

ⓓ Which do you prefer, having a meal or taking a break?

ⓔ What is that?

|   | (A) | (B) |
|---|-----|-----|
| ① | ⓐ | ⓒ |
| ② | ⓑ | ⓒ |
| ③ | ⓑ | ⓔ |
| ④ | ⓓ | ⓐ |
| ⑤ | ⓓ | ⓔ |

12. 다음 빈칸에 들어갈 알맞은 말은?　　　　　　　(3점)

| It is easy _____ me to make bulgogi. |

① of　　　　　② in　　　　　③ with
④ for　　　　　⑤ at

13. 다음 우리말에 맞도록 주어진 단어를 이용하여 문장을 완성하시오.　　　　　　　(5점)

(1) 벤치에서 책을 읽고 있는 두 소년이 있다.
　(read / the bench)
　• There ＿＿＿＿＿＿＿＿＿＿＿＿＿.

(2) 거리에서 뛰고 있는 한 여자가 있다.
　(run / the street)
　• There ＿＿＿＿＿＿＿＿＿＿＿＿＿.

(1) ＿＿＿＿＿＿＿＿＿＿＿＿＿＿＿
(2) ＿＿＿＿＿＿＿＿＿＿＿＿＿＿＿

14. 다음 〈보기〉와 같이 두 문장을 한 문장으로 쓰시오.　(4점)

┌ 보기 ┐
There is a boy reading a book on the bench.

| There is a girl. She is watering the flowers.
→ ＿＿＿＿＿＿＿＿＿＿＿＿＿＿＿ |

정답: ＿＿＿＿＿＿＿＿＿＿＿＿＿＿＿

[15~16] 다음 글을 읽고 물음에 답하시오.

**Spork:** On a recent trip, I have found that it is best to use a spoon and fork. A spoon is best for grains and soup, and a fork is good for eating meat.

**Knork:** No! It is ⓐ_____ better to use a knife and a fork instead. Don't you think it is easier for you to hold a fork in one hand and a knife in ⓑ_____? What can be ⓒ_____ elegant than using them to cut meat on a plate!

**Chopsticks:** Why do you use two different kinds of utensils when you can use two of the same utensil? Plus, you can use chopsticks with just one hand!

**Barehands:** No way! When I eat with my (A)_____, of course I can see and smell the food, but I can also touch it. Because I use my sense of touch when I eat, I get to enjoy my food more.

They raised and argued many points, and nobody wanted to give up. It was not easy for their host, Ms. Disher, to listen to their arguments patiently. So, she hurriedly, yet quietly, left.

**15.** 위 글의 빈칸 (A)에 들어갈 가장 알맞은 말은? (3점)

① hands     ② forks     ③ spoons
④ knives     ⑤ chopsticks

**16.** 위 글의 빈칸 ⓐ, ⓑ, ⓒ에 들어갈 말이 바르게 짝지어진 것은? (4점)

|   | ⓐ | ⓑ | ⓒ |
|---|------|-----------|------|
| ① | very | the other | more |
| ② | much | another | most |
| ③ | much | the other | more |
| ④ | very | the other | most |
| ⑤ | much | other | more |

**[17~19]** 다음 글을 읽고 물음에 답하시오.

They raised and argued many points, and nobody wanted to give up. (가)It was not easy for Ms. Disher listen to their arguments. So, she hurriedly, yet quietly, left.

Spork: Where is Ms. Disher? She has disappeared.

Knork: What should we do? Without Ms. Disher, this dinner is not complete.

Chopsticks: Where did she go?

Barehands: Let's go out to find her!

After hours of searching all over the Dining Republic, (나)they found Ms. Disher sat under a huge tree.

**Spork, Knork, Chopsticks, Barehands:** We're sorry we became (다)뽐내는 and (라)너를 무시했

어. Please forgive us and come back and join us.

**Ms. Disher:** It's okay. I forgive you. Let's go back to my home.

Since then, every time they meet, (마)another / allow / they / one / eat in the manner that they please. In their hearts they now know that food will always be delicious regardless of which utensils they use to eat it with.

**17.** 위 글의 밑줄 친 (가), (나)에서 공통으로 틀린 곳을 고쳐 쓰시오. (6점)

(가) _____
(나) _____

**18.** 위 글의 밑줄 친 (다), (라)의 표현을 영어로 쓰시오. (다)는 b로 시작할 것. (4점)

(다): _____     (라): _____ you

**19.** 위 글의 밑줄 친 (마)를 알맞게 배열하고, 한 단어를 추가하여 쓰시오. (4점)

정답: _____

**[20~23]** 다음 글을 읽고 물음에 답하시오.

ⓐSpork and Chopsticks, Knork, Barehands, Ms. Disher are close friends in the Dining Republic. Spork, Chopsticks, Knork, and Barehands travel a lot with their families, (A)_____ Ms. Disher's family does not travel much. ⓑUnderline She makes up for this by host a dinner for her friends coming back from their trips. ⓒShe always is eager to listen to their adventures. ⓓThey talk often about what they learned from their recent trips. ⓔThe most recent topic was about the best way to eat and Ms. Disher's guests began to arguing.

**Spork:** On a recent trip, I have found that it is best to use a spoon and fork. A spoon is best for grains and soup, and a fork is good for eating meat.

**Knork:** No! It is much better to use a knife and a fork instead. Don't you think it is easier for you to hold a fork in one hand and a knife in the other? What can be more elegant than using them to cut meat on a plate!

**Chopsticks:** Why do you use two different kinds of utensils when you can use two of the same utensil? Plus, you can use chopsticks with just one hand!

**Barehands:** No way! When I eat with my hands, of course I can see and smell the food, but I can also touch it. Because I use my sense of touch when I eat, I get to enjoy my food more.

They raised and argued many points, and nobody wanted to give up. (B)_____. So, she hurriedly, yet quietly, left.

20. 위 글의 등장인물들이 말한 내용과 일치하는 것은?　　(4점)

① Spork: 숟가락은 야채와 밥을 먹기에 최고이고, 포크는 고기를 자르는 데 좋아.
② Knork: 네가 한 손으로 포크와 나이프를 드는 것이 더 쉽다고 생각하지 않니?
③ Spork: 최근 여행에서 나이프와 포크를 사용하는 것이 가장 좋다는 것을 알았어.
④ Chopsticks: 서로 다른 도구 두 개를 쓸 수 있는데 왜 같은 종류의 도구를 사용한단 말이야?
⑤ Barehands: 음식을 먹을 때 촉각을 사용하기 때문에 음식을 더 즐기게 돼.

21. 위 글의 빈칸 (A)에 들어갈 적절한 말은?　　(3점)

① But　　② And　　③ Then
④ So　　⑤ Or

22. 위 글의 밑줄 친 ⓐ~ⓔ 중 어법상 옳은 문장은?　　(4점)

① ⓐ　　② ⓑ　　③ ⓒ　　④ ⓓ　　⑤ ⓔ

23. 위 글의 빈칸 (B)에 들어갈 문장으로 가장 알맞은 것은?　(4점)

① It was easy of their host, Ms. Disher, to listen to their arguments patiently.
② It was easy for their host, Ms. Disher, to listen to their arguments patiently.
③ It was not easy for their host, Ms. Disher, listen to their arguments patiently.
④ It was not easy of their host, Ms. Disher, to listen to their arguments patiently.
⑤ It was not easy for their host, Ms. Disher, to listen to their arguments patiently.

**Spork:** On a recent trip. I have found that it is best to use a spoon and fork. A spoon is best ⓐ_____ grains and soup, and a fork is good for eating meat.

**Knork:** No! It is ⓑ_____ better to use a knife and a fork instead. Don't you think (A)네가 한 손에는 포크를 나머지 다른 한 손에는 나이프를 드는 것이 더 쉽다고? What can be more elegant ⓒ_____ using them to cut meat on a plate!

**Chopsticks:** Why do you use two different kinds of utensils when you can use two of the same utensil? Plus, you can use chopsticks ⓓ_____ just one hand!

**Barehands:** No way! When I eat with my hands, of course I can see and smell the food, but I can also touch it. ⓔ_____ I use my sense of touch when I eat, I get to enjoy my food more.

They raised and argued many points, and nobody wanted to give up. (B)그들의 주최자인 Ms. Disher가 그들의 논쟁들을 참을성 있게 듣는 것은 쉽지 않았다. So, she hurriedly, yet quietly, left.

[충북 ○○중]

**24.** 위 글의 밑줄 친 (A)를 가장 바르게 영작한 것은? (4점)

네가 한 손에는 포크를 나머지 다른 한 손에는 나이프를 드는 것이 더 쉽다.

① it is easier you to hold a fork in one hand and a knife in the other

② it is easy of you to hold a fork in one hand and a knife in the other

③ it is easier for you hold a fork in one hand and a knife in the other

④ it is easy for you to hold a fork in one hand and a knife in another

⑤ it is easier for you to hold a fork in one hand and a knife in the other

[충북 ○○중]

**25.** 위 글의 ⓐ~ⓔ에 들어갈 표현으로 알맞지 않은 것은? (4점)

① ⓐ – for  　　② ⓑ – very

③ ⓒ – than  　　④ ⓓ – with

⑤ ⓔ – Because

[충북 ○○중]

**26.** 위 글의 밑줄 친 (B)를 〈조건〉에 맞게 문장으로 영작하시오. (4점)

그들의 주최자인 Ms. Disher가 그들의 논쟁들을 참을성 있게 듣는 것은 쉽지 않다.

┌─ 조건 ┤
- 가주어 it, 의미상 주어, 진주어 to부정사 구문을 이용할 것.
- 동격 구문을 사용할 것.
- 'listen', 'patient', 'arguments'를 사용할 것. (필요한 경우 형태 변형 가능)
- 과거시제를 사용할 것.

정답: _____

◎ 선택형 문항의 답안은 컴퓨터용 수정 싸인펜을 사용하여 OMR 답안지에 바르게 표기하시오.
◎ 서술형 문제는 답을 답안지에 반드시 검정 볼펜으로 쓰시오.
◎ 총 26문항 100점 만점입니다. 문항별 배점은 각 문항에 표시되어 있습니다.

[영등포구 ○○중]

**1. 다음 관용어구의 뜻이 어색한 것은?**          (3점)

① as a result: 그 결과
② regardless of: ~ 때문에
③ make up for: ~을 보상하다
④ come up with: ~을 생각해 내다
⑤ be eager to: ~하고 싶어하다

[충북 ○○중]

**2. 다음 주어진 대화 다음에 이어질 대화의 순서로 알맞은 것은?**
          (4점)

A: What time is it now?
B: It's already 8 p.m.
A: Why don't we stop now and have a meal?
B: Good idea. We need to take a break at this point.
A: Which do you prefer, having a meal early or late in the evening?

(A) I usually go to bed early, so I eat my last meal early too. How about you?
(B) What is the reason?
(C) I prefer having a meal early.
(D) I have meals late in the evening, because I work late at night.

① (A)–(B)–(D)–(C)     ② (A)–(C)–(B)–(D)
③ (B)–(D)–(A)–(C)     ④ (C)–(B)–(A)–(D)
⑤ (C)–(D)–(A)–(B)

[충북 ○○중]

**3. 다음 대화의 밑줄 친 ⓐ~ⓔ 중 흐름상 어색한 것은?**          (4점)

G: What can we do to stay healthy?
B: ⓐI think having healthy food is important.
G: My brother exercises every day for his health.
B: ⓑWhich do you prefer, having healthy food or exercising?
G: I can't control which food I eat. ⓒSo, I prefer to have healthy food.
B: ⓓBoth of them seem to be important for our health.
G: But if you can't do both, it might be better to focus on just one.
B: I think you are right. ⓔI'm going to exercise first.

① ⓐ     ② ⓑ     ③ ⓒ     ④ ⓓ     ⑤ ⓔ

[충북 ○○중]

**4. 다음 대화의 내용과 일치하는 것은?**          (4점)

A: It seems to me that you don't like the food.
B: No, I enjoyed the food. I usually leave some food on my plate. That's good table manners in my country, China.
A: Why is that?
B: We think finishing everything on the plate means that you are still hungry.
A: It is more polite to finish everything on your plate in Korea, though.
B: Different cultures have different rules.

① B는 A가 준 음식이 마음에 들지 않았다.
② B는 중국의 식사 예절에 따라 접시의 음식을 모두 먹었다.

③ 한국에서는 접시에 음식을 남기면 아직 배가 고프다는 의미이다.

④ 한국에서는 접시의 음식을 모두 먹는 것이 더 예의 바른 행동이다.

⑤ 다른 문화라도 비슷한 예절을 따르는 경우가 많다.

**[5~6]** 다음 대화를 읽고 물음에 답하시오.

> M: We need to take a break at this point.
> W: Which do you prefer, (가)<u>or / late / meal / early / a / having</u> (일찍 또는 늦게 밥 먹는 것 중) in the evening?
> M: I prefer having a meal early.
> W: What is the reason?
> M: I usually go to bed early, so I eat my last meal early, too. (나)<u>넌 어떠니?</u>
> W: I have meals late in the evening because I work late at night.

**5. 밑줄 친 (가)를 우리말에 맞게 배열하시오.** (4점)

정답: _____

**6. 밑줄 친 (나)를 3 단어의 영어로 쓰시오. (how로 시작할 것.)** (4점)

정답: _____

**7. 다음 대화의 내용과 일치하는 것은?** (4점)

> Girl: What can we do to stay healthy?
> Boy: I think having healthy food is important.
> Girl: My brother exercises every day for his health.
> Boy: Which do you prefer, having healthy food or exercising, Emma?
> Girl: I can't control which food I eat. So, I prefer to exercise.
> Boy: Both of them seem to be important for our health.
> Girl: But if you can't do both, it might be better to focus on just one.
> Boy: I think you are right. I'm going to exercise first.

① 여학생은 음식 조절을 잘하는 편이다.

② 남학생은 운동과 음식 조절을 동시에 할 계획이다.

③ 여학생의 오빠는 건강을 위해 매일 음식 조절을 한다.

④ 남학생은 끝까지 여학생의 말에 동의하지 않고 있다.

⑤ 여학생은 운동과 음식 조절 중 한 가지에 집중하는 것이 좋다고 말한다.

8. 다음 대화를 요약한 글에서 밑줄 친 부분이 올바르지 <u>않은</u> 것은?

(4점)

W: It seems to me that it's time for dinner. Are you hungry?

B: Yes. Can we order pizza for dinner?

W: I'm going to cook fish, Jacob. Cooking at home is much healthier than ordering pizza.

B: But we can save time by ordering pizza. I'm so hungry.

W: Dinner will be ready soon. So, please be patient.

B: Okay.

*W: mom B: son

↓

Jacob wants to ⓐorder pizza for dinner. But his mom plans to ⓑcook pizza at home. His mom thinks ⓒcooking at home is much better for the health than ordering pizza. But Jacob thinks ⓓordering food can ⓔsave time.

① ⓐ  ② ⓑ  ③ ⓒ  ④ ⓓ  ⑤ ⓔ

9. 다음 대화의 빈칸에 우리말에 해당하는 영어 문장을 3단어로 쓰시오.

(3점)

A: Which do you prefer, fish or steak?

B: _____ (나는 생선이 더 좋아.)

정답: _____

10. 다음 대화가 자연스럽게 이어지도록 주어진 부분 다음에 이어질 내용을 순서대로 배열한 것은?

(4점)

A: Claire, which do you prefer, fish or steak?

B: I prefer fish, Jinho.

A: There is fish on the menu.

ⓐ Both are on the menu.

ⓑ Then I will have sushi. It seems to me that fish tastes better when it's uncooked.

ⓒ That's good. Is it sushi or fried?

ⓓ Okay. Then you get sushi and I'll get fried fish. Let's order.

① ⓐ － ⓑ － ⓓ － ⓒ

② ⓐ － ⓒ － ⓑ － ⓓ

③ ⓑ － ⓓ － ⓐ － ⓒ

④ ⓒ － ⓑ － ⓓ － ⓐ

⑤ ⓒ － ⓐ － ⓑ － ⓓ

11. 다음 우리말에 맞도록 주어진 단어를 사용하여 〈보기〉와 같이 영어로 쓰시오.

(4점)

┌ 보기 ┐

It is difficult for me to solve the problem.

(necessary, is, people, recycle)

사람들이 재활용하는 것이 필요하다.

정답: _____

**12. 다음 주어진 단어를 배열하여 문장을 완성하시오.**　　(4점)

> It seems to me that (it, time, is, for, dinner).

정답: It seems to me that ＿＿＿＿＿＿＿＿＿＿.

**14. 다음 조건에 맞게 영어 문장을 만드시오.**　　(4점)

> ┌─ 조건 ┤
> 1. "네가 내 생일을 기억해 주다니 정말 친절하구나."와 의미가 같을 것.
> 2. It, very nice, remember, birthday를 사용할 것.
> 3. 문장으로 쓸 것.

→ ＿＿＿＿＿＿＿＿＿＿＿＿＿＿＿＿＿＿

**13. 다음 주어진 단어를 활용하여 〈보기〉와 같이 영어로 쓰시오.**　　(4점)

> ┌─ 보기 ┤
> People are recycling. (necessary)
> → It is necessary for people to recycle.

> Children are riding a bike without a helmet. (dangerous)

정답: ＿＿＿＿＿＿＿＿＿＿＿＿＿＿＿＿

**15. 다음 (1), (2)의 우리말을 주어진 단어를 활용하여 알맞게 영작하시오. (필요시 형태를 바꿀 것.)**　　(5점)

> (1) 나는 그가 달아나는 것을 보았다. (과거형) (see / run away)
> (2) 나는 그녀가 피아노 연주하는 것을 들었다. (과거형) (hear / the piano)

(1) ＿＿＿＿＿＿＿＿＿＿＿＿＿＿＿＿
(2) ＿＿＿＿＿＿＿＿＿＿＿＿＿＿＿＿

**[16~19]** 다음 글을 읽고 물음에 답하시오.

Spork, Chopsticks, Knork, Barehands, and Ms. Disher are close friends in the Dining Republic. Spork, Chopsticks, Knork, and Barehands travel a lot with their families, but Ms. Disher's family does not travel much. She makes up for this by hosting a dinner for her friends coming back from their trips. She is always eager to listen to their adventures. 그들은 최근 여행에서 배운 것에 대해 자주 이야기합니다. The most recent topic was about the best way to eat and Ms. Disher's guests began to argue.

**Spork:** On a recent trip, I have found that it is best to use a spoon and fork. A spoon is best for grains and soup, and a fork is good for eating meat.

**Knork:** No! It is much better to use a knife and a fork instead. Don't you think it is easier for you to hold a fork in one hand and a knife in the other? What can be more elegant than using them to cut meat on a plate!

**Chopsticks:** Why do you use two different kinds of utensils _____ you can use two of the same utensil? Plus, you can use chopsticks with just one hand!

**Barehands:** No way! _____ I eat with my hands, of course I can see and smell the food, but I can also touch it. Because I use my sense of touch _____ I eat, I get to enjoy my food more.

They raised and argued many points, and nobody wanted to give up. It was not easy for their host, Ms. Disher, to listen to their arguments patiently. So, she hurriedly, yet quietly, left.

16. 위 글의 내용과 일치하는 것은? (4점)

① Spork hosts a dinner for Ms. Disher.

② Ms. Disher loves to talk about her trip.

③ Ms. Disher travels a lot with her family.

④ Four friends had an argument on what is the best way to eat.

⑤ Spork, Chopsticks, Knork, Barehands, and Ms. Disher are close cousins in the Dining Republic.

17. 위 글의 빈칸에 공통으로 들어갈 말은? (3점)

① who / Who      ② where / Where

③ how / How      ④ when / When

⑤ what / What

18. 위 글을 읽고 대답할 수 <u>없는</u> 질문은? (4점)

① Why does Ms. Disher host a dinner for her friends?

② Why did Ms. Disher leave?

③ According to Chopsticks, what is the disadvantage of using chopsticks?

④ What is the reason that Knork believes that it is much better to use a knife and a fork?

⑤ What is the reason that Spork believes that it is best to use a spoon and fork?

**19.** 위 글의 밑줄 친 우리말에 맞는 영어 문장으로 올바른 것은?

(4점)

① They talk often about which they learned from their recent trips.

② They often talk about which they learned from their recent trips.

③ They talk often about they learned what from their recent trips.

④ They often talk about what they learned from their recent trips.

⑤ They talk about often what they learned from their recent trips.

**20.** 다음은 식사도구에 대한 설명이다. 내용상 <u>틀린</u> 부분을 고쳐 쓰시오.

(6점)

> Spork: On a recent trip, I have found that it is best to use a spoon and fork. A spoon is best for grains and soup, and a fork is good for eating meat.
>
> Knork: No! It is much better to use a knife and a fork instead. Don't you think it is easier for you to hold a fork in one hand and a knife in the other? What can be more elegant than using them to cut meat on a plate!
>
> Chopsticks: Why do you use two different kinds of utensils when you can use two of the same utensil? Plus, you can use chopsticks with just one hand!
>
> Barehands: No way! When I eat with my hands, of course I can see and smell the food, but I can also touch it. Because I use my sense of touch when I eat, I get to enjoy my food more.

(1) Spork: A spoon is best for eating meat.

정답: _____

(2) Chopsticks: You can use forks with just one hand.

정답: _____

(3) Barehands: I can see, smell, and cook the food.

정답: _____

**[21~22]** 다음 글을 읽고 물음에 답하시오.

> Knork: No! It is (A)[much / very] better to use a knife and a fork instead. Don't you think it is easier to hold a fork in one hand and a knife in (B)[the other / another]? What can be more elegant than using them to cut meat on a plate!
>
> Chopsticks: Why do you use two different kinds of utensils when you can use two of the same utensil? ⓐ_____, you can use chopsticks with just one hand!
>
> Barehands: No way! When I eat with my hands, of course I can see and smell the food, but I can also touch (C)[it / them]. Because I use my sense of touch when I eat, I get to enjoy my food more.

**21. 위 글의 괄호 (A), (B), (C) 안에서 바르게 짝지어진 것은? (4점)**

| | (A) | (B) | (C) |
|---|---|---|---|
| ① | very | another | it |
| ② | very | the other | it |
| ③ | very | another | them |
| ④ | much | the other | them |
| ⑤ | much | the other | it |

**22. 위 글의 빈칸 ⓐ에 들어갈 연결사로 적절하지 않은 것은? (3점)**

① Also    ② Besides    ③ Plus
④ However    ⑤ Moreover

**[23~25]** 다음 글을 읽고 물음에 답하시오.

They raised and argued many points, and nobody wanted to give up. Ms. Disher found it difficult to listen to their arguments patiently. So, she hurriedly, yet (A)[quietly / quite], left.

**Spork:** Where is Ms. Disher? She has disappeared.
**Knork:** What should we do? Without Ms. Disher, this dinner is not complete.
**Chopsticks:** Where did she go?
**Barehands:** Let's go out to find her!
After discovering Ms. Disher had (B)[disappeared / appeared], the friends searched all over the Dining Republic for her. When they found her, she sat under a huge tree.

**Spork, Knork, Chopsticks, Barehands:** We're sorry we became (C)[boastful / modest]

and ignored you. Please forgive us and come back and join us.
**Ms. Disher:** It's okay. I forgive you. Let's go back to my home.

Since then, every time they meet, ⓐ그들은 서로가 좋아하는 방식으로 음식을 먹는 것을 허용한다. In their hearts they now know that food will always be delicious regardless of which utensils they use to eat it with.

**23. 위 글을 읽고, 다음 질문에 대한 답을 알 수 있는 것은? (3점)**

① Where was Ms. Disher?
② Is Ms. Disher sad often?
③ Is Ms. Disher good at cooking?
④ Who does Ms. Disher like the most?
⑤ Why did Ms. Disher plant the huge tree?

**24. 위 글의 괄호 (A), (B), (C) 안에서 바르게 짝지어진 것은? (3점)**

| | (A) | (B) | (C) |
|---|---|---|---|
| ① | quite | appeared | boastful |
| ② | quite | appeared | modest |
| ③ | quietly | disappeared | boastful |
| ④ | quietly | disappeared | modest |
| ⑤ | quietly | appeared | boastful |

**25. 위 글의 밑줄 친 ⓐ의 우리말을 바르게 영작한 것은?** (4점)

① they allow one another eat in the manner which they please

② they allow one another to eat in the manner that they please

③ they allow each other eating in the manner that they please

④ they allow each other to eating in the manner what they please

⑤ they allow one another to eat in the manner what they please

**26. 다음 글의 흐름과 관계없는 문장을 하나 쓰시오.** (3점)

Spork, Chopsticks, Knork, Barehands, and Ms. Disher are close friends in the Dining Republic. Spork, Chopsticks, Knork, and Barehands travel a lot with their families, but Ms. Disher's family does not travel much. She makes up for this by hosting a dinner for her friends coming back from their trips. She is always eager to listen to their adventures. She joined an adventure club recently. They often talk about what they learned from their recent trips. The most recent topic was about the best way to eat and Ms. Disher's guests began to argue.

정답: _____

# 3학년 영어 1학기 기말고사(3과) 1회

문항수 : 선택형(23문항)  서술형(1문항)  20 .  .  .

◎ 선택형 문항의 답안은 컴퓨터용 수정 싸인펜을 사용하여 OMR 답안지에 바르게 표기하시오.
◎ 서술형 문제는 답을 답안지에 반드시 검정 볼펜으로 쓰시오.
◎ 총 24문항 100점 만점입니다. 문항별 배점은 각 문항에 표시되어 있습니다.

[부산 ○○중]

**1. 다음 중 뜻풀이가 잘못된 것은?** (4점)

① wake up: 일어나다
② turn away: 외면하다
③ scare away: 쫓아내다
④ float away: 멀리 던지다
⑤ be afraid of: ~을 두려워하다

[영등포구 ○○중]

**2. 다음 중 단어의 뜻풀이가 올바른 것을 모두 골라 묶은 것은?** (4점)

ⓐ polite – having good manners for other people
ⓑ creative – to touch something
ⓒ patient – staying calm for a long time and not annyoyed
ⓓ inspire – to give someone a new idea
ⓔ control – to say what food you want in a restaurant

① ⓐ, ⓑ, ⓓ   ② ⓐ, ⓒ, ⓓ   ③ ⓐ, ⓓ, ⓔ
④ ⓑ, ⓒ, ⓔ   ⑤ ⓒ, ⓓ, ⓔ

[영등포구 ○○중]

**3. 다음 대화의 내용과 일치하지 않는 것은?** (4점)

W: Today, we have a special guest, Thomas Thwaites, the Goat Man. Hello, Thomas.
M: Hello, Anna. Great to be here.
W: Thomas, I'm so fascinated by the fact that you lived like a goat in the Alps for three days. Why did you do that?
M: One day, I saw goats playing on the mountain. They looked so peaceful that I wanted to live like them.
W: Didn't you have any problems being a goat?
M: Walking on all four legs was very difficult for me.
W: Do you have any plans to live like a goat again?
M: Sure. I'm planning my second visit to the Alps.
W: I can't wait to hear about your next adventure. Thank you, Thomas, for your time.

① Goat Man은 Thomas Thwaites의 별명이다.
② Thomas는 알프스 산에서 3일 동안 염소처럼 살았다.
③ Anna는 Thomas의 경험에 매우 흥미 있어 한다.
④ 네 다리로 걷는 것은 Thomas에게 문제가 되지 않았다.
⑤ Thomas는 다시 알프스 산에 가려고 계획하고 있다.

**4. 두 대화의 빈칸에 공통으로 들어갈 표현은?** (4점)

(A) B: ( ) this noodle cooling fan.

G: A noodle cooling fan? I've never heard of it.

B: This little fan will cool noodles when they're very hot.

G: That looks funny but useful.

(B) G: This candle holder can make candles last twice as long.

B: Really? How's that possible?

G: When a candle burns, it melts into the tube below the holder to form a new candle.

B: Wow, ( ) the idea! Now we can use candles longer.

① It is fascinated by

② I'm really impressed by

③ I'm not impressed by

④ I have heard about

⑤ I'm really interested in

**5. 다음 밑줄 친 ⓐ～ⓔ 중 흐름상 어색한 것은?** (4점)

G: ⓐYou know that Leonardo da Vinci painted the Mona Lisa, don't you?

B: ⓑNo, I don't. I think he was a really great artist.

G: ⓒHe was also a great inventor.

B: What did he invent?

G: He dreamed of flying like a bird. ⓓSo, he drew a flying machine that looked like a bird.

B: Did he also make that machine?

G: ⓔNo, but his creative idea inspired many other inventors.

① ⓐ     ② ⓑ     ③ ⓒ     ④ ⓓ     ⑤ ⓔ

**6. ⓐ～ⓓ를 대화의 흐름에 맞게 배열한 것은?** (4점)

A: Have you heard of a mosquito needle, Jian?

B: A mosquito needle? Can you explain it to me?

A: Some scientists made this new needle by imitating a mosquito's mouth.

ⓐ That's interesting. So how will that help?

ⓑ That's great. How come it's less painful?

ⓒ You know mosquito bites are not very painful, don't you? The new needle will also cause less pain.

ⓓ Like a mosquito's mouth, it makes less contact with our skin.

B: Wow, I think that there's nothing useless in the world!

① ⓐ-ⓑ-ⓒ-ⓓ
② ⓐ-ⓒ-ⓑ-ⓓ
③ ⓑ-ⓒ-ⓐ-ⓓ
④ ⓑ-ⓓ-ⓐ-ⓒ
⑤ ⓒ-ⓐ-ⓓ-ⓑ

**8. 다음 밑줄 친 ①~⑤ 중 대화의 흐름상 어색한 것을 고르시오. (4점)**

> B: Have you heard of a mosquito needle, Jian?
>
> G: A mosquito needle? ①Can you explain it to me?
>
> B: Some scientists made this new needle by imitating a mosquito's mouth.
>
> G: That's interesting. ②So how will that help?
>
> B: ③You know mosquito bites are not very painful, don't you? The new needle will also cause less pain.
>
> G: That's great. ④How come it's less painful?
>
> B: Like a mosquito's mouth, it makes less contact with our skin.
>
> G: ⑤Wow, I think that there's nothing useful in the world!

**7. 다음 중 밑줄 친 부분을 바르게 고친 것은? (3점)**

① There is a bench to sit.
  → There is a bench to sit under.
② There are two boys walk in the park.
  → There are two boys walked in the park.
③ Not only James but also his sister being good at math.
  → Not only James but also his sister are good at math.
④ My father likes not only hiking but also to fish.
  → My father likes not only hiking but also to fishing.
⑤ I wonder when did she leave here.
  → I wonder when she left here.

**9. 다음 중 어법상 올바른 것은? (4점)**

① He gave me not only advice but also money.
② Not only have I play the guitar but also the drums.
③ Not only he but also you is wrong.
④ Not only James but also his sisters is good at math.
⑤ She enjoys not only running but also to swim in the pool.

**10.** 다음 중 어법상 올바른 문장을 <u>모두</u> 고른 것은?  (5점)

ⓐ She knows exactly what she is doing.

ⓑ Can you tell me why are you upset?

ⓒ He is not only smart but also friendly.

ⓓ Not only do I study a lot, but I also play a lot.

ⓔ Do you think where she is from?

ⓕ Not only children but also adults likes his new song.

① ⓐ, ⓒ, ⓓ  ② ⓐ, ⓔ, ⓕ  ③ ⓑ, ⓒ, ⓓ

④ ⓑ, ⓒ, ⓔ  ⑤ ⓒ, ⓓ, ⓕ

**11.** 다음 대화의 흐름상 빈칸 (A)에 알맞은 것을 2개 고르시오.  (4점)

Henry: What are you doing, Mina?

Mina: I'm reading an article about a bug robot.

Henry: A bug robot? Is it interesting?

Mina: Yes. _____(A)_____

Henry: Can you tell me more about it?

Mina: You know that some bugs can slip into narrow spaces, don't you?

Henry: Yeah. That's why it's hard to catch them.

Mina: A bug robot can do the same. It can help to find survivors after earthquakes or big fires.

Henry: That's really fascinating!

① I'm so good at this thing.

② This thing is really impressive.

③ This thing impresses you a lot.

④ I'm really fascinated by this thing.

⑤ It is less interesting than other articles.

**12.** 다음 중 어법상 적절한 것은?  (4점)

① What he didn't do it was his science homework.

② He heard Amber to walk into the room.

③ She not only likes reading books in her room but also enjoys hanging out with her friends.

④ It is very kind for you to help your grandfather!

⑤ Can you guess what did I get for my birthday?

**[13~16]** 다음 글을 읽고 물음에 답하시오.

One day, a Swiss engineer, George de Mestral, was hiking in the woods with his dog. On his way home, he saw that burrs were stuck to his clothes and his dog's hair. ( ① ) He took a closer look at the burrs and noticed that the ends of the burr needles were not straight. ( ② ) He wondered if he could apply ⓐthat to make something useful. ( ③ ) After a lot of testing, he finally invented ⓑtwo new materials. ( ④ ) One had many tiny needles like those of burrs and the other had a hairy surface. ( ⑤ ) When ⓒthey were pressed together, they became a very good fastener. 그것은 튼튼할 뿐만 아니라, 사용하기도 쉬웠다. Since then, many people have used ⓓhis invention in many different ways. It is often used for clothing, shoes, and bags. Some people use it to play a number of different games. In space, ⓔit keeps things from floating away.

**13.** 위 글의 흐름으로 보아, 주어진 문장이 들어가기에 가장 적절한 곳을 고르시오. (4점)

> He wanted to know how that happened.

①      ②      ③      ④      ⑤

**14.** 위 글의 내용과 일치하지 않는 것은? (4점)

① 산책을 다녀온 후, 스위스 공학자의 옷과 개의 털은 가시 식물의 가시로 덮여 있었다.
② 가시 식물의 가시 끝은 일직선이었다.
③ 잠금장치(fastener)는 가시 식물에서 영감을 얻어 개발되었다.
④ 잠금장치(fastener)의 한쪽은 표면이 털로 되어 있다.
⑤ 잠금장치(fastener)는 다양한 놀이에도 사용되고 있다.

**15.** 위 글의 밑줄 친 @~@ 중 가리키는 대상이 다른 하나는? (4점)

① @    ② ⓑ    ③ ⓒ    ④ ⓓ    ⑤ ⓔ

**16.** 위 글의 밑줄 친 우리말을 조건에 따라서 영어로 옮기시오. (4점)

┌─ 조건 ─┐
- 10단어로 쓰시오.
- only, also, easy, to를 이용하시오.

정답: _____

**17.** 다음 주어진 문장을 빈칸에 넣을 때 알맞은 형태로 바꿔 쓰시오. (5점)

(1) Why does an elephant have a trunk?
→ Do you know _____?

(2) Will he come back soon?
→ I'm wondering _____.

**[18~20]** 다음 글을 읽고 물음에 답하시오.

> <Learning from a Bird: Moving Fast and Quietly>
> The high-speed train was first made in Japan. But it had one problem. When the train entered a tunnel, the sudden increase in air pressure created a very loud sound. It often woke people up and caused headaches. @A team of engineers tried to solve the problem, but they didn't know how they could reduce the noise. One day, one of the engineers was watching a bird (㉠ ~을 찾고 있는) a meal. ⓑHe saw the bird quickly and quietly diving into the water. He wondered how the bird entered the water so gracefully. So, he studied more about the bird and discovered its long, narrow beak. He redesigned the front of the train by imitating the bird's beak. It was successful. ⓒNow the new train travels not only more quietly but also 10% fast with 15% less electricity.
>
> <Learning from Burrs: Inventing an All-Purpose Fastener>
> One day, a Swiss engineer, George de Mestral, was hiking in the woods with his dog. (㉡그가

집으로 가는 도중에), he saw that burrs were stuck to his clothes and his dog's hair. He wanted to know how that happened. He (ⓒ ~을 자세히 살펴봤다) the burrs and noticed that the ends of the burr needles were not straight. ⓓHe wondered if he could apply that to make something useful. After a lot of testing, he finally invented two new materials. One had many tiny needles like those of burrs and the other had a hairy surface. When they were pressed together, they became a very good fastener. ⓔIt was not only strong but also easy to use. Since then, many people have used his invention in many different ways. It is often used for clothing, shoes, and bags. Some people use it to play a number of different games. In space, it keeps things from (ⓔ떠다니는 것).

[강동구 ○○중]

**18. 위 글의 밑줄 친 ⓐ~ⓔ 중 어법상 어색한 것을 고르시오. (4점)**

① ⓐ  ② ⓑ  ③ ⓒ  ④ ⓓ  ⑤ ⓔ

[강동구 ○○중]

**19. 위 글의 ㉠~㉣에 들어갈 표현이 시제, 어법에 맞게 바르게 연결된 것을 고르시오. (5점)**

① in search of – on him way home – took a closer look at – floating away

② in search for – on his way home – took a closer look – float away

③ in search of – on him way home – took a closer look – floating away

④ in search at – on his way home – took a closer look at – to float away

⑤ in search of – on his way home – took a closer look at – floating away

[강동구 ○○중]

**20. 위 글의 내용과 일치하지 않는 것을 고르시오. (4점)**

① 고속 열차는 처음 일본에서 만들어졌다.

② 새의 부리를 모방하여 열차의 앞면을 다시 디자인한 것이 성공적이었다.

③ 자연 재해를 극복해야만 자연 현상을 활용한 발명품을 만들 수 있다.

④ George는 자연을 주의 깊게 관찰해서 발명에 대한 좋은 아이디어를 얻었다.

⑤ 자연으로부터 아이디어를 얻어서 발명한 것들은 다양한 방식으로 사용될 수 있다.

**[21~22] 다음 글을 읽고 물음에 답하시오.**

(A) Polar Bears, North Pole

Polar bears survive the cold because they have black skin to easily absorb the heat from the sun. Each of their hairs has an air space. This also helps them stay warm.

(B) Wolves, Canada

Wolves are great hunters. Their wide feet help them travel a long way in the snow. Leadership is also important for their survival. The lead wolf decides when the group will travel and hunt. It also decides where to go and knows what to do when there is danger.

(C) Sahara Desert Ants, North Africa

ⓐ The Sahara Desert is located in north Africa. ⓑ The Sahara Desert is not only the driest but also the hottest place on earth. ⓒ But even at the hottest time of day, Sahara Desert ants go hunting. ⓓ Their bodies are covered with unique hairs that reflect the heat from the sun. ⓔ

21. 위 글의 내용으로 바른 것끼리 짝지어진 것을 고르시오. (5점)

> ㉠ 통솔력은 늑대의 생존에 별로 중요하지 않다.
> ㉡ 북극곰의 검은색 피부는 북극곰이 추위에서 생존하도록 도와준다.
> ㉢ 사하라 사막 개미들은 하루 중 가장 기온이 낮은 시간에 사냥을 간다.
> ㉣ 이 글은 극한의 자연환경에서 살아남은 동물들의 생존법을 다루고 있다.
> ㉤ 사하라 사막 개미들의 몸을 덮고 있는 독특한 털은 태양으로부터 열기를 반사해내는 역할을 한다.

① ㉡,㉢,㉤    ② ㉡,㉣,㉤    ③ ㉢,㉣,㉤
④ ㉠,㉡,㉢,㉣    ⑤ ㉠,㉡,㉢,㉤

22. 위 글의 (C) ⓐ~ⓔ 중 다음 문장이 들어가기 가장 알맞은 자리를 고르시오. (4점)

> Do you know how they survive the heat?

① ⓐ    ② ⓑ    ③ ⓒ    ④ ⓓ    ⑤ ⓔ

(A) The high-speed train was first made in Japan. But it had one problem. When the train entered a tunnel, the ⓐ[sudden / suddenly] increase in air pressure created a very loud sound. (B) It often woke people up and caused headaches. A team of engineers tried to solve the problem, but they didn't know how they could reduce the noise. (C) One day, one of the engineers was watching a bird in search of a meal. He saw the bird quickly and quietly ⓑ[to dive / diving] into the water. He wondered how the bird entered the water so gracefully. (D) He redesigned the front of the train by imitating the bird's beak. It was successful. (E) Now the new train travels not only more quietly but also 10% ⓒ[fast / faster] with 15% less electricity.

23. 위 글의 (A)~(E) 중 다음 주어진 문장이 들어갈 위치로 가장 적절한 곳은? (4점)

> So, he studied more about the bird and discovered its long, narrow beak.

① (A)    ② (B)    ③ (C)    ④ (D)    ⑤ (E)

24. 위 글의 괄호 ⓐ~ⓒ 안에 들어갈 말이 바르게 짝지어진 것은? (5점)

| | ⓐ | ⓑ | ⓒ |
|---|---|---|---|
| ① | sudden | to dive | faster |
| ② | suddenly | diving | fast |
| ③ | sudden | diving | faster |
| ④ | suddenly | to dive | fast |
| ⑤ | sudden | diving | fast |

# 3학년 영어 1학기 기말고사(3과) 2회

문항수 : 선택형(23문항)  서술형(2문항)  20 .  .  .

◎ 선택형 문항의 답안은 컴퓨터용 수정 싸인펜을 사용
  하여 OMR 답안지에 바르게 표기하시오.
◎ 서술형 문제는 답을 답안지에 반드시 검정 볼펜으로
  쓰시오.
◎ 총 25문항 100점 만점입니다. 문항별 배점은 각
  문항에 표시되어 있습니다.

[강동구 ○○중]

1. 다음 중 영영 풀이가 바른 것끼리 짝지어진 것을 고르시오.  (4점)

ⓐ needle: a small, very thin object that is used in sewing
ⓑ wing: a part of an animal's body that is used for walking
ⓒ imitate: to copy what someone does or produces
ⓓ genius: someone who shows a lack of good judgement
ⓔ fastener: a device such as a button or small hook that fastens something

① ⓐ, ⓒ, ⓓ  ② ⓐ, ⓒ, ⓔ  ③ ⓒ, ⓓ, ⓔ
④ ⓑ, ⓒ, ⓔ  ⑤ ⓐ, ⓑ, ⓒ

[영등포구 ○○중]

2. 다음 중 어느 빈칸에도 들어갈 수 없는 단어는? (대·소문자 무시)  (4점)

• The beauty of nature always _____ humans.
• _____ is 1% talent and 99% hard work.
• Necessity is the mother of _____.
• Boys try to _____ their fathers.

① fascinates  ② invention
③ genius  ④ imitate
⑤ beak

[강동구 ○○중]

3. 다음 문장의 빈칸에 알맞은 말로 짝지어진 것은?  (3점)

• I saw Tom _____ my way to school.
• She went into the kitchen in search _____ a drink.

① on – of  ② to – from
③ on – to  ④ at – for
⑤ in – with

[영등포구 ○○중]

4. 다음 중 짝지어진 대화가 어색한 것은?  (4점)

① A: Why don't we stop now and have a meal?
  B: Good idea. We need to take a break at this point.
② A: How about writing about the problem on the community website?
  B: That's a good idea.
③ A: A bug robot? Is it interesting?
  B: Yes, I'm really fascinated by this thing.
④ A: Have you heard of a mosquito needle, Jian?
  B: That's great. How come it's less painful?
⑤ A: I love our stickers!
  B: Me, too. I hope these stickers will be helpful.

[5~6] 다음 대화를 읽고 물음에 답하시오.

B: Have you heard of a mosquito needle, Jian?

G: ⓐ A mosquito needle? Can you explain it to me?

B: Some scientists made this new needle by imitating a mosquito's mouth.

G: That's interesting. ⓑ So how will that help?

B: ⓒ The new needle will also cause less pain.

G: That's great. ⓓ How come it's less painful?

B: Like a mosquito's mouth, it makes less contact with our skin.

G: ⓔ Wow, I think that there's nothing useless in the world!

[B: Tom / G: Jian]

[강동구 ○○중]

**5. 위 대화의 흐름상 주어진 문장이 들어갈 가장 알맞은 곳은?(4점)**

You know mosquito bites are not very painful, don't you?

① ⓐ     ② ⓑ     ③ ⓒ     ④ ⓓ     ⑤ ⓔ

[영등포구 ○○중]

**6. 위 대화를 읽고 나눈 대화 중 바르지 않은 것 두 개는? (3점)**

① A: 모기 주삿바늘은 왜 덜 고통스럽나요?
　 B: 우리의 피부와 덜 닿기 때문에요.

② A: 모기의 어떤 부분을 모방해서 주삿바늘을 만들었나요?
　 B: 모기의 입모양요.

③ A: Jian은 누구에게서 모기 주삿바늘에 대해 들었나요?
　 B: Tom에게서요.

④ A: 어느 나라에서 모기 주삿바늘이 처음 만들어졌나요?
　 B: 스위스요.

⑤ A: 세상에 쓸모없는 것에 대한 Jian의 생각은 무엇인가요?
　 B: 너무 많다고 생각해요.

[영등포구 ○○중]

**7. 다음 중 대화에 관한 설명으로 옳지 않은 것은? (5점)**

Anna: Today, we have a special guest, Thomas Thwaites, the Goat Man. Hello, Thomas.

Thomas: Hello, Anna. Great to be here.

Anna: Thomas, I'm so fascinated by the fact that you lived like a goat in the Alps for three days. Why did you do that?

Thomas: One day, I saw goats playing on the mountain. They looked so peaceful that I wanted to live like them.

Anna: Didn't you have any problems being a goat?

Thomas: Walking on all four legs was very difficult for me.

Anna: Do you have any plans to live like a goat again?

Thomas: Sure. I'm planning my second visit to the Alps.

Anna: I can't wait to hear about your next adventure. Thank you, Thomas, for your time.

① Anna는 진행자로서 참가자에 대한 소개를 하고 있다.

② Anna와 Thomas는 인터뷰에 앞서 서로에게 인사를 건네고 있다.

③ Thomas는 자신이 염소처럼 생활하게 된 배경에 대해 설명한다.

④ Thomas는 별 어려움 없이 3일 동안 염소처럼 살 수 있었다.

⑤ Anna는 인터뷰를 위해 시간을 내 준 Thomas에게 감사 인사를 하고 있다.

[8~9] 다음 대화를 읽고 물음에 답하시오.

---

Henry: What are you doing, Mina?

Mina: I'm reading an article about a bug robot.

Henry: A bug robot? Is it interesting?

Mina: Yes, I'm really fascinated by this thing.

Henry: Can you tell me more about it?

Mina: You know that some bugs can slip into narrow spaces, don't you?

Henry: Yes. That's why it's hard to catch them.

Mina: A bug robot can do the same. It can help to find survivors after earthquakes or big fires.

Henry: That's really fascinating!

---

[영등포구 ○○중]

8. 위 대화의 내용에서 유추한 것으로 옳지 <u>않은</u> 것은? (4점)

① Henry is wondering what Mina is doing.

② The bug robot in the article is really interesting to Mina.

③ Henry already knows a lot about the bug robot.

④ Mina is comparing the bug robot to real bugs.

⑤ Henry becomes interested in the bug robot.

[영등포구 ○○중]

9. 다음은 위 대화에 소개된 기사 내용의 일부이다. 대화에 근거했을 때 〈보기〉의 ⓐ~ⓔ 중 적절하지 <u>않은</u> 것은? (4점)

┌─ 보기 ┐

This Tiny Friend Can Save People's Life!

A team of scientists from London University invented a new robot named "Rolly." This ⓐbird robot is so small that it can ⓑslip into narrow spaces ⓒjust like some real bugs. If you're wondering why this is so fascinating, check this out: When ⓓearthquakes or big fires happen, Rolly can ⓔhelp find survivors trapped under destroyed buildings.

(The article continues ...)

└──────────┘

[영등포구 ○○중]

10. 다음 중 밑줄 친 것과 같은 문장 구조를 사용하는 목적으로 옳지 <u>않은</u> 것은? (4점)

① It is important <u>for you</u> to understand this problem.

Why you use it — to say who understands this problem

② That bird <u>flying in the sky</u> is an eagle.

Why you use it — to add more meaning to the phrase "That bird"

③ I don't know <u>where I can find him</u>.

Why you use it — to put a question inside another sentence

④ <u>Which do you prefer</u>, orange or apple?

Why you use it — to ask what you like more between the two things

⑤ You know mosquito bites are not that painful, <u>don't you</u>?

Why you use it — to ask why you don't know the answer to the question

[영등포구 ○○중]

11. 다음 중 어법상 적절하지 <u>않은</u> 것은? (3점)

① The girl standing on the stage is my sister.

② She saw Jack running across the field.

③ I understand why he had to tell a lie.

④ It is difficult for my son tie his shoelaces yet.

⑤ I have no idea why they are here.

**[12~14]** 다음 글을 읽고 물음에 답하시오.

Learning from Burrs: Inventing an All-Purpose Fastener

One day, a Swiss engineer, George de Mestral, was hiking in the woods with his dog. On his way home, he saw that burrs were stuck to his clothes and his dog's hair. He wanted to know how that happened. He took a closer look at the burrs and noticed that the ends of the burr needles were not straight. He wondered if he could apply that to make something useful. (A)_____, he invented two new materials after a lot of testing. One had many tiny needles like those of burrs and the other had ⓐa hairy surface. When they were pressed together, they became ⓑa very good fastener. It was not only strong but also easy to use. Since then, many people have used his invention in many different ways. (B)_____ ⓒit is often used for clothing, shoes, and bags. Some people use ⓓit to play a number of different games. In space, ⓔit keeps things from floating away.

There is nothing useless in nature. We just have to become curious and ask questions.

12. 위 글의 빈칸 (A), (B)에 들어갈 말로 알맞게 연결한 것은? (3점)

|   | (A) | (B) |
|---|-----|-----|
| ① | But | Finally |
| ② | So | But |
| ③ | For example | Finally |
| ④ | Finally | For example |
| ⑤ | For example | So |

13. 위 글의 밑줄 친 ⓐ~ⓔ 중 가리키는 대상이 <u>다른</u> 것은? (4점)

① ⓐ      ② ⓑ      ③ ⓒ      ④ ⓓ      ⑤ ⓔ

14. 위 글을 읽고 답할 수 <u>없는</u> 것은? (4점)

① How do people use the new fastener?

② Why are burrs easily stuck to clothes and hair?

③ What did the ends of the burr needles look like?

④ Is an all-purpose fastener used in many different ways?

⑤ How many times did the Swiss engineer take a test to make a fastener?

**[15~16]** 다음 글을 읽고 물음에 답하시오.

From flying birds to self-cleaning plants, the way nature works fascinates us. Some people not only use nature but also ( ⓐ ) it to find solutions to their problems. Leonardo da Vinci (1452–1519) was one such person. 그는 새들이 어떻게 날 수 있는지 궁금했다. He closely watched birds, made notes, and ( ⓑ ) pictures of them. Even though his invention was not successful, he imitated a bird's wings to make a flying machine.

15. 밑줄 친 우리말을 주어진 단어를 사용하여 영작할 때, ◆의 위치에 올 단어는? (4점)

fly, wondered, how, could, birds
→ He _____ _____ _____ ◆ _____ _____.

① fly      ② wondered      ③ how

④ could      ⑤ birds

**16.** 빈칸 ⓐ, ⓑ에 들어갈 말이 알맞게 짝지어진 것은? (4점)

|   | ⓐ | ⓑ |
|---|---|---|
| ① | imitate | drew |
| ② | imitate | to draw |
| ③ | to imitate | drew |
| ④ | to imitate | to draw |
| ⑤ | to imitate | drawing |

**18.** 위 글의 제목으로 가장 알맞은 것은? (4점)

① Imitating Nature to Find a Solution
② How to Avoid Headache in a Tunnel
③ Why the Train Caused a Loud Sound
④ Imitation: Creating High Air Pressure
⑤ The Best Way to Dive into the Water

**[17~19]** 다음 글을 읽고 물음에 답하시오.

The high-speed train was first made in Japan. But it had one problem. When the train entered a tunnel, the sudden increase in air pressure created a very loud sound. It often woke people up and caused headaches. A team of engineers tried to solve the problem, but they didn't know how they could ( ⓐ ) the noise. One day, one of the engineers was watching a bird in search of a meal. He saw the bird quickly and quietly diving into the water. He wondered how the bird entered the water so gracefully. So, he studied more about the bird and discovered its long, narrow beak. He redesigned the front of the train by ( ⓑ ) the bird's beak. It was successful.

**17.** 위 글의 빈칸 ⓐ, ⓑ에 들어갈 말이 맞게 짝지어진 것은? (4점)

|   | ⓐ | ⓑ |
|---|---|---|
| ① | reduce | ignoring |
| ② | reduce | imitating |
| ③ | reduce | inventing |
| ④ | increase | ignoring |
| ⑤ | increase | imitating |

**19.** 위 글의 내용과 일치하지 <u>않는</u> 것은? (4점)

① 초기의 고속 열차는 터널에 들어갈 때 큰 소음이 났다.
② 기술자 팀은 해결책을 찾는 데 실패한 적이 있다.
③ 초기의 고속 열차가 터널에서 나올 때 큰 소음이 발생했다.
④ 고속 열차는 처음 일본에서 만들었다.
⑤ 한 기술자가 새의 부리를 모방해서 소음 문제의 해결책을 찾았다.

**20.** 다음 글의 밑줄 친 ⓐ~ⓔ 중 옳은 표현은? (5점)

---

### Nature's Genius Around the World

#### Polar Bears, North Pole
Polar bears survive the cold because they have black skin to easily ⓐreflect the heat from the sun. Each of their hairs has an air space. This also helps them ⓑstay warm.

#### Wolves, Canada
Wolves are great hunters. Their wide feet help them travel a long way in the snow. Leadership is also important for their ⓒsurvive. The lead wolf decides when the group will travel and hunt. It also decides where to go and knows what to do when there is danger.

#### Sahara Desert Ants, North Africa
The Sahara Desert is not only the driest but also the hottest place on Earth. But even at the hottest time of day, Sahara Desert ants go hunting. Do you know how they ⓓsurvival the heat? Their bodies are covered with unique hairs that ⓔabsorb the heat from the sun.

---

① ⓐ ② ⓑ ③ ⓒ ④ ⓓ ⑤ ⓔ

---

**[21~23]** 다음 글을 읽고 물음에 답하시오.

---

One day, a Swiss engineer, George de Mestral, was hiking in the woods with his dog. On his way home, he saw that burrs were stuck to his clothes and his dog's hair. He wanted to know how (가)that happened. He took a closer look at the burrs and noticed that the ends of the burr needles were not straight. He wondered if he could apply ⓐthat to make something useful. After a lot of testing, he finally invented ⓑtwo new materials. One had many tiny needles like those of burrs and the other had a hairy surface. When they were pressed together, ⓒthey became a very good fastener. It was not only strong but also easy to use. Since then, many people have used ⓓhis invention in many different ways. It is often used for clothing, shoes, and bags. Some people use it to play a number of different games. In space, ⓔit keeps things from floating away.

---

**21.** 위 글의 제목으로 가장 알맞은 것은? (4점)

① Moving Fast and Quietly
② We Can Make a Difference
③ Invent by Imitating Nature
④ Be Cautious and Answer Questions
⑤ Necessity Is the Mother of Invention

---

**22.** 위 글의 밑줄 친 ⓐ~ⓔ 중 의미하는 것이 <u>다른</u> 하나는? (4점)

① ⓐ ② ⓑ ③ ⓒ ④ ⓓ ⑤ ⓔ

**23.** 위 글의 밑줄 친 (가)가 가리키는 것을 우리말로 쓰시오. (5점)

정답: _____

**25.** 위 글의 밑줄 친 우리말을 〈조건〉에 맞도록 문장을 완성하시오.

(5점)

┌─ 조건 ├─────────────────────────────┐
- how, wonder, birds, can을 사용하되, 필요시 어형을 바꿀 것.
- 간접 의문문을 사용할 것.
- 과거시제를 사용할 것.
└────────────────────────────────────┘

→ _____

**[24~25]** 다음 글을 읽고 물음에 답하시오.

From flying birds to self-cleaning plants, the way nature works fascinates us. Some people not only use nature but also imitate it to find solutions to their problems. Leonardo da Vinci (1452-1519) was one (A)such person. 그는 새들이 어떻게 날 수 있는지 궁금했다. He closely watched birds, made notes, and drew pictures of them. Even though his invention was not successful, he imitated a bird's wings to try to make a flying machine. Since then, more and more people have successfully imitated the surprising abilities of nature's genius. Let's explore some of them.

**24.** 위 글의 밑줄 친 (A)such person의 의미로 가장 적절한 것은?

(4점)

① 새를 관찰하는 것을 좋아하는 사람
② 스스로 깨끗하게 하는 식물을 기른 사람
③ 천연자원을 낭비하여 환경을 파괴한 사람
④ 자연을 모방하여 문제를 해결하려고 한 사람
⑤ 자연을 보호하기 위한 법을 만들어 낸 사람

# 3학년 영어 1학기 기말고사(4과) 1회

| 반 | | 점수 |
|---|---|---|
| 이름 | | |

문항수 : 선택형(23문항)   서술형(1문항)　　　20 .  .  .

◎ 선택형 문항의 답안은 컴퓨터용 수정 싸인펜을 사용하여 OMR 답안지에 바르게 표기하시오.
◎ 서술형 문제는 답을 답안지에 반드시 검정 볼펜으로 쓰시오.
◎ 총 24문항 100점 만점입니다. 문항별 배점은 각 문항에 표시되어 있습니다.

[영등포구 ○○중]

1. 다음 빈칸에 들어갈 수 없는 단어는?　　　(4점)

> • If you catch a cold, you _____ often.
> • Don't _____ your friends when they are studying.
> • I can _____ you my book if you want to borrow it.
> • Some people think it is _____ to ask someone's age.

① lend　　　② bother　　　③ sneeze
④ happen　　⑤ impolite

[영등포구 ○○중]

2. 다음 중 단어의 영영 풀이가 옳은 것은?　　　(4점)

① inspire – to get close to something and touch it
② melt – a person who makes new things
③ creative – alone; without other people
④ frightening – causing someone to become scared
⑤ match – being uncomfortable and in pain

[영등포구 ○○중]

3. 다음 중 단어의 영영 풀이가 올바르지 <u>않은</u> 것은?　　　(4점)

① crime: activities that involve breaking the law
② grab: to quickly hold someone or something with your hand or arms
③ norrow: long and not wide
④ apology: an act of saying that you are sorry for something wrong you have done
⑤ independent: confident but being able to do things only with the help of others

[영등포구 ○○중]

4. 다음 대화의 내용과 일치하는 것은?　　　(5점)

Title: Fountain
Artist: Marcel Duchamp

**Ms. Parker:** Now, take a look at this work of art. How do you like it?
**Jinho:** Well, is it even art?
**Henry:** To me, it isn't more than a toilet.
**Ms. Parker:** It is not just art. I think it is the greatest piece of art of the 20th century.
**Mina:** Why do you think so?
**Ms. Parker:** It is a perfect example of a different point of view. The artist used real-life objects to create art.
**Claire:** So, he didn't create something new?
**Ms. Parker:** That's right. He simply wanted people to look at the objects in a different way.
**Mina:** Thank you so much, Ms. Parker. I learned a lot today!

① Henny thinks Fountain is great art.
② The artist made new objects to create art.
③ The artist imitated real-life objects to make something new.
④ The artist wanted people to look at the objects in a different way.
⑤ Jinho thinks Fountain is the greatest piece of art of the 20th century.

**6. 위 대화의 내용과 일치하지 <u>않는</u> 것은?** (4점)

① Taeho read the book about Heungbu and Nolbu.
② Nolbu tells the story from his point of view in the book.
③ Nolbu didn't help Heungbu because Heungbu made money by himself.
④ Nolbu hoped that Heungbu would be independent.
⑤ Anna liked the story of the book that Taeho read.

**[5~6] 다음 대화를 읽고 물음에 답하시오.**

> G: Have you finished the book, Taeho?
> B: Yes. I finished it yesterday, Anna.
> G: _____
> B: It was interesting.
> G: What is the book about?
> B: You know the story of Heungbu, right? In the book, Nolbu tells the story from his point of view.
> G: What does he say?
> B: Well, he says he didn't help Heungbu for a reason. He wanted Heungbu to make money on his own and be independent.
> G: Wow, it's a unique story! I can't wait to read the book. Thanks. Taeho.

**5. 위 대화의 빈칸에 알맞은 표현은?** (4점)

① What do you like?
② How did you like it?
③ Which do you prefer?
④ What does it look like?
⑤ Why did you think so?

**7. 다음 대화의 흐름상 빈칸에 알맞은 것은?** (4점)

> W: You look worried, Juwon.
> B: I think we will lose the soccer game tomorrow, Ms. Kim.
> W: _____
> B: We will have a match against Class 3. They have the strongest players in the school.
> W: Look on the bright side. They might have strong players, but your class has the best teamwork.
> B: You're right. I didn't think about it that way. I'll go and practice!

① Why not? I'll try it.
② Why do you think so?
③ What do you think they did?
④ You know what your problem is?
⑤ I don't think you will lose the match.

**8. 다음 짝지어진 대화가 <u>어색한</u> 것을 고르시오.** (4점)

① A: Why don't we stop now and have a meal?

　B: Good idea. We need to take a break at this point.

② A: It seems to me that it's time for dinner. Are you hungry?

　B: Yes. Can we order pizza for dinner?

③ A: Which did you like better, soccer or baseball?

　B: Well, I liked soccer.

④ A: What do you think about my drawing, Prince?

　B: Wow, this picture is very great!

⑤ A: How did you like the soccer game?

　B: I think we will lose the soccer game tomorrow.

① ⓐ − ⓑ − ⓓ − ⓒ　② ⓐ − ⓒ − ⓑ − ⓓ

③ ⓑ − ⓒ − ⓐ − ⓓ　④ ⓑ − ⓐ − ⓓ − ⓒ

⑤ ⓒ − ⓓ − ⓐ − ⓑ

**9. 다음 대화의 빈칸 Ⓐ에 들어갈 말의 순서로 알맞은 것은?** (5점)

A: How did you like the movie *Good Friends*, Yura?

B: I liked it. It was fun to compare the movie with the original book.

< Ⓐ >

A: You're right.

ⓐ That's interesting. To me, the movie was better because it was easier to understand the story.

ⓑ Which did you like better, the movie or the book?

ⓒ I liked the movie, but I think I enjoyed the book more. It helped me understand the characters better.

ⓓ That's true. I guess they both have their own advantages.

**10. 다음 대화의 빈칸에 알맞은 표현으로 짝지어진 것은?** (4점)

B: (A)_____ the movie *Good Friends*, Yura?

G: I liked it. It was fun to compare the movie with the original book.

B: (B)_____ better, the movie or the book?

G: Well, I liked the movie, but I think I enjoyed the book more. The book helped me understand the characters better.

B: That's interesting. To me, the movie was better because it was easier to understand the story.

G: That's true. I guess they both have their own advantages.

B: You're right.

|                    (A)                    |              (B)              |
| --- |

① How did you like — Which did you like

② How did you like — What did you think about

③ What did you like — Which did you like

④ Why did you like — How did you feel

⑤ Which did you like — What did you like

[충북 ㅇㅇ중]

**11. 다음 중 밑줄 친 부분의 용법이 나머지 넷과 <u>다른</u> 것은?**　(4점)

① I study hard <u>to get a good grade</u>.

② I was excited <u>to see the special lunch menu</u>.

③ I am sad <u>to see my friend in the hospital</u>.

④ I am proud <u>to be on the school soccer team</u>.

⑤ I felt happy <u>to have her as my homeroom teacher</u>.

[충북 ㅇㅇ중]

**12. 다음 문장 중 올바른 것은?**　(4점)

① I had moved to Busan when I was twelve.

② I realized that I have made a big mistake.

③ I had been very tired because I didn't sleep well.

④ We did a good job because we had prepared a lot.

⑤ She has gone out when I arrived at the office.

---

**[13~15] 다음 글을 읽고 물음에 답하시오.**

R: Thank you, Mr. Pig. Now, let's meet our second guest, the wolf. Mr. Wolf, could you tell us what happened?

W: This whole "Big Bad Wolf" thing is wrong. The real story is about a sneeze from ⓐ<u>a terrible cold</u> and a cup of sugar.

R: What do you mean?

W: ⓑ<u>Back then</u>, I was making a birthday cake for my dear old grandmother. I ⓒ <u>ran out of</u> sugar. I walked down the street to ask my neighbor for a cup of sugar. When I knocked on the door, it fell down. Then I called, "Little pig, are you in?" I had just grabbed ⓓ<u>the broken door</u> when I felt a sneeze coming on. I sneezed a great sneeze and you know what? The whole straw house fell down. I was very surprised by ⓔ<u>what had happened</u>. Unfortunately, the same thing happened to the second little pig's house.

R: Reporter, W: Wolf

[영등포구 ㅇㅇ중]

**13. 위 글의 밑줄 친 ⓐ~ⓔ의 의미가 <u>틀린</u> 것은?**　(4점)

① ⓐ a terrible cold: 지독한 감기

② ⓑ Back then: 그 당시에

③ ⓒ ran out of: ~이 다 떨어졌다

④ ⓓ the broken door: 부서진 문

⑤ ⓔ what had happened: 무슨 일이 일어났는지

**14. 위 글의 내용과 일치하는 것은?** (4점)

① 기자는 늑대를 첫 번째 손님으로 소개한다.

② 늑대는 설탕을 구해서 생일 케이크를 만들었다.

③ 늑대의 할머니는 생일 케이크를 만들고 있었다.

④ 늑대의 재채기로 인해 짚으로 만들어진 돼지의 집이 무너졌다.

⑤ 다행스럽게도 둘째 돼지의 집은 늑대에 의해 무너지지 않았다.

**15. 위 글을 읽고 (A)~(D)를 사건이 일어난 순서대로 바르게 배열한 것은?** (4점)

(A) The whole house fell down.

(B) The wolf sneezed a great sneeze.

(C) The wolf walked to the pig's house.

(D) The wolf grabbed the broken door.

① (B)–(A)–(C)–(D)   ② (B)–(D)–(C)–(A)

③ (C)–(B)–(D)–(A)   ④ (C)–(D)–(B)–(A)

⑤ (D)–(B)–(C)–(A)

**16. 다음 대화의 괄호 (A), (B), (C) 안에 들어갈 알맞은 표현으로 짝지어진 것은?** (4점)

M: (A)[What / Why] do you think about my drawing, Prince?

B: Wow, this picture is very frightening!

M: (B)[What / Why] do you think so?

B: I mean the picture shows a snake that ate an elephant.

M: You're right. Actually, many people thought it was a picture of a hat.

B: Really? That's interesting.

M: I know. That's why I decided to become a pilot instead of a painter.

B: Haha. At least I can understand (C)[what / why] you mean.

M: Thank you, Prince.

|     | (A)    | (B)   | (C)   |
| --- | ------ | ----- | ----- |
| ①   | What   | Why   | what  |
| ②   | Why    | Why   | what  |
| ③   | Why    | What  | what  |
| ④   | What   | Why   | why   |
| ⑤   | What   | What  | why   |

**[17~18]** 다음 글을 읽고 물음에 답하시오.

Reporter: Welcome to Animal World News. Last Sunday, a wolf ⓐ경찰서로 연행되었습니다 for blowing down pigs' houses. Today, we have the third little pig and the wolf with us. Mr. Pig, could you explain ⓑ무슨 일이 일어났는지 to you and your brothers?

(A)

Reporter: How are your brothers doing now?

(B)

Pig: They ⓒ그들의 집을 잃어버려서 너무 충격을 받았습니다. They are resting in my house.

(C)

Pig: Yes. My brothers and I thought it was time to build our own houses, so we ⓓ짚, 나무 막대기, 벽돌로 집을 지었습니다. One day, the wolf came and completely blew down my brothers' houses. He almost blew down my house, but it ⓔ벽돌로 만들어졌습니다, so he couldn't.

17. 주어진 글 다음에 이어질 글의 순서로 가장 적절한 것은? (4점)

① (A)–(B)–(C)  ② (A)–(C)–(B)
③ (B)–(A)–(C)  ④ (B)–(C)–(A)
⑤ (C)–(A)–(B)

18. 위 글의 밑줄 친, ⓐ~ⓔ 중 영어로 옮긴 것 중 어색한 것은? (4점)

① ⓐ was taken to the police station
② ⓑ what occurred
③ ⓒ are so shocked to lost their houses
④ ⓓ built houses with straw, sticks, and bricks
⑤ ⓔ was made of bricks

[19~20] 다음 글을 읽고 물음에 답하시오.

Reporter: Thank you, Mr. Pig. Now, let's meet our second guest, the wolf. Mr. Wolf, could you tell us what happened?

Wolf: This whole "Big Bad Wolf" thing is wrong. The real story is about a sneeze from a terrible cold and a cup of sugar.

Reporter: What do you mean?

Wolf: Back then, I was ⓐmade a birthday cake for my dear old grandmother. I ran out of sugar. I walked down the street ⓑasked my neighbor for a cup of sugar. When I knocked on the door, it fell down. Then I called, "Little pig, are you in?" I had just ⓒgrabbed the broken door when I felt a sneeze ⓓcame on. I sneezed a great sneeze and you know what? The whole straw house fell down. 나는 일어난 일에 매우 놀랐다. ⓔUnfortunate, the same thing happened to the second little pig's house.

19. 위 글의 밑줄 친 ⓐ~ⓔ 중 쓰임이 올바른 것은? (4점)

① ⓐ made  ② ⓑ asked
③ ⓒ grabbed  ④ ⓓ came
⑤ ⓔ Unfortunate

20. 위 글의 밑줄 친 우리말을 주어진 표현을 모두 배열하여 영작하시오. (5점)

나는 일어난 일에 매우 놀랐다.

(was / I / happened / very / had / by / surprised / what)

정답: _____

**[21~23]** 다음 글을 읽고 물음에 답하시오.

---

**Reporter:** Thank you, Mr. Pig. Now, let's meet our second guest, the wolf. ⓐ <u>Mr. Wolf, could you tell us what happened?</u>

**Wolf:** This whole "Big Bad Wolf" thing is wrong. ⓑ<u>The real story is about a sneeze from a terrible cold and a cup of sugar.</u>

**Reporter:** What do you mean?

**Wolf:** Back then, I was making a birthday cake for my dear old grandmother. I ran out of sugar. ⓒ<u>I walked down the street asking my neighbor a cup of sugar.</u> ⓓ <u>When I knocked on the door, it fell down.</u> Then I called, "Little pig, are you in?" ⓔ<u>I had just grabbed the broken door when I felt a sneeze to come on.</u> I sneezed a great sneeze and you know what? The whole straw house fell down. ⓕ<u>I was very surprising by what had happened.</u> Unfortunately, the same thing happened to the second little pig's house.

---

21. 위 글 바로 앞에 가장 자연스럽게 올 수 있는 내용으로 옳은 것은? **(4점)**

① A talk with Mr. Pig
② A conversation with the wolf
③ An interview with news reporters
④ A conversation with police officers
⑤ An interview with the pigs' neighbors

---

22. 위 글을 읽고, 〈보기〉의 문장들을 사건이 일어난 순서대로 배열한 것은? **(4점)**

> ┌ 보기 ────────────────
> a. The wolf sneezed a great sneeze.
> b. The wolf walked to the pig's house.
> c. The wolf grabbed the broken door.
> d. The whole house fell down.
> └────────────────────

① a – b – d - c
② b – d – a - c
③ b – c – a - d
④ c – a – b - d
⑤ c – b – d - a

---

23. 위 글의 ⓐ~ⓕ 중 어법이 옳은 문장의 개수는? **(4점)**

① 0개  ② 1개  ③ 2개  ④ 3개  ⑤ 4개

24. 다음 글을 읽고 대답할 수 <u>없는</u> 질문은? (5점)

> **Reporter:** Welcome to Animal World News. Last Sunday, a wolf was taken to the police station for blowing down pigs' houses. Today, we have the third little pig and the wolf with us. Mr. Pig, could you explain what happened to you and your brothers?
>
> **Pig:** Yes. My brothers and I thought it was time to build our own houses, so we built houses with straw, sticks, and bricks. One day, the wolf came and completely blew down my brothers' houses. He almost blew down my house, but it was made of bricks, so he couldn't.
>
> **Reporter:** How are your brothers doing now?
>
> **Pig:** They are so shocked to lose their houses. They are resting in my house.

① What did the pigs build their houses with?
② Why couldn't the wolf blow down the last house?
③ How are the first and the second little pigs doing?
④ Why was the wolf taken to the police station?
⑤ What did the wolf run out of when he was making a cake?

# 3학년 영어 1학기 기말고사(4과) 2회

| 반 | | 점수 | |
|---|---|---|---|
| 이름 | | | |

문항수 : 선택형(21문항) 서술형(2문항)　　20 ．　．　．

◎ 선택형 문항의 답안은 컴퓨터용 수정 싸인펜을 사용
하여 OMR 답안지에 바르게 표기하시오.

◎ 서술형 문제는 답을 답안지에 반드시 검정 볼펜으로
쓰시오.

◎ 총 23문항 100점 만점입니다. 문항별 배점은 각
문항에 표시되어 있습니다.

[영등포구 ○○중]

1. 다음 중 단어의 영영 풀이로 옳은 것은?　　(4점)

① narrow: short and wide

② all-purpose: unsuitable for many uses

③ similar: having features that are the same

④ genius: someone who shows a lack of good judgement

⑤ independent: confident and free to do things with needing help from other people

[영등포구 ○○중]

2. 다음 중 단어의 영영 풀이로 잘못된 것은?　　(4점)

① imitate: to copy what someone does or produces

② headache: a pain in someone's head

③ crime: an illegal action or activity for which a person can be punished by law

④ unfortunately: used to say that something good or lucky has happened

⑤ object: anything that has a fixed shape or form, which you can touch or see, and which is not alive

[강동구 ○○중]

3. 다음 밑줄 친 부분의 우리말 표현이 어색한 것을 고르시오.　　(4점)

① Nolbu tells the story from his point of view. (관점, 견해)

② He wanted Heungbu to make money on his own. (혼자 힘으로)

③ When the police came, they thought I was breaking into the pig's house. (무너져 내리다)

④ Last Sunday, a wolf was taken to the police station for blowing down pigs' houses. (끌려갔다)

⑤ The club welcomes all new members regardless of age. (~에 관계없이)

[울산 ○○중]

4. 다음 대화의 내용과 일치하는 것은?　　(5점)

> B: How did you like the movie 'Good Friends', Yura?
>
> G: I liked it. It was fun to compare the movie with the original book.
>
> B: Which did you like better, the movie or the book?
>
> G: Well, I liked the movie, but I think I enjoyed the book more. The book helped me understand the characters better.
>
> B: That's interesting. To me, the movie was better because it was easier to understand the story.
>
> G: That's true. I guess they both have their own advantages.
>
> B: You're right.
>
> B: Boy, G: Girl

① B는 책을 영화로 만드는 작업은 재미있다고 생각한다.

② B는 영화 'Good Friends'는 봤지만 책은 읽지 않았다.

③ 영화 'Good Friends'와 책 'Good Friends'는 서로 다른 내용이다.

④ G는 원작과 원작을 영화화한 작품을 비교하는 것은 어려운 일이라고 말한다.

⑤ G는 영화 'Good Friends'보다 책이 등장인물들을 더 잘 이해하게 해줬다고 말한다.

[강동구 ○○중]

6. 위 대화의 흐름상 (B)가 의미하는 바로 가장 적절한 것은?    (4점)

① to be mean

② not to be fair

③ to wake up the rabbit

④ not to take a responsibility

⑤ to leave the rabbit sleeping

**[5~6]** 다음 대화를 읽고 물음에 답하시오.

> B: Do you know the story *The Rabbit and the Turtle*?
>
> G: Of course, I do.
>
> B: I think the turtle in the story is mean.
>
> G: _____(A)_____
>
> B: The turtle sees the rabbit sleeping but doesn't wake him up. It is not fair.
>
> G: I don't see it that way. Why should the turtle be responsible for the rabbit? I don't think he should be (B)that.
>
> B: That's interesting.

[충북 ○○중]

7. 다음 대화에서 <보기>의 표현이 들어가기에 가장 알맞은 곳은?    (5점)

┌ 보기 ┐

> I don't think he should be.

> A: Do you know the story *The Rabbit and the Turtle*?
>
> B: Of course, I do. (A)
>
> A: I think the turtle in the story is mean.
>
> B: Why do you think so? (B)
>
> A: The turtle sees the rabbit sleeping but doesn't wake him up. It is not fair. (C)
>
> B: I don't see it that way. Why should the turtle be responsible for the rabbit? (D)
>
> A: That's interesting. (E)

① (A)    ② (B)    ③ (C)    ④ (D)    ⑤ (E)

[강동구 ○○중]

5. 위 대화의 흐름상 (A)에 들어갈 말로 가장 적절한 것은?    (4점)

① Why do you think so?

② What should the turtle do?

③ What does the rabbit need?

④ What's wrong with the story?

⑤ What is the meaning of "mean?"

8. 다음 대화의 내용과 일치하지 <u>않는</u> 것은?　　　　(5점)

Ms. Parker: Now, take a look at this work of art. How do you like it?

Jinho: Well, is it even art?

Henry: To me, it isn't more than a toilet.

Ms. Parker: It is not just art. I think it is the greatest piece of art of the 20th century.

Mina: What makes you think so?

Ms. Parker: It is a perfect example of a different point of view. The artist used real-life objects to create art.

Claire: So, he didn't create something new?

Ms. Parker: That's right. He simply wanted people to look at the objects in a different way.

Mina: Thank you so much. Ms. Parker. I learned a lot today!

① Henry doesn't think that the work is art.

② Mina learned a lot from Mr. Parker.

③ The artist just wanted people to have a different point of view on real-life objects.

④ Ms. Parker thinks the work is the greatest piece of art in the 20th century.

⑤ The artist imitated real-life objects to make something new.

9. 다음 대화의 빈칸에 들어갈 문장으로 적절한 것은?　　　　(4점)

Jisun: Have you finished the book, Daron?

Daron: Yes, I finished it yesterday, Jisun.

Jisun: How did you like it?

Daron: It was interesting.

Jisun: What is the book about?

Daron: You know the story of Heungbu, right? In the book, Nolbu tells the story from his point of view.

Jisun: What does he say?

Daron: He says he didn't help Heungbu for a reason. _____

Jisun: Wow, it's a unique story! I can't wait to read the book. Thanks, Daron!

① He didn't love Heungbu.

② He has already made a lot of money.

③ He helped Heungbu, so he can become a kind person.

④ He wanted to make a lot of money to help Heungbu.

⑤ He wanted Heungbu to make money on his own and be independent.

**10.** 다음 대화의 밑줄 친 ⓐ~ⓔ 중에서 가리키는 대상이 나머지 넷과 다른 것은? (4점)

---

G: Have you finished the book, Taeho?

B: Yes. I finished it yesterday, Anna.

G: How did you like it?

B: It was interesting.

G: What is the book about?

B: You know the story of Heungbu, right? In the book, ⓐNolbu tells the story from ⓑhis point of view.

G: What does he say?

B: Well, ⓒhe says he didn't help Heungbu for a reason. He wanted Heungbu to make money on ⓓhis own. Finally Heungbu could be independent and thanked ⓔhim.

G: Wow, it's a unique story! I can't wait to read the book. Thanks, Taeho.

---

① ⓐ  ② ⓑ  ③ ⓒ  ④ ⓓ  ⑤ ⓔ

**11.** 다음 대화의 밑줄 친 문장의 의미로 알맞은 것은? (4점)

---

Ms. Kim: You look worried, Juwon.

Juwon: I think we will lose the soccer game tomorrow, Ms. Kim.

Ms. Kim: Why do you think so?

Juwon: We will have a match against Class 3. They have the strongest players in our school.

Ms. Kim: Look on the bright side. They might have strong players, but your class has the best teamwork.

Juwon: You're right. I didn't think about it that way. I'll go and practice!

---

① Look into the light.

② Be positive about the situation.

③ Look at the other side of the soccer field.

④ Think about your future.

⑤ Be kind to your friends in your class.

**12.** 다음 우리말을 조건에 맞게 영작하시오. (6점)

---

My uncle visited my house yesterday.

(1) 그는 홍콩에 있었다 before he came to Korea.
(조건: 'had'를 반드시 사용할 것.)

---

(2) 나는 나의 숙제를 끝냈다 when he arrived at my house.
(조건: 'had'를 반드시 사용할 것.)

---

(3) 나는 그를 다시 만나서 매우 기뻤다.
(조건: 과거시제, 'see'를 반드시 사용할 것.)

---

(1) _____

(2) _____

(3) _____

Reporter: Thank you for explaining what you have experienced, Mr. Pig. Please wait your turn. Now, let's meet our second guest, the wolf. Mr. Wolf, could you (가)[tell us what happened / tell what happened us]?

Wolf: This whole "Big Bad Wolf" thing is wrong. The real story is about a sneeze from a terrible cold and a cup of sugar.

Reporter: What do you mean?

Wolf: Back then, I was (나)[making / made] a birthday cake for my dear old grandmother. I ran out of sugar. I walked down the street to ask my neighbor for a cup of sugar. When I knocked on the door, it fell down. Then I called, "Little pig, are you in?" I had just grabbed the broken door when I felt a sneeze coming on. I sneezed a great sneeze and you know what? The whole straw house fell down. I was very surprised by what had happened. (다)[Unfortunately / Fortunately], the same thing happened to the second little pig's house.

[강동구 ○○중]

**13. 위 글의 내용과 일치하지 않는 것은?** (4점)

① 기자는 돼지와 늑대를 인터뷰하고 있다.
② 재채기로 인해 두 돼지 형제 집이 무너졌다.
③ 늑대가 케이크를 만드는 데 설탕이 다 떨어졌다.
④ 첫째 아기 돼지 집은 나무 막대기로 지어졌다.
⑤ 늑대는 문을 움켜잡았을 때 재채기가 나오는 것을 느꼈다.

**14. 위 글의 (가), (나), (다)에 들어갈 말로 가장 적절한 것은?** (4점)

(가) — (나) — (다)

① tell us what happened — made — Fortunately
② tell us what happened — making — Unfortunately
③ tell us what happened — making — Fortunately
④ tell what happened us — made — Unfortunately
⑤ tell what happened us — making — Fortunately

**15. 다음은 위 인터뷰 후, 일어난 일에 대한 두 인물간의 대화이다. 밑줄 친 부분에 들어갈 말을 조건에 모두 맞추어 영작하시오.** (5점)

A: The wolf came to say sorry to me. Did you see him?

B: No, I didn't. What did he say?

A: I heard he didn't blow down our houses on purpose. At that time, 그는 일어난 일에 의해 매우 놀랐어.

B: Um, I don't believe how it could happen in a row.

[A: the first little pig / B: the second little pig]

┤ 조건 ├
• 문장에 시간의 흐름이 나타나게 할 것.
• 주어진 단어를 활용할 것.
  - surprise, by, what, happen
• 형태 변형 가능 및 시제 유의.
• 8 단어로 문장을 작성할 것.

Q: 그는 일어난 일에 의해 매우 놀랐어.

→ _____

R: Welcome to Animal World News. Last Sunday, a wolf was taken to the police station for blowing down pigs' houses. Today, we have the third little pig and the wolf with us. Mr. Pig, could you explain what happened to you and your brothers?

P: Yes. My brothers and I thought it was time to build our own houses, so we built houses with straw, sticks, and bricks. One day, the wolf came and completely blew down my brothers' houses. He almost blew down my house, but it was made of bricks, so he couldn't.

R: How are your brothers doing now?

P: They are so (A)_____ to lose their houses. They are resting in my house.

R: Reporter, P: Pig

[울산 ○○중]

**16. 위 글의 종류는?** (5점)

① Diary     ② Report     ③ Journal
④ Article     ⑤ Interview

[울산 ○○중]

**17. 위 글의 흐름상 빈칸 (A)에 들어갈 말로 어색한 것은?** (4점)

① sad     ② upset     ③ surprised
④ impressed     ⑤ shocked

[강동구 ○○중]

**18. 위 글을 읽고 답할 수 없는 것은?** (4점)

① Whose house was made of bricks?
② What is the name of the News program?
③ When did the three pigs build their houses?
④ What did the pigs build their houses with?
⑤ Why was the wolf taken to the police station?

[충북 ○○중]

**19. 다음 글은 Mr. Pig가 쓴 글의 일부이다. 빈칸 (가), (나)에 들어갈 말로 알맞게 연결한 것은?** (4점)

One day, the wolf came and completely blew down my brothers' houses. (가)_____, my house was fine (나)_____ it was made of bricks. My brothers lost their houses, so they are resting in my house.

    (가)          (나)
① So            if
② However     because
③ As a result     because of
④ In addition     when
⑤ Besides       whether

20. 다음 글의 빈칸 (A)~(C)에 들어갈 말이 바르게 짝지어진 것을 고르시오. (4점)

> Today, Sarah and I danced in a contest. We danced to a K-pop song. We ___(A)___ (practice) for 6 months before we ___(B)___ (dance) in the contest. When we arrived, people had set up the stage already. We were a little worried, but we did a good job because we ___(C)___ (prepare) a lot. And, we won! We were the best dancers in the contest. It was a great day!

　　　　(A)　–　(B)　–　(C)
① practiced – had danced – had prepared
② had practiced – had danced – prepared
③ practice – dance – had prepared
④ practiced – danced – prepare
⑤ had practiced – danced – had prepared

**[21~22]** 다음 글을 읽고 물음에 답하시오.

> Reporter: Then why did you go to the third little pig's house?
>
> Wolf: I still needed a cup of sugar, so I went to the next house. The third little pig had built his house of bricks. I called out, "I'm sorry to trouble you, but are you in?" And do you know what he answered? "Go away. Don't bother me again!" How impolite! I thought I deserved an apology, so I kept knocking. When the police came, of course they thought I was breaking into this pig's house.
>
> Reporter: Do you think you were framed?
>
> Wolf: Yes. The news reporters of the town thought a sick wolf going to borrow a cup of sugar didn't sound very exciting. So, they made me the "Big Bad Wolf." Could you maybe lend me a cup of sugar?
>
> Reporter: Thank you for your time. Everyone, which do you think is the true story, the pig's or the wolf's?

21. According to the passage above, which one cannot be answered? (5점)

① Why was the wolf sick?
② Why did the wolf keep knocking?
③ How much sugar did the wolf need?
④ Who made the wolf the "Big Bad Wolf"?
⑤ What did the third little pig make his house of?

22. 위 글에서 셋째 아기 돼지 집에 찾아갔을 때 Wolf의 심경의 변화로 가장 적절한 것은? (3점)

① interested → lonely
② sorry → upset
③ delighted → frightened
④ sad → glad
⑤ relieved → satisfied

23. 다음 글의 내용과 일치하는 것은?　　　　(5점)

> ### Cinder Edna
>
> This story has Cinder Edna who is a neighbor of the famous Cinderella. Both of them work all day for their stepmothers and stepsisters. But while Cinderella is saved by a fairy, Edna saves herself. She makes money and gets herself a nice dress. Then she goes to the party by bus. Cinder Edna meets Prince Rupert and falls in love with him. They live happily ever after in a small house outside of the palace.
>
> ### Prince Cinders
>
> This story has a quiet and skinny teenage boy named Prince Cinders. His only wish is to be like his big hairy brothers. One evening a fairy comes and tries to help him, but she changes him into a huge monkey. Prince Cinders meets the princess, but he frightens her because he looks like a monkey. Fortunately, when he changes back to a boy at midnight, the princess thinks he has saved her from the monkey. Prince Cinders and the princess live happily ever after.

① Cinder Edna meets Prince Cinders and falls in love with him.

② Cinder Edna is a cousin of Cinderella.

③ Cinderella makes money and gets herself a nice dress.

④ Prince Cinders is a big hairy boy.

⑤ A fairy changes Prince Cinders into a huge monkey.

# 정답 및 해설

## Lesson 1 (중간)  1회

| | | | |
|---|---|---|---|
| 01 ⑤ | 02 ⑤ | 03 ③ | 04 ⑤ |
| 05 ④ | 06 ④ | 07 ⑤ | 08 ⑤ |

09 look down  10 signed up  11 ④

12 He heard the baby crying.

13 (1) What's the matter?

   (2) I hope you find another fun club.

14 ④  15 they can have more parks

| | | | |
|---|---|---|---|
| 16 ⑤ | 17 ② | 18 ② | 19 ③ |
| 20 ③ | 21 ①, ⑤ | 22 ② | |

23 ⓐ I finally made what I called "lion lights."

   ⓑ This is exactly what we wanted.

24 ①  25 ③

26 I could find what I needed to make the lights.

27 so  28 I woke up and saw our cow lying

---

**01** sort: 분류하다, 구분하다

**02** (A) fall off: ~에서 떨어지다 (B) bump: (도로의) 튀어나온 부분[요철] (C) 그 문제에 대해 '쓰는 것'이 적절하다.

**03** (A)에서 스티커가 아주 좋다고 하자 (C)에서 스티커가 도움이 되길 바란다고 하고 (E)에서 도움이 될 거라고 확신한다고 하자 (D)에서 효과가 있는지 내일 다시 오자고 하고 (B)에서 좋다고 하는 순서가 자연스럽다.

**04** 'Why don' you ~?'는 '~하는 게 어때?'라는 의미로 권유할 때 쓰인다.

**05** ④번은 '계속하는 게 어때?'라는 의미로 상대방의 걱정 또는 염려를 묻는 표현인 'What's the matter?'와는 다르다.

**06** 'Why don't we make a video that shows the famous places in our town and put it on the Internet?'이라고 했다.

**07** 앞에서 'Both of them seem to be important for our health.'라고 했고 뒤에서는 'I think you are right. I'm going to exercise first.'라고 했으므로 ⑤번이 적절하다.

**08** ① rang → ring[ringing] ② The things what → What, 또는 The things what he said was true. → The things that he said were true. ③ to run → run[running] ④ danced → dance[dancing]

**09** look down: 우울해 보이다

**10** sign up for: ~에 신청(가입)하다, ~에 등록하다

**11** what은 선행사를 포함하고 있는 관계대명사이므로 선행사가 나와 있는 ④번은 어색하다.

**12** 지각동사 heard의 목적격 보어로 동사원형이나 현재분사를 쓴다.

**13** (1) What's the matter?: 무슨 일이니? (2) 'I hope'로 '소망'을 나타낼 수 있다.

**14** 지각동사 look at의 목적격 보어로 동사원형이나 현재분사를 쓴다.

**15** 'I hope'로 '소망'을 나타낼 수 있다.

**16** (D)에서 소가 죽어 있는 것을 보고 문제를 무시하면 안 된다는 것을 깨닫고 (A)에서 첫 번째 아이디어로 실패하고 (C)에서 사자들이 움직이는 불빛을 두려워한다는 것을 발견하고 (B)에서 마침내 '사자 전등'을 만들게 되는 순서가 적절하다.

**17** 'I realized I shouldn't ignore the problem.'이라고 했다.

**18** ⓐ to protect ⓑ cows move ⓒ were turned away ⓓ made what ⓔ from being ⓕ electronically ⓖ cow lie[lying]

**19** Richard가 15살에 무엇을 만들었는지는 알 수 없다.

**20** (가)에는 complain(당신이 불행하거나, 아프거나, 불편하다는 것 등을 말하거나 쓰다)이 들어간다.

**21** ㉠, ①, ⑤: to부정사의 부사적 용법 ②, ③, ④: 명사적 용법

**22** 주어진 문장의 then이 (B) 앞에서 '사자 전등'이라고 불렸던 것을 만든 때를 말하므로 (B)가 적절하다.

**23** ⓐ made와 called의 목적어 역할을 하도록 that을 what으로 고쳐야 한다. ⓑ is의 보어와 wanted의 목적어 역할을 하도록 that을 what으로 고쳐야 한다.

**24** 기대했던 결과가 안 나왔으므로 Sadly가 적절하다.

**25** 'I discovered that lions were afraid of a moving light.'라고 했다.

**26** 나는 찾을 수 있었다: I could find 내가 필요했던 것들: what I needed 전등을 만들기 위해: to make the lights

**27** 문맥상 결과를 나타내는 so가 적절하다.

**28** 과거의 일이므로 woke이며 saw의 목적격 보어로 lie의 현재분사 lying이 적절하다.

## Lesson 1 (중간)

01 ④　　02 What's the matter?　　03 ③

04 (가) What's the matter?

05 (나) I'm sorry to hear that.

06 Because he fell off his bike at Hangang Park this afternoon.

07 How about writing about the problem on the community website?

08 ①

09 ⓐ 나는 나의 교과서를 가져오는 것을 잊어버렸다.
　ⓑ 제발 인내심이 있어라.
　ⓒ 건강을 유지하기 위해서 우리는 무엇을 할 수 있을까?
　ⓓ 우리는 그것에 대해 무언가를 해야 한다.
　ⓔ 그 말을 들으니 유감이다.

10 what they need

11 ⑤　　12 ⑤　　13 ②　　14 ③

15 ④　　16 ①

17 I hope that every child in the world can get an education.

18 ⑤　　19 ④　　20 ③　　21 ①

22 ③　　23 saw our cow lying on the ground

24 that → what

25 prevent lions from being killed

26 Our ideas can make a difference in people's lives.

27 ④　　28 ③　　29 ⑤

30 Then I had another idea.

---

01 (A) What's the matter?: 무슨 일이니? (B) 유감을 나타내는 sorry (C) 소망하는 것을 나타내는 hope가 적절하다.

02 What's the matter?: 무슨 일이니?

03 앞에서 'I'm going to help people try flower tea.'라고 했으므로 ③번이 적절하다.

04 (가) 뒤에서 'I'm worried about this dog.'이라고 했으므로 'What's the matter?'

05 (나) 앞에서 'I don't think it has a home.'이라고 했으므로 'I'm sorry to hear that.'이 적절하다.

06 'I fell off my bike at Hangang Park this afternoon.'이라고 했다.

07 about의 목적어로 동명사 writing이 되어야 한다.

08 (A) 'Look at these comments, Henry.' (B) 'Why don't we make a video that shows the famous places in our town and put it on the Internet?'이라고 했다.

09 ⓐ forget+to부정사: ~할 것을 잊다 ⓑ patient: 인내심 있는 ⓒ stay healthy: 건강을 유지하다 ⓓ should do something: 무언가를 해야 한다 ⓔ I am sorry ~: 유감의 표

---

현

10 관계대명사 'what'은 선행사를 포함하는 것으로 the thing(s) that/which로 바꿔 쓸 수 있다.

11 각각 (A) ③ (B) ② (C) ① (D) ④가 들어간다.

12 영작하면 'I'm worried about this dog'이다.

13 첫 번째 빈칸: 의문형용사 What, 두 번째 빈칸: 관계대명사 What이 적절하다.

14 ③번은 what이 보어가 되는 명사절을 이끌고, 나머지는 목적어가 되는 명사절을 이끈다.

15 지각동사 saw의 목적격 보어로 동사원형이나 현재분사를 쓴다.

16 이어지는 내용으로 보아 ⓐ는 'there were some people who believed that girls do not need to go to school'이 적절하다.

17 저는 바랍니다: I hope 세상의 모든 아이들: every child in the world 교육을 받을 수 있다: can get an education

18 'Thanks to the support from many people, an education law was finally passed in my country.'라고 했다.

19 At first, I thought I couldn't do anything because I was only eleven. Then I realized I shouldn't ignore the problem.'이라고 했다.

20 불을 사용하는 것은 효과가 없었다. - (B) 대신에 불이 사자들이 소들을 더 잘 보도록 도왔다. - (A) 다른 아이디어를 생각해 냈다. - (C) 첫날에는 사자들이 돌아갔지만 둘째 날에는 사자들이 더 많은 동물들을 죽였다.

21 be동사 다음에 진행형을 만드는 현재분사가 적절하다.

22 야생 동물들이 얼마나 많은 가축들을 죽였는지는 알 수 없다.

23 saw의 목적격 보어로 현재분사 lying을 쓴다.

24 (가) made와 called의 목적어 역할을 하도록 that을 what으로 고쳐야 한다. (나) is의 보어와 wanted의 목적어 역할을 하도록 that을 what으로 고쳐야 한다.

25 prevent ... from -ing: …을 ~하는 것으로부터 막다. 죽임을 당하는 것: being killed

26 make a difference: 변화를 가져오다, 차이를 만들다

27 ⓐ free → freely ⓑ to lie → lying ⓒ badly → bad ⓔ helping → to help

28 (A)는 wild animals (B)는 farmers를 가리킨다.

29 ⓔ는 'I hope every child in the world can get an education.'으로 쓰는 것이 적절하다.

30 보기의 It이 가리키는 것이 'another idea'이다.

## Lesson 2 (중간)

---

01 ②　　　02 ③　　　03 ⑤　　　04 ④

05 (A) (She is the girl) watering the flowers.

　　(B) (He is the boy) reading a book on the bench.

06 (가) Are you hungry?

07 (나) be patient

08 It seems to me that you don't like the food.

09 ②　　　10 ①　　　11 ②　　　12 ④

13 (1) are two boys reading books on the bench

　　(2) is a woman running on the street

14 There is a girl watering the flowers.

15 ①　　　16 ③

17 (가) It was not easy for Ms. Disher to listen to their arguments.

　　(나) they found Ms. Disher sitting under a huge tree

18 (다) boastful　(라) ignored

19 they allow one another to eat

20 ⑤　　　21 ①　　　22 ⑤　　　23 ⑤

24 ⑤　　　25 ②

26 It was not easy for their host, Ms. Disher, to listen to their arguments patiently.

---

01 '곡물, 특히 밀, 옥수수 또는 쌀'을 뜻하는 말은 'grain(곡물)'이다.

02 음식을 다 먹으면 여전히 배가 고프다고 생각한다고 했으므로 ③번이 적절하다.

03 한국과 중국의 식사 예절의 차이를 말하고 있으므로 ⑤번이 적절하다.

04 'I go to bed early, so I eat my last meal early, too.'라고 했다.

05 (A) watering the flowers가 the girl을 수식하도록 쓰고 (B) reading a book이 the boy를 수식하도록 쓴다.

06 (가) 뒤에서 'Yes. Can we order pizza for dinner?'라고 했으므로 Are you hungry?가 적절하다.

07 (나) 앞에서 'Dinner will be ready soon.'이라고 했으므로 be patient가 적절하다.

08 나에게는 ~인 것 같다: It seems to me that ~

09 (A)에서 뭘 좀 먹자고 하자 (C)에서 선호하는 것을 묻고 (B)에서 국수를 좋아 한다고 하자 (D)에서 좋은 국수 식당이 있다고 하는 순서가 자연스럽다.

10 'It seems to me that you don't like the food.'라고 했다.

11 (A) 'I prefer having a meal early.'라고 답하고 있으므로 ⓑ (B) 'I usually go to bed early, so I eat my last meal early, too.'라고 답하고 있으므로 ⓒ가 적절하다.

12 'to make'의 의미상의 주어로 'for+목적격'이 적절하다.

13 (1) reading books가 two boys를 수식하도록 쓴다. (2) running이 a woman을 수식하도록 쓴다.

14 watering the flowers가 a girl을 수식하도록 쓴다.

15 'can also touch it'이라고 했으므로 ①번이 적절하다.

16 ⓐ 비교급을 수식하는 much ⓑ one에 호응하는 the other ⓒ 뒤에 than이 나오므로 more가 적절하다.

17 (가) 진주어로 to listen이 되어야 한다. (나) sitting이 Ms. Disher를 수식하도록 써야 한다.

18 (다) boastful: 자랑하는, 뽐내는 (라) ignore: 무시하다

19 allow의 목적격 보어로 to부정사가 나와야 하므로 to를 추가한다.

20 'Because I use my sense of touch when I eat, I get to enjoy my food more.'라고 했다.

21 상반되는 내용이 이어지므로 but이 적절하다.

22 ⓐ Spork, Chopsticks, Knork, Barehands, and Ms. Disher ⓑ by hosting ⓒ is always eager ⓓ often talk about

23 뒤에서 'So, she hurriedly, yet quietly, left.'라고 했으므로 ⑤번이 적절하다.

24 가주어 it을 쓰고 진주어로 'to hold a fork in one hand and a knife in the other'를 쓰며 의미상 주어로 for you를 쓴다.

25 very는 비교급을 수식하지 않는다.

26 가주어 It을 쓰고 진주어로 'to listen to their arguments patiently'를 쓰며 의미상 주어로 for their host, Ms. Disher를 쓴다.

## Lesson 2 (중간)

```
01 ②        02 ④        03 ③        04 ④
05 having a meal early or late
06 How about you?
07 ⑤        08 ②        09 I prefer fish.
10 ⑤        11 It is necessary for people to recycle.
12 it is time for dinner
13 It is dangerous for children to ride a bike without
   a helmet.
14 It is very nice of you to remember my birthday.
15 (1) I saw him running away.
   (2) I heard her playing the piano.
16 ④        17 ④        18 ③        19 ④
20 (1) A spoon is best for eating grains and soup.
   (2) You can use chopsticks with just one hand.
   (3) I can see and smell and touch the food.
21 ⑤        22 ④        23 ①        24 ③
25 ②
26 She joined an adventure club recently.
```

01 regardless of …에 상관없이
02 '선호하는 것을 질문받자 (C)에서 선호하는 것을 말하고 (B)에서 이유를 묻자 (A)에서 이유를 설명하고 (D)에서 질문한 본인의 경우를 말한다.
03 앞에서 음식 통제가 안 된다고 했으므로 'So, I prefer to exercise.'가 적절하다.
04 'It is more polite to finish everything on your plate in Korea, though.'라고 했다.
05 밥 먹는 것: having a meal 일찍 또는 늦게: early or late
06 How about you?: 넌 어떠니?
07 'But if you can't do both, it might be better to focus on just one.'이라고 했다.
08 엄마는 'I'm going to cook fish, Jacob.'이라고 했다.
09 prefer: (다른 것보다) ~을 (더) 좋아하다, 선호하다
10 메뉴에 생선이 있다고 하자 ⓒ에서 좋다며 초밥인지 구이인지 묻고 ⓐ에서 둘 다 있다고 하자 ⓑ에서 초밥을 먹겠다고 하고 ⓓ에서 자기는 구이를 먹겠다고 하는 순서이다.
11 가주어 It을 쓰고 진주어로 'to recycle'을 쓰며 'for people'을 의미상의 주어로 쓴다.
12 비인칭 주어 it과 동사 is를 쓴 후 time for dinner를 쓴다.
13 가주어 It을 쓰고 진주어로 'to ride a bike without a helmet'을 쓰며 'for children'을 의미상의 주어로 쓴다.
14 가주어 It을 쓰고 진주어로 'to remember my birthday'를 쓰며 'of you'를 의미상의 주어로 쓴다.
15 (1) saw의 목적격 보어로 running (2) heard의 목적격 보어

로 playing을 쓴다.
16 'The most recent topic was about the best way to eat and Ms. Disher's guests began to argue.'라고 했다.
17 '때'를 나타내는 접속사 when이 적절하다.
18 Chopsticks는 단점에 대해서는 말하지 않았다.
19 빈도부사 often을 talk 앞에 쓰고, about과 learned 두 개의 목적어 역할을 할 수 있는 what을 이용한다.
20 (1) 'A spoon is best for grains and soup, and a fork is good for eating meat.'라고 했다. (2) 'Plus, you can use chopsticks with just one hand!'라고 했다. (3) 'I can see and smell the food, but I can also touch it.'라고 했다.
21 (A) 비교급을 수식하는 much (B) one에 호응하는 the other (C) the food를 가리키므로 it이 적절하다.
22 모두 '추가'의 내용 앞에 나오지만 ④번은 상반되는 내용 앞에 나온다.
23 'When they found her, she sat under a huge tree.'라고 했다.
24 (A) hurriedly와 병렬로 quietly (B) disappear: 사라지다 (C) boastful: 자랑하는, 뽐내는 modest: 겸손한
25 셋 이상이므로 one another를 쓰고 allow의 목적격 보어로 to eat을 쓴다.
26 친구들을 위해 저녁 식사를 주최해서 모험담을 듣고 싶어한다는 내용 다음에 갑자기 모험 동아리에 가입했다는 말이 나오는 것은 어색하다.

## Lesson 3 (기말)

```
01 ④        02 ②        03 ④        04 ②
05 ②        06 ②        07 ⑤        08 ⑤
09 ①        10 ①        11 ②, ④     12 ③
13 ①        14 ②        15 ①
16 It was not only strong but also easy to use.
17 (1) why an elephant has a trunk
   (2) if[whether] he will come back soon
18 ③        19 ⑤        20 ③        21 ②
22 ④        23 ④        24 ③
```

01 float away: 떠다니다
02 creative: having or showing an ability to make new things or think of new ideas, control: to direct the behavior of (a person or animal), to cause (a person or

animal) to do what you want

03 'Walking on all four legs was very difficult for me.'라고 했다.

04 'be fascinated by'는 '나는 …에 매료되었다.'라는 뜻으로 높은 관심을 나타내는 표현이다. 'be impressed by'로 쓸 수 있다.

05 뒤에서 'I think he was a really great artist.'라고 했으므로 ⓑ의 'No, I don't.'는 'Sure'나 'Yes, I do.' 정도로 고쳐야 한다.

06 모기의 입을 모방해서 만들었다고 하자 ⓐ에서 어떻게 도움이 되는지 묻고 ⓒ에서 새 주삿바늘이 통증을 덜 유발할 거라고 답하고 ⓑ에서 왜 덜 아픈지 묻고 ⓓ에서 모기의 입처럼 피부와 덜 접촉한다고 답하는 순서가 적절하다.

07 ① to sit on[in] ② walking in the park ③ is good at math ④ not only hiking but also fishing

08 ⑤에서 'nothing useful'을 'nothing useless'로 바꾸는 것이 적절하다.

09 ② play → played ③ is → are. ④ is → are ⑤ to swim → swimming

10 ⓑ are you → you are ⓔ Do you think where → Where do you think ⓕ likes → like

11 be fascinated by ~ = ~ impress me a lot = ~ is really impressive = be (really) impressed by ~

12 ① it 삭제 ② to walk → walk[walking] ④ for → of ⑤ did I get → I got

13 ①번 다음에서 'He took a closer look at ~ were not straight.'라고 했으므로 ①번이 적절하다.

14 'noticed that the ends of the burr needles were not straight'라고 했다.

15 ⓐ의 that은 '가시 식물의 가시 끝이 곧지 않다는 것'을 가리키고 나머지는 모두 그가 발명한 것을 가리킨다.

16 not only A but also B: A뿐만 아니라 B도

17 간접의문문은 '의문사(또는 if나 whether)+주어+동사'의 순서다.

18 ⓒ not only에서 비교급 more quietly가 쓰였으므로 but also 뒤에서도 10% faster가 되는 것이 적절하다.

19 ㉠ in search of: ~을 찾고 있는 ㉡ on his way home: 그가 집으로 가는 도중에 ㉢ took a closer look at: ~을 자세히 살펴봤다 ㉣ floating away: 떠다니는 것

20 '자연 재해를 극복해야만 자연 현상을 활용한 발명품을 만들 수 있다.'라는 내용은 나오지 않는다.

21 'Leadership is also important for their survival.'과 'But even at the hottest time of day, Sahara Desert ants go hunting.'이라고 했다.

22 주어진 문장의 they가 ⓓ 앞에 나온 Sahara Desert ants를 가리키므로 ⓓ가 적절하다.

23 주어진 문장의 'So'에 유의하면 (D) 앞의 내용의 결과가 나오므로 (D)가 적절하다.

24 ⓐ 명사 increase를 수식하는 sudden ⓑ saw의 목적격 보어로 diving ⓒ not only 다음의 more quietly에 맞춰 비교급 faster가 적절하다.

## Lesson 3 (기말) 2회

| | | | |
|---|---|---|---|
| 01 ② | 02 ⑤ | 03 ① | 04 ④ |
| 05 ③ | 06 ④, ⑤ | 07 ④ | 08 ③ |
| 09 ① | 10 ⑤ | 11 ④ | 12 ④ |
| 13 ① | 14 ⑤ | 15 ④ | 16 ① |
| 17 ② | 18 ① | 19 ③ | 20 ② |
| 21 ③ | 22 ① | | |
| 23 껍질이 꺼끌꺼끌한 씨앗이 그의 옷과 개의 털에 붙은 것 | | | |
| 24 ④ | | 25 He wondered how birds could fly. | |

01 ⓑ wing: a part of an animal's body that is used for flying or gliding ⓓ genius: a very smart or talented person

02 순서대로 fascinates, genius, invention, imitate가 들어간다.

03 on one's way to: ~에 가는 길에 in search of: ~을 찾아

04 모기 주삿바늘에 대해 들어 본 적이 있는지 물었는데 왜 그것이 덜 아픈지 묻는 것은 어색하다.

05 ⓒ 다음에 나오는 'also'에 주목하면 그 앞에도 유사한 설명이 있어야 함을 알 수 있다.

06 스위스에서 모기 주삿바늘이 처음 만들어졌다는 말은 없고 'I think that there's nothing useless in the world!'라고 했다.

07 'Walking on all four legs was very difficult for me.'라고 했다.

08 'A bug robot? Is it interesting?'이라고 묻고 있다.

09 ⓐ의 bird robot을 bug robot으로 고쳐야 한다.

10 부가의문문은 사실을 확인하거나 동의를 구할 때 쓴다.

11 It is difficult for my son to tie his shoelaces yet.

12 (A) 결과가 나오므로 Finally (B) 예가 이어지므로 For example이 적절하다.

13 ⓐ는 '털로 덮인 표면'이고 나머지는 모두 그의 발명품이다.

14 스위스 공학자가 얼마나 많이 실험을 했는지는 알 수 없다.

15 바르게 배열하면 'wondered how birds could fly'이다.

**16** ⓐ not only 다음에 use가 쓰였으므로 imitate ⓑ watched, made와 병렬 관계로 drew가 적절하다.

**17** ⓐ 소음을 줄여야 했으므로 reduce ⓑ 새의 부리를 모방한 것이므로 imitating이 적절하다.

**18** 자연에서 모방하여 해결책을 찾은 이야기이므로 ①번이 적절하다.

**19** 'When the train entered a tunnel, the sudden increase in air pressure created a very loud sound.'라고 했다.

**20** 각각 ⓐ absorb ⓒ survival ⓓ survive ⓔ reflect가 적절하다.

**21** 자연을 모방하여 새로운 발명품을 만들었다는 글이다.

**22** ⓐ의 that은 '가시 식물의 가시 끝이 곧지 않다는 것'을 가리키고 나머지는 모두 그가 발명한 것을 가리킨다.

**23** that은 바로 앞 문장의 내용을 받고 있다.

**24** (A)의 such person은 앞에서 말한 'Some people not only use nature but also imitate it to find solutions to their problems.'이다.

**25** 간접의문문은 '의문사(또는 if나 whether)+주어+동사'의 어순이다. 그는 궁금했다: He wondered 새들이 어떻게 날 수 있는지: how birds could fly

## Lesson 4 (기말)

1회

| | | | |
|---|---|---|---|
| 01 ④ | 02 ④ | 03 ⑤ | 04 ④ |
| 05 ② | 06 ③ | 07 ② | 08 ⑤ |
| 09 ③ | 10 ① | 11 ① | 12 ④ |
| 13 ⑤ | 14 ④ | 15 ④ | 16 ① |
| 17 ⑤ | 18 ③ | 19 ③ | |
| 20 I was very surprised by what had happened. | | | |
| 21 ① | 22 ③ | 23 ④ | 24 ⑤ |

**01** 순서대로 • sneeze • bother • lend • impolite가 들어간다.

**02** inspire: to give somebody the desire or enthusiasm to do something well / melt: to cause something to change from a solid to a liquid usually because of heat / creative: having or showing an ability to make new things or think of new ideas / match: a contest between two or more players or teams

**03** independent: confident and free to do things without needing help from other people

**04** Mr. Parker는 'He simply wanted people to look at the objects in a different way.'라고 말했다.

**05** 'It was interesting.'이라고 답했으므로 책이 어땠는지 묻는 ②번이 적절하다.

**06** B는 'Well, he says he didn't help Heungbu for a reason. He wanted Heungbu to make money on his own and be independent.'라고 말했다.

**07** 앞에서 경기에서 질 것이라고 했고 뒤에서 그 이유를 설명하고 있으므로 이유를 묻는 ②번이 적절하다.

**08** 축구 경기가 어땠는지 묻는데 내일 질 거라고 생각한다는 답은 어색하다.

**09** 영화와 원작을 비교하는 것이 재미있었다는 말에 이어 ⓑ에서 영화와 책 중에 어느 것이 더 좋았는지 묻고 ⓒ에서 책이 더 좋았다고 하자 ⓐ에서 자기는 이해하기 쉬워서 영화가 더 나았다고 하고 ⓓ에서 동의하며 각자 장점이 있다고 하는 순서가 적절하다.

**10** (A) 'I liked it.'이라고 답했으므로 어땠는지 묻는 'How did you like' (B) 빈칸 뒤에서 'better, the movie or the book'이라고 했으므로 선호하는 것을 묻는 'Which did you like'가 적절하다.

**11** ①은 부사적 용법의 '목적'이고, 나머지는 모두 부사적 용법의 '감정의 원인'이다.

**12** ① moved ② had made ③ was very tired, hadn't slept ⑤ had gone

**13** ⓔ의 'what had happened'는 '일어난 일'을 말한다.

**14** 'I sneezed a great sneeze and you know what? The whole straw house fell down.'이라고 했다.

**15** 늑대가 돼지 집으로 가고(C) 늑대가 부서진 문을 움켜잡고(D) 늑대가 재채기를 아주 크게 하고(B) 집 전체가 무너졌다(A)

**16** (A) think의 목적어로 What (B) 이유를 묻는 Why (C) mean의 목적어로 what이 적절하다.

**17** 무슨 일이 일어났는지 설명해 달라고 하자 (C)에서 설명을 하고 (A)에서 형제들은 지금 어떻게 지내고 있는지 묻자 (B)에서 집에서 쉬고 있다고 답하는 순서가 적절하다.

**18** ⓒ to lose가 적절하다.

**19** ⓐ making, ⓑ to ask, ⓓ coming, ⓔ Unfortunately가 적절하다.

**20** 감정을 느끼는 것이므로 과거분사로 쓴다. what had happened: 일어난 일

**21** 글의 맨 앞부분에 'let's meet our second guest'라고 했으므로 다른 사람과 먼저 이야기했음을 알 수 있다.

**22** 늑대가 돼지 집으로 가고(b) 늑대가 부서진 문을 움켜잡고(c) 늑대가 재채기를 아주 크게 하고(a) 집 전체가 무너졌다(d)

**23** ⓒ asking → to ask ⓔ to come → coming ⓕ surprising → surprised

**24** 늑대가 케이크를 만들고 있을 때 무엇이 떨어졌는지는 알 수 없다.

## Lesson 4 (기말)

| | | | |
|---|---|---|---|
| 01 ③ | 02 ④ | 03 ③ | 04 ⑤ |
| 05 ① | 06 ③ | 07 ④ | 08 ⑤ |
| 09 ⑤ | 10 ④ | 11 ② | |

12 (1) He had been in Hong Kong
   (2) I had finished my homework
   (3) I was very[so] glad[happy/pleased] to see him again.

| | |
|---|---|
| 13 ④ | 14 ② |

15 he was very surprised by what had happened

| | | | |
|---|---|---|---|
| 16 ⑤ | 17 ④ | 18 ③ | 19 ② |
| 20 ⑤ | 21 ① | 22 ② | 23 ⑤ |

01 narrow: long and not wide / all-purpose: suitable for many uses / genius: a very smart or talented person / independent: confident and free to do things without needing help from other people

02 unfortunately: used to say that something bad or unlucky has happened

03 break into: ~에 침입하다

04 G는 'The book helped me understand the characters better.'라고 말했다.

05 뒤에서 이유를 설명하고 있으므로 이유를 묻는 ①번이 적절하다.

06 (B)의 that은 앞에 나온 'responsible for the rabbit'을 대신하고 있으므로 ③번이 적절하다.

07 <보기>의 표현은 '그래야 한다고 생각하지 않는다'라는 말인데 이것은 (D) 앞의 질문(일종의 수사의문문)에 대한 부연 설명이므로 (D)가 적절하다.

08 Ms. Parker는 'The artist used real-life objects to create art.'라고 말했고 'So, he didn't create something new?'라는 질문에 'That's right.'라고 말했다.

09 Heungbu를 돕지 않은 이유가 나와야 하는데 ⑤번이 적절하다.

10 ⓓ는 Heungbu이고 나머지는 모두 Nolbu이다.

11 밝은 면을 보라고 하는 것은 긍정적으로 생각하라는 뜻이다.

12 (1), (2) 과거보다 앞선 시제의 일을 과거완료로 쓴다.

13 'The whole straw house fell down.'이라고 했다.

14 (가) tell+간접목적어(us)+직접목적어(what happened) (나) a birthday cake이 목적어로 나와 있으므로 was에 이어지는 making (다) 안 좋은 일이 반복되고 있으므로 Unfortunately가 적절하다.

15 그가 놀란 것이므로 'was surprised'가 되어야 하고 '일어난 일'이 놀란 것보다 앞서므로 과거완료로 쓴다.

16 인터뷰하는 글이다.

17 'impressed'는 '인상 깊은, 감명[감동]을 받은' 정도의 뜻이다. 나머지는 놀라움이나 슬픔을 나타낸다.

18 세 돼지가 언제 집을 지었는지는 알 수 없다.

19 (가) 앞의 내용과 상반되므로 However (나) 이유를 언급하고 있으므로 because가 적절하다.

20 (A) 과거 이전에 6개월 동안 연습해 왔던 것이므로 과거완료 (B) 과거의 일이므로 과거시제 (C) 'did a good job'보다 앞선 시제이므로 과거완료로 쓴다.

21 늑대가 왜 아팠는지는 알 수 없다.

22 'I'm sorry to trouble you, but are you in?' → 'How impolite!'

23 'One evening a fairy comes and tries to help him, but she changes him into a huge monkey.'라고 했다.

MEMO